# Classic Readings in Organizational Behavior

## Second Edition

# Classic Readings in Organizational Behavior

## Second Edition

J. Steven Ott
*University of Utah*

Wadsworth Publishing Company

 An International Thomson Publishing Company

Belmont • Albany • Bonn • Boston • Cincinnati • Detroit • London • Madrid • Melbourne
Mexico City • New York • Paris • San Francisco • Singapore • Tokyo • Toronto • Washington

Public Administration Editor: Jason Moore
Production: The Wheetley Company
Print Buyer: Karen Hunt
Permissions Editor: Jeanne Bosschart
Copy Editor: The Wheetley Company
Cover: Andrew Ogus
Compositor: TCSystems, Inc.

COPYRIGHT © 1996 by Wadsworth Publishing Company
A Division of International Thomson Publishing Inc.

 The ITP logo is a trademark under license.

Printed in the United States of America
1 2 3 4 5 6 7 8 9 10—02 01 00 99 98 97 96

For more information, contact Wadsworth Publishing Company:

Wadsworth Publishing Company
10 Davis Drive
Belmont, California 94002, USA

International Thomson Publishing Europe
Berkshire House 168-173
High Holborn
London, WC1V 7AA, England

Thomas Nelson Australia
102 Dodds Street
South Melbourne 3205
Victoria, Australia

Nelson Canada
1120 Birchmount Road
Scarborough, Ontario
Canada M1K 5G4

International Thomson Editores
Campos Eliseos 385, Piso 7
Col. Polanco
11560 México D.F. México

International Thomson Publishing GmbH
Königswinterer Strasse 418
53227 Bonn, Germany

International Thomson Publishing Asia
221 Henderson Road
#05-10 Henderson Building
Singapore 0315

International Thomson Publishing Japan
Hirakawacho Kyowa Building, 3F
2-2-1 Hirakawacho
Chiyoda-ku, Tokyo 102, Japan

**Library of Congress Cataloging-in-Publication Data**
Classic readings in organizational behavior / [edited by] J. Steven
   Ott. — 2nd ed.
        p.    cm.
   Includes bibliographical references.
   ISBN 0-534-50413-2 (alk. paper)
    1. Organizational behavior.    I. Ott, J. Steven.
HD58.7.C52   1996
658.3—dc20                                                                    95–18087
                                                                                        CIP

*This book is printed on acid-free recycled paper.*

# Foreword

Who has not come across the master's theses, dissertations, or journal articles that start by telling us that nobody in the whole world has ever thought of the brilliant new hypothesis, much less seen the earth-shaking results, to be unfolded to our amazed and unbelieving eyes? All too often, as it turns out, this happens to be hyperbole. In fact, if the truth be told, the history of psychology begins for many budding organizational psychologists on the day they enroll in their first psychology course. They are amazed that Nicole Machiavelli's treatise, *The Prince*, was only one early version of the "How to lead" books, and few graduate students in I/O psychology know that they owe anything to people with such strange names as Chester Barnard, Elton Mayo or Hugo Muensterberg who gave industrial and organizational psychology its start.

And why, one might ask, should students be concerned with these names, which they are no longer required to know on tests? Most of us feel that we don't have the time to dig up "old," outdated, and in some cases, superseded articles. Going into the stacks to rummage among old journals is not everyone's favorite occupation, especially when passing exams, preparing for the next class, or preparing another article for publication are more pressing.

Nevertheless, we do need to remember that we are building on the work of others. To think otherwise is not only a mark of arrogance but also of folly. Moreover, there is a lot of scientific pay-dirt in "them thar hills:" One good example is the sudden re-emergence of Max Weber's articles on the topic of charisma. This old chestnut has suddenly sprouted into one of the most active current topics in the organizational literature. It is almost embarrassing to note how many points old Max Weber made that we are now rediscovering.

Another concept that has recently come to life again is the work on leader intelligence. The problem of how the leader's intelligence contributes to leadership status or effectiveness, interestingly enough, was the topic of the very first empirical paper in leadership. In "A Preliminary Study of the Psychology and Pedagogy of Leadership," Lewis Terman (1904) anticipated current contingency theories of leadership by pointing out that the selection of a leader depends not only on the leader's own attributes but on the needs of the group. Quite apart from the scholarly tradition of citing one's predecessors when it comes to theory building, many of the great insights about how organizations work, are to be found in papers which, today, are considered classics. I am reminded of Mark Twain's little story about how dumb his father was when Mark Twain was growing up, how much dumber the old man got year after year, and even more surprising, how much the old man learned in the few years of his son's absence.

Professor Ott's thoughtfully assembled collection of classic papers makes a major contribution to our thinking. It is not only a welcome reminder that the field of organizational behavior did not begin the first year we entered college, but that these early papers became classics because their insights are still valid today. They contain wisdom that has not gone out of style, and they represent a rich source of hypotheses that are yet to be tested. This selection undoubtedly will find a useful place in the graduate school curriculum, as well as provide the researcher with a valuable and convenient collection of papers that are not always easily obtained from the nearest library, spanning the field of organizational behavior.

**Fred E. Fiedler**
**University of Washington**

# Preface

*Classic Readings in Organizational Behavior* has been designed to meet several purposes: (1) to be a stand-alone collection of the most important writings about organizational behavior, (2) to supplement any of several excellent college and graduate-level texts in organizational behavior and administrative practice, and (3) to mesh with and to supplement Jay Shafritz's and Steve Ott's fourth edition of *Classics of Organization Theory* (1996). Only one chapter in *Classics of Organization Theory* is devoted to organizational behavior and, as Shafritz and Ott explain in their *Introduction,* "organizational behavior is a very large field of study unto itself with an enormous body of literature . . . . It is impossible to do much more than provide a 'flavor' of this body of theory and research in a single chapter."

As the title, *Classic Readings in Organizational Behavior* implies, this book is a collection of previously published *classics.* Although several important recent articles are included, no attempt has been made to incorporate selections that reflect all of the recent trends and developments in the field. Current trends are not the purpose of this book. Rather, this collection presents the most enduring themes and works of organizational behavior, organized in a way that is conceptually sound, useful in practice, and that allows the reader to track the historical development of the most important topics.

The older works have not been included simply because they are interesting relics, reminders of quaint but outdated thinking. Although organizational behavior has experienced marked growth and maturation over the decades, many of the *basics* remain the same. In fact, this is a field in which it sometimes feels as though the more we learn about the important things, the less we truly know. (For a good example, see Warren Bennis' lamentful 1990 piece, which is reprinted in Chapter III, "Why Leaders Can't Lead.") The laws of physics and gravity do not change with intellectual fashions or technological advances, nor do the basic psychological, cultural, or social characteristics of people. Just as those who would build spaceships have to start by studying Newton, those who would work with people in organizations must start with 1930s writers such as Mary Parker Follett and Chester I. Barnard. The future will always build upon what is enduring from the past. That is the rationale for this book—to provide those who seek to understand and/or to advance organization theory with a convenient place to find the essentials, indeed the classics, of organizational behavior's past. Once-dominant ideas and perspectives on organizations may lose the center stage, but they do not die. Their thinking influences subsequent writers, even those who may reject their basic assumptions and tenets. However old some of the articles may be, they are not dated. A classic *is* a classic because it continues to be of value to each new generation of students and practitioners.

Inherently, organizations are part of the society and the culture in which they are situated and operate. Human behavior—and thus organizational behavior—is heavily influenced by culturally rooted beliefs, values, assumptions, and behavioral norms affecting all aspects of organizational life. For this reason, a society's ways of thinking about how people behave in organizations do not develop in a vacuum. They reflect what is going on in the contemporary world of the time. Thus, contributions to organizational behavior vary by what was happening when and where, and in different cultures and subcultures. The advent of World War II, the American P.O.W.s who defected following the Korean war, the "flower child"/antiestablishment/self-development era of the 1960s, the computer/information society of the 1970s, and the competitive scare from Japanese industry in the late 1970s all substantially influenced the evolution of our thinking, our theories, and our research about people in organizations. In order to truly understand organizational behavior as it exists today, one must appreciate the historical contexts through which it developed and the cultural milieux during and in which important contributions were made to its body of knowledge. In order to help readers place writings in their historical contexts, A *Chronology of Organizational Behavior*, a review of the most important events and publications in the field, follows the *Introduction*.

## CRITERIA FOR SELECTION

Several criteria were used to select these particular classics of organizational behavior for inclusion. The first was the answer to the question: "Should the serious student of organizational behavior be expected to be able to identify this author and his or her basic themes?" If the answer was yes, then it was so because such a contribution has long been, or is increasingly being recognized as, an important theme by a significant writer. While I expect to be criticized for excluding other articles and writers, it will be more difficult to honestly criticize my inclusions. The writers and pieces chosen are among the most widely quoted and reprinted by students and theorists in the field of organizational behavior. Some of the recent pieces had to be exceptions. I felt that it was important to include a sprinkling of *potentially important* current articles along with the time-tested classics. Obviously, these newer articles have not been cited as extensively as those written twenty or thirty years earlier. Thus, more subjective judgments were required about their inclusion.

The second criterion is related to the first: Each article or chapter from a book had to make a basic statement that has been consistently echoed or attacked over the years. The selection had to be acknowledged as important—significant—in the sense that it must have been (or will become) an integral part of the foundation for the subsequent building of the field of organizational behavior.

The third criterion was that articles had to be readable. Fortunately, this was a relatively easy criterion to meet. Much of the literature on organizational behavior is easily understandable and interesting. However, many of the truly great works are of a length which, in my judgment, detracts from their major themes. Consequently, articles have been shortened for this book, but the only editing has been "editing out": No sentences have been changed or added to the original.

## ORGANIZATION OF THE BOOK

This book is structured around the most important topics in the field of organizational behavior. Then, the readings within each topical chapter are organized chronologically. An author's choice of major topics and the sequence of their presentation reflects his or her conceptual framework of a field. Thus, the structure of a book, in and of itself, communicates the author's implicit perspective of the field; this collection is no exception. The readings are grouped in six chapters that reflect the most pervasive themes in the literature of organizational behavior:

- Motivation;
- Group and intergroup behavior;
- Leadership;
- Work teams and empowerment;
- Effects of the work environment on individuals;
- Power and influence; and
- Organizational change (including the subfield of organization development [O.D.]).

The development of behavioral science theory tends to be cumulative, but almost never in a straight line. Sometimes the cumulative building of theory is accomplished through adoption of prior theorists' logic and research findings; in other instances, it is by trying unsuccessfully to use prior theorists' works, rejecting them, and veering off in a new exploratory direction. The chronological sequencing of readings within topics should allow the reader to track some of the important ebbs and flows of theory development over the decades. For those who are interested in a quick overview of the historical evolution of organizational behavior, a *Chronology* follows the *Introduction*.

## CHANGES FROM THE FIRST EDITION

This second edition attempts to retain the essence of the first edition. It has not changed in level of presentation, point of view, purpose, or emphasis. Its scope has been expanded to incorporate important developments in the field, including: individual and group empowerment (including self-managing work teams), cultural diversity, applications of chaos theory, the "new science," and learning organizations.

It is hoped that several changes make the book's structure "hold together" better conceptually. Chapter IV in the first edition, *People in Organizations: The Context*, has been eliminated. A new Chapter V has been added, *Effects of the Work Environment on Individuals*. Two selections have been moved from the old Chapter

II, *Group and Intergroup Behavior,* to the new Chapter V: Solomon Asch, "Effects of Group Pressure Upon the Modification and Distortion of Judgments," and Irving L. Janis, "Groupthink: The Desperate Drive for Consensus at Any Cost." Three readings have been moved from the old Chapter IV, *People in Organizations: The Context,* to the new Chapter V: Robert Merton, "Bureaucratic Structure and Personality," Eric Trist and Kenneth Bamforth, "Some Social and Psychological Consequences of the Longwall Method of Coal-Getting," and "William H. Whyte, Jr., "The Organization Man: Conclusion."

A number of people who have used the first edition asked that we "update" the book's coverage—to include readings that "bring the book into the 1990s." Other reviewers have disagreed, urging us to resist the temptation to venture into untested new writing that has not withstood the test of time. We should keep *Classic Readings* true to its title. Until now, and with only a few exceptions, *Classic Readings* has sided with the latter viewpoint. After all, this is intended to be a collection of enduring works by the great writers, not paperbacks about modern fads that disappear as quickly as they appear on the racks in airport newsstands.

This second edition attempts to walk a line. It tries to retain its *classics* focus and identity while presenting a sprinkling of newer important works. For example, the new Chapter IV is about work teams and empowerment—two themes that have influenced the field of organizational behavior markedly during the past 15 years. Thus, the readings in Chapter IV tend to be recent. And, there are no "older" articles about work force diversity (in its current usage) or applications of chaos theory and quantum mechanics to organizational behavior.

Chapter-by-chapter, the following selections have been added or deleted from the first to the second edition:

## CHAPTER I: MOTIVATION

Deletions from the First Edition

David C. McClelland, "That Urge to Achieve" (1966)

John P. Campbell, Marvin D. Dunnette, Edward E. Lawler III, and Karl E. Weick, Jr. "Expectancy Theory" (1970)

Steven Kerr, "On the Folly of Rewarding A, While Hoping for B" (1975)

Barry M. Staw, "Motivation in Organizations: Toward Synthesis and Redirection" (1977)

New Additions in the Second Edition

Victor H. Vroom, "Work and Motivation" (1964)

Edwin A. Locke, "The Ubiquity of the Technique of Goal Setting in the Theories of and Approaches to Employee Motivation" (1978)

Richard T. Mowday, "Equity Theory Predictions of Behavior in Organizations" (1983)

## CHAPTER II: GROUP AND INTERGROUP BEHAVIOR

Deletions from the First Edition

Richard E. Walton and John M. Dutton, "The Management of Interdepartmental Conflict: A Model and Review" (1969)

Edgar H. Schein, "Group and Intergroup Relationships" (1970)

Jeffrey Pfeffer, "Coalitions" (1981)

New Additions in the Second Edition

Robert R. Blake, Herbert A. Shepard, and Jane S. Mouton, "Foundations and Dynamics of Intergroup Behavior" (1964)

Clayton P. Alderfer, "An Intergroup Perspective on Group Dynamics" (1987)

Taylor H. Cox, Jr., "Cultural Diversity in Organizations: Intergroup Conflict" (1993)

## CHAPTER III: LEADERSHIP

Deletions from the First Edition

Douglas M. McGregor, "An Analysis of Leadership" (1960)

Robert L. Kahn and Daniel Katz, "Leadership Practices in Relation to Productivity and Morale" (1962)

Warren G. Bennis, "Mortal Stakes: Where Have All the Leaders Gone?" (1976)

Thomas J. Sergiovanni, "Leadership as Cultural Expression" (1984)

New Additions in the Second Edition

Warren G. Bennis, "Why Leaders Can't Lead" (1990)

Edgar H. Schein, "The Learning Leader as Culture Manager" (1992)

Margaret J. Wheatley, "Leadership and the New Science: Searching for a Simpler Way to Lead Organizations" (1992)

## CHAPTER IV: TEAMWORK AND EMPOWERMENT

Deletions from the First Edition

Alvin W. Gouldner, "Cosmopolitans and Locals: Toward an Analysis of Latent Social Roles" (1957)

Frederick C. Thayer, " 'Democracy' as Hierarchy and Alienation" (1981)

New Additions in the Second Edition

> J. Richard Hackman and Greg R. Oldham, "The Design of Work for Groups and Groups for Work" (1980)

> Ian I. Mitroff, "Business NOT as Usual: Building the Organization of the Future" (1987)

> Jack D. Orsburn, Linda Moran, Ed Musselwhite, John H. Zenger, and Craig Perrin, "Self Directed Work Teams: The New American Challenge" (1990)

> Marvin R. Weisbord, "Transforming Teamwork: Work Relationships in a Fast-Changing World" (1991)

> David E. Bowen and Edward E. Lawler III, "The Empowerment of Service Workers: What, Why, How, and When" (1992)

## CHAPTER V: EFFECTS OF THE WORK ENVIRONMENT ON INDIVIDUALS

New Additions in the Second Edition

> Lyman W. Porter, Edward E. Lawler III, and J. Richard Hackman, "Social Influences on Work Effectiveness" (1975)

> Nancy E. Bell and Barry M. Staw, "People as Sculptors versus Sculpture: The Roles of Personality and Personal Control in Organizations" (1989)

## CHAPTER VI: POWER AND INFLUENCE

Deletions from the First Edition

> Mason Haire, "The Concept of Power and the Concept of Man" (1962)

> Douglas Yates, Jr., "Identifying and Using Political Resources" (1985)

New Addition in the Second Edition

> David Mechanic, "Sources of Power of Lower Participants in Complex Organizations" (1962)

## CHAPTER VII: ORGANIZATIONAL CHANGE

Deletions from the First Edition

> Harold J. Leavitt, "Applied Organizational Change in Industry: Structural, Technological and Humanistic Approaches" (1965)

> Warren G. Bennis, "Applying Behavioral Sciences to Planned Organizational Change" (1966)

New Additions in the Second Edition

Peter M. Senge, "The Fifth Discipline: The Art and Practice of the Learning Organization" (1990)

Richard Beckhard and Wendy Pritchard, "Focusing the Effort: Crucial Themes that Drive Change" (1992)

## ACKNOWLEDGMENTS

Many people have contributed invaluable insights and assistance that have allowed me to assemble, edit, and write this second edition. I am always reluctant to list names in an acknowledgment, for any listing is certain to overlook some people who should be recognized. Also, a mere listing of names is entirely inadequate thanks. Nevertheless, some individuals simply must be acknowledged. First and foremost is Jay Shafritz, at the University of Pittsburgh, who is a part of this book in so many ways.

Breena E. Coates, also at the University of Pittsburgh, was absolutely indispensable in writing and editing this edition. Breena had a major voice in deciding which articles to include and delete, as well as identifying what to edit out of articles. She also was my primary source of ideas for new entries in the "Chronology of Organizational Behavior" that follows the *Introduction*. Working with her has been a delightful, creative experience.

Sam Overman and Bob Gage at the University of Colorado-Denver provided numerous ideas; Al Hyde, American University, provided inspiration and motivation. David Sullivan helped with the first edition's chapter on leadership; Alice Kaiser-Drobney, Slippery Rock University, prepared many Chronology entries for the first edition.

Bruce H. Johnson, Gustavus Adolphus College; Carl J. Bellone, California State University, Hayward; Edward J. Conlon, University of Iowa; Andrew McNitt, Eastern Illinois University; and Susan J. B. Cox, University of North Carolina-Greensboro reviewed the first edition. Richard Simpson, Associate Dean of Continuing Education at the University of Utah, not only served as a reviewer for the second edition but also provided many useful suggestions about approach and contents, as did Michael Jennings, University of Alaska, Fairbanks; Frank Piff, Johns Hopkins University; and Frank Capuzzi, Johns Hopkins University.

Finally, we want to put readers on notice that changed standards of language are evident in some of the readings. Many terms and phrases that are sexist and racist by today's standards, were in common use twenty or thirty years ago. When it was possible to do so, offensive language was removed from articles by editing out sentences or paragraphs. Some words and phrases, however, are essential to the text and could not be deleted.

J. Steven Ott
University of Utah

# Contents

**Chapter III**
## Leadership, 163

**Chapter IV**
## Teamwork and Empowerment, 244

# Introduction

## DEFINING ORGANIZATIONAL BEHAVIOR

O*rganizational behavior* seeks to understand human behavior in organizational contexts. It examines the ways people cope with the problems and opportunities of organizational life. It asks questions such as:

- Why do people behave the way they do when they are in organizations?
- Under what circumstances will peoples' behavior in organizations change?
- What impacts do organizations have on the behavior of individuals, formal groups (such as departments), and informal groups (such as people from several departments who meet regularly in the company lunchroom)?
- Why do different groups in the same organization develop different behavioral norms?

Organizational behavior results from the many complex interactions that occur daily between humans, groups of humans, and the organizational environment in which they spend their workday. Therefore, in order to understand these interactions, it is first necessary to know something about:

- The behavior of people and groups in general;
- Organizations and organizational environments; and
- The behavior of people and groups when they are in organizations.

*Organizational behavior* has at least two very different meanings, and these differences are important. First, organizational behavior (or "OB") is the actual behavior of individuals and groups in and around purposeful organizations. It is the application of the theories, methods, and research findings of the behavioral sciences—particularly of psychology, social psychology, sociology, cultural anthropology, and to a lesser degree of economics and political science—to understanding the behavior of humans in organizations. However, understanding is not the sole goal of organizational behavior. OB practitioners apply knowledge, understanding, and techniques from the behavioral sciences in attempts to improve the functioning of organizations and to improve the fit between organizations' and their members' needs and wants.

Although behavioral scientists are interested in human behavior in any organization setting, their primary focus always has been on behavior in the work-place—on employment-related organizational behavior. Organizational behavior is mostly

*1*

about behavior in settings where there tend to be constraints on people; where there is an economic relationship between individuals and their organizations. People are not as free to establish and terminate employment relationships as they are other types of relationships with organizations. Usually there is a structured set of roles, a hierarchy of relations, and ongoing goal-related activities (although the goals may or may not be organizationally sanctioned).

Second, organizational behavior is one of several frameworks or *perspectives* on what makes an organization work. A perspective defines the organizational variables that are important enough to warrant the attention of managers and students of organizations. Perspectives identify what a person sees when looking at an organization and, therefore, almost prescribes what *levers* to use when trying to change or stabilize an organization. But a perspective is more than a way of seeing and approaching an organization. It is also a set of bedrock beliefs and values about, for example, the basic purposes for organizations, their fundamental right to existence, the nature of their links to the surrounding environment, and—most important for organizational behavior—the whole of their relationships with the people who work in them.

Students and practitioners of management have always been interested in and concerned with the behavior of people in organizations. But, fundamental assumptions about the behavior of people at work did not change dramatically from the beginnings of humankind's attempts to organize until only a few decades ago. Using the traditional "the boss knows best" mind-set (set of assumptions), Hugo Münsterberg (1863-1916), the German-born psychologist whose later work at Harvard would earn him the title of "father" of industrial or applied psychology, pioneered the application of psychological findings from laboratory experiments to practical matters. He sought to match the abilities of new hires with a company's work demands, to positively influence employee attitudes toward their work and their company, and to understand the impact of psychological conditions on employee productivity (H. Münsterberg, 1913; M. Münsterberg, 1922). Münsterberg's approach characterized how the behavioral sciences tended to be applied in organizations well into the 1950s. During and following World War II, the armed services were particularly active in conducting and sponsoring research into how the military could best *find and shape people to fit its needs*. This theme or quest became known as *Industrial Psychology* and more recently as *industrial/organizational psychology* or *I/O psychology*.

In contrast to the Hugo Münsterberg-type perspective on organizational behavior, the 1960s and 1970s "modern breed" of applied behavioral scientists have focused their attention to seeking to answer questions such as how organizations could and should allow and encourage their people to grow and develop. From this perspective, it was *assumed* that organizational creativity, flexibility, and prosperity would flow naturally from employee growth and development. The essence of the relationship between organization and people was redefined from dependence to codependence. People were considered to be as or more important than the organization itself. The organizational behavior methods and techniques of the 1960s and

1970s could not have been used in Münsterberg's days, *because we didn't believe (assume) that codependence was the "right" relationship between an organization and its employees.* All of this is what is meant by a perspective.

Although practitioners and researchers have been interested in the behavior of people inside organizations for a very long time, it has only been since about 1957—when our basic assumptions about the relationship between organizations and people truly began to change—that the *organizational behavior perspective* came into being. Those who *see* organizations through the *lenses* of the organizational behavior perspective focus on people, groups, and relationships among them and the organizational environment. For example, when organizational behaviorists contemplate the introduction of a new technology, they will immediately start thinking about and planning:

- How to minimize fear of change by involving people at all levels in designing the introduction of the changes;
- How to minimize the negative impacts of the change on groups of workers (such as older, less-skilled, or younger);
- How to coopt informal leaders, especially those who might become antagonistic; and
- Alternatives for employees who do not see the changes being consistent with their personal goals.

Because the organizational behavior perspective places a very high value on humans as individuals, things typically are done very openly and honestly, providing employees with maximum amounts of accurate information, so they can make informed decisions with free will about their future (Argyris, 1970).

But there are other perspectives as well, each with its own assumptions, values, and *levers*—ways of approaching issues such as organizational change and stabilization (Shafritz & Ott, 1996). The systems perspective focuses on things such as an organization's information systems and its decision processes (Kast & Rosenzweig, 1970; Thompson, 1967); the structural perspective emphasizes things like the structural arrangement of the organization, the organization of work within the structure, and the procedures and rules that maintain order (Blau & Scott, 1962; Burns & Stalker, 1961; Mintzberg, 1979); and, the power perspective looks mostly at managing conflict, building, maintaining, and using coalitions, and the nature of real and perceived power relationships (Kotter, 1985; Pfeffer, 1981; Pfeffer, 1992; Salancik & Pfeffer, 1977).

Thus, as a perspective of organization theory, organizational behavior is one of several ways of looking at and thinking about organizations (and people) which is defined by a set of basic assumptions about people, organizations, and the relationships, dynamics, and tensions between and among them. It is common to refer to this second use of the phrase, *organizational behavior* as the *human relations* or *human resources school, perspective,* or *frame* of organization theory. In order to distinguish clearly between the two meanings and thus to avoid confusion, the phrase, *organiza-*

*tional behavior* is used throughout this book to mean *the behavior of individuals and groups in and around purposeful organizations.* To differentiate, the phrase *organizational behavior perspective*, or *human relations perspective*, refers to the school or perspective of organization theory that reflects basic managerial assumptions about employees similar to those of Theory X and Theory Y, as articulated by Douglas McGregor. (See Chapter I, *Motivation.*)

Organizational behavior is solidly grounded in theory and in empirical research. It uses applications of theory, methods, and findings about the behavior of people and groups in general, about social organizations, and about people in purposeful social organizations, adapted from long-established behavioral science disciplines. No other perspective of organizations has ever had such a wealth of research findings and methods at its disposal.

It is difficult to draw a clear distinction between what behavior is and is not *organizational*, since out-of-organizational behavior affects behavior in organizations and vice versa. In general, however, behavior is considered organizational if something associated with the organization causes or enhances the behavior, the behavior results from an organizational activity or function, or organizational meaning is attached to the behavior.

Assumptions about human behavior are crucial for understanding how managers and workers interact in organizations. Each perspective on organizations has its own fundamental tenets or assumptions which are very different. The tenets of the "modern" structural perspective and the organizational behavior perspective (as they are articulated by Bolman and Deal, 1991[1]) are presented side-by-side in Table 1—to emphasize the differences and to highlight how the differences cause these two schools to differ with respect to almost everything!

Assumptions are more than beliefs or values: They are givens or truths that are held so strongly that they are no longer questioned nor even consciously thought about. They are the foundation and the justification (Sathe, 1985) for the perspective's beliefs, truths, values, and ways of doing things.

The assumptions of the Münsterberg–early I/O psychology perspective continued well into the 1950s. It was assumed that people should be fit to the organization: The organization had set needs to be filled. Thus, during the "classical era" of organization theory—from the late 1800s through the 1940s—the organizational role of the applied behavioral sciences largely consisted of helping organizations find and shape people to serve as *replacement parts* for *organizational machines.* The dominant theorists of organizations during these years were people such as Frederick Winslow Taylor (1911) and his disciples in *scientific management*, and Max Weber (1922), the brilliant theorist of *bureaucracy* (Shafritz & Ott, 1996).

Although the Münsterberg–I/O psychology theme provided important early background for organizational behavior, its more important direct genealogy lies in social psychology. The one most significant set of events that led to a conscious field of organizational behavior was the multilayer work done by the Elton Mayo team at the Hawthorne plant of the Western Electric Company beginning in 1927 (Mayo, 1933; Roethlisberger & Dixon, 1939). Three other significant threads or

## TABLE 1 · TENETS OF THE "MODERN" STRUCTURAL PERSPECTIVE AND THE ORGANIZATIONAL BEHAVIOR PERSPECTIVE SIDE-BY-SIDE FOR COMPARISON

| "Modern" Structural School | Organizational Behavior Perspective |
|---|---|
| 1. Organizations are rational institutions whose primary purpose is to accomplish established objectives; rational organizational behavior is achieved best through systems of defined rules and formal authority. Organizational control and coordination are key to maintaining organizational rationality. | 1. Organizations exist to serve human needs. Humans do not exist to serve organizational needs. |
| 2. There is a "best" structure for any organization in light of its given objectives, the environmental conditions surrounding it, the nature of its products and/or services, and the technology of the production processes. | 2. Organizations and people need each other. Organizations need the ideas, energy, and talent that people provide, while people need the careers, salaries, and work opportunities that organizations provide. |
| 3. Specialization and the division of labor increase the quality and quantity of production—particularly in highly skilled operations and professions. | 3. When the fit between the individual and the organization is poor, one or both will suffer. The individual will be exploited or will seek to exploit the organization or both. |
| 4. Most problems in an organization result from structural flaws and can be solved by changing the structure (pp. 48–49). | 4. When the fit is good between the individual and the organization, both benefit. Humans are able to do meaningful and satisfying work while providing the resources the organization needs to accomplish its mission (p. 121). |

*Adapted from:* Lee G. Bolman and Terrence E. Deal (1991). *Reframing Organizations.* San Francisco: Jossey-Bass.

forces also accounted for a great deal of the direction of industrial social psychology research and practice into the 1950s (Haire, 1954):

1. The late 1930s contributions by Kurt Lewin in group dynamics, with important contributions by Lippitt and White (group climate and leadership) and Bavelas (leadership as a group problem);

2. Jacob Moreno's work on sociometry (the network of relations among people in a group) and sociodrama (role playing); and

3. The rapid rise of industry and government willingness to ask social psychologists for help during World War II. This trend was a start toward establishing a role for social scientist (*process*) consultants that differed substantially from *content consultants*.

During these early years, industrial social psychology differed quite markedly from I/O psychology in its interests and premises. Whereas I/O psychology was busily engaged in trying to solve organizational problems (for example, selecting people to fit into positions), industrial social psychology developed an early concern for creating a psychological—rather than an institutional or technical—definition of the work setting. In this arena, the Hawthorne studies of Mayo and his collaborators were extraordinary contributions.

Once again, the difference between the I/O psychology approach and the work of Mayo, Roethlisberger, and their associates at the Hawthorne plant, lay in their *assumptions*. The I/O psychologists adopted the assumptions of classical organization theory and shaped their field to fit its tenets. Those assumptions are:

1. Organizations exist to accomplish production-related and economic goals.
2. There is one best way to organize for production, and that way can be found through systematic, scientific inquiry (in this instance, systematic, scientific, *psychological inquiry*).
3. Production is maximized through specialization and division of labor.
4. People and organizations act in accordance with rational economic principles.

It is important to note that the Mayo team—like the I/O psychology groups—began its work trying to fit into the mold of classical organization theory thinking. The team phrased its questions in the language and concepts industry was accustomed to using, to see and explain problems such as: productivity in relationship to such factors as the amount of light, the rate of flow of materials, and alternative wage payment plans. The Mayo team succeeded in making significant breakthroughs in understanding only after it redefined the Hawthorne problems as social psychological problems—problems conceptualized in such terms as interpersonal relations in groups, group norms, control over one's own environment, and personal recognition. It was only after the Mayo team achieved this breakthrough that it became the "grandfather"—the direct precursor—of the field of organizational behavior and of the human relations perspective of organization theory. The Hawthorne studies laid the foundation for a set of assumptions that would be fully articulated and would displace the assumptions of classical organization theory 20 years later.

Despite their later start, the industrial social psychologists were years ahead of the industrial psychologists in understanding that behavior in organizations could not be understood nor controlled by viewing behavior solely as an organizational phenomenon or solely from an organizational vantage point. The organization is not the independent variable to be manipulated in order to change behavior (as a dependent variable)—even though organizations pay employees to help them achieve organizational goals. Instead, the organization must be seen as the context in which behavior occurs. It is both an independent and a dependent variable. The organization influences human behavior just as behavior shapes the organization. The interactions shape conceptualizations of jobs, human communication and interaction in work groups, the impacts of participation in decisions about one's own work, roles (in general), and the roles of leaders.

Between 1957 and 1960, the organizational behavior perspective literally exploded onto the organization scene. On April 9, 1957, Douglas M. McGregor delivered the Fifth Anniversary Convocation address to the School of Industrial Management at the Massachusetts Institute of Technology. He titled his address, "The Human Side of Enterprise." Three years later, McGregor expanded his talk into what has become one of the most influential books on organizational behavior and organization theory. In *The Human Side of Enterprise*, McGregor articulated how managerial assumptions about employees become self-fulfilling prophesies. He labeled his two sets of contrasting assumptions *Theory X* and *Theory Y*, but they are more than just theories. McGregor had articulated the basic assumptions of the organizational behavior perspective.

The organizational behavior perspective is the most optimistic of all perspectives of orgnization. Building from Douglas McGregor's Theory X and Theory Y assumptions, organizational behavior has assumed that under the right circumstances, people and organizations will grow and prosper together. The ultimate worth of people is an overarching value of the human relations movement—a worthy end in-and-of-itself—not simply a means or process for achieving a higher-order organizational end. Individuals and organizations are not necessarily antagonists. Managers can learn to unleash previously stifled energies and creativities. The beliefs, values, and tenets of organizational behavior are noble, uplifting, and exciting. They hold a promise for humankind, especially those who will spend their lifetime working in organizations.

As one would expect of a very optimistic and humanistic set of assumptions and values, they (and the strategies of organizational behavior) became strongly normative (prescriptive). For many organizational behavior practitioners of the 1960s, 1970s, and 1980s, the perspective's assumptions and methods became a cause. Hopefully, through the choice of articles and the introductions to each chapter, this volume communicates these optimistic tenets and values, and articulates the logical and emotional reasons why the organizational behavior perspective developed into a virtual movement. This is the true essence of *organizational behavior*.

## CHAPTER NOTE

1. Bolman and Deal (1991) use the labels, "Human Resources Frame" and "Structural Frame."

## REFERENCES

Allport, G. W. (1954). The historical background of modern social psychology. In, G. Lindzey (Ed.), *Handbook of social psychology: Volume II: Special fields and applications* (pp. 3–56). Reading, MA: Addison-Wesley Publishing Co.

Argyris, C. (1970). *Intervention theory and method.* Reading, MA: Addison-Wesley Publishing Co.

Bell, D. (1956). *Work and its discontents.* Boston: Beacon Press.

Bennis, W. G. (1976). *The unconscious conspiracy: Why leaders can't lead.* New York: AMACOM.

Berelson, B., & Steiner, G. A. (1964). *Human behavior: An inventory of scientific findings.* New York: Harcourt, Brace & World.

Blau, P. M., & Scott, W. R. (1962). *Formal organizations: A comparative approach.* San Francisco: Chandler Publishing.

Bolman L. G., & Deal, T. E. (1991). *Reframing organizations: Artistry, choice, and leadership.* San Francisco: Jossey-Bass.

Burns, T., & Stalker, G. M. (1961). *The management of innovation.* London, UK: Tavistock Publications.

Cohen, A. R., Finks, S. L., Gadon, H., & Willits, R. D. (1984). *Effective behavior in organizations* (3d ed.). Homewood, IL: Richard D. Irwin.

Dunham, R. B. (1984). *Organizational behavior.* Homewood, IL: Richard D. Irwin.

Gantt, H. L. (1908). Training workmen in habits of industry and cooperation. Paper presented to the American Society of Mechanical Engineers.

George, C. S., Jr. (1972). *The history of management thought* (2d ed.). Englewood Cliffs, NJ: Prentice-Hall, Inc.

Haire, M. (1954). Industrial social psychology. In, G. Lindzey (Ed.), *Handbook of social psychology: Volume II: Special fields and applications* (pp. 1104–1123). Reading, MA: Addison-Wesley Publishing Company.

Hampton, D. R., Summer, C. E., & Webber, R. A. (1987). *Organizational behavior and the practice of management* (5th ed.). Glenview, IL: Scott, Foresman and Company.

Hersey, P., & Blanchard, K. H. (1982). *Management of organizational behavior: Utilizing human resources* (4th ed.). Englewood Cliffs, NJ: Prentice-Hall.

Kast, F. E., & Rosenzweig, J. E. (1970). *Organization and management: A systems approach.* New York: McGraw-Hill.

Kotter, J. P. (1985). *Power and influence: Beyond formal authority.* New York: Free Press.

Kuhn, T. S. (1970). *The structure of scientific revolutions* (2d ed., enlarged). Chicago: University of Chicago Press.

Lewin, K. (1947). Frontiers in group dynamics: Concept, method and reality in social science: Social equilibrium and social change. *Human Relations, 1,* 5–41.

Lewin, K. (1948). *Resolving social conflicts.* New York: Harper.

Luthans, F. (1972). *Contemporary readings in organizational behavior.* New York: McGraw-Hill.

Mayo, G. E. (1933). *The human problems of an industrial civilization.* Boston, MA: Harvard Business School, Division of Research.

McGregor, D. M. (1957, April). The human side of enterprise. Address to the Fifth Anniversary Convocation of the School of Industrial Management, Massachusetts Institute of Technology. In, *Adventure in thought and action.* Cambridge, MA: M.I.T. School of Industrial Management, 1957. Reprinted in W. G. Bennis, E. H. Schein, & C. McGregor (eds.), (1966), *Leadership and motivation: Essays of Douglas McGregor* (pp. 3–20). Cambridge, MA: The M.I.T. Press.

McGregor, D. M. (1960). *The human side of enterprise.* New York: McGraw-Hill.

Mintzberg, H. (1979). *The structuring of organizations.* Englewood Cliffs, NJ: Prentice-Hall.

Münsterberg, H. (1913). *Psychology and industrial efficiency.* Boston: Houghton Mifflin Company.

Münsterberg, M. (1922). *Hugo Münsterberg, his life and work.* New York: D. Appleton and Company.

Organ, D. W., & Bateman, T. (1986). *Organizational behavior: An applied psychologial approach* (3d ed.). Plano, TX: Business Publications, Inc.

Pfeffer, J. (1981). *Power in organizations.* Boston: Pitman Publishing.

Pfeffer, J. (1992). *Managing with power: Politics and influence in organizations.* Boston: Harvard Business School Press.

Reitz, H. J. (1987). *Behavior in organizations* (3d ed.). Homewood, IL: Richard D. Irwin.

Roethlisberger, F. J., & Dixon, W. J. (1939). *Management and the worker.* Cambridge, MA: Harvard University Press.

Salancik, G. R., & Pfeffer, J. (1977). Who gets power—and how they hold on to it: A strategic-contingency model of power. *Organizational Dynamics, 5,* 2–21.

Sathe, V. (1985). *Culture and related corporate realities.* Homewood, IL: Richard D. Irwin.

Shafritz, J. M., & Ott, J. S. (1996). *Classics of organization theory* (4th ed.). Belmont, CA: Wadsworth.

Taylor, F. W. (1911). *The principles of scientific management.* New York: W. W. Norton.

Thompson, J. D. (1967). *Organizations in action.* New York: McGraw-Hill.

Weber, M. (1922). Bureaucracy. In H. Gerth & C. W. Mills (Eds.), *Max Weber: Essays in sociology.* Oxford, UK: Oxford University Press.

Wilson, J. A. (1951). *The culture of ancient Egypt.* Chicago: University of Chicago Press.

Wren, D. A. (1972). *The evolution of management thought.* New York: Ronald Press.

# A CHRONOLOGY OF ORGANIZATIONAL BEHAVIOR

**2100 B.C.**   Hammurabi, King of Babylon, establishes a written code of 282 laws which control every aspect of Babylonian life including individual behavior, interpersonal relations, and other societal matters. This may have been the first employee policy handbook.

**1750 B.C.**   Ancient Egyptians assign ten workers to each supervisor while building the pyramids. This may have been the earliest recorded use of the span of control concept.

**1491 B.C.**   During the exodus from Egypt, Jethro, the father-in-law of Moses, urges Moses to delegate authority over the tribes of Israel along hierarchical lines.

**525 B.C.**   Confucius writes that obedience to the organization (government) is the most "respectable goal of citizenship." This becomes the basic justification for authority systems.

**1200**   Medieval European guilds function as quality circles to ensure fine craftsmanship.

**1490**   John Calvin, Protestant religious reformer, promotes the merit system by promising a reward "of eternal life in His (God's) kingdom to the faithful who do God's work." The Puritan movement champions the concepts of time management, duty to work, and motivation theories; wasting time is considered the "deadliest of sins."

**1527**   Machiavelli's *The Prince* offers managers practical advice for developing authoritarian structures within organizations. His justification is that "all men are bad and ever ready to display their vicious nature."

**1651**   In his essay, *Leviathan,* Thomas Hobbes advocates strong centralized leadership as a means of bringing "order to the chaos created by man." He provides a justification for autocratic rule, thereby establishing the pattern for organizations through the nineteenth century.

**1690**   In his *Two Treatises of Government,* John Locke provides the philosophical framework for the justification of the U.S. Declaration of Independence. In effect, John Locke advocates participatory management when he argues that leadership is granted by the governed.

**1762**   Jean Jacques Rousseau in *The Social Contract* postulates that governments work best when they are chosen and controlled by the governed. This concept furthers the idea of participatory management.

**1776**   Adam Smith in *The Wealth of Nations* revolutionizes economic and organizational thought by suggesting the use of centralization of labor and equipment in factories, division of specialized labor, and management of specialization in factories.

1800    In Britain, the Roebuck and Garrett Company seeks to maintain organizational harmony by putting factories only in locations where workers are perceived to be "reliable, loyal, and controllable."

1811    The Luddites, workers in English textile mills, seek to destroy new textile machinery that is displacing them. This is an early example of management's need to plan for organizational change.

1813    In his "Address to the Superintendents of Manufactures," Robert Owens encourages managers to provide their *vital machines* (employees) with as much attention as they do their *inanimate machines*.

1832    In the first managerial textbooks, *The Carding and Spinning of Masters' Assistant* and *The Cotton Spinners' Manual*, James Montgomery promotes the control function of management: Managers must be "just and impartial, firm and decisive, and always alert to prevent rather than check employee faults."

1883    Frederick W. Taylor begins experiments in Midvale and Bethlehem Steel plants that eventually lead to his concepts of *scientific management*.

1902    Vilfredo Pareto becomes the "father" of the concept of *social systems*; his societal notions would later be applied by Elton Mayo and the human relationists in an organizational context.

1903    In Frederick W. Taylor's book, *Shop Management*, he explains the role of management in motivating workers to avoid "natural soldiering," the natural tendency of people to "take it easy."

1909    Hugo Münsterberg, considered the "father of organizational psychology," writes, "The Market and Psychology," in which he cautions managers to be concerned with "all the questions of the mind . . . like fatigue, monotony, interest, learning, work satisfaction, and rewards." He is the first to encourage government funded research in the area of industrial psychology.

1911    Frederick W. Taylor's book, *The Principles of Scientific Management*, investigates the influence of salary, mechanical design, and work layout on individual job performance to discover the "one best way" of accomplishing a given task.

       Walter D. Scott's series of articles, "The Psychology of Business," published in *System Magazine* are some of the first to apply principles of psychology to motivation and productivity in the workplace.

1912    Edward Cadbury, using his chocolate factories as a laboratory, pioneers the field of industrial psychology with his book, *Experiments in Industrial Organization*.

1913    Hugo Münsterberg's book, *Psychology and Industrial Efficiency*, addresses personnel selection, equipment design, product packaging, and other concerns in an attempt to match the "best man" with the "best work" in order to get the "best possible effect."

Lillian M. Gilbreth's "The Psychology of Management," published in *Industrial Engineering Magazine*, becomes one of the earliest contributions to the understanding of human behavior in the industrial setting.

**1924**  As a joint project, the National Research Council, Massachusetts Institute of Technology, and Harvard University begin their investigations of group behavior and worker sentiments at the Hawthorne works of the Western Electric Company in Chicago.

Elton Mayo explains in "The Basis of Industrial Psychology," published by the *Bulletin of the Taylor Society*, that short work breaks improve worker motivation and decrease employee turnover rates; this notion supports the importance of *social environment* in the workplace.

**1926**  Mary Parker Follett's chapter, "The Giving of Orders," is one of the very first calls for the use of a participatory leadership style, in which employees and employers cooperate to assess the situation and collaboratively decide what should be done.

**1933**  Elton Mayo makes the first significant call for the human relations movement in his Hawthorne studies interim report entitled, *The Human Problems of an Industrial Civilization*.

**1937**  The American Association for Applied Psychology is organized to study industrial and organizational psychology.

Walter C. Langer publishes his book, *Psychology and Human Living*, in which he provides the first significant discussion of human needs, repression, and integration of personality, and their application to the workplace.

**1938**  *Functions of the Executive*, by Chester I. Barnard, suggests that the purpose of a manager is to balance organizational and workers' needs. This encourages and foreshadows the postwar revolution in thinking about organizational behavior.

**1939**  Kurt Lewin, Ronald Lippett, and Ralph K. White's article, "Patterns of Aggressive Behavior in Experimentally Created Social Climates," published in the *Journal of Social Psychology*, is the first empirical study of the effects of various leadership styles. Their work becomes the basis of the popularity of participative management techniques.

F. J. Roethlisberger and W. J. Dickson publish *Management and the Worker*, the definitive account of the Hawthorne studies.

**1940**  Robert K. Merton's *Social Forces* article, "Bureaucratic Structure and Personality," explains how bureaucratic structures exert pressures on people to conform to patterns of obligations, and eventually cause people to adhere to rules as a matter of blind conformance.

**1942**  Carl Rogers's *Counseling and Psychotherapy* offers human relations training as a method to overcome communication barriers and enhance interpersonal skills. These techniques lead to "control through leadership rather than force."

**1943**  Abraham Maslow's *needs hierarchy* first appears in his *Psychological Review* article, "A Theory of Human Motivation."

**1945**  Kurt Lewin forms the Research Center for Group Dynamics at MIT to perform experiments in group behavior. In 1948, Lewin's research center moves to the University of Michigan and becomes a branch of the Institute for Social Research.

**1946**  Rensis Likert develops the Institute for Social Research at the University of Michigan to conduct studies in the social sciences.

**1947**  The National Training Laboratory for Group Development, the predecessor to the National Training Laboratory Institute for Applied Behavioral Science, is established in Bethel, Maine, to conduct experimentation and training in group behavior.

**1948**  In their *Human Relations* article, "Overcoming Resistance to Change," Lester Coch and John R. P. French, Jr., note that employees resist change less when the need for it is effectively communicated to them and when the workers are involved in planning the changes.

Kenneth D. Benne and Paul Sheats's article, "Functional Role of Group Members," published in *Journal of Social Issues*, identifies three group role categories: *group task; group building and maintenance;* and *nonparticipatory.* These become the basis for future leadership research and training programs.

**1949**  In his *Public Administration Review* article, "Power and Administration," Norton E. Long finds that power is the lifeblood of administration, and that managers have to do more than simply apply the scientific method to problems—they have to attain, maintain, and increase their power, or risk failing in their mission.

The term *behavioral sciences* is first put into use by the Ford Foundation to describe its fundings for interdisciplinary research in the social sciences; and the term is later adopted by a group of University of Chicago scientists seeking such funding.

**1950**  Ralph M. Stogdill in his *Psychological Bulletin* article, "Leadership, Membership, and Organization," identifies the importance of the leader's role in influencing group efforts toward goal setting and goal achievement. His ideas become the basis for modern leadership research.

**1951**  Alex Bavelas and Dermot Barrett's article, "An Experimental Approach to Organizational Communication," appearing in *Personnel*, recognizes that the effectiveness of an organization is based on the availability of information and that communication is "the basic process out of which all other functions derive."

Eric. L. Trist and K. W. Bamforth's pioneering sociotechnical systems study of British miners, "Some Social and Psychological Consequences of the Longwall Method of Coal-getting," demonstrates that the introduction of new structural and technological systems can destroy important social systems.

"Effects of Group Pressure upon the Modification and Distortion of Judgments," by Solomon Asch, describes his experiments showing that a sizable minority of subjects alter their judgment to match that of the majority, even when the facts clearly demonstrate the majority is wrong.

Kurt Lewin proposes a general model of change consisting of three phases, *unfreezing, change,* and *refreezing,* in his *Field Theory in Social Science.* This model becomes the conceptual frame for organization development.

**1953**   Dorwin Cartwright's address to the Society for the Psychological Study of Social Issues, titled "Power: A Neglected Variable in Social Psychology," identifies leadership and social roles, public opinion, rumor, propaganda, prejudice, attitude change, morale, communications, race relations, and conflicts of value, as leading social issues that cannot be understood except through the concept of power.

**1954**   *The Practice of Management,* written by Peter F. Drucker, outlines his famous *management by objectives* (MBO) approach; a way that management might give "full scope to individual strength and responsibility, and at the same time give direction of vision and effort, establish teamwork, and harmonize the goals of the individual."

Bernard M. Bass's *Psychological Bulletin* article, "The Leaderless Group Discussion," identifies a leadership training program in which a leader is not selected but rather emerges from the group's task.

In their *American Sociological Review* article, "Some Findings Relevant to the Great Man Theory of Leadership," Edgar F. Borgatta, Robert F. Bales, and Authur S. Couch promote the concept of leader assessment centers as a way to recognize individual leadership ability.

**1955**   Arthur H. Brayfield and Walter H. Crockett's *Psychological Bulletin* article, "Employee Attitudes and Employee Performance," claims that there is no direct influence of job satisfaction on worker performance; in other words, a happy worker is not necessarily a better worker.

*The Organization Man* by William H. Whyte, Jr., describes empirical findings about individuals who accept organizational values and find harmony in conforming to all policies.

**1957**   Chris Argyris asserts in his first major book, *Personality and Organization,* that there is an inherent conflict between the personality of a mature adult and the needs of modern organizations.

Philip Selznick in *Leadership in Administration* anticipates many of the 1980s notions of *transformational leadership* when he asserts that the function of an institutional leader is to help shape the environment in which the institution operates and to define new institutional directions through recruitment, training, and bargaining.

The first organization development (OD) program is designed by Herbert Shepard and Robert Blake, and is implemented at (Esso) Standard Oil Company.

On April 9, Douglas M. McGregor delivers the Fifth Anniversary Convocation address to the School of Industrial Management at the Massachusetts Institute of Technology. His address, "The Human Side of Enterprise," was expanded into a book by the same title in 1960.

Leon Festinger's *A Theory of Cognitive Dissonance* suggests that dissonance is a motivator of human behavior.

Alvin W. Gouldner's *Administrative Science Quarterly* study, "Cosmopolitans and Locals: Toward an Analysis of Latent Social Roles," finds that people with different role orientations differ in their degree of influenceability, level of participation in the organization, willingness to accept organizational rules, and informal relations at work.

**1958**   Robert Tannenbaum and Warren H. Schmidt's *Harvard Business Review* article, "How to Choose a Leadership Pattern," describes "democratic management" and devises a leadership continuum ranging from authoritarian to democratic.

*Organizations* by James G. March and Herbert Simon provides an overview of the behavioral sciences' influence in organization theory.

Leon Festinger, the father of cognitive dissonance theory, writes "The Motivating Effect of Cognitive Dissonance," which becomes the theoretical foundation for the "inequity theories of motivation."

**1959**   John R. P. French and Bertram Raven identify five bases of power (expert, referent, reward, legitimate, and coercive) in their article, "The Bases of Social Power." They argue that managers should not rely on coercive and expert power bases, since they are least effective.

Herzberg, Mausner, and Snyderman's *The Motivation to Work* puts forth the motivation-hygiene theory of worker motivation.

In *Modern Organizational Theory*, Cyert and March prepare a chapter, "A Behavioral Theory of Organizational Objectives," which postulates that power and politics impact on the formation of organizational goals. Their work is an early precursor of the power and politics school.

**1960**   Herbert Kaufman's *The Forest Ranger* describes how employee conformity can be increased through organizational and professional socialization efforts.

Donald F. Roy's *Human Organization* study, "Banana Time: Job Satisfaction and Informal Interaction," finds that workers in monotonous jobs survive psychologically through informal interaction; they keep from "going nuts" by talking and fooling around in a nonstop, highly stylized, and ritualistic manner.

Douglas M. McGregor's book, *The Human Side of Enterprise*, articulates the basic assumptions of the organizational behavior perspective and becomes perhaps the single most influential work in organizational behavior and organizational theory.

**1961**   Burns and Stalker's *The Management of Innovation* advocates a contingency model of leadership when it articulates the need for different types of management systems (organic and mechanistic) under differing circumstances.

Rensis Likert's *New Patterns of Management* offers an empirically based defense of participatory management and organization development techniques.

**1962**   In his *Administrative Science Quarterly* article, "Control In Organizations: Individual Adjustment and Organizational Performance," Arnold S. Tannenbaum explains that distributing control more broadly within the organization helps to encourage involvement and adherence to the group norms by its members.

David Mechanic's *Administrative Science Quarterly* article, "Sources of Power of Lower Participants in Complex Organizations," explores factors that account for the power of lower-level participants in organizations over those above them.

Robert L. Kahn and Daniel Katz report their findings on the supervisor's role, the closeness of supervision, the quality of supportiveness, and the amount of group cohesiveness on the productivity and level of morale of organizational groups, in "Leadership Practices in Relation to Productivity and Morale."

In "The Concept of Power and the Concept of Man," Mason Haire traces the change in the ultimate sources of organizational authority from the state to organizational ownership, and forecasts an eventual shift to the authority of the work group.

Robert Prethus's work, *The Organizational Society*, presents his threefold classification of patterns of organizational accommodations: *upward-mobiles*, those who accept goals and values of the organization as their own; *indifferents*, those who reject organizational values and seek personal satisfaction off the job; and *ambivalents*, those unable to cope with organizational demands but who still desire its rewards.

Blau and Scott write *Formal Organizations: A Comparative Approach*, in which they argue that all organizations have both an informal and formal structure, and that one cannot understand formal structure without first understanding the informal workings of an organization.

**1964**  Considered the father of Transactional Analysis (TA), Eric Berne in his book, *Games People Play: The Psychology of Human Relationships*, identifies three *ego states*: the *parent*, the *adult*, and the *child*; he further suggests that successful managers should strive for adult-adult relationships.

Robert Blake, Herb Shepard, and Jane S. Mouton, in *Managing Intergroup Conflict in Industry*, assert that the behavior of two members of an organization in relation to each other is determined by three factors: the requirements of formal role, their backgrounds of training and experience, and the role they feel themselves to be in as representatives of particular groups in the organization.

*The Management Grid: Key Orientations for Achieving Production Through People*, by Robert Blake and Jane Mouton, is a diagnostic device for leadership development programs which provides a *grid* of leadership style possibilities based on managerial assumptions about people and production.

**1965**  Robert L. Kahn's *Organizational Stress* is the first major study of the mental health consequences of organizational role conflict and ambiguity.

James G. March prepares *Handbook of Organizations*, a series of essays which attempts to consolidate all scientific knowledge about organizations and organizational behavior.

**1966**  *Think Magazine* publishes David C. McClelland's article, "That Urge to Achieve," in which he identifies two groups of people: the majority group, who aren't concerned about achieving, and the minority group, who are challenged by the opportunity to achieve. This notion becomes a premise for future motivation studies.

*The Social Psychology of Organizations* by Daniel Katz and Robert L. Kahn seeks to unify the findings of behavioral science on organizational behavior through open systems theory.

Fred Fiedler, in "The Contingency Model: A Theory of Leadership Effectiveness," argues that organizations should not try to change leaders to fit them, but instead should change their situations to mesh with the style of their leaders.

In "Applying Behavioral Sciences to Planned Organizational Change," a chapter from his book, *Changing Organizations*, Warren Bennis describes planned change as a link between theory and practice and as a deliberate and collaborative process involving change agents and client-systems who are brought together to solve a problem.

**1967**  The *Personnel Administration* article, "Organizations of the Future," by Warren Bennis states that bureaucracy will disappear due to rapid and unexpected change, unprecedented growth in organizational size, increasing complexity in modern technology, and philosophical changes in managerial controls and behaviors.

In their *Personnel Administration* article, "Grid Organization Development," Robert A. Blake and Jane S. Mouton explain that organizational goals determine managers' actions; they offer an innovative, systematic approach to "organizational development."

Fred E. Fiedler publishes his work, A *Theory of Leadership Effectiveness*, which proposes that leadership style must fit the circumstances; there is no one best way to perform leadership tasks.

Norman Maier in his *Psychological Review* article, "Assets and Liabilities in Group Problem-Solving," explains that the benefits of group versus individual problem-solving depends on the "nature of the problem, the goals to be achieved, and the skill of the discussion leader."

Anthony Downs's *Inside Bureaucracy* seeks to develop laws and propositions that would aid in predicting the behavior of bureaus and bureaucrats.

William G. Scott's *Organization Theory: A Behavioral Analysis for Management* suggests that an "individual's opportunity for self-realization at work" can be actualized by applying "industrial humanism" concepts such as reducing authoritarian tendencies in organizations, encouraging participatory decision making on all levels, and integrating individual and corporate goals.

Anthony Jay's *Management and Machiavelli* applies Machiavelli's political principles (from *The Prince*) to modern organizational management.

1968   In *Group Dynamics*, Dorwin Cartwright and Alvin Zander propose that the systematic study of group dynamics would advance knowledge of the nature of groups; how they are organized; and relationships among individuals, other groups, and larger institutions.

John P. Campbell and M. D. Dunnette's "Effectiveness of T-Group Experiences in Managerial Training and Development," appearing in *Psychological Bulletin*, provides a critical review of T-Group literature. They conclude that "an individual's positive feelings about his T-Group experiences" cannot be scientifically measured, nor should they be based entirely on "existential grounds."

Frederick Herzberg's *Harvard Business Review* article, "One More Time, How Do You Motivate Employees?" catapults *motivators* or *satisfiens* and *hygiene factors* into the forefront of organizational motivaton theory.

1969   In Fred E. Fiedler's *Psychology Today* article, "Style or Circumstance: The Leadership Enigma," three elements of effective leadership are identified: power of the leader; the task at hand; and the leader-member relationships. He determines that jobs should be designed to fit individual leadership styles rather than the reverse.

Paul Hersey and Kenneth R. Blanchard's "Life Cycle Theory of Leadership," appearing in *Training and Development Journal*, asserts that the appropriate leadership style for a given situation depends upon the employee's education and experience levels, achievement motivation, and willingness to accept responsibility by the subordinates.

Wendell French, in his *California Management Review* article, "Organization Development: Objectives, Assumptions, and Strategies," defines organization development as a total system of planned change.

Harold M. F. Rush's *Behavioral Science: Concepts and Management Application* challenges managers to better understand the behavioral sciences so they can more effectively motivate the "new breed of employee," who is better educated, more politically, socially, and economically astute, and more difficult to control.

Richard E. Walton and John M. Dutton's *Administrative Science Quarterly* article, "The Management of Interdepartmental Conflict: A Model and Review," provides a diagnostic model for managers to determine what needs changing in order to prevent or terminate interdepartmental conflicts.

**1970** In his book, *Organizational Psychology*, Edgar H. Schein distinguishes between formal and informal groups within organizations and indicates that effective group work is a result of considering the "characteristics of the members and assessing the likelihood of their being able to work with one another and serve one another's needs."

In "Expectancy Theory," John P. Campbell, Marvin D. Dunnette, Edward E. Lawler III, and Karl E. Weick, Jr., articulate the *expectancy theories of motivation*. People are motivated by calculating how much they want something, how much of it they think they will get, how likely it is their actions will cause them to get it, and how much others in similar circumstances have received.

Chris Argyris writes *Intervention Theory and Methods*, which becomes one of the most widely cited and enduring works on organizational consulting for change that is written from the organizational behavior/organization development perspective.

**1971** Rensis Likert's *Michigan Business Review* article, "Human Organizational Measurements: Key to Financial Success," emphasizes that assessing human elements of an organization can identify organizational problems before they occur; he argues that implementing human organizational measurements can help ensure an organization's long-term success.

B. F. Skinner, in *Beyond Freedom and Dignity*, demands a change in the contemporary views of people and how they are motivated in an organization; his alternative includes using *behavior modification* strategies by applying operant conditioning principles to improve employee motivation.

In their *Journal of Applied Psychology* article, "Employee Reactions to Job Characteristics," J. Richard Hackman and Edward E. Lawler III identify four core job dimensions, variety, autonomy, task identity, and feedback, which, they claim, relate to job satisfaction, motivation, quality of work, and decreased absenteeism.

Irving Janis's "Groupthink," first published in *Psychology Today*, proposes that group cohesion can lead to the deterioration of effective group decision-making efforts.

**1974** Robert J. House and Terrance R. Mitchell's *Journal of Contemporary Business* article, "Path-Goal Theory of Leadership," offers path-goal theory as a useful tool for explaining the effectiveness of certain leadership styles in given situations.

Victor H. Vroom's *Organizational Dynamics* article, "A New Look at Managerial Decision-Making," develops a useful model whereby leaders can perform a diagnosis of a situation to determine which leadership style is most appropriate.

Steven Kerr's *Academy of Management Journal* article, "On the Folly of Rewarding A, While Hoping for B," substantiates that many organizational reward systems are "fouled up"—they pay off for behaviors other than those they are seeking.

**1975** *Behavior in Organizations*, by Lyman Porter, Edward Lawler III, and Richard Hackman, focuses on the interaction between individuals and work organizations. It examines how individual-organizational relationships emerge and grow, including how groups can exert influence on individuals in organizations and how such social influences relate to work effectiveness.

**1976** Douglas W. Bray's "The Assessment Center Method," part of the *Training and Development Handbook*, promotes the idea of observing individual behaviors in simulated job-related situations (assessment centers) for evaluative purposes.

Michael Maccoby psychoanalytically interviews 250 corporate managers and discovers *The Gamesman*, a manager whose main interest lies in "competitive activity where he can prove himself a winner."

In "Moral Stakes: Where Have All the Leaders Gone?" Warren Bennis coins the phrase *social architects* to describe what he considers to be the most important roles of organizational leaders: understanding the organizational culture, having a sense of vision, and encouraging people to be innovative.

**1977** The *American Psychologist* article, "Job Satisfaction Reconsidered," by Walter R. Nord explains that a revision of accepted economic and political ideologies is necessary if distribution of power in organizations is to be altered.

Gerald Salancik and Jeffrey Pfeffer's *Organizational Dynamics* article, "Who Gets Power—And How They Hold on to It: A Strategic-contingency Model of Power," views the power by subunits as an important means by which organizations align themselves with their critical needs; thus, suppression of the use of power reduces organizational adaptability.

John P. Kotter's *Harvard Business Review* article, "Power, Dependence, and Effective Management," describes how successful managers build their power by creating a sense of obligation in others, creating images, fostering unconscious identification with these images, and feeding people's beliefs that they are dependent upon the images.

**1978** Daniel Katz and Robert L. Kahn publish *The Social Psychology of Organizations*, in which they coin the term *open system approach*. They advocate creating organizations that are open to change.

Edwin A. Locke's article, "The Ubiquity of the Technique of Goal Setting in Theories of and Approaches to Employee Motivation," argues that goals motivate. His review of the Hawthorne study data, for example, demonstrates that workers are more responsive to the goals-based financial incentives than to the widely reported social influences.

William G. Ouchi and Alfred M. Jaeger popularize a third *ideal type organization* in their *Academy of Management Review* article, "Type Z Organization: Stability in the Midst of Mobility." The three types include: Type A (American); Type J (Japanese); and Type Z (one that combines the best of both types). This article becomes the first of many dealing with Japanese management strategies

Thomas J. Peter's *Organizational Dynamics* article, "Symbols, Patterns, and Settings: An Optimistic Case for Getting Things Done," is the first major analysis of symbolic management in organizations to gain significant attention in the mainstream literature of organization theory.

Herbert C. Kelman and Donald P. Warwick examine stages in organizational interventions that are likely to surface important ethical issues, in *The Ethics of Social Intervention*.

**1980** J. Richard Hackman and Greg R. Oldham attempt to answer the oft-asked question, "Which is better, individuals or groups?" Some tasks should be done by individuals and some by groups. In the latter case, though, tasks should be redesigned for groups and groups for the nature of the tasks; in *Work Redesign*.

**1981** *Power in Organizations* by Jeffrey Pfeffer proposes that intergroup conflicts are inevitable in organizations because of inherent differences between perspectives and ongoing competition for scarce organizational resources; coalitions are the means through which people muster power for political contests.

In "'Democracy' as Hierarchy and Alienation," Frederick Thayer proposes that employee alienation can be ended by eradicating hierarchy, and alienation cannot be eradicated so long as hierarchy remains.

**1982** Barry Staw's chapter, "Motivation in Organizations: Toward Synthesis and Redirection," echoes wide disenchantment with the usefulness of existing theories of motivation and attempts to broaden the conceptualization of motivation through viewing individuals as actors who change the "rules" of traditional motivation theories.

**1983**   Henry Mintzberg, in *Power in and Around Organizations*, proposes that "everyone exhibits a lust for power" and the dynamic of the organization is based on the struggle between various *influencers* to control the organization. As a result, he molds the power and politics school of organizational theory into an integrative theory of management policy.

"In Equity Theory of Predictions of Behavior in Organizations," Richard T. Mowday argues that the presence of inequity motivates individuals to change the situation through behavioral or cognitive means to return to a condition of equity.

Daniel C. Feldman and Hugh J. Arnold's *Managing Individual and Group Behavior in Organizations* concludes that individual motivation is based on the sum of intrinsic and extrinsic motivation sources and not merely upon a manager's ability to motivate.

In *The Change Masters*, Rosabeth Moss Kanter defines *change masters* as architects of organizational change; they are the right people in the right places at the right time.

**1984**   Thomas J. Sergiovanni's "Leadership as Cultural Expression," proposes that organizational leadership is a cultural artifact: The shape and style of leadership results from the unique mixture of organizational culture and the *density* of leadership competence.

Tichy and Ulrich's *Sloan Management Review* article, "The Leadership Challenge—A Call for the Transformational Leader," describes the functions of a transformational leader as those of a cheerleader and a belief model during radical organizational change.

Caren Siehl and Joanne Martin report the findings of the first major quantitative and qualitative empirical study of organizational culture in their "The Role of Symbolic Management: How Can Managers Effectively Transmit Organizational Culture?"

In *Goal Setting: A Motivational Technique That Works*, Edwin A. Locke and Gary P. Latham encourage managers to set goals based on their findings that an individual worker's performance increases as goal difficulty increases (assuming the person is willing and has the ability to do the work).

**1985**   Edgar Schein writes his comprehensive and integrative statement of the organizational culture school in *Organizational Culture and Leadership*.

In a chapter from *The Politics of Management*, Douglas Yates, Jr., describes the management of political conflict as the process of managing strategic conflict between actors who possess different forms of resources, and reminds managers that using power is costly: It depletes one's reservoir of credible power.

Warren Bennis and Burt Nanus reemphasize the importance of vision, power, and context for establishing leadership in organizations, in *Leaders: The Strategies for Taking Charge*.

**1986**   S. G. Harris and R. I. Sutton's *Academy of Management Journal* article, "Functions of Parting Ceremonies in Dying Organizations," focuses on the particular importance of symbolic leadership during periods of organizational decline.

In *The Transformational Leader*, Noel Tichy and Mary Anne Devanna propose a Lewin-type "three-act framework" for transformational leadership—the "leadership of change, innovation, and entrepreneurship."

**1987**   Research findings by Edward Lawler and Susan Morhrman suggest that in the long term, quality cricles have difficulty coexisting with traditional management approaches. Quality circles require basic management changes, or they will not be effective, and alternative strategies should be used; in the *Organizational Dynamics* piece, "Quality Circles: After the Honeymoon."

Clayton P. Alderfer's analysis, "An Intergroup Perspective on Group Dynamics," explores the influence on intergroup analysis of the persistently problematic relationship between individuals and collective social processes. He asserts that intergroup theory provides interpretations for individual, interpersonal, group, intergroup, and organizational relations.

**1988**   Ralph Kilmann and Teresa Joyce Covin publish the first comprehensive collection of research studies and practitioner papers targeting the implementation of transformational change, in *Corporate Transformation*.

In *The Leadership Factor*, John Kotter expands upon his prior studies of power and leadership in organizations, to explain why organizations often do not have adequate leadership capacity, and proposes steps to rectify the problems.

**1989**   In "People as Sculptors versus Sculpture: The Roles of Personality and Personal Control in Organizations," Nancy E. Bell and Barry M. Staw provide evidence that people may not be as malleable or open to organizational influence as they have been depicted, particularly in the literature on organizational socialization. People may shape their work environments as much or more than they are shaped by their environments.

**1990**   Warren Bennis concludes that we have never needed leaders more but held them in lower regard. Circumstances and the American people conspire against them without meaning to. *Why Leaders Can't Lead: The Unconscious Conspiracy Continues* predicts that change for the better is possible, but the outlook for leadership is not optimistic.

Jack Orsburn, Linda Moran, Ed Musselwhite, and John Zenger write their extensive analysis of self-directed work teams—highly trained groups of employees that are fully responsible for turning out a well-defined segment of finished work; in *Self-Directed Work Teams: The New American Challenge*.

Peter Senge's book, *The Fifth Discipline: The Art and Practice of the Learning Organization*, argues that we should—and can—build organizations where people continually expand their capacity to create, where collective aspiration is set free, and where people are continually learning how to learn together.

**1991**    Marvin R. Weisbord's book, *Productive Workplaces*, examines the importance of effective teamwork in a fast-changing world. Teams get much "lip service," but the term rivals "quality" as a business cliché. Managers must consciously strive to transform individuals and groups into effective teams.

**1992**    In *Changing the Essence*, Richard Beckhard and Wendy Pritchard identify the leadership behaviors necessary for initiating and managing fundamental change in organizations. They also attempt to find ways to manage the tension between dealing with short-term pressures and addressing the long-term strategic management of organizations' identities and destinies.

In "The Empowerment of Service Workers: What, Why, How, and When," David Bowen and Edward Lawler III assess the key business characteristics that determine whether empowerment of service workers is beneficial. Managers need to be certain that there is a good fit between organizational needs and their approach before deciding to empower front-line service employees.

In the second edition of *Leadership and Organizational Culture*, Edgar H. Schein shows how leaders create, embed, develop, and sometimes deliberately attempt to change cultural assumptions during different phases of an organization's development and maturation.

Margaret J. Wheatley's book, *Leadership and the New Science*, proposes that managers need to look to the "new sciences" of quantum physics, self-ordering systems, and chaos theory to find clues about how to improve their leadership behavior in organizations.

**1993**    "Intergroup Conflict," a chapter in *Cultural Diversity in Organizations*, by Taylor Cox, Jr., examines the potential benefits and the difficulties that may accrue to an organization from cultural diversity. Cox identifies various sources of conflict among culture identity groups and how intergroup conflict is manifested in organizations. He suggests ways in which intergroup conflict can be minimized.

# CHAPTER I

# *Motivation*

For hundreds of years, the motivation of workers has been the proverbial "pot of gold to be found at the end of the rainbow" for management practitioners and students of organizational behavior. If employees could be motivated to produce just slightly more, the economic rewards to individual organizations and to societies would be immense. Although there always has been consensus about the need for motivated employees, the same cannot be said for beliefs about how to induce higher levels of motivation. Not only have prevailing views (or theories) of motivation changed radically over the course of organizational history, but incompatible theories usually have competed with each other at the same points in time. Some theories of motivation have been developed from empirical research, but most have not. Some theories assume that employees act rationally: Managers simply need to manipulate rewards and punishments rationally, fairly, and consistently. Other theories start from the position that managerial assumptions about employees—which undergird such systems of rewards and punishments—actually stifle employee motivation.

Even today, widely divergent views remain about the essence of motivation in organizations. This chapter attempts to sort, organize, and summarize some of the more important theories that have been proposed over the years. As in all chapters of this book, the readings are organized chronologically. For purposes of perspective, the chapter starts its analysis in the 1760s, at the beginning of the Industrial Revolution.

## MOTIVATION THEORY PRIOR TO THE HAWTHORNE STUDIES

Even in the early years of the Industrial Revolution (beginning about 1760), *employee discipline* was one of the most vexing problems confronting managers in the factory system of mass production. Motivating employees and strategic use of negative sanctions were integral tactics for maintaining production and discipline. Prior to the Industrial Revolution, most workers worked under craft traditions or were agrarains and had some degree of independence (Wren, 1972, Chapter 3). But, the new style factories needed workers who fit into the factory systems' production concept which was driven by the principle of the *division of labor* (Smith 1776). Workers had to produce on a schedule not of their own choosing. Expensive machines had to be kept busy. Production shifted from labor-intensive to capital-intensive; and society's basic concept of humans at work changed with this shifting economic base (Haire, 1962). Although some early industrialists reportedly threw periodic feasts in attempts to build company loyalty, reduce absenteeism, and thereby keep production high, the backbone of motivational strategy was the incentive piece-rate system of compensation. Workers were paid for production output rather than for hours at work.

The twentieth-century scientific management movement of Frederick Winslow Taylor, Lillian and Frank Gilbreth, Henry Gantt, and others followed naturally from the piece-rate payment system ethic of the industrial revolution/factory system of production (see Shafritz & Ott, 1996, Chapter 1). Under scientific management principles, motivational methods were rooted in the concept of workers as *rational economic men*. People work for money: Tie compensation to production, and employees produce more (Gantt, 1910). Deal only with individual employees, and try to prevent the formation of groups because they restrict output and lead to unions. Beyond restricting output, Taylor saw productivity limited primarily by workers' ignorance of how to maximize production. To Taylor, scientific study of production processes (what he called *scientific management*) was the answer. It would provide for standardization, for the improvement of practices, and for techniques that would reduce worker fatigue. With better procedures and less fatigue, employee income and company profits would increase (Taylor, 1911).

## THE HAWTHORNE STUDIES

In 1924, a team of researchers under the aegis of the National Academy of Sciences' National Research Council went to the Hawthorne plant of the Western Electric Company, near Chicago, to study ways for improving productivity. The research team began its work from the perspective—the assumptions, precepts, and principles—of scientific management. Scientific investigative procedures (including control groups) were used to find and identify environmental changes which would increase worker productivity. Their investigations focused on room temperature, humidity, and illumination levels (Pennock, 1930). Interestingly, illumination was included as an experimental variable because scientific management studies by Frederick Winslow Taylor (1911) fifteen years earlier had identified illumination as an easily controlled variable for influencing productivity. The early Hawthorne studies caused confusion. Worker output continued to increase even as illumination decreased.

By 1927, the results were so snarled that Western Electric and the National Research Council were ready to abandon the entire endeavor. In that year, George Pennock, Western Electric's superintendent of inspection, heard Harvard professor Elton Mayo speak at a meeting and invited him to take a team to Hawthorne. Team members eventually included Fritz Roethlisberger, George Homans, and T. N. Whitehead. The results are legendary. However, it was not until the Mayo-led Hawthorne team discarded its rational economic man/scientific management assumptions about people at work that the groundwork was laid for what we have been calling in this volume the field of *organizational behavior*—a perspective with its own very different set of assumptions. (See the *Introduction* to this book.) The long-held assumptions of Industrial/Organizational psychology, that people could and should be fit to organizations, had been challenged. The process had begun that would render obsolete scientific management's assumptions about people and how to motivate them.

The Hawthorne experiments were the emotional and intellectual wellspring of the organizational behavior perspective and modern theories of motivation. The Hawthorne experiments showed that complex, interactional variables make the difference in motivating people—things like attention paid to workers as individuals, workers' control over their own work, differences between individuals' needs, management willingness to listen, group norms, and direct feedback.

Fritz J. Roethlisberger, of the Harvard Business School, is the best known chronicler of the Hawthorne studies. Roethlisberger, with William J. Dickson of the Western Electric Company, wrote the most comprehensive account of the Hawthorne studies, *Management and the Worker* (1939). Roethlisberger's chapter, which is reprinted here, "The Hawthorne Experiments," is from his shorter 1941 book, *Management and Morale*.

## NEED THEORIES OF MOTIVATION

All discussions of *need theories of motivation* start with Abraham Maslow. His *hierarchy of needs* stands alongside the Hawthorne experiments and Douglas McGregor's *Theory* X and *Theory* Y as *the* departure points for studying motivation in organizations. An overview of Maslow's basic theory of needs is presented here from his 1943 *Psychological Review* article, "A Theory of Human Motivation." Maslow's theoretical premises can be summarized in a few phrases:

- All humans have needs which underlie their motivational structure;
- As lower levels of needs are satisfied, they no longer "drive" behavior;
- Satisfied needs are not motivators; and
- As lower level needs of workers become satisfied, higher order needs take over as the motivating forces.

Maslow's theory has been attacked frequently. Few empirical studies have supported it, and it oversimplifies the complex structure of human needs and motivations (for example, see Wahba & Bridwell, 1973). Several modified needs hierarchies have been proposed over the years which reportedly are better able to withstand empirical testing (for example, Alderfer, 1969). But, despite the criticisms and the continuing advances across the spectrum of applied behavioral sciences, Abraham Maslow's theory continues to occupy a most honored and prominent place in organizational behavior and management textbooks.

## THEORY X AND THEORY Y

Douglas McGregor's *The Human Side of Enterprise* is about much more than the motivation of people at work. In its totality, it is a cogent articulation of the basic assumptions of the organizational behavior perspective. Theory X and Theory Y are contrasting basic managerial assumptions about employees which, in McGregor's words, become self-fulfilling prophesies. Managerial assumptions *cause* employee behavior. Theory X and Theory Y are ways of seeing and thinking about people which, in turn, affect their behavior. Thus, "The Human Side of Enterprise" (1957b), which is reprinted in this chapter, is a landmark theory of motivation.

Theory X assumptions represent a restatement of the tenets of the scientific management movement. For example, human beings inherently dislike work and will avoid it if possible. Most people must be coerced, controlled, directed, or threatened with punishment to get them to work toward the achievement of organizational objectives; and, humans prefer to be directed, to avoid responsibility, and will seek security above all else. These assumptions serve as polar opposites to McGregor's Theory Y.

Theory Y assumptions postulate, for example: People do not inherently dislike work; work can be a source of satisfaction. People will exercise self-direction and self-control if they are committed to organizational objectives. People are willing to seek and to accept responsibility; avoidance of responsibility is not natural, it is a consequence of experiences. The intellectual potential of most humans is only partially utilized at work.

## COGNITIVE DISSONANCE AND INEQUITY THEORIES OF MOTIVATION

When two or more people or things around a person are in a state of disharmony, imbalance, or incongruity, that imbalance causes *dissonance* (or discomfort). According to *cognitive dissonance theory*, people will act—*will do something*—to reduce or eliminate dissonance. For example, I like two people, "A" and "B," but "A" does not like "B." An imbalance exists which causes dissonance, and I will act to eliminate it. The theory of cognitive dissonance cannot predict what I will do, but it says that I will be motivated to do something. I might try to change "A's" feelings toward "B"; or I might change my feelings about either "A" or "B" and then sever my relationship with the out-of-favor person. Similarly, if I believe that wearing a seat belt will not save my life in the event of a car accident, but I fasten my seat belt anyway because state law says I must, dissonance is created by the incongruity between my belief and my behavior. Cognitive dissonance theory predicts that I will be motivated to reduce or eliminate the dissonance. I might stop wearing a seat belt (for example, by convincing myself that the probability of getting caught violating the law is low or the legal penalty is too minimal to worry about) or, as the authors of the state law hope, I could allow my belief to be altered. If my belief does change, I probably will continue to "buckle up" even if the seat belt law is repealed some day.

Cognitive dissonance theory has many practical managerial applications for motivating employees. For example, management can require workers to do certain things in the hope that attitudes or beliefs will follow—just as in the seat belt example. On the other hand, management can attempt to change peoples' attitudes or beliefs (Zimbardo & Ebbesen, 1970) in hope that the resulting cognitive dissonance will motivate a behavior change. In contrast, under cognitive dissonance theories, motivation is *engineered* by intentionally creating dissonance and then not allowing the desired state to change (in the examples used here, beliefs or behavior).

Cognitive dissonance provides the theoretical basis for what are known as *equity theories of motivation*. Equity theories postulate that workers are motivated to act (for example, to produce more or less) by their perceptions of inequities in the environment (such as between *their* levels of work and compensation, and *others'* levels of work and compensation) (Mowday, 1983, reprinted as the last reading in this chapter). The theory of cognitive dissonance assumes that a worker performing the same work as another but being paid significantly less will do something to relieve this dissonance. Among the worker's options are asking for a raise, restricting output, or seeking another job. The 1958 article, "The Motivating Effect of Cognitive Dissonance," by Leon Festinger, the "father" of cognitive dissonance theory, is reprinted in this chapter.

## EXPECTANCY THEORY OF MOTIVATION

*Expectancy theory* holds that people are motivated by two dynamics: How much they want certain rewards (or to avoid negative sanctions) and the expectancy (probability) that their actions will garner the rewards. Victor Vroom (1964; 1969), the most respected expectancy theorist, identifies four classes of variables that comprise expectancy theory:

1. The amounts of particular classes of outcomes such as pay, status, acceptance, and influence, attained by the person.
2. The strength of the person's desire or aversion for outcomes.
3. The amounts of these outcomes believed by the person to be received by comparable others.
4. The amounts of these outcomes which the person expected to receive or has received at earlier points in time (1969, p. 207).

Very simply, expectancy theory claims that people are motivated by calculating how much they want something, how much of it they think they will get, how likely it is their actions will cause them to get it, and how much others in similar circumstances have received. (Notice how this last calculation resembles *equity theories* as described by Mowday later in this chapter.)

## ANOTHER NEED THEORY

Frederick Herzbeg is one of the most widely cited of the numerous students and theorists who studied and wrote about motivation in organizations during the 1960s.

Herzberg began the construction of his motivation theory with Abraham Maslow's need theory, and was also influenced substantially by the Theory X and Theory Y assumptions of Douglas McGregor.

Herzberg's theory of motivation evolved from extensive empirical research. Herzberg and his collaborating researchers would ask people to identify situations when they felt particularly satisfied and dissatisfied with their job (Herzberg, Mausner & Snyderman, 1959). From thousands of responses, Herzberg developed the motivation-hygiene theory which holds:

- *Motivators* or *satisfiers* are variables centered in the work (or work content) which satisfy self-actualization-type needs (Maslow, 1943) and lead to higher motivation. Examples of Herzberg's motivators include achievement, recognition for achievement, and opportunities for self-development.
- In contrast, *hygiene factors* are maintainers—preventers of dissatisfaction. A few examples of hygiene factors are supervision, administrative practices, and (in most respects) pay.

According to Herzberg's theory, which is described here in his 1968 article, "One More Time: How Do You Motivate Employees?" motivators and hygiene factors are on different dimensions or planes. They are not extreme points on a single scalar continuum. The presence of hygiene factors does not motivate, it only prevents dissatisfaction; and the absence of motivators does not cause employees to be dissatisfied, it only yields nonmotivated employees. If managers want satisfied employees, they should pay attention to hygiene factors, like pay and working conditions. However, hygiene factors do not "turn employees on": They only neutralize negative sentiments. In order to increase motivation, managers must work with motivators.

Herzberg's work has been attacked with great vigor on two fronts. First, numerous behavioral researchers have tried unsuccessfully to replicate his findings, which has raised serious questions about the validity of his research methods (Vroom, 1964). The second line of criticism directed at Herzberg has essentially been an argument against any and all simplistic, static, one- or two-dimensional theories of motivation, and for more complex, contingency-type theories (Behling, Labovitz, & Kosmo, 1968; Schein, 1980). Despite the sometimes bitter criticisms of motivation-hygiene theory, its popularity continues among management practitioners and trainers. Its greatest weakness—simplicity—also gives it credibility.

## REINFORCEMENT AND GOALS THEORIES

Virtually all organizations attempt to motivate employees through combinations of rewards and punishments. Reinforcement theories of motivation assume that people at work seek rewards and try to avoid punishments. By rewarding activities the organization wants done and punishing counterproductive behavior, managers *engineer* the accomplishment of organizational goals. "Whether dealing with monkeys, rats, or human beings, . . . most organisms seek information concerning what activities are rewarded, and then seek to do (or at least pretend to do) those things. . . . Nevertheless, numerous examples exist of reward systems that are fouled up in that behaviors which are rewarded are those which the rewarder is trying to *discourage*" (Kerr, 1975, p. 769). Reinforcement theories of motivation focus on the behavioral effects of rewards and punishments.

The goals theory of motivation is predicated on the assumption that people respond positively to goals—that goals motivate. Edwin A. Locke's article, "The Ubiquity of the Technique of Goal Setting in Theories of and Approaches to Employee Motivation" (1978), which is reprinted here, argues that virtually all major theories of motivation except Scientific Management and Management by objectives have overlooked the importance of goals. Locke acknowledges that needs and values—not goals—are the most fundamental factors in motivation, because needs and values are determinants of goals. "Goal setting is simply the most directly useful motivational approach in a managerial context . . ." (p. 599).

Locke arrives at some surprising conclusions. For example: "It was asserted by the Hawthorne researchers that employees were either too stupid or too irrational to understand incentive systems or too disinterested in money, in comparison to social rewards, for it to be a motivator of production." Further, "despite the fact that actual evidence from the Hawthorne studies themselves supported the view that the workers were most responsive to financial incentives and restricted output, quite rationally in their context, so as not to lose future earnings, the main conclusion drawn from the studies was that social incentives (such as belonging to a cohesive work group) were more potent than monetary ones" (p. 596). And, in conclusion: "It would not be unjustified to view [Frederick Winslow] Taylor as the father of employee motivation theory. Despite the decades of outrageous criticisms which Taylor's theories have had to endure, made often by writers who seem not to have read his actual writings, he has had the last word" (p. 600).

## EQUITY THEORY

As the readings that are included in this chapter demonstrate, a great deal of research has attempted to identify the important influences on the motivation of individuals and why these influences are important. Richard T. Mowday's article, "Equity Theory Predictions of Behavior in organizations" (1983), uses theories of social exchange processes to explain Adams's (1963; 1965) theory of equity. Exchange theories imply that people behave much as the "rational economic men" of classical economics and organization theory, but with limited and imperfect information. Mowday describes the major postulates of equity theory as: "(1) perceived inequity creates tension in the individual; (2) the amount of tension is proportional to the magnitude of the inequity; (3) the tension created in the individual will motivate him or her to reduce it; and (4) the strength of the motivation to reduce inequity is proportional to the perceived inequity" (p. 94. Mowday cites Adams, 1965).

The concept of equity in work motivation usually has involved the "equity norm"—a belief that people who contribute more to an organization should receive a larger share of rewards. The core question, then, for equity theory has been how people react to perceived inequity in the distribution of rewards. Until recently, most equity theorists limited their studies to monetary rewards. Instead, Mowday explains, "the utility of equity theory may be greatest for increasing our understanding of interpersonal interactions at work (e.g., supervisory-subordinate relationships)" (p. 110).

## CONCLUSION

This chapter tries to present a balanced sampling of the more important theories of motivation both in this *Introduction* and in the eight selected readings. If the result is confusing and inconclusive, I apologize. However, in many ways, motivation *is* "the proverbial pot of gold at the end of the rainbow." We may never totally unlock its mysteries. Humans are complicated, ever-changing beings. Organizations are complex social systems. Understanding and predicting either is extremely difficult (Schein, 1980, Chapters 6 and 11). Discovering universal truths about what motivates people in the context of organizations may be an unrealistic "pot of gold" to seek. On the other hand, much has been learned about what does and does not cause people to "turn on" or "tune out" at work.

## REFERENCES

Adams, J. S. (1963). Toward an understanding of inequity. *Journal of Abnormal Social Psychology, 67,* 422–436.

Adams, J. S. (1965). Inequity in social exchange. In L. Berkowitz (Ed.), *Advances in experimental social psychology. Vol. 2* (pp. 267–299). New York: Academic Press.

Alderfer, J. S. (1969). An empirical test of a new theory of human needs. *Organizational Behavior and Human Performance, 4,* 142–175.

Atkinson, J. W., & Raynor, J. O. (1974). *Motivation and achievement.* New York: John Wiley.

Behling, O., Labovitz, G., & Kosmo, R. (1968). The Herzberg controversy: A critical reappraisal. *Academy of Management Journal, 11(1),* 99–108.

Behling, O., & Starke, F. (1973). The postulates of expectancy theory. *Academy of Management Journal, 16,* 373–388.

Campbell, J. P., Dunnette, M. D., Lawler, E. E. III, & Weick, K. E., Jr. (1970). Expectancy theory. In J. P. Campbell, M. D. Dunnette, E. E. Lawler, III, & K. E. Weick, Jr. (Eds.), *Managerial behavior, performance and effectiveness* (pp. 343–348). New York: McGraw-Hill.

Cohen, A. R., Fink, S. L., Gadon, H., & Willits, R. D. (1988). *Effective behavior in organizations* (4th ed.). Homewood, IL: Richard D. Irwin.

Deci, E. L. (1971). The effects of externally mediated rewards on intrinsic motivation. *Journal of Personality and Social Psychology, 18,* 105–115.

Festinger, L. (1954). Motivations leading to social behavior. In, M. R. Jones (Ed.), *Nebraska symposium on motivation*. Lincoln, NE: University of Nebraska Press.

Festinger, L. (1957). *A theory of cognitive dissonance*. Standord, CA: Stanford University Press.

Festinger, L. (1958). The motivating effect of cognitive dissonance. In G. Lindzey (Ed.), *Assessment of human motives* (pp. 69–86). New York: Holt, Rinehart & Co.

Fink, S. L. (1992). *High commitment workplaces*. New York: Quorum Books.

Gantt, H. L. (1910). *Work, wages, and profit*. New York: Engineering Magazine Company.

Hackman, J. R., & Oldham, G. R. (1976). Motivation through the design of work. *Organizational Behavior and Human Performance, 16*, 250–279.

Haire, M. (1962). The concept of power and the concept of man. In G. B. Strother (Ed.), *Social science approaches to business behavior* (pp. 163–183). Homewood, IL: Richard D. Irwin.

Herzberg, F. (January/February 1968). One more time: How do you motivate employees?" *Harvard Business Review 46* (1).

Herzberg, F., Mausner, B., & Snyderman, B. B. (1959). *The motivation to work*. New York: John Wiley & Sons.

Katzenbach, J. R., & Smith, D. K. (1993). *The wisdom of teams: Creating the high-performance organization*. Boston: Harvard Business School Press.

Kerr, S. (December 1975). On the folly of rewarding A, while hoping for B. *Academy of Management Journal, 18*(4), 769–782.

Lawler, E. E., III, & Porter, L. W. (1963). Perceptions regarding management compensation. *Industrial Relations, 3*, 41–49.

Litwin, G. H., & Stringer, R. A., Jr. (1968). *Motivation and organizational climate*. Boston: Harvard University Press.

Locke, E. A. (July 1978). The ubiquity of the technique of goal setting in theories of and approaches to employee motivation. *Academy of Management Review*, 594–601.

Maslow, A. H. (1943). A theory of human motivation. *Psychological Review, 50*.

Mayo, E. (1933). *The human problems of an industrial civilization*. New York: Macmillan.

McClelland, D. C. (1961). *The achieving society*. Princeton, NJ: Van Nostrand.

McClelland, D. C. (1966). That urge to achieve. *Think* (published by International Business Machines Corporation), 82–89.

McGregor, D. M. (April 1957a). The human side of enterprise. Address to the Fifth Anniversary Convocation of the School of Industrial Management, Massachusetts Institute of Technology. In *Adventure in thought and action*. Cambridge, MA: M.I.T. School of Industrial Management, 1957. Reprinted in W. G. Bennis, E. H. Schein, & C. McGregor (Eds.), *Leadership and motivation: Essays of Douglas McGregor* (pp. 3–20). Cambridge, MA: The M.I.T. Press, 1966.

McGregor, D. M. (November, 1957b). The human side of enterprise. *Management Review*, 22–28, 88–92.

McGregor, D. M. (1960). *The human side of enterprise*. New York: McGraw-Hill.

Mowday, R. T. (1983). Equity theory predictions of behavior in organizations. In R. W. Steers & L. W. Porter (Eds.), *Motivation and work behavior* (3d. ed.) (pp. 91–113). New York: McGraw-Hill.

Organ, D. W., & Bateman, T. (1986). *Organizational behavior: An applied psychological approach* (3rd ed.). Plano, TX: Business Publications, Inc.

Pennock, G. (1930). Industrial research at Hawthorne. *The Personnel Journal, 8,* 296.

Roethlisberger, F. I. (1941). *Management and morale.* Cambridge, MA: Harvard University Press.

Roethlisberger, F. J., & Dickson, W. J. (1939). *Management and the worker.* Cambridge, MA: Harvard University Press.

Ross, I. C., & Zander, A. (1957). Need satisfactions and employee turnover. *Personnel Psychology, 10,* 327–338.

Schein, E. H. (1980). *Organizational psychology* (3rd ed.). Englewood Cliffs, NJ: Prentice-Hall.

Shafritz, J. M., & Ott, J. S. (1996). *Classics of organization theory,* (4th ed.). Belmont, CA: Wadsworth.

Smith, A. (1776). Of the division of labor. In, A. Smith, *The wealth of nations* (Chapter 1).

Staw, B. M. (1982). Motivation in organizations: Toward synthesis and redirection. In B. M. Staw & G. R. Salancik (Eds.), *New directions in organizational behavior* (pp. 55–95). Malabar, FL: Robert E. Krieger Publishing Company.

Taylor, F. W. (1903). *Shop management.* New York: Harper & Row.

Taylor, F. W. (1911). *The principles of scientific management.* New York: Harper & Row.

Urwick, L. (Ed.). (1956). *The golden book of management.* London, UK: Newman Neame.

Vroom, V. H. (1964). *Work and motivation.* New York: John Wiley & Sons.

Vroom, V. H. (1969). Industrial social psychology. In G. Lindzey & E. Aronson (Eds.). *The handbook of social psychology* (Vol. 5) (2d ed.) (pp. 200–208). Reading, MA: Addison-Wesley Publishing Co.

Vroom, V. H., & Deci, E. L. (Eds.) (1970). *Management and motivation.* Harmondsworth, UK: Penguin Books.

Wahba, M. A., & Bridwell, L. G. (1973). Maslow reconsidered: A review of research on the need hierarchy theory. Boston: *Proceedings of the 1973 meetings of the Academy of Management.*

Wren, D. A. (1972). *The evolution of management thought.* New York: The Ronald Press.

Zaleznik, A., Christensen, C. R., & Roethlisberger, F. J. (1958). *The motivation, productivity and satisfaction of workers: A prediction study.* Cambridge, MA: Harvard University, Graduate School of Business Administration.

Zimbardo, P., & Ebbesen, E. B. (1970). *Influencing attitudes and changing behavior* (rev. printing). Reading, MA: Addison-Wesley Publishing Co.

# 1

# The Hawthorne Experiments

## Frederick J. Roethlisberger

There seems to be an assumption today that we need a complex set of ideas to handle the complex problems of this complex world in which we live. We assume that a big problem needs a big idea; a complex problem needs a complex idea for its solution. As a result, our thinking tends to become more and more tortuous and muddled. Nowhere is this more true than in matters of human behavior. It seems to me that the road back to sanity—and here is where my title comes in—lies

1. In having a few simple and clear ideas about the world in which we live.
2. In complicating our ideas, not in a vacuum, but only in reference to things we can observe, see, feel, hear, and touch. Let us not generalize from verbal definitions; let us know in fact what we are talking about.
3. In having a very simple method by means of which we can explore our complex world. We need a tool which will allow us to get the idea from which our generalizations are to be drawn. We need a simple skill to keep us in touch with what is sometimes referred to as "reality."
4. In being "tough-minded," i.e., in not letting ourselves be too disappointed because the complex world never quite fulfills our most cherished expectations of it. Let us remember that the concrete phenomena will always elude any set of abstractions that we can make of them.
5. In knowing very clearly the class of phenomena to which our ideas and

methods relate. Now, this is merely a way of saying, "Do not use a saw as a hammer." A saw is a useful tool precisely because it is limited and designed for a certain purpose. Do not criticize the usefulness of a saw because it does not make a good hammer. . . .

It is my simple thesis that a human problem requires a human solution. First, we have to learn to recognize a human problem when we see one; and, second, upon recognizing it, we have to learn to deal with it as such and not as if it were something else. Too often at the verbal level we talk glibly about the importance of the human factor; and too seldom at the concrete level of behavior do we recognize a human problem for what it is and deal with it as such. A *human problem to be brought to a human solution requires human data and human tools.* It is my purpose to use the Western Electric researchers as an illustration of what I mean by this statement, because, if they deserve the publicity and acclaim which they have received, it is because, in my opinion, they have so conclusively demonstrated this point. In this sense they are the road back to sanity in management-employee relations.

## EXPERIMENTS IN ILLUMINATION

The Western Electric researches started about sixteen years ago, in the Haw-

*Source:* Reprinted by permission of the publishers from *Management and Morale* by F. J. Roethlisberger, Cambridge, Massachusetts: Harvard University Press, Copyright © 1941 by the President and Fellows of Harvard College; © 1969 by F. J. Roethlisberger.

thorne plant, with a series of experiments on illumination. The purpose was to find out the relation of the quality and quantity of illumination to the efficiency of industrial workers. These studies lasted several years, and I shall not describe them in detail. It will suffice to point out that the results were quite different from what had been expected.

In one experiment the workers were divided into two groups. One group, called the "test group," was to work under different illumination intensities. The other group, called the "control group," was to work under an intensity of illumination as nearly constant as possible. During the first experiment, the test group was submitted to three different intensities of illumination of increasing magnitude, 24, 46, and 70 foot candles. What were the results of this early experiment? Production increased in both rooms—in both the test group and the control group—and the rise in output was roughly of the same magnitude in both cases.

In another experiment, the light under which the test group worked was decreased from 10 to 3 foot candles, while the control group worked, as before, under a constant level of illumination intensity. In this case the output rate in the test group went up instead of down. It also went up in the control group.

In still another experiment, the workers were allowed to believe that the illumination was being increased, although, in fact, no change in intensity was made. The workers commented favorably on the improved lighting condition, but there was no appreciable change in output. At another time, the workers were allowed to believe that the intensity of illumination was being decreased, although again, in fact, no actual change was made. The workers complained somewhat about the poorer lighting, but

again there was no appreciable effect on output.

And finally, in another experiment, the intensity of illumination was decreased to .06 of a foot candle, which is the intensity of illumination approximately equivalent to that of ordinary moonlight. Not until this point was reached was there any appreciable decline in the output rate.

What did the experimenters learn? Obviously, as Stuart Chase said, there was something "screwy," but the experimenters were not quite sure who or what was screwy—they themselves, the subjects, or the results. One thing was clear: the results were negative. Nothing of a positive nature had been learned about the relation of illumination to industrial efficiency. If the results were to be taken at their face value, it would appear that there was no relation between illumination and industrial efficiency. However, the investigators were not yet quite willing to draw this conclusion. They realized the difficulty of testing for the effect of a single variable in a situation where there were many uncontrolled variables. It was thought therefore that another experiment should be devised in which other variables affecting the output of workers could be better controlled.

A few of the tough-minded experimenters already were beginning to suspect their basic ideas and assumptions with regard to human motivation. It occurred to them that the trouble was not so much with the results or with the subjects as it was with their notion regarding the way their subjects were supposed to behave—the notion of a simple cause-and-effect, direct relationship between certain physical changes in the workers' environment and the responses of the workers to these changes. Such a notion completely ignored the human meaning of these changes to the people who were subjected to them.

In the illumination experiments, therefore, we have a classic example of trying to deal with a human situation in nonhuman terms. The experimenters had obtained no human data; they had been handling electric-light bulbs and plotting average output curves. Hence their results had no human significance. That is why they seemed screwy. Let me suggest here, however, that the results were not screwy, but the experimenters were—a "screwy" person being by definition one who is not acting in accordance with the customary human values of the situation in which he finds himself.

## THE RELAY ASSEMBLY TEST ROOM

Another experiment was framed, in which it was planned to submit a segregated group of workers to different kinds of working conditions. The idea was very simple: A group of five girls were placed in a separate room where their conditions of work could be carefully controlled, where their output could be measured, and where they could be closely observed. It was decided to introduce at specified intervals different changes in working conditions and to see what effect these innovations had on output. . . . Under these conditions of close observation the girls were studied for a period of five years. Literally tons of material were collected. Probably nowhere in the world has so much material been collected about a small group of workers for such a long period of time.

But what about the results? They can be stated very briefly. When all is said and done, they amount roughly to this: A skillful statistician spent several years trying to relate variations to output with variations in the physical circumstances of these five operators. . . . The attempt to relate changes in physical circumstances to variations in output resulted in not a single correlation of enought statistical significance to be recognized by any competent statistician as having any meaning.

Now, of course, it would be misleading to say that this negative result was the only conclusion reached. There were positive conclusions, and it did not take the experimenters more than two years to find out that they had missed the boat. After two years of work, certain things happened which made them sit up and take notice. Different experimental conditions of work, in the nature of changes in the number and duration of rest pauses and differences in the length of the working day and week, had been introduced in this Relay Assembly Test Room. For example, the investigators first introduced two five-minute rests, one in the morning and one in the afternoon. Then they increased the length of these rests, and after that they introduced the rests at different times of the day. During one experimental period they served the operators a specially prepared lunch during the rest. In the later periods, they decreased the length of the working day by one-half hour and then by one hour. They gave the operators Saturday morning off for a while. Altogether, thirteen such periods of different working conditions were introduced in the first two years.

During the first year and a half of the experiment, everybody was happy, both the investigators and the operators. The investigators were happy because as conditions of work improved the output rate rose steadily. Here, it appeared, was strong evidence in favor of their preconceived hypothesis that fatigue was the major factor limiting output. The operators were happy because their conditions of work were being improved, they were earning more money, and they were objects of considerable attention from top management. But then one investigator—one of those tough-minded fellows—suggested that they restore the original conditions of work, that is, go back to a full forty-eight-hour week without rests, lunches and what not. This was Period XII. Then the happy state of affairs, when everything was going along as it theoretically should, went sour. Output, instead of taking the expected nose dive, maintained its high level.

Again the investigators were forcibly reminded that human situations are likely to be complex. In any human situation, whenever a simple change is introduced—a rest pause, for example—other changes, unwanted and unanticipated, may also be brought about. What I am saying here is very simple. If one experiments on a stone, the stone does not know it is being experimented upon—all of which makes it simple for people experimenting on stones. But if a human being is being experimented upon, he is likely to know it. Therefore, his attitudes toward the experiment and toward the experimenters become very important factors in determining his responses to the situation.

Now that is what happened in the Relay Assembly Test Room. To the investigators, it was essential that the workers give their full and whole-hearted coöperation to the experiment. They did not want the operators to work harder or easier depending upon their attitude toward the conditions that were imposed. They wanted them to work as they felt, so that they could be sure that the different physical conditions of work were solely responsible for the variations in output. For each of the experimental changes, they wanted subjects whose responses would be uninfluenced by so-called "psychological factors."

In order to bring this about, the investigators did everything in their power to secure the complete coöperation of their subjects, with the result that almost all the practices common to the shop were altered. The operators were consulted about the changes to be made, and, indeed, several plans were abandoned because they met with the disapproval of the girls. They were questioned sympathetically about their reactions to the conditions imposed, and many of these conferences took place in the office of the superintendent. The girls were allowed to talk at work; their "bogey" was eliminated. Their physical health and well-being became matters of great concern. Their opinions, hopes, and fears were eagerly sought. What happened was that in the very process of setting the conditions for the test—a so-called "controlled" experiment—the experimenters had completely altered the social situation of the room. Inadvertently a change had been introduced which was far more important than the planned experimental innovations: the customary supervision in the room had been revolutionized. This accounted for the better attitudes of the girls and their improved rate of work.

## THE DEVELOPMENT OF A NEW AND MORE FRUITFUL POINT OF VIEW

After Period XII in the Relay Assembly Test Room, the investigators decided to change their ideas radically. What all their experiments had dramatically and conclusively demonstrated was the importance of employee attitudes and sentiments. It was clear that the responses of workers to what was happening about them were dependent upon the significance these events had for them. In most work situations the meaning of a change is likely to be as important, if not more so, than the change itself. This was the great *éclaircissement*, the new illumination, that came from the research. It was an illumination quite different from what they had expected from the illumination studies. Curiously enough, this discovery is nothing very new or startling. It is something which anyone who has had some concrete experience in handling other people intuitively recognizes and practices.

Whether or not a person is going to give his services whole-heartedly to a group depends, in good part, on the way he feels about his job, his fellow workers, and supervisors—the meaning for him of what is happening about him.

However, when the experimenters began to tackle the problem of employee attitudes and the factors determining such attitudes—when they began to tackle the problem of "meaning"—they entered a sort of twilight zone where things are never quite what they seem. Moreover, overnight, as it were, they were robbed of all the tools they had so carefully forged; for all their previous tools were nonhuman tools concerned with the measurement of output, temperature, humidity, etc., and these were no longer useful for the human data that they now wanted to obtain. What the experimenters now wanted to know was how a person felt, what his intimate thinking, reflections, and preoccupations were, and what he liked and disliked about his work environment. In short, what did the whole blooming business—his job, his supervision, his working conditions—mean to him? Now this was human stuff, and there were no tools, or at least the experimenters knew of none, for obtaining and evaluating this kind of material.

Fortunately, there were a few courageous souls among the experimenters. These men were not metaphysicians, psychologists, academicians, professors, intellectuals, or what have you. They were men of common sense and of practical affairs. They were not driven by any great heroic desire to change the world. They were true experimenters, that is, men compelled to follow the implications of their own monkey business. All the evidence of their studies was pointing in one direction. Would they take the jump? They did.

## EXPERIMENTS IN INTERVIEWING WORKERS

A few tough-minded experimenters decided to go into the shops and—completely disarmed and denuded of their elaborate logical equipment and in all humility—to see if they could learn how to get the workers to talk about things that were important to them and could learn to understand what the workers were trying to tell them. This was a revolutionary idea in the year 1928, when this interviewing program started—the idea of getting a worker to talk to you and to listen sympathetically, but intelligently, to what he had to say. In that year a new era of personnel relations began. It was the first real atttempt to get human data and to forge human tools to get them. In that year a novel idea was born; dimly the experimenters perceived a new method of human control. In that year the Rubicon was crossed from which there could be no return to the "good old days." Not that the experimenters ever wanted to return, because they now entered a world so exciting, so intriguing, and so full of promise that it made the "good old days" seem like the prattle and play of children.

When these experimenters decided to enter the world of "meaning," with very few tools, but with a strong sense of curiosity and a willingness to learn, they had many interesting adventures. It would be too long a story to tell all of them, or even a small part of them. They made plenty of mistakes, but they were not afraid to learn.

At first, they found it difficult to learn to give full and complete attention to what a person had to say without interrupting him before he was through. They found it difficult to learn not to give advice, not to make or imply moral judgments about the speaker, not to argue, not to be too clever, not to dominate the conversation, not to ask leading questions. They found it difficult to get the person to talk about matters which were important to him and not to the interviewer. But, most important of all, they found it difficult to learn that perhaps the thing most significant to a person was not something in his immediate work situation.

Gradually, however, they learned these things. They discovered that sooner or later a person tends to talk about what is uppermost in his mind to a sympathetic and skillful listener, and they became more proficient in interpreting what a person is saying or trying to say. Of course they protected the confidences given to them and made absolutely sure that nothing an employee said could ever be used against him. Slowly they began to forge a simple human tool—imperfect, to be sure—to get the kind of data they wanted. They called this method "interviewing." I would hesitate to say the number of manhours of labor which went into the forging of this tool. There followed from studies made through its use a gradually changing conception of the worker and his behavior.

## A NEW WAY OF VIEWING EMPLOYEE SATISFACTION AND DISSATISFACTION

When the experimenters started to study employee likes and dislikes, they assumed, at first, that they would find a simple and logical relation between a simple and logical relation between a person's likes or dislikes and certain items and events in his immediate work situation. They expected to find a simple connection, for example, between a person's complaint and the object about which he was complaining. Hence, the solution would be easy: Correct the object of the complaint, if possible, and presto! the complaint would disappear. Unfortunately, however, the world of human behavior is not so simple as this conception of it; and it took the investigators several arduous and painful years to find this out. I will mention only a few interesting experiences they had.

Several times they changed the objects of the complaint only to find that the attitudes of the complainants remained unchanged. In these cases, correcting the object of the complaint did not remedy the complaint or the attitude of the person expressing it. A certain complaint might disappear, to be sure, only to have another one arise. Here the investigators were running into so-called "chronic kickers," people whose dissatisfactions were more deeply rooted in factors relating to their personal histories. . . .

Many times they found that people did not really want anything done about the things of which they were complaining. What they did want was an opportunity to talk about their troubles to a sympathetic listener. It was astonishing to find the number of instances in which workers complained about things which had happened many, many years ago, but which they described as vividly as if they had happened just a day before.

Here again, something was "screwy," but this time the experimenters realized that it was their assumptions which were screwy. They were assuming that the meanings which people assign to their experience are essentially logical. They were carrying in their heads the notion of the "economic man," a man primarily motivated by economic interest, whose logical capacities were being used in the service of this self-interest.

Gradually and painfully in the light of the evidence, which was overwhelming, the experimenters had been forced to abandon this conception of the worker and his behavior. Only with a new working hypothesis could they make sense of the data they had collected. The conception of the worker which they developed is actually nothing very new or startling; it is one which any effective administrator intuitively recognizes and practices in handling human beings.

First, they found that the behavior of workers could not be understood apart from their feelings or sentiments. I shall use the word "sentiment" hereafter to refer not only to such things as feelings and emotions, but also to a much wider range of phenomena which may not be expressed in violent feelings or emotions—phenomena that are referred to by such words as "loyalty," "integrity," "solidarity."

Secondly, they found that sentiments are easily disguised, and hence are difficult to recognize and to study. Manifestations of sentiment take a number of different forms. Feelings of personal integrity, for example, can be expressed by a handshake; they can also be expressed, when violated, by a sitdown strike. Moreover, people like to rationalize their sentiments and to objectify them. We are not so likely to say "I feel bad," as to say "The world is bad." In other words, we like to endow the world with those attributes and qualities which will justify and account for the feelings and sentiments we have toward it; we tend to project our sentiments on the outside world.

Thirdly, they found that manifestations of sentiment could not be understood as things in and by themselves, but only in terms of the total situation of the person. To comprehend why a person felt the way he did, a wider range of phenomena had to be explored. The following three diagrams illustrate roughly the development of this point of view.

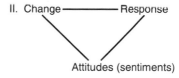

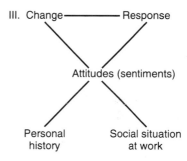

It will be remembered that at first the investigators assumed a simple and direct relation between certain physical changes in the worker's environment and his responses to them. This simple state of mind is illustrated in diagram I. But all the evidence of the early experiments showed that the responses of employees to changes in their immediate working environment can be understood only in terms of their attitudes—the "meaning" these changes have for them. This point of view is represented in diagram II. However, the "meaning" which these changes have for the worker is not strictly and primarily logical, for they are fraught with human feelings and values. The "meaning," therefore, which any individual worker assigns to a particular change depends upon (I) his social "conditioning," or what sentiments (values, hopes, fears, expectations, etc.) he is bringing to the work situation because of his previous family and group associations, and hence the relation of the change to these sentiments; and (2) the kind of human satisfaction he is deriving from his social participation with other workers and supervisors in the immediate work group of which he is a member, and hence the effect of the change on his customary interpersonal relations. This way of regarding the responses of workers (both verbal and overt) is represented in diagram III. It says briefly: Sentiments do not appear in a vacuum; they do not come out of the blue; they appear in a social context. They have to be considered in terms of that context, and apart from it they are likely to be misunderstood.

One further point should be made about that aspect of the worker's environment designated "Social Situation at Work" in diagram III. What is meant is that the worker is not an isolated, atomic individual; he is a member of a group, or of groups. Within each of these groups the individuals have feelings and sentiments toward each other, which bind them together in collaborative effort. Moreover, these collective sentiments can, and do, become attached to every item and object in the industrial environment—even to output. Material goods, output, wages, hours of work, and so on, cannot be treated as things in themselves. Instead, they must be interpreted as carriers of social value.

## OUTPUT AS A FORM OF SOCIAL BEHAVIOR

That output is a form of social behavior was well illustrated in a study made by the Hawthorne experimenters, called the Bank Wiring Observation Room. This room contained fourteen workmen representing three occupational groups—wiremen, soldermen, and inspectors. These men were on group piecework, where the more they turned out the more they earned. In such a situation one might have expected that they would have been interested in maintaining total output and that the faster workers would have put pressure on the slower workers to improve their efficiency. But this was not the case. Operating within this group were four basic sentiments, which can be expressed briefly as follows: (1) You should not turn out too much work; if you do, you are a "rate buster." (2) You should not turn out too little work; if you do, you are a "chiseler." (3) You should not say anything to a supervisor which would react to the detriment of one of your associates; if you do, you are a "squealer." (4) You should not be too officious; that is, if you are an inspector you should not act like one.

To be an accepted member of the group a man had to act in accordance with these social standards. One man in this group exceeded the group standard of what constituted a fair day's work. Social pressure was put on him to conform, but without avail, since he enjoyed doing things the others disliked. The best-liked person in the group was the one who kept his output exactly where the group agreed it should be.

Inasmuch as the operators were agreed as to what constituted a day's work, one might have expected rate of output to be about the same for each member of the group. This was by no means the case; there were marked differences. At first the experimenters thought that the differences in individual performance were related to differences in ability, so they compared each worker's relative rank in output with his relative rank in intelligence and dexterity as measured by certain tests. The results were interesting: The lowest producer in the room ranked first in intelligence and third in dexterity; the highest producer in the room was seventh in dexterity and lowest in intelligence. Here surely was a situation in which the native capacities of the men were not finding expression. From the viewpoint of logical, economic behavior, this room did not make sense. Only in terms of powerful sentiments could these individual differences in output level be explained. Each worker's level of output reflected his position in the informal organization of the group.

## WHAT MAKES THE WORKER NOT WANT TO COÖPERATE

As a result of the Bank Wiring Observation Room, the Hawthorne researchers became more and more interested in the informal employee groups which tend to form within the formal organization of the company, and which are not likely to be represented in the organization chart. They became interested in the beliefs and creeds which have the effect of making each individual feel an integral part of the group and which make the group appear as a single unit, in the social codes and norms of behavior by means of which employees automatically work together in a group without any conscious choice as to whether they will or will not coöperate. They studied the important social functions these groups perform for their members, the histories of these informal work groups, how they spontaneously appear, how they tend to perpetuate themselves, multiply, and disappear, how they are in constant jeopardy from technical change, and hence how they tend to resist innovation. In particular, they became interested in those groups whose norms and codes of behavior are at variance with the technical and economic objectives of the company as a whole. They examined the social conditions under which it is more likely for the employee group to separate itself out in opposition to the remainder of the groups which make up the total organization. In such phenomena they felt that they had at last arrived at the heart of the problem of effective collaboration. They obtained a new enlightenment of the present industrial scene; from this point of view, many perplexing problems became more intelligible.

Some people claim, for example, that the size of the pay envelope is the major demand which the employee is making of his job. All the worker wants is to be told what to do and to get paid for doing it. If we look at him and his job in terms of sentiments, this is far from being as generally true as we would like to believe. Most of us want the satisfaction that comes from being accepted and recognized as people of worth by our friends and work associates. Money is only a small part of this social recognition. The way we are greeted by our boss, being asked to help a newcomer, being asked to keep an eye on a difficult operation, being given a job requiring special skill—all of these are acts of social recognition. They tell us how we stand in our work group. We all want tangible evidence of our social importance. We want to have a skill that is socially recognized as useful. We want the feeling of security that comes not so much from the amount of money we have in the bank as from being an accepted member of a group. A man whose job is without social function is like a man without a country; the activity to which he has to give the major portion of his life is robbed of all human meaning and significance. . . .

In summary, therefore, the Western Electric researchers seem to me like a beginning on the road back to sanity in employee relations because (1) they offer a fruitful working hypothesis, a few simple and relatively clear ideas for the study and understanding of human situations in business; (2) they offer a simple method by means of which we can explore and deal with the complex human problems in a business organization—this method is a human method: it deals with things which are important to people; and (3) they throw a new light on the precondition for effective collaboration. Too often we think of collaboration as something which can be logically or legally contrived. The Western Electric studies indicate that it is far more a matter of sentiment than a matter of logic. Workers are not isolated, unrelated individuals; they are social animals and should be treated as such.

This statement—the worker is a social animal and should be treated as such—is simple, but the systematic and consistent practice of this point of view is not. If it were systematically practiced, it would revolutionize present-day personnel work. Our technological development in the past hundred years has been tremendous. Our methods of handling people are still archaic. If this civilization is to survive, we must obtain a new understanding of human motivation and behavior in business organizations—an understanding which can be simply but effectively practiced. The Western Electric researchers contribute a first step in this direction.

# 2
# A Theory of Human Motivation
## Abraham H. Maslow

## I. INTRODUCTION

In a previous paper (13) various propositions were presented which would have to be included in any theory of human motivation that could lay claim to being definitive. These conclusions may be briefly summarized as follows:

1. The integrated wholeness of the organism must be one of the foundation stones of motivation theory.
2. The hunger drive (or any other physiological drive) was rejected as a centering point or model for a definitive theory of motivation. Any drive that is somatically based and localizable was shown to be atypical rather than typical in human motivation.
3. Such a theory should stress and center itself upon ultimate or basic goals rather than partial or superficial ones, upon ends rather than means to these ends. Such a stress would imply a more central place for unconscious than for conscious motivations.
4. There are usually available various cultural paths to the same goal. Therefore conscious, specific, local-cultural desires are not as fundamental in motivation theory as the more basic, unconscious goals.
5. Any motivated behavior, either preparatory or consummatory, must be understood to be a channel through which many basic needs may be simultaneously expressed or satisfied. Typically an act has *more* than one motivation.
6. Practically all organismic states are to be understood as motivated and as motivating.

7. Human needs arrange themselves in hierarchies of prepotency. That is to say, the appearance of one need usually rests on the prior satisfaction of another, more prepotent need. Man is a perpetually wanting animal. Also no need or drive can be treated as if it were isolated or discrete; every drive is related to the state of satisfaction or dissatisfaction of other drives.
8. *Lists* of drives will get us nowhere for various theoretical and practical reasons. Furthermore any classification of motivations must deal with the problem of levels of specificity or generalization of the motives to be classified.
9. Classifications of motivations must be based upon goals rather than upon instigating drives or motivated behavior.
10. Motivation theory should be human-centered rather than animal-centered.
11. The situation or the field in which the organism reacts must be taken into account but the field alone can rarely serve as an exclusive explanation for behavior. Furthermore the field itself must be interpreted in terms of the organism. Field theory cannot be a substitute for motivation theory.
12. Not only the integration of the organism must be taken into account, but also the possibility of isolated, specific, partial or segmental reactions.

It has since become necessary to add to these another affirmation.

*Source:* From "A Theory of Human Motivation," by Abraham H. Maslow, *Psychological Review, 50.* Copyright 1943 by the American Psychological Association. Reprinted by permission.

13. Motivation theory is not synonymous with behavior theory. The motivations are only one class of determinants of behavior. While behavior is almost always motivated, it is also almost always biologically, culturally and situationally determined as well.

The present paper is an attempt to formulate a positive theory of motivation which will satisfy these theoretical demands and at the same time conform to the known facts, clinical and observational as well as experimental. . . . The present theory then must be considered to be a suggested program or framework for future research and must stand or fall, not so much on facts available or evidence presented, as upon researches yet to be done, researches suggested perhaps, by the questions raised in this paper.

## II. THE BASIC NEEDS

*The "Physiological" Needs.* The needs that are usually taken as the starting point for motivation theory are the so-called physiological drives. Two recent lines of research make it necessary to revise our customary notions about these needs, first, the development of the concept of homeostasis, and second, the finding that appetites (preferential choices among foods) are a fairly efficient indication of actual needs or lacks in the body.

Homeostasis refers to the body's automatic efforts to maintain a constant, normal state of the blood stream. Cannon (2) has described this process for (1) the water content of the blood, (2) salt content, (3) sugar content, (4) protein content, (5) fat content, (6) calcium content, (7) oxygen content, (8) constant hydrogen-ion level (acid-base balance) and (9) constant temperature of the blood. Obviously this list can be extended to include other minerals, the hormones, vitamins, etc.

Young in a recent article (21) has summarized the work on appetite in its relation to body needs. If the body lacks some chemical, the individual will tend to develop a specific appetite or partial hunger for that food element. . . .

It should be pointed out again that any of the physiological needs and the consummatory behavior involved with them serve as channels for all sorts of other needs as well. That is to say, the person who thinks he is hungry may actually be seeking more for comfort, or dependence, than for vitamins or proteins. Conversely, it is possible to satisfy the hunger need in part by other activities such as drinking water or smoking cigarettes. In other words, relatively isolable as these physiological needs are, they are not completely so.

Undoubtedly these physiological needs are the most prepotent of all needs. What this means specifically is that, in the human being who is missing everything in life in an extreme fashion, it is most likely that the major motivation would be the physiological needs rather than any others. A person who is lacking food, safety, love, and esteem would most probably hunger for food more strongly than for anything else.

If all the needs are unsatisfied, and the organism is then dominated by the physiological needs, all other needs may become simply nonexistent or be pushed into the background. . . . For the man who is extremely and dangerously hungry, no other interests exist but food. He dreams food, he remembers food, he thinks about food, he emotes only about food, he perceives only food and he wants only food. The more subtle determinants that ordinarily fuse with the physiological drives in organizing even feeding, drinking or sexual behavior, may now be so completely overwhelmed as to allow us to speak at this time (but *only* at this time) of pure hunger drive and behavior, with the one unqualified aim of relief.

Another peculiar characteristic of the human organism when it is dominated by a certain need is that the whole philosophy of the future tends also to change. For our chronically and extremely hungry man, Utopia can be defined very simply as a place where there is plenty of food. He tends to think that, if only he is guaranteed food for the rest of his life, he will be perfectly happy and will never want anything more. Life itself tends to be defined in terms of eating. Anything else will be defined as unimportant. Freedom, love, community feeling, respect, philosophy, may all be waved aside as fripperies which are useless since they fail to fill the stomach. Such a man may fairly be said to live by bread alone.

It cannot possibly be denied that such things are true but their *generality* can be denied. Emergency conditions are, almost by definition, rare in the normally functioning peaceful society. . . .

At *once other (and "higher") needs emerge* and these, rather than physiological hungers, dominate the organism. And when these in turn are satisfied, again new (and still "higher") needs emerge and so on. This is what we mean by saying that the basic human needs are organized into a hierarchy of relative prepotency.

One main implication of this phrasing is that gratification becomes as important a concept as deprivation in motivation theory, for it releases the organism from the domination of a relatively more physiological need, permitting thereby the emergence of other more social goals. The physiological needs, along with their partial goals, when chronically gratified cease to exist as active determinants or organizers of behavior. They now exist only in a potential fashion in the sense that they may emerge again to dominate the organism if they are thwarted. But a want that is satisfied is no longer a want. The organism is dominated and its behavior organized only by unsatisfied needs. If hunger is satisfied, it becomes unimportant in the current dynamics of the individual. . . .

*The Safety Needs.* If the physiological needs are relatively well gratified, there then emerges a new set of needs, which we may categorize roughly as the safety needs. . . .

Although in this paper we are interested primarily in the needs of the adult, we can approach an understanding of his safety needs perhaps more efficiently by observation of infants and children, in whom these needs are much more simple and obvious. One reason for the clearer appearance of the threat or danger reaction in infants is that they do not inhibit this reaction at all, whereas adults in our society have been taught to inhibit it at all costs. Thus even when adults do feel their safety to be threatened we may not be able to see this on the surface. Infants will react in a total fashion and as if they were endangered, if they are disturbed or dropped suddenly, startled by loud noises, flashing light, or other unusual sensory stimulation, by rough handling, by general loss of support in the mother's arms, or by inadequate support.[1]

In infants we can also see a much more direct reaction to bodily illnesses of various kinds. Sometimes these illnesses seem to be immediately and *per se* threat-

---

[1] As the child grows up, sheer knowledge and familiarity as well as better motor development make these "dangers" less and less dangerous and more and more manageable. Throughout life it may be said that one of the main cognitive functions of education is this neutralizing of apparent dangers through knowledge, *e.g.*, I am not afraid of thunder because I know something about it.

ening and seem to make the child feel unsafe. For instance, vomiting, colic, or other sharp pains seem to make the child look at the whole world in a different way. At such a moment of pain, it may be postulated that, for the child, the appearance of the whole world suddenly changes from sunniness to darkness, so to speak, and becomes a place in which anything at all might happen, in which previously stable things have suddenly become unstable. Thus a child who because of some bad food is taken ill may, for a day or two, develop fear, nightmares, and a need for protection and reassurance never seen in him before his illness.

Another indication of the child's need for safety is his preference for some kind of undisrupted routine or rhythm. He seems to want a predictable, orderly world. For instance, injustice, unfairness, or inconsistency in the parents seems to make a child feel anxious and unsafe. This attitude may be not so much because of the injustice *per se* or any particular pains involved, but rather because this treatment threatens to make the world look unreliable, or unsafe, or unpredictable. Young children seem to thrive better under a system which has at least a skeletal outline of rigidity, in which there is a schedule of a kind, some sort of routine, something that can be counted upon, not only for the present but also far into the future. Perhaps one could express this more accurately by saying that the child needs an organized world rather than an unorganized or unstructured one. . . .

From these and similar observations, we may generalize and say that the average child in our society generally prefers a safe, orderly, predictable, organized world, which he can count on, and in which unexpected, unmanageable or other dangerous things do not happen, and in which, in any case, he has all-

powerful parents who protect and shield him from harm.

That these reactions may so easily be observed in children is in a way a proof of the fact that children in our society, feel too unsafe (or, in a word, are badly brought up). Children who are reared in an unthreatening, loving family do *not* ordinarily react as we have described above (17). In such children the danger reactions are apt to come mostly to objects or situations that adults too would consider dangerous.[2]

The healthy, normal, fortunate adult in our culture is largely satisfied in his safety needs. The peaceful, smoothly running, "good" society ordinarily makes its members feel safe enough from wild animals, extremes of temperature, criminals, assault and murder, tyranny, etc. Therefore, in a very real sense, he no longer has any safety needs as active motivators. Just as a sated man no longer feels hungry, a safe man no longer feels endangered. . . .

Other broader aspects of the attempt to seek safety and stability in the world are seen in the very common preference for familiar rather than unfamiliar things, or for the known rather than the unknown. The tendency to have some religion or world-philosophy that organizes the universe and the men in it into some sort of satisfactorily coherent, meaningful whole is also in part motivated by safety-seeking. Here too we may

---

[2] A "test battery" for safety might be confronting the child with a small exploding firecracker, or with a bewhiskered face, having the mother leave the room, putting him upon a high ladder, [with] a hypodermic injection, having a mouse crawl up to him, etc. Of course I cannot seriously recommend the deliberate use of such "tests" for they might very well harm the child being tested. But these and similar situations come up by the score in the child's ordinary day-to-day living and may be observed. There is no reason why these stimuli should not be used with, for example, young chimpanzees.

list science and philosophy in general as partially motivated by the safety needs (we shall see later that there are also other motivations to scientific, philosophical or religious endeavor).

Otherwise the need for safety is seen as an active and dominant mobilizer of the organism's resources only in emergencies, e.g., war, disease, natural catastrophes, crime waves, societal disorganization, neurosis, brain injury, chronically bad situation. . . .

*The Love Needs.* If both the physiological and the safety needs are fairly well gratified, then there will emerge the love and affection and belongingness needs, and the whole cycle already described will repeat itself with this new center. Now the person will feel keenly, as never before, the absence of friends, or a sweetheart, or a wife, or children. He will hunger for affectionate relations with people in general, namely, for a place in his group, and he will strive with great intensity to achieve this goal. He will want to attain such a place more than anything else in the world and may even forget that once, when he was hungry, he sneered at love. . . .

One thing that must be stressed at this point is that love is not synonymous with sex. Sex may be studied as a purely physiological need. Ordinarily sexual behavior is multi-determined, that is to say, determined not only by sexual but also by other needs, chief among which are the love and affection needs. Also not to be overlooked is the fact that the love needs involve both giving *and* receiving love.[3]

*The Esteem Needs.* All people in our society (with a few pathological exceptions) have a need or desire for a stable, firmly based, (usually) high evaluation of themselves, for self-respect, or self-esteem, and for the esteem of others. By

firmly based self-esteem, we mean that which is soundly based upon real capacity, achievement and respect from others. These needs may be classified into two subsidiary sets. These are, first, the desire for strength, for achievement, for adequacy, for confidence in the face of the world, and for independence and freedom.[4] Secondly, we have what we may call the desire for reputation or prestige (defining it as respect or esteem from other people), recognition, attention, importance or appreciation.[5] These needs have been relatively stressed by Alfred Adler and his followers, and have been relatively neglected by Freud and the psychoanalysts. More and more today however there is appearing widespread appreciation of their central importance.

Satisfaction of the self-esteem need leads to feelings of self-confidence, worth, strength, capability and adequacy of being useful and necessary in the world. But thwarting of these needs produces feelings of inferiority, of weakness and of helplessness. These feelings in turn give rise to either basic discourage-

[3] For further details see (12) and (16, Chap. 5).

[4] Whether or not this particular desire is universal we do not know. The crucial question, especially important today, is "Will men who are enslaved and dominated, inevitably feel dissatisfied and rebellious?" We may assume on the basis of commonly known clinical data that a man who has known true freedom (not paid for by giving up safety and security but rather built on the basis of adequate safety and security) will not willingly or easily allow his freedom to be taken away from him. But we do not know that this is true for the person born into slavery. The events of the next decade should give us our answer. See discussion of this problem in (5).

[5] Perhaps the desire for prestige and respect from others is subsidiary to the desire for self-esteem or confidence in oneself. Observation of children seems to indicate that this is so, but clinical data give no clear support for such a conclusion.

ment or else compensatory or neurotic trends. An appreciation of the necessity of basic self-confidence and an understanding of how helpless people are without it can be easily gained from a study of severe traumatic neurosis (8).[6]

*The Need for Self-Actualization.* Even if all these needs are satisfied, we may still often (if not always) expect that a new discontent and restlessness will soon develop, unless the individual is doing what he is fitted for. A musician must make music, an artist must paint, a poet must write, if he is to be ultimately happy. What a man *can* be, he *must* be. This need we may call self-actualization.

This term, first coined by Kurt Goldstein, is being used in this paper in a much more specific and limited fashion. It refers to the desire for self-fulfillment, namely, to the tendency for him to become actualized in what he is potentially. This tendency might be phrased as the desire to become more and more what one is, to become everything that one is capable of becoming.

The specific form that these needs will take will of course vary greatly from person to person. In one individual it may take the form of the desire to be an ideal mother, in another it may be expressed athletically, and in still another it may be expressed in painting pictures or in inventions. It is not necessarily a creative urge although in people who have any capacities for creation it will take this form.

The clear emergence of these needs rests upon prior satisfaction of the physiological, safety, love and esteem needs. We shall call people who are satisfied in these needs, basically satisfied people, and it is from these that we may expect

the fullest (and healthiest) creativeness.[7] Since, in our society, basically satisfied people are the exception, we do not know much about self-actualization, either experimentally or clinically. It remains a challenging problem for research.

*The Preconditions for the Basic Need Satisfactions.* There are certain conditions which are immediate prerequisites for the basic need satisfactions. Danger to these is reacted to almost as if it were a direct danger to the basic needs themselves. Such conditions as freedom to speak, freedom to do what one wishes so long as no harm is done to others, freedom to express one's self, freedom to investigate and seek for information, freedom to defend one's self, justice, fairness, honesty, orderliness in the group are examples of such preconditions for basic need satisfactions. Thwarting in these freedoms will be reacted to with a threat or emergency response. These conditions are not ends in themselves but they are *almost* so since they are so closely related to the basic needs, which are apparently the only ends in themselves. . . .

We must therefore introduce another hypothesis and speak of degrees of closeness to the basic needs, for we have already pointed out that *any* conscious desires (partial goals) are more or less

[6] For more extensive discussion of normal self-esteem, as well as for reports of various researches, see (11).

[7] Clearly creative behavior, like painting, is like any other behavior in having multiple determinants. It may be seen in 'innately creative' people whether they are satisfied or not, happy or unhappy, hungry or sated. Also it is clear that creative activity may be compensatory, ameliorative or purely economic. It is my impression (as yet unconfirmed) that it is possible to distinguish the artistic and intellectual products of basically satisfied people from those of basically unsatisfied people by inspection alone. In any case, here too we must distinguish, in a dynamic fashion, the overt behavior itself from its various motivations or purposes.

important as they are more or less close to the basic needs. The same statement may be made for various behavior acts. An act is psychologically important if it contributes directly to satisfaction of basic needs. The less directly it so contributes, or the weaker this contribution is, the less important this act must be conceived to be from the point of view of dynamic psychology. A similar statement may be made for the various defense or coping mechanisms. Some are very directly related to the protection or attainment of the basic needs; others are only weakly and distantly related. Indeed if we wished, we could speak of more basic and less basic defense mechanisms, and then affirm that danger to the more basic defenses (always remembering that this is so only because of their relationship to the basic needs). . . .

## III. FURTHER CHARACTERISTICS OF THE BASIC NEEDS

*The Degree of Fixity of the Hierarchy of Basic Needs.* We have spoken so far as if this hierarchy were a fixed order but actually it is not nearly as rigid as we may have implied. It is true that most of the people with whom we have worked have seemed to have these basic needs in about the order that has been indicated. However, there have been a number of exceptions.

1. There are some people in whom, for instance, self-esteem seems to be more important than love. This most common reversal in the hierarchy is usually due to the development of the notion that the person who is most likely to be loved is a strong or powerful person, one who inspires respect or fear, and who is self confident or aggressive. Therefore such people who lack love and seek it may try hard to put on a front of aggressive, confident behavior. But essentially they seek high self-esteem and its behavior expressions more as a means-to-an-end than for its own sake; they seek self-assertion for the sake of love rather than for self-esteem itself.

2. There are other, apparently innately creative people in whom the drive to creativeness seems to be more important than any other counter-determinant. Their creativeness might appear not as self-actualization released by basic satisfaction, but in spite of lack of basic satisfaction.

3. In certain people the level of aspiration may be permanently deadened or lowered. That is to say, the less prepotent goals may simply be lost, and may disappear forever, so that the person who has experienced life at a very low level, *i.e.,* chronic unemployment, may continue to be satisfied for the rest of his life if only he can get enough food.

4. The so-called "psychopathic personality" is another example of permanent loss of the love needs. These are people who, according to the best data available (9), have been starved for love in the earliest months of their lives and have simply lost forever the desire and the ability to give and to receive affection (as animals lose sucking or pecking reflexes that are not exercised soon enough after birth).

5. Another cause of reversal of the hierarchy is that when a need has been satisfied for a long time, this need may be underevaluated. . . .

6. Another partial explanation of *apparent* reversals is seen in the fact that we have been talking about the hierarchy of prepotency in terms of consciously felt wants or desires rather than of behavior. Looking at behavior itself may give us the wrong impression. What we have claimed is that the person will *want* the more basic of two needs when deprived in both. There is no necessary implication here that he will act upon his de-

sires. Let us say again that there are many determinants of behavior other than the needs and desires.

7. Perhaps more important than all these exceptions are the ones that involve ideals, high social standards, high values and the like. With such values people become martyrs; they will give up everything for the sake of a particular ideal, or value. These people may be understood, at least in part, by reference to one basic concept (or hypothesis) which may be called "increased frustration-tolerance through early gratification." People who have been satisfied in their basic needs throughout their lives, particularly in their earlier years, seem to develop exceptional power to withstand present or future thwarting of these needs simply because they have strong, healthy character structure as a result of basic satisfaction. They are the "strong" people who can easily weather disagreement or opposition, who can swim against the stream of public opinion and who can stand up for the truth at great personal cost. It is just the ones who have loved and been well loved, and who have had many deep friendships who can hold out against hatred, rejection or persecution.

. . . In respect to this phenomenon of increased frustration tolerance, it seems probable that the most important gratifications come in the first two years of life. That is to say, people who have been made secure and strong in the earliest years, tend to remain secure and strong thereafter in the face of whatever threatens.

*Degrees of Relative Satisfaction.* So far, our theoretical discussion may have given the impression that these five sets of needs are somehow in a step-wise, all-or-none relationships to each other. We have spoken in such terms as the following: "If one need is satisfied, then another emerges." This statement might give the false impression that a need must be satisfied 100 per cent before the next need emerges. In actual fact, most members of our society who are normal are partially satisfied in all their basic needs and partially unsatisfied in all their basic needs at the same time. A more realistic description of the hierarchy would be in terms of decreasing percentages of satisfaction as we go up the hierarchy of prepotency. For instance, if I may assign arbitrary figures for the sake of illustration, it is as if the average citizen is satisfied perhaps 85 per cent in his physiological needs, 70 per cent in his safety needs, 50 per cent in his love needs, 40 per cent in his self-esteem needs, and 10 per cent in his self-actualization needs.

As for the concept of emergence of a new need after satisfaction of the prepotent need, this emergence is not a sudden, saltatory phenomenon but rather a gradual emergence by slow degrees from nothingness. For instance, if prepotent need A is satisfied only 10 per cent then need B may not be visible at all. However, as this need A becomes satisfied 25 per cent, need B may emerge 5 per cent, as need A becomes satisfied 75 per cent need B may emerge 90 per cent, and so on.

*Unconscious Character of Needs.* These needs are neither necessarily conscious nor unconscious. On the whole, however, in the average person, they are more often unconscious rather than conscious. . . .

*Cultural Specificity and Generality of Needs.* This classification of basic needs makes some attempt to take account of the relative unity behind the superficial differences in specific desires from one culture to another. Certainly in any particular culture an individual's conscious motivational content will usually be extremely different from the conscious motivational content of an individual in another society. However, it is the common experience of anthropologists that people, even in different societies, are much more alike than we would think from our first contact with them, and that as we know them better we seem to find more and more of this commonness. . . .

*Multiple Motivations of Behavior.* . . . Most behavior is multi-motivated. Within the sphere of motivational determinants any behavior tends to be determined by several or *all* of the basic needs simultaneously rather than by only one of them. The latter would be more an exception than the former. Eating may be partially for the sake of filling the stomach, and partially for the sake of comfort and amelioration of other needs. One may make love not only for pure sexual release, but also to convince one's self of one's masculinity, or to make a conquest, to feel powerful, or to win more basic affection. . . .

*Multiple Determinants of Behavior.* Not all behavior is determined by the basic needs. We might even say that not all behavior is motivated. There are many determinants of behavior other than motives.[8] For instance, one other important class of determinants is the so-called "field" determinants. Theoretically, at least, behavior may be determined completely by the field, or even by specific isolated external stimuli, as in association of ideas, or certain conditioned reflexes. If in response to the stimulus word "table," I immediately perceive a memory image of a table, this response certainly has nothing to do with my basic needs.

Secondly, we may call attention again to the concept of "degree of closeness to the basic needs" or "degree of motivation." Some behavior is highly motivated, other behavior is only weakly motivated. Some is not motivated at all (but all behavior is determined).

Another important point[9] is that there is a basic difference between expressive behavior and coping behavior (functional striving, purposive goal seeking). An expressive behavior does not try to do anything; it is simply a reflection of the personality. A stupid man behaves stupidly, not because he wants to, or tries to, or is motivated to, but simply because he *is* what he is. . . .

We may then ask, is *all* behavior expressive or reflective of the character structure? The answer is "No." Rote, habitual, automatized, or conventional behavior may or may not be expressive. The same is true for most "stimulus-bound" behaviors.

It is finally necessary to stress that expressiveness of behavior, and goal-directedness of behavior are not mutually exclusive categories. Average behavior is usually both.

*Goals as Centering Principle in Motivation Theory.* It will be observed that the basic principle in our classification has been neither the instigation nor the motivated behavior but rather the functions, effects, purposes, or goals of the behavior. It has been proven sufficiently by various people that this is the most suitable point for centering in any motivation theory.[10]

*Animal- and Human-Centering.* This theory starts with the human being rather than any lower and presumably

[8] I am aware that many psychologists and psychoanalysts use the term "motivated" and "determined" synonymously, e.g., Freud. But I consider this an obfuscating usage. Sharp distinctions are necessary for clarity of thought, and precision in experimentation.

[9] To be discussed fully in a subsequent publication.

[10] The interested reader is referred to the very excellent discussion of this point in Murray's *Explorations in Personality* (15).

"simpler" animal. Too many of the findings that have been made in animals have been proven to be true for animals but not for the human being. There is no reason whatsoever why we should start with animals in order to study human motivation. . . .

*Motivation and the Theory of Psychopathogenesis.* The conscious motivational content of everyday life has, according to the foregoing, been conceived to be relatively important or unimportant accordingly as it is more or less closely related to the basic goals. A desire for an ice cream cone might actually be an indirect expression of a desire for love. If it is, then this desire for the ice cream cone becomes extremely important motivation. If however the ice cream is simply something to cool the mouth with, or a casual appetitive reaction, then the desire is relatively unimportant. Everyday conscious desires are to be regarded as symptoms, as *surface indicators of more basic needs.* If we were to take these superficial desires at their face value we would find ourselves in a state of complete confusion which could never be resolved, since we would be dealing seriously with symptoms rather than with what lay behind the symptoms.

Thwarting of unimportant desires produces no psychopathological results; thwarting of a basically important need does produce such results. Any theory of psychopathogenesis must then be based on a sound theory of motivation. A conflict or a frustration is not necessarily pathogenic. It becomes so only when it threatens or thwarts the basic needs, or partial needs that are closely related to the basic needs (10).

*The Role of Gratified Needs.* It has been pointed out above several times that our needs usually emerge only when more prepotent needs have been gratified. Thus gratification has an important role in motivation theory. Apart from this, however, needs cease to play an active determining or organizing role as soon as they are gratified.

What this means is that, e.g., a basically satisfied person no longer has the needs for esteem, love, safety, etc. . . .

It is such considerations as these that suggest the bold postulation that a man who is thwarted in any of his basic needs may fairly be envisaged simply as a sick man. This is a fair parallel to our designation as "sick" of the man who lacks vitamins or minerals. Who is to say that a lack of love is less important than a lack of vitamins? Since we know the pathogenic effects of love starvation, who is to say that we are invoking value-questions in an unscientific or illegitimate way, any more than the physician does who diagnoses and treats pellagra or scurvy? If I were permitted this usage, I should then say simply that a healthy man is primarily motivated by his needs to develop and actualize his fullest potentialities and capacities. If a man has any other basic needs in any active, chronic sense, then he is simply an unhealthy man. He is as surely sick as if he had suddenly developed a strong salt-hunger or calcium hunger.[11]

If this statement seems unusual or paradoxical the reader may be assured that this is only one among many such paradoxes that will appear as we revise our ways of looking at man's deeper motiva-

[11] If we were to use the word "sick" in this way, we should then also have to face squarely the relations of man to his society. One clear implication of our definition would be that (1) since a man is to be called sick who is basically thwarted, and (2) since such basic thwarting is made possible ultimately only by forces outside the individual, then (3) sickness in the individual must come ultimately from a sickness in the society. The "good" or healthy society would then be defined as one that permitted man's highest purposes to emerge by satisfying all his prepotent basic needs.

tions. When we ask what man wants of life, we deal with his very essence.

## IV. SUMMARY

1. There are at least five sets of goals, which we may call basic needs. These are briefly physiological, safety, love, esteem, and self-actualization. In addition, we are motivated by the desire to achieve or maintain the various conditions upon which these basic satisfactions rest and by certain more intellectual desires.

2. These basic goals are related to each other, being arranged in a hierarchy of prepotency. This means that the most prepotent goal will monopolize consciousness and will tend of itself to organize the recruitment of the various capacities of the organism. The less prepotent needs are minimized, even forgotten or denied. But when a need is fairly well satisfied, the next prepotent ("higher") need emerges, in turn to dominate the conscious life and to serve as the center of organization of behavior, since gratified needs are not active motivators.

Thus man is a perpetually wanting animal. Ordinarily the satisfaction of these wants is not altogether mutually exclusive, but only tends to be. The average member of our society is most often partially satisfied and partially unsatisfied in all of his wants. The hierarchy principle is usually empirically observed in terms of increasing percentages of nonsatisfaction as we go up the hierarchy. Reversals of the average order of the hierarchy are sometimes observed. Also it has been observed that an individual may permanently lose the higher wants in the hierarchy under special conditions. There are not only ordinarily multiple motivations for usual behavior, but in addition many determinants other than motives.

3. Any thwarting or possibility of thwarting of these basic human goals, or danger to the defenses which protect them, or to the conditions upon which they rest, is considered to be a psychological threat. With a few exceptions, all psychopathology may be partially traced to such threats. A basically thwarted man may actually be defined as a "sick" man, if we wish.

4. It is such basic threats which bring about the general emergency reactions. . . .

## REFERENCES

1. Adler, A. *Social interest.* London: Faber & Faber, 1938.

2. Cannon, W. B. *Wisdom of the body.* New York: Norton, 1932.

3. Freud, A. *The ego and the mechanisms of defense.* London: Hogarth, 1937.

4. Freud, S. *New introductory lectures on psychoanalysis.* New York: Norton, 1933.

5. Fromm, E. *Escape from freedom.* New York: Farrar and Rinehart, 1941.

6. Goldstein, K. *The organism.* New York: American Book Co., 1939.

7. Horney, K. *The neurotic personality of our time.* New York: Norton, 1937.

8. Kardiner, A. *The traumatic neuroses of war.* New York: Hoeber, 1941.

9. Levy, D. M. Primary affect hunger. *Amer. J. Psychiat.,* 1937, 94, 643–652.

10. Maslow, A. H. Conflict, frustration, and the theory of threat. *J. Abnorm. (soc.) Psychol.,* 1943, 38, 81–86.

11. ———. Dominance, personality and social behavior in women. *J. Soc. Psychol.,* 1939, 10, 3–39.

12. ———. The dynamics of psychological security-insecurity. *Character & Pers.,* 1942, 10, 331–344.

13. ———. A preface to motivation theory. *Psychosomatic Med.,* 1943, 5, 85–92.

14. ———, & Mittelmann, B. *Principles of abnormal psychology.* New York: Harper & Bros., 1941.

15. Murray, H. A., et al. *Explorations in personality.* New York: Oxford University Press, 1938.

16. Plant, J. *Personality and the cultural pattern.* New York: Commonwealth Fund, 1937.

17. Shirley, M. Children's adjustments to a strange situation. *J. Abnorm. (soc.) Psychol.*, 1942, 37, 201–217.

18. Tolman, E. C. *Purposive behavior in animals and men.* New York: Century, 1932.

19. Wertheimer, M. Unpublished lectures at the New School for Social Research.

20. Young, P. T. *Motivation of behavior.* New York: John Wiley & Sons, 1936.

21. ———. The experimental analysis of appetite. *Psychol. Bull.*, 1941, 38, 129–164.

# 3

# The Human Side of Enterprise

## Douglas Murray McGregor

To a degree, the social sciences today are in a position like that of the physical sciences with respect to atomic energy in the thirties. We know that past conceptions of the nature of man are inadequate and, in many ways, incorrect. We are becoming quite certain that, under proper conditions, unimagined resources of creative human energy could become available within the organizational setting. . . .

## MANAGEMENT'S TASK: THE CONVENTIONAL VIEW

The conventional conception of management's task in harnessing human energy to organizational requirements can be stated broadly in terms of three propositions. In order to avoid the complications introduced by a label, let us call this set of propositions "Theory X":

1. Management is responsible for organizing the elements of productive enterprise—money, materials, equipment, people—in the interest of economic ends.
2. With respect to people, this is a process of directing their efforts, motivating them, controlling their actions, modifying their behavior to fit the needs of the organization.
3. Without this active intervention by management, people would be passive—even resistant—to organizational needs. They must therefore be persuaded, rewarded, punished, controlled—their activities must be directed. This is management's task. We often sum it up by saying that management consists of getting things done through other people.

Behind this conventional theory there are several additional beliefs—less explicit, but widespread:

4. The average man is by nature indolent—he works as little as possible.
5. He lacks ambition, dislikes responsibility, prefers to be led.
6. He is inherently self-centered, indifferent to organizational needs.
7. He is by nature resistant to change.
8. He is gullible, not very bright, the ready dupe of the charlatan and the demagogue.

The human side of economic enterprise today is fashioned from propositions and beliefs such as these. Conventional organization structures and managerial policies, practices, and programs reflect these assumptions.

In accomplishing its task—with these assumptions as guides—management has conceived of a range of possibilities.

At one extreme, management can be "hard" or "strong." The methods for directing behavior involve coercion and threat (usually disguised), close supervision, tight controls over behavior. At the other extreme, management can be

Source: Reprinted, by permission of the publisher, from "The Human Side of Enterprise," by Douglas Murray McGregor, 1957, Management Review. Copyright 1957 by the American Management Association, New York. All rights reserved.

Note: This article is based on an address by Dr. McGregor before the Fifth Anniversary Convocation of the M.I.T. School of Industrial Management.

"soft" or "weak." The methods for directing behavior involve being permissive, satisfying people's demands, achieving harmony. Then they will be tractable, accept direction.

This range has been fairly completely explored during the past half century, and management has learned some things from the exploration. There are difficulties in the "hard" approach. Force breeds counter-forces: restriction of output, antagonism, militant unionism, subtle but effective sabotage of management objectives. This "hard" approach is especially difficult during times of full employment.

There are also difficulties in the "soft" approach. It leads frequently to the abdication of management—to harmony, perhaps, but to indifferent performance. People take advantage of the soft approach. They continually expect more, but they give less and less. . . .

## IS THE CONVENTIONAL VIEW CORRECT?

The social scientist does not deny that human behavior in industrial organization today is approximately what management perceives it to be. He has, in fact, observed it and studied it fairly extensively. But he is pretty sure that this behavior is *not* a consequence of man's inherent nature. It is a consequence rather of the nature of industrial organizations, of management philosophy, policy, and practice. The conventional approach of Theory X is based on mistaken notions of what is cause and what is effect.

Perhaps the best way to indicate why the conventional approach of management is inadequate is to consider the subject of motivation.

## PHYSIOLOGICAL NEEDS

Man is a wanting animal—as soon as one of his needs is satisfied, another ap-

pears in its place. This process is unending. It continues from birth to death. . . .

*A satisfied need is not a motivator of behavior!* This is a fact of profound significance that is regularly ignored in the conventional approach to the management of people. Consider your own need for air: Except as you are deprived of it, it has no appreciable motivating effect upon your behavior.

## SAFETY NEEDS

When the physiological needs are reasonably satisfied, needs at the next higher level begin to dominate man's behavior—to motivate him. These are called *safety needs*. They are needs for protection against danger, threat, deprivation. . . .

The fact needs little emphasis that, since every industrial employee is in a dependent relationship, safety needs may assume considerable importance. Arbitrary management actions, behavior which arouses uncertainty with respect to continued employment or which reflects favoritism or discrimination, unpredictable administration of policy— these can be powerful motivators of the safety needs in the employment relationship *at every level*, from worker to vice president.

## SOCIAL NEEDS

When man's physiological needs are satisfied and he is no longer fearful about his physical welfare, his *social needs* become important motivators of his behavior— needs for belonging, for association, for acceptance by his fellows, for giving and receiving friendship and love.

Management knows today of the existence of these needs, but it often assumes quite wrongly that they represent a threat to the organization.

. . . When man's social needs—and perhaps his safety needs, too—are thus thwarted, he behaves in ways which tend to defeat organizational objectives. He becomes resistant, antagonistic, uncooperative. But this behavior is a consequence, not a cause.

## EGO NEEDS

Above the social needs—in the sense that they do not become motivators until lower needs are reasonably satisfied— are the needs of greatest significance to management and to man himself. They are the *egoistic needs,* and they are of two kinds:

1. Those needs that relate to one's self-esteem—needs for self-confidence, for independence, for achievement, for competence, for knowledge.
2. Those needs that relate to one's reputation—needs for status, for recognition, for appreciation, for the deserved respect of one's fellows.

. . . The typical industrial organization offers few opportunities for the satisfaction of these egoistic needs to people at lower levels in the hierarchy. The conventional methods of organizing work, particularly in mass-production industries, give little heed to these aspects of human motivation. If the practices of scientific management were deliberately calculated to thwart these needs, they could hardly accomplish this purpose better than they do.

## SELF-FULFILLMENT NEEDS

Finally—a capstone, as it were, on the hierarchy of man's needs—there are what we may call the *needs for self-fulfillment.* These are the needs for realizing one's own potentialities, for continued self-development, for being creative in the broadest sense of that term.

It is clear that the conditions of modern life give only limited opportunity for these relatively weak needs to obtain expression. The deprivation most people experience with respect to other lower-level needs diverts their energies into the struggle to satisfy *those* needs, and the needs for self-fulfillment remain dormant.

## MANAGEMENT AND MOTIVATION

. . . The man whose needs for safety, association, independence, or status are thwarted is sick just as surely as the man who has rickets. And his sickness will have behavioral consequences. We will be mistaken if we attribute his resultant passivity, his hostility, his refusal to accept responsibility to his inherent "human nature." These forms of behavior are *symptoms* of illness—of deprivation of his social and egoistic needs.

The man whose lower-level needs are satisfied is not motivated to satisfy those needs any longer. For practical purposes they exist no longer. Management often asks, "Why aren't people more productive? We pay good wages, provide good working conditions, have excellent fringe benefits and steady employment. Yet people do not seem to be willing to put forth more than minimum effort."

The fact that management has provided for these physiological and safety needs has shifted the motivational emphasis to the social and perhaps to the egoistic needs. Unless there are opportunities *at work* to satisfy these higher-level needs, people will be deprived; and their behavior will reflect this deprivation. Under such conditions, if management continues to focus its attention on physiological needs, its efforts are bound to be ineffective.

People *will* make insistent demands for more money under these conditions. It becomes more important than ever to buy the material goods and services which can provide limited satisfaction of the thwarted needs. Although money has only limited value in satisfying many higher-level needs, it can become the focus of interest if it is the *only* means available.

## THE CARROT-AND-STICK APPROACH

The carrot-and-stick theory of motivation (like Newtonian physical theory) works reasonably well under certain circumstances. The *means* for satisfying man's physiological and (within limits) his safety needs can be provided or withheld by management. Employment itself is such a means, and so are wages, working conditions, and benefits. By these means the individual can be controlled so long as he is struggling for subsistence. . . .

. . . And so management finds itself in an odd position. The high standard of living created by our modern technological known-how provides quite adequately for the satisfaction of physiological and safety needs. The only significant exception is where management practices have not created confidence in a "fair break"—and thus where safety needs are thwarted. But by making possible the satisfaction of low-level needs, management has deprived itself of the ability to use as motivators the devices on which conventional theory has taught it to rely—rewards, promises, incentives, or threats and other coercive devices.

The philosophy of management by direction and control—*regardless of whether it is hard or soft*—is inadequate to motivate because the human needs on which this approach relies are today unimportant motivators of behavior. Direction and control are essentially useless in motivating people whose important needs are social and egoistic. Both the hard and the soft approach fail today because they are simply irrelevant to the situation.

People, deprived of opportunities to satisfy at work the needs which are now important to them, behave exactly as we might predict—with indolence, passivity, resistance to change, lack of responsibility, willingness to follow the demagogue, unreasonable demands for economic benefits. It would seem that we are caught in a web of our own weaving.

## A NEW THEORY OF MANAGEMENT

For these and many other reasons, we require a different theory of the task of managing people based on more adequate assumptions about human nature and human motivation. I am going to be so bold as to suggest the broad dimensions of such a theory. Call it "Theory Y," if you will.

1. Management is responsible for organizing the elements of productive enterprise—money, materials, equipment, people—in the interest of economic ends.

2. People are *not* by nature passive or resistant to organizational needs. They have become so as a result of experience in organizations.

3. The motivation, the potential for development, the capacity for assuming responsibility, the readiness to direct behavior toward organizational goals are all present in people. Management does not put them there. It is a responsibility of management to make it possible for people to recognize and develop these human characteristics for themselves.

4. The essential task of management is to arrange organizational conditions and

methods of operation so that people can achieve their own goals *best* by directing *their own* efforts toward organizational objectives.

This is a process primarily of creating opportunities, releasing potential, removing obstacles, encouraging growth, providing guidance. It is what Peter Drucker has called "management by objectives" in contrast to "management by control." It does *not* involve the abdication of management, the absence of leadership, the lowering of standards, or the other characteristics usually associated with the "soft" approach under Theory X.

## SOME DIFFICULTIES

It is no more possible to create an organization today which will be a full, effective application of this theory than it was to build an atomic power plant in 1945. There are many formidable obstacles to overcome.

The conditions imposed by conventional organization theory and by the approach of scientific management for the past half century have tied men to limited jobs which do not utilize their capabilities, have discouraged the acceptance of responsibility, have encouraged passivity, have eliminated meaning from work. Man's habits, attitudes, expectations—his whole conception of membership in an industrial organization—have been conditioned by his experience under these circumstances. . . .

Another way of saying this is that Theory X places exclusive reliance upon external control of human behavior, while Theory Y relies heavily on self-control and self-direction. It is worth noting that this difference is the difference between treating people as children and treating them as mature adults. After generations of the former, we cannot expect to shift to the latter overnight.

## STEPS IN THE RIGHT DIRECTION

Before we are overwhelmed by the obstacles, let us remember that the application theory is always slow. Progress is usually achieved in small steps. Some innovative ideas which are entirely consistent with Theory Y are today being applied with some success.

### Decentralization and Delegation

These are ways of freeing people from the too-close control of conventional organization, giving them a degree of freedom to direct their own activities, to assume responsibility, and, importantly, to satisfy their egoistic needs. . . .

### Job Enlargement

This concept, pioneered by IBM and Detroit Edison, is quite consistent with Theory Y. It encourages the acceptance of responsibility at the bottom of the organization; it provides opportunities for satisfying social and egoistic needs. In fact, the reorganization of work at the factory level offers one of the more challenging opportunities for innovation consistent with Theory Y.

### Participation and Consultative Management

Under proper conditions, participation and consultative management provide encouragement to people to direct their creative energies toward organizational objectives, give them some voice in decisions that affect them, provide significant opportunities for the satisfaction of social and egoistic needs. The Scanlon Plan is the outstanding embodiment of these ideas in practice.

### Performance Appraisal

Even a cursory examination of conventional programs of performance appraisal within the ranks of management will reveal how completely consistent they are with Theory X. In fact, most such programs tend to treat the individual as though he were a product under inspection on the assembly line.

A few companies—among them General Mills, Ansul Chemical, and General Electric—have been experimenting with approaches which involve the individual in setting "targets" or objectives *for himself* and in a *self*-evaluation of performance semiannually or annually. . . .

The individual is encouraged to take a greater responsibility for planning and appraising his own contribution to organizational objectives; and the accompanying effects on egoistic and self-fulfillment needs are substantial.

## APPLYING THE IDEAS

The not infrequent failure of such ideas as these to work as well as expected is often attributable to the fact that a man-

agement has "bought the idea" but applied it within the framework of Theory X and its assumptions.

Delegation is not an effective way of exercising management by control. Participation becomes a farce when it is applied as a sales gimmick or a device for kidding people into thinking they are important. . . .

## THE HUMAN SIDE OF ENTERPRISE

The ingenuity and the perseverance of industrial management in the pursuit of economic ends have changed many scientific and technological dreams into commonplace realities. It is now becoming clear that the application of these same talents to the human side of enterprise will not only enhance substantially these materialistic achievements, but will bring us one step closer to "the good society."

# 4

# The Motivating Effect of Cognitive Dissonance
## Leon Festinger

## COGNITIVE DISSONANCE AS A MOTIVATING STATE

I should like to postulate the existence of *cognitive dissonance* as a motivating state in human beings. Since most of you probably never heard of cognitive dissonance, I assume that so far I have been no more informative than if I had said that I wish to postulate X as a motivating state. I will try, then, to provide a conceptual definition of cognitive dissonance.

*Definition of Dissonance.* The word "dissonance" was not chosen arbitrarily to denote this motivating state. It was chosen because its ordinary meaning in the English language is close to the technical meaning I want to give it. The synonyms which the dictionary gives for the word "dissonant" are "harsh," "jarring," "grating," "unmelodious," "inharmonious," "inconsistent," "contradictory," "disagreeing," "incongruous," "discrepant." The word, in this ordinary meaning, specifies a relation between two things. In connection with musical tones, where it is usually used, the relation between the tones is such that they sound unpleasant together. In general, one might say that a dissonant relation exists between two things which occur together, if, in some way, they do not belong together or fit together.

Cognitive dissonance refers to this kind of relation between cognitions which exist simultaneously for a person. If a person knows two things, for example, something about himself and something about the world in which he lives, which somehow do not fit together, we will speak of this as cognitive dissonance. Thus, for example, a person might know that he is a very intelligent, highly capable person. At the same time, let us imagine, he knows that he meets repeated failure. These two cognitions would be dissonant—they do not fit together. In general, two cognitions are dissonant with each other if, considering these two cognitions alone, the obverse of one follows from the other. Thus, in the example we have given, it follows from the fact that a person is highly capable that he does not continually meet with failure. . . .

*How Cognitive Dissonance Resembles Other Need States.* Thus far I have said nothing about the motivating aspects of cognitive dissonance. This is the next step. I wish to hypothesize that the existence of cognitive dissonance is comparable to any other need state. Just as hunger is motivating, cognitive dissonance is motivating. Cognitive dissonance will give rise to activity oriented toward reducing or eliminating the dissonance. Successful reduction of dissonance is rewarding in the same sense that eating when one is hungry is rewarding.

In other words, if two cognitions are dissonant with each other there will be

*Source:* From: "The Motivating Effect of Cognitive Dissonance," by Leon Festinger, from *Assessment of Human Motives,* edited by Gardner Lindzey (New York: Holt, Rinehart & Winston, 1958), pp. 69–85. Reprinted by permission.

some tendency for the person to attempt to change one of them so that they do fit together, thus reducing or eliminating the dissonance. . . .

*Data Needed to Demonstrate the Motivating Character of Cognitive Dissonance.* Before proceeding, let us consider for a moment the kinds of data one would like to have in order to document the contention that cognitive dissonance is a motivating state. One would like to have at least the following kinds of data:

1. Determination at Time 1 that a state of cognitive dissonance exists. This could be done either by measurement or by experimental manipulation.
2. Determination at Time 2 that the dissonance has been eliminated or reduced in magnitude.
3. Data concerning the behavioral process whereby the person has succeeded in changing some cognition, thus reducing the dissonance.

Actually, the above three items are minimal and would probably not be sufficient to demonstrate cogently the validity of the theory concerning cognitive dissonance. . . .

The kind of data that would be more convincing concerning the motivating aspects of dissonance would be data concerning instances where the dissonance was reduced in the other direction, such as is exemplified in the old joke about the psychiatrist who had a patient who believed he was dead. After getting agreement from the patient that dead men do not bleed, and being certain that the patient understood this, the psychiatrist made a cut on the patient's arm and, as the blood poured out, leaned back in his chair, smiling. Whereupon the patient, with a look of dismay on his face, said, "Well, what do you know, dead men *do* bleed." This kind of thing, if it

occurred actually, would be harder to explain in alternative ways.

In other words, one has to demonstrate the effects of dissonance in circumstances where these effects are not easily explainable on the basis of other existing theories. Indeed, if one cannot do this, then one could well ask what the usefulness was of this new notion that explained nothing that was not already understood. . . .

[An] intriguing example of the reduction of dissonance in a startling manner comes from a study I did together with Riecken and Schachter (1956) of a group of people who predicted that, on a given date, a catastrophic flood would overwhelm most of the world. This prediction of the catastrophic flood had been given to the people in direct communications from the gods and was an integral part of their religious beliefs. When the predicted date arrived and passed there was considerable dissonance established in these people. They continued to believe in their gods and in the validity of the communications from them, and at the same time they knew that the prediction of the flood had been wrong. We observed the movement as participants for approximately two months preceding and one month after this unequivocal disproof of part of their belief. The point of the study was, of course, to observe how they would react to the dissonance. Let me give a few of the details of the disproof and how they reacted to it.

For some time it had been clear to the people in the group that those who were chosen were to be picked up by flying saucers before the cataclysm occurred. Some of the believers, these mainly college students, were advised to go home and wait individually for the flying saucer that would arrive for each of them.

This was reasonable and plausible, since the data of the cataclysm happened to occur during an academic holiday. Most of the group, including the most central and most heavily committed members, gathered together in the home of the woman who received the messages from the gods to wait together for the arrival of the saucer. For these latter, disproof of the prediction, in the form of evidence that the messages were not valid, began to occur four days before the predicted event was to take place. A message informed them that a saucer would land in the back yard of the house at 4:00 P.M. to pick up the members of the group. With coat in hand they waited, but no saucer came. A later message told them there had been a delay—the saucer would arrive at midnight. Midst absolute secrecy (the neighbors and press must not know), they waited outdoors on a cold and snowy night for over an hour, but still no saucer came. Another message told them to continue waiting, but still no saucer came. At about 3:00 A.M. they gave up, interpreting the events of that night as a test, a drill, and a rehearsal for the real pickup which would still soon take place.

Tensely, they waited for the final orders to come through—for the messages which would tell them the time, place, and procedure for the actual pickup. Finally, on the day before the cataclysm was to strike, the messages came. At midnight a man would come to the door of the house and take them to the place where the flying saucer would be parked. More messages came that day, one after another, instructing them in the passwords that would be necessary in order to board the saucer, in preparatory procedures such as removal of metal from clothing, removal of personal identification, maintaining silence at certain times, and the like. The day was spent by the group in preparation and rehearsal of the necessary procedures and, when midnight came, the group sat waiting in readiness. But no knock came at the door, no one came to lead them to the flying saucer.

From midnight to five o'clock in the morning the group sat there struggling to understand what had happened, struggling to find some explanation that would enable them to recover somewhat from the shattering realization that they would not be picked up by a flying saucer and that consequently the flood itself would not occur as predicted. It is doubtful that anyone alone, without the support of the others, could have withstood the impact of this disproof of the prediction. Indeed, those members of the group who had gone to their homes to wait alone, alone in the sense that they did not have other believers with them, did not withstand it. Almost all of them became skeptics afterward. In other words, without easily obtainable social support to begin reducing the dissonance, the dissonance was sufficient to cause the belief to be discarded in spite of the commitment to it. But the members of the group that had gathered together in the home of the woman who received the messages could, and did, provide social support for one another. They kept reassuring one another of the validity of the messages and that some explanation would be found.

At fifteen minutes before five o'clock that morning an explanation was found that was at least temporarily satisfactory. A message arrived from God which, in effect, said that He had saved the world and stayed the flood because of this group and the light and strength this group had spread throughout the world that night.

The behavior of these people from that moment onwards presented a revealing contrast to their previous behavior. These people, who had been disinterested in publicity and even avoided it, became avid publicity seekers. . . .

There were almost no lengths to which these people would not go to attract publicity and potential believers in the validity of the messages. If, indeed, more and more converts could be found, more and more people who believed in the messages and the things the messages said, then the dissonance between their belief and the knowledge that the messages had not been correct could be reduced. . . .

*An Experimental Investigation.* In this experiment, we created dissonance in the subjects by inducing them to say something which was at variance with their private opinion. It is clear that this kind of situation does produce dissonance between what the person believes and what he knows he has said. There are also cognitive consonances for the person. His cognitions concerning the things that induced him to make the public statement are consonant with his knowledge of having done it. The total magnitude of the dissonance between all other relevant cognitions taken together and the knowledge of what he has publicly said will, of course, be a function of the number and importance of the dissonances in relation to the number and importance of the consonances. One could, then, manipulate the total magnitude of dissonance experimentally by holding everything constant and varying the strength of the inducement for the person to state something publicly which was at variance with his private opinion. The *stronger* the inducement to do this, the *less* would be the over-all magnitude of dissonance created. . . .

Now for the details of the experiment. I will describe it as it proceeded for the subject, with occasional explanatory comments. Each subject had signed up for a two hour experiment on "measures of performance." The subjects were all students from the Introductory Psychology course at Stanford where they are required to serve a certain number of hours as subjects in experiments. When the student arrived he was met by the experimenter and, with a minimum of explanation, was given a repetitive motor task to work on. . . .

From our point of view, the purpose of this initial part was to provide for each subject an experience which was rather dull, boring, and somewhat fatiguing. The student, however, believed this to be the whole experiment. The explanation of the experiment given to the student was that the experiment was concerned with the effect of preparatory set on performance. He was told that there were two conditions in the experiment, one of these being the condition he had experienced where the subject was told nothing ahead of time. The other condition, the experimenter explained, was one in which the subject, before working on the tasks, was led to expect that they were very enjoyable, very interesting, and lots of fun. The procedure for subjects in this other condition, the experimenter explained, proceeded in the following manner. A person working for us is introduced to the waiting subject as someone who has just finished the experiment and will tell the prospective subject a little about it. This person who works for us then tells the waiting subject that the experiment is very enjoyable, interesting, and lots of fun. In this way, the subjects in the other condition are given the set we want them to have. This concluded the false explanation of the experiment to the student and, in the control group, nothing more was done at this point.

In the experimental groups, however, the experimenter continued by telling the subject that he had a rather unusual proposal to make. It seems that the next subject is scheduled to be in that condition where he is to be convinced in advance that the experiment is enjoyable and a lot of fun. The person who works for us and usually does this, however, although very reliable, could not do it today. We thought we would take a chance and ask him (the student) to do it for us. We would like, if agreeable to him, to hire him on the same basis that the other person was hired to work for us. We would like to put him on the payroll and pay him a lump sum of money to go tell the waiting subject that the experiment is enjoyable, interesting, and fun; and he was also to be on tap for us in case this kind of emergency arises again.

There were two experimental conditions which we actually conducted. The procedure was absolutely identical in both except for the amount of money that the subjects were paid as "the lump sum." In one condition they were paid one dollar for their immediate and possible future services. In the other condition they were paid twenty dollars. When the student agreed to do this, he was actually given the money and he signed a receipt for it. He was then taken into the room where the next subject was waiting and introduced to her by the experimenter, who said that the student had just been a subject in the experiment and would tell her a bit about it. The experimenter then went out, leaving student and the waiting subject together for two and a half minutes. The waiting subject was actually a girl in our employ. Her instructions were very simple. After the student had told her that the experiment was interesting, enjoyable and lots of fun, she was to say something like, "Oh, a friend of mine who took it yesterday told me it was dull and that if I could I should get out of it." After that she was simply supposed to agree with whatever the student said. If, as almost always happened, the student reaffirmed that the experiment was fun, she was to say that she was glad to hear it. . . .

The experimenter then thanked the subject and made a brief speech in which he said that most subjects found the experimental tasks very interesting and enjoyed them, and that, when he thinks about it, he will probably agree. The purpose of this brief speech is to provide some cognitive material which the subject can use to reduce dissonance, assuming that such dissonance exists. The identical speech is, of course, made to the control subjects, too.

The only remaining problem in the experiment was to obtain a measure of what each subject honestly thought privately about the tasks on which he had worked for an hour. It seemed desirable, naturally, to obtain this measure in a situation where the subject would be inclined to be very frank in his statements. . . .

The student was told that someone from Introductory Psychology probably wanted to interview him. The experimenter confessed ignorance about what this impending interview was about but said he had been told that the subject would know about it. Usually at this point the subject nodded his head or otherwise indicated that he did, indeed, know what it was about. The experimenter then took him to an office where the interviewer was waiting, said goodbye to the subject, and left.

The interview itself was rather brief. Four questions were asked, namely, how interesting and enjoyable the experiment was, how much the subject learned from it, how important he thought it was scientifically, and how much he would like to participate in a similar experiment again. The important question, for us, is the first one concerning how interesting and enjoyable the experiment was, since this was the content area in which dissonance was established for the experimental subjects.

Let us look, then, at what the results show. . . .

In the One Dollar experimental condition there is a definite increase over the control group. Here the average rating is +1.35, definitely on the positive side of the scale and significantly different from the control group at the 1 per cent level of confidence. In other words, in the One Dollar condition the dissonance between their private opinion of the experiment and their knowledge of what they had said to the waiting subject was reduced significantly by changing their private opinion somewhat, to bring it closer to what they had overtly said.

But now let us turn our attention to the Twenty Dollar condition. Here the magnitude of dissonance experimentally created was less than in the One Dollar condition because of the greater importance of the cognition that was consonant with what they knew they had done. It seems undeniable that twenty dollars is a good deal more important then one dollar. There should hence be less pressure to reduce the dissonance, and indeed, the average rating for the Twenty Dollar condition is −.05, only slightly above the Control condition and significantly different from the One Dollar condition at the 2 per cent level of confidence.

## SUMMARY AND CONCLUSION

The evidence for the validity and usefulness of conceiving cognitive dissonance as motivating is as follows:

1. Evidence that the existence of cognitive dissonance sometimes leads to behavior that appears very strange indeed when viewed only from the standpoint of commonly accepted motives. Here I have had time only to give two examples illustrating this phenomenon.
2. Evidence that the amount of reduction of dissonance is a direct function of the magnitude of dissonance which exists. I illustrated this by describing a laboratory experiment where, under controlled conditions, the magnitude of dissonance was experimentally manipulated.

## REFERENCES

Festinger, Leon. A *theory of cognitive dissonance*. Evanston, Ill.: Row-Peterson, 1957.

———, Riecken, H. W., and Schachter, S. *When prophecy fails*. Minneapolis: University of Minnesota Press, 1956.

Janis, I. L., and King, B. T. The influence of role-playing on opinion change. *J. Abnorm. (soc.) Psychol.*, 1954, 49, 211–218.

King, B. T., and Janis, I. L. Comparison of the effectiveness of improvised versus nonimprovised role-playing in producing opinion changes. *Human Relations*, 1956, 9, 177–186.

Prasad, J. A comparative study of rumors and reports in earthquakes. *Brit. J. Psychol.*, 1950, 41, 129–144.

Sinha, D. Behavior in a catastrophic situation: a psychological study of reports and rumors. *Brit. J. Psychol.*, 1952, 43, 200–209.

# 5

# Work and Motivation

## *Victor H. Vroom*

### THE NATURE OF MOTIVATION

There are two somewhat different kinds of questions which are typically dealt with in discussions of motivation. One of these is the question of the arousal or energizing of the organism. Why is the organism active at all? What conditions instigate action, determine its duration or persistence and finally its cessation? The phenomena to be explained include the level of activity of the organism and the vigor of amplitude of its behavior. The second question involves the direction of behavior. What determines the form that activity will take? Under what conditions will an organism choose one response or another or move in one direction or another? The problem is to explain the choices made by an organism among qualitatively different behaviors.

The latter question—concerning direction or choice—is probably the more important of the two to the psychologist. . . .

Is all behavior motivated? The answer to this question depends somewhat on the range of processes which are subsumed under the heading of motivation. We will follow the relatively common practice of viewing as motivated only the behaviors that are under central or voluntary control. . . .

To sum up, we view the central problem of motivation as the explanation of choices made by organisms among different voluntary responses. Although some behaviors, specifically those that are not under voluntary control, are defined as unmotivated, these probably constitute a rather small proportion of the total behavior of adult human beings. It is reasonable to assume that most of the behavior exhibited by individuals on their jobs as well as their behavior in the "job market" is voluntary, and consequently motivated.

### AN OUTLINE OF A COGNITIVE MODEL

In the remainder of this chapter, we outline a conceptual model which will guide our discussion and interpretation of research in the remainder of the book. The model to be described is similar to those developed by other investigators including Lewin (1938), Rotter (1955), Peak (1955), Davidson, Suppes, and Siegel (1957), Atkinson (1958b), and Tolman (1959). It is basically ahistorical in form. We assume that the choices made by a person among alternative courses of action are lawfully related to psychological events occurring contemporaneously with the behavior. We turn now to consider the concepts in the model and their interrelations.

*The Concept of Valence.* We shall begin with the simple assumption that, at any given point in time, a person has preferences among outcomes or states of nature. For any pair of outcomes, x and y, a person prefers x to y, prefers y to x, or is indifferent to whether he receives x or y. Preference, then, refers to a relationship between the strength of a person's desire for, or attraction toward, two outcomes. . . . In our system, an outcome is positively valent when the person prefers attaining it to not attaining it (i.e., he prefers x to not x). An outcome has a valence of zero when the person is indifferent to attaining or not attaining it (i.e., he is indifferent to x or not x), and it is negatively valent when he prefers not attaining it to attaining it (i.e., he prefers not x to x). It is assumed that valence can take a wide range of both positive and negative values.

We use the term motive whenever the referent is a preference for a class of outcomes. A positive (or approach) motive signifies that outcomes which are members of the class have positive valence, and a negative (or avoidance) motive signifies that outcomes in the class have negative valence.

It is important to distinguish between the valence of an outcome to a person and its value to that person. An individual may desire an object but derive little satisfaction from its attainment—or he may strive to avoid an object which he later finds to be quite satisfying. At any given time there may be a substantial discrepancy between the anticipated satisfaction from an outcome (i.e., its valence) and the actual satisfaction that it provides (i.e., its value).

There are many outcomes which are positively or negatively valent to persons, but are not in themselves anticipated to be satisfying or dissatisfying. The strength of a person's desire or aversion for them is based not on their intrinsic properties but on the anticipated satisfaction or dissatisfaction associated with other outcomes to which they are expected to lead. People may desire to join groups because they believe that

membership will enhance their status in the community, and they may desire to perform their jobs effectively because they expect that it will lead to a promotion.

In effect, we are suggesting that means acquire valence as a consequence of their expected relationship to ends. . . . If an object is believed by a person to lead to desired consequences or to prevent undesired consequences, the person is predicted to have a positive attitude toward it. If, on the other hand, it is believed by the person to lead to undesired consequences or to prevent desired consequences, the person is predicted to have a negative attitude toward it. . . .

We do not mean to imply that all the variance in the valence of outcomes can be explained by their expected consequences. We must assume that some things are desired and abhorred "for their own sake." Desegregation may be opposed "on principle" not because it leads to other events which are disliked, and people may seek to do well on their jobs even though no externally mediated rewards are believed to be at stake.

Without pretending to have solved all of the knotty theoretical problems involved in the determinants of valence, we can specify the expected functional relationship between the valence of outcomes and their expected consequences in the following proposition.

*Proposition 1. The valence of an outcome to a person is a monotonically increasing function of the algebraic sum of the products of the valences of all other outcomes and his conceptions of its instrumentality for the attainment of these other outcomes.*

In equation form the same proposition reads as follows:

$$V_j = f_j [\sum_{k=1}^{n} (V_k I_{jk})] \, (j = 1 \ldots n)$$
$$f_j' > O; \, I_{jj} = O$$

where $V_j$ = the valence of outcome $j$

$I_{jk}$ = the cognized instrumentality $(-1 \leq I_{jk} \leq 1)$ of outcome $j$ for the attainment of outcome $k$

*The Concept of Expectancy.* The specific outcomes attained by a person are dependent not only on the choices that he makes but also on events which are beyond his control. For example, a person who elects to buy a ticket in a lottery is not certain of winning the desired prize. Whether or not he does so is a function of many chance events. Similarly, the student who enrolls in medical school is seldom certain that he will successfully complete the program of study; the person who seeks political office is seldom certain that he will win the election; and the worker who strives for a promotion is seldom certain that he will triumph over other candidates. Most decision-making situations involve some element of risk, and theories of choice behavior must come to grips with the role of these risks in determining the choices that people do make.

Whenever an individual chooses between alternatives which involve uncertain outcomes, it seems clear that his behavior is affected not only by his preferences among these outcomes but also by the degree to which he believes these outcomes to be probable. . . .

Expectancy is an action-outcome association. It takes values ranging from zero, indicating no subjective probability that an act will be followed by an outcome, to 1, indicating certainty that the act will be followed by an outcome. Instrumentally, on the other hand, is an outcome-outcome association. It can take values ranging from $-1$, indicating a belief that attainment of the second outcome is certain without the first outcome and impossible with it, to $+1$, indicating that the first outcome is believed to be a necessary and sufficient condition

for the attainment of the second outcome.

*The Concept of Force.* It remains to be specified how valences and expectancies combine in determining choices. The directional concept in our model is the Lewinian concept of force. Behavior on the part of a person is assumed to be the result of a field of forces each of which has direction and magnitude. . . .

There are many possible ways of combining valences and expectancies mathematically to yield these hypothetical forces. On the assumption that choices made by people are subjectively rational, we would predict the strength of forces to be a monotonically increasing function of the *product* of valences and expectancies. Proposition 2 expresses this functional relationship.

*Proposition 2. The force on a person to perform an act is a monotonically increasing function of the algebraic sum of the products of the valences of all outcomes and the strength of his expectancies that the act will be followed by the attainment of these outcomes.*

We can express this proposition in the form of the following equation:

$$F_i = f_i \left[ \sum_{j=1}^{n} (E_{ij} V_j) \right] (i = n + 1 \ldots m)$$
$$f_i' > 0; \, i \cap j = \Phi, \, \Phi \text{ is the null set}$$

where $F_i$ = the force to perform act $i$

$E_{ij}$ = the strength of the expectancy $(0 \leq E_{ij} \leq 1)$ that act $i$ will be followed by outcome $j$

$V_j$ = the valence of outcome $j$

It is also assumed that people choose from among alternative acts the one corresponding to the strongest positive (or weakest negative) force. This formulation is similar to the notion in decision theory that people choose in a way that maximizes subjective expected utility.

Expressing force as a monotonically increasing function of the product of valence and expectancy has a number of implications which should be noted. An outcome with high positive or negative valence will have no effect on the generation of a force unless there is some expectancy (i.e., some subjective probability greater than zero) that the outcome will be attained by some act. As the strength of an expectancy that an act will lead to an outcome increases, the effect of variations in the valence of the outcome on the force to perform the act will also increase. Similarly, if the valence of an outcome is zero (i.e., the person is indifferent to the outcome), neither the absolute value nor variations in the strength of expectancies of attaining it will have any effect on forces.

Our two propositions have been stated in separate terms, but are in fact highly related to one another. Insofar as the acts and outcomes are described in different terms the separation is a useful one. We have in the first proposition a basis for predicting the valence of outcomes, and in the second proposition a basis for predicting the actions that a person will take with regard to the outcome. . . .

In practice we will find it useful to maintain the separation between the two propositions by defining sets of actions and sets of outcomes independently of one another. We will use the term action to refer to behavior which might reasonably be expected to be within the repertoire of the person, e.g., seeking entry into an occupation, while the term outcomes will be reserved for more temporally distant events which are less likely to be under complete behavioral control, e.g., attaining membership in an occupation.

## TESTING THE MODEL

The model, as outlined so far, is untestable, for its concepts have not been related to observable events. In order to derive empirical hypotheses from the model, we must specify operational definitions for the formal concepts. Some further assumptions must be made which will permit the measurement or experimental manipulation of the concepts. . . .

The only concept in the model that has been directly linked with potentially observable events is the concept of force. We have assumed that the acts performed by a person reflect the relative strength of forces acting upon him. If a person performs act x rather than y the force corresponding to x is assumed to be stronger than y and vice versa.

We have, however, said nothing about observable events that would lead us to infer either that an outcome has a certain valence for a person, or that the strength of a person's expectancy that an act will lead to an outcome has a particular value. It is this kind of problem to which we now turn.

Our approach to this problem is "eclectic." Instead of proposing a single operational definition for each of the concepts, we outline a series of broad approaches to their measurement and/or experimental manipulation.

*The Measurement of Valence.* What approaches can be taken to the measurement of valence? What observations of behavior need to be made in order to permit us to conclude that one outcome is positively valent and a second negatively valent, or that one is more positively valent than a second?

One approach is to use *verbal reports*. If an individual states that an event is attractive or desirable, it might be assumed to have positive valence. If he states that a second event is unattractive or undesirable, it might be assumed to have negative valence. This procedure can be extended to provide measures of the relative attractiveness or unattractiveness of a series of events or outcomes by requesting the person to make comparative judgments or by using a standard judgmental scale. . . .

The most convincing argument against the use of self-report measures is a theoretical one. If a person's reports of his desires and aversions are voluntary responses, it should be possible to explain them in terms of processes similar to those involved in other kinds of voluntary behavior. A person's statement that he prefers outcome x to outcome y should, therefore, be a more reliable indicator of the expected consequences of making this statement than of the expected consequences of attaining outcomes x and y. Investigators who use self-report measures of motivation are aware of this problem, and they try to minimize or eliminate "faking" by structuring the testing situation in such a way that the subject believes his responses are confidential or anonymous.

A second approach is found in the work of Atkinson, McClelland, and their associates (McClelland et al., 1953; Atkinson, 1958a). They assume that the motives of a person can be inferred from the *analysis of fantasy*. The thematic apperception method (Murray, 1938) is the principal device used for eliciting this fantasy. Subjects are requested to tell stories about pictures, and the content of their stories is scored according to the frequency with which different kinds of imagery appear. The achievement motive has been most frequently studied by this method, but work has also been carried out on a number of other motives including affiliation, power, and sex.

This method has both strong supporters and detractors. . . .

A third approach to the measurement of valence involves the use of outcomes to create new learning. If an outcome strengthens a response tendency, it could be assumed to be positively valent; if it weakens a response tendency, it could

be assumed to be negatively valent. The measure of valence is the *amount or rate of change in response probability* when the outcome is made contingent on the response. We would expect such data to be a reliable indicator of whether an outcome is positively valent or negatively valent but not to be especially sensitive to differences in degree of positive or negative valence.

A fourth approach rests on the assumption that the valence of outcomes can be inferred from *the choices that persons make* among alternative courses of action. If a person is given a free choice between two outcomes x and y, under conditions in which his expectancies of attaining them are equal (e.g., certain), his choice between them may be assumed to reflect their relative valence. Choice of x is assumed to indicate that x is more positively valent than y, whereas choice of y is assumed to indicate that y is more positively valent than x. This approach will easily permit the ordering of a set of outcomes on an ordinal or relative scale. If we introduce differential risks into the choice situation, interval measurement becomes a possibility. Following ideas originally introduced by Von Neumann and Morgenstern (1947), Mosteller and Nogee (1951) and Davidson, Suppes, and Siegel (1957) have outlined methods for obtaining interval measurements of the utility of different amounts of money.

A fifth approach involves observation of *consummatory behavior*. It is consequently applicable primarily to those outcomes such as food, water, and sexual activity where consummation takes place. We might assume that the hungrier a person is, i.e., the greater valence of food, the more food he will eat. Thus, measures of amount or rate of eating, drinking, or copulation could be used to indicate the extent to which the consumed outcomes were positively valent.

Finally, we might be able to use "*decision time*" as a behavioral indication of differences in valence of outcomes. If a person is given a "free choice" among two outcomes, x and y, the length of time elapsing before he makes his choice could be assumed to reflect the extent to which the outcomes differ in valence. Instantaneous choice of one over the other would indicate a substantial difference in their valence, whereas a long decision time would indicate much less difference. A theory relating decision time to differences in the strength of forces acting on the person has been advanced by Cartwright (1941). It should be noted that, at best, decision time can be used to indicate the amount of difference in valence among outcomes, not which outcome is more positively valent. However, observations of decision time and of the choice can typically be made concurrently, permitting inferences concerning both the amount and direction of difference in the valence of outcomes. . . .

*The Measurement of Expectancy.* How is the strength of expectancy to be measured? What behaviors can be taken as evidence that a person believes that the probability of an outcome following a response is 0, or .50, or 1.00? This problem is by no means simple. A number of different approaches are available, but each presents certain problems.

One possible approach rests on the assumption that expectancies are reflected in *verbal reports* by individuals about the probability of outcomes. Just as verbal reports may be taken as evidence for the valence of outcomes, they may also constitute the main form of evidence for expectancies. If a person states that an outcome is certain to follow an act, we assume an expectancy value of 1.00, whereas if he states that an

outcome has a 50-50 chance of following that act, we assume an expectancy value of .50. This approach has not received enthusiastic support from decision theorists (Davidson, Suppes, and Siegel, 1957). The arguments against it are similar to those noted earlier in connection with self-reports of motives. . . .

Other investigators have assumed that expectancies are best inferred from *actual choices or decisions made by the person.* For example, Preston and Barrata (1948) assumed a linear relationship between psychological probabilities of attaining a given prize and the amount that the subject was willing to wager to get a chance at the prize. If a subject was willing to wager $5.00 for a possible prize of $50, his psychological probability was assumed to be .10. Psychological probabilities measured by this procedure were generally related to mathematical probabilities. However, they tended to be larger than mathematical probabilities at low values of probability, and smaller than mathematical probabilities at higher values.

The problem with this approach is to disentangle the roles of expectancies and preferences in actual decisions. . . .

## BIBLIOGRAPHY

Atkinson, J. W. (Ed.) *Motives in fantasy, action, and society.* Princeton: Van Nostrand, 1958a.

Atkinson, J. W. Towards experimental analysis of human motivation in terms of motives, expectancies, and incentives. In Atkinson, J. W. (Ed.) *Motives in fantasy, action, and society.* Princeton: Van Nostrand, 1958b, pp. 288–305.

Cartwright, D. Decision-time in relation to the differentiation of the phenomenal field. *Psychol. Rev.,* 1941, 48, 425–442.

Davidson, D., Suppes, P., and Siegel, S. *Decision making: An experimental approach.* Stanford: Standford University Press, 1957.

Lewin, K. The conceptual representation and the measurement of psychological forces.

*Contr. psychol. Theory*. Durham, N.C.: Duke University Press, 1938, 1, No. 4.

McClelland, D. C., Atkinson, J. W., Clark, R. A., and Lowell, E. L. *The achievement motive*. New York: Appleton-Century-Crofts, 1953.

Mosteller, F., and Nogee, P. An experimental measurement of utility. *J. pol. Econ.*, 1951, 59, 371–404.

Murray, H. A. *Explorations in personality*. New York: Oxford University Press, 1938.

Peak, Helen. Attitude and motivation. In Jones, M. R. (Ed.) *Nebraska symposium on motivation*. Lincoln: University of Nebraska Press, 1955, pp. 149–188.

Preston, M. G., and Baratta, P., An experimental study of the auction-value of an uncertain outcome. *Amer. J. Psychol.*, 1948, 61, 183–193.

Rotter, J. B. The role of the psychological situation in determining the direction of human behavior. In Jones, M. R. (Ed.) *Nebraska symposium on motivation*. Lincoln: University of Nebraska Press, 1955, pp. 245–268.

Tolman, E. C. Principles of purposive behavior. In Koch, S. (Ed.) *Psychology: A study of a science*. Vol. 2. New York: McGraw-Hill, 1959, pp. 92–157.

Von Neumann, J., and Morgenstern, O. *Theory of games and economic behavior*. Princeton: Princeton University Press, 1947, 2nd ed.

# 6

# One More Time: How Do You Motivate Employees?

## Not By Improving Work Conditions, Raising Salaries, or Shuffling Tasks

*Frederick Herzberg*

## "MOTIVATING" WITH KITA

In lectures to industry on the problem, I have found that the audiences are anxious for quick and practical answers, so I will begin with a straightforward, practical formula for moving people.

What is the simplest, surest, and most direct way of getting someone to do something? Ask him? But if he responds that he does not want to do it, then that calls for a psychological consultation to determine the reason for his obstinacy. Tell him? His response shows that he does not understand you, and now an expert in communication methods has to be brought in to show you how to get through to him. Give him a monetary incentive? I do not need to remind the reader of the complexity and difficulty involved in setting up and administering an incentive system. Show him? This means a costly training program. We need a simple way.

Every audience contains the "direct action" manager who shouts, "Kick him!" And this type of manager is right. The surest and least circumlocuted way of getting someone to do something is to kick him in the pants—give him what might be called the KITA.

There are various forms of KITA, and here are some of them:

*Negative Physical KITA.* This is a literal application of the term and was frequently used in the past. It has, however, three major drawbacks: (1) it is inelegant; (2) it contradicts the precious image of benevolence that most organizations cherish; and (3) since it is a physical attack, it directly stimulates the autonomic nervous system, and this often results in negative feedback—the employee may just kick you in return. These factors give rise to certain taboos against negative physical KITA. . . .

*Negative Psychological KITA.* This has several advantages over negative physical KITA. First, the cruelty is not visible; the bleeding is internal and comes much later. Second, since it affects the higher cortical centers of the brain with its inhibitory powers, it reduces the possibility of physical backlash. Third, since the number of psychological pains that a person can feel is almost infinite, the direction and site possibility of the KITA are

*Source:* Reprinted by permission of the *Harvard Business Review.* "One More Time: How Do You Motivate Employees?" by Frederick Herzberg (January/February 1968). Copyright© 1968 by the President and Fellows of Harvard College; all rights reserved.

*Author's note:* I should like to acknowledge the contribution that Robert Ford of the American Telephone and Telegraph Company has made to the ideas expressed in this paper, and in particular to the successful application of these ideas in improving work performance and the job satisfaction of employees.

increased many times. Fourth, the person administering the kick can manage to be above it all and let the system accomplish the dirty work. Fifth, those who practice it receive some ego satisfaction (one upmanship), whereas they would find drawing blood abhorrent. Finally, if the employee does complain, he can always be accused of being paranoid, since there is no tangible evidence of an actual attack.

Now, what does negative KITA accomplish? If I kick you in the rear (physically or psychologically), who is motivated? *I* am motivated; you move! Negative KITA does not lead to motivation, but to movement. So:

*Positive KITA.* Let us consider motivation. If I say to you, "Do this for me or the company and in return I will give you a reward, an incentive, more status, a promotion, all the quid pro quos that exist in the industrial organization," am I motivating you? The overwhelming opinion I receive from management people is "Yes, this is motivation.". . .

Why is it that managerial audiences are quick to see that negative KITA is not motivation while they are almost unanimous in their judgment that positive KITA is motivation? It is because negative KITA is rape, and positive KITA is seduction. But it is infinitely worse to be seduced than to be raped; the latter is an unfortunate occurrence, while the former signifies that you were a party to your own downfall. This is why positive KITA is so popular: it is a tradition; it is in the American way. The organization does not have to kick you; you kick yourself.

## MYTHS ABOUT MOTIVATION

With this in mind, we can review some positive KITA personnel practices that were developed as attempts to instill "motivation":

1. *Reducing time spent at work*—This represents a marvelous way of motivating people to work—getting them off the job! We have reduced (formally and informally) the time spent on the job over the last 50 to 60 years until we are finally on the way to the "63-day weekend." An interesting varient of this approach is the development of off-hour recreation programs. The philosophy here seems to be that those who play together, work together. The fact is that motivated people seek more hours of work, not fewer.

2. *Spiraling wages*—Have these motivated people? Yes, to seek the next wage increase. . . .

3. *Fringe benefits*—Industry has outdone the most welfare-minded of welfare states in dispensing cradle-to-the grave succor. . . .

   These benefits are no longer rewards; they are rights. . . .

   Unless the ante is continuously raised, the psychological reaction of employees is that the company is turning back the clock.

4. *Human relations training*—Over 30 years of teaching and, in many instances, of practicing psychological approaches to handling people have resulted in costly human relations programs and, in the end, the same question: How do you motivate workers? . . .

   The failure of human relations training to produce motivation led to the conclusion that the supervisor or manager himself was not psychologically true to himself in his practice of interpersonal decency. So an advanced form of human relations KITA, sensitivity training, was unfolded.

5. *Sensitivity training*—Do you really, really understand yourself? Do you really, really, really trust the other man? Do you really, really, really, really cooperate? The failure of sensitivity training is now being explained, by those who have become opportunistic exploiters of the technique, as a failure to really (five times) conduct proper sensitivity training courses. . . .

6. *Communications*—The professor of communications was invited to join the faculty of management training programs and help in making employees understand what management was doing for them. House organs, briefing sessions, supervisory instruction on the importance of communication, and all sorts of propaganda have proliferated until today there is even an International Council of Industrial Editors. But no motivation resulted, and the obvious thought occurred that perhaps management was not hearing what the employees were saying. That led to the next KITA.

7. *Two-way communication*—Management ordered morale surveys, suggestion plans, and group participation programs. Then both employees and management were communicating and listening to each other more than ever, but without much improvement in motivation.

The behavioral scientists began to take another look at their conceptions and their data, and they took human relations one step further. A glimmer of truth was beginning to show through in the writings of the so-called higher-order-need psychologists. People, so they said, want to actualize themselves. Unfortunately, the "actualizing" psychologists got mixed up with the human relations psychologists, and a new KITA emerged.

8. *Job participation*—Though it may not have been the theoretical intention, job participation often became a "give them the big picture" approach. For example, if a man is tightening 10,000 nuts a day on an assembly line with a torque wrench, tell him he is building a Chevrolet. Another approach had the goal of giving the employee a *feeling* that he is determining, in some measure, what he does on his job. The goal was to provide a *sense* of achievement rather than a substantive achievement in his task. Real achievement, of course, requires a task that makes it possible.

9. *Employee counseling*—The initial use of this form of KITA in a systematic fashion can be credited to the Hawthorne experiment of the Western Electric Company during the early 1930s. At that time, it was found that the employees harbored irrational feelings that were interfering with the rational operation of the factory. Counseling in this instance was a means of letting the employees unburden themselves by talking to someone about their problems. Although the counseling techniques were primitive, the program was large indeed. . . .

Since KITA results only in short-term movement, it is safe to predict that the cost of these programs will increase steadily and new varieties will be developed as old positive KITA reach their satiation points.

## HYGIENE VS. MOTIVATORS

Let me rephrase the perennial question this way: How do you install a generator in an employee? A brief review of my motivation hygiene theory of job attitudes is required before theoretical and practical suggestions can be offered. The theory was first drawn from an examination of events in the lives of engineers and accountants. At least 16 other investigations, using a wide variety of populations including some in the Communist countries have since been completed, making the original research one of the most replicated studies in the field of job attitudes.

The findings of these studies, along with corroboration from many other investigations using different procedures, suggest that the factors involved in producing job satisfaction and motivation are separate and distinct from the factors that lead to job dissatisfaction. Since separate factors need to be considered, depending on whether job satisfaction or job dissatisfaction is being examined, it follows that these two feelings are not opposites of each other. The opposite of job satisfaction is not job dissatisfaction but, rather, *no* job satisfaction; and similarly, the opposite of job dissatisfaction is not job satisfaction, but *no* job dissatisfaction. . . .

Two different needs of man are involved here. One set of needs can be thought of as stemming from his animal nature—the built-in drive to avoid pain from the environment, plus all the learned drives which become conditioned to the basic biological needs. For example, hunger, a basic biological drive, makes it necessary to earn money, and then money becomes a specific drive. The other set of needs relates to that antique human characteristic, the ability to achieve and, through achievement, to experience psychological growth. The stimuli for the growth needs are tasks that induce growth; in the industrial setting, they are the *job content.* Contrariwise, the stimuli inducing pain-avoidance behavior are found in the *job environment.*

The growth or *motivator* factors that are intrinsic to the job are: achievement, recognition for achievement, the work itself, responsibility, and growth oradvancement. The dissatisfaction-avoidance or *hygiene* (KITA) factors that are extrinsic to the job include: company policy and administration, supervision, interpersonal relationships, working conditions, salary, status, and security.

A composite of the factors that are involved in causing job satisfaction and job dissatisfaction [is] drawn from samples of 1,685 employees. The results indicate that motivators were the primary cause of satisfaction, and hygiene factors the primary cause of unhappiness on the job. The employees, studied in 12 different investigations, included lower-level supervisors, professional women, agricultural administrators, men about to retire from management positions, hospital maintenance personnel, manufacturing supervisors, nurses, food handlers, military officers, engineers, scientists, housekeepers, teachers, technicians, female assemblers, accountants, Finnish foremen, and Hungarian engineers.

They were asked what job events had occurred in their work that had led to extreme satisfaction or extreme dissatisfaction on their part. Their responses are broken down in the exhibit into percentages of total "positive" job events and of total "negative" job events. . . .

To illustrate, a typical response involving achievement that had a negative effect for the employee was, "I was unhappy because I didn't do the job successfully." A typical response in the small number of positive job events in the Company Policy and Administration grouping was, "I was happy because the company reorganized the section so that I didn't report any longer to the guy I didn't get along with."

As the lower right-hand part of *Exhibit I* shows, of all the factors contributing to job satisfaction, 81% were motivators. And of all the factors contributing to the employees' dissatisfaction over their work, 69% involved hygiene elements.

## ETERNAL TRIANGLE

There are three general philosophies of personnel management. The first is based on organizational theory, the second on industrial engineering, and the third on behavioral science.

The organizational theorist believes that human needs are either so irrational or so varied and adjustable to specific situations that the major function of personnel management is to be as pragmatic as the occasion demands. If jobs are organized in a proper manner, he reasons, the result will be the most efficient job

# EXHIBIT I • FACTORS AFFECTING JOB ATTITUDES, AS REPORTED IN 12 INVESTIGATIONS

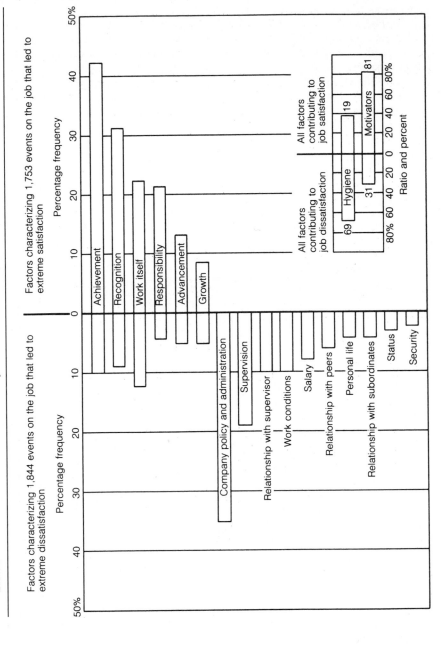

Factors characterizing 1,844 events on the job that led to extreme dissatisfaction

Factors characterizing 1,753 events on the job that led to extreme satisfaction

Percentage frequency

Percentage frequency

Achievement
Recognition
Work itself
Responsibility
Advancement
Growth

Company policy and administration
Supervision
Relationship with supervisor
Work conditions
Salary
Relationship with peers
Personal life
Relationship with subordinates
Status
Security

All factors contributing to job dissatisfaction

All factors contributing to job satisfaction

Hygiene 69
31

Motivators 19
81

Ratio and percent

structure, and the most favorable job attitudes will follow as a matter of course.

The industrial engineer holds that man is mechanistically oriented and economically motivated and his needs are best met by attuning the individual to the most efficient work process. The goal of personnel management therefore should be to concoct the most appropriate incentive system and to design the specific working conditions in a way that facilitates the most efficient use of the human machine. By structuring jobs in a manner that leads to the most efficient operation, the engineer believes that he can obtain the optimal organization of work and the proper work attitudes.

The behavioral scientist focuses on group sentiments, attitudes of individual employees, and the organization's social and psychological climate. According to his persuasion, he emphasizes one or more of the various hygiene and motivator needs. His approach to personnel management generally emphasizes some form of human relations education, in the hope of instilling healthy employee attitudes and an organizational climate which he considers to be felicitous to human values. He believes that proper attitudes will lead to efficient job and organizational structure.

The three philosophies can be depicted as a triangle, as is done in *Exhibit II*, with each persuasion claiming the apex angle. The motivation-hygiene theory claims the same angle as industrial engineering, but for opposite goals. Rather than rationalizing the work to increase efficiency, the theory suggests that work be enriched to bring about effective utilization of personnel. Such a systematic attempt to motivate employees by manipulating the motivator factors is just beginning.

The term *job enrichment* describes this embryonic movement. An older term, job enlargement should be avoided because it is associated with past failures stemming from a misunderstanding of the problem. Job enrichment provides the opportunity for the employee's psychological growth, while job enlargement merely makes a job structurally bigger. Since scientific job enrichment is very new, this article only suggests the principles and practical steps that have recently emerged from several successful experiments in industry.

## JOB LOADING

In attempting to enrich an employee's job, management often succeeds in reducing the man's personal contribution, rather than giving him an opportunity for growth in his accustomed job. Such an endeavor, which I shall call horizontal job loading (as opposed to vertical loading, or providing motivator factors), has been the problem of earlier job enlargement programs. This activity merely enlarges the meaningless of the job. Some examples of this approach, and their effect, are:

- Challenging the employee by increasing the amount of production expected of him. If he tightens 10,000 bolts a day, see if he can tighten 20,000 bolts a day. The arithmetic involved shows that multiplying zero by zero still equals zero.
- Adding another meaningless task to the existing one, usually some routine clerical activity. The arithmetic here is adding zero to zero.
- Rotating the assignments of a number of jobs that need to be enriched. This means washing dishes for a while, then washing silverware. The arithmetic is substituting one zero for another zero.
- Improving the most difficult parts of the assignment in order to free the worker to accomplish more of the less challenging assignment. This traditional industrial engineering approach amounts to subtraction in the hope of accomplishing addition.

EXHIBIT II · TRIANGLE OF PHILOSOPHIES OF
PERSONNEL MANAGEMENT

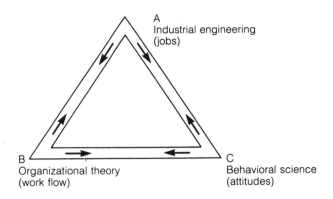

A
Industrial engineering
(jobs)

B
Organizational theory
(work flow)

C
Behavioral science
(attitudes)

These are common forms of horizontal loading that frequently come up in preliminary brain-storming sessions on job enrichment. The principles of vertical loading have not all been worked out as yet, and they remain rather general, but I have furnished seven useful starting points for consideration in *Exhibit III. . . .*

## STEPS TO JOB ENRICHMENT

Now that the motivator idea has been described in practice, here are the steps that managers should take in instituting the principle with their employees:

1. Select those jobs in which (a) the investment in industrial engineering does not make changes too costly, (b) attitudes are poor, (c) hygiene is becoming very costly, and (d) motivation will make no difference in performance.
2. Approach these jobs with the conviction that they can be changed. Years of tradition have led managers to believe that the content of the jobs is sacrosanct and the only scope of action that they have is in ways of stimulating people.

3. Brainstorm a list of changes that may enrich the jobs, without concern for their practicality.
4. Screen the list to eliminate suggestions that involve hygiene, rather than actual motivation.
5. Screen the list for generalities, such as "give them more responsibility," that are rarely followed in practice. This might seem obvious, but the motivator words have never left industry; the substance has just been rationalized and organized out. Words like "responsibility," "growth," "achievement," and "challenge," for example, have been elevated to the lyrics of the patriotic anthem for all organizations. It is the old problem typified by the pledge of allegience to the flag being more important than contributions to the country—of following the form, rather than the substance.
6. Screen the list to eliminate any *horizontal* loading suggestions.
7. Avoid direct participation by the employees whose jobs are to be enriched. Ideas they have expressed previously certainly constitute a valuable source for recommended changes, but their direct involvement contaminates the process with human relations *hygiene*

### EXHIBIT III · PRINCIPLES OF VERTICAL JOB LOADING

| Principle | Motivators Involved |
|---|---|
| A. Removing some controls while retaining accountability | Responsibility and personal achievement |
| B. Increasing the accountability of individuals for own work | Responsibility and recognition |
| C. Giving a person a complete natural unit of work (module, division, area, and so on) | Responsibility, achievement, and recognition |
| D. Granting additional authority to an employee in his activity; job freedom | Responsibility, achievement, and recognition |
| E. Making periodic reports directly available to the worker himself rather than to the supervisor | Internal recognition |
| F. Introducing new and more difficult tasks not previously handled | Growth and learning |
| G. Assigning individuals specific or specialized tasks, enabling them to become experts | Responsibility, growth, and advancement |

and, more specifically, gives them only a *sense* of making a contribution. The job is to be changed, and it is the content that will produce the motivation, not attitudes about being involved or the challenge inherent in setting up a job. That process will be over shortly, and it is what the employees will be doing from then on that will determine their motivation. A sense of participation will result only in short-term movement.

8. In the initial attempts at job enrichment, set up a controlled experiment. At least two equivalent groups should be chosen, one an experimental unit in which the motivators are systematically introduced over a period of time, and the other one a control group in which no changes are made. For both groups, hygiene should be allowed to follow its natural course for the duration of the experiment. Pre- and post-installation tests of performance and job attitudes are necessary to evaluate the effectiveness of the job enrichment program. The attitude test must be limited to motivator items in order to divorce the employee's view of the job he is given from all the surrounding hygiene feelings that he might have.

9. Be prepared for a drop in performance in the experimental group the first few weeks. The changeover to a new job may lead to a temporary reduction in efficiency.

10. Expect your first-line supervisors to experience some anxiety and hostility over the changes you are making. The anxiety comes from their fear that the changes will result in poorer performance for their unit. Hostility will arise when the employees start assuming what the supervisors regard as their own responsibility for performance. The supervisor without checking duties to perform may then be left with little to do.

After a successful experiment, however, the supervisor usually discovers the supervisory and managerial functions he has neglected, or which were never his because all his time was given over to

EXHIBIT IV · ENLARGEMENT VS. ENRICHMENT OF
CORRESPONDENTS' TASKS IN COMPANY EXPERIMENT

| Horizontal Loading Suggestions (Rejected) | Vertical Loading Suggestions (Adopted) | Principle |
|---|---|---|
| Firm quotas could be set for letters to be answered each day, using a rate which would be hard to reach. | Subject matter experts were appointed within each unit for other members of the unit to consult with before seeking supervisory help. (The supervisor had been answering all specialized and difficult questions.) | G |
| The women could type the letters themselves as well as compose them, or take on any other clerical functions. | Correspondents signed their own names on letters. (The supervisor had been signing all letters.) | B |
| All difficult or complex inquiries could be channeled to a few women so that the remainder could achieve high rates of output. These jobs could be exchanged from time to time. | The work of the more experienced correspondents was proofread less frequently by supervisors and was done at the correspondents' desks, dropping verification from 100% to 10%. (Previously, all correspondents' letters had been checked by the supervisor.) | A |
| The women could be rotated through units handling different customers, and then sent back to their own units. | Production was discussed, but only in terms such as "full day's work is expected." As time went on, this was no longer mentioned. (Before, the group had been constantly reminded of the number of letters that needed to be answered.) | D |
| | Outgoing mail went directly to the mailroom without going over supervisors' desks. (The letters had always been routed through the supervisors.) | A |
| | Correspondents were encouraged to answer letters in a more personalized way. (Reliance on the form-letter approach had been standard practice.) | C |
| | Each correspondent was held personally responsible for the quality and accuracy of letters. (This responsibility had been the province of the supervisor and the verifier.) | B, E |

checking the work of his subordinates. . . .

What has been called an employee-centered style of supervision will come about not through education of supervisors, but by changing the jobs that they do.

## CONCLUDING NOTE

Job enrichment will not be a one-time proposition, but a continuous management function. The initial changes, however, should last for a very long period of time. . . .

Not all jobs can be enriched, nor do all jobs need to be enriched. If only a small percentage of the time and money that is now devoted to hygiene, however, were given to job enrichment efforts, the return in human satisfaction and economic gain would be one of the largest dividends that industry and society have ever reaped through their efforts at better personnel management.

The argument for job enrichment can be summed up quite simply: If you have someone on a job, use him. If you can't use him on the job, get rid of him, either via automation or by selecting someone with lesser ability. If you can't use him and you can't get rid of him, you will have a motivation problem.

# 7

# The Ubiquity of the Technique of Goal Setting in Theories of and Approaches to Employee Motivation[1]

## *EDWIN A. LOCKE*

In an earlier article, this author wrote:

> A cardinal attribute of the behavior of living organisms is goal-directedness. It may be observed at all levels of life: in the assimilation of food by an amoeba, in the root growth of a tree or a plant, in the stalking of prey by a wild animal, and in the activities of a scientist in a laboratory (20, p. 991).

Goal-directedness can also be observed in the behavior of an employee at work. Most employee behavior is not only goal directed, it is *consciously* goal directed, i.e., purposeful. . . . While purposeful action is required for a human being to survive, such action is not automatic; it is determined neither by instinct nor by environmental conditioning (24). To consciously direct one's actions toward an end requires an act of choice. One must focus one's thought on what one wants to achieve and on the means to attain it.

Since productive work requires purposeful action and since the setting of conscious purpose is a volitional process, all organizations face the necessity of

[1] This is a revised and expanded version of a paper delivered at the American Psychological Association meetings, Washington, D.C., 1976.

persuading employees to set goals which will further organizational objectives. While virtually all existing theories of and approaches to work motivation have recognized this necessity, the nature, degree, and form of this recognition has varied widely from theory to theory. One can divide such theories and approaches into three categories based on the degree to which they have emphasized explicitly goal-setting as a method of directing employee activities. . . .

One group of theories, Scientific Management and Management by Objectives (MBO), has explicitly recognized the importance of goal-setting in both theory and practice. A second group, Human Relations and Valence-Instrumentality-Expectancy (VIE) theory, denied the importance of goal-setting in earlier versions but acknowledged its importance, in both theory and practice, in later versions. The third group, Job Enrichment and Organizational Behavior Modification (OB Mod), has consistently refused to concede the relevance of goal setting informal theoretical statements, but has acknowledged its importance implicitly by actually encouraging goal-setting when these theories are put into practice.

*Source:* From "The Ubiquity of the Technique of Goal Setting in Theories of and Approaches to Employee Motivation," by Edwin A. Locke, in *Academy of Managment Review* (July 1978), pp. 594–601. Reprinted by permission of the publisher.

Let us examine each group of theories in turn.

## SCIENTIFIC MANAGEMENT AND MANAGEMENT BY OBJECTIVES

Nowhere was the importance of goal setting more explicitly recognized than in Scientific Management which attained popularity in the first two decades of this century. Its founder, Frederick W. Taylor, preferred the term "task" to "goal" (38). Task referred to the specific amount of work assigned to the worker each day.

Taylor wrote:

Perhaps the most important law belonging to this class (pertaining to the motives which influence people), in its relation to scientific management, is the effect which the task idea has upon the efficiency of the workman. This, in fact, has become such an important element of the mechanism of scientific management, that by a great number of people scientific management has come to be known as "task management" (38, p. 120). . . .

The original contribution of Taylor and other advocates of Scientific Management to the task concept lay in the development of methods of estimating a proper day's task for a worker. Motion study, popularized by Gilbreth, focused on eliminating wasted motions from the work, while time study, systematized by Taylor, enabled experts to determine how much work should be accomplished by a carefully selected and trained worker using the most efficient motions (the "one best way"). Each worker was given daily feedback regarding performance in relation to task with respect to both quantity and quality. This was supplemented when necessary with coaching and encouragement by supervisors (38).

To obtain the workers' commitment to the assigned task, which involved learning radically new work methods as well as attaining substantially higher productivity, a differential, or two-tiered, piece rate system was employed. This method of payment resulted in a substantially higher rate of pay (e.g., 70%) for attaining the task than for failure to attain it. Since attaining the task resulted, in effect, in the worker's receiving a monetary bonus, Taylor's colleague, Henry Gantt, called it a "task and bonus" system. . . .

Management by Objectives (6), which stresses goal setting by definition, did not become popular until about forty years after the alleged demise of Scientific Management. MBO can be viewed, in large part, as Scientific Management applied to a managerial context. For example, the tasks or goals of managers under MBO are determined by organizational goals rather than by time study, a procedure which is not applicable to managerial work. Similarly, in line with the longer range time perspective of managerial jobs, the goals under MBO programs refer to the work to be accomplished within the following three to twelve months rather than the work to be accomplished each day as in the case of manual work.

The counterpart, in MBO, of training the worker in the use of standardized tools and motions, is the action plan which is tailored to each manager's unique skills and problems. In contrast to repetitive manual work, the "one best way" to accomplish managerial objectives cannot always be known in advance since it will differ with each manager's particular circumstances.

Like Scientific Management, an effective MBO program integrates the MBO system with the reward system so that individuals are rewarded for reaching their goals. Due to the greater complexity of the manager's job, MBO does not usually employ pre-determined bonuses for specific accomplishments.

## HUMAN RELATIONS AND VIE THEORY

Scientific Management reached the peak of its popularity by about 1920. The following decade saw a continuing interest in bonuses but markedly less interest in tasks, the main exception being the laboratory work on goal-setting by Mace (28). The British Industrial Health and Fatigue Research Boards (as well as American Industrial Psychologists of the 1920s) did extensive studies of the effects of incentives, illumination, rest pauses, hours of work, ventilation, noise, and music on performance and morale (23).

The following two decades ushered in a shift in emphasis from physical conditions of work to social conditions, due, of course, to the influence of the Hawthorne studies (33) which marked the beginning of the Human Relations school. To the degree that goal-setting was considered at all by the Hawthorne investigators, it was viewed primarily as a factor, which *limited* production rather than one which motivated production, and such limiting, in turn, was seen as being caused by the social conditions of work, e.g., group norms.

The well documented existence of restriction of output (30, 33, 43) was widely interpreted by Human Relations advocates as showing the inadequacy of "task and bonus" systems in industry. It was asserted by the Hawthorne researchers that employees were either too stupid or too irrational to understand incentive systems or too disinterested in money, in comparison to social rewards, for it to be a motivator of production (33, pp. 531ff). Despite the fact that actual evidence from the Hawthorne studies themselves supported the view that the workers were most responsive to finan-cial incentives (5) and restricted output, quite rationally in their context, so as not to lose future earnings (37), the main conclusion drawn from the studies was that social incentives (such as belonging to a cohesive work group) were more potent than monetary ones.

While more recent advocates of the Human Relations school necessarily share this emphasis on the importance of social factors, some acknowledge the importance of "task and bonus" factors as well. . . .

Most contemporary Human Relations advocates openly concede the importance of task and bonus factors. A recent book on the Scanlon Plan, a participative, Human Relations oriented plan which uses economic rewards to motivate employees, asserts that:

. . . standards are not inconsistent with a Scanlon Plan if they are used as a tool for meeting the cost and not for restrictive control. Everyone needs a benchmark and a set of criteria to evaluate himself . . . (10, p. 121).

Similarly, Likert, while emphasizing the importance of managers acting supportively toward subordinates, acknowledges that:

Superiors in System 4 organizations . . . should have high performance aspirations, but this is not enough. Every *member* should have high performance aspirations as well (18, p. 51). . . .

The main difference between the theories of Likert and Taylor with respect to goals lies in the methods by which they are set. Taylor attempted to use a scientific approach, time and motion study, while Likert favors participation, e.g., group decision-making. These different methods reflect the different theoretical orientations of the Scientific Management and Human Relations philosophies. Scientific Management was primarily concerned with facts, i.e., the best way to do the job, including the objective determination of a proper day's work, while the Human Relations school has been primarily concerned with feelings, i.e., what will make the worker happiest.

Most contemporary Human Relations advocates acknowledge that successful managers must be concerned with both facts, (concern for production), and feelings (concern for people) (3).

VIE, or valence-instrumentality-expectancy theory, which became popular in the 1960s, also failed to recognize the importance of goal setting in its early versions (41). Its initial disregard of goal setting is probably explained by its hedonistic emphasis. Its major focus was on the way in which people's beliefs and feelings (allegedly) lead them to choose a particular course of action. (In this respect, VIE theory resembles Human Relations theory.) The major premise of VIE theory is that in making choices, an individual mentally sums the expected pleasures to be derived from each possible alternative, subtracts the sum of the expected pains, and chooses the alternative with the highest positive net value.

The hedonistic and other assumptions of VIE theory have been sufficiently criticized in detail elsewhere (22). Suffice it to say that more recent models have put less stress on hedonism, and, more pertinent to the present discussion, have expanded VIE theory to include an explicit goal setting stage (4, pp. 345ff). Recent research has shown that one possible way to integrate some of the VIE constructs with goal setting is to view values and expectancies as factors "which influence the goals an individual chooses, while viewing goals themselves as the more direct determinants of action (7). (Even this model of motivation is grossly incomplete, and there are still unresolved conflicts between VIE theory and goal setting theory, e.g., the relationship of expectancy of success to level of performance.)

## COGNITIVE GROWTH AND OB MOD

The last two theories of employee motivation to be discussed have never shown any explicit theoretical recognition of the relevance of goal setting to employee motivation. Both schools have recognized its importance implicitly, since when these theories are put into practice, goal setting is virtually always involved, directly or indirectly.

The Cognitive Growth School, associated mainly with Maslow and Herzberg (12, 14), began in the early 1960s and emphasized man's psychological or growth needs (e.g., knowing more, integrating one's knowledge, being creative, being effective in ambiguity, developing a genuine sense of self-worth, etc.). It was asserted that this need could be best satisfied through work. According to Herzberg, jobs which did not allow for such growth needed to be enriched by providing the employee with increased responsibility and autonomy.

Herzberg never mentioned goal setting as an element of job enrichment. In fact, the idea was rejected by him (13, pp. 98–99) and his followers (9, p. 28), due probably to its association with Scientific Management whose emphasis on extreme division of labor Herzberg disparages (12).

In practice, goal setting was smuggled into the procedure of job enrichment under another name, namely, feedback. The explicit purpose of feedback in job enrichment programs is to increase the employee's feeling of achievement and to provide him or her with a sense of personal responsibility for the work. Two obvious questions that arise in this context are: How does an employee know when he or she has achieved something? How does he or she know when he or she has adequately or successfully fulfilled his/her responsibility? The answer must be: When the feedback is compared, by management or by the employee, with some standard of appropriate performance, i.e., when the feedback is appraised in terms of some goal. Thus whenever management gives its employees feedback, one can be confident that some performance standard is involved, implicitly if not explicitly.

Numerous studies have shown that feedback, in itself, does *not* have the power to motivate performance directly (1, 25). It has been argued that feedback motivates action only indirectly, through its relationship to goal setting. For example, if the feedback shows that one's prior performance was below the desired standard, one can increase one's subsequent effort, or change one's tactics, in order to meet the standard in the future.

In practice, job enrichment has involved so many different types of job changes, often within the same study, that isolating specific effects of the different elements is virtually impossible (22). . . .

If the practice of goal smuggling has been subtle and inconspicuous among advocates of the Cognitive Growth School, it is much more obvious among advocates of a more recent school, Organizational Behavior Modification, which became popular as a method of motivating employees in the 1970s. The OB Mod technique of goal smuggling consists of openly advocating the use of "performance standards," a term used as a synonym for goal, accompanied by feedback and possibly praise and/or money, but describing these procedures at the theoretical level in behavioristic language. Thus performance standards or goals become "controlling stimuli" or "discriminative stimuli," and feedback, praise, and money become "reinforcers" (2, 24, 27).

While this behavioristic jargon adds nothing to our understanding of how or why these techniques actually modify employee behavior (21), it enables OB Mod advocates to pretend that they are basing their procedures on Skinner's model of man. By removing any reference to human consciousness (e.g., human knowledge, values, feelings) when discussing terms like goals, feedback, and money and by asserting that these "stimuli" or "reinforcers" automatically *condition* employees to behave in a certain way, Behavior Mod advocates can remain, theoretically, within a behavioristic framework.

## CONCLUSION

The most striking aspect of the history of the technique of goal setting in theories of employee motivation is that none of them were able to escape it. Theories which rejected it initially were compelled to acknowledge its importance later. Approaches which denied its importance in theory inevitably recognized it in practice.

The ubiquity of goal setting in these theories is no accident. It is not due to coincidence nor to the irresistible power of social pressures within the scientific community, but to an explicit or implicit recognition of a basic fact of reality: rational human action is goal directed. All competent managers recognize this and quite logically attempt to influence (by instructions, persuasion, etc.) the nature and difficulty of the goals their employees set in order to further organizational goals.

This should not be taken to imply that goal setting is the only element in these theories that helps to motivate employee performance, but only that it is *one* very important element. . . .

The concept of goal is *not* the most fundamental motivational concept; it does not provide an ultimate explanation of human action. The concepts of need and value are the more fundamental concepts (23) and are, along with the individual's knowledge and premises, what determine goals. Goal setting is simply the most directly useful motivational approach in a *managerial* context, since goals are the most immediate regulators of human action and are more easily modified than values of sub-conscious premises. The impressive results obtained by Latham and others in increasing productivity through the use of goal setting in industrial settings testifies to the practical utility of this concept (15).

Many people (including the author) have been surprised at the ease with which employers have been able to get employees to accept assigned goals (as in the field studies summarized by Latham and Yukl (15). Many of us assumed that most employees would reject assigned goals unless they were accompanied by substantial monetary incentives or by "good" Human Relations techniques such as participation. We failed to realize that the "demand characteristics" (32) involved in the employer-employee relationship are very similar to, if not stronger than, those involved in an experimenter-subject relationship. Just as a subject is hired to do the bidding of an experimenter, an employee is hired to perform tasks for an employer. The employee's mental "set" upon accepting a job is: "What do you want me to do?" In short, it is the same mental set as that of an experimental subject.

This is not to say that the employer's power is unlimited. It is not. The ease with which employers can get employees to accept assigned goals depends upon numerous factors, including: fairness and difficulty of the goals, values of the employees, their trust of management, and the perceived legitimacy of management's demands.

Nor should it be assumed that setting specific quantitative goals is inevitably

beneficial. For example, stressing goal achievement in certain areas might lead to neglect of performance in other areas where the results are not so easily measurable. It may also lead to falsifying data. If the process of setting goals and formulating action plans does not include a measure of the costs of achieving the goals, they may be attained at a greater cost than the organization is really willing to pay. The process of goal setting must always be considered in relation to the wider organizational context.

In conclusion, Latham's studies of goal setting were stimulated by the laboratory work of Locke (19), who was in turn influenced by Ryan (34, 35) whose basic motivational concept, the task or intention, is almost identical to Taylor's (38). In view of his widespread influence, it would not be unjustified to view Taylor as the father of employee motivation theory. Despite the decades of outrageous criticisms which Taylor's theories have had to endure, made often by writers who seem not to have read his actual writings, he has had the last word.

## REFERENCES

1. Annett, J. *Feedback and Human Behaviour* (Baltimore: Penguin, 1969).

2. "At Emery Air Freight: Positive Reinforcement Boosts Performance," *Organizational Dynamics*, Vol. 1, No. 3 (1973), 41–50.

3. Blake, R. R., and J. S. Mouton. *The Managerial Grid* (Houston: Gulf Publishing Co., 1964).

4. Campbell, J. P., M. D. Dunnette, E. E. Lawler, and K. E. Weick. *Managerial Behavior, Performance, and Effectiveness* (New York: McGraw-Hill, 1970).

5. Carey, A. "The Hawthorne Studies: A Radical Criticism," *American Sociological Review*, Vol. 32 (1967), 403–416.

6. Carroll, S. J., and H. L. Tosi. *Management by Objectives* (New York: Macmillan, 1973).

7. Cartledge, N. D. "An Experimental Study of the Relationship Between Expectancies,

Goal Utility, Goals and Task Performance" (Ph.D. Thesis, University of Maryland, 1973).

8. Dowling, W. F. "At General Motors: System-4 Builds Performance and Profits," *Organizational Dynamics*, Vol. 3, No. 3 (1975), 23–38.

9. Ford, R. N. *Motivation Through the Work Itself* (New York: American Management Association, 1969).

10. Frost, C. F., J. H. Wakeley, and R. A. Ruh. *The Scanlon Plan for Organizational Development: Identity, Participation, and Equity* (East Lansing, Mich.: Michigan State University, 1974).

11. Hannan, R. L. "The Effects of Participation in Goal Setting on Goal Acceptance and Performance: A Laboratory Experiment" (Master's Thesis, University of Maryland, 1975).

12. Herzberg, F. *Work and the Nature of Man* (Cleveland: World Publishing Co., 1966).

13. Herzberg, F. "One More Time: How Do You Motivate Employees?" in R. M. Steers and L. W. Porter (Eds.), *Motivation and Work Behavior* (New York: McGraw-Hill, 1975).

14. Herzberg, F., B. Mausner, and B. B. Snyderman. *The Motivation to Work* (New York: Wiley, 1959).

15. Latham, G. P., and G. A. Yukl. "A Review of Research on the Application of Goal Setting in Organizations," *Academy of Management Journal*, Vol. 18 (1975), 824–845.

16. Lawler, E. E. "Job Design and Employee Motivation," in V. H. Vroom and E. L. Deci (Eds.) *Management and Motivation* (Baltimore: Penguin, 1970).

17. Lawrence, L. C., and P. C. Smith. "Group Decision and Employee Participation," *Journal of Applied Psychology*, Vol. 39 (1955), 334–337.

18. Likert, R. *The Human Organization* (New York: McGraw-Hill, 1967).

19. Locke, E. A. "Toward a Theory of Task Motivation and Incentives," *Organizational Behavior and Human Performance*, Vol. 3 (1968), 157–189.

20. Locke, E. A. "Purpose without Consciousness: A Contradiction," *Psychological Reports*, Vol. 25 (1969), 991–1009.

21. Locke, E. A. "Critical Analysis of the Concept of Casuality in Behavioristic Psychology," *Psychological Reports*, Vol. 31 (1972), 175–197.

22. Locke, E. A. "Personnel Attitudes and Motivation," *Annual Review of Psychology*, Vol. 26 (1975), 457–480.

23. Locke, E. A. "The Nature and Causes of Job Satisfaction," in M. D. Dunnette (Ed), *Handbook of Industrial and Organizational Psychology* (Chicago: Rand McNally, 1976).

24. Locke, E. A. "The Myths of Behavior Mod in Organizations," *Academy of Management Review*, Vol. 2 (1977), 543–553.

25. Locke, E. A., N. Cartledge, and J. Koeppel. "Motivational Effects of Knowledge of Results: A Goal Setting Phenomenon?" *Psychological Bulletin*, Vol. 70 (1968), 474–485.

26. Locke, E. A., D. Sirota, and A. D. Wolfson. "An Experimental Case Study of the Successes and Failures of Job Enrichment in a Government Agency," *Journal of Applied Psychology*, Vol. 61 (1976), 701–711.

27. Luthans, F., and R. Kreitner. *Organizational Behavior Modification* (Glenview, Ill.: Scott Foresman, 1975).

28. Mace, C. A. "Incentives: Some Experimental Studies," *Report No. 72* (Great Britain: Industrial Health Research Board, 1935).

29. Marrow, A. J., D. G. Bowers, and S. E. Seashore. *Management by Participation* (New York: Harper, 1967).

30. Mathewson, S. B. *Restriction of Output Among Unorganized Workers* (New York: Viking, 1931).

31. Meyer, H. H., E. Kay, and J. R. P. French. "Split Roles in Performance Appraisal," *Harvard Business Review*, Vol. 43 (Jan./Feb. 1965), 123–129.

32. Orne, M. T. "On the Social Psychology of the Psychological Experiment with Particular Reference to Demand Characteristics," *American Psychologist*, Vol. 17 (1962), 776–783.

33. Roethlisberger, F. J., and W. J. Dickson. *Management and the Worker* (Cambridge: Harvard University Press, 1939).

34. Ryan, T. A. *Intentional Behavior* (New York: Ronald, 1970).

35. Ryan, T. A., and P. C. Smith. *Principles of Industrial Psychology* (New York: Ronald, 1954).

36. Sorcher, M. *Motivating the Hourly Employee* (General Electric: Behavioral Research Service, 1967).

37. Sykes, A. J. M. "Economic Interest and the Hawthorne Researches," *Human Relations*, Vol. 18 (1965), 253–263.

38. Taylor, F. W. *The Principles of Scientific Management* (New York: Norton, 1911/1967).

39. Umstot, D. D., C. H. Bell, and T. R. Mitchell. "Effects of Job Enrichment and Task Goals on Satisfaction and Productivity: Implications for Job Design," *Journal of Applied Psychology*, Vol. 61 (1976), 379–394.

40. Viteles, M. S. *Motivation and Morale in Industry* (New York: Norton, 1953).

41. Vroom, V. H. *Work and Motivation* (New York: Wiley, 1964).

42. Walters, R. W. "Job Enrichment: Challenge of the Seventies," in W. W. Suoganen, M. J. McDonald, G. L. Swallow, and W. W. Suojanen (Eds.), *Perspectives on Job Enrichment and Productivity* (Atlanta: Georgia State Univ., 1975).

43. Whyte, W. F. *Money and Motivation* (New York: Harper, 1955).

# 8

# Equity Theory Predictions of Behavior in Organizations

*Richard T. Mowday*

Employees are seldom passive observers of the events that occur in the workplace. They form impressions of others and the events that affect them and cognitively or behaviorally respond based on their positive or negative evaluations. A great deal of theory and research in the social sciences has been devoted to understanding these evaluative processes. More specifically, research has attempted to uncover the major influences on individual reactions in social situations and the processes through which these reactions are formed. One useful framework for understanding how social interactions in the workplace influence employee reactions to their jobs and participation in the organization is provided by theories of social exchange processes (Adams, 1965; Homans, 1961; Jaques, 1961; Patchen, 1961; Simpson, 1972).

Exchange theories are based on two simple assumptions about human behavior. First, there is an assumed similarity between the process through which individuals evaluate their social relationships and economic transactions in the market. Social relationships can be viewed as exchange processes in which individuals make contributions (investments) for which they expect certain outcomes. Individuals are assumed to have expectations about the outcomes that should result when they contribute their time or resources in interaction with others.

The second assumption concerns the process through which individuals decide whether or not a particular exchange is satisfactory. Most exchange theories assign a central role to social comparison processes in terms of how individuals evaluate exchange relationships. Information gained through interaction with others is used to determine whether an exchange has been advantageous. For example, individuals may compare their outcomes and contributions in an exchange with the outcomes and contributions of the person with whom they are interacting. Where there is relative equality between the outcomes and contributions of both parties to an exchange, satisfaction is likely to result from the interaction.

The popularity of social exchange theories may be attributable to their agreement with commonsense observations about human behavior in social situations. Exchange theories suggest that individuals in social interaction behave in a manner similar to the "economic man" of classical economics. Most theories of

*Source:* Richard T. Mowday, "Equity Theory Predictions of Behavior in Organizations" by Richard T. Mowday. Pages 91–112 in Richard M. Steers and Lyman W. Porter (Eds.), *Motivation and Work Behavior* (Third Edition) (McGraw-Hill, 1993). Reprinted with permission of the publisher.

motivation assume that individuals are motivated to maximize their rewards and minimize their costs (Vroom, 1964; Walster, Bercheid, & Walster, 1976). The major difference between assumptions made about economic man and social exchange theories is that the latter recognize that individuals exist in environments characterized by limited and imperfect information. The ambiguity present in most social situations results in individuals relying heavily on information provided by others to evaluate their actions and those of others (Darley & Darley, 1973). Social interactions therefore play a central role in providing information to individuals on the quality of their relationships with others. Our reliance upon others for valued information, however, may place constraints on how we behave in our interactions with others. In order to maintain our social relationships it may be necessary to conform to certain social norms that prevent us from maximizing our outcomes without regard to the outcome of others.

The purpose of this paper is to examine one prominent theory of social exchange processes: Adams' (1963, 1965) theory of equity. . . .

## EQUITY THEORY

### Antecedents of Inequity

The major components of exchange relationships in Adams' theory are inputs and outcomes. Inputs or investments are those things a person contributes to the exchange. In a situation where a person exchanges his or her services for pay, inputs may include previous work experience, education, effort on the job, and training. Outcomes are those things that result from the exchange. In the employment situation, the most important outcome is likely to be pay. In addition, other outcomes such as supervisory treatment, job assignments, fringe benefits, and status symbols may also be considered in evaluating the exchange. To be considered in evaluating exchange relationships, inputs and outcomes must meet two conditions. First, the existence of an input or outcome must be recognized by one or both parties to the exchange. Second, an input or outcome must be considered relevant to the exchange (i.e., have some marginal utility). Unless inputs or outcomes are both recognized and considered relevant, they will not be considered in evaluating an exchange relationship.

Adams suggests that individuals weigh their inputs and outcomes by their importance to the individual. Summary evaluation of inputs and outcomes are developed by separately summing the weighted inputs and weighted outcomes. In the summation process, inputs and outcomes are treated as independent even though they may be highly related (e.g., age and previous work experience would be considered as separate inputs). The ratio of an individual's (called "person's") outcomes to inputs is compared to the ratio of outcomes to inputs of another individual or group (called "other"). Other may be a person with whom you are engaged in a direct exchange, another individual engaged in an exchange with a common third party, or person in a previous or anticipated work situation. The selection of comparison others is discussed in more detail below. The important consideration at this point is that person evaluates his or her outcomes and inputs by comparing them with those of others.

Equity is said to exist whenever the ratio of person's outcomes to inputs is equal to the ratio of other's outcomes and inputs.

$$\frac{O_p}{I_p} = \frac{O_o}{I_o}$$

Inequity exists whenever the two ratios are unequal.

$$\frac{O_p}{I_p} < \frac{O_o}{I_o} \text{ or } \frac{O_p}{I_p} > \frac{O_o}{I_o}$$

Several important aspects of this definition should be recognized. First, the conditions necessary to produce equity or inequity are based on the individual's perceptions of inputs and outcomes. In behavioral terms, the objective characteristics of the situation are of less importance than the person's perceptions. Second, inequity is a relative phenomenon. Inequity does not necessarily exist if person has high inputs and low outcomes as long as the comparison other has a similar ratio. Employees may therefore exhibit satisfaction on a job that demands a great deal and for which they receive very little if their comparison other is in a similar position. Third, inequity exists when a person is relatively underpaid and relatively overpaid. It is this implication of Adams' theory that has generated the most attention since it suggests that people will react in a counterintuitive fashion when they are overpaid. Research evidence indicates, however, that the threshold for underpayment is lower than that associated with overpayment (Levanthal, Weiss, & Long, 1969). As might be expected, individuals are somewhat more willing to accept overpayment in an exchange relationship than they are to accept underpayment. The relationship between the ratios of outcomes to inputs of person and other might best be considered along a continuum reflecting different degrees of inequity ranging from overpayment on one extreme to underpayment on the other. The midpoint of the continuum represents the point at which the two ratios are equal. Equity is defined as a zone which is asymmetric about the midpoint. The asymmetry reflects the fact that the thresholds for overpayment and underpayment may differ.

One final aspect of Adams' formulation should be mentioned. Walster et al. (1976) have shown that the formula relating the two ratios of person and other is inadequate in situations where inputs might be negative. Following their example, consider the situation where person's inputs have a value of 5 and outcomes are $-10$ while other's inputs and outcomes are $-5$ and 10, respectively. Using Adams' formula, these two ratios are equal and thus a condition of equity would be said to exist.

$$\frac{O_p}{I_p} = \frac{-10}{5} = -2 \text{ and } \frac{O_o}{I_o} = \frac{10}{-5} = -2$$

Obviously, a situation in which person makes positive inputs but receives negative outcomes is inequitable when compared to another who makes negative inputs but receives positive outcomes. Walster et al. (1976) have proposed an alternative formulation that overcomes this problem. Equity and inequity are defined by the following relationship.

$$\frac{\text{Outcomes}_p - \text{Inputs}_p}{(|\text{Inputs}_p|)^{k_p}} \text{ compared with}$$
$$\frac{\text{Outcomes}_o - \text{Inputs}_o}{(|\text{Inputs}_o|)^{k_o}}.$$

The reader interested in pursuing this subject further can find a more detailed discussion of this formula and its terms in Walster et al. (1976).

## Consequence of Inequity

The motivational aspects of Adams' theory are derived from the hypothesized consequences of perceived inequity. The major postulates of the theory can be summarized simply: (1) perceived inequity creates tension in the individual; (2) the amount of tension is proportional to the magnitude of the inequity; (3) the tension created in the individual will motivate him or her to reduce it; and (4) the strength of the motivation to reduce inequity is proportional to the perceived inequity (Adams, 1965). In other words, the presence of inequity motivates the individual to change the situation through behavioral or cognitive means to return to a condition of equity.

The methods through which individuals reduce inequity are referred to as methods of inequity resolution. Adams describes six alternative methods of restoring equity: (1) altering inputs; (2) altering outcomes; (3) cognitively distorting inputs or outcomes; (4) leaving the field; (5) taking actions designed to change the inputs or outcomes of the comparison other; or (6) changing the comparison other. The choice of a particular method of restoring equity will depend upon the characteristics of the inequitable situation. Adams suggests, however, that the person will attempt to maximize positively valent outcomes and minimize increasingly effortful inputs in restoring equity. In addition, person will resist changing the object of comparison and distorting inputs that are considered central to the self-concept. In general, it is considered easier to distort other's inputs and outcomes than the person's own inputs or outcomes. Finally, leaving the field (e.g., turnover from an organization) as a method of reducing inequity will only be considered in extreme cases of inequity. . . .

. . . Since theories or models of social processes are ways of making sense out of our environment by simplifying relationships between variables, it should not be surprising that any given theory fails to capture the complexity we know to exist in the real world. Consequently, there are usually a number of limitations that can be pointed out in any given theory, and equity theory is

no different from other motivation approaches in this regard. The conceptual issues to be discussed below point to several limitations of the present formulation of equity theory, and they should be viewed as areas in which the theory may be clarified or extended through further research.

## Concept of Equity

The concept of equity is most often interpreted in work organizations as a positive association between an employee's effort or performance on the job and the pay he or she receives (Goodman, 1977). In other words, it is believed that employees who contribute more to the organization should receive higher amounts of the rewards the organization has to offer. This belief is often referred to as the "equity norm." Adams (1965) suggests that individual expectations about equity or "fair" correlations between inputs and outcomes are learned during the process of socialization (e.g., in the home or at work) and through comparison with the inputs and outcomes of others. Although few would question the existence of an equity norm governing social relationships, the derivation of this norm and its pervasiveness remain somewhat unclear. In addition, it is important to determine the extent to which the equity norm is defined by an individual's effort and performance or by other types of contributions they may make to organizations. . . .

The equity norm appears to be only one of several norms that govern the distribution of rewards in social relationships. An important question concerns what factors influence the extent to which rewards are distributed equitably or allocated on some other basis. In an analysis of reward allocation in small groups, Leventhal (1976) suggests that the particular distribution rule adopted in allocating rewards is related to both the goals of the reward system and characteristics of the allocator. Table 1 contrasts three decision rules that can be used in allocating rewards (equity, equality, and responsiveness to needs) and the situations where each rule is most likely to be used. The equity norm appears to be most closely associated with the goal of maximizing productivity in a group, while rewards are most likely to be distributed equally when the goal is to minimize group conflict.

Distribution rules represent an important concept in understanding reward systems (Cook, 1975; Goodman, 1977). Distribution rules identify the association between any dimension of evaluation and the levels of outcomes to

## TABLE 1 · DISTRIBUTION RULES FOR ALLOCATING REWARDS

| Distribution rule | Situations where distribution rule is likely to be used | Factors affecting use of distribution rule |
|---|---|---|
| Equity/contributions (outcomes should match contributions) | 1 Goal is to maximize group productivity<br><br>2 A low degree of cooperation is required for task performance. | 1 What receiver is expected to do<br><br>2 What others receive<br>3 Outcomes and contributions of person allocating rewards<br>4 Task difficulty and perceived ability<br>5 Personal characteristics of person allocating rewards and person performing |
| Social responsibility/needs (outcomes distributed on the basis of needs) | 1 Allocator of rewards is a close friend of the receiver, feels responsible for the well-being of the receiver, or is successful or feels competent. | 1 Perceived legitimacy of needs<br>2 Origin of need (e.g., beyond control of the individual) |
| Equality (equal outcomes given to all participants | 1 Goal is to maximize harmony, minimize conflict in group.<br>2 Task of judging performer's needs or contribution is difficult.<br>3 Person allocating rewards has a low cognitive capacity.<br>4 A high degree of cooperation is required for task performance.<br>5 Allocator anticipates future interactions with low-input member. | 1 Sex of person allocating rewards (e.g., females more likely to allocate rewards equally than males)<br>2 Nature of task |

*Source:* Adapted from Leventhal (1976).

be distributed. A consideration of distribution rules suggests both that different norms may govern the distribution of rewards in organizations and that different factors may weight more heavily in allocating rewards using any given norm. For example, in organizations where an equity norm is followed, it is common to find that an individual's contribution in terms of seniority is a more important basis for rewards than is actual job performance. Our ability to predict how individuals react to reward systems therefore depends upon identifying the particular norm they believe should be followed and the specific dimension (i.e., input) they feel is most important in allocating rewards. Equity theory often assumes that rewards should be given in relation to a person's contribution and, further, that performance is the most important contribution in the work setting. The accuracy of our predictions of employee reactions to reward systems can be increased, however, by recognizing the existence of several norms governing the distribution of rewards and the differential importance that may be attached to employee inputs.

## Choice of a Method of Inequity Resolution

Although the several factors Adams (1965) suggested individuals will take into consideration in choosing among alternative methods of reducing inequity make the theory more testable, they do not allow a totally unequivocal set of predictions to be made from the theory (Wicklund & Brehm, 1976). In any situation, a given method of restoring inequity may satisfy one of these rules while at the same time violating another. Cognitively distorting inputs as a method of reducing inequity, for example, may allow the individual to maximize positively valent outcomes, but at the expense of threatening aspects central to

his or her self-concept. When such a conflict occurs, it is difficult to specify how an individual will react to inequity. . . .

. . . Research also suggests that strategies for reducing inequity are dynamic and may change over time.

## Choice of a Comparison Other

One area of recent concern in equity theory is to develop a greater understanding of how individuals choose comparison standards against which to evaluate inputs and outcomes. Adams (1965) suggested that comparison others may be the other party to the exchange or another individual involved in an exchange with the same third party. Until recently, little has been known about the actual comparison standards people use or the process through which alternative comparisons are chosen.

Goodman (1974) differentiated between three classes of referents: (1) others, (2) self-standards, and (3) system referents. Others are people who may be involved in a similar exchange either with the same organization or with some other organization. Self-standards are unique to the individual but different from his or her current ratio of outcomes and inputs; for example, individuals may compare their current ratio against inputs and outcomes associated with an earlier job. System referents are implicit or explicit contractual expectations between an employer and employee. At the time of being hired, an employee may be promised future rewards and this can become a basis for evaluating the exchange. In a study of 217 managers, Goodman (1974) found each of these referents was used in determining the degree of satisfaction with pay. Perhaps his most important finding was that a majority of managers reported using multiple referents in assessing their satisfaction. For example, 28 percent of the managers indicated they compared their present situation against both those of others and self-standards. He also found that higher levels of education were associated with choosing a comparison referent outside the organization . . .

## CONCLUSIONS AND DIRECTIONS FOR FUTURE RESEARCH

Has equity theory largely outlived its usefulness as a theory of motivation in organizations, or is it a theory capable of providing general explanations of behavior in a number of different social settings? This is a difficult question to answer at the present time. However, it appears that equity theory has more to contribute to our understanding of organizational behavior than previous research would suggest. The early emphasis of organizational research on equity theory predictions of employee reactions to pay was perhaps both its greatest strength and weakness. On the positive side, focusing on monetary rewards provided a research setting in which the variables were easily quantifiable and the predictions were relatively unambiguous (or so it seemed at the time). On the negative side, exclusive interest in employee reactions to pay prevented the extension of equity theory to other areas of social relationships in organizations. Adams (1965) was careful to note that equity theory was relevant to any social situations in which exchanges may take place (e.g., between coworkers, between superiors and subordinates, etc.). With the exception of Goodman's (1977) recent work on social comparison process in organizations, the extension of the theory to a broad range of social relationships has been left to social psychologists (see Berkowitz & Walster, 1976). Several areas of behavior in organiza-

tions that might profitably be examined in equity theory terms are discussed below.

Previous research on equity theory has largely been concerned with individual reactions to perceived inequity. What appears to have been neglected are the instrumental uses of inequity in interpersonal relationships (Adams & Freedman, 1976). Individuals in organizations, for example, may purposely create perceived inequity in social relationships as a way of improving their situation or achieving certain goals. Supervisors may routinely attempt to convince employees that they are not contributing as much as another employee or at a level expected for the pay they receive. Creating perceptions of overpayment inequity may therefore be viewed as a strategy designed to increase the level of employee performance. Just as routinely, employees may attempt the same strategy, but in reverse. Ingratiation attempts (Wortman & Linsenmeier, 1977) may be viewed as strategies on the part of lower-status employees to increase the outcomes of those in higher level positions. To the extent that those in higher positions perceive an inequity in their social relationships with lower-level employees, they will feel obligated to reciprocate. . . .

Campbell, Dunnette, Lawler, and Weick (1970) have suggested the importance of viewing leadership processes in terms of exchanges between superiors and subordinates. In describing what they call the "unilateral fiction" in leadership research, they point out that managers are most often viewed as initiating the action of others and that superior-subordinate interactions are assumed to end when the manager issues a directive. Relationships between superiors and subordinates in organizations, however, are more accurately characterized by reciprocal-influence processes. A great deal of interaction between managers and employees in organizations may involve bargaining processes in which the terms of an exchange are established to the satisfaction of each party. When the manager issues a directive that is carried out by the employee, it is reasonable to assume that expectations of repayment are formed in the employee. Furthermore, when employees do a favor for the manager it may result in a perceived obligation to reciprocate on the part of the manager. Reciprocal relationships between managers and employees can be described in terms of equity theory; taking such a perspective may increase our understanding of the leadership process.

Equity theory appears to offer a useful approach to understanding a wide variety of social relationships in the workplace. Additional research is needed to extend predictions from the theory beyond simple questions about how employees react to their pay. As Goodman and Friedman (1971) have noted, equity theory predictions about employee performance levels may be one of the less interesting and useful applications of the theory. The effects of perceived inequity on employee performance levels are often slight and of limited time duration. The utility of equity theory may be greatest for increasing our understanding of interpersonal interactions at work (e.g., supervisory-subordinate relationships). In this regard, researchers interested in organizations may want to follow the lead of social psychologists in extending applications of the theory.

# REFERENCES

Adams, J. S. Toward an understanding of inequity. *Journal of Abnormal and Social Psychology*, 1963, **67**, 422–436. (a)

Adams, J. S. Inequity in social exchange. In L. Berkowitz (Ed.), *Advances in experimental social psychology*. Vol. 2. New York: Academic Press, 1965. Pp. 267–299.

Adams, J. S., & Freedman, S. Equity theory revisited: Comments and annotated bibliography. In L. Berkowitz & E. Walster (Eds.), *Advances in experimental social psychology*, Vol. 9. New York: Academic Press, 1976. Pp. 43–90.

Berkowitz, L., & Walster, E. (Eds.), *Advances in experimental social psychology*, Vol. 9. New York: Academic Press, 1976.

Campbell, J. P., Dunnette, M. D., Lawler, E. E., & Weick, K. E. *Managerial behavior, performance, and effectiveness.* New York: McGraw-Hill, 1970.

Cook, K. S. Expectations, evaluations and equity. *American Sociological Review,* 1975, **40**, 372–388.

Darley, J. M., & Darley, S. A. *Conformity and deviation.* Morristown, N.J.: General Learning Press, 1973.

Goodman, P. S. An examination of referents used in the evaluation of pay. *Organizational Behavior and Human Performance,* 1974, **12**, 170–195.

Goodman, P. S. Social comparison processes in organizations. In B. Staw & G. Salancik (Eds.), *New directions in organizational behavior.* Chicago: St. Clair, 1977. Pp. 97–132.

Goodman, P. S., & Friedman, A. An examination of Adams' theory of inequity. *Administrative Science Quarterly,* 1971, **16**, 271–288.

Homans, G. C. *Social behavior: Its elementary forms.* New York: Harcourt, Brace & World, 1961.

Jaques, E. *Equitable payment.* New York: Wiley, 1961.

Leventhal, G. S. Fairness in social relationships. In J. Thibaut, J. Spence, & R. Carson (Eds.), *Contemporary topics in social psychology.* Morristown, N.J.: General Learning Press, 1976.

Leventhal, G. S., Weiss, T., & Long, G. Equity, reciprocity, and reallocating rewards in the dyad. *Journal of Personality and Social Psychology,* 1969, **13**, 300–305.

Patchen, M. *The choice of wage comparisons.* Englewood Cliffs, N.J.: Prentice-Hall, 1961.

Simpson, R. L. *Theories of social exchange*. Morristown, N.J.: General Learning Press, 1972.

Vroom, V. H. *Work and motivation*. New York: Wiley, 1964.

Walster, E., Bercheid, E., & Walster, G. W. New directions in equity research. In L. Berkowitz & E. Walster (Eds.), *Advances in experimental social psychology*, Vol. 9. New York: Academic Press, 1976. Pp. 1–42.

Wicklund, R. A., & Brehm, J. W. *Perspectives on cognitive dissonance*. Hillsdale, N.J.: Lawrence Erlbaum, 1976.

Wortman, C. B., & Linsenmeier, J. A. W. Interpersonal attraction and methods of ingratiation in organizational settings. In B. M. Staw & G. R. Salancik (Eds.), *New directions in organizational behavior*. Chicago: St. Clair, 1977. Pp. 133–178.

# CHAPTER II

# Group and
# Intergroup Behavior

People are social beings at work as well as at play. We form and associate in groups, and groups create their own norms, values, sentiments, membership criteria, roles, and aspirations. Most work groups also develop shared beliefs and attitudes about such things as the nature of the relationship between members and their employing organization, expectations about levels of work output and pay, what it takes to get ahead, and positive and negative consequences of trusting the organization or exhibiting loyalty to it.

Deciding whether to become a member of a group usually poses an *approach-avoidance conflict* for people. Joining has plus and minus connotations. Groups are a primary way people satisfy their desire for affiliation, their need for belonging. People working with and near each other form bonds—relationships—of friendship, camaraderie, and conversation. Yet, group membership always requires relinquishing some individuality—of personal identity and freedom of behavior—at least temporarily. Although groups vary, most norms demand some degree of conforming behavior, of acquiescence to "claims" made by other members or by the group, as one "price" of membership and thus for satisfying affiliation wants. As the result, decisions to join groups at work often are made with tentativeness and feelings of ambiguity.

The formation of groups in the workplace is more than just a way for people to satisfy their desires for affiliation. Ever since the days of the Industrial Revolution, workplace organizations have been constructed on the foundation principles of *specialization* and *division of labor* (Smith, 1776). In our complex organizations of today, few jobs can be done from start to finish by one person. Specialization allows an organization to use people's skills and efforts more systematically and to focus their knowledge and energy on a limited number of tasks. Employee learning curves are minimized.

With division of labor, people who perform a set of specialized functions are organizationally clustered in work groups, work groups in units or branches, branches in divisions or departments, divisions in companies or agencies, and so forth. Work groups attract people with like backgrounds; for example, professional training, socialization, and experience as accountants, teachers, production managers, or human resources managers; or, perhaps, people from similar sociodemographic backgrounds, for example, from "old line" New England families, or particular ethnic groups. All such shared backgrounds involve the socialization of people into common value/belief/behavior systems. We learn how to think and act like doctors, teachers, accountants, or credit managers; and, like Texans, Mainers, or Southern Californians.

Virtually all groups, and particularly purposeful, specialized, organizational groups, develop their own sets of norms (behavioral rules), values, stories, heroes, sagas, legends, myths, beliefs about their realities, and assumptions about things like the nature of their organizational environment and appropriate relations with other groups. When a group becomes institutionalized in an organization, such as a production unit or a branch office, these shared beliefs, values, and assumptions become the essence of an organizational subculture (Martin & Siehl, 1983). Most group subcultures have a resemblance to the overall organizational culture but also contain unique elements that form through the impacts of events, circumstances, and personalities, including (Ott, 1989, Ch. 4):

- The nature or type of business in which the organization is engaged,
- The *psychological script* or basic personality of the founder or other dominant early leaders, and
- The general culture of the society where the organization is located.

A specific group subculture develops from the learning members accumulate through their shared successes and failures experienced in solving problems that threatened the survival of the group and its identity or independence (Schein, 1992).

Putting aside the question of why work groups have at least partially unique subcultures, the fact remains that they usually are distinctive. Then, considering the normal loyalties that groups demand and the affiliational needs they meet, it becomes easy to understand why *ingroups* and *outgroups* and feelings of *we* and *they* and *we* versus *they* are so characteristic of life in organizations.

*Group dynamics* is the subfield of organization behavior "dedicated to achieving knowledge about the nature of groups, the laws of their development, and their interrelations with individuals, other groups, and larger institutions" (Cartwright & Zander, 1968). Kurt Lewin, perhaps the most influential social psychologist of this century (Marrow, 1969), is widely credited with creating and naming this field in which he has been a most influential contributor.

Lewin's group dynamics perspective was subsumed under the general heading *field theory*, which holds that a person's behavior is a function of the individual and her or his immediate environment—the group and the organizational context. (Excerpts from Lewin's chapter, "Group Decision and Social Change" are in Chapter VII.) For much of the decade of the 1940s, Lewin and his associates at the Massachusetts Institute of Technology's Research Center for Group Dynamics introduced concepts like *fields, force fields,* and *field forces* into the study of human behavior, focusing on things such as resistance to change and the effects of leadership on group performance. Perhaps Lewin's greatest single contribution, however, was to move the focus of behavioral theory and research from individuals to groups.

But the field of group dynamics has been more than Kurt Lewin. It has represented the first comprehensive pulling together of theories, research methods, and empirical findings from myriad social sciences. It is the acquisition of "knowledge about the . . . psychological and social forces associated with groups. . . . It refers to a field of inquiry dedicated to achieving knowledge about the nature of groups, the laws of their development, and their interrelations with individuals, other groups, and larger institutions" (Cartwright & Zander, 1968). Group dynamics is the accumulated contributions of many notable social scientists including R. F. Bales (1950), Alex Bavelas (1942), Dorwin Cartwright and Alvin Zander (1968), George Homans (1950), Jake Moreno (1934), T. M. Newcomb (1943), M. Sherif (1936), and William F. Whyte (1943, 1948).

Although definitions of a *group* vary, there is less disagreement here than there is about definitions of most other concepts of organizational behavior, such as *leader* and *motivation*. Usually, the term *group* refers to what is more technically known as a *primary group*—a group small enough to permit face-to-face interaction among its members and which remains in existence long enough for some personal relations, sentiments, and feelings of identification or belongingness to develop. Schein (1980) uses the term *psychological group* to mean much the same thing: "Any number of people who [1] interact with one another, [2] are psychologically aware of one another, and [3] perceive themselves to be a group." Over the years, many labels have been used to describe different types of groups, but for understanding organizational behavior, the most important types of groups probably are (Ivancevich & Matteson, 1993, pp. 287–289):

- *Formal Groups:* Groups that are formally sanctioned, usually for the purpose of accomplishing tasks. Employees are assigned to formal groups based upon their position in the organization. There are two basic types of formal groups:
  - *Command groups:* Formal groups that are specified in the organization chart—groups that include supervisors and the people who report directly to them. Groups of this type are the *building blocks* of organization structure, for example, a production work group, the staff of a small branch office, a product marketing group, or a military flight crew.
  - *Task groups:* Formally sanctioned, task-oriented groups with short lives. Employees who work together to complete a particular project or task, such as solving a problem or capitalizing on a specific opportunity, and then are disbanded. Examples include task forces and committees.
- *Informal Groups:* Natural groupings of people in the work situation. People who associate voluntarily, primarily to satisfy social needs. Although informal groups at work may have goals and tasks (for example, ethnic support groups, investment clubs, and luncheon bridge groups), their primary reasons for existence are friendship, affiliation, and shared interests. Although informal groups seldom are formally sanctioned, they are extremely important to the working of organizations. Their norms, values, beliefs and expectations have significant impacts on work-related behavior and attitudes.

Groups in organizations of all types are of high importance and interest to students and practioners of organizational behavior, both for what happens *in* them (and why) and what happens *between* them. Thus, this chapter contains five important readings about diverse aspects of group and intergroup dynamics.

Groups cannot be discussed without considering important variables that are the subjects of other chapters, most importantly leadership, motivation, and the organizational context. However, to avoid repetition, subjects that are the topics of other chapters are introduced only tangentially.

## DYNAMICS IN GROUPS

In this chapter's first reading, " 'Banana Time': Job Satisfaction and Informal Interaction," Donald F. Roy examines workers' *psychological survival* in monotonous jobs (p. 158), but Roy's true interest is the workplace relationship among group cohesiveness, group goals, and job satisfaction. In "Banana Time," Roy focuses on interaction and job satisfaction. (In 1961, he followed this article with, "Efficiency and 'the Fix': Informal Intergroup Relations in a Piecework Machine Shop.") Roy took a job—by his description, a monotonous, repetitive, simple job—as a machine operator in order to collect information for the two studies. He concludes that workers in monotonous jobs survive psychologically through informal interaction. He watched machine operators keep from "going nuts" by talking and fooling around in a nonstop, highly stylized, and ritualistic manner. Roy found no evidence to support the then-prevailing belief that informal interaction on the job boosts productivity. In fact, quite the contrary. Roy predicts that productivity would increase if the "fooling around" were to cease. "As far as achievement of managerial goals is concerned, the most that could be suggested is that leavening the deadly boredom of individualized work routines with a concurrent flow of group festivities had a negative effect on turnover" (p. 166). Roy's article provides an important reminder that common sense expectations about people in groups aren't always valid. What would appear to be obviously correlated factors—informal interaction with coworkers, job satisfaction, and productivity—are not.

Dorwin Cartwright and Alvin Zander's contribution here is the introductory chapter "Origins of Group Dynamics" from their landmark volume, *Group Dynamics*. Cartwright and Zander define group dynamics as "a field of inquiry dedicated to advancing knowledge about the nature of groups, the laws of their development, and their interrelations with individuals, other groups, and larger institutions" (p. 7). The distinguishing characteristics of group dynamics—what separates group dynamics from numerous other groups of behavioral sciences that have investigated groups over the years—are:

1.  Emphasis on theoretically significant empirical research; conceptual theories and personal observations are not adequate.

2.  Interest in the dynamics and interdependence of phenomena. The dynamics are more important than static elements, single-variable theories, and structural schemes.

3. Broad interdisciplinary relevance, the importance of incorporating methods and knowledge from all of the social sciences, including sociology, psychology, and cultural anthropology.

4. "Potential applicability of its findings in efforts to improve the functioning of groups and their consequences on individuals and society" (p. 7). The results must be useful in social practice.

"Origins of Group Dynamics" provides a thorough analysis of the historical development of the field including the positive impetus provided by advancements in other professions, most notably group psychotherapy, education, and social group work, and social research techniques such as controlled observation and sociometry. Cartwright and Zander are *the* premiere chroniclers of group dynamics, and "Origins of Group Dynamics" is *the* outstanding overview of this field.

## INTERGROUP DYNAMICS

Robert Blake, Herb Shepard, and Jane Mouton's chapter, "Foundations and Dynamics of Intergroup Behavior" (1964) (reprinted here) approaches conflict within and among groups from a different perspective than Donald Roy's. Blake, Shepard, and Mouton identify sets of forces that affect behavior between two or more members of an organization: formal roles and responsibilities, personal backgrounds, and the roles they feel (themselves) to be in as representatives of particular groups in the organization. This three-forces framework is used to distinguish between conflict in organizations that is caused by personal matters and conflict that is caused by intergroup matters. The authors offer three sets of assumptions about intergroup disagreement and discuss strategies for managing disagreement under each: (1) Disagreement is inevitable and permanent, (2) conflict can be avoided since interdependence between groups is unnecessary, and (3) agreement and maintaining interdependence is possible.

In, "An Intergroup Perspective on Group Dynamics" (1987) (included in this chapter), Clayton P. Alderfer proposes a theory of intergroup relations that incorporates individual, interpersonal, group, intergroup, and organizational relations interpretations. Alderfer argues that an intergroup perspective "can explain a broader range of phenomena than just what go on at the intersection of two or more groups" (p. 190). His theory relates the status of intergroup relations to the larger organizational system in which groups are embedded. It has application in a wide variety of organizational problems and opportunities, including "the development of effective work teams, the definition and management of organizational culture, the analysis and implementation of affirmative action, and the teaching of organizational behavior in management schools" (p. 219).

The final reading in this chapter, "Intergroup Conflict" (1993), by Taylor Cox, Jr., is a chapter from his groundbreaking book, *Cultural Diversity in Organizations: Theory, Research & Practice*. "Intergroup Conflict" suggests that a great deal of interpersonal conflict in organizations may be analyzed from an intergroup perspective, because "group identities are an integral part of the individual personality.

Therefore, much of what is commonly referred to as 'personality clash' may actually be a manifestation of group identity-related conflict" (p. 138). Five sources of intergroup conflict are particularly important in the context of cultural diversity in organizations: competing goals, competition for resources, cultural differences, power discrepancies, and assimilation versus preservation of microcultural identity. Cox concludes with a listing of approaches for managing intergroup conflict in organizations and an assessment of the sources of diversity-related conflict that each of the approaches is most effective in addressing.

## REFERENCES

Alderfer, C. P. (1987). An intergroup perspective on group dynamics. In, J. W. Lorsch (Ed.), *Handbook of organizational behavior* (pp. 190–222). Englewood Cliffs, NJ: Prentice-Hall.

Asch, S. E. (1951). Effects of group pressure upon the modification and distortion of judgments. In, H. S. Guetzkow (Ed.), *Groups, leadership, and men* (pp. 177–190). Pittsburgh, PA: Carnegie Press.

Bales, R. F. (1950). *Interaction process analysis: A method for the study of small groups.* Reading, MA: Addison-Wesley.

Bavelas, A. (1942). Morale and training of leaders. In, G. Watson (Ed.), *Civilian morale.* Boston: Houghton Mifflin.

Blake, R. R., Shepard, H. A., & Mouton, J. S. (1964). *Managing intergroup conflict in industry.* Houston: Gulf.

Cartwright, D., & Zander, A. (Eds.). (1968). *Group dynamics: Research and theory* (3d ed.). New York: Harper & Row.

Cohen, A. R., Fink, S. L., Gadon, H., & Willits, R. D. (1988). *Effective behavior in organizations* (4th ed.). Homewood, IL: Richard D. Irwin.

Cox, T. H., Jr. (1993). *Cultural diversity in organizations: Theory, research & practice.* San Francisco: Berrett-Koehler.

Davis, S. M., & Lawrence, P. R. (1977). *Matrix.* Reading, MA: Addison-Wesley.

Gouldner, A. (1960). The norm of reciprocity. *American Sociological Review, 25,* 161–178.

Harvard Business Review (Eds.) (1994). *Differences that work: Organizational excellence through diversity.* Boston: Harvard Business Review Publishing Corporation.

Homans, G. C. (1950). *The human group.* New York: Harcourt, Brace.

Ivancevich, J. M., & Matteson, M. T. (1993). *Organizational behavior and management* (3d ed.). Homewood, IL: Irwin.

Janis, I. L. (November 1971). Groupthink. *Psychology Today,* 44–76.

Lewin, K. (1943). Forces behind food habits and methods of change. Washington, D.C.: *Bulletin of the National Research Council, 108,* 35–65.

Lewin, K. (June 1947). Frontiers in group dynamics: Concept, method and reality in social science; Social equilibria and social change. *Human Relations, 1* (1).

Lewin, K. (1951). *Field theory in social science.* New York: Harper & Row.

Lewin, K. (1952). Group decision and social change. In, G. E. Swanson, T. N. Newcomb, & E. L. Hartley (Eds.), *Reading in social psychology* (rev. ed.) (pp. 207–211). New York: Holt, Rinehart & Winston.

Lindzey, G. W. (Ed.). (1954). *The handbook of social psychology.* Cambridge, MA: Addison-Wesley.

Marrow, A. J. (1969). *The practical theorist: The life and work of Kurt Lewin.* New York: Basic Books.

Martin, J., & Siehl, C. (Autumn 1983). Organizational culture and counterculture: An uneasy symbiosis. *Organizational Dynamics,* 52–64.

Moreno, J. L. (1934). *Who shall survive?: A new approach to human interrelations.* Washington, D.C.: Nervous and Mental Disease Publishing Co.

Newcomb, T. M. (1943). *Personality and social change.* New York: Dryden.

Ott, J. S. (1989). *The organizational culture perspective.* Belmont, CA: Wadsworth.

Pfeffer, J. (1981). *Power in organizations.* Boston: Pitman Publishing Company.

Pondy, L. R. (1967). Organizational conflict: Concepts and models. *Administrative Science Quarterly, 12,* 296–320.

Roy, D. F. (1960). "Banana time": Job satisfaction and informal interaction. *Human Organization, 18,* 158–168.

Roy, D. F. (1961). Efficiency and "the fix": Informal intergroup relations in a piecework machine shop. In, S. M. Lipset & N. J. Smelser (Eds.), *The progress of a decade.* Englewood Cliffs, NJ: Prentice-Hall.

Schein, E. H. (1980). *Organizational psychology* (3d ed.). Englewood Cliffs, NJ: Prentice-Hall.

Schein, E. H. (1992). *Organizational culture and leadership* (2d ed.). San Francisco: Jossey-Bass.

Seashore, S. E. (1954). *Group cohesiveness in the industrial work group.* Ann Arbor: University of Michigan Press.

Shafritz, J. M., & Ott, J. S. (Eds.). (1996). *Classics of organization theory* (4th ed.). Belmont, CA: Wadsworth.

Sherif, M. (1936). *The psychology of social norms.* New York: Harper.

Sherif, M., Harvey, O. J., White, B. J., & Sherif, C. (1961). *Intergroup conflict and cooperation: The robbers' cave experiment.* Norman, OK: University Book Exchange.

Smith, A. (1776). *The wealth of nations* (Chapter 1, Of the division of labor).

Strauss, G. (1962). Tactics of lateral relationship: The purchasing agent. *Administrative Science Quarterly, 7,* 161–186.

Thibaut, J., & Kelly, H. (1959). *The social psychology of groups.* New York: John Wiley & Sons.

Thorndike, E. L. (1935). *The psychology of wants, interests, and attitudes.* New York: Appleton-Century.

Walton, R. E., & Dutton, J. M. (March, 1969). The management of interdepartmental conflict: A model and review. *Administrative Science Quarterly, 14* (1).

Walton, R. E., Dutton, J. M., & Fitch, H. G. (1966). A study of conflict in the process, structure, and attitudes of lateral relationships. In, A. H. Rubenstein & C. J. Haberstroh (Eds.), *Some theories of organization* (rev. ed.) (pp. 444–465). Homewood, IL: Richard D. Irwin.

Whyte, W. F., Jr. (1943). *Street corner society.* Chicago: University of Chicago Press.

Whyte, W. F., Jr. (1948). *Human relations in the restaurant industry.* New York: McGraw-Hill.

Zander, A. (1971). *Motives and goals in groups.* New York: Academic Press.

Zander, A. (1982). *Making groups effective.* San Francisco: Jossey-Bass.

## 9

# "Banana Time": Job Satisfaction and Informal Interaction

*Donald F. Roy**

This paper undertakes description and exploratory analysis of the social interaction which took place within a small work group of factory machine operatives during a two-month period of participant observation. The factual and ideational materials which it presents lie at an intersection of two lines of research interest and should, in their dual bearings, contribute to both. Since the operatives were engaged in work which involved the repetition of very simple operations over an extra-long workday, six days a week, they were faced with the problem of dealing with a formidable "beast of monotony." Revelation of how the group utilized its resources to combat that "beast" should merit the attention of those who are seeking solution to the practical problem of job satisfaction, or employee morale. It should also provide insights for those who are trying to penetrate the mysteries of the small group. . . .

My account of how one group of machine operators kept from "going nuts" in a situation of monotonous work activity attempts to lay bare the tissues of interaction which made up the content of their adjustment. The talking, fun, and fooling which provided solution to the elemental problem of "psychological

survival" will be described according to their embodiment in intra-group relations. In addition, an unusual opportunity for close observation of behavior involved in the maintenance of group equilibrium was afforded by the fortuitous introduction of a "natural experiment." My unwitting injection of explosive materials into the stream of interaction resulted in sudden, but temporary, loss of group interaction.

My fellow operatives and I spent our long days of simple, repetitive work in relative isolation from other employees of the factory.

. . . Face-to-face contact with members of the managerial hierarchy were few and far between. No one bearing the title of foreman ever came around. The only company official who showed himself more than once during the two-month observation period was the plant superintendent. . . . Although no observable consequences accrued from the peculiar visitations of this silent fellow, it was assumed that he was some sort of efficiency expert, and he was referred to as "The Snooper." . . .

Our work group was thus not only abandoned to its own resources for creating job satisfaction, but left without that basic reservoir of ill-will toward management which can sometimes be counted on to stimulate the development of interesting activities to occupy hand and

* Dr. Roy is in the Department of Sociology, Duke University, Durham, North Carolina.

*Source:* From "'Banana Time': Job Satisfaction and Informal Interaction" by Donald F. Roy in *Human Organization*, 18 (1960). Reproduced by permission of the Society for Applied Anthropology.

brain. Lacking was the challenge of intergroup conflict, that periennial source of creative experience to fill the otherwise empty hours of meaningless work routine. . . .[1]

## THE WORK GROUP

Absorbed at first in three related goals of improving my clicking skill, increasing my rate of output, and keeping my left hand unclicked, I paid little attention to my fellow operatives save to observe that they were friendly, middle aged, foreign-born, full of advice, and very talkative. Their names, according to the way they addressed each other, were George, Ike, and Sammy.[2] George, a stocky fellow in his late fifties, operated the machine at the opposite end of the line; he, I later discovered, had emigrated in early youth from a country in Southeastern Europe. Ike, stationed at George's left, was tall, slender, in his early fifties, and Jewish; he had come from Eastern Europe in his youth. Sammy, number three man in the line, and my neighbor, was heavy set, in his late fifties, and Jewish; he had escaped from a country in Eastern Europe just before Hitler's legions had moved in. All three men had been downwardly mobile as to occupation in recent years. George and Sammy had been proprietors of small businesses; the former had been "wiped out" when his uninsured establishment burned down; the latter had been entrepreneuring on a small scale before he left all behind him to flee the Germans. According to his account, Ike had left a highly skilled trade which he had practiced for years in Chicago.

[1] Donald F. Roy, "Work Satisfaction and Social Reward in Quota Achievement: An Analysis of Piecework Incentive," *American Sociological Review*, XVIII (October, 1953), 507–514.

[2] All names used are fictitious.

I discovered also that the clicker line represented a ranking system in descending order from George to myself. George not only had top seniority for the group, but functioned as a sort of leadman. His superior status was marked in the fact that he received five cents more per hour than the other clickermen, put in the longest workday, made daily contact, outside the workroom, with the superintendent on work matters which concerned the entire line, and communicated to the rest of us the directives which he received. The narrow margin of superordination was seen in the fact that directives were always relayed in the superintendent's name. . . .

Ike was next to George in seniority, then Sammy. I was, of course, low man on the totem pole. Other indices to status differentiation lay in informal interaction, to be described later.

## THE WORK

It was evident to me, before my first workday drew to a weary close, that my clicking career was going to be a grim process of fighting the clock, the particular timepiece in this situation being an old-fashioned alarm clock which ticked away on a shelf near George's machine. I had struggled through many dreary rounds with the minutes and hours during the various phases of my industrial experience, but never had I been confronted with such a dismal combination of working conditions as the extra-long workday, the infinitesimal cerebral excitation, and the extreme limitation of physical movement. . . . This was standing all day in one spot beside three old codgers in a dingy room looking out through barred windows at the bare walls of a brick warehouse, leg movements largely restricted to the shifting of body weight from one foot to the other, hand and arm movements confined, for the most part, to a simple repetitive sequence of place the die,———punch the clicker,———place the die,——— punch the clicker, and intellectual activity reduced to computing the hours to quitting time. . . .

The next day was the same: the monotony of the work, the tired legs and sore feet and thoughts of quitting.

## THE GAME OF WORK

In discussing the factory operative's struggle to "cling to the remnants of joy in work," Henri de Man makes the general observations that "it is psychologically impossible to deprive any kind of work of all its positive emotional elements," that the worker will find *some* meaning in any activity assigned to him, a "certain scope for initiative which can satisfy after a fashion the instinct for play and the creative impulse," that "even in the Taylor system there is found luxury of self-determination."[3]

. . . I did find a "certain scope for initiative," and out of this slight freedom to vary activity, I developed a game of work.

The game developed was quite simple, so elementary, in fact, that its playing was reminiscent of rainy-day preoccupations in childhood, when attention could be centered by the hour on colored bits of things of assorted sizes and shapes. But this adult activity was not mere pottering and piddling; what it lacked in the earlier imaginative content, it made up for in clean-cut structure. Fundamentally involved were: a) variation in color of the materials cut, b) variation in shapes of the dies used, and c) a process called "scraping the block." The basic procedure which ordered the particular

[3] Henri de Man, *The Psychology of Socialism*, Henry Holt and Company, New York, 1927, pp. 80–81.

combination of components employed could be stated in the form: "As soon as I do so many of these, I'll get to do those." If, for example, production scheduled for the day featured small, rectangular strips in three colors, the game might go: "As soon as I finish a thousand of the green ones, I'll click some brown ones." And, with success in attaining the objective of working with brown materials, a new goal of "I'll get to do the white ones" might be set. Or the new goal might involve switching dies. . . .

But a hasty conclusion that I was having lots of fun playing my clicking game should be avoided. These games were not as interesting in the experiencing as they might seem to be from the telling. Emotional tone of the activity was low, and intellectual currents weak. . . . Before the first week was out this adjustment to the work situation was complicated by other developments. The game of work continued, but in a different context. Its influence became decidedly subordinated to, if not completely overshadowed by, another source of job satisfaction.

## INFORMAL SOCIAL ACTIVITY OF THE WORK GROUP: TIMES AND THEMES

The change came about when I began to take serious note of the social activity going on around me; my attentiveness to this activity came with growing involvement in it. What I heard at first, before I started to listen, was a stream of disconnected bits of communication which did not make much sense. Foreign accents were strong and referents were not joined to coherent contexts of meaning. It was just "jabbering." What I saw at first, before I began to observe, was occasional flurries of horseplay so simple and unvarying in pattern and so childish in quality that they made no strong bid for attention. . . .

But, as I began to pay closer attention, as I began to develop familiarity with the communication system, the disconnected became connected, the nonsense made sense, the obscure became clear, and the silly actually funny. And, as the content of the interaction took on more and more meaning, the interaction began to reveal structure. There were "times" and "themes," and roles to serve their enaction. The interaction had subtleties, and I began to savor and appreciate them. I started to record what hitherto had seemed unimportant.

## Times

This emerging awareness of structure and meaning included recognition that the long day's grind was broken by interruptions of a kind other than the formally instituted or idiosyncratically developed disjunctions in work routine previously described. These additional interruptions appeared in daily repetition in an ordered series of informal interactions. They were, in part, but only in part and in very rough comparison, similar to those common fractures of the production process known as the coffee break, the coke break, and the cigarette break. Their distinction lay in frequency of occurrence and in brevity. As phases of the daily series, they occurred almost hourly, and so short were they in duration that they disrupted work activity only slightly. . . . The major significance of the interactional interruptions lay in such a carryover of interest. The physical interplay which momentarily halted work activity would initiate verbal exchanges and thought processes to occupy group members until the next interruption. The group interactions thus not only marked off the time; they gave it content and hurried it along.

Most of the breaks in the daily series were designated as "times" in the parlance of the clicker operators, and they featured the consumption of food or drink of one sort or another. There was coffee time, peach time, banana time, fish time, coke time, and, of course, lunch time. Other interruptions, which formed part of the series but were not verbally recognized as times, were window time, pickup time, and the staggered quitting times of Sammy and Ike. These latter unnamed times did not involve the partaking of refreshments.

My attention was first drawn to this times business during my first week of employment when I was encouraged to join in the sharing of two peaches. It was Sammy who provided the peaches; he drew them from his lunch box after making the announcement, "Peach time!" . . .

Banana time followed peach time by approximately an hour. Sammy again provided the refreshments, namely, one banana. There was, however, no four-way sharing of Sammy's banana. Ike would gulp it down by himself after surreptitiously extracting it from Sammy's lunch box, kept on a shelf behind Sammy's work station. Each morning, after making the snatch, Ike would call out, "Banana time!" and proceed to down his prize while Sammy made futile protests and denunciations. George would join in with mild remonstrances, sometimes scolding Sammy for making so much fuss. The banana was one which Sammy brought for his own consumption at lunch time; he never did get to eat his banana, but kept bringing one for his lunch. At first this daily theft startled and amazed me. Then I grew to look forward to the daily seizure and the verbal interaction which followed.

Window time came next. It followed banana time as a regular consequence of Ike's castigation by the indignant

Sammy. After "taking" repeated references to himself as a person badly lacking in morality and character, Ike would "finally" retaliate by opening the window which faced Sammy's machine, to let the "cold air" blow in on Sammy. . . . Sammy would protest, argue, and make claims that the air blowing in on him would give him a cold; he would eventually have to leave his machine to close the window. Sometimes the weather was slightly chilly, and the draft from the window unpleasant; but cool or hot, windy or still, window time arrived each day. (I assume that it was originally a cold season development.) George's part in this interplay, in spite of the "good daddy" laudations, was to encourage Ike in his window work. He would stress the tonic values of fresh air and chide Sammy for his unappreciativeness.

Following window time came lunch time, a formally designated half-hour for the midday repast and rest break. . . .

Pickup time, fish time, and coke time came in the afternoon. I name it pickup time to represent the official visit of the man who made daily calls to cart away boxes of clicked materials. . . .

About mid-afternoon came fish time. George and Ike would stop work for a few minutes to consume some sort of pickled fish which Ike provided. Neither Sammy nor I partook of this nourishment, nor were we invited. . . .

Coke time came late in the afternoon, and was an occasion for total participation. The four of us took turns in buying the drinks and in making the trip for them to a fourth floor vending machine. Through George's manipulation of the situation, it eventually became my daily chore to go after the cokes; . . .

## Themes

To put flesh, so to speak, on this interactional frame of "times," my work group had developed various "themes" of verbal interplay which had become standardized in their repetition. These topics of conversation ranged in quality from an extreme of nonsensical chatter to another extreme of serious discourse. Unlike the times, these themes flowed one into the other in no particular sequence of predictability. Serious conversation could suddenly melt into horseplay, and vice versa. In the middle of a serious discussion on the high cost of living, Ike might drop a weight behind the easily startled Sammy, or hit him over the head with a dusty paper sack. Interaction would immediately drop to a low comedy exchange of slaps, threats, guffaws, and disapprobations which would invariably include a ten-minute echolalia of "Ike is a bad man, a very bad man! George is a good daddy, a very fine man!" Or, on the other hand, a stream of such invidious comparisons as followed a surreptitious switching-off of Sammy's machine by the playful Ike might merge suddenly into a discussion of the pros and cons of saving for one's funeral.

"Kidding themes" were usually started by George or Ike, and Sammy was usually the butt of the joke. Sometimes Ike would have to "take it," seldom George. One favorite kidding theme involved Sammy's alleged receipt of $100 a month from his son. The points stressed were that Sammy did not have to work long hours, or did not have to work at all, because he had a son to support him. George would always point out that he sent money to his daughter; she did not send money to him. . . .

Serious themes included the relating of major misfortunes suffered in the past by group members. George referred again and again to the loss, by fire, of his business establishment. Ike's chief complaints centered around a chronically ill wife who had undergone various operations and periods of hospital care. Ike spoke with discouragement of the expenses attendant upon hiring a housekeeper for himself and his children; he referred with disappointment and disgust to a teen-age son, an inept lad who "couldn't even fix his own lunch. He couldn't even make himself a sandwich!" Sammy's reminiscences centered on the loss of a flourishing business when he had to flee Europe ahead of Nazi invasion.

There was one theme of especially solemn import, the "professor theme." This theme might also be termed "George's daughter's marriage theme"; for the recent marriage of George's only child was inextricably bound up with George's connection with higher learning. The daughter had married the son of a professor who instructed in one of the local colleges. This professor theme was not in the strictest sense a conversation piece; when the subject came up, George did all the talking. . . . It was monologue, but there was listening, there was communication, the sacred communication of a temple, when George told of going for Sunday afternoon walks on the Midway with the professor, or of joining the professor for a Sunday dinner. Whenever he spoke of the professor, his daughter, the wedding, or even of the new son-in-law, who remained for the most part in the background, a sort of incidental like the wedding cake, . . . I came to the conclusion that it was the professor connection, not the straw-boss-ship or extra nickel an hour, which provided the fount of George's superior status in the group.

If the professor theme may be regarded as the cream of verbal interaction, the "chatter themes" should be classed as the dregs. The chatter themes were hardly themes at all; perhaps they should be labeled "verbal states," or "oral autisms." . . . "George is a good daddy, a very fine man! Ike is a bad man, a very

bad man!" Also, Sammy's repetition of "Don't bother me! Can't you see I'm busy? I'm a very busy man!" for ten minutes after Ike had dropped a weight behind him would fit the classification. Ike would shout "Mamariba!" at intervals between repetition of bits of verse, such as:

> Mama on the bed,
> Papa on the floor,
> Baby in the crib
> Says giver some more!

Sometimes the three operators would pick up one of these simple chatterings in a sort of chorus. "Are you man or mouse? I ask you, are you man or mouse?" was a favorite of this type.

So initial discouragement with the meagerness of social interaction I now recognized as due to lack of observation. The interaction was there, in constant flow. It captured attention and held interest to make the long day pass. The twelve hours of "click,——move die,——click,——move die" became as easy to endure as eight hours of varied activity in the oil fields or eight hours of playing the piecework game in a machine shop. The "beast of boredom" was gentled to the harmlessness of a kitten.

## BLACK FRIDAY: DISINTEGRATION OF THE GROUP

But all this was before "Black Friday." Events of that dark day shattered the edifice of interaction, its framework of times and mosaic of themes, and reduced the work situation to a state of social atomization and machine-tending drudgery. The explosive element was introduced deliberately, but without prevision of its consequences.

On Black Friday, Sammy was not present; he was on vacation. . . .

Suddenly I was possessed of an inspiration for modification of the professor theme. When the idea struck, I was working at Sammy's machine, clicking out leather parts for billfolds. It was not difficult to get the attention of close neighbor Ike to suggest *sotto voce*, "Why don't you tell him you saw the professor teaching in a barber college on Madison Street? . . . Make it near Halsted Street."

Ike thought this one over for a few minutes, and caught the vision of its possibilities. After an interval of steady application to his clicking, he informed the unsuspecting George of his near West Side discovery; he had seen the professor busy at his instructing in a barber college in the lower reaches of Hobohemia.

George reacted to this announcement with stony silence. The burden of questioning Ike for further details on his discovery fell upon me. Ike had not elaborated his story very much before we realized that the show was not going over. George kept getting redder in the face, and more tight-lipped; he slammed into his clicking with increased vigor. I made one last weak attempt to keep the play on the road by remarking that barber colleges paid pretty well. George turned to hiss at me, "You'll have to go to Kankakee with Ike!" I dropped the subject. Ike whispered to me, "George is sore!"

George was indeed sore. He didn't say another word the rest of the morning. There was no conversation at lunchtime, nor was there any after lunch. A pall of silence had fallen over the clicker room. Fish time fell a casualty. George did not touch the coke I brought for him. A very long, very dreary afternoon dragged on. Finally, after Ike left for home, George broke the silence to reveal his feelings to me:

Ike acts like a five-year-old, not a man! He doesn't even have the respect of the niggers. But he's got to act like a man around here! He's always fooling around! I'm going to stop that! I'm going to show him his place! . . .

For three days, George would not speak to Ike. Ike made several weak attempts to break the wall of silence which George had put between them, but George did not respond; it was as if he did not hear. George would speak to me, on infrequent occasions, and so would Ike. They did not speak to each other.

On the third day George advised me of his new communication policy, designed for dealing with Ike, and for Sammy, too, when the latter returned to work. Interaction was now on a "strictly business" basis, with emphasis to be placed on raising the level of shop output. . . .

Twelve-hour days were creeping again at snail's pace. The strictly business communications were of no help, and the sporadic bursts of distaste or enthusiasm for Sammy's clicking ability helped very little. With the return of boredom, came a return of fatigue. My legs tired as the afternoons dragged on, and I became engaged in conscious efforts to rest one by shifting my weight to the other. . . .

In desperation, I fell back on my game of work, my blues and greens and whites, my ovals and trapezoids, and my scraping the block. . . .

When Sammy returned to work, discovery of the cleavage between George and Ike left him stunned. "They were the best of friends!" he said to me in bewilderment. . . .

Then, thirteen days after Black Friday, came an abrupt change in the pattern of interaction. George and Ike spoke to each other again, in friendly conversation:

I noticed Ike talking to George after lunch. The two had newspapers of fish at George's cabinet. Ike was excited; he said, "I'll pull up a chair!" The two ate for ten minutes. . . . It seems that they went up to the 22nd Street Exchange together during lunch period to cash pay checks.

That afternoon Ike and Sammy started to play again, and Ike burst once more into song. Old themes reappeared as suddenly as the desert flowers in spring. At first, George managed to maintain some show of the dignity of superordination. When Ike started to sing snatches of "You Are My Sunshine," George suggested that he get "more production." . . .

George was for a time reluctant to accept fruit when it was offered to him, and he did not make a final capitulation to coke time until five days after renewal of the fun and fooling. . . .

Of course, George's demand for greater production was metamorphized into horseplay. His shout of "Production please!" became a chatter theme to accompany the varied antics of Ike and Sammy.

The professor theme was dropped completely. George never again mentioned his Sunday walks on the Midway with the professor.

# CONCLUSIONS

Speculative assessment of the possible significance of my observations on information interaction in the clicking room may be set forth in a series of general statements.

## Practical Application

First, in regard to possible practical application to problems of industrial management, these observations seem to support the generally accepted notion that one key source of job satisfaction lies in the informal interaction shared by members of a work group. . . .

In regard to another managerial concern, employee productivity, any appraisal of the influence of group interaction upon clicking-room output could be no more than roughly impressionistic. I obtained no evidence to warrant a claim that banana time, or any of its accompaniments in consumatory interaction, boosted production. . . . As far as achievement of managerial goals is concerned, the most that could be suggested is that leavening the deadly boredom of individualized work routines with a concurrent flow of group festivities had a negative effect on turnover. . . .

## Theoretical Considerations

Secondly, possible contribution to ongoing sociological inquiry into the behavior of small groups in general, and factory work groups, in particular, may lie in one or more of the following ideational products of my clicking-room experience:

1. In their day-long confinement together in a small room spatially and socially isolated from other work areas of the factory the Clicking Department employees found themselves ecologically situated for development of a "natural" group. Such a development did take place; from worker intercommunications did emerge the full-blown sociocultural system of consumatory interactions which I came to share, observe, and record in the process of my socialization.

2. These interactions had a content which could be abstracted from the total existential flow of observable doings and sayings for labelling and objective consideration. That is, they represented a distinctive sub-culture, with its recurring patterns of reciprocal influencings which I have described as times and themes.

3. From these interactions may also be abstracted a social structure of statuses and roles. This structure may be discerned in the carrying out of the various informal activities which provide the content of the sub-culture of the group. The times and themes were performed with a system of roles which formed a sort of pecking hierarchy. Horseplay had its initiators and

its victims, its amplifiers and its chorus; kidding had its attackers and attacked, its least attacked and its most attacked, its ready acceptors of attack and its strong resistors to attack. The fun went on with the participation of all, but within the controlling frame of status, a matter of who can say or do what to whom and get away with it.

4. In both the cultural content and the social structure of clicker group interaction could be seen the permeation of influences which flowed from the various multiple group memberships of the participants. Past and present "other-group" experiences or anticipated "outside" social connections provided significant materials for the building of themes and for the establishment and maintenance of status and role relationships. . . .

5. Stability of the clicking-room social system was never threatened by immediate outside pressures. Ours was not an instrumental group, subject to disintegration in a losing struggle against environmental obstacles or oppositions. It was not striving for corporate goals; nor was it faced with the enmity of other groups. It was strictly a consumatory group, devoted to the maintenance of patterns of self-entertainment. Under existing conditions, disruption of unity could come only from within. . . .

6. Although both George and I were solidly linked in other-group affiliations with the higher learning, there was not enough agreement in our attitudes toward university professors to prevent the interactional development which shattered our factory play group. George perceived my offered alterations as a real attack, and he responded with strong hostility directed against Ike, the perceived assailant, and Sammy, a fellow traveler.

My innovations, if accepted, would have lowered the tone of the sacred professor theme . . . Such a downgrading of George's reference group would, in turn, have downgraded George. His status in the shop group hinged largely upon his claimed relations with the professor.

7. Integration of our group was fully

restored after a series of changes in the patterning and quality of clicking-room interaction. It might be said that reintegration took place in these changes, that the series was a progressive one of step-by-step improvement in relations, that re-equilibration was in process during the three weeks that passed between initial communication collapse and complete return to "normal" interaction. . . .

The group had disintegrated when George withdrew from participation; and, since the rest of us were at all times ready for rapprochement, reintegration was dependent upon his "return." Therefore, each change of phase in interaction on the road to recovery could be said to represent an increment of return on George's part. Or, conversely, each phase could represent an increment of reacceptance of punished deviants. Perhaps more generally applicable to description of a variety of reunion situations would be conceptualization of the phase changes as increments of reassociation without an atomistic differentiation of the "movements" of individuals.

8. . . . The clicking-room group regained equilibrium under certain undetermined conditions. One of a number of other possible outcomes could have developed had conditions not been favorable for recovery.

For purposes of illustration, and from reflection on the case, I would consider the following as possibly necessary conditions for reintegration of our group: a) continued monotony of work operations; b) continued lack of a comparatively adequate substitute for the fun and fooling release from work tensions; c) inability of the operatives to escape from the work situation or from each other, within the work situation. George could not fire Ike or Sammy to remove them from his presence, and it would have been difficult for the three middle-aged men to find other jobs if they were to quit the shop. Shop space was small; and the machines close together. Like a submarine crew, they had to "live together"; d) Lack of conflicting definitions of the situation after Ike's perception of George's reaction to the "barber college" attack. George's anger and his punishment of the offenders was perceived as justified; e) Lack of introduction of new issues or causes which might have carried justification for new attacks and counterattacks, thus leading interaction into a spiral of conflict and crystallization of conflict norms. . . .

9. Whether or not the particular patterning of interactional change previously noted is somehow typical of a "re-equilibration process" is not a major question here. My purpose in discriminating the seven changes is primarily to suggest that re-equilibration, when it does occur,

may be described in observable phases and that the emergence of each succeeding phase should be dependent upon the configuration of conditions of the preceding one. Alternative eventual outcomes may change in their probabilities, as the phases succeed each other, just as prognosis for recovery in sickness may change as the disease situation changes.

10. Finally, discrimination of phase changes in social process may have practical as well as scientific value. Trained and skillful administrators might follow the practice in medicine of introducing aids to re-equilibration when diagnosis shows that they are needed.

## 10

# Foundations and Dynamics of Intergroup Behavior

## Robert R. Blake, Herbert A. Shepard, and Jane S. Mouton

## BEHAVIOR AT THE INTERPERSONAL LEVEL

When a man speaks as a group representative, his behavior is to some extent dictated by the fact that he is a member of that group. In contrast, when a man speaks from the framework of his job responsibilities, he speaks only for himself. In the latter case, disagreement between the parties is a *personal* matter. . . .

## FACTORS INFLUENCING THE RESOLUTION OF A DISPUTE WHEN DISAGREEMENT IS AN INTERGROUP MATTER

Significant differences appear when a person's interactions with another are dictated by his membership in or leadership of a group. Under these conditions, *the individual is not free* in the same sense as the person who acts independently out of job description or rank alone. Now the person's behavior is determined by many additional factors.[1]

## The Dynamics of Group Interplay in Resolution of Disputes

In situations where an individual is interacting with another and both are representatives of groups, additional forces, quite complex, come into play. Acting as an individual, a man is free to change his mind on the basis of new evidence. But as a group representative, if he changes his thinking or position from that of his group's and capitulates to an outside point of view, *he is likely to be perceived by them as a traitor.*[2] On the other hand, if as a representative, he is able to persuade a representative of the other group to capitulate to his point of view, *his group receives him as a hero.* In other words, when a man is acting as a representative of one group in disagreement with another, the problem is no longer a personal affair. It is an *intergroup* problem. And as such, it can become a significant factor in accounting for his actions—as we will see.

## Group Responsibilities of Individual Members

Often, men are quite aware that they have responsibilities as group representatives as well as individual job responsibilities. But formal organizational practices and attitudes often prevent this awareness from being discussed or from being openly considered.

As an example, consider the situation where the Vice President of sales speaks with the Vice President of operations. Formal organizational theory commonly

*Source:* From *Foundations and Dynamics of Intergroup Behavior,* by Robert R. Blake, Herbert A. Shepard, and Jane S. Mouton, Gulf Publishing Company, 1964, pp. 1–17. Reprinted by permission of Scientific Methods.

assumes that each man speaks for himself, out of the background of his individual job and responsibilities. In practice, however, each may be keenly aware that he is representing the goals, values and convictions of his own group, and furthermore, when he speaks for them, he also speaks for himself. When problems between sales and operations seem difficult to resolve, it is not, as a rule, a sign of rigidity, incompetence, or personality conflict.[3] Rather, it is more likely to be a product of the complex task of seeking resolutions which will not violate the attitudes, values, and interests of the many other persons that each represents.

## Incompatible Group Norms, Goals and Values

Just as formal organizational theory, as written, recognizes only that the individual speaks for himself out of his job responsibilities, similarly it may fail to recognize other facts of organizational life. Formal organization theory assumes that the goals, norms and procedures of different functional groups in the organization are, by definition, similar, complementary or identical. . . .

There is increasing recognition, however, that neither of these circumstances accurately describes many situations in modern industrial life. This recognition has led to an acknowledgment that men, in fact, are group representatives within the framework of an organization. In turn, it has led to an awareness and appreciation of how an individual acting as a member, or as a leader, of a group, is confronted with a host of additional problems.[4] These problems must be dealt with in terms of their genuine complexities if unity of organizational purpose is to be achieved.

The roots of these complex problems which group representatives face are characteristic of groups and of individuals. As will be seen, group membership is complicated further by the characteristics of intergroup relations. After looking briefly at these characteristics of groups, we will turn our attention to the dynamics of intergroup relations.

## THE STRUCTURE AND PROCESS OF GROUPS-IN-ISOLATION

There are a number of ways of describing the characteristics of groups-in-isolation which we should consider prior to dealing with industrial intergroup relations.[5, 6]

### Regulation of the Interdependent Behavior of Members of Groups-in-Isolation

Fundamentally, a group consists of a number of individuals bound to each other in some stage or degree of interdependence or shared "stake." Their problem is to guarantee the survival of the group in order to attain some *purpose or goal*. Taking for granted that the group's goals are clearly understood by its members, the interdependence among individuals, then, must be regulated to insure partial or entire achievement of these goals.

### The Emergence of Group Structure, Leadership and Normative Rules

The need to regulate interdependence leads to three further properties of groups. When these properties emerge in group life they become additional forces which influence individual behavior. Let us look at each of these.

1. *Group Structure*. A differentiation of individual roles often is needed to accomplish group objectives. Differentiation inevitably results in some individuals who have varying degrees of power to influence the actions of others. The result is that some group members carry

greater weight than others in determining the direction of group action, it norms, values and attitudes.

2. *Leadership.* When the power system among members of an informal group is crystallized, it is common to speak of *that individual with the most power as the leader.* In some groups, he is boss, or supervisor; other members are subordinates. The leader is looked to by the members for guidance and direction. The power and influence of the leader varies according to his ability to aid the group in achieving its goals.[7] Where the leader is appointed by a more powerful group rather than being selected by his own group, the above generalizations must be qualified. For instance, if the goals of the subordinate group clash with those of the group by which he is appointed, he will be received not as leader, but as a representative of a different group.

3. *Normal Rules Guiding Group Behavior.* Along with the emerging set of power relations is the evolution of a normal set of "rules of the game," which specifies the conditions of interaction between group members. In other words, varying degrees of familiarity, influence, interaction and other relationships between members are sanctioned by the group according to an individual's role and position in the group hierarchy. Deviations from the rules and procedures by a member can lead to subtle but potent pressures by his fellow members to insure that the deviant "swings back into line."[7] Such pressures act quite differently on each person as a function of his status and personality, but they do act.

### Identification with One's Group

The preceding three characteristics of group formation and operation—goals, leadership and norms—lead to varying degrees of identification with one's group. When feelings of identification are strong, the group is said to have high morale; it is highly cohesive.[8] The opposite is true when feelings of identification with group goals are low. Under circumstances of unacceptable power distribution or inappropriate norms, for example, the result is feelings of low morale, demoralization, low cohesion or possibly alienation. The greater the sense of identification a member has with his group, the greater are the pressures on him to follow, at times blindly, the direction and will of the group position.[9, 10]

These are all common properties of organized groups. A representative of a group, whether leader or member, is compelled to acknowledge in some way these group properties as he comes in contact with members of other groups whose interests support or violate those of his own. For a representative to agree to actions which other members feel are contrary to group goals can result in his being seen to have acted in a betraying way, or in poor faith. On the other hand, acting effectively against opposition and in support of group purpose and goals, and consistent with internal norms and values, insures retention or enhancement of his status.[11]

## THE RELATIONSHIP OF THE ORGANIZATION FRAMEWORK TO INDIVIDUAL AND GROUP RELATIONS

The internal properties of a group are only one of the significant matters involved in understanding and managing intergroup relations. When the actions of individuals and groups are viewed within the framework of a complex organization, we can identify additional determinants of behavior.[12]

### A Framework of Interdependent Organizational Subgroups

Consider the following circumstance in a large and complex organization: the total membership of the organization is subdivided into many smaller groups. Each subgroup has its own leadership and its own rules and regulations. Each has its own goals which may or may not be in accord with overall organizational goals.[13] Each operates with its own degree of cohesion which varies with feelings of failure or accomplishment.[14] In an organization, these groups are interdependent with one another. They may be interdependent in performing a complex task requiring coordination of effort, in geographical proximity, or in terms of the reward system of the organization. Differences among them immediately become apparent to members.

*Comparison Between Groups.* Perception of differences between groups leads spontaneously to a comparison and to a "we-they" orientation.[5] Attention quickly focuses on similarities and differences. Furthermore, these spontaneous comparisons are intensified by the tendency of higher levels of authority to evaluate and reward by group comparison. For example, group incentive plans, awarding of plaques or other symbols of organization success to the highest selling group, the group with the highest safety record, and so forth, all tend to highlight group differences.[15] Thus, in a sense, "winning" and "losing" groups are help up for all to see. The organization's rationale is that a spirit of competition is a "healthy" motivating force for achieving organizational ends.[16, 17]

On the other hand, these comparisons sometimes lead to the discovery of common values and mutually supportive opportunities which can result in greater intergroup cohesion. When this happens, it is possible to achieve an intergroup atmosphere that can lead to effective problem-solving and cooperation. Feelings of shared responsibility may then lead to identification with overall organizational goals, and to heightened recognition of similarities with resulting reduction of differences and tensions between them.[18]

*Pitfalls of Comparisons Across Groups.* There is no assurance, however, that comparisons between groups inevitably lead to favorable outcomes. Instead, in the process of comparison, groups may discover discrepancies in treatment and privileges,[19] points of view, objectives, values, and so on. Then a different process unfolds. Comparisons tend to become invidious.[5] Differences are spotlighted and come to the focus of attention. Distortions in perception occur which favor the ingroup and deprecate the outgroup.[20, 21, 22] Each group finds in the other's performances an obstacle to attaining some or all of its own goals. When this situation extends beyond some critical point, each group may view the other as a threat to its own survival. At this point, disagreements are seen as permanent and inevitable, and the only possible resolution seems to lie in defeat of the other group in order to gain one's own objectives. Then all of the tools of common power struggles are brought into play.[23]

The manner in which representatives of groups interact, then, is colored by the background and history of agreements or disagreements of the groups they represent. The forces involved are powerful. The individual group's representative does not act only in terms of his job description or his specific background of training. Nor does he act solely within the context of his position within the group. Rather, he must be governed to some extent, depending on circumstances, by pre-existing relationships between the group he represents and the opposing group or representative of it that he is addressing.

Evaluated in terms of the forces acting in intergroup life, effective management of intergroup relations is a dimension of management that requires more analysis, more theory, and more skills than has been traditional in industrial life. To gain the necessary perspective, managers must focus not only on effective methods of resolving intergroup differences, but also on dysfunctional methods which lead to undesirable and disruptive side effects. Many dysfunctional methods for resolving conflicts have become common. These common practices have become embedded in the traditions of groups and organizations and must be understood to avoid their unthoughtful repetition.

## THREE BASIC ASSUMPTIONS TOWARD INTERGROUP DISAGREEMENT

Three basic assumptions or attitudes toward intergroup disagreements and its management can be identified.

### 1. Disagreement Is Inevitable and Permanent

One identifiable basic assumption is that disagreement is inevitable and permanent. When A and B disagree, the assumption is that the disagreement must be resolved in favor of A or in favor of B, one way or the other. Under this assumption there seems to be no other alternative. If two points of view are seen to be mutually exclusive, and if neither party is prepared to capitulate, then any of three major mechanisms of resolution may be used:

A. *Win-lose* power struggle to the point of capitulation by one group.

B. Resolution through a *third-party* decision.

C. Agreement *not* to determine the outcome, namely, *fate* arbitration.

### 2. Conflict Can Be Avoided Since Interdependence Between Groups Is Unnecessary

A second orientation to intergroup relations rests on the assumption that while

intergroup disagreement is not inevitable, neither is intergroup agreement possible. If these assumptions can be made, then interdependence is not necessary. Hence, when points of conflict arise between groups, they can be resolved by reducing the interdependence between parties. This reduction of interdependence may be achieved in three ways.

A. One group withdrawing from the scene of action.

B. Maintaining, or substituting *indifference* when it appears there is a conflict of interest.

C. *Isolating* the parties from each other; or the parties isolating themselves.

All of these (A, B, and C) share in common the maintenance of independence, rather than any attempt to achieve interdependence.

### 3. Agreement and Maintaining Interdependence Is Possible

The third orientation to intergroup disagreement is that agreement is possible and that a means of resolving it must be found. Resolving conflict in this way is achieved by smoothing over the conflict while retaining interdependence. For example, visible though trivial reference may be made to overall organizational goals to which both parties are in some degree committed. Then attention is shifted away from real issues with surface harmony maintained. Alternatively, agreement may be achieved by bargaining, trading, or compromising. In a general sense, this is splitting the difference that separates the parties while at the same time retaining their interdependence. Finally, an effort may be made to resolve the disagreement by a genuine problem-solving approach. Here the effort is not devoted to determining who is right and who is wrong. Nor is it devoted to yielding something to gain something. Rather, a genuine effort is made to discover a creative resolution of fundamental points of difference.

As mentioned earlier, each of these three orientations is related to another dimension which determines the specific approach to be used in managing disagreement. This dimension might be pictured as extending from a *passive* attitude or low stakes to an *active* orientation involving high stakes.

## FRAMEWORK FOR VIEWING INTERGROUP CONFLICT

Figure 1 pictures the possibilities within each of the three major orientations just described. These orientations (three vertical columns in Figure 1) are:

1. Conflict inevitable. Agreement impossible.
2. Conflict not inevitable, yet agreement not possible.
3. Agreement possible in spite of conflict.

At the bottom of each orientation is the method of resolution likely to be used where stakes in the outcome are low. The middle shows mechanisms employed where stakes in the outcome are moderate, and the upper end shows mechanisms likely to be adopted where stakes in the outcome of the conflict are high.

All the approaches in the left-hand orientation (column) *presume a condition of win-lose between the contesting parties*. Fate strategies come into force when stakes in the outcome are low, arbitration when the stakes are moderate, and win-lose power struggles when the stakes are high.

The right-hand vertical column of the graph reflects three opposite approaches to resolving disagreement. These approaches assume that though disagreement is present, agreement can be found.

The most passive orientation here is identified as "smoothing over." This approach involves such well-known cultural phenomena as efforts to achieve intergroup cohesion and co-existence without really solving problems. The assumption is that somehow or another, peaceful co-existence will arise and that people will act in accordance with it.

The more active agreement contains the element of splitting differences. This is a more positive (active) approach than smoothing over differences, but it leaves much to be desired for it often produces only temporary resolution.

In the upper right-hand corner is the orientation of problem solving. This position identifies the circumstances under which the contesting parties search out the rationale of their agreements as well as the bases of their disagreements. It also identifies the causes for reservations and doubts of both parties. Here, the parties work toward the circumstances which will eliminate reservations. This climate affords the opportunity to actively explore means for achieving true agreement on issues without "smoothing over" or compromising differences. . . .

## SUMMARY

As a group member, whether leader or member, *an individual is a representative of his group* whenever he interacts with others in different groups, provided the groups are in some way interdependent. As a representative, a group member's opinions and attitudes are shaped by the goals, norms and values he shares with others of his group. Normal rules of conduct and the expectations of others in his group do not allow him to act independently of his group's interests when areas of disagreement arise between his group and another.

FIGURE I · THE THREE BASIC ASSUMPTIONS TOWARD INTERGROUP
DISAGREEMENTS AND THEIR MANAGEMENT.

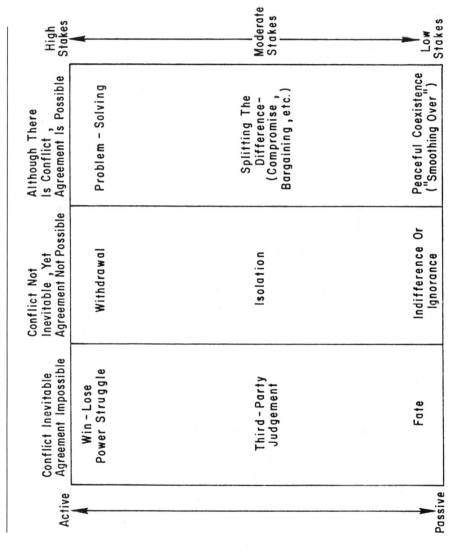

Large organizations are composed of many small groups. Because of the size, complexity and nature of present-day organizations, group comparisons, particularly of an invidious character, are bound to occur. Under such circumstances, differences, rather than similarities and commonness of purpose, are highlighted, with conflict the inevitable result. The result is that organizational needs for interdependence and cooperation among groups are not met as well as they might have been, had managerial personnel applied greater understanding to intergroup relations.

Three basic orientations to intergroup disagreement, in combination with these different degrees of "stake in the outcome," and their accompanying approaches for achieving resolution were outlined. . . .

# REFERENCES

1. Sheppard, H. L. "Approaches to conflict in American industrial Sociology." *Brit. J. Sociol.*, 5, 1954, 324–341.

2. Blake, R. R. "Psychology and the Crisis of Statesmanship." *Amer. Psychologist*, 14, 1959, 87–94. Blake R. R. and Mouton, J. S., *Group Dynamics–Key to Decision Making*. Houston: Gulf Publishing Co., 1961, 87.

3. Faris, R. E. L. "Interaction Levels and Intergroup Relations." In. M. Sherif, (Ed.) *Intergroup Relations and Leadership*. New York: John Wiley and Sons, Inc., 1962, 24–45.

4. Stogdill, R. M. Intragroup-Intergroup Theory and Research. In M. Sherif (ed.), *Intergroup Relations and Leadership*. New York: John Wiley and Sons, Inc., 1962, 48–65.

5. Sherif, M. and Sherif C. *Outline of Social Psychology* (revised). New York: Harper & Bros., 1956.

6. Cartwright, D. and Zander, A. *Group Dynamics: Research and Theory* (2nd edition). Evanston, Illinois: Row, Peterson & Co., 1960.

7. Hamblin, R. L., Miller, K. and Wiggins, J. A. "Group Morale and Competence of the Leader," *Sociometry*, 24 (3), 1961, 295–311.

8. Sherif, M. and Sherif, C. W. *Outline of Social Psychology* (revised), *op. cit.*

9. Cartwright, D. and Zander, A. *Group Dynamics: Research and Theory* (1st edition). Evanston, Ill. Row, Peterson & Co., 1953.

10. Gerard, H. B. "The Anchorage of Opinion in Face to Face Groups," *Human. Relat.*, 7, 1954, 313–325; and Kelley, H. H. and Volkart, E. H., "The Resistance to Change of Group Anchored Attitudes," *Amer. Sociol. Rev.*, 17, 1952, 453–465.

11. Pryer, M. W., Flint, A. W., and Bass, B. M. "Group Effectiveness and Consistency of Leaderhip," *Sociometry*, 25 (4), 1962, 391; and Sherif, M. and Sherif, C. W. *Outline of Social Psychology* (revised), *op. cit.*

12. Arensberg, C. H. "Behavior and Organization: Industrial Studies." In J. H. Rohrer and M. Sherif (eds.), *Social Psychology at the Crossroads*. New York: Harper & Bros., 1951.

13. Cooper, H. C. "Perception of Subgroup Power and Intensity of Affiliation with a Large Organization." *Amer. Sociol. Rev.*, 26 (2) 1961, 272–274.

14. Wolman, B. B. "Impact of Failure on Group Cohesiveness," *J. Soc. Psychol.*, 51, 1960, 409–418.

15. Sherif, M. and Sherif, C. W. *Outline of Social Psychology* (revised), *op. cit.*

16. Sayles, L. R. "The Impact of Incentives on Intergroup Relations: Management and Union Problem," *Personnel*, 28, 1952, 483–490.

17. Spriegel, W. R. and Lansburgh, R. H. *Industrial Management*, (5th edition). New York: John Wiley, 1955; and Strauss, G. and Sayles, L. R. *Personnel*. Englewood Cliffs, N. J.: Prentice-Hall, 1960.

18. Sherif, M. "Superordinate Goals in the Reduction of Intergroup Conflict," *Amer. J. Sociol.*, 43, 1958, 394–356.

19. Strauss, G. "Group Dynamics and Intergroup Relations." In W. F. White (ed.), *Money and Motivation*. New York: Harper & Bros., 1955, 90–96.

20. Sherif, M. and Sherif, C. W. *Outline of Social Psychology* (revised), *op. cit.*

21. Cohen, A. R. "Upward Communication in Experimentally Created Hierarchies," *Human Relat.*, 11, 1958, 41–53; Kelley, H. H. "Communication in Experimentally Created Hierarchies," *Human Relat.*, 4, 1951, 39–56; and Thibaut, J. "An Experimental Study of the Cohesiveness of Under-Privileged Groups," *Human Relat.*, 3, 1950, 251–278.

22. Blake, R. R. and Mouton, J. S. "Comprehension of Own and Outgroup Position Under Intergroup Competition," *J. Confl. Resolut.*, 5 (3), 1961, 304–310.

# 11
# Origins of Group Dynamics
## *Dorwin Cartwright & Alvin Zander*

Whether one wishes to understand or to improve human behavior, it is necessary to know a great deal about the nature of groups. . . .

What, then, is group dynamics? The phrase has gained popular familiarity since World War II but, unfortunately, with its increasing circulation its meaning has become imprecise. According to one rather frequent usage, group dynamics refers to a sort of political ideology concerning the ways in which groups should be organized and managed. This ideology emphasizes the importance of democratic leadership, the participation of members in decisions, and the gains both to society and to individuals to be obtained through cooperative activities in groups. The critics of this view have sometimes caricatured it as making "togetherness" the supreme virtue, advocating that everything be done jointly in groups that have and need no leader because everyone participates fully and equally. A second popular usage of the term group dynamics has it refer to a set of techniques, such as role playing, buzz-sessions, observation and feedback of group process, and group decision, which have been employed widely during the past decade or two in training programs designed to improve skill in human relations and in the management of conferences and committees. These techniques have been identified most closely with the National Training Laboratories whose annual training programs at

Bethel, Maine, have become widely known. According to the third usage of the term group dynamics, it refers to a field of inquiry dedicated to achieving knowledge about the nature of groups, the laws of their development, and their interrelations with individuals, other groups, and larger institutions.

. . . [We] shall limit our usage of the term group dynamics to refer to the field of inquiry dedicated to advancing knowledge about the nature of group life.

Group dynamics, in this sense, is a branch of knowledge or an intellectual specialization. Being concerned with human behavior and social relationships, it can be located within the social sciences. And yet it cannot be identified readily as a subpart of any of the traditional academic disciplines. . . .

In summary, then, we have proposed that group dynamics should be defined as a field of inquiry dedicated to advancing knowledge about the nature of groups, the laws of their development, and their interrelations with individuals, other groups, and larger institutions. It may be identified by four distinguishing characteristics: (a) an emphasis on theoretically significant empirical research, (b) an interest in dynamics and the interdependence among phenomena, (c) a broad relevance to all the social sciences, and (d) the potential applicability of its findings in efforts to improve the functioning of groups and their consequences on individuals and society.

*Source:* From *Group Dynamics*, 3rd ed., by Dorwin Cartwright and Alvin Zander, pp. 4–21. Copyright © 1968 by Dorwin Cartwright and Alvin Zander. Reprinted by permission of HarperCollins Publishers, Inc.

Thus conceived, group dynamics need not be associated with any particular ideology concerning the ways in which groups should be organized and managed nor with the use of any particular techniques of group management. In fact, it is a basic objective of group dynamics to provide a better scientific basis for ideology and practice.

## CONDITIONS FOSTERING THE RISE OF GROUP DYNAMICS

Group dynamics began, as an identifiable field of inquiry, in the United States toward the end of the 1930s. Its origination as a distinct specialty is associated primarily with Kurt Lewin (1890–1947) who popularized the term group dynamics, made significant contributions to both research and theory in group dynamics, and in 1945 established the first organization devoted explicitly to research on group dynamics. Lewin's contribution was of great importance, but, as we shall see in detail, group dynamics was not the creation of just one person. It was, in fact, the result of many developments that occurred over a period of several years and in several different disciplines and professions. Viewed in historical perspective, group dynamics can be seen as the convergence of certain trends within the social sciences and, more broadly, as the product of the particular society in which it arose. . . .

## A SUPPORTIVE SOCIETY

. . . In the 1930s significant resources were being allotted to the social sciences. The dramatic use of intelligence testing during World War I had stimulated research on human abilities and the application of testing procedures in school systems, industry, and government. "Scientific management," though slow to recognize the importance of social factors, was laying the groundwork for a scientific approach to the management of organizations. The belief that the solution of "social problems" could be facilitated by systematic fact-finding was gaining acceptance. . . . Thus, when the rapid expansion of group dynamics began after World War II, there were important segments of American society prepared to provide financial support for such research. Support came not only from academic institutions and foundations but also from business, the Federal Government, and various organizations concerned with improving human relations.

## DEVELOPED PROFESSIONS

. . . Before considering the social scientific background of group dynamics, we will describe briefly some of the developments within the professions that facilitated its rise.

By the 1930s a large number of distinct professions had come into existence in the United States, probably more than in any other country. Many of these worked directly with groups of people, and as they became concerned with improving the quality of their practice they undertook to codify procedures and to discover general principles for dealing with groups. It gradually became evident, more quickly in some professions than in others, that generalizations from experience can go only so far and that systematic research is required to produce a deeper understanding of group life. Thus, when group dynamics began to emerge as a distinct field, the leaders of some of the professions were well prepared to foster the idea that systematic research on group life could make a significant contribution to their professions. As a result, several professions helped to create a favorable atmosphere for the financing of group dynamics research, provided from their accumulated experience a broad systematic conception of group functioning from which hypotheses for research could be drawn, afforded facilities in which research could be conducted, and furnished the beginnings of a technology for creating and manipulating variables in experimentation on groups. Four professions played an especially important part in the origin and growth of group dynamics.

1. Social Group Work
2. Group Psychotherapy
3. Education
4. Administration

## DEVELOPED SOCIAL SCIENCE

. . . A basic premise of group dynamics is that the methods of science can be employed in the study of groups. This assumption could be entertained seriously only after the more general belief had gained acceptance that man, his behavior, and his social relations can be properly subjected to scientific investigation. . . . Not until the last decades of the nineteenth century were there many people actually observing, measuring, or conducting experiments on human behavior. The first psychological laboratory was established only in 1879.

*The Reality of Groups.* An important part of the early progress in school science consisted in clarifying certain basic assumptions about the reality of social phenomena. The first extensions of the scientific method of human behavior occurred in close proximity to biology. Techniques of experimentation and measurement were first applied to investigations of the responses of organisms to stimulation of the sense organs and to modification of responses due to repeated stimulation. There was never much doubt about the "existence" of individual organisms, but when attention

turned to groups of people and to social institutions, a great confusion arose. Discussion of these matters invoked terms like "group mind," "collective representations," "collective unconscious," and "culture." And people argued heatedly as to whether such terms refer to any real phenomena or whether they are mere "abstractions" or "analogies." On the whole, the disciplines concerned with institutions (anthropology, economics, political science, and sociology) have freely attributed concrete reality to supra-individual entities, whereas psychology, with its interest in the physiological bases of behavior, has been reluctant to admit existence to anything other than the behavior of organisms. But in all these disciplines there have been conflicts between "institutionalists" and "behavioral scientists."

It may appear strange that social scientists should get involved in philosophical considerations about the nature of reality. As a matter of fact, however, the social scientist's view of reality makes a great deal of difference to his scientific behavior. In the first place, it determines what things he is prepared to subject to empirical investigation. Lewin pointed out this fact succinctly in the following statement (22, 190):

> Labeling something as "nonexistent" is equivalent to declaring it "out of bounds" for the scientist. Attributing "existence" to an item automatically makes it a duty of the scientist to consider this item as an object of research; it includes the necessity of considering its properties as "facts" which cannot be neglected in the total system of theories; finally, it implies that the terms with which one refers to the item are acceptable as scientific "concepts" (rather than as "mere words").

Secondly, the history of science shows a close interaction between the techniques of research which at any time are available and the prevailing assumptions about reality. Insistence on the existence of phenomena that cannot at that time be objectively observed, measured, or experimentally manipulated accomplishes little of scientific value if it does not lead to the invention of appropriate techniques of empirical research. . . .

*Development of Techniques of Research.* Of extreme importance for the origin of group dynamics, then, was the shaping of research techniques that could be extended to research on groups. This process, of course, took time. It began in the last half of the nineteenth century with the rise of experimental psychology. Over the subsequent years more and more aspects of human experience and behavior were subjected to techniques of measurement and experimentation. . . . These advances were important, of course, not only for the rise of group dynamics but for progress in all the behavioral sciences.

Within this general development we may note three methodological gains contributing specifically to the rise of group dynamics.

1. Experiments on individual behavior in groups. As noted above, research in group dynamics is deeply indebted to experimental psychology for the invention of techniques for conducting experiments on the conditions affecting human behavior. But experimental psychology did not concern itself, at first, with social variables; it was only toward the beginning of the present century that a few investigators embarked upon experimental research designed to investigate the effects of social variables upon the behavior of individuals.

2. Controlled observation of social interaction. . . . The first serious attempts to refine methods of observation, so that objective and quantitative data might be obtained, occurred around 1930 in the field of child psychology. A great amount of effort went into the construction of categories of observation that would permit an observer simply to indi-

cate the presence or absence of a particular kind of behavior or social interaction during the period of observation. Typically, reliability was heightened by restricting observation to rather overt interactions whose "meaning" could be revealed in a short span of time and whose classification required little interpretation by the observer. Methods were also developed for sampling the interactions of a large group of people over a long time so that efficient estimates of the total interaction could be made on the basis of more limited observations. By use of such procedures and by careful training of observers quantitative data of high reliability were obtained. The principal researchers responsible for these important advances were Goodenough (15), Jack (19), Olson (34), Parten (35), and Thomas (44).

3. Sociometry. . . . Of the many devices for obtaining information from group members one of the earliest and most commonly used is the sociometric test, which was invented by Moreno (30). Although based essentially on subjective reports of individuals, the sociometric test provides quantifiable data about patterns of attractions and repulsions existing in a group. The publication by Moreno (30) in 1934 of a major book based on experience with the test and the establishment in 1937 of a journal, *Sociometry*, ushered in a prodigious amount of research employing the sociometric test and numerous variations of it.

The significance of sociometry for group dynamics lay both in the provision of a useful technique for research on groups and in the attention it directed to such features of groups as social position, patterns of friendship, subgroup formation, and, more generally, informal structure.

## BEGINNINGS OF GROUP DYNAMICS

By the mid-1930s conditions were ripe within the social sciences for a rapid advance in empirical research on groups.

And, in fact, a great burst of such activity did take place in America just prior to the entry of the United States into World War II. This research, moreover, began to display quite clearly the characteristics that are now associated with work in group dynamics. Within a period of approximately five years several important research projects were undertaken, more or less independently of one another but all sharing these distinctive features. We now briefly consider four of the more influential of these.

## EXPERIMENTAL CREATION OF SOCIAL NORMS

In 1936 Sherif (42) published a book containing a systematic theoretical analysis of the concept *social norm* and an ingenious experimental investigation of the origin of social norms among groups of people. Probably the most important feature of this book was its bringing together of ideas and observations from sociology and anthropology and techniques of laboratory experimentation from experimental psychology. . . .

In formulating his research problem, Sherif drew heavily upon the findings of Gestalt psychology in the field of perception. He noted that this work had established that there need not necessarily be a fixed point-to-point correlation between the physical stimulus and the experience and behavior it arouses. The frame of reference a person brings to a situation influences in no small way how he sees that situation. Sherif proposed that psychologically a social norm functions as such a frame of reference. Thus, if two people with different norms face the same situation (for example, a Mohammedan and a Christian confront a meal of pork chops), they will see it and react to it in widely different ways. For each, however, the norm serves to give meaning and to provide a stable way of reacting to the environment.

Having thus related social norms to the psychology of perception, Sherif proceeded to ask how norms arise. It occurred to him that he might gain insight into this problem by placing people in a situation that had no clear structure and in which they would not be able to bring to bear any previously acquired frame of reference or social norm. . . .

. . . Sherif's experiment consisted of placing subjects individually in the darkened room and getting judgments of the extent of apparent motion. He found that upon repeated test the subject establishes a range within which his judgments fall and that this range is peculiar to each individual. Sherif then repeated the experiment, but this time having groups of subjects observe the light and report aloud their judgments. Now he found that the individual ranges of judgment converged to a group range that was peculiar to the group. In additional variations Sherif was able to show that (42, 104):

> When the individual, in whom a range and a norm within that range are first developed in the individual situation, is put into a group situation, together with other individuals who also come into the situation with their own ranges and norms established in their own individual sessions, the ranges and norms tend to converge.

Moreover, "when a member of a group faces the same situation subsequently *alone*, after once the range and norm of his group have been established, he perceives the situation in terms of the range and norm that he brings from the group situation" (42, 105).

Sherif's study did much to establish the feasibility of subjecting group phenomena to experimental investigation. . . . And his research helped establish among psychologists the view that certain properties of groups have reality, for, as he concluded, "the fact that the norm thus established is peculiar to the group suggests that there is a factual psychological basis in the contentions of social psychologists and sociologists who maintain that new and supra-individual qualities arise in the group situations" (**42**, 105).

## SOCIAL ANCHORAGE OF ATTITUDES

During the years 1935–39, Newcomb (**32**) was conducting an intensive investigation of the same general kind of problem that interested Sherif but with quite different methods. Newcomb selected a "natural" rather than a "laboratory" setting in which to study the operation of social norms and social influence processes, and he relied primarily upon techniques of attitude measurement, sociometry, and interviewing to obtain his data. Benninton College was the site of his study, the entire student body were his subjects, and attitudes toward political affairs provided the content of the social norms. . . .

Newcomb's study showed that the attitudes of individuals are strongly rooted in the groups to which people belong, that the influence of a group upon an individual's attitudes depends upon the nature of the relationship between the individual and the group, and that groups evaluate members, partially at least, on the basis of their conformity to group norms. Although most of these points had been made in one form or another by writers in the speculative era of social science, this study was especially significant because it provided detailed, objective, and quantitative evidence. It thereby demonstrated, as Sherif's study did in a different way, the feasibility of conducting scientific research on important features of group life.

## GROUPS IN STREET CORNER SOCIETY

The sociological and anthropological background of group dynamics is most apparent in the third important study of this era. In 1937 W. F. Whyte moved into one of the slums of Boston to begin a three and one-half year study of social clubs, political organizations, and racketeering. His method was that of "the participant observer," which had been most highly developed in anthropological research. More specifically, he drew upon the experience of Warner and Arensberg which was derived from the "Yankee City" studies. In various ways he gained admittance to the social and political life of the community and faithfully kept notes of the various happenings that he observed or heard about. In the resulting book, Whyte (**51**) reported in vivid detail on the structure, culture, and functioning of the Norton Street gang and the Italian Community Club. The importance of these social groups in the life of their members and in the political structure of the larger society was extensively documented. . . .

The major importance of this study for subsequent work in group dynamics was three-fold: (*a*) It dramatized, and described in painstaking detail, the great significance of groups in the lives of individuals and in the functioning of larger social systems. (*b*) It gave impetus to the interpretation of group properties and processes in terms of interactions among individuals. (*c*) It generated a number of hypotheses concerning the relations among such variables as initiation of interaction, leadership, status, mutual obligations, and group cohesion. These hypotheses have served to guide much of Whyte's later work on groups as well as the research of many others.

## EXPERIMENTAL MANIPULATION OF GROUP ATMOSPHERE

By far the most influential work in the emerging study of group dynamics was that of Lewin, Lippitt, and White (**23**,

**25,** Chap. 25). Conducted at the Iowa Child Welfare Research Station between 1937 and 1940, these investigations of group atmosphere and styles of leadership accomplished a creative synthesis of the various trends and developments considered above. . . .

The basic objective of this research was to study the influences upon the group as a whole and upon individual members of certain experimentally induced "group atmospheres," or "styles of leadership." Groups of ten- and eleven-year-old children were formed to meet regularly over a period of several weeks under the leadership of an adult, who induced the different group atmospheres. In creating these groups care was taken to assure their initial comparability; by utilizing the sociometric test, playground observations, and teacher interviews, the structural properties of the various groups were made as similar as possible; on the basis of school records and interviews with the children, the backgrounds and individual characteristics of the members were equated for all the groups; and the same group activities and physical setting were employed in every group.

The experimental manipulation consisted of having the adult leaders behave in a prescribed fashion in each experimental treatment, and in order to rule out the differential effects of the personalities of the leaders, each one led a group under each of the experimental conditions. Three types of leadership, or group atmosphere, were investigated: democratic, autocratic, and laissez-faire. . . . Each group, moreover, developed a characteristic level of aggressiveness, and it was demonstrated that when individual members were transferred from one group to another their aggressiveness changed to approach the new group level. An interesting insight into the dynamics of aggression was provided by the rather violent emotional "explosion" which took place when some of the groups that had reacted submissively to autocratic leadership were given a new, more permissive leader. . . .

Of major importance for subsequent research in group dynamics was the way in which Lewin formulated the essential purpose of these experiments. The problem of leadership was chosen for investigation, in part, because of its practical importance in education, social group work, administration, and political affairs. Nevertheless, in creating the different types of leadership in the laboratory the intention was not to mirror or to simulate any "pure types" that might exist in society. The purpose was rather to lay bare some of the more important ways in which leader behavior may vary and to discover how various styles of leadership influence the properties of groups and the behavior of members. As Lewin put it (**21,** 74), the purpose "was not to duplicate any given autocracy or democracy or to study an 'ideal' autocracy or democracy, but to create set-ups which would give insight into the underlying group dynamics." This statement, published in 1939, appears to be the earliest use by Lewin of the phrase group dynamics.

It is important to note rather carefully how Lewin generalized the research problem. He might have viewed this research primarily as a contribution to the technology of group management in social work or education. Or he might have placed it in the context of research on leadership. Actually, however, he stated the problem in a most abstract way as one of learning about the underlying dynamics of group life. He believed that it was possible to construct a coherent body of empirical knowledge about the nature of group life that would be meaningful when specified for any particular kind of group. Thus, he envisioned a general theory of groups that could be brought to bear on such apparently diverse matters as family life, work groups, classrooms, committees, military units, and the community. Furthermore, he saw such specific problems as leadership, status, communication, social norms, group atmosphere, and intergroup relations as part of the general problem of understanding the nature of group dynamics. . . .

upon the prevailing group atmosphere had been established. And different styles of leadership had been created experimentally and shown to produce marked consequences on the functioning of groups. After the interruption imposed by World War II, rapid advances were made in constructing a systematic, and empirically based, body of knowledge concerning the dynamics of group life.

## SUMMARY

Group dynamics is a field of inquiry dedicated to advancing knowledge about the nature of groups, the laws of their development, and their interrelations with individuals, other groups, and larger institutions. It may be identified by its reliance upon empirical research for obtaining data of theoretical significance, its emphasis in research and theory upon the dynamic aspects of group life, its broad relevance to all the social sciences, and the potential applicability of its findings to the improvement of social practice. . . .

By the end of the 1930s several trends converged with the result that a new field of group dynamics began to take shape. The practical and theoretical importance of groups was by then documented empirically. The feasibility of conducting objective and quantitative research on the dynamics of group life was no longer debatable. And the reality of groups had been removed from the realm of mysticism and placed squarely within the domain of empirical social science. Group norms could be objectively measured, even created experimentally in the laboratory, and some of the processes by which they influence the behavior and attitudes of individuals had been determined. The dependence of certain emotional states of individuals

## REFERENCES

1. Allport, F. H. *Social psychology.* Boston: Houghton Mifflin, 1924.

2. Allport, G. W. The historical background of modern social psychology. In G. Lindzey (Ed.), *Handbook of social psychology.* Cambridge, Mass.: Addison-Wesley, 1954. Pp. 3–56.

3. Bach, G. R. *Intensive group psychotherapy.* New York: Ronald Press, 1954.

4. Bales, R. F. *Interaction process analysis.* Cambridge, Mass.: Addison-Wesley, 1950.

5. Barnard, C. I. *The functions of the executive.* Cambridge, Mass.: Harvard Univ. Press, 1938.

6. Bavelas, A. Morale and training of leaders. In G. Watson (Ed.), *Civilian morale.* Boston: Houghton Mifflin, 1942.

7. Bion, W. R. Experiences in groups. I–VI. *Human Relations,* 1948–1950, **1,** 314–320, 487–496; **2,** 13–22, 295–303; **3,** 3–14, 395–402.

8. Bogardus, E. S. Measuring social distance. *Journal of Applied Sociology,* 1925, 9, 299–308.

9. Busch, H. M. *Leadership in group work.* New York: Association Press, 1934.

10. Chapple, E. D. Measuring human relations: An introduction to the study of interaction of individuals. *Genetic Psychology Monographs,* 1940, **22,** 3–147.

11. Coyle G. L. *Social process in organized groups.* New York: Rinehart, 1930.

12. Dashiell, J. F. Experimental studies of the influence of social situations on the behavior of individual human adults. In C. C. Murchison (Ed.), *Handbook of social psychology,*

Worcester, Mass.: Clark Univ. Press, 1935. Pp. 1097–1158.

13. Follett, M. P. *The new state, group organization, the solution of popular government.* New York: Longmans, Green, 1918.

14. Follett, M. P. *Creative experience.* New York: Longmans, Green, 1924.

15. Goodenough, F. L. Measuring behavior traits by means of repeated short samples. *Journal of Juvenile Research,* 1928, **12,** 230–235.

16. Gordon, K. Group judgments in the field of lifted weights. *Journal of Experimental Psychology,* 1924, **7,** 398–400.

17. Haire, M. Group dynamics in the industrial situation. In A. Kornhauser, R. Dubin, & A. M. Ross (Eds.), *Industrial conflict.* New York: McGraw-Hill, 1954. Pp. 373–385.

18. Homans, G. C. *The human group.* New York: McGraw-Hill, 1954. Pp. 373–385.

19. Jack, L. M. An experimental study of ascendent behavior in preschool children. *Univ. of Iowa Studies in Child Welfare,* 1934, **9,** (3).

20. Lewin, K. Forces behind food habits and methods of change. *Bulletin of the National Research Council,* 1943, **108,** 35–65.

21. Lewin, K. *Resolving social conflicts.* New York: Harper, 1948.

22. Lewin, K. *Field theory in social science.* New York: Harper, 1951.

23. Lewin, K., Lippitt, R., & White, R. Patterns of aggressive behavior in experimentally created "social climates." *Journal of Social Psychology,* 1939, **10,** 271–299.

24. Likert, R. A technique for the measurement of attitudes. *Archives of Psychology,* 1932, No. 140.

25. Lippitt, R. An experimental study of authoritarian and democratic group atmospheres. *Univ. of Iowa Studies in Child Welfare,* 1940, **16** (3), 43–195.

26. Marrow, A. J. *Making management human.* New York: McGraw-Hill, 1957.

27. Mayo, E. *The human problems of an industrial civilization.* New York: Macmillan, 1933.

28. Moede, W. *Experimentelle massenpsychologie.* Leipzig: S. Hirzel, 1920.

29. Moore, H. T. The comparative influence of majority and expert opinion. *American Journal of Psychology,* 1921, **32,** 16–20.

30. Moreno, J. L. *Who shall survive?* Washington, D. C.: Nervous and Mental Diseases Publishing Co., 1934.

31. Myrdal, G. *An American dilemma.* New York: Harper, 1944.

32. Newcomb, T. M. *Personality and social change.* New York: Dryden, 1943.

33. Newstetter, W., Feldstein, M., & Newcomb, T. M. *Group adjustment, a study in experimental sociology.* Cleveland: Western Reserve Univ., School of Applied Social Sciences, 1938.

34. Olson, W. C., & Cunningham, E. M. Time-sampling techniques. *Child Development,* 1934, **5,** 41–58.

35. Parten, M. B. Social participation among preschool children. *Journal of Abnormal and Social Psychology,* 1932, **27,** 243–269.

36. Radke, M., & Klisurich, D. Experiments in changing food habits. *Journal of American Dietetics Association,* 1947, **23,** 403–409.

37. Redl, F., & Wineman, D. *Children who hate.* Glencoe, Ill.: Free Press, 1951.

38. Roethlisberger, F. J., & Dickson, W. J. *Management and the worker.* Cambridge, Mass.: Harvard Univ. Press, 1939.

39. Scheidlinger, S. *Psychoanalysis and group behavior.* New York: Norton, 1952.

40. Shaw, C. R. *The jack roller.* Chicago: Univ. of Chicago Press, 1939.

41. Shaw, M. E. A comparison of individuals and small groups in the rational solution of complex problems. *American Journal of Psychology.* 1932, **44,** 491–504.

42. Sherif, M. *The psychology of social norms.* New York: Harper, 1936.

43. Slavson, S. R. *Analytic group psychotherapy.* New York: Columbia Univ. Press. 1950.

44. Thomas, D. S. An attempt to develop precise measurement in the social behavior field. *Sociologus,* 1933, **9,** 1–21.

45. Thomas, W. I., & Znaniecki, F. *The Polish peasant in Europe and America.* Boston: Badger, 1918.

46. Thrasher, F. *The gang.* Chicago: Univ. of Chicago Press, 1927.

47. Thurstone, L. L. Attitudes can be measured. *American Journal of Sociology,* 1928, **33,** 529–554.

48. Thurstone, L. L., & Chave, E. J. *The measurement of attitude.* Chicago: Univ. of Chicago Press, 1929.

49. Triplett, N. The dynamogenic factors in pacemaking and competition. *American Journal of Psychology*, 1897, **9**, 507–533.

50. Watson, G. B. Do groups think more effectively than individuals? *Journal of Abnormal and Social Psychology*, 1928, **23**, 328–336.

51. Whyte, W. F., Jr. *Street corner society*. Chicago: Univ. of Chicago Press, 1943.

52. Whyte, W. H., Jr. *The organization man*. New York: Simon and Schuster, 1956.

53. Wilson, A. T. M. Some aspects of social process. *Journal of Social Issues*, 1951 (Suppl. Series 5).

54. Wilson, G., & Ryland, G. *Social group work practice*. Boston: Houghton Mifflin, 1949.

# 12
# An Intergroup Perspective on Group Dynamics
*Clayton P. Alderfer*

## INTRODUCTION

The study of intergroup relations brings to bear a variety of methods and theories from social science on a diverse set of difficult social problems (Allport 1954; Merton 1960; Sherif and Sherif 1969; Van Den Berge 1972; Pettigrew 1981). Taken literally, intergroup relations refer to activities *between* and *among* groups. Note that the choice of preposition is significant. Whether people observe groups only two at a time or in more complex constellations has important implications for action and for understanding. Intergroup concepts can explain a broader range of phenomena than just what go on at the intersection of two or more groups. The range of concern is from how individuals think as revealed in studies of prejudice and stereotyping to how nation states deal with each other in the realm of international conflict. A central feature of virtually all intergroup analysis is the persistently problematic relationship between individual people and collective social processes. . . .

## A THEORY OF INTERGROUP RELATIONS AND ORGANIZATIONS

In the two preceding sections I sought to establish two metatheoretical points. The first was to establish intergroup theory in general as a way of thinking about

problems of human behavior; the aim was to distinguish intergroup theory from nonintergroup theory. The second was to determine dimensions on which particular versions of intergroup theory varied from one another; the objective was to differentiate among versions of intergroup theories. This section now presents a particular version of intergroup theory.

According to the dimensions of difference among intergroup theories, it has the following properties:

1. The group is the primary level of analysis.
2. Groups appear embedded in social systems.
3. The orientation toward research is clinical.
4. Concepts from the theory apply to researchers as well as to respondents. . . .

## Definition of Groups in Organizations

Within the social psychology literature there is no shortage of definitions of groups, but there is also no clear consensus among those who propose definitions (Cartwright and Zander, 1968). Because much of the work leading to these definitions has been done by social psychologists studying internal properties of groups in laboratories, the resulting concepts have been comparatively limited in recognizing the external properties of groups. Looking at groups in organiza-

*Source:* From *Handbook of Organizational Behavior*, Jay W. Lorsch, ed., Prentice-Hall, Inc., 1987. Reprinted by permission of the author. This research was sponsored by the Organizational Effectiveness Research Programs, Office of Naval Research (Code 442OE, Contract No. N00014-82-K-0715).

tions, however, produce a definition that gives more balanced attention to both functional and external properties.

A human group is a collection of individuals (1) who have significantly interdependent relations with each other, (2) who perceive themselves as a group, reliably distinguishing members from nonmembers, (3) whose group identity is recognized by nonmembers, (4) who, as group members acting alone or in concert, have significantly interdependent relations with other groups, and (5) whose roles in the group are therefore a function of expectations from themselves, from other group members, and from non-group members (Alderfer 1977a).

This idea of a group begins with individuals who are interdependent, moves to the sense of the group as a significant social object whose boundaries are confirmed from inside and outside, recognizes that the group as a whole is an interacting unit through representatives or by collective action, and returns to the individual members whose thoughts, feelings, and actions are determined by forces within the individual and from both group members and nongroup members. This conceptualization of a group makes every individual member into a group representative wherever he or she deals with members of other groups and treats transactions among individuals as at least, in part, intergroup events (Rice 1969; Smith 1977).

Figure 1 shows an "intergroup transaction between individuals." This is another way of reconceptualizing what may usually be thought of as an interpersonal transaction. In the diagram, there are three classes of forces corresponding to intrapersonal, intragroup, and intergroup dynamics. The general point is that any exchange between people is subject to all three kinds of forces; most people (including behavioral scientists) tend to understand things mainly in intrapersonal or interpersonal terms.

Which class of forces becomes most dominant at any time depends on how the specific dimensions at each level of analysis differentiate the individuals. Suppose $I_1$ is a male engineering supervisor and $I_2$ is a female union steward. Intrapersonally $I_1$ prefers abstract thinking and demonstrates persistent difficulty in expressing feelings; $I_2$ prefers concrete thinking and shows ease in expressing feelings. $G_1$ is a predominantly male professional group that communicates to $I_1$ that he at all times should stay in control and be rational. $G_2$ is a predominantly female clerical group that communicates to $I_2$ that she should be more assertive about the needs of the $G_2$s. The $I$-$G_{1-2}$ relationship includes ten years of labor-management cooperation punctuated by a series of recent strike (from the labor side) and termination (from the management side) threats. The tradition in much of behavioral-science intervention is to focus on the $I$ dynamics and to give little or no attention to $G$ or $I$-$G$ forces (Argyris 1962; Walton 1969).

By viewing transactions between individuals from an intergroup perspective, an observer learns to examine the condition of each participant's group, the relationship of participants to their groups, and the relationship between groups represented by participants as well as their personalities in each "interpersonal" relationship. . . .

## Properties of Intergroup Relations

Research on intergroup relations has identified a number of properties characteristic of intergroup relations, regardless of the particular groups or the specific setting where the relationship occurs (Sumner 1906; Coser 1956; Van Den Berge 1972; Levine and Campbell 1972; Billig 1976; Alderfer 1977). These phenomena include

1. Group boundaries. Group boundaries, both physical and psychological, de-

FIGURE 1 • INTERGROUP TRANSACTION BETWEEN INDIVIDUALS

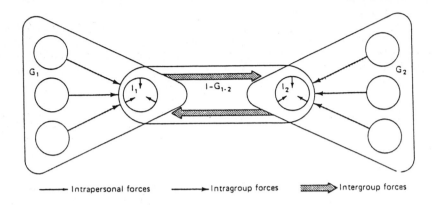

————► Intrapersonal forces        ————►Intragroup forces        ▨▨▨▨▨►Intergroup forces

termine who is a group member and regulate transactions among groups by variations in their permeability (Alderfer 1977b). Boundary permeability refers to the ease with which boundaries can be crossed.

2. Power differences. Groups differ in the types of resources they can obtain and use (Lasswell and Kaplan 1950). The variety of dimensions on which there are power differences and the degree of discrepancy among groups on these dimensions influence the degree of boundary permeability among groups.

3. Affective patterns. The permeability of group boundaries varies with the polarization of feeling among the groups; that is, to the degree that group members split their feelings so that mainly positive feelings are associated with their own group and mainly negative feelings are projected onto other groups (Sumner 1906; Coser 1956; Levine and Campbell 1972).

4. Cognitive formations, including "distortions." As a function of power differences and affective patterns, groups tend to develop their own language (or elements of language, including social categories), condition their members' perceptions of objective and subjective phenomena, and transmit sets of propositions—including theories and ideologies—to explain the nature of experiences encountered by members and to influence rela-

tions with other groups (Sherif and Sherif 1969; Blake, Shepard, and Mouton 1964; Tajfel 1970; Billig 1976).

5. Leadership behavior. The behavior of group leaders and of members representing a group reflects the boundary permeability, power differences, affective patterns, and cognitive formations of their group in relation to other groups. The behavior of group representatives, including formally designated leaders, is both cause and effect of the total pattern of intergroup behavior in a particular situation.

## Group Relations in Organizations

Every organization consists of a large number of groups, and every organization member represents a number of these groups in dealing with other people in the organization. The full set of groups in an organization can be divided into two broad classes: identify groups and organizational groups. An identity group may be thought of as a group whose members share some common biological characteristic (such as gender), have participated in equivalent historical experiences (such as migration), currently are subjected to similar social forces (such as unemployment), and as a result have consonant world views. The coming together of world views by people who are in the same group occurs because of their having like experiences *and* developing shared meanings of these experiences through exchanges with other group members. As people enter organizations they carry with them their ongoing membership in identity groups based on variables such as their ethnicity, gender, age, and family. An organizational group may be conceived of as one whose members share (approximately) common organizational positions, participate in equivalent work experiences, and, as a consequence, have consonant organizational views. Organizations assign their members to organizational groups based on division of labor and hierarchy of authority. One critical factor in understanding intergroups in organizations is that identity-group membership and organizational-group membership are frequently highly related. Depending on the nature of the organization and the culture in which it is embedded, certain organizational groups tend to be populated by members of particular identity groups. In the United States, for example, upper-management positions tend to be held by older white males, and certain departments and ranks tend to be more accepting of females and minorities than others (Loring and Wells 1972; Purcell and Cavanagh 1972).

Considering the definition of a human group given above, we can observe how both identity groups and organizational groups fit the five major criteria. First, identity-group members have significant interdependencies because of their common historical experiences, and organizational groups, because of their equivalent work or organizational experiences, which result in their sharing similar fates even though members may be unaware of their relatedness or even actively deny it. Second, organization-group and identity-group members can reliably distinguish themselves as members from nonmembers on the basis of either identity factors (ethnicity, gender, etc.) or of location in the organization. However, the precision of this identification process can vary, depending on both the permeability of group boundaries and the fact that many groups overlap significantly, with individuals having multiple group memberships. A similar point applies to the third definitional characteristic, the ability of nonmembers to recognize members; this again will vary, depending on the permeability of the group's boundaries. The less permeable the boundaries, the more easily recognizable are members. The fourth and fifth aspects of the definition are highly linked when applied to identity and organizational groups. For example, members may be more or less aware of the extent to which they are acting, or being seen, as group representatives when relating to individuals from other groups. Every person has a number of identity- and organizational-group memberships. At any given moment an individual may be simultaneously a member of a large number, if not all, of these groups. However, which group will be focal at the moment will depend on who else representing which other groups is present and what identity-group and organizational-group issues are critical in the current intergroup exchanges. A white person in a predominantly black organization, for example, can rarely escape representing "white people" at some level, regardless of performance. But the same white person placed in a predominantly white organization will not be seen as representing "white people," but rather some other group, such as a particular hierarchical level. Rarely are individuals "just people" when they act in organizations. When there are no other group representatives present, individuals may experience themselves as "just people" in the context of their own group membership, but this subjective experience will quickly disappear when the individual is placed in a multiple-group setting. How group members relate to each other within their group, and to the expectations placed upon them by others, is highly dependent on the nature of both the intragroup and intergroup forces active at that time. . . .

*Organizational Groups*. The essential characteristic of organizational groups is that individuals belong to them as a function of negotiated exchange between the person and the organization. Often the exchange is voluntary, as when a person decides to work to earn a living or volunteers to work for a community agency. But the exchange may also be involuntary, as when children must attend school, draftees must join the military, and convicted criminals must enter a prison. Regardless of whether the exchange about entry is mainly voluntary or involuntary, becoming an organizational member assigns a person to membership in both a task group and a hierarchical group. A person who stops being an organization member, for whatever reason, also gives up membership in the task and hierarchical groups. In this way task-group and hierarchical-group memberships differ from identity-group affiliations.

*Task*-group membership arises because of the activities (or, in some unusual cases, such as prisons or hospitals, the inactivities) members are assigned to perform. The activities typically have a set of objectives, role relationships, and other features that shape the task-group members' experiences. As a result, people develop a perspective on their own group, other groups, and the organization as a whole, which in turn shapes their behavior and attitudes.

Membership in task groups also tends to be transferable from one organization to another because people can carry the knowledge and skills necessary to perform particular tasks with them if they leave one system and attempt to join another. As a function of developing and maintaining certain knowledge and skills, people may belong to known professional or semiprofessional organizations outside their employing (or confining) organizations. Support from these "outside interest groups" may help people achieve more power within the system where they are working, and it may make it more possible for them to leave one system and join another.

*Hierarchical*-group membership is assigned by those in the system with the authority to determine rank in the system. The determination of a member's hierarchical position in an organization is typically a carefully controlled, and often highly secret, process. One's place in the hierarchy determines one's legitimate authority, decision-making autonomy, scope of responsibility, and, frequently, access to benefits of membership. Group effects of the hierarchy arise from the nature of the work required of people who occupy the different levels, from the various personal attributes that the work calls for from incumbents, and from the relations that develop between people who occupy different positions in the hierarchy (Smith 1982; Oshry 1977). . . .

No one who belongs to an organization escapes the effects of hierarchy. Finer differentiations than the three offered here (e.g., upper upper, lower middle, etc.) can be made, but the same basic structure will be repeated within the microcosm of finer distinctions. The effects of hierarchy are "system" characteristics; anyone occupying a particular position in the hierarchy will tend to show the traits associated with that level.

Figure 2 provides a schematic to show the intersection of identity and organization groups. There is an inevitable tension between the two classes of groups as long as there are systematic processes that allocate people to organization groups as a function of their identity groups. Sometimes these processes are called "institutional discrimination." (Thought question: how many 30-year-old [age group too young] Greek [ethnic group nondominant] women do you know of who are presidents of major corporations?) There is usually enough tension among organization groups to occupy the emotional energies of the top group, who have the task of managing group boundaries and transactions. Thus, unless there are special forces to strengthen the boundaries of identity groups within organizations (i.e., give

them more authority), the inclination of those in senior positions will be to manage only in terms of organization groups. The manner in which an organization is embedded in its environment and the relations among identity groups in that environment will affect the degree to which management processes respond to identity *and* organization groups or just to organization groups. . . .

## Embedded-Intergroup Relations

Any intergroup relationship occurs within an environment shaped by the suprasystem in which it is embedded. In observing an intergroup relationship one has several perspectives.

1. The effects on individuals who represent the groups in relation to one another
2. The consequences for subgroups within groups as the groups deal with one another

## FIGURE 2 • IDENTITY AND ORGANIZATION GROUPS

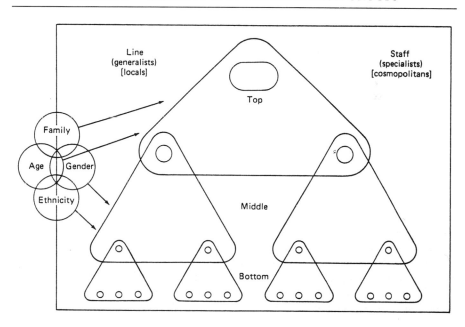

3. The outcomes for groups as a whole when they relate to significant other groups
4. The impact of suprasystem forces on the intergroup relationship in question

Regardless of which level one observes, the phenomenon of "interpenetration" among levels will be operating. Individuals carry images of their own and other groups as they serve in representational roles (Berg 1978; Wells 1980). Subgroup splits within face-to-face groups reflect differing degrees of identification and involvement with the group itself, which are in turn shaped by the relationship of the group as a whole to other groups. Then the groups as a whole develops a sense—which may be more or less unconscious—of how its interests are cared for or abused by the suprasystem. The concept of embedded-intergroup relations applies to both identity and task groups (Alderfer and Smith 1982). . . .

Figure 3 shows how intergroup dynamics might be exhibited in the dynamics within a ten-person work group. The work group has four subgroups identified by dashed lines. Viewed exclusively from the perspective of intragroup dynamics, the work group is affected only by the individual and subgroup processes inside the group. An intergroup perspective, however, suggests that the subgroups inside the work group represent memberships in groups that exist beyond the boundaries of the work unit as indicated by the dotted lines. Suppose $I_3$ is a new female group leader, having recently joined the group from outside; $I_1$ and $I_2$ are men closely associated with the former male group leader; $I_4$, $I_5$, and $I_6$ are junior male members of the work team; and $I_7$, $I_8$, $I_9$, and $I_{10}$ are junior female members of the work team. During the period of transition, and probably subsequent to it as well, embedded-intergroup theory would predict that the

relationship between the new female leader and the senior men would be affected by the authority of women in the total system, and that the relationship between the junior men and junior women in the work group would be changed by the group as a whole gaining a female leader. . . .

## APPLICATION OF THE INTERGROUP THEORY TO SELECTED PROBLEMS

As a general perspective on group behavior in organizations, the intergroup theory may be used to address a variety of human problems. In this concluding section. . . . I selected each of the problems because it has been a subject of my attention during the last several years. The problems are,

understanding organizational culture; responding to minorities and white women in predominantly white male organizations.

### Understanding Organizational Culture

As investigators and consultants have shifted their concerns from small groups to the organization as a whole, there has been a corresponding search for concepts that offer the possibility of giving a holistic formulation to the total system. The notion of an organizational culture has, in part, emerged from this quest.[1] From the standpoint of this paper, the key question is What sort of intellectual conversation might occur between the theorist of organizational culture and the intergroup theorist? . . .

Martin and Siehl (1982) . . . use the concept of subculture. In their case, they

---

[1] The concept of organizational culture serves other functions as well, and not all organizational culture researchers are concerned with viewing organizations holistically.

## FIGURE 3 • INTERGROUP DYNAMICS EMBEDDED IN A SMALL GROUP

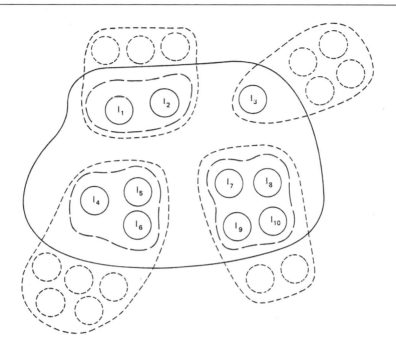

propose the notion of a "counterculture" formed around a charismatic figure who provides a sensitivity balanced set of assumptions and behaviors that offer an alternative to the dominant culture. Their empirical material is drawn from the activities of John DeLorean when he was a senior executive with General Motors.

The notion of subcultures, of course, suggests an intergroup perspective, but it does not explicitly propose that view. Rather the term *sub*culture implies that the diversity of cultures is really *subordinate* to the main culture, or perhaps, that subculture is the theorist's way of accommodating to data that are obviously present but do not quite fit a "one-group" view of cultural dynamics. What if the idea of organizational culture were viewed as a multiple-group phenomenon?

A study by McCollom (1983) provides data that were gathered and analyzed from a multiple-group perspective. Her work is especially interesting because she initially expected to find a single culture but emerged from her research to write about the cultures of the BCD School. Her own words state,

> I began this study expecting to be able to identify a culture which typified BCD. Instead, I found a number of distinct subcultures residing in the major groups in the School (students, faculty, and staff). The interaction of these cultures seemed to produce an organizational culture that was far from homogeneous. In fact, conflict between the groups seemed to become part of the culture of the whole system (e.g., the generally held expectation that staff and faculty would disagree). My hypothesis is that the relative power of each of the groups over time in the organization is a major factor in determining the culture.

This statement exemplifies an intergroup view of organizational culture. It makes the culture of the whole system a product of the cultures of key groups in the system *in interaction with one another*. In McCollom's study the predominant pattern of interaction between at least two of these groups was conflictual. Conflict, however, need not be the major style of intergroup transaction for the organization culture to be usefully conceptualized as dynamic intergroup pattern.

An important difference between the work of McCollom and that of . . . Martin and Siehl (1982) may be their own roles and group memberships in relation to the cultures they described. . . . Martin and Siehl were outsiders who read published materials about GM and DeLorean and who interviewed people who had been close to the scene. McCollom was a member of the organizations she studied and was committed to examining the perspectives her group memberships gave her on the system she studied. It is likely that . . . Martin and Siehl were prevented from fully seeing the multiple-group qualities of the organizations they studied, because they permitted themselves to become mainly associated with just one group. I suggest again that the intergroup relationships of investigators and how those relationships are managed are likely to shape the data they obtain and the concepts derived from those findings. . . .

## Responding to White Women and Minorities in Predominantly White Male Organizations

An intergroup perspective on affirmative action notably heightens the complexity of thinking and of action. Perhaps the beginning is to recognize and to accept that a white male is not only an individual but also a group condition (see Figure 1). The term *affirmative action* interpreted progressively means recognizing and changing the exclusively white-male domination of a large proportion of U.S. institutions. Acknowledging only the individual differences among white men (or any other group) and denying the group effects seriously limits what can be understood and what can be done. These limits often serve the material interests of certain groups and individuals—perhaps especially white men but also individual white women and individual members of minority groups who unconsciously or consciously have decided to cope with their group's position by using white men as models (see Davis and Watson 1982; Davis 1983; Joseph and Lewis 1981).

However, once one begins to take a multiple group perspective, the answers do not come easily nor do the actions become obvious. In fact, there is probably an increase in group-level psychic pain associated with an increase in consciousness about both the historical and contemporary relations of one's own group to other groups. For some, there may be a wish that all oppressed groups can unit in challenging the oppressor group of white males. But then new awareness develops. An historical examination of the relation between white woman and blacks reveals some periods of serious cooperation *and also* many evidences of deep-seated racism in the (white) women's movement (Joseph and Lewis 1981; Davis 1983). History also includes episodes when black men spoke against immediately developing voting rights for women (Davis 1983). Contemporary research shows evidence of black women ready to capitalize on the difficulties of black men in order to advance in predominantly white male corporate cultures (Davis and Watson 1982) and of white women in totally female interracial organizations apparently oblivious to racial dynamics unless directly confronted with the issues (Van Steenberg 1983). . . .

## CONCLUSION

Intergroup perspectives began to shape the understanding of human behavior from the beginning of the twentieth century. Scholars reflecting upon such diverse events as political revolution, tribal warfare, labor-management relations, and mental illness showed an awareness of group-to-group relations in their thinking and action. In the last thirty years, numerous intergroup theories have evolved and shaped methodological traditions. Currently, these theory-method combinations can be distinguished by their relative focus on group-level concepts, attention to groups in context or in isolation, acceptance of interventionist behavior by researchers, and tendency toward examining the individual and group behavior of investigators.

Intergroup theory provides interpretations for individual, interpersonal, group, intergroup, and organizational relations. The version of intergroup theory given here uses a definition of group that is concerned with both internal and external properties. It explains intergroup dynamics in terms of group boundaries, power, affect, cognition, and leadership behavior. It examines the nature of identity and organization groups. It relates the state of intergroup relations to the suprasystem in which they are embedded. It presents an understanding of the changing relations among interdependent groups and their representatives through the operation of parallel and unconscious processes.

The theory relates to a wide array of social and organizational problems, including the development of effective work teams, the definition and management of organizational culture, the analysis and implementation of affirmative action, and the teaching of organizational behavior in management schools.

The most important implication of intergroup theory may be the reorientation it offers to those who study and teach about human behavior in groups and organizations. Mannheim was among the most prominent of twentieth-century scholars who connected the sociology of knowledge with the group memberships of writers.

> Accordingly, the products of the cognitive process are already . . . differentiated because not every possible aspect of the world comes within the purview of the members of a group, but only those out of which difficulties and problems for the group arise. And even this common world (not shared by any outside groups in the same way) appears differently to subordinate groups within the larger group. It appears differently because the subordinate groups and strata in a functionally differentiated society have a different experiential approach . . . (Mannheim 1936, 29).

Intergroup theory proposes that both organization groups (e.g., being a researcher versus being a respondent) and identity groups (e.g., being a person of particular gender, age, ethnicity and family) affect one's intergroup relations and thereby shape one's cognitive formations. The body of data supporting this general proposition grows as changes in society broaden the range of identity groups who access to research roles (see Balmary 1981; Eagly and Carli 1981; Herman 1981), and consequently the content of "well-established" empirical generalizations and conceptual frameworks are called into question. These new developments affect research and development as well as clinical methods. None of the accepted methods in their implementation escapes potential intergroup effects between researchers and respondents. Investigators who accept this idea cannot avoid questioning the part they and their groups play in the knowledge-making process. Understanding one's intergroup relationships may become a key ingredient for all who wish to study people effectively.

# REFERENCES

Alderfer, C. P. 1977a. "Group and Intergroup Relations." In *Improving Life at Work*, ed. J. R. Hackman and J. L. Suttle, pp. 227–96. Santa Monica: Goodyear.

———. 1977b. "Improving Organizational Communication through Long-Term, Intergroup Intervention." *Journal of Applied Behavioral Science* 13:193–210.

Alderfer, C. P., and K. K. Smith. 1982. "Studying Intergroup Relations Embedded in Organizations." *Administrative Science Quarterly* 27:35–65.

Allport, G. W. 1954. *The Nature of Prejudice*, New York: Doubleday.

Argyris, C. 1962. *Interpersonal Competence and Organizational Effectiveness.* Homewood, Ill.: Richard D. Irwin.

Balmary, M. 1981. *Psychoanalyzing Psychoanalysis.* Baltimore: Johns Hopkins University Press.

Berg, D. N. 1978. "Intergroup Relations in Out Patient Psychiatric Facility." Ann Arbor, Mich.: University of Michigan.

Billig, M. 1976. *Social Psychology and Intergroup Relations.* London: Academic Press.

Blake, R. R., H. A. Shepard, and J. Mouton. 1964. *Managing Intergroup Conflict in Industry.* Houston: Gulf.

Cartwright, D., and A. Zander. 1968. *Group Dynamics.* 3d ed. Evanston, Ill.: Row-Peterson.

Coser, L. A. 1956. *The Functions of Social Conflict.* Glencoe, Ill.: Free Press.

Davis, A. Y. 1983. *Women, Race, and Class.* New York: Vintage Books.

Davis, G., and G. Watson. 1982. *Black Life in Corporate America.* Garden City, N.Y.: Anchor Press/Doubleday.

Eagly, A. H., and L. L. Carli. 1981. "Sex of Researchers and Sex-Typed Communications as Determinants of Sex Differences in Influenceability: A Meta-Analysis of Social Influence Studies." *Psychological Bulletin* 90:1–20.

Herman, J. L. 1981. *Father-Daughter Incest.* Cambridge, Mass.: Harvard University Press.

Joseph, G. I., and J. Lewis. 1981. *Common Differences: Conflicts in Black and White Feminist Perspectives.* Garden City, N.Y.: Anchor Press/Doubleday.

Lasswell, H. D., and A. Kaplan. 1950. *Power and Society.* New Haven: Yale.

Levine, R. A., and D. T. Campbell. 1972. *Ethnocentrism.* New York: Wiley.

Loring, R., and T. Wells. 1972. *Breakthrough: Women into Management.* New York: Van Nostrand Reinhold.

Mannheim, Karl. 1936. *Ideology and Utopia.* New York: Harcourt Brace Jovanovich.

Martin, J., and C. Siehl. 1982. "Organizational Culture and Counterculture: An Uneasy Symbiosis." Working paper, Stanford University.

McCollom, M. 1983. "Organizational Culture: A Cast Study of the BCD School." Yale School of Organization and Management Working Paper.

Merton, R. K. 1960. "The Ambivalences of Le Bon's *The Crowd.*" In *The Crowd*, ed. G. Le Bon, pp. v–xxxix. New York: Viking.

Oshry, B. 1977. *Power and Position.* Boston: Power and Systems Training.

Pettigrew, T. P. 1981. "Extending the Stereotype Concept." In *Cognitive Processes in Stereotyping and Intergroup Behavior*, ed. D. Hamilton, pp. 303–32. Hillsdale, N.J.: Lawrence Erlbaum Associates.

Purcell, T. V., and G. F. Cavanagh. 1972. *Blacks in the Industrial World.* New York: Free Press.

Rice, A. K. 1969. "Individual, Group, and Intergroup Processes." *Human Relations* 22:565–84.

Sherif, M., and C. Sherif. 1969. *Social Psychology.* New York: Harper and Row.

Singer, E. 1965. *Key Concepts in Psychotherapy.* New York: Random House.

Smith, K. K. 1977. "An Intergroup Perspective on Individual Behavior." In *Perspectives on Behavior in Organizations.* 2d ed., ed. J. R. Hackman, E. E. Lawler, and L. W. Porter, pp. 397–407. New York: McGraw-Hill.

———. 1982. *Groups in Conflict: Prisons in Disguise.* Dubuque, Iowa: Kendall-Hunt.

Sumner, W. J. 1906. *Folkways*. New York: Ginn.

Tajfel, H. 1970. "Experiments in Intergroup Discrimination." *Scientific American* 223:96–102.

Van Den Berge, P., ed. 1972. *Intergroup Relations*. New York: Basic Books.

Van Steenberg, V. 1983. "Within White Group Differences on Race Relations at CTCGS."

Yale School of Organization and Management Working Paper.

Walton, R. E. 1969. *Interpersonal Peacemaking*. Reading, Mass.: Addison-Wesley.

Wells, L. J. 1980. "The Group-as-a-Whole." In *Advances in Experiential Social Processes*, vol. 2, ed. C. P. Alderfer and C. L. Cooper, pp. 165–200. London: Wiley.

## 13
# Cultural Diversity in Organizations: Intergroup Conflict
*Taylor Cox, Jr.*

## INTERGROUP CONFLICT DEFINED

Although writers have offered numerous different definitions of conflict, they seem to agree that conflict is an overt expression of tensions between the goals or concerns of one party and those of another. Thus the core of conflict is opposing interests of the involved parties (Rummell, 1976). In this chapter we are concerned with conflict between groups. Since all groups are composed of individuals and conflict behavior is frequently enacted by individuals, intergroup conflict may be conceived as a special case of interpersonal conflict. Intergroup conflict in the context of cultural diversity has two distinguishing features: (1) group boundaries and group differences are involved, and (2) the conflict is directly or indirectly related to culture group identities.

Concerning the second point, there are at least two reasons why a great deal of observed interpersonal conflict may be analyzed from an intergroup perspective. First, as group identities are an integral part of the individual personality. Therefore, much of what is commonly referred to as "personality clash" may actually be a manifestation of group identity-related conflict. Second, there are clear cases in which the basis of conflict is endemic to the groups as well as,

or instead of, the individuals involved. For example, considerable conflict has arisen in parts of Florida and California over the extent to which education will be conducted exclusively in English. The main parties to the conflict are Hispanic Americans (the majority of whom are bilingual but have Spanish as their first language) and non-Hispanic Americans, who by and large are monolingual English speakers. In this instance, the source of the conflict itself has roots in the different culture identities of the parties.

Also in the context of cultural diversity in organizations, it may be useful to note that intergroup conflict occurs between the majority group and the various minority groups represented as well as among the minority groups themselves. In the following section, sources of intergroup conflict in the context of cultural diversity in organizations will be addressed.

## SOURCES OF INTERGROUP CONFLICT

As indicated in the definition above, the core element of conflict is opposing interests. A study of literature on intergroup dynamics in organizations reveals myriad issues, attitudes, and behaviors around which opposing interest may de-

*Source:* Reprinted with permission of the publisher. *Cultural Diversity in Organizations: Theory, Research & Practice,* Copyright © 1993 by Taylor H. Cox, Jr., Berret-Koehler Publishers, Inc., San Francisco, CA 94104.

velop (Alderfer, Alderfer, Tucker, & Tucker, 1980; Landis & Boucher, 1987; Arnold & Feldman, 1986; Daft & Steers, 1986). In the context of cultural diversity in organizations, however, five stand out to me as particularly important. They are:

1. Competing goals
2. Competition for resources
3. Cultural differences
4. Power discrepancies
5. Assimilation versus preservation of microcultural identity . . .

## Competing Goals

As previously indicated, common goals is one of the defining characteristics of culture groups. Indeed, this characteristic applies to groups of any kind. In multicultural social systems, the various groups represented may develop competing goals which then become the basis of intergroup conflict. This insight into intergroup conflict has been addressed extensively by Campbell (1965) and by Sherif (1966) in their discussions of "realistic group conflict theory. . . ."

. . . The point to be made here is that organizational functions are often characterized by very different systems of norms, goal priorities, work styles, and so on. In other words, they may be viewed as having different occupational cultures. The difference in cultures between them, partly manifested in different goals, sets the stage for intergroup conflict.

## Competition for Resources

A second source of intergroup conflict is disagreement about the allocation of resources. In some cases, such as conflict between American Indians and white Americans, the bases of these conflicts are embedded in the history of intergroup relations. In other cases, such as tensions between men and women over

access to executive jobs, the conflict is more directly embedded in organizational issues. Several examples will be offered.

Intergroup conflict over resources is illustrated by a recent consulting project I was involved in at a plant site of a large international telecommunications company. Several years ago, the plant hired a significant number of Laotian immigrants. Subsequently there was a major downsizing in which several hundred employees were relocated or lost their jobs. Many of the local Laotian workers survived these cuts. In interviews with African American, Hispanic Americans, and white American workers at the plant, all of whom are native-born, a great deal of resentment was expressed toward the plant's management and toward the Laotians themselves over the loss of jobs to "outsiders." The Laotians that I talked to were also aware of this resentment and held a certain amount of hostility of their own toward what they regarded as unfair treatment by the native-born Americans. The conflict had persisted over a period of several years and was a hindrance to the effective functioning of self-managed work-teams that the plant was trying to implement.

The resource in contention in the above example (jobs) is frequently a source of intergroup conflict related to diversity. This can be seen, for example, in the recent events in European cities where immigrants, most of them non-white, are increasingly being harassed by natives who view them as unwelcome outsiders who are threatening their access to employment (see, for example, "Germans," 1991). It has also been identified as a major source of conflict between black and white Americans as well as between blacks and other racioethnic minorities. . . .

## Cultural Differences

Intergroup conflict between diverse groups may also occur because of misunderstandings and misperceptions that are related to the different worldviews of culture groups. For example, Alderfer and Smith (1982) and Daft and Steers (1986) are among those citing cognitive differences between groups as a primary source of potential conflict. Alderfer and Smith describe the nature of these differences in the following way: "[Groups] condition their members' perceptions of objective and subjective phenomena and transmit a set of propositions . . . to explain the nature of experiences encountered by members and to influence relations with other groups" (p. 40).

Alderfer and Smith provide one of the most startling examples of different cognitive orientations between groups from their data on perceptions of race relations in a large organization. In a study of 2,000 managers in a large corporation, they found that perceptions between whites and blacks were dramatically different. For example, they found that while 62 percent of black men and 53 percent of black women agreed that qualified whites were promoted in the company more rapidly than equally qualified blacks, the percent agreement among whites was only 4 and 7 percent respectively for men and women. They also asked the same subjects if they agreed that qualified blacks are promoted more rapidly than equally qualified whites. Here the percentages tended to be reversed, with agreement by only 12 to 13 percent of blacks versus 75 to 82 percent of whites. Since the statements are mutually exclusive, these data give a striking portrayal of how members of different groups in the same organization can see events very differently. Another revealing finding from this study concerns perceptions of the nature of two

support groups in the organization. The Black Managers Association was composed of black managers of all organization levels and restricted its membership to blacks. The Foreman's Club was composed of first-level supervisors, nearly all of whom were white; however, membership was open to anyone at the specified organization level. Nearly half of the white women (45 percent) and more than half of the white men (64 percent) viewed the Black Manager's Association as "essentially a racist organization." This compared to only 25 and 16 percent respectively for black women and men. Alternatively, a majority of blacks (both men and women) viewed the Foreman's Club as essentially racist, while less than 20 percent of whites held this view. One could argue that the differences in eligibility criteria between the two support groups left the Black Managers Association more vulnerable to charges of racism, but the point here is to note how differently whites and blacks viewed the two organizations.

These types of organizational support groups have become increasingly common in recent years (Cox, 1991) and therefore these data are relevant to one of the most ubiquitous consequences of cultural diversity in organizations. I contend that it is not the existence of such organizational support groups per se that creates conflict but rather the differences in how they are perceived. Reconciling such differences in perceptions therefore is a critical challenge for organization development work related to cultural diversity. . . .

## Power Discrepancies

Majority groups as defined in this book hold advantages over minority groups in the power structure of organizations. As numerous writers have noted, this discrepancy of power is a primary source of potential conflict (Landis & Boucher,

1987; Alderfer & Smith, 1982; Randolph & Blackburn, 1989). The logic of this is straightforward. Stated simply, the "power approach" argues that intergroup hostility and antagonism are natural results of competition between groups for control of the economic, political, and social structures of social systems (Giles & Evans, 1986). On a general level, a core manifestation of the power perspective is tension between minority groups and the majority group over whether to change or preserve the status quo. . . .

. . . The power approach to explaining intergroup conflict is illustrated in tensions between majority and minority group members over the use of affirmative action in promotion decisions. Most minority group members are favorable toward affirmative action as one method to promote a redistribution of power in organizations, while many majority group members oppose it as an unwarranted and misguided policy of reverse discrimination. . . . Suffice to say, however, majority group backlash against affirmative action and similar practices are among the most serious forms of intergroup conflict in organizations. . . .

*Minority Group Density.* Minority *group density* refers to the percentage representation of a minority group in the total population of a social system. A considerable amount of research in the political science and social science fields has addressed the effects of minority group density on majority-minority relations in diverse groups (Blalock, 1967; Giles & Evans, 1986). Much of the research has focused on how minority group density affects the behavior of majority group members toward minorities. Specifically of interest has been the "minority-group-size-inequality hypothesis" (MGSI) which holds that majority group members tend to lower levels of

support for, and increase levels of discrimination against, minorities when their percentage representation increases beyond a certain, relatively low, threshold (Blalock, 1967; Blau, 1977). The essence of the argument is that majority members are less favorable toward minorities when their numbers are relatively large because they perceive them as a threat to their established power.

Blalock's empirical data on the MGSI hypothesis were largely taken from records of voting behavior among whites, and on educational and economic inequality between blacks and whites in the southern United States. He concluded that the level of educational and economic disadvantage for blacks, and the level of support for politically conservative candidates among whites, was systematically related to the percentage representation of blacks in the local area. Consistent with the MGSI hypothesis, Blalock concluded that the aforementioned conditions were more favorable toward blacks in those areas where they had small representations (Blalock, 1967). . . .

A second example is Ott's study (1989) of 297 women in two Dutch police departments. Ott found that male attitudes toward the presence of women shifted from neutral to negative when their numbers reached a critical mass (15–20 percent).

In another relevant study, Hoffman (1985) examined communications patterns in ninety-six groups with varying percentages of black and white government-agency supervisors. He predicted that communication would improve in higher-density groups because there would be less isolation and stereotyping of blacks in groups where they represented a larger percentage of the group. He found, however, that only formal communications such as in staff meetings increased in the higher-density groups. Communication on the interpersonal level actually declined as the percent non-white increased. . . .

Collectively the theory and research of MGSI provide considerable support for the idea that the distribution of power is key to majority-minority group conflict. Promotion decisions are a primary mechanism by which organizations define participation in the formal influence structure, and therefore changes here simultaneously pose a threat to the existing power structure and an opportunity for those who are relatively powerless.

## Conformity Versus Identity Affirmation

The final source of interconflict to be discussed here is the tension between majority and minority group members over the preservation of minority group identity. One perspective on this source of conflict that I have found very useful is provided by Ashforth and Mael (1989) in their discussion of high-status versus low-status groups in organization: "The identity of a low-status group is implicitly threatened by a high-status group. . . . A high-status group, however, is less likely to feel threatened and thus less in need of positive affirmation. Accordingly, while a low-status group may go to great lengths to differentiate itself from a high-status group, the latter may be relatively unconcerned about such comparisons and form no strong impression about the low-status group. This indifference of the high-status group is, perhaps, the greatest threat to the identity of the low-status group because the latter's identity remains socially unvalidated" (p.33).

Status is not defined by the authors but, based on the examples they give, appears to be closely related to the relative power and prestige of groups. Thus the majority group in an organization

has higher status than minority groups by definition. Having made this clarification, we can identify several important insights in the above quotation. First, it points out that minority groups will usually be much more aware of, and more concerned with, the preservation of group identity than majority group members will. Not feeling a need for "positive affirmation" themselves, they often will not understand or appreciate that members of minority groups do feel this need. The constant efforts of minority groups to affirm themselves may annoy majority group members, who view these efforts as needless differentiations that serve no useful purpose. A prime example of this in organizations is the reaction of majority group members to support groups formed by minority group members. . . . Many majority group members view these organizations with disdain. The difference in perspective regarding the need for, and desirability of, such groups often becomes the focus of intergroup tensions.

The prevalence of minority support groups throughout history attests to the fact that minority group members in majority organizations often feel a need to form such groups and their purposes are often expressly understood to include protection against a perceived threat to survival of the group (i.e., the groups are to some degree a reaction to being in a lower-status situation). Thus, in the groups of which I have been a member or had occasion to observe, the role of the group in identity affirmation has been explicitly acknowledged. On the other hand, my experience has been that majority group members often fail to realize that their opposition to minority support groups is, in part, a result of their insensitivity to the identity threat that minorities feel. The last statement of the Ashforth and Mael quotation gets at this. They refer to the indifference of the high-status group toward efforts of minority groups to differentiate and affirm themselves. As suggested previously, I have observed numerous cases where the attitude has gone beyond indifference to a hostility toward efforts of the minority group to differentiate itself. The refusal by members of a majority group to acknowledge the need for support groups leaves differences unvalidated, which minorities are quite sensitive to but majorities, by and large, are not. Thus Ashforth and Mael have hit upon an important, albeit subtle, insight into sources of intergroup conflict in organizations related to identity preservation. . . .

A final example of intergroup conflict related to identity preservation is the frequent disagreement over the use of non-majority-group languages in organizations. In my own work, this was illustrated most recently in interviews at the plant site of a large telecommunications company, referred to earlier, that employs a significant number of Laotians. Considerable tensions between Laotian and non-Laotian members of the organization existed. As previously reported some of this was due to conflict over jobs. However, a second dimension was the preference among many of the non-Laotian members for the use of English only in communications in the workplace. Some Laotians felt that this represented an unwarranted denial of their opportunity for cultural expression as well as simply a loss of communication facility when conversing with others who knew their native language. The basis of concern among some about the use of the Laotian language revolved around a discomfort with not being able to understand proximate communication, even when it was directed to someone else, and a concern that it tended to interfere with developing English language skills. . . .

## APPROACHES TO MANAGING INTERGROUP CONFLICT

Thus far in this chapter I have reviewed five primary sources of intergroup conflict related to cultural diversity in organizations. There is no question that the potential for increased conflict is a possible downside of increased diversity in workgroups. However, since diversity in many situations is a fact of life and not a choice, and since the potential benefits of diversity appear to be greater than the potential costs (Cox & Blake, 1991), the challenge for organizations is to manage the conflict. In this final section, I will briefly discuss suggestions for minimizing diversity-related intergroup conflict.

Management writers have identified common approaches to the resolution of intergroup conflict in organizations (Arnold & Feldman, 1986; Randolph & Blackburn, 1989). Table 1 shows a list of the most commonly mentioned strategies, along with my assessment of the sources of diversity-related conflict that they are most effective in addressing.

### Competing Goals

As Table 1 indicates, most of the strategies offer some potential for addressing conflict resulting from competing goals. I will discuss two examples. Competing goals between marketing and manufacturing might be addressed by restructuring the organization into cross-functional workteams whose organizational rewards depend upon collaboration and joint outcomes. One of the most promising resolution techniques is to get both departments to focus attention on superordinate organizational goals such as profits and market share rather than on those of their individual departments. As a final example, bargaining and mediation have historically been used to resolve competing interests

### TABLE 1 · MANAGING CONFLICT IN DIVERSE WORKGROUPS.

| Resolution Strategies | Source of Conflict | | | | |
|---|---|---|---|---|---|
| | Competitive Goals | Resources | Cultural Differences | Power Discrepancies | Identity Affirmation |
| Collaboration/ negotiation/ bargaining | X | | | X | X |
| Alter situation/ context (e.g., organization redesign) | X | X | | X | X |
| Procedures/ rules/policies | | X | | X | X |
| Alter personnel | | | X | | X |
| Alter/redefine the issues of contention | X | | X | X | |
| Hierarchical appeal | X | | | | |
| Smoothing (emphasize similarities, play down conflict) | X | | | | |
| Superordinate goals | X | X | | | |
| Structured interactions | X | X | X | X | X |
| Integrative problem solving (mediation + compromise) | X | | | | X |

of management and labor groups, although not always successfully, especially in recent years.

An application of superordinate goals and of smoothing that seems especially pertinent to gender, racioethnic, and nationality diversity in organizations is to capitalize on the shared group identity of the common employer. To do this successfully, minority as well as majority members of organizations have to iden-tify with the employer and have some degree of confidence that the goals of the organization and those of the micro-culture group are compatible if not mutually supportive.

## Competition for Resources

As noted earlier, one of the most common manifestations of resource competition in the context of cultural diversity is competition over jobs. Obviously a great deal of conflict potential is eliminated when jobs are more plentiful. Thus to the extent that overall job opportunities can be expanded, the climate of intergroup relations will be improved immeasurably. Unfortunately, the expansion of resources is often not possible, especially in the short term.

In many organizations, hiring policies—such as Xerox's Balanced Workforce Plan—attempt to formally acknowledge group identities such as gender, racioethnicity, and nationality in regulating the competition for jobs. The goal is to ensure equal competition, although, as noted in previous chapters, the reaction to such plans among majority group members often heightens intergroup conflict related to job competition. Xerox has been somewhat successful at minimizing and resolving conflict related to their plan partly by paying a lot of attention to how the plan has been communicated.

The utility of superordinate goals for resolving resource-based conflict can be illustrated by considering the case of two departments vying for a larger share of a limited training budget. If both can be encouraged to plan on the basis of the training priorities of the overall organization, it may help to resolve the conflict.

Finally, as with all of the sources of conflict, structured interaction to discuss the points of contention, gain a better appreciation of the other party's perspective, and promote mutual understanding is a potentially valuable tool for resolving conflict based on resource competition.

## Cultural Differences

Here I recommend three strategies for conflict resolution related to cultural differences, beginning with altering personnel. One way to achieve this goal is by educating existing personnel to obtain a better knowledge of cultural differences. Another way is to hire and promote persons with tolerant and flexible personalities who will productively support cultural-diversity change initiatives in the organization. Stated simply, people who are more tolerant and accepting of difference will produce less conflict when confronted with cultural differences than people who are not. The problem of intergroup conflict is partly due to emotional or affective reactions of individuals.

Redefining issues can also aid in cultural conflict resolution. An example of this is promoting the mindset that cultural differences present opportunities rather than problems to be solved. For example, Blau (1977) argues that increased intergroup experience stimulates intellectual endeavors. One way that this kind of redefinition is illustrated in the language of organizational relations is in the preference for the "valuing" of diversity rather than "tolerating" diversity.

Structured interaction is also usable in resolving conflict related to cultural differences. An example is the use of interdepartmental task forces. Although such groups normally have a specific work task to accomplish, time may be spent initially on activities designed to help representatives of the various departments get to know the culture of the other departments better. Familiarity with the language and norms of the other groups is likely to facilitate the work on the task. Even informal meetings may be of great value. For example, during a recent consulting project with a research and development firm, several engineers and scientists spoke about how some of them had used cross-disciplinary meetings as a means of gaining understanding about the differences between their functions and how they viewed their role in the overall mission of the firm. These persons reported that the meetings had proved valuable in reducing misconceptions between the groups and that joint projects and cross-functional communications had increased as a result.

## Power Discrepancies

The earlier discussion of this factor made it clear that power differences between majority and minority members of organizations are perhaps the most deadly of the conflict sources. Power discrepancies are sometimes resolved by negotiations, such as those currently under way between the government of South Africa and the African National Congress over representation of Black and White South Africans in the new government under a democratic model. Power differences may also be resolved by policies, such as designated representation of minority groups in government bodies. For example, a minimum of four seats are reserved for Maoris in the New Zealand legislature.

Another policy with obvious power redistribution objectives is affirmative action in promotion decisions. Although controversial, there is no denying the impact of affirmative action in changing and diversifying the authority structure of an organization. The substantial results of Xerox's Balanced Workforce Plan and U.S. West's Pluralism Performance Effort are two cases in point.

An example of an organization redesign to assist in resolving intergroup power conflicts is the creation of diverse groups of advisers to give direct input to senior management. U.S. West and Equitable Life Insurance are examples of companies that have created these. To the extent that such groups address issues beyond diversity, they hold the potential to make modest shifts in the power structure of organizations, even though they do not change the fundamental authority hierarchy per se.

It may also be useful to redefine issues as a means of conflict reduction. For example, what is the primary motive for using affirmative action in promotion decisions? Is it to right the wrongs of past discrimination, to address the discrimination of the present, to meet social responsibility objectives, or to meet economic responsibilities of the organization? . . . I submit that how these questions are answered, and the extent to which their answers are understood and embraced by members of organizations, has much to do with the success in resolving power-based conflict in organizations.

Finally, planned interactions between groups to discuss the existence of power discrepancies, their effects, and what to do about them are advised for majority-minority situations of all kinds.

## Conflict over Conformity Versus Affirmative Identity

In this last category, a number of strategies are indicated in Table 1 as potentially effective. First, since some combination of assimilation to majority group norms and preservation of microculture norms is expected, the techniques of negotiation and compromise seem at least theoretically relevant. One example is the extent to which organizations adapt the work environment to accommodate a particular disability of an employee or potential employee. In many instances the level of accommodation will not eliminate all barriers to full participation. However, some compromise may be reached that reduces the potential for conflict between persons with disabilities seeking accommodation and fully able members who may feel that the cost of accommodations places an undue burden on the financial and social resources of the firm.

In some instances, mediation may be of help in resolving intergroup differences related to conformity. One example is when consultants on workforce diversity are asked to assist in improving relations between identity-based employee support groups and the senior management of organizations. This work includes increasing awareness among senior management of the importance of identity affirmation by members of minority groups, as well increasing sensitivity among support-group members of senior management concerns over the existence and purposes of these groups.

An example of a structural/environmental change that organizations can make to alter conflict potential related to conformity is the selection of a mode of acculturation. . . . But suffice to say here that an organization's choice of whether to approach acculturation using a pluralism or a traditional assimilation model has many implications for the identity-based conflict under discussion here.

Another type of identity-related conflict that was discussed above is disagreement over the use of alternative languages. Organizations may wish to address this type of conflict by establishing a policy statement about the use of alternative languages in the workplace that is sensitive to the concerns of both groups. Companies such as Esprit De Corp., Economy Color Card, and Pace Foods are examples of firms that have taken what I consider to be a sound approach by supporting the learning of alternative languages by English-only speakers and the formal use of non-English languages under some conditions such as in published policy manuals (Cox, 1991).

Concerning altering personnel, the same points made earlier in this section about cultural differences apply here. Intolerant, narrow-minded people will tend to expand the scope of behaviors for which pressure is applied to conform to the norms of the majority group. It is true that restricting the hiring of persons in minority groups to those who do not have a strong concern with the preservation of microcultural identity may eliminate some potential intergroup conflict by creating a more culturally homogeneous organization. This approach is not recommended, however, because it is out of step with worldwide labor-force demographic trends and because it brings other, unaffordable costs, such as the loss of divergent cultural perspectives to enhance problem solving.

# REFERENCES

Alderfer, C. P., Alderfer, C. J., Tucker, L., & Tucker, R. (1980). Diagnosing race relations in management. *Journal of Applied Behavioral Science, 16*, 135–166.

Alderfer, C. P., & Smith, K. K. (1982). Studying intergroup relations embedded in organizations. *Administrative Science Quarterly, 27*, 5–65.

Arnold, H., & Feldman, D. (1986). *Organizational behavior*. New York: McGraw-Hill.

Ashforth, B., & Mael, F. (1989). Social identity theory and the organization. *Academy of Management Review, 14*(1), 20–39.

Blalock, H., Jr. (1967). *Toward a theory of minority-group relations*. New York: Wiley.

Blau, P. M. (1977). A macrosociological theory of social structure. *American Journal of Sociology, 83*, 26–54.

Campbell, D. T. (1965). Ethnocentric and other altruistic motives. In D. Levine (Ed.), *Nebraska symposium on motivation* (pp. 283–311). Lincoln: University of Nebraska Press.

Cox, T. H. (1991). The multicultural organization. *The Executive, 5*(2), 34–47.

Cox, T. H., & Blake, S. (1991). Managing cultural diversity: Implications for organizational competitiveness. *The Executive, 5*(3), 45–56.

Daft, R., & Steers, R. (1986). *Organizations: A micro/macro approach*. Glenview, IL: Scott-Foresman.

Germans try to stem right wing attacks against foreigners. (1991, December 4). *Wall Street Journal*.

Giles, M. W., & Evans, A. (1986). The power approach to intergroup hostility. *Journal of Conflict Resolution, 30*(3), 469–486.

Hoffman, E. (1985). The effect of race ratio composition on the frequency of organizational communication. *Social Psychology Quarterly, 48*(1), 17–26.

Landis, D., & Boucher, J. (1987). Themes and models of conflict. In J. Boucher, D. Landis, & K. A. Clark (Eds.), *Ethnic conflict: International perspectives* (pp. 18–32). Newbury Park, CA: Sage.

Ott, E. M. (1989). Effects of the male-female ratio. *Psychology of Women Quarterly, 13,* 41–57.

Randolph, W. A., & Blackburn, R. S. (1989). *Managing organizational behavior.* Homewood, IL: Richard D. Irwin.

Rummell, R. J. (1976). *Understanding conflict and war.* New York: Wiley.

Sherif, M. (1966). *Group conflict and cooperation.* London: Routledge & Kegan Paul.

# CHAPTER III

# *Leadership*

## WHAT IS LEADERSHIP?

Over the years, the importance attributed to the position of leaders has led innumerable practitioners and theorists to ask the seemingly unanswerable question: "What does it take to be an effective leader?" and almost as many behavioral scientists have tried to offer answers. This chapter discusses some of the more important approaches that have been proposed in answer to this most basic but elusive question of leadership.

Although we need to have an understanding of what leadership is in order to discuss it, it is important to realize that there are no clear-cut, universally accepted definitions of what it is. Lombardo and McCall (1978, p. 3) describe the situation well. "'Leadership' is one of the most magnetic words in the English language. Mention it, and a perceptible aura of excitement, almost mystical in nature appears . . . [Yet] if leadership is bright orange, leadership research is slate gray." Complicating this is the fact that we also need to distinguish between *leadership* (or *leader*) and *management* (or *manager*). Although the two functions and roles overlap substantially, *manager* implies that authority has been formally granted to an individual by an organization. *Management* involves power (usually formal authority) bestowed on the occupant of a position by a higher organizational authority. With the power of management comes responsibility and accountability for the use of organizational resources. In contrast, *leader* implies effective use of influence that is rather independent of the authority granted to one because of position. Leadership cannot be bestowed upon a person by a higher authority. Effective managers also must be leaders, and many leaders become managers, but the two sets of roles and functions differ.

One group of authors recently began defining a successful leader as one who is able to transform an organization when situations call for such action (Bennis, 1984; Bennis & Nanus, 1985; Tichy, 1983; Tichy & Devanna, 1986). Probably the most widely accepted current definitions view leadership as an interpersonal process through which one individual influences the attitudes, beliefs, and especially the behavior of one or more other people.

The subject of leadership raises many complex issues that have plagued behavioral scientists for generations: For example, what gives a manager or a leader legitimacy? Shafritz (1988, p. 324) describes *legitimacy* as "a characteristic of a social institution, such as a government or a family [or an organization], whereby it has both a legal and a perceived right to make binding decisions." Thus, managers presumably have legitimacy because of the legal and perceived rights that accompany their organizational positions. In contrast, the legitimacy of a leader—separate and distinct from the legitimacy of a manager—cannot be addressed without introducing the concept of *charisma*. Charisma is "leadership based on the compelling personality of the leader rather than on formal position" (Shafritz 1988, p. 89).

The concept was first articulated by the German sociologist, Max Weber, who distinguished charismatic authority from the traditional authority of a monarch and the legal authority one receives by virtue of law—such as the authority that legitimizes organizational executives.

Despite the differences and the unresolved questions, two important definitional givens are evident: First, leadership involves a relationship between people in which influence and power are unevenly distributed on a legitimate basis; and second, a leader cannot function in isolation. In order for there to be a leader, someone must follow (Fiedler and Chemers, 1974, p. 4). In his enduring chapter, "The Executive Functions" (1938), which is reprinted in this chapter, Chester Barnard defines three essential functions of leaders of executives: to provide a system of communication, to promote the securing of essential efforts, and to formulate and define the purposes and goals of an organization. He was decades ahead of his times in arguing that the most critical function of a chief executive is to establish and communicate a system of organizational values among organizational members. If the value system is clear and strong, the day-to-day concerns will take care of themselves.

## TRAIT THEORIES

Over the years, studies of leadership have taken different approaches based on divergent perspectives. The trait approach to leadership dominated into the 1950s. The trait theories assume that leaders possess traits which are fundamentally different from followers. A *trait* is a "personality attribute or a way of interacting with others which is independent of the situation, that is, a characteristic of the person rather than of the situation" (Fiedler and Chemers, 1974, p. 22). Advocates of trait theory believe that some individuals have characteristics and qualities which enable them to "rise above the population," to assume responsibilities not everyone can execute, and therefore to become leaders (Hampton et al., 1982, p. 566). Under trait theory, the task of the behavioral sciences is to identify those traits and learn how to identify people who possess them.

It is no longer fashionable to contend that people will be effective leaders because they possess certain traits—without also considering other variables that influence leadership effectiveness. The arguments against trait theory are persuasive and come from a number of points of view. First, trait theory has largely fallen out of favor because reality never matched the theory. Instead, starting in the late

1950s, it started to become standard practice to view leadership as a relationship, an interaction between individuals. The interaction was called a *transaction,* so the term *transactional leadership* became the umbrella label encompassing many theories of leadership of the 1950s, 1960s, and 1970s. Second, the situation strongly influences leadership. As Stogdill (1948) stated, the situation has an active influence in determining the qualities, characteristics, and skills needed in a leader.

Probably the most damaging criticism of trait theory, however, has been its lack of ability to identify which traits make an effective leader. Even among the traits that have been most commonly cited—intelligence, energy, achievement, dependability, and socioeconomic status—there is a lack of consensus across studies. Leadership involves more than possessing certain traits. A leader may be effective in one setting and ineffective in another. It depends on the situation (Fiedler, 1969).

## TRANSACTIONAL APPROACHES TO LEADERSHIP

The transactional approaches to leadership had early beginnings in the 1930s but did not emerge as the dominant view of leadership until the 1950s. Two primary forces were behind the ascendancy: (1) frustration and disappointment with the trait theories, and (2) dramatic post–World War II advances in the applied behavioral sciences.

Whereas the trait approaches view leadership as something(s) inherent in a leader, the transactional approaches see leadership as a set of functions and roles that develop from an interaction between two or more people. The interaction between a person who leads and those who follow is labeled a *transaction*—much the same as in *Transactional Analysis* (Berne, 1964; Harris, 1969; James & Jongeward, 1971). Although there are vast differences in emphasis among groupings of transactional leadership theories, all of them focus on the transaction—what happens and why, and what directly and indirectly influences or shapes it. Thus, for example, the transactional theorist Fiedler (1966) emphasizes the leader—but in the context of the match between leaders and followers. In contrast, Hersey and Blanchard (1969) focus on subordinates—but in a leader-follower context.

### Leadership Style Theories

The early transactional leadership theories tended to assume that people have relatively fixed styles and thus were often labeled *leadership style theories.* Many of the more recent theories also involve leadership styles, but because the earlier assumption of style inflexibility has been abandoned, they usually are called *situational* or *contingency approaches.* But once again in both cases, leadership is seen as a transaction. Whereas the central question for the trait approach is, *who exerts leadership?* the quest of the transactional approaches is to determine *how leadership is established and exerted.*

Leadership style-oriented transactional approaches all follow in the tradition of the famous Lewin, Lippitt, and White (1939) studies of the effectiveness of leadership styles on group productivity. Lewin, Lippitt, and White studied groups of 10-year-old children engaged in hobby activities. The leader in each group was classified as authoritarian, democratic, or laissez-faire oriented. Authoritarian leaders determined all policies, set all work assignments, and were personal in their criticisms. They were product (or task) oriented and practiced initiating structure. Democratic-oriented leaders shared decision-making powers with subordinates, decisions about assignments were left to the group, and they participated in group activities but tried not to monopolize. They used high levels of consideration. Laissez-faire-oriented leaders allowed freedom for individual and group decision making, provided information (or supplies) only when requested, and did not participate in the group except when called upon. They function more as facilitators.

Groups with democratic-oriented leaders were the most satisfied and productive. The authoritarian-led groups showed the most aggressive behavior and were the least satisfied, but they were highly productive (possibly because of fear of the leader.) The groups with laissez-faire-oriented leaders showed low satisfaction, low production, and were behaviorally aggressive toward group members and other groups.

The leadership style-oriented transactional approaches attempt to identify styles of leader behavior which result in effective group performance. Probably the best known groups of studies using this approach were conducted at the University of Michigan and at Ohio State University. They were widely known as *the Michigan studies* and *the Ohio State studies*.

Most of the Michigan studies analyzed two extreme leadership styles, *product-oriented* and *employee-oriented*. A product-oriented leadership style focuses on accomplishing the task of the organization producing the product. This style is exhibited in such activities as setting organizational or group goals, assigning work to subordinates, and constantly evaluating performance. The employee-oriented leadership style pays more attention to how well subordinates are doing and to their feelings and attitudes.

Typically, the Michigan studies had subordinates rate their supervisors on the degree to which "he treats people under him without considering their feelings," or "he does personal favors for the people under him" (Fleishman and Harris, 1962, p. 10). Findings from the Michigan studies have shown that high productivity may be associated with either style of leadership, but product-oriented leaders tend to be confronted more often and their employees have more job dissatisfaction, high turnover rates, and higher absenteeism rates (Fleishman and Harris, 1962, p. 53). Finally, other studies have shown that work output is correlated with the freedom supervisors give to workers, and employees produce more under loose supervision than under close supervision.

Like the University of Michigan studies, the Ohio State studies classified leader behavior as either product-oriented or employee-oriented, but they used different terminology: *initiation of structure* and *consideration*. The Ohio State studies treat the two behaviors as independent dimensions rather than as scalar opposites. In other words, a leader can rank high on consideration and either high or low on initiation of structure. Thus, leaders can be grouped into four quadrants.

*Initiation of structure* is "the leader's behavior in delineating the relationship between himself and members of the work group and in endeavoring to establish well-defined patterns of organization, channels of command, and methods of procedure" (Bozeman, 1979, p. 208). It is a variety of leader actions used "to get the work out." The leader plans, directs, sets standards, and controls the work of subordinates.

*Consideration* is "any action which the leader takes to perceive the human needs of his subordinates and to support the subordinates in their own attempts to satisfy their needs" (Hampton et al., 1982, p. 569). Or as stated by Stogdill, consideration is "any behavior indicative of friendship, mutual trust, respect, and warmth in the relationship between the leader and a member of his staff" (Bozeman, 1979, p. 208).

The Ohio State studies found the productivity of individuals and groups to be higher when the leader initiates structure than when they do not. Some studies have found consideration positively related to productivity, while others show a negative effect or no effect at all. As far as satisfaction, studies have shown the initiation of structure to be received differently by different people in different situations. For example, House's (1971) work illustrated that the larger the organization, the more employees need some stability, order, and direction. At the other extreme, considerate behavior has almost always been shown to increase employee satisfaction (Fleishman and Harris, 1962, p. 47).

The Ohio State studies contain interesting parallels to the Michigan studies. In their 1969 article, "Life Cycle Theory of Leadership," (included in this chapter), Hersey and Blanchard emphasize that leadership should be appropriate for a given situation. They use the maturity of the work groups as a variable influencing the effectiveness of the style used. Using *initiation of structure* and *consideration* for dimensions, they develop a matrix with four leadership styles: telling, selling, participating, and delegating. When a work group is not mature enough to assume a task, the leader needs to be high in initiation (task) and low in consideration (relationship) behavior, in order to help the group understand what is required of them. On the other hand, when a group is mature, the leader should be high in consideration (relationship) and low in initiation (task) behavior, because the group is able to complete its task without much guidance. Although the model is conceptually intriguing, a major weakness is its lack of a "systematic measurement device to measure maturity" (Schein, 1980).

## Situational or Contingency Approaches

Probably, the earliest situationist was the classical organizational philosopher, Mary Parker Follett. In her 1926 article, "The Giving of Orders," Follett discusses how orders should be given in any organization: They should be depersonalized "to unite all concerned in a study of the situation, to discover the law of the situation and obey that" (p. 33). Follett thus argues for a *participatory leadership style* where employees and employers cooperate to assess the situation and decide what should be done at that moment—in that situation. Once the *law of the situation* is discovered, "the employee can issue it to the employer as well as employer to employee" (p.

33). This manner of giving orders facilitates better attitudes within an organization because nobody is necessarily under another person; rather all take their cues from the situation.

The early style approach to transactional leadership assumed that leaders could be trained to act in the appropriate way as called for by their organization. This has proven to be a major weakness. When leaders return to their organization after leadership training sessions, they seldom exhibit behavior changes. Despite training, department heads will not necessarily act considerately toward subordinates if their own supervisors do not act supportively toward them. One obvious implication is that changes must be introduced into an organization as a whole—not just to certain employees.

In practice, leaders apply different styles in different situations. Thus, the "pure" leadership style emphasis has given way to the contingency approaches. Unlike the trait theory and leadership style approaches, the contingency approaches take into consideration many factors that may influence a leader's style. It recognizes that a successful leader in one type of organization may not be successful in another simply because it differs from the previous one. Its situation (or context) is different, and the choice of a style needs to be contingent upon the situation. As Stogdill (1974) notes, the contingency theories stress:

1.  The type, structure, size, and purpose of the organization;
2.  The external environment in which the organization functions;
3.  The orientation, values, goals, and expectations of the leader, his superiors, and subordinates; and
4.  The expert or professional knowledge required of the position.

The contingency approaches assert that different leadership styles will differ in their effects in different situations. The situation (not traits or styles themselves) determines whether a leadership style or a particular leader will be effective. Thus, contingency theorists maintain that there is no "one best way" of effective leadership.

Tannenbaum and Schmidt (1958, 1973) conducted one of the first studies that actually indicated a need for leaders to evaluate the situational factors prior to the implementation of a particular leadership style (Blunt, 1981). Tannenbaum and Schmidt grouped leader decision-making behavior into seven categories along a continuum from *boss-centered* to *subordinate-centered*. Each category is based on a single variable: the degree of participation in making decisions that is allowed to subordinates. For example:

- Category 1 assumes that the leader makes all decisions and announces them to subordinates.
- Category 7 assumes that the leader defines limits but allows the group to define the problem and to make the final decision.

Tannenbaum and Schmidt also specify three factors that influence where along their continuum a decision will be made. These factors are: forces in the leader, forces of the subordinates, and forces in the situation.

The successful manager of men can be primarily characterized neither as a strong leader nor as a permissive one. Rather, he is one who maintains a high batting average in accurately assessing the forces that determine what his most appropriate behavior at any given time should be and in actually being able to behave accordingly (Tannenbaum and Schmidt, 1973, p. 180).

Whereas Tannenbaum and Scmidt have focused mostly on variables involving followers, Fred Fiedler has emphasized the leader (but still from a transactional perspective). In "The Contingency Model: A Theory of Leadership Effectiveness" (included in this chapter), Fiedler discusses a study done with the Belgian Naval Forces. Some earlier leadership theorists had believed that leaders could be trained to adopt styles that are suitable for situations, but Fielder found the opposite to be true. It is easier to change the work environment, the situation, to fit a leader's style. A person's underlying leadership style depends upon one's personality. According to Fiedler, a leader's personality is not likely to change because of a few lectures or a few weeks of intensive training. Therefore, an organization should not choose a leader who fits a situation, but should change the situation to mesh with the style of its leader. (See also, Cooper & Robertson, 1988, p. 84.)

## CULTURAL AND TRANSFORMATIVE THEORIES

A growing number of leadership theorists recently have moved past the transactional approaches to write about leadership from an organizational culture perspective or, as it is sometimes called, a symbolic management perspective (Shafritz & Ott, 1996; Ott, 1989). Without question, Edgar Schein is the best known writer about organizational culture, and his book, *Organizational Culture and Leadership,* has been the most widely cited source on the topic since publication of the first edition in 1985. "The Learning Leader as Culture Manager," a chapter from the second edition (1992), is reprinted here. In it, Schein argues "that leadership and culture are closely connected. . . . leaders create, embed, develop, and sometimes deliberately attempt to change cultural assumptions" (p. 374). Different kinds of culture management are needed at different stages in an organization's development and maturation: culture creation, at organizational midlife, and in mature and potentially declining organizations. Schein examines how these stages of culture management affect organizational strategy formation and discusses the implications for the selection and development of leaders.

Like Bennis (in this chapter) and Senge (in Chapter VII), Schein concludes that leaders of the future will have to be perpetual learners. "If the leaders of today want to create organizational cultures that will themselves be more amenable to learning, they will have to set the example by becoming learners themselves and involving others in the learning process. . . . In the end, cultural understanding and cultural learning start with self-insight" (p. 392).

*Transformational leadership* or *transformative leadership* is a somewhat recent slant on leadership that is theoretically consistent with the organizational culture perspective. Whereas the transactional theories of leadership apply primarily to leadership roles, functions, and behavior *within* an existing organizational culture, transformative leadership is about leadership to *change* a culture. *Transactional leadership focuses on incremental change: Transformative leadership is about radical change*. Lee Iacocca (1984) is the most visible current embodiment of a transformative leader. It is interesting to note that transformational leadership theories have many similarities with the trait theories of leadership. Transformational leadership borders on "great man" theory: Leaders are born, not made. In many ways, leadership theory is once again involved in seeking to find the basis of leadership in traits— rather than in relational and cultural factors.

Noel Tichy and David Ulrich's 1984 *Sloan Management Review* article, "The Leadership Challenge—A Call for the Transformational Leader" (reprinted in this chapter) describes a transformational leader as "one who must develop and communicate a new vision and get others not only to see the vision but also to commit themselves to it" (p. 59). They describe transformational leaders as those rare individuals who can lead employees through their fears and uncertainties to the realization of the vision. This requires transformational leadership—leadership that successfully changes peoples' perceptions of the organization. Transformational change is more than a rational, technical, incremental approach to change. The leader's primary function is to lead and support through carefully conceived change stages, acting as a *cheerleader* and as a *belief model*—verbally and nonverbally communicating belief in the benefits to all that will accrue from the changes.

## Continuing Concerns About Leadership

Warren Bennis seems always to have astutely led theory into transitional stages. Leadership is not an exception. His work in the late 1950s and early 1960s was traditionally transactional: for example, his 1961 *Harvard Business Review* article, "Revisionist Theory of Leadership." But, as reflected in his writings about organizations in general during the late 1960s and 1970s, Bennis started to question generally accepted views about leadership. Were we really learning anything new or of use about leadership that had practical value? A chapter from Bennis's 1976 book, *The Unconscious Conspiracy: Why Leaders Can't Lead*, titled "Mortal Stakes: Where have all the Leaders Gone?" was in the first edition of *Classic Readings in Organizational Behavior* (1989). In it, Bennis pondered why we no longer have leaders like those of old. He argued that the leaders of the day were confused: The gap between expectations and reality was widening. However, he remained optimistic that managers could learn to lead, to have a perspective of the future, and to practice the strategic functions of leadership.

In 1990, Bennis published his updated views on leadership in *Why Leaders Can't Lead: The Unconscious Conspiracy Continues*, parts of which are included in this chapter. Unfortunately, Bennis could not maintain his optimistic views of 1976. "In America Today, it is harder than ever to lead. . . . Though we need leaders as much as ever, we have never held them in lower regard. Circumstances conspire against them. And so—without meaning to—do the American people" (p. xi). An unconscious conspiracy prevents leaders from taking charge and making changes. His views coincide with those of Peter Senge's (Chapter VII). Change is possible as people, "one by one," make conscious choice to live up to their potential. However, he concludes: "The best hope I have for this book is that twelve years from now I will look back on it and muse, 'Where have all the leaders come from?' "

## Leadership: Where from Here?

During the last fifty years, leadership theory has wound its way torturously over twisting and often seemingly fruitless paths. For every gain in understanding, there have been more new questions to answer. The search for a comprehensive theory of leadership is a seemingly never-ending quest. Since the 1940s, the search has led us through trait theories, myriad transactional approaches, and now transformative/cultural theories. No one truly believes that the answers to the most basic questions of leadership have been found. Many of us, when confronted with the practical realities of leading, particularly in complex organizations, share Bennis's frustrations. We find ourselves asking: Why can't leaders lead? Where have all the leaders gone?

Margaret J. Wheatley, among others, has been arguing that we will continue to struggle with fundamental leadership problems until we begin to "see" organizations, people, *and leadership* in very different ways than we do now. Her 1992 book, *Leadership and the New Science*, is "an exploration" into ways in which "new science"—quantum physics, chaos theory, theories on self-organizing or dissipative systems, and "new" biology—may provide new insights for "comprehending the issues that trouble organizations most: chaos, order, control, autonomy, structure, information, participation, planning, and prediction" (p. xi). Her chapter, "Searching for a Simpler Way to Lead Organizations" (reprinted here), opens the exploration by rejecting the use of Newtonian images of the universe as our basis for understanding and managing organizations. "The new physics cogently explains that there is no objective reality out there waiting to reveal its secrets. . . . There is only what we create through our engagement with others and with events" (p. 7). Relationships are the key to understanding organizational realities and managing in complex organizations.

Perhaps the "new science" will provide us with the insights needed to frame answers to Warren Bennis's questions (or perhaps to reframe his questions) and allow him to regain his lost optimism.

## REFERENCES

Allaire, Y., & Firsirotu, M. (Spring, 1985). How to implement radical strategies in large organizations. *Sloan Management Review*, 26(3), 19–34.

Barnard, C. I. (1968). *The functions of the executive*. Cambridge, MA: Harvard University Press. (Originally published in 1938.)

Beckhard, R. (1988). The executive management of transformational change. In R. H. Kilmann & T. J. Covin (Eds.), *Corporate transformation* (pp. 89–101). San Francisco: Jossey-Bass.

Bennis, W. G. (1961). Revisionist theory of leadership. *Harvard Business Review, 39*.

Bennis, W. G. (1976). Mortal stakes: Where have all the leaders gone? In W. G. Bennis, *The unconscious conspiracy: Why leaders can't lead* (pp. 143–156). New York: AMACOM.

Bennis, W. G. (1984). Transformative power and leadership. In T. J. Sergiovanni & J. E. Corbally (Eds.), *Leadership and organizational culture* (pp. 64–71). Urbana, IL: University of Illinois Press.

Bennis, W. G. (1990). *Why leaders can't lead: The unconscious conspiracy continues.* San Francisco: Jossey-Bass.

Bennis, W. G., & Nanus, B. (1985). *Leaders: The strategies for taking charge.* New York: Harper & Row.

Bergquist, W. (1993). *The postmodern organization: Mastering the art of irreversible change.* San Francisco: Jossey-Bass.

Berne, E. (1964). *Games people play.* New York: Grove Press.

Block, P. (1991). *The empowered manager: Positive political skills at work.* San Francisco: Jossey-Bass.

Blunt, B. E. (1981). *Organizational leadership.* Ann Arbor, MI: University Microfilm International.

Bozeman, B. (1979). *Public management and policy analysis.* New York: St. Martin's Press.

Cattell, R. B. (1951). New concepts for measuring leadership in terms of group syntality. *Human Relations, 4,* 161–184.

Cooper, C. L., & Robertson, I. (Eds.). (1988). *International review of industrial and organizational psychology.* New York: John Wiley.

Deal, T. E. (1985). Cultural change: Opportunity, silent killer, or metamorphosis? In R. H. Kilmann, M. J. Saxton, & R. Serpa (Eds.), *Gaining control of the corporate culture* (pp. 292–331). San Francisco: Jossey-Bass.

Dublin, R. (1951). *Human relations in administration.* Englewood Cliffs, NJ: Prentice-Hall.

Dunnette, M. D. (1976). *Handbook of industrial and organizational psychology.* Chicago: Rand McNally.

Fiedler, F. E. (1966). The contingency model: A theory of leadership effectiveness. In C. W. Backman & P. F. Secord (Eds.), *Problems in social psychology* (pp. 278–289). New York: McGraw-Hill.

Fielder, F. E. (1967). *A theory of leadership effectiveness.* New York: McGraw-Hill.

Fiedler, F. E. (March, 1969). Style or circumstance: The leadership enigma. *Psychology Today 2*(10), 38–43.

Fiedler, F. E., & Chemers, M. M. (1974). *Leadership style and effective management.* Glenview, IL: Scott, Foresman and Company.

Fiedler, F. E., Chemers, M. M., & Mahar, L. (1976). *Improving leadership effectiveness: The leader match concept.* New York: John Wiley & Sons.

Fleishman, E. A., & Harris, E. F. (1962). Patterns of leadership behavior related to employee grievances and turnover. *Personnel Psychology, 15,* 43–56.

Fleishman, E. A., & Hunt, J. G. (1973). *Current developments in the study of leadership.* Carbondale, IL: Southern Illinois University Press.

Follett, M. P. (1926). The giving of orders. In H. C. Metcalf (Ed.), *Scientific foundations of business administration.* Baltimore, MD: Williams & Wilkins Company.

Hampton, D. R., Summer, C. E., & Webber, R. A. (1982). *Organizational behavior and the practice of management*. Glenview, IL: Scott: Foresman and Company.

Harris, T. A. (1969). *I'm OK—You're OK*. New York: Harper & Row.

Hemphill, J. K. (1950). *Leader behavior description*. Columbus, OH: Ohio State University Press.

Hersey, P., & Blanchard, K. H. (May, 1969). Life cycle theory of leadership. *Training and Development Journal*, 26–34.

House, R. J. (1971). Path-goal theory of leadership effectiveness. *Administrative Sciences Quarterly, 16*, 321–338.

House, R. J., & Mitchell, T. M. (Autumn, 1974). Path-goal theory of leadership. *Journal of Contemporary Business, 3*(4), 81–97.

Iacocca, L. (1984). *Iacocca, an autobiography*. Toronto: Bantam Books.

James, M., & Jongeward, D. (1971). *Born to win*. Reading, MA: Addison-Wesley.

Kahn, R. L., & Katz, D. (1962). Leadership practices in relation to productivity and morale. In D. Cartwright & A. Zander (Eds.), *Group dynamics* (2d ed.) (pp. 554–570). New York: Harper & Row.

Kouzes, J. M., & Posner, B. Z. (1993). *Credibility: How leaders gain and lose it, and why people demand it*. San Francisco: Jossey-Bass.

Leavitt, H. J. (June, 1962). Applied organizational change: A summary and evaluation of the power equalization approaches. Seminar in the Social Science of Organizations. Pittsburgh, PA.

Lewin, K., Lippitt, R., & White, R. K. (1939). Patterns of aggressive behavior in experimentally created social climates. *Journal of Social Psychology, 10*, 271–299.

Likert, R. (1961). *New patterns of management*. New York: McGraw-Hill.

Lombardo, M. M., & McCall, M. W., Jr., (1978). Leadership. In M. W. McCall, Jr., & M. M. Lombardo (Eds.), *Leadership: Where else can we go?* (pp. 3–34). Durham, NC: Duke University Press.

Ott, J. S. (1989). *The organizational culture perspective*. Chicago: The Dorsey Press.

Schein, E. H. (1980). *Organizational psychology* (3d ed.). Englewood Cliffs, NJ: Prentice-Hall.

Schein, E. H. (1992). *Organizational culture and leadership* (2d ed.). San Francisco: Jossey-Bass.

Schön, D. A. (1984). Leadership as reflection-in-action. In T. J. Sergiovanni & J. E. Corbally (Eds.), *Leadership and organizational culture* (pp. 36–63). Urbana, IL: University of Illinois Press.

Selznick, P. (1957). *Leadership in administration: A sociological interpretation*. New York: Harper & Row.

Sergiovanni, T. J. (1984). Leadership as cultural expression. In T. J. Sergiovanni & J. E. Corbally (Eds.), *Leadership and organizational culture* (pp. 105–114). Urbana, IL: University of Illinois Press.

Shafritz, J. M. (1988). *The Dorsey dictionary of politics and government*. Chicago: The Dorsey Press.

Shafritz, J. M., & Ott, J. S. (1996). *Classics of organization theory* (4th ed.) Belmont, CA: Wadsworth.

Stogdill, R. M. (1948). Personal factors associated with leadership: A survey of the literature. *Journal of Pscyhology, 25*, 35–71.

Stogdill, R. M. (1974). *Handbook of leadership: A study of theory and research.* New York: The Free Press.

Stogdill, R. M., & Coons, A. E. (Eds.). (1957). *Leader behavior: Its description and measurement.* Columbus, OH: Ohio State University Press.

Tannenbaum, R. J., & Schmidt, W. H. (March–April, 1958). How to choose a leadership pattern. *Harvard Business Review, 36*(2), 95–101.

Tannenbaum, R. J., & Schmidt, W. H. (May–June, 1973). How to choose a leadership pattern. *Harvard Business Review, 51*(3), 1–10.

Tannenbaum, R. J., Weschler, I. R., & Massarik, F. (1961). *Leadership and organization.* New York: McGraw-Hill.

Tichy, N. M. (1983). *Managing strategic change: Technical, political and cultural dynamics.* New York: John Wiley & Sons.

Tichy, N. M., & Devanna, M. A. (1986). *The transformational leader.* New York, John Wiley & Sons.

Tichy, N. M., & Ulrich, D. O. (1984). The leadership challenge—a call for the transformational leader. *Sloan Management Review, 26*, 59–68.

Vroom, W. H. (Winter, 1976). Can leaders learn to lead? *Organizational Dynamics.*

Vroom, Victor, H., & Yetton, P. W. (1973). *Leadership and decision making.* Pittsburgh, PA: University of Pittsburgh Press.

Wheatley, M. J. (1992). *Leadership and the new science: Learning about organization from an orderly universe.* San Francisco: Berrett-Koehler.

Zaleznik, A. (1967). *Human dilemmas of leadership.* New York: Harper & Row.

## 14
# The Giving of Orders
## *Mary Parker Follett*

To some men the matter of giving orders seems a very simple affair; they expect to issue their own orders and have them obeyed without question. Yet, on the other hand, the shrewd common sense of many a business executive has shown him that the issuing of orders is surrounded by many difficulties; that to demand an unquestioning obedience to orders not approved, not perhaps even understood, is bad business policy. Moreover, psychology, as well as our own observation, shows us not only that you cannot get people to do things most satisfactorily by ordering them or exhorting them; but also that even reasoning with them, even convincing them intellectually, may not be enough. Even the "consent of the governed" will not do all the work it is supposed to do, an important consideration for those who are advocating employee representation. For all our past life, our early training, our later experience, all our emotions, beliefs, prejudices, every desire that we have, have formed certain habits of mind that the psychologists call habit-patterns, action-patterns, motor-sets.

Therefore it will do little good merely to get intellectual agreement; unless you change the habit-patterns of people, you have not really changed your people. . . .

If we analyse this matter a little further we shall see that we have to do three things. I am now going to use psychologi-

cal language [to]: (1) build up certain attitudes; (2) provide for the release of these attitudes; (3) augment the released response as it is being carried out. What does this mean in the language of business? A psychologist has given us the example of the salesman. The salesman first creates in you the attitude that you want his article; then, at just the "psychological" moment, he produces his contract blank which you may sign and thus release that attitude; then if, as you are preparing to sign, some one comes in and tells you how pleased he has been with his purchase of this article, that augments the response which is being released.

If we apply this to the subject of orders and obedience, we see that people can obey an order only if previous habit-patterns are appealed to or new ones created. . . .

This is an important consideration for us, for from one point of view business success depends largely on this—namely, whether our business is so organized and administered that it tends to form certain habits, certain mental attitudes. It has been hard for many old-fashioned employers to understand that *orders will not take the place of training*. I want to italicize that. Many a time an employer has been angry because, as he expressed it, a workman "wouldn't" do so and so, when the truth of the matter was that the workman couldn't, actually

*Source:* From "The Giving of Orders" by Mary Parker Follett, in *Scientific Foundations of Business Administration* (Baltimore: Williams & Wilkins Co., 1926). Copyright © 1926 The Williams and Wilkins Company. Reproduced by permission.

couldn't, do as ordered because he could not go contrary to life-long habits. This whole subject might be taken up under the heading of education, for there we could give many instances of the attempt to make arbitrary authority take the place of training. In history, the aftermath of all revolutions shows us the results of the lack of training.

. . . A boy may respond differently to the same suggestion when made by his teacher and when made by his schoolmate. Moreover, he may respond differently to the same suggestion made by the teacher in the schoolroom and made by the teacher when they are taking a walk together. Applying this to the giving of orders, we see that the place in which orders are given, the circumstances under which they are given, may make all the difference in the world as to the response which we get. Hand them down a long way from President or Works Manager and the effect is weakened. One might say that the strength of favourable response to an order is in inverse ratio to the distance the order travels. Production efficiency is always in danger of being affected whenever the long-distance order is substituted for the face-to-face suggestion. There is, however, another reason for that which I shall consider in a moment.

. . . I should say that the giving of orders and the receiving of orders ought to be a matter of integration through circular behavior, and that we should seek methods to bring this about.

Psychology has another important contribution to make on this subject of issuing orders or giving directions: before the integration can be made between order-giver and order-receiver, there is often an integration to be made within one or both of the individuals concerned. There are often two dissociated paths in the individual; if you are clever enough to recognize these, you can

sometimes forestall a Freudian conflict, make the integration appear before there is an acute stage. . . .

Business administration has often to consider how to deal with the dissociated paths in individuals or groups, but the methods of doing this successfully have been developed much further in some departments than in others. We have as yet hardly recognized this as part of the technique of dealing with employees, yet the clever salesman knows that it is the chief part of his job. The prospective buyer wants the article and does not want it. The able salesman does not suppress the arguments in the mind of the purchaser against buying, for then the purchaser might be sorry afterwards for his purchase, and that would not be good salesmanship. Unless he can unite, integrate, in the purchaser's mind, the reasons for buying and the reasons for not buying, his future sales will be imperilled, he will not be the highest grade salesman.

Please note that this goes beyond what the psychologist whom I quoted at the beginning of this section told us. He said, "the salesman must create in you the attitude that you want his article." Yes, but only if he creates this attitude by integration, not by suppression.

Apply all this to orders. An order often leaves the individual to whom it is given with two dissociated paths; an order should seek to unite, to integrate, dissociated paths. Court decisions often settle arbitrarily which of two ways is to be followed without showing a possible integration of the two, that is, the individual is often left with an internal conflict on his hands. This is what both courts and business administration should try to prevent, the internal conflicts of individuals or groups. . . .

. . . Probably more industrial trouble has been caused by the manner in which orders are given than in any other way.

In the *Report on Strikes and Lockouts*, a British government publication, the cause of a number of strikes is given as "alleged harassing conduct of the foreman," "alleged tyrannical conduct of an under-foreman," "alleged overbearing conduct of officials." The explicit statement, however, of the tyranny of superior officers as the direct cause of strikes is I should say, unusual, yet resentment smoulders and breaks out in other issues. And the demand for better treatment is often explicit enough. We find it made by the metal and woodworking trades in an aircraft factory, who declared that any treatment of men without regard to their feelings of self-respect would be answered by a stoppage of work. We find it put in certain agreements with employers that "the men must be treated with proper respect, and threats and abusive language must not be used."

What happens to man, *in* a man, when an order is given in a disagreeable manner by foreman, head of department, his immediate superior in store, bank or factory? The man addressed feels that his self-respect is attacked, that one of his most inner sanctuaries is invaded. He loses his temper or becomes sullen or is on the defensive; he begins thinking of his "rights"—a fatal attitude for any of us. In the language we have been using, the wrong behaviour pattern is aroused, the wrong motor-set; that is, he is now "set" to act in a way which is not going to benefit the enterprise in which he is engaged.

There is a more subtle psychological point here, too; the more you are "bossed" the more your activity of thought will take place within the bossing-pattern, and your part in that pattern seems usually to be opposition to the bossing.

This complaint of the abusive language and the tyrannical treatment of the one just above the worker is an old story to us all, but there is an opposite extreme which is far too little considered. The immediate superior officer is often so close to the worker that he does not exercise the proper duties of his position. Far from taking on himself an aggressive authority, he has often evaded one of the chief problems of his job: how to do what is implied in the fact that he has been put in a position over others. . . .

Now what is our problem here? How can we avoid the two extremes: too great bossism in giving orders, and practically no orders given? I am going to ask how *you* are avoiding these extremes. My solution is to depersonalize the giving of orders, to unite all concerned in a study of the situation, to discover the law of the situation and obey that. Until we do this I do not think we shall have the most successful business administration. This is what does take place, what has to take place, when there is a question between two men in positions of equal authority. The head of the sales departments does not give orders to the head of the production department, or vice versa. Each studies the market and the final decision is made as the market demands. This is, ideally, what should take place between foreman and rank and file, between any head and his subordinates. One *person* should not give orders to another *person*, but both should agree to take their orders from the situation. If orders are simply part of the situation, the question of someone giving and someone receiving does not come up. Both accept the orders given by the situation. Employers accept the orders given by the situation; employees accept the orders given by the situation. This gives, does it not, a slightly different aspect to the whole of business administration through the entire plant?

We have here, I think, one of the largest contributions of scientific management: it tends to depersonalize orders. From one point of view, one might call the essence of scientfic management the attempt to find the law of the situation. With scientific management the managers are as much under orders as the workers, for both obey the law of the situation. Our job is not how to get people to obey orders, but how to devise methods by which we can best *discover* the order integral to a particular situation. When that is found, the employee can issue it to the employer, as well as employer to employee. This often happens easily and naturally. My cook or my stenographer points out the law of the situation, and I, if I recognize it as such, accept it, even although it may reverse some "order" I have given.

If those in supervisory positions should depersonalize orders, then there would be no overbearing authority on the one hand, nor on the other that dangerous *laissez-aller* which comes from the fear of exercising authority. Of course we should exercise authority, but always the authority of the situation. I do not say that we have found the way to a frictionless existence, far from it, but we now understand the place which we mean to give to friction. . . .

I call it depersonalizing because there is not time to go any further into the matter. I think it really is a matter of *repersonalizing*. We, persons, have relations with each other, but we should find them in and through the whole situation. We cannot have any sound relations with each other as long as we take them out of that setting which gives them their meaning and value. This divorcing of persons and the situation does a great deal of harm. I have just said that scientific management depersonalizes; the deeper philosophy of scientific management show us personal relations within the whole setting of that thing of which they are a part. . . .

I said above that we should substitute for the long-distance order the face-to-face suggestion. I think we can now see a more cogent reason for this than the one then given. It is not the face-to-face suggestion that we want so much as the joint study of the problem, and such joint study can be made best by the employee and his immediate superior or employee and special expert on that question.

I began this talk by emphasizing the advisability of preparing in advance the attitude necessary for the carrying out of orders, as in the previous paper we considered preparing the attitude for integration; but we have now, in our consideration of the joint study of situations, in our emphasis on obeying the law of the situation, perhaps got a little beyond that, or rather we have now to consider in what sense we wish to take the psychologist's doctrine of prepared-in-advance attitudes. . . .

We should not try to create the attitude we *want*, although that is the usual phrase, but the attitude required for co-operative study and decision. This holds good even for the salesman. We said above that when the salesman is told that he should create in the prospective buyer the attitude that he wants the article, he ought also to be told that he should do this by integration rather than by suppression. We have now a hint of *how* he is to attain this integration.

I have spoken of the importance of changing some of the language of business personnel relations. We considered whether the words "grievances," "complaints," or Ford's "trouble specialists" did not arouse the wrong behaviour-patterns. I think "order" certainly does. If that word is not to mean any longer external authority, arbitrary authority, but the law of the situation, then we need a new word for it. It is often the order that people resent as much as the thing ordered. People do not like to be ordered even to take a holiday. I have often seen instances of this. The wish to govern one's own life is, of course, one of the most fundamental feelings in every human being. To call this "the instinct of self-assertion," "the instinct of initiative," does not express it wholly. . . .

We have here something far more profound than "the egoistic impulse" or "the instinct of self-assertion." We have the very essence of the human being.

This subject of orders has led us into the heart of the whole question of authority and consent. When we conceive of authority and consent as parts of an inclusive situation, does that not throw a flood of light on this question? The point of view here presented gets rid of several dilemmas which have seemed to puzzle people in dealing with consent. The feeling of being "under" someone, of "subordination," of "servility," of being "at the will of another," comes out again and again in the shop stewards movement and in the testimony before the Coal Commission. One man said before the Coal Commission, "It is all right to work *with* anyone; what is disagreeable is to feel too distinctly that you are working *under* anyone." *With* is a pretty good preposition, not because it connotes democracy, but because it connotes functional unity, a much more profound conception than that of democracy as usually held. The study of the situation involves the *with* preposition. . . .

Twice I have had a servant applying for a place ask me if she would be treated as a menial. When the first woman asked me that, I had no idea what she meant, I thought perhaps she did not want to do the roughest work, but later I came to the conclusion that to be treated as a menial meant to be obliged to be under someone, to follow orders without using one's own judgment. If we believe that

what heightens self-respect increases efficiency, we shall be on our guard here.

Very closely connected with this is the matter of pride in one's work. If an order goes against what the craftsman or the clerk thinks is the way of doing his work which will bring the best results, he is justified in not wishing to obey that order. Could not that difficulty be met by a joint study of the situation? It is said that it is characteristic of the British workman to feel, "I know my job and won't be told how." The peculiarities of the British workman might be met by a joint study of the situation, it being understood that he probably has more to contribute to that study than anyone else. . . .

There is another dilemma which has to be met by everyone who is in what is called a position of authority: how can you expect people merely to obey orders and at the same time to take that degree of responsibility which they should take? Indeed, in my experience, the people who enjoy following orders blindly, without any thought on their own part, are those who like thus to get rid of responsibility. But the taking of responsibility, each according to his capacity, each according to his function in the whole . . ., this taking of responsibility is usually the most vital matter in the life of every human being, just as the allotting of responsibility is the most important part of business administration.

A young trade unionist said to me, "How much dignity can I have as a mere employee?" He can have all the dignity in the world if he is allowed to make his fullest contribution to the plant *and to assume definitely the responsibility therefor*.

I think one of the gravest problems before us is how to make the reconciliation between receiving orders and taking responsibility. And I think the reconciliation can be made through our conception of the law of the situation. . . .

We have considered the subject of symbols. It is often very apparent that an order is a symbol. The referee in the game stands watch in hand, and says "Go." It is an order, but order only as symbol. I may say to an employee, "Do so and so," but I should say it only because we have both agreed, openly or tacitly, that that which I am ordering done is the best thing to be done. The order is then a symbol. And if it is a philosophical and psychological truth that we owe obedience only to a functional unity to which we are contributing, we should remember that a more accurate way of stating that would be to say that our obligation is to a unifying, to a process.

This brings us now to one of our most serious problems in this matter of orders. It is important, but we can touch on it only briefly; it is what we spoke of . . . as the evolving situation. I am trying to show here that the order must be integral to the situation and must be recognized as such. But we saw that the situation was always developing. If the situation is never stationary, then the order should never be stationary, so to speak; how to prevent it from being so is our problem. The situation is changing while orders are being carried out, because, by and through orders being carried out. How is the order to keep up with the situation? External orders never can, only those drawn fresh from the situation.

Moreover, it taking a *responsible* attitude toward experience involves recognizing the evolving situation, a *conscious* attitude toward experience means that we note the change which the developing situation makes in ourselves; the situation does not change without changing us. . . .

. . . When I asked a very intelligent girl what she thought would be the result of profit sharing and employee representation in the factory where she worked,

she replied joyfully, "We shan't need foremen any more." While her entire ignoring of the fact that the foreman has other duties than keeping workers on their jobs was amusing, one wants to go beyond one's amusement and find out what this objection to being watched really means. . . .

I have seen similar instances cited. Many workmen feel that being watched is unbearable. What can we do about it? How can we get proper supervision without this watching which a worker resents? Supervision is necessary; supervision is resented—how are we going to make the integration there? Some say "Let the workers elect the supervisors." I do not believe in that.

There are . . . other points closely connected with the subject of this paper which I should like merely to point out. First, when and how do you point out mistakes, misconduct? One principle can surely guide us here: don't blame for the sake of blaming, make what you have to say accomplish something; say it in that form, at that time, under those circumstances, which will make it a real education to your subordinate. Secondly, since it is recognized that the one who gives the orders is not as a rule a very popular person, the management sometimes tries to offset this by allowing the person who has this onus upon him to give any pleasant news to the workers, to have the credit of any innovation which the workers very much desire. One manager told me that he always tried to do this. I suppose that this is good behaviouristic psychology, and yet I am not sure that it is a method I wholly like. It is quite different, however, in the case of a mistaken order having been given; then I think the one who made the mistake should certainly be the one to rectify it, not as a matter of strategy, but because it is better for him too. . . .

# 15
# The Executive Functions
## Chester I. Barnard

The coördination of efforts essential to a system of coöperation requires, as we have seen, an organization system of communication. Such a system of communication implies centers or points of interconnection and can only operate as these centers are occupied by persons who are called executives. It might be said, then, that the function of executives is to serve as channels of communication so far as communications must pass through central positions. But since the object of the communication system is coördination of all aspect of organization, it follows that the functions of executives relate to all the work essential to the vitality and endurance of an organization, so far, at least, as it must be accomplished through formal coördination.

The executive functions serve to maintain a system of cooperative effort. They are impersonal. The functions are not, as so frequently stated, to manage a group of persons. I do not think a correct understanding of executive work can be had if this narrower, convenient, but strictly speaking erroneous, conception obtains. It is not even quite correct to say that the executive functions are to manage the system of coöperative efforts. As a whole it is managed by itself, not by the executive organization, which is a part of it. The functions with which we are concerned are like those of the nervous system, including the brain, in

relation to the rest of the body. It exists to maintain the bodily system by directing those actions which are necessary more effectively to adjust to the environment, but it can hardly be said to manage the body, a large part of whose functions are independent of it and upon which it in turn depends.

The essential executive functions, as I shall present them, correspond to the elements of organization. . . .

They are, first, to provide the system of communication; second, to promote the securing of essential efforts; and, third, to formulate and define purpose. Since the elements of organization are interrelated and interdependent, the executive functions are so likewise; nevertheless they are subject to considerable specialization and as functions are to a substantial degree separable in practice. We shall deal with them only as found in complex, though not necessarily large, organizations.

## I. THE MAINTENANCE OF ORGANIZATION COMMUNICATION

We have noticed in previous chapters that, when a complex of more than one unit is in question, centers of communication and corresponding executives are necessary. The need of a definite system of communication creates the first task of the organizer and is the immediate

Source: Reprinted by permission of the publishers from *The Functions of the Executive* by Chester I. Barnard, Cambridge, Massachusetts: Harvard University Press, Copyright © 1938, 1968 by the President and Fellows of Harvard College; © 1966 by Grace F. Noera Barnard.

origin of executive organization. If the purpose of an organization is conceived initially in the mind of one person, he is likely very early to find necessary the selection of lieutenants; and if the organization is spontaneous its very first task is likely to be the selection of a leader. Since communication will be accomplished only through the agency of persons, the selection of persons for executive functions is the concrete method of establishing the *means* of communication, though it must be immediately followed by the creation of positions, that is, a *system* of communication; and, especially in established organizations, the positions will exist to be filled in the event of vacancies. . . .

Therefore, the problem of the establishment and maintenance of the system of communication, that is, the primary task of the executive organization, is perpetually that of obtaining the coalescence of the two phases, executive personnel and executive positions. Each phase in turn is the strategic factor of the executive problem—first one, then the other phase, must be adjusted. This is the central problem of the executive functions. Its solution is not in itself sufficient to accomplish the work of all these functions; but no others can be accomplished without it, and none well unless it is well done. . . .

## 1. The Scheme of Organization

Let us call the first phase of the function—the definition of organization positions—the "scheme of organization." This is the aspect of organization which receives relatively excessive formal attention because it can apparently be reduced to organization charts, specifications of duties, and descriptions of divisions of labor, etc. It rests upon or represents a coördination chiefly of the work to be done by the organization, that is, its purposes broken up into subsidiary purposes, specializations, tasks, etc., which will be discussed in [the third section] of this chapter; the kind and quantity of *services* of personnel that can be obtained; the kind and quantity of *persons* that must be included in the coöperative system for this purpose; the inducements that are required; and the places at which and the times when these factors can be combined, which will not be specifically discussed here.

It is evident that these are mutually dependent factors, and that they all involve other executive functions which we shall discuss later. So far as the *scheme* of organization is separately attacked, it is always on the assumption that it is then the strategic factor, the other factors of organization remaining fixed for the time being; but since the underlying purpose of any change in a scheme of organization is to affect these other factors as a whole favorably, any scheme of organization at any given time represents necessarily a result of previous successive approximations through a period of time. It has always necessarily to be attacked on the basis of the present situation.

## 2. Personnel

The scheme of organization is dependent not only upon the general factors of the organizations as a whole, but likewise, as we have indicated, on the availability of various kinds of services for the executive positions. This becomes in its turn the strategic factor. In general, the principles of the economy of incentives apply here as well as to other more general personnel problems. The balance of factors and the technical problems of this special class, however, are not only different from those generally to be found in other spheres of organization economy but are highly special in different types of organizations.

The most important single contribution required of the executive, certainly the most universal qualification, is loyalty, domination by the organization personality. This is the first necessity because the lines of communication cannot function at all unless the personal contributions of executives will be present at the required positions, at the times necessary, without default or ordinary personal reasons. This, as a personal qualification, is known in secular organizations as the quality of "responsibility"; in political organizations as "regularity"; in governmental organizations as fealty or loyalty; in religious organizations as "complete submission" to the faith and to the hierarchy of objective religious authority.

The contribution of personal loyalty and submission is least susceptible to tangible inducements. It cannot be bought either by material inducements or by other positive incentives, except all other things be equal. This is as true of industrial organizations, I believe, as of any others. It is rather generally understood that although money or other material inducements must usually be paid to responsible persons, responsibility itself does not arise from such inducements.

However, love of prestige is, in general, a much more important inducement in the case of executives than with the rest of the personnel. Interest in work and pride in organization are other incentives that usually must be present. These facts are much obscured as respects commerical organizations, where material inducements appear to be the effective factors partly because such inducements are more readily offered in such organizations and partly because, since the other incentives are often equal as between such organizations, material inducements are the only available differential factor. It also becomes an important secondary factor to individuals in many cases, because prestige and official responsibilities impose heavy material burdens on them. Hence neither churches nor socialistic states have been able to escape the necessity of direct or indirect material inducements for high dignitaries or officials. But this is probably incidental and superficial in all organizations. It appears to be true that in all of them adequate incentives to executive services are difficult to offer. Those most available in the present age are tangible, materialistic; but on the whole they are both insufficient and often abortive.[1]

Following loyalty, responsibility, and capacity to be dominated by organization personality, come the more specific personal abilities. They are roughly divided into two classes: relatively general abilities, involving general alertness, comprehensiveness of interest, flexibility, faculty of adjustment, poise, courage, etc; and specialized abilities based on particular aptitudes and acquired techniques. The first kind is relatively difficult to appraise because it depends upon innate characteristics developed through general experience. It is not greatly susceptible of immediate inculcation. The second kind may be less rare because the division of labor, that is,

---

[1] After much experience, I am convinced that the most ineffective services in a continuing effort are in one sense those of volunteers, or of semi-volunteers; for example, half-pay workers. What appears to be inexpensive is in fact very expensive, because non-material incentives— such as prestige, toleration of too great personal interest in the work with its accompanying fads and "pet" projects, the yielding to exaggerated conceptions of individual importance—are causes of internal friction and many other undesirable consequences. Yet in many emergency situations, and in a large part of political, charitable, civic, educational, and religious organization work, often indispensable services cannot be obtained by material incentives.

organization itself, fosters it automatically, and because it is susceptible to development (at a cost) by training and education. We deliberately and more and more turn out specialists; but we do not develop general executives well by specific efforts, and we know very little about how to do it.

The higher the positions in the line of authority, the more general the abilities required. The scarcity of such abilities, together with the necessity for keeping the lines of authority as short as feasible, controls the organization of executive work. It leads to the reduction of the number of formally executive positions to the minimum, a measure made possible by creating about the executives in many cases staffs of specialists who supplement them in time, energy, and technical capacities. This is made feasible by elaborate and often delicate arrangements to correct errors resulting from the faults of over-specialization and the paucity of line executives. . . .

Thus, jointly with the development of the scheme of organization, the selection, promotion, demotion, and dismissal of men becomes the essence of maintaining the system of communication without which no organization can exist. The selection in part, but especially the promotion, demotion, and dismissal of men, depend upon the exercise of supervision or what is often called "control."

Control relates directly, and in conscious application chiefly, to the work of the organization as a whole rather than to the work of executives as such. But so heavily dependent is the success of coöperation upon the functioning of the executive organization that practically the control is over executives for the most part. If the work of an organization is not successful, if it is inefficient, if it cannot maintain the services of its personnel, the conclusion is that its

"management" is wrong; that is, that the scheme of communication or the associated personnel or both, that is, the executive department directly related, are at fault. This is, sometimes at least, not true, but often it is. Moreover, for the correction of such faults the first reliance is upon executive organization. The methods by which control is exercised are, of course, numerous and largely technical to each organization, and need not be further discussed here.

## 3. Informal Executive Organizations

The general method of maintaining an informal executive organization is so to operate and to select and promote executives that a general condition of compatibility of personnel is maintained. Perhaps often and certainly occasionally men connot be promoted or selected, or even must be relieved, because they cannot function, because they "do not fit," where there is no question of formal competence. This question of "fitness" involves such matters as education, experience, age, sex, personal distinctions, prestige, race, nationality, faith, politics, sectional antecedents; and such very special personal traits as manners, speech, personal appearance, etc. It goes by few if any rules, except those based at least nominally on other, formal, considerations. It respresents in its best sense the political aspects of personal relationship in formal organization. I suspect it to be most highly developed in political, labor, church, and university organizations, for the very reason that the intangible types of personal services are relatively more important in them than in most other, especially industrial, organizations. But it is certainly of major importance in all organizations.

This compatibility is promoted by educational requirements (armies, navies, churches, schools); by requirement of certain background (European armies, navies, labor unions, Soviet and Fascist governments, political parties); by conferences and conventions; by specifically social activities; by class distinctions connected with privileges and "authority" (in armies, navies, churches, universities). A certain conformity is required by unwritten understanding that can sometimes be formally enforced, expressed for its negative aspect by the phrase "conduct unbecoming a gentleman and an officer." There are, however, innumerable other processes, many of which are not consciously employed for this purpose.

It must not be understood that the desired degree of compatibility is always the same or is the maximum possible. On the contrary it seems to me to be often the case that excessive compatibility or harmony is deleterious, resulting in "single track minds" and excessively crystallized attitudes and in the destruction of personal responsibility; but I know from experience in operating with new emergency organizations, in which there was no time and little immediate basis for the growth of an informal organization properly coördinated with formal organization that it is almost impossible to secure effective and efficient coöperation without it.

The functions of informal executive organizations are the communication of intangible facts, opinions, suggestions, suspicions, that cannot pass through formal channels without raising issues calling for decisions, without dissipating dignity and objective authority, and without overloading executive positions; also to minimize excessive cliques of political types arising from too great divergence of interests and views; to promote self-discipline of the group; and to make possible the development of important personal influences in the organization. There are probably other functions.

I shall comment on only two functions of informal executive organization. The necessity for avoiding formal issues, that is, for avoiding the issuance of numerous formal orders except on routine matters and except in emergencies, is important.[2] I know of major executives who issue an order or judgement settling an important issue rather seldom, although they are functioning all the time. The obvious desire of politicians to avoid important issues (and to impose them on their opponents) is based upon a thorough sense of organization. Neither authority nor coöperative disposition (largely the same things) will stand much overt division on formal issues in the present stage of human development. Hence most laws, executive orders, decisions, etc., are in effect formal notice that all is well—there is agreement, authority is not questioned.

The question of personal influence is very subtle. Probably most good organizations have somewhere a Colonel House; and many men not only exercise beneficent influence far beyond that implied by their formal status, but most of them, at the time, would lose their influence if they had corresponding formal status. The reason may be that many men have personal qualifications of high order that will not operate under the stress of commensurate official responsibility. By analogy I may mention the golfers of first class skill who cannot "stand up" in public tournaments. . . .

[2] When writing these lines I tried to recall an important general decision made by me on my initiative as a telephone executive within two years. I could recall none, although on reviewing the record I found several. On the other hand, I can still recall without any record many major decisions made by me "out of hand" when I was a Relief Administrator. I probably averaged at least five a day for eighteen months. In the latter case I worked with a very noble group but a very poor informal organization under emergency conditions.

## II. THE SECURING OF ESSENTIAL SERVICES FROM INDIVIDUALS

The second function of the executive organization is to promote the securing of the personal services that constitute the material of organizations.

The work divides into two main divisions: (I) the bringing of persons into coöperative relationship with the organization; (II) the eliciting of the services after such persons have been brought into that relationship.

### 1.

The characteristic fact of the first division is that the organization is acting upon persons who are in every sense outside it. Such action is necessary not merely to secure the personnel of new organizations, or to supply the material for the growth of existing organizations, but also to replace the losses that continually take place by reason of death, resignation, "backsliding," emigration, discharge, excommunication, ostracism. These factors of growth or replacement of contributors require bringing persons by organization effort within range of the consideration of the incentives available in order to induce some of these persons to attach themselves to the organization. Accordingly the task involves two parts: (*a*) bringing persons within reach of specific effort to secure services, and (*b*) the application of that effort when they have been brought near enough. Often both parts of the task occupy the efforts of the same persons or parts of an organization; but they are clearly distinct elements and considerable specialization is found with respect to them.

(*a*) Bringing persons within reach of recruiting or proselyting influence is a task which differs in practical emphasis among organizations in respect both to scope and to method. Some religious organizations—especially the Catholic Church, several Protestant Churches, the Mormon Church, for example—have as ideal goals the attachment of all persons to their organizations, and the wide world is the field of proselyting propaganda. During many decades the United States of America invited all who could reach its shores to become American citizens. Other organizations, having limits on the volume of their activities, restrict the field of propaganda. Thus many nations in effect now restrict substantial growth to those who acquire a national status by birth; the American Legion restricts its membership to those who have acquired a status by certain type of previous service, etc. Others restrict their fields practically on the basis of proportions. Thus universities "in principle" are open to all or to all with educational and character qualifications but may restrict their appeals to geographical, racial, and class proportions so as to preserve the cosmopolitan character of their bodies, or to preserve predominance of nationals, etc. Industrial and commercial organizations are theoretically limited usually by considerations of social compatibility and additionally by the costs of propaganda. They usually attempt no appeal when the geographic remoteness makes it ineffective. . . .

(*b*) The effort to induce specific persons who by the general appeal are brought into contact with an organization actually to become identified with it constitutes the more regular and routine work of securing contributors. This involves in its general aspects the method of persuasion which has already been described, the establishment of inducements and incentives, and direct negotiation. The methods required are indefinitely large in number and of very wide variety. . . .[3]

## 2.

Although the work of recruiting is important in most organizations, and especially so in those which are new or rapidly expanding or which have high "turnover," nevertheless in established and enduring organizations the eliciting of the quantity and quality of efforts from their adherents is usually more important and occupies the greater part of personnel effort. Because of the more tangible character of "membership," being an "employee," etc., recruiting is apt to receive more attention as a field of personnel work than the business of promoting the actual output of efforts and influences, which are the real material of organization.[4] Membership, nominal adherence, is merely the starting point; and the minimum contributions which can be conceived as enabling retention of such connection would generally be insufficient for the survival of active or productive organization. . . . In short, every organization to survive must deliberately attend to the maintenance and growth of its authority to do the things necessary for coördination, effectiveness, and efficiency. This, as we have seen, depends upon its appeal to persons who are already related to the organization. . . .

[3] I must repeat that although the emphasis is on the employee group of contributors, so far as industrial organizations are concerned, nevertheless "customers" are equally included. The principles broadly discussed here relate to salesmanship as well as employing persons.

[4] As an instance, note the great attention in civil service regulations, and also in political appointments, to obtaining and retaining employment, and the relatively small attention to services.

## III. THE FORMULATION OF PURPOSE AND OBJECTIVES

The third executive function is to formulate and define the purposes, objectives, ends, of the organization. It has already been made clear that, strictly speaking, purpose is defined more nearly by the aggregate of action taken than by any formulation in words; but that the aggregate of action is a residuum of the decisions relative to purpose and the environment, resulting in closer and closer approximations to the concrete acts. It has also been emphasized that purpose is something that must be accepted by all the contributors to the system of efforts. Again, it has been stated that purpose must be broken into fragments, specific objectives, not only ordered in time so that detailed purpose and detailed action follow in the series of progressive coöperation, but also ordered contemporaneously into the specializations—geographical, social, and functional—that each unit organization implies. It is more apparent here than with other executive functions that it is an entire executive organization that formulates, redefines, breaks into details, and decides on the innumerable simultaneous and progressive actions that are the stream of syntheses constituting purpose or action. No single executive can under any conditions accomplish this function alone, but only that part of it which relates to his position in the executive organization.

Hence the critical aspect of this function is the assignment of responsibility—the delegation of objective authority. Thus in one sense this function is that of the scheme of positions, the system of communication, already discussed. That is its potential aspect. Its other aspect is the actual decisions and conduct which make the scheme a working system. Accordingly, the general executive states that "this is the purpose, this the objective, this the direction, in general terms, in which we wish to move, before next year." His department heads, or the heads of his main territorial divisions, say to their departments or suborganizations: "This means for us these things now, then others next month, then others later, to be better defined after experience." Their subdepartment or division heads say: "This means for us such and such operations now at these places, such others at those places, something today here, others tomorrow there." Then district or bureau chiefs in turn become more and more specific, their sub-chiefs still more so. . . .

The formulation and definition of purpose is then a widely distributed function only the more general part of which is executive. In this fact lies the most important inherent difficulty in the operation of coöperative systems—the necessity for indoctrinating those at the lower levels with general purposes, the major decisions, so that they remain cohesive and able to make the ultimate detailed decisions coherent; and the necessity, for those at the higher levels, of constantly understanding the concrete conditions and the specific decisions of the "ulti-

mate" contributors from which and from whom executives are often insulated. Without that up-and-down-the-line coördination of purposeful decisions, general decisions and general purposes are mere intellectual processes in an organization vacuum, insulated from realities by layers of misunderstanding. The function of formulating grand purposes and providing for their redefinition is one which needs sensitive systems of communication, experience in interpretation, imagination, and delegation of responsibility.

Perhaps there are none who could consider even so extremely condensed and general a description of the excutive functions as has here been presented without perceiving that these functions are merely elements in an organic whole. It is their combination in a working system that makes an organization.

This combination involves two opposite incitements to action. First, the concrete interaction and mutual adjustment of the executive functions are partly to be determined by the factors of the environment of the organization—the specific coöperative system as a whole and its environment. This involves fundamentally the logical processes of analysis and the discrimination of the strategic factors. . . .

## 16
# Life Cycle Theory of Leadership
*Paul Hersey & Kenneth H. Blanchard*

The recognition of task and relationships as two important dimensions of leader behavior has pervaded the works of management theorists[1] over the years. These two dimensions have been variously labeled as "autocratic" and "democratic"; "authoritarian" and "equalitarian"; "employee-oriented" and "production-oriented"; "goal achievement" and "group maintenance"; "task-ability" and "likeability"; "instrumental" and "expressive"; "efficiency" and "effectiveness." The difference between these concepts and task and relationships seems to be more semantic than real. . . .

## OHIO STATE LEADERSHIP STUDIES

In more recent years, the feeling that task and relationships were either/or leadership styles has been dispelled. In particular, the leadership studies initiated in 1945 by the Bureau of Business Research at Ohio State University[2] questioned whether leader behavior could be depicted on a single continuum.

In attempting to describe *how* a leader carries out his activities, the Ohio State staff identified "Initiating Structure" (task) and "Consideration" (relationships) as the two most important dimensions of leadership. "Initiating Structure" refers to "the leader's behavior in delineating the relationship between himself and members of the work-group

and in endeavoring to establish well-defined patterns of organization, channels of communication, and methods of procedure." On the other hand, "Consideration" refers to "behavior indicative of friendship, mutual trust, respect, and warmth in the relationship between the leader and the members of his staff."[3]

In the leadership studies that followed the Ohio State staff found that leadership styles vary considerably from leader to leader. The behavior of some leaders is characterized by rigidly structuring activities of followers in terms of *task* accomplishments, while others concentrate on building and maintaining good personal *relationships* between themselves and their followers. Other leaders have styles characterized by both task and relationships behavior. There are even some individuals in leadership positions whose behavior tends to provide little structure or development of interpersonal relationships. No dominant style appears. Instead, various combinations are evident. Thus, task and relationships are not either/or leadership styles as an authoritarian-democratic continuum suggests. Instead, these patterns of leader behavior are separate and distinct dimensions which can be plotted on two separate axes, rather than a single continuum. Thus, the Ohio State studies resulted in the development of four quadrants to illustrate leadership styles in terms of Initiating Structure

*Source:* This article is reprinted as originally presented in the May 1969 issue of *Training and Development Journal.* The model has been updated several times since 1969. The current information is available from The Center for Leadership Studies, Inc., Escondido, California.

(task) and Consideration (relationships) as shown in Figure. 1.

## THE MANAGERIAL GRID

Robert R. Blake and Jane S. Mouton[4] in their Managerial Grid have popularized the task and relationships dimensions of leadership and have used them extensively in organization and management development programs.

In the Managerial Grid [Figure 2], five different types of leadership based on concern for production (task) and concern for people (relationships) are located in the four quadrants identified by the Ohio State studies.

Concern for *production* is illustrated on the horizontal axis. Production becomes more important to the leader as his rating advances on the horizontal scale. A leader with a rating of 9 has a maximum concern for production.

Concern for people is illustrated on the vertical axis. People become more important to the leader as his rating progresses up the vertical axis. A leader with a rating of 9 on the vertical axis has a maximum concern for people.

The Managerial Grid, in essence, has given popular terminology to five points within the four quadrants identified by the Ohio State studies.

## SUGGESTING A "BEST" STYLE OF LEADERSHIP

After identifying task and relationships as two central dimensions of any leadership situation, some management writers have suggested a "best" style of leadership. Most of these writers have supported either an integrated leader behavior style (high task and high relationships) or a permissive, democratic, human relations approach (high relationships).

Andrew W. Halpin,[5] of the original Ohio State staff, in a study of school superintendents, pointed out that according to his findings "effective or desirable leadership behavior is characterized by high ratings on both Initiating Structure and Consideration. Conversely, ineffective or undesirable leadership behavior is marked by low ratings on both dimensions." Thus, Halpin seemed to conclude that the high Consideration

## FIGURE 1 • THE OHIO STATE LEADERSHIP QUADRANTS

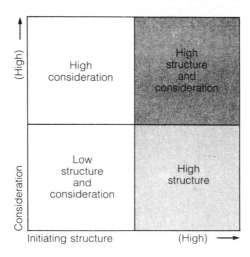

## FIGURE 2 · THE MANAGERIAL GRID LEADERSHIP STYLES

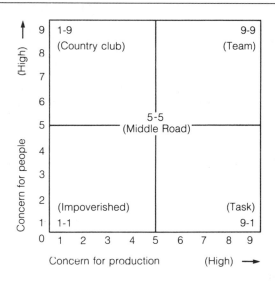

and high Initiating Structure style is theoretically the ideal or "best" leader behavior, while the style low on both dimensions is theoretically the "worst."

Blake and Mouton in their Managerial Grid also imply that the most desirable leadership style is "team management" (maximum concern for production and people) and the least desirable is "impoverished management" (minimum concern for production and people). In fact, they have developed training programs designed to change the behavior of managers toward this "team" style.[6]

## LEADERSHIP STYLE SHOULD VARY WITH THE SITUATION

Some of the most convincing evidence which dispels the idea of a single "best" style of leader behavior was gathered and published by A. K. Korman[7] in 1966. Korman attempted to review all the studies which examined the relationship between the Ohio State behavior dimensions of Initiating Structure (task)

and Consideration (relationships) and various measures of effectiveness, including group productivity, salary, performance under stress, administrative reputation, work group grievances, absenteeism, and turnover. . . .

Thus, Korman found the use of Consideration and Initiating Structure had no significant predictive value in terms of effectiveness as situations changed. *This suggests that since situations differ, so must leader style.*

Fred E. Fiedler,[8] in testing his contingency model of leadership in over fifty studies covering a span of fifteen years (1951–1967), concluded that both directive, task-oriented leaders and non-directive, human relations-oriented leaders are successful under some conditions. . . .

In summary, empirical studies tend to show that there is no normative (best) style of leadership; that successful leaders are those who can adapt their leader behavior to meet the needs of their followers and the particular situation. Effectiveness is dependent upon the leader, the followers, and other situational elements. In managing for effectiveness a leader must be able to diagnose his own leader behavior in light of his environment. Some of the variables other than his followers which he should examine include the organization, superiors, associates, and job demands. This list is not all inclusive, but contains interacting components which used to be important to a leader in many different organizational settings.

## ADDING AN EFFECTIVENESS DIMENSION

To measure more accurately how well a leader operates within a given situation, an "effectiveness dimension" should be added to the two-dimension Ohio State model. This is illustrated in Figure 3.

By adding an effectiveness dimension to the Ohio State model, a three-dimensional model is created.[9] This Leader Effectiveness Model attempts to integrate the concepts of leader style with situational demands of a specific environment. When the leader's style

is appropriate in a given environment measured by results, it is termed *effective*; when his style is inappropriate to a given environment, it is termed *ineffective*.

If a leader's effectiveness is determined by the interaction of his style and environment (followers and other situational variables), it follows that any of the four styles depicted in the Ohio State model may be effective or ineffective depending on the environment. . . .

While a high task style might be effective for a combat officer, it might not be effective in other situations even within the military. This was pointed out when the officers trained at West Point were sent to command outposts in the Dew Line, which was part of an advanced warning system. The scientific personnel involved, living in close quarters in an Arctic region, did not respond favorably to the task-oriented behavior of these combat trained officers. The level of education and maturity of these people was such that they did not need a great deal of structure in their work. In fact, they tended to resent it.

Other studies of scientific and research-oriented personnel show also

FIGURE 3 • ADDING AN EFFECTIVENESS DIMENSION

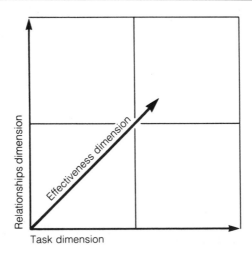

that many of these people desire, or need, only a limited amount of socio-emotional support. Therefore, there are situations in which the low task and relationships style, which has been assumed by some authors to be theoretically a poor leadership style, may be an appropriate style.

In summary, an effective leader must be able to *diagnose* the demands of the environment and then either *adapt* his leader style to fit these demands, or develop the means to *change* some or all of the other variables.

## ATTITUDINAL VS. BEHAVIORAL MODELS

In examining the dimensions of the Managerial Grid (*concern* for production and *concern* for people), one can see that these are attitudinal dimensions. That is, concern is a feeling or emotion toward something. On the other hand, the dimensions of the Ohio State Model (Initiating Structure and Consideration) and the Leader Effectiveness Model (task and relationships) are dimensions of *observed* behavior. Thus, the Ohio State and Leader Effectiveness Models measure *how* people behave, while the Managerial Grid measures *predisposition* toward production and people. As discussed earlier, the Leader Effectiveness Model is an outgrowth of the Ohio State Model but is distinct from it in that it adds an effectiveness dimension to the two dimensions of behavior.

Although the Managerial Grid and the Leader Effectiveness Model measure different aspects of leadership, they are not incompatible. A conflict develops, however, because behavioral assumptions have often been drawn from analysis of the attitudinal dimensions of the Managerial Grid.[10] While high *concern* for both production and people is desirable in many organizations, managers

having a high concern for both people and production do not always find it appropriate in all situations to initiate a high degree of structure and provide a high degree of socio-emotional support. . . .

. . . Korman suggests the possibility of a curvilinear relationship rather than a simple linear relationship between Structure and Consideration and other variables. The Life Cycle Theory of Leadership which we have developed is based on a curvilinear relationship between task and relationships and "maturity." This theory will attempt to provide a leader with some understanding of the relationship between an effective style of leadership and the level of maturity of one's followers. The emphasis in the Life Cycle Theory of Leadership will be on the followers. As Fillmore H. Sanford has indicated, there is some justification for regarding the followers, "as the most crucial factor in any leadership event."[11] Followers in any situation are vital, not only because individually they accept or reject the leader, but as a group they actually determine whatever personal power he may have.

According to Life Cycle Theory, as the level of maturity of one's followers continues to increase, appropriate leader behavior not only requires less and less structure (task) but also less and less socio-emotional support (relationships). This cycle can be illustrated in the four quadrants of the basic styles portion of the Leader Effectiveness Model as shown in Figure 4.

Maturity is defined in Life Cycle Theory by the relative independence,[12] ability to take responsibility, and achievement-motivation[13] of an individual or group. These components of maturity are often influenced by level of education and amount of experience. While age is a factor, it is not directly related

### FIGURE 4 · LIFE CYCLE THEORY OF LEADERSHIP

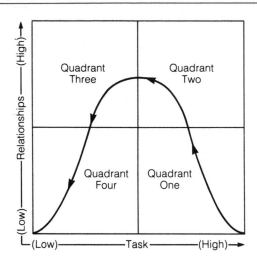

to maturity as used in the Life Cycle. Our concern is for psychological age, not chronological age. Beginning with structured task behavior which is appropriate for working and immature people, Life Cycle Theory suggests that leader behavior should move from: (1) high task–low relationships behavior to (2) high task–high relationships and (3) high relationships–low task behavior to (4) low task–low relationships behavior, if one's followers progress from immmaturity to maturity.

An illustration of this Life Cycle Theory familiar to everyone is the parent-child relationship. As a child begins to mature, it is appropriate for the parent to provide more socio-emotional support and less structure. Experience shows us that if the parent provides too much relationships before a child is somewhat mature, this behavior is often misinterpreted by the child as permissiveness. Thus it is appropriate to increase one's relationships behavior as the child is able to increase his maturity or capacity to take responsibility. . . .

## OTHER ASPECTS OF THE LIFE CYCLE

The parent-child relationship is only one example of the Life Cycle. This cycle is also discernible in other organizations in the interaction between superiors and subordinates. An interesting example is found in Research and Development work. In working with highly trained and educated Research and Development personnel, the most effective leader behavior style might be low task–low relationships. However, during the early stages of a particular project, the director must impose a certain amount of structure as the requirements and limitations of the project are established. Once these limitations are understood, the R & D director moves rapidly through the *"project cycle"* back to the mature low task-low relationships style.

We realize that most groups in our society do not reach the backward bending aspect of the cycle. But there is some evidence that as the level of education and experience of a group increases, appropriate movement in this direction will take place. However, the demands of the job may often be a limiting factor on the development of maturity in workers. For example, an assembly line operation in an automobile plant is so highly structured that it offers little opportunity for the maturing process to occur. With such monotonous tasks, workers are given minimal control over their environment and are often encouraged to be passive, dependent, and subordinate.

## LIFE CYCLE AND SPAN OF CONTROL

For years it has been argued by many management writers that one man can *supervise* only a relatively few people; therefore, all managers should have a limited span of control. . . .

. . .Yet the Life Cycle Theory of Leadership suggests that span of control may not depend on the level of the management hierarchy but should be a function of the maturity of the individuals being supervised. The more independent, able to take responsibility, and achievement-motivated one's subordinates are, the more people a manager can supervise. It is theoretically possible to supervise an infinite number of subordinates if everyone is completely mature and able to be responsible for his own job. This does not mean there is less control, but these subordinates are self-controlled rather than externally controlled by their superior. Since people occupying higher level jobs in an organization tend to be more "mature" and therefore need less close supervision than people occupying lower level jobs, it seems reasonble to assume that top managers should be able to supervise more subordinates than their counterparts at lower levels.[14]

## CONCLUSIONS

Rensis Likert[15] found in his research that supervisors with the best records of per-formance were employee-centered (high relationships), while job-centered (high task) supervisors were found more often to have low-producing sections. While this relationship seemed to exist, Likert raised the question of which variable was the causal factor. Is the style of the supervisor causing the level of production or is the level of production encouraging the style of the managers? As Likert suggests, it may very well be that high-producing sections allow for general supervision rather than close supervision and relationship behavior rather than task behavior. The supervisor soon learns that his subordinates are mature enough to structure their own environment, thus leaving him time for other kinds of activities. At the same time a low-producing section may leave the supervisor with no choice but to be job-centered. If he attempted to use a relationships style this may be misunderstood and interpreted as reinforcement for their low level of performance. The point is, the supervisor must change appropriately.

## CHANGING STYLE

The problem with the conclusions of Likert and other behavioral scientists comes in implementation. Practitioners read that employee-centered supervisors tend to have higher-producing sections than job-centered supervisors. Wanting to implement these findings overnight, they encourage all supervisors to become more employee-oriented. Consequently, a foreman who has been operating as a task-oriented authoritarian leader for many years may be encouraged to change his style—"get in step with the times." Upon returning from a "human relations" training program, the foreman will probably try to utilize some of the new relationships techniques he has recently been taught. The problem is that his personality is not compatible with the new concepts, but he tries to use them anyway. As long as things are running smoothly, there is no difficulty. However, the minute an important issue or crisis develops he tends to revert to his old basic style and becomes inconsistent, vacillating between the new relationships style he has been taught, and his old task style which has the force of habit behind it.

This idea was supported in a study conducted by the General Electric Company at one of its turbine and generator plants. In this study, the leadership styles of about 90 foremen were analyzed and rated as "democratic," "authoritarian" or "mixed." In discussing the findings, Saul W. Gellerman[16] reported that:

> The lowest morale in the plant was found among those men whose foremen were rated *between* the democratic and authoritarian extremes. The GE research team felt that these foremen might have varied inconsistently in their tactics, permissive at one moment and hard-fisted the next, in a way that left their men frustrated and unable to anticipate how they would be treated. The naturally autocratic supervisor who is exposed to human relations training may behave in exactly such a manner . . . . a pattern which will probably make him even harder to work for than he was before being "enlightened."

Thus, changing the style of managers is a difficult process, and one that takes considerable time to accomplish. Expecting miracles overnight will only lead to frustration and uneasiness for both managers and their subordinates. Yet industry invests many millions of dollars annually for training and development programs which concentrate on effecting change in the style of managers. As Fiedler[17] suggests:

> A person's leadership style . . . reflects the individual's basic motivational and need structure. At best it takes one, two, or three years of intensive psychotherapy to

effect changes in personality structure. It is difficult to see how we can change in more than a few cases an equally important set of core values in a few hours of lectures and role playing or even in the course of a more intensive training program of one or two weeks.

Fiedler's point is well-taken. It is indeed difficult to effect changes in the styles of managers overnight. However, it is not completely hopeless. But, at best, it is a slow and expensive process which requires creative planning and patience. In fact, Likert[18] found that it takes from three to seven years, depending on the size and complexity of the organization, to effectively implement a new management theory.

## CHANGING PERFORMANCE

Not only is it difficult to effect changes in the styles of managers overnight, but the question that we raise is whether it is even appropriate. It is questionable whether a work group whose performance has been continually low would suddenly leap to high productivity with the introduction of an employee-centered supervisor. In fact, they might take advantage of him and view him as a "soft-touch." These workers lack maturity and are not ready for more responsibility. Thus the supervisor must bring them along slowly, becoming more employee-centered and less job-centered as they mature. When an individual's performance is low, one cannot expect drastic changes overnight, regardless of changes in expectations or other incentives. The key is often reinforcing positively *"successive approximations."* By successive approximations we mean behavior which comes closer and closer to the supervisor's expectations of good performance. Similar to the child learning some new behavior, a manager should not expect high levels of performance at the outset. As a parent or teacher, we would use positive reinforcement as the child's behavior approaches the desired level of performance. Therefore, the manager must be aware of any progress of his subordinates so that he is in a position to reinforce appropriately improved performance.

Change through the cycle from quadrant 1 to quadrant 2, 3, and then 4 [Figure 4] must be gradual. This process by its very nature cannot be revolutionary but must be evolutionary—gradual developmental changes, a result of planned growth and the creation of mutual trust and respect.

## REFERENCES

1. As examples see the following: Robert F. Bales, "Task Roles and Social Roles in Problem-Solving Groups," in *Readings in Social Psychology*, E. E. Maccoby, T. M. Newcomb and E. L. Hartley (eds.), Holt, Rinehart and Winston, 1958; Chester I. Barnard, *The Functions of the Executive*, Harvard University Press, 1938; Dorwin Cartwright and Alvin Zander (eds.), *Group Dynamics: Research and Theory*, second edition, Row, Peterson and Co., 1960; D. Katz, N. Maccoby, and Nancy C. Morse, *Productivity Supervision, and Morale in an Office Situation*, The Darel Press, Inc., 1950; Talcott Parsons, *The Social System*, The Free Press, 1951.

2. Roger M. Stogdill and Alvin E. Coons (eds.), *Leader Behavior: Its Description and Measurement*, Research Monograph No. 88, Bureau of Business Research, The Ohio State Univ., 1957.

3. Stogdill and Coons, *Leader Behavior* . . . See also Andrew W. Halpin. *The Leadership Behavior of School Superintendents*, Midwest Administration Center, The University of Chicago, 1959.

4. Robert R. Blake and Jane S. Mouton, *The Managerial Grid*, Gulf Publishing, 1964.

5. Halpin, *The Leadership Behavior of School Superintendents*.

6. Robert R. Blake, *et al.*, "Breakthrough in Organization Development," *Harvard Business Review*, Nov.–Dec. 1964.

7. A. K. Korman, " 'Consideration,' 'Initiating Structure,' and Organizational Criteria—A Review," *Personnel Psychology: A Journal of Applied Research*, Vol. 19, No. 4 (Winter, 1966), pp. 349–361.

8. Fred E. Fiedler, *A Theory of Leadership Effectiveness*. McGraw-Hill, 1967.

9. Paul Hersey and Kenneth H. Blanchard, *Leader Behavior*, Management Education & Development, Inc., 1967; see also Hersey and Blanchard, *Management of Organizational Behavior: Utilizing Human Resources*, Prentice-Hall, Inc., and William J. Reddin, "The 3-D Management Style Theory," *Training and Development Journal*, Apr. 1967.

10. Fred E. Fiedler in his Contingency Model of Leadership Effectiveness (Fiedler, *A Theory of Leadership Effectiveness*) tends to make behavioral assumptions from data gathered from an attitudinal measure of leadership style. A leader is asked to evaluate his least preferred co-worker (LPC) on a series of Semantic Differential type scales. Leaders are classified as high or low LPC depending on the favorableness with which they rate their LPC.

11. Fillmore H. Sanford, *Authoritarianism and Leadership*, Institute for Research in Human Relations, 1950.

12. Chris Argyris, *Personality and Organization*, Harper & Row, Publishers, Inc., 1957; *Interpersonal Competence and Organizational Effectiveness*, Dorsey Press, 1962; and *Integrating the Individual and the Organization*, Wiley, 1964.

13. David C. McClelland, J. W. Atkinson, R. A. Clark, and E. L. Lowell, *The Achievement Motive*, Appleton-Century-Crafts, Inc., 1953, and *The Achieving Society*, D. Van Nostrand Co., 1961.

14. Support for this discussion is provided by Peter F. Drucker, *The Practice of Management*, Harper & Bros., 1954, pp. 139–40.

15. Rensis Likert, *New Patterns of Management*, McGraw-Hill, 1961.

16. Saul Gellerman, *Motivation and Productivity*, American Management Assn., 1963.

17. Fiedler, *A Theory of Leadership Effectiveness*.

18. Likert, *New Patterns of Management*.

# 17
# The Contingency Model: A Theory of Leadership Effectiveness[1]
## Fred E. Fiedler

Leadership, as a problem in social psychology, has dealt primarily with two questions, namely, how one becomes a leader, and how one can become a *good* leader, that is, how one develops effective group performance. Since a number of excellent reviews (e.g., Stogdill, 1948; Gibb, 1954; Mann, 1959; Bass, 1960), have already dealt with the first question we shall not be concerned with it in the present paper.

The second question, whether a given leader will be more or less effective than others in similar situations, has been a more difficult problem of research and has received correspondingly less attention in the psychological literature. The theoretical status of the problem is well reflected by Browne and Cohn's (1958) statement that ". . . leadership literature is a mass of content without coagulating substances to bring it together or to produce coordination. . . ." Mc-

Grath (1962), in making a similar point, ascribed this situation to the tendency of investigators to select different variables and to work with idiosyncratic measures and definitions of leadership. He also pointed out, however, that most researchers in this area have gravitated toward two presumably crucial clusters of leadership attitudes and behaviors. These are the critical, directive, autocratic, task-oriented versus the democratic, permissive, considerate, person-oriented type of leadership. While this categorization is admittedly oversimplified, the major controversy in this area has been between the more orthodox viewpoint, reflected in traditional supervisory training and military doctrine that the leader should be decisive and forceful, that he should do the planning and thinking for the groups, and that he should coordinate, direct and evaluate his men's actions. The other viewpoint, reflected in the newer human relations oriented training and in the philosophy behind non-directive and brainstorming technique stresses the need for democratic, permissive, group-oriented leadership techniques. Both schools of thought have strong adherents and there is evidence supporting both points of view (Gibb, 1954; Hare, 1962).

While one can always rationalize that contradictory findings by other investigators are due to poor research design,

[1] The present paper is mainly based on research conducted under Office of Naval Research Contracts 170–106, N6-ori-07135 (Fred E. Fiedler, Principal Investigator) and RN 177–472, Noor 1834(36). (Fred E. Fiedler, C. E. Osgood, L. M. Stolurow, and H. C. Triandis, Principal Investigators.) The writer is especially indebted to his colleagues, A. R. Bass, L. J. Cronbach, M. Fishbein, J. E. McGrath, W. A. T. Meuwese, C. E. Osgood, H. C. Triandis, and L. R. Tucker, who offered invaluable suggestions and criticisms at various stages of the work.

*Source:* From "The Contingency Model: A Theory of Leadership Effectiveness" by Fred E. Fiedler, in *Problems in Social Psychology,* edited by Carl W. Backman and Paul F. Secord, pp. 279–289. New York: McGraw-Hill Book Company, 1970. Reprinted by permission of the author.

or different tests and criteria, such problems present difficulties if they appear in one's own research. We have, during the past thirteen years, conducted a large number of studies on leadership and group performance, using the same operational definitions and essentially similar leader attitude measures. The inconsistencies which we obtained in our own research program demanded an integrative theoretical formulation which would adequately account for the seemingly confusing results.

The studies which we conducted used as the major predictor of group performance an interpersonal perception or attitude score which is derived from the leader's description of his most and of his least preferred co-workers. He is asked to think of all others with whom he has ever worked, and then to describe first the person with whom he worked best (his most preferred coworker) and then the person with whom he could work least well (his least preferred co-worker, or *LPC*). These descriptions are obtained, wherever possible, before the leader is assigned to his team. However, even when we deal with already existing groups, these descriptions tend to be of individuals whom the subject has known in the past rather than of persons with whom he works at the time of testing.

The descriptions are typically made on 20 eight-point bi-polar adjective scales, similar to Osgood's Semantic Differential (Osgood, et al., 1957), e.g.,

Pleasant _:_:_:_:_:_:_:_ Unpleasant

Friendly _:_:_:_:_:_:_:_ Unfriendly

These items are scaled on an evaluative dimension, giving a score of 8 to the most favorable pole (i.e., Friendly, Pleasant) and a score of 1 to the least favorable pole. Two main scores have been derived from these descriptions. The first one, which was used in our earlier studies, is based on the profile similarity measure *D* (Cronbach and Gleser, 1953) between the descriptions of the most and of the least preferred co-worker. This core, called the Assumed Similarity between Opposites, or *ASo*, indicates the degree to which the individual perceives the two opposites on his co-worker continuum as similar or different. The second score is simply based on the individual's description of his least preferred co-worker, *LPC*, and indicates the degree to which the subject evaluates his *LPC* in a relatively favorable or unfavorable manner. The two measures are highly correlated (.80 to .95) and will here be treated as interchangeable.

We have had considerable difficulty in interpreting these scores since they appear to be uncorrelated with the usual personality and attitude measures. They are, however, related to the Ohio State University studies' "Initiation of structure" and "Consideration" dimensions (Stogdill and Coons, 1957). Extensive content analysis (Meuwese and Oonk, 1960; Julian and McGrath, 1963; Morris and Fiedler, 1964) and a series of studies by Hawkins (1962) as well as research by Bass, Fiedler, and Krueger (1964) have given consistent results. These indicate that the person with high *LPC* or *ASo*, who perceives his least preferred co-worker in a relatively favorable, accepting manner, tends to be more accepting, permissive, considerate, and person-oriented in his relations with group members. The person who perceives his most and least preferred co-workers as quite different, and who sees his least preferred coworker in a very unfavorable, rejecting manner tends to be directive, task-oriented and controlling on task relevant group behaviors in his interactions. . . .

The results of these investigations clearly showed that the direction and magnitude of the correlations were contingent upon the nature of the group-task situation with which the leader had to deal. Our problem resolved itself then into (a) developing a meaningful system for categorizing group-task situations; (b) inducing the underlying theoretical model which would integrate the seemingly inconsistent results obtained in our studies, and (c) testing the validity of the model by adequate research.

## DEVELOPMENT OF THE MODEL

*Key Definitions.* We shall here be concerned solely with "interacting" rather than "co-acting" task groups. By an interacting task group we mean a face-to-face team situation (such as a basketball team) in which the members work *interdependently* on a common goal. In groups of this type, the individual's contributions cannot readily be separated from total group performance. In a co-acting group, however, such as a bowling or a rifle team, the group performance is generally determined by summing the members' individual performance scores. . . .

The leader's effectiveness is here defined in terms of the group's performance on the assigned primary task. . . .

*The Categorization of Group-Task Situations.* Leadership is essentially a problem of wielding influence and power. When we say that different types of groups require different types of leadership we imply that they require a different relationship by which the leader wields power and influence. Since it is easier to wield power in some groups than in others, an attempt to categorize groups might well begin by asking what conditions in the group-task situation will facilitate or inhibit the leader's exercise of power. On the basis of our previous work we postulated three important aspects in the total situation which influence the leader's role.

1. *Leader-member relations.* The leader who is personally attractive to his group members, and who is respected by his group, enjoys considerable power (French, 1956). In fact, if he has the confidence and loyalty of his men he has less need of official rank. This dimension can generally be measured by means of sociometric indices or by group atmosphere scales (Cf. Fiedler, 1962) which indicate the degree to which the leader experiences the groups as pleasant and well disposed toward him.

2. *Task structure.* The task generally implies an order "from above" which incorporates the authority of the superior organization. The group member who refuses to comply must be prepared to face disciplinary action by the higher authority. For example, a squad member who fails to perform a lawful command of his sergeant may have to answer to his regimental commander. However, compliance with a task order can be enforced only if the task is relatively well structured, i.e., if it is capable of being programmed, or spelled out step by step. One cannot effectively force a group to perform well on an unstructured task such as developing a new product or writing a good play.

Thus, the leader who has a structured task can depend on the backing of his superior organizations, but if he has an unstructured task the leader must rely on his own resources to inspire and motivate his men. The unstructured task thus provides the leader with much less effective power than does the highly structured task.

We operationalized this dimension by utilizing four of the aspects which Shaw (1962) recently proposed for the classification of group task. These are, (a) decision *verifiability*, the degree to which the correctness of the solution can be demonstrated objectively; (b) *good clarity*, the degree to which the task requirements are clearly stated or known to the group; (c) *goal path multiplicity*, the degree to which there are many or few procedures available for performing the task (reverse scoring); and (d) *solution specificity*, the degree to which there is one rather than an infinite number of correct solutions (e.g., writing a story vs. solving an equation). Ratings based on these four dimensions have yielded interrater reliabilities of .80 to .90.

3. *Position power.* The third dimension is defined by the power inherent in the position of leadership irrespective of the occupant's personal relations with his members. This includes the rewards and punishments which are officially or traditionally at the leader's disposal, his authority as defined by the group's rules and bylaws, and the organizational support given to him in dealing with his men. . . .

*A Three-Dimensional Group Classification.* Group-task situations can now be rated on the basis of the three dimensions of leader-member relations, task structure, and position power. This locates each group in a three dimensional space. A rough categorization can be accomplished by halving each of the dimensions so that we obtain an eight celled

cube (Fig. 1). We can now determine whether the correlations between leader attitudes and group performance within each of these eight cells, or octants, are relatively similar in magnitude and direction. If they are, we can infer that the group classification has been successfully accomplished since it shows that groups falling within the same octant require similar leader attitudes.

An earlier paper has summarized 52 group-task situations which are based on our previous studies (Fiedler, 1964). These 52 group-task situations have been ordered into the eight octants. As can be seen from Table 1, groups falling within the same octant show correlations between the leader's *ASo* or *LPC* score and the group performance criterion which are relatively similar in magnitude and direction. We can thus infer that the group classification has been accomplished with at least reasonable success.

FIGURE 1 • A MODEL FOR THE CLASSIFICATION OF
GROUP-TASK SITUATIONS.

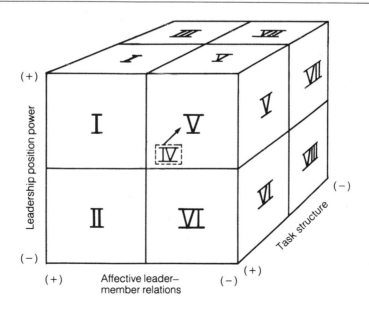

TABLE 1 • MEDIAN CORRELATION BETWEEN LEADER LPC AND
GROUP PERFORMANCE IN VARIOUS OCTANTS

| | Leader-Member Relations | Task Structure | Position Power | Median Correlation | Number of Relations Included in Median |
|---|---|---|---|---|---|
| Octant I | Good | Structured | Strong | −.52 | 2 |
| Octant II | Good | Structured | Weak | −.58 | 3 |
| Octant III | Good | Unstructured | Strong | −.41 | 4 |
| Octant IV | Good | Unstructured | Weak | .47 | 10 |
| Octant V | Mod. poor | Structured | Strong | .42 | 6 |
| Octant VI | Mod. poor | Structured | Weak | | 0 |
| Octant VII | Mod. poor | Unstructured | Strong | .05 | 10 |
| Octant VIII | Mod. poor | Unstructured | Weak | −.43 | 12 |

Consideration of Figure 1 suggests a further classification of the cells in term of the effective power which the group-task situation places at the leader's disposal, or more precisely, the favorableness of the situation for the leader's exercise of his power and influence.

Such an ordering can be accomplished without difficulty at the extreme poles of the continuum. A liked and trusted leader with high rank and a structured task is in a more favorable position than is a disliked and powerless leader with an ambiguous task. . . . In the present instance we have postulated that the most important dimension in the system is the leader-member relationship since the highly liked and respected leader is less in need of position power or the power of the higher authority incorporated in the task structure. The second-most important dimension in most group-task situations is the task structure since a leader with a highly structured task does not require a powerful leader position. . . . This leads us here to order the group-task situations first on leader-member relations, then on task structure, and finally on position power. While admittedly not a unique solution,

the resulting ordering constitutes a reasonable continuum which indicates the degree of the leader's effective power in the group.[2]

As was already apparent from Table 1, the relationship between leader attitudes and group performance is contingent upon the accurate classification of the group-task situation. A more meaningful model of this contingency relationship emerges when we now plot the correlation between LPC or ASo and group performance on the one hand, against the octants ordered on the effective power, or favorableness-for-the-leader dimension on the other. This is shown on Figure 2. Note that each point in the plot is a *correlation* predicting leadership performance or group effectiveness. The plot therefore represents 53 *sets of groups* totalling over 800 separate groups.

As Figure 2 shows, managing, controlling, directive (low LPC) leaders perform most effectively either under very

[2] Another cell should be added which contains real-life groups which reject their leader. Exercise of power would be very difficult in this situation and such a cell should be placed at the extreme negative end of the continuum. Such cases are treated in the section on validation.

# FIGURE 2 • CORRELATIONS OF LEADER LPC AND GROUP PERFORMANCE PLOTTED AGAINST OCTANTS

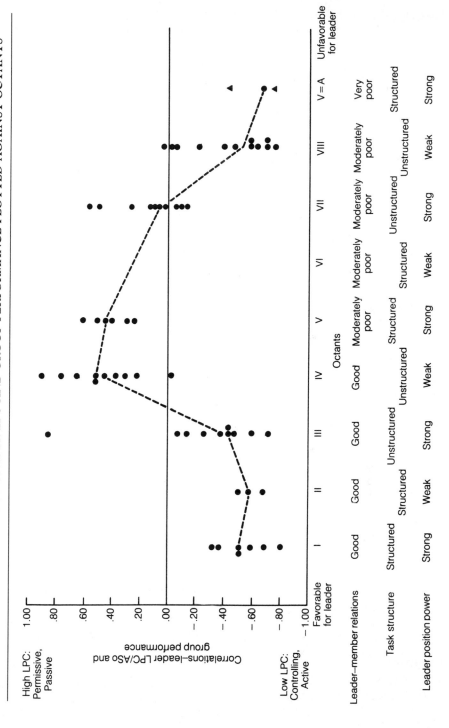

favorable or under very unfavorable situations. Hence we obtain negative correlations between *LPC* and group performance scores. Considerate, permissive, accepting leaders obtain optimal group performance under situations intermediate in favorableness. These are situations in which (*a*) the task is structured, but the leader is disliked and must, therefore, be diplomatic; (*b*) the liked leader has an ambiguous, unstructured task and must, therefore, draw upon the creativity and cooperation of his members. Here we obtain positive correlations between *LPC* and group performance scores. Where the task is highly structured and the leader is well-liked, non-directive behavior or permissive attitudes (such as asking how the group ought to proceed with a missile count-down) is neither appropriate nor beneficial. Where the situation is quite unfavorable, e.g., where the disliked chairman of a volunteer group faces an ambiguous task, the leader might as well be autocratic and directive since a positive, non-directive leadership style under these conditions might result in complete inactivity on the part of the group. This model, thus, tends to shed some light on the apparent inconsistencies in our own data as well as in data obtained by other investigators.

## EMPIRICAL TESTS EXTENSION OF THE MODEL

The basic hypothesis of the model suggests that the directive, controlling, task oriented (low *LPC*) leader will be most successful in group-task situations which are either very favorable or else very unfavorable for the leader. The permissive, considerate, human relations oriented (high *LPC*) leader will perform best under conditions which are intermediate in favorableness. . . .

### Experimental Test of the Contingency Model

In cooperation with the Belgian Naval Forces we recently conducted a major

study which served in part as a specific test of the model. Only aspects immediately relevant to the test are here described. The investigation was conducted in Belgium where the French and Dutch speaking (or Flemish) sectors of the country have been involved in a long standing and frequently acrimonious dispute. This conflict centers about the use of language, but it also involves a host of other cultural factors which differentiate the 60 per cent Flemish and 40 per cent French speaking population groups in Wallonie and Brussels. This "linguistic problem" which is rooted in the beginning of Belgium's national history, has in recent years been the cause of continuous public controversy, frequent protest meetings, and occasional riots.

The linguistic problem is of particular interest here since a group, consisting of members whose mother tongue, culture, and attitudes differ, will clearly present a more difficult problem in leadership than a group whose members share the same language and culture. We were thus able to test the major hypothesis of the model as well as to extend the research by investigating the type of leadership which linguistically and culturally heterogeneous groups require.

*Design.* The experiment was conducted at the naval training center at Ste. Croix-Bruges.[3] It utilized 48 career

[3] This investigation was conducted in collaboration with Dr. J. M. Nuttin (Jr.) and his students while the author was Ford Faculty Research Fellow at the University of Louvain, 1963–1964. The experiment, undertaken with permission of Commodore L. Petitjean, then Chief of Staff of the Belgian Naval Forces, was carried out at the Centre de Formation Navale, Ste. Croix-Bruges. The writer wishes to express his especial gratitude and appreciation to the commandant of the center, Captain V. Van Laethem, who not only made the personnel and the facilities of the center available to us, but whose active participation in the planning and the execution of the project made this study possible. We are also most grateful to Dr. U.

petty officers and 240 recruits who had been selected from a pool of 546 men on the basis of a pre-test in which we obtained *LPC*, intelligence, attitude, and language comprehension scores.

The experiment was specifically designed to incorporate the three major group classification dimensions shown on Figure 1, namely, leader-member relations, position power, and task structure. It also added the additional dimension of group homogeneity vs. heterogeneity. Specifically, 48 groups had leaders with high position power (petty officers) while 48 had leaders with low position power (recruits); 48 groups began with the unstructured task, while the other 48 groups began with two structured tasks; 48 groups were homogeneous, consisting of three French or three Dutch speaking men, while the other 48 groups were heterogeneous, consisting of a French speaking leader and two Flemish members, or a Dutch speaking, Flemish leader and two French speaking members. The quality of the leader-member relations was measured as in our previous studies by means of a group atmosphere scale which the leader completed after each task session.

*Group Performance Criteria.* Two essentially identical structured tasks were administered. Each lasted 25 minutes and required the groups to find the shortest route for a ship which, given certain fuel capacity and required ports of call, had to make a round trip calling at respectively ten or twelve ports. The tasks were objectively scored on the basis of sea miles required for the trip. Appro-

Bouvier, Director of the Center for Social Studies, Ministry of Defense, to Capt. W. Cafferata, USN, the senior U.S. Naval representative of the Military Assistance and Advisory Group, Brussels, and to Cmdr. J. Robison, U.S. Naval Attache in Brussels, who provided liaison and guidance.

priate corrections and penalties were assigned for errors.

The unstructured task required the groups to compose a letter to young men of 16 and 17 years, urging them to choose the Belgian Navy as a career. The letter was to be approximately 200 words in length and had to be completed in 35 minutes. Each of the letters, depending upon the language in which it was written, was then rated by Dutch or by French speaking judges on style and use of language, as well as interest value, originality, and persuasiveness. Estimated reliabilty was .92 and .86 for Dutch and French speaking judges, respectively.

It should be noted in this connection that the task of writing a letter is not as unstructured as might have been desirable for this experiment. . . High and low task-structure is, therefore, less well differentiated in this study than it has been in previous investigations.

*Results.* The contingency model specifies that the controlling, managing, low *LPC* leaders will be most effective either in very favorable or else in relatively unfavorable group-task situations, while the permissive, considerate, high *LPC* leaders will be more effective in situations intermediate in difficulty. . . .

The hypothesis can be tested most readily with correlations of leader *LPC* and group performance in homogeneous groups on the more reliably scorable second structured task. . . We have here made the fairly obvious assumption that the powerful leader or the leader who feels liked and accepted faces an easier group-task situation than low ranking leaders and those who see the groups as unpleasant and tense. Each situation is represented by two cells of six groups, each. Since there were two orders of presentation—half the groups worked first on the structured task, the other half on the unstructured task, arranging the group-task situations in order of favorableness for the leader then gives us the following results:

|                                                  | Order 1 | Order 2 |
|--------------------------------------------------|---------|---------|
| High group atmosphere and high position power    | −.77    | −.77    |
| High group atmosphere and low position power     | +.60    | +.50    |
| Low group atmosphere and high position power     | +.16    | +.01    |
| Low group atmosphere and low position power      | −.16    | −.43    |

These are, of course, the trends in size and magnitude of correlations which the model predicts. Low *LPC* leaders are again most effective in favorable and unfavorable group-task situations: the more permissive, considerate high *LPC* leaders were more effective in the intermediate situations. . . .

The resulting weighting system leads to a scale from 12 to 0 points, with 12 as the most favorable pole. If we now plot the median correlation coefficients of the 48 group-task situations against the scale indicating the favorableness of the situation for the leader, we obtain the curve presented on Figure 3.

As can be seen, we again obtain a curvilinear relationship which resembles that shown on Figure 2. Heterogeneous groups with low position power and/or poor leader-member relations fall below point 6 on the scale, and thus tend to perform better with controlling, directive, low *LPC* leaders. Only under otherwise very favorable conditions do heterogeneous groups perform better with permissive, considerate high *LPC* leaders, that is, in group-task situations char-

acterized by high group atmosphere as well as high position power, four of the six correlations (66%) are positive, while only five of eighteen (28%) are positive in the less favorable group-task situations.

It is interesting to note that the curve is rather flat and characterized by relatively low negative correlations as we go toward the very unfavorable end of the scale. This result supports Meuwese's (1964) recent study which showed that correlations between leader *LPC* as well as between leader intelligence and group performance tend to become attenuated under conditions of relative stress. These findings suggest that the leader's ability to influence and control the group decreases beyond a certain point of stress and difficulty in the group-task situation.

## DISCUSSION

The contingency model seeks to reconcile results which up to now had to be considered inconsistent and difficult to understand. . . .

The model has a number of important implications for selection and training, as well as for the placement of leaders and organizational strategy. Our research suggests, first of all, that we can utilize a very broad spectrum of individuals for positions of leadership. The problem becomes one of placement and training rather than of selection since both the permissive, democratic, human-relations oriented, and the managing, autocratic, task-oriented leader can be effectively utilized. Leaders can be trained to recognize their own style of leadership as well as the conditions which are most compatible with their style.

The model also points to a variety of administrative and supervisory strategies which the organization can adopt to fit the group-task situation to the needs of

# FIGURE 3 • MEDIAN CORRELATIONS BETWEEN LEADER LCP AND GROUP PERFORMANCE SCORES PLOTTED AGAINST FAVORABLENESS-FOR-LEADER SCALE IN THE BELGIAN NAVY STUDY.

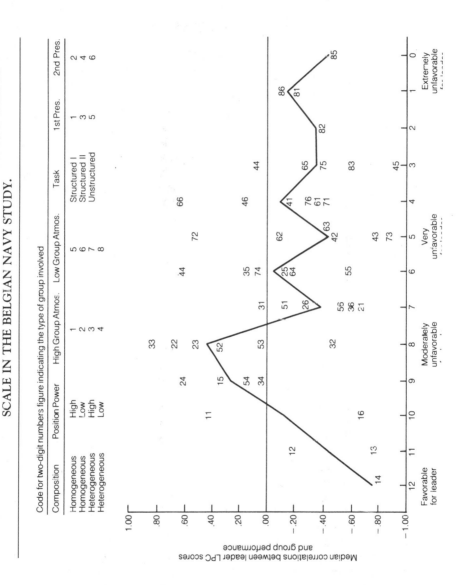

the leader. Tasks can, after all, be structured to a greater or lesser extent by giving very specific and detailed, or vague and general instructions; the position power of the group leader can be increased or decreased and even the congeniality of a group, and its acceptance of the leader can be affected by appropriate administration action, such as for instance increasing or decreasing the group's homogeneity.

The model also throws new light on phenomena which were rather difficult to fit into our usual ideas about measurement in social psychology. Why, for example, should groups differ so markedly in their performance on nearly parallel tasks? The model—and our data— shows that the situation becomes easier for the leader as the group moves from the novel to the already known group-task situations. The leaders who excel under relatively novel and therefore more difficult conditions are not necessarily those who excel under those which are more routine, or better known and therefore more favorable. Likewise, we find that different types of task structure require different types of leader behavior. Thus, in a research project's early phases the project director tends to be democratic and permissive; everyone is urged to contribute to the plan and to criticize all aspects of the design. This situation changes radically in the more structured phase when the research design is frozen and the experiment is underway. Here the research director tends to become managing, controlling, and highly autocratic and woe betide the assistant who attempts to be creative in giving instructions to subjects, or in his timing of tests. A similar situation is often found in business organizations where the routine operation tends to be well structured and calls for a managing, directive leadership. The situation becomes suddenly unstructured when a crisis occurs. Under these conditions the number of discussions, meetings, and conferences increases sharply so as to give everyone an opportunity to express his views.

At best, this model is of course only a partial theory of leadership. The leader's intellectual and task-relevant abilities, and the members' skills and motivation, all play a role in affecting the group's performance. It is to be hoped that these other important aspects of group interaction can be incorporated into the model in the not too distant future.

# REFERENCES

Bass, A. R., Fiedler, F. E., and Krueger, S. Personality correlates of assumed similarity (ASo) and related scores. Urbana, Ill.: Group Effectiveness Research Laboratory, University of Illinois, 1964.

Bass, B. M. *Leadership psychology and organizational behavior.* New York: Harper Brothers, 1960.

Browne, C. G., and Cohn, T. S. (Eds.) *The study of leadership.* Danville, Illinois. The Interstate Printers and Publishers, 1958.

Cleven, W. A., and Fiedler, F. E. Interpersonal perceptions of open hearth foremen and steel production. *J. Appl. Psychol.* 1956. 40, 312–314.

Cronbach, J. J., and Gleser, Goldene C. Assessing similarity between profiles. *Psychol. Bull.,* 1953, 50, 456–473.

Fiedler, F. E. Assumed similarity measures as predictors of team effectiveness. *J. Abnorm. Soc. Psychol.* 1954, 49, 381–388.

Fiedler, F. E. Leader attitudes, group climate, and group creativity. *J. Abnorm. Soc. Psychol.,* 1962, 64. 308–318.

Fiedler, F. E. A contingency model of leadership effectiveness. In L. Berkowitz (Ed.) *Advances in Experimental Social Psychology.* New York: Academic Press, 1964. Vol. I.

Fiedler, F. E., and Meuwese, W. A. T. The leader's contribution to performance in cohesive and uncohesive groups. *J. Abnorm. Soc. Psychol.* 1963, 67, 83–87.

Fiedler, F. E., Meuwese, W. A. T., and Oonk, Sophie. Performance of laboratory tasks requiring group creativity. *Acta Psychologica,* 1961, 18, 100–119.

French, J. R. P., Jr. A formal theory of social power. *Psychol. Rev.*, 1956, 63, 181–194.

Gibb, C. A. "Leadership" in G. Lindzey (Ed.) *Handbook of Social Psychology*, Vol. II, Cambridge, Mass.: Addison-Wesley, 1954.

Godfrey, Eleanor P., Fiedler, F. E., and Hall, D. M. *Boards, Management, and Company Success*. Danville, Illinois: Interstate Printers and Publishers, 1959.

Hare, A. P. *Handbook of Small Group Research*. New York: Free Press, 1962.

Hawkins, C. A study of factors mediating a relationship between leader rating behavior and group productivity. Unpublished Ph. D. dissertion, University of Minnesota, 1962.

Hutchins, E. B., and Fiedler, F. E. Task-oriented and quasi-therapeutic role functions of the leader in small military groups. *Sociometry*, 1960, 23, 293–406.

Julian, J. W., and McGrath, J. E. The influence of leader and member behavior on the adjustment and task effectiveness of negotiation groups. Urbana, Ill.: Group Effectiveness Research Laboratory, University of Illinois, 1963.

McGrath, J. E. A summary of small group research studies. Arlington, Va.: Human Sciences Research Inc., 1962 (Litho.).

Mann, R. D. A review of the relationship between personality and performance in small groups. *Psychol. Bull.*, 1959, 56, 241–270.

Meuwese, W. A. T. The effect of the leader's ability and interpersonal attitudes on group creativity under varying conditions of stress. Unpublished doctoral dissertation, University of Amsterdam, 1964.

Morris, C. G., and Fiedler, F. E. Application of a new system of interaction analysis to be relationships between leader attitudes and behavior in problem solving groups. Urbana, Ill.: Group Effectiveness Research Laboratory, University of Illinois, 1964.

Osgood, C. A., Suci, G. A., and Tannenbaum, P. H. *The Measurement of Meaning*. Urbana, Ill.: University of Illinois Press, 1957.

Shaw, M. E. Annual Technical Report, 1962. Gainesville, Florida: University of Florida, 1962 (Mimeo.).

Stogdill, R. Personal factors associated with leadership: a survey of the literature. *J. of Psychol*. 1948, 25, 35–71.

Stogdill, R. M., and Coons, A. E. Leader behavior: its description and measurement. Columbus, Ohio: Ohio State University, *Research Monograph*, No. 88, 1957.

# 18

# The Leadership Challenge—A Call for the Transformational Leader

*Noel M. Tichy & David O. Ulrich*

Some optimists are heralding in the age of higher productivity, a transition to a service economy, and a brighter competitive picture for U.S. corporations in world markets. We certainly would like to believe that the future will be brighter, but our temperament is more cautious. We feel that the years it took for most U.S. companies to get "fat and flabby" are not going to be reversed by a crash diet for one or two years. Whether we continue to gradually decline as world competitive economy will largely be determined by the quality of leadership in the top echelons of our business and government organizations. Thus, it is our belief that now is the time for organizations to *change* their corporate lifestyles.

To revitalize organizations such as General Motors, American Telephone and Telegraph, General Electric, Honeywell, Ford, Burroughs, Chase Manhattan Bank, Citibank, U.S. Steel, Union Carbide, Texas Instruments, and Control Data—just to mention a few companies currently undergoing major transformations—a new brand of leadership is necessary. Instead of managers who continue to move organizations along historical tracks, the new leaders must *transform* the organizations and head them down new tracks. What is required of this kind of leader is an ability to help the organization develop a vision of what it can be, to mobilize the organization

to accept and work toward achieving the new vision, and to institutionalize the changes that must last over time. Unless the creation of this breed of leaders becomes a national agenda, we are not very optimistic about the revitalization of the U.S. economy.

We call these new leaders transformational leaders, for they must create something new out of something old: out of an old vision, they must develop and communicate a new vision and get others not only to see the vision but also to commit themselves to it. Where transactional managers make only minor adjustments in the organization's mission, structure, and human resource management, transformational leaders not only make major changes in these three areas but they also evoke fundamental changes in the basic political and cultural systems of the organization. The revamping of the political and cultural systems is what most distinguishes the transformational leader from the transactional one.

## LEE IACOCCA: A TRANSFORMATIONAL LEADER

One of the most dramatic examples of transformational leadership and organizational revitalization in the early 1980s has been the leadership of Lee Iacocca, the chairman of Chrysler Corporation.

*Source:* Reprinted from "The Leadership Challenge—A Call for the Transformational Leader" by N. M. Tichy and D. O. Ulrich in *Sloan Management Review* (Fall 1984), pp. 59–68, by permission of the publisher. Copyright © 1984 by the Sloan Management Review Association. All rights reserved.

He provided the leadership to transform a company from the brink of bankruptcy to profitability. He created a vision of success and mobilized large factions of key employees toward enacting that vision while simultaneously downsizing the workforce by 60,000 employees. As a result of Iacocca's leadership, by 1984 Chrysler had earned record profits, had attained high levels of employee morale, and had helped employees generate a sense of meaning in their work.

Until Lee Iacocca took over at Chrysler, the basic internal political structure had been unchanged for decades. It was clear who reaped what benefits from the organization, how the pie was to be divided, and who could exercise what power. Nonetheless, Mr. Iacocca knew that he needed to alter these political traditions, starting with a new definition of Chrysler's link to external stakeholders. Therefore, the government was given a great deal of control over Chrysler in return for the guaranteed loan that staved off bankruptcy. Modification of the political system required other adjustments, including the "trimming of fat" in the management ranks, limiting financial rewards for all employees, and receiving major concessions for the UAW. An indicator of a significant political shift was the inclusion of Douglas Frazer on the Chrysler Board of Directors as part of UAW concessions.

Equally dramatic was the change in the organization's cultural system. First, the company had to recognize its unique status as a recipient of a federal bailout. This bailout came with a stigma, thus Mr. Iacocca's job was to change the company's cultural values from a loser's to a winner's feeling. Still, he realized that employees were not going to be winners unless they could, in cultural norms, be more efficient and innovative than their competitors. The molding and shaping of the new culture was clearly and visibly led by Mr. Iacocca, who not only used internal communication as a vehicle to signal change but also used his own personal appearance in Chrysler ads to reinforce these changes. Quickly, the internal culture was transformed to that of a lean and hungry team looking for victory. Whether Chrysler will be able to sustain this organizational phenomenon over time remains to be seen. If it does, it will provide a solid corporate example of what Burns referred to as a transforming leader.[1]

Lee Iacocca's high visibility and notoriety may be the *important* missing elements in management today: there seems to be a paucity of transformational leader role models at all levels of the organization.

## ORGANIZATIONAL DYNAMICS OF CHANGE

### Assumption One: Trigger Events Indicate Change Is Needed

Organizations do not change unless there is a trigger which indicates change is needed. This trigger can be as extreme as the Chrysler impending bankruptcy or as moderate as an abstract future-oriented fear that an organization may lose its competitiveness. For example, General Electric's trigger for change is a view that by 1990 the company will not be world competitive unless major changes occur in productivity, innovation, and marketing. . . . For General Motors, economic factors of world competition, shifting consumer preferences, and technological change have driven it to change.

In a decade of increased information, international competition, and technological advances, triggers for change have become commonplace and very pressing. However, not all potential trigger events lead to organizational responses, and not all triggers lead to change. Nonetheless, the trigger must create a *felt need* in organizational leaders. Without this felt need, the "boiled frog phenomenon" is likely to occur.

*The Boiled Frog.* This phenomenon is based on a classic experiment in biology. A frog which is placed in a pan of cold water but which still has the freedom to jump out can be boiled if the temperature change is gradual, for it is not aware of the barely detectable changing heat threshold. In contrast, a frog dropped in a pot of boiling water will immediately jump out: it has a felt need to survive. In a similar vein, many organizations that are insensitive to gradually changing organizational thresholds are likely to become "boiled frogs"; they act in ignorant bliss of environmental triggers and eventually are doomed to failure. This failure, in part, is a result of the organization having no felt need to change.

## Assumption Two: A Change Unleashes Mixed Feelings

A felt need for change unleashes a mix of forces, both a positive impetus for change as well as a strong negative individual and organizational resistance. These forces of resistance are generated in each of three interrelated systems— technical, political, cultural—which must be managed in the process of organizational transitions (see Table 1).[2] Individual and organizational resistance to change in these three systems must be overcome if an organization is to be revitalized.[3]

Managing technical systems refers to managing the coordination of technology, capital information, and people in order to produce products or services desired and used in the external marketplace. Managing political systems refers to managing the allocation of organizational reward such as money, status, power, and career opportunities and to exercising power so employees and de-

partments perceive equity and justice. Managing cultural systems refers to managing the set of shared values and norms which guides the behavior of members of the organization.

When a needed change is perceived by the organizational leaders, the dominant group in the organization must experience a dissatisfaction with the status quo. . . .

The technical, political, and cultural resistances are most evident during early stages of an organizational transformation. At GM the early 1980s were marked by tremendous uncertainty concerning many technical issues such as marketing strategy, production strategy, organization design, factory automation, and development of international management. Politically, many powerful coalitions were threatened. The UAW was forced to make wage concessions and accept staffing reductions. The white-collar workers saw their benefits being cut and witnessed major layoffs within the managerial ranks. Culturally, the once dominant managerial style no longer fit the environmental pressures for change: the "GM way" was no longer the right way.

One must be wary of these resistances to change as they can lead to organizational stagnation rather than revitalization. In fact, some managers at GM in late 1983 were waiting for "the good old days" to return. Such resistance exemplifies a dysfunctional reaction to the felt need. As indicated in Figure 1, a key to whether resistant forces will lead to little or inadequate change and hence organizational decline or revitalization lies in an organization's leadership. Defensive, transactional leadership will not rechannel the resistant forces. . . .

## Assumption Three: Quick-Fix Leadership Leads to Decline

Overcoming resistance to change requires transformational leadership, not

## TABLE 1 • A LIST OF TECHNICAL, POLITICAL, AND CULTURAL SYSTEM RESISTANCES

### Technical System Resistances Include:

Habit and inertia. Habit and inertia cause task-related resistance to change. Individuals who have always done things one way may not be politically or culturally resistant to change, but may have trouble, for technical reasons, changing behavior patterns. Example: some office workers may have difficulty shifting from electric typewriters to word processors.

Fear of the unknown or loss of organizational predictability. Not knowing or having difficulty predicting the future creates anxiety and hence resistance in many individuals. Example: the introduction of automated office equipment has often been accompanied by such resistances.

Sunk costs. Organizations, even when realizing that there are potential payoffs from a change, are often unable to enact a change because of the sunk costs of the organizations' resources in the old way of doing things.

### Political System Resistances Include:

Powerful coalitions. A common threat is found in the conflict between the old guard and the new guard. One interpretation of the exit of Archie McGill, former president of the newly formed AT&T American Bell, is that the backlash of the old-guard coalition exacted its price on the leader of the new-guard coalition.

Resource limitations. In the days when the economic pie was steadily expanding and resources were much less limited, change was easier to enact as every part could gain—such was the nature of labor management agreements in the auto industry for decades. Now that the pie is shrinking decisions need to be made as to who shares a smaller set of resources. These zero-sum decisions are much more politically difficult. As more and more U.S. companies deal with productivity, downsizing, and divestiture, political resistance will be triggered.

Indictment quality of change. Perhaps the most significant resistance to change comes from leaders having to indict their own past decisions and behaviors to bring about a change. Example: Roger Smith, chairman and CEO of GM, must implicitly indict his own past behavior as a member of senior management when he suggests changes in GM's operations. Psychologically, it is very difficult for people to change when they were party to creating the problems they are trying to change. It is much easier for a leader from the outside, such as Lee Iacocca, who does not have to indict himself every time he says something is wrong with the organization.

### Cultural System Resistances Include:

Selective perception (cultural filters). An organization's culture may highlight certain elements of the organization, making it difficult for members to conceive of other ways of doing things. An organization's culture channels that which people perceive as possible; thus, innovation may come from outsiders or deviants who are not as channeled in their perceptions.

Security based on the past. Transition requires people to give up the old ways of doing things. There is security in the past, and one of the problems is getting people to overcome the tendency to want to return to the "good old days." Example: today, there are still significant members of the white-collar workforce at GM who are waiting for the "good old days" to return.

Lack of climate for change. Organizations often vary in their conduciveness to change. Cultures that require a great deal of conformity often lack much receptivity to change. Example: GM with its years of internally developed managers must overcome a limited climate for change.

FIGURE 1 · TRANSFORMATIONAL LEADERSHIP

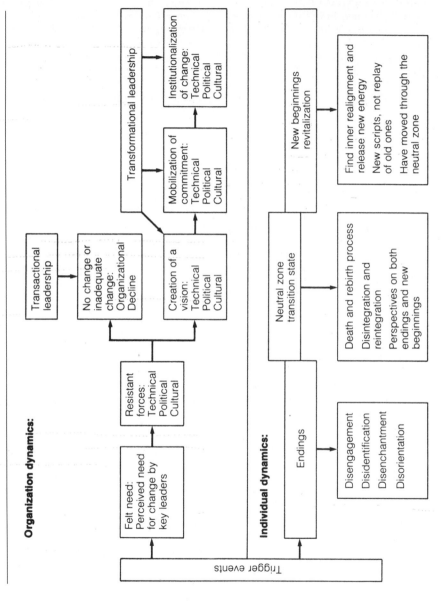

defensive, transactional managers who are in search of the one minute quick fix. The transformational leader needs to avoid the trap of simple, quick-fix solutions to major organizational problems. Today, many versions of this quick-fix mentality abound: the book, *The One Minute Manager*, has become a best seller in companies in need of basic transformation.[4] Likewise, *In Search of Excellence* has become a cookbook for change.[5] In fact, a number of CEOs have taken the eight characteristics of the "excellent" companies and are trying to blindly impose them on their organizations without first examining their appropriateness. For example, many faltering organizations try to copy such company practices as Hewlett-Packard's (HP) statement of company values. Because they read that HP has a clearly articulated statement of company values—the HP equivalent of the ten commandments—they want to create their list of ten commandments. . . .

The problem with the ten-commandments quick fix is that the CEOs tend to overlook the lesson Moses learned several thousand years ago—namely, getting the ten commandments written down and communicated is the easy part; getting them implemented is the challenge. How many thousands of years has it been since Moses received the ten commandments, and yet today there still seems to be an implementation challenge. Transformational leadership is different from defensive, transactional leadership. Lee Iacocca did not have to read about what others did to find a recipe for his company's success.

## Assumption Four: Revitalization Requires Transformational Leadership

There are three identifiable programs of activity associated with transformational leadership.

*1. Creation of a Vision.* The transformational leader must provide the organization with a vision of a desired future state. While this task may be shared with other key members of the organization, the vision remains the core responsibility of the transformational leader. The leader needs to integrate analytic, creative, intuitive, and deductive thinking. Each leader must create a vision which gives direction to the organization while being congruent with the leader's and the organization's philosophy and style.

For example, in the early 1980s at GM, after several years of committee work and staff analysis, a vision of the future was drafted which included a mission statement and eight objectives for the company. This statement was the first articulation of a strategic vision for General Motors since Alfred Sloan's leadership. This new vision was developed consistently with the leadership philosophy and style of Roger Smith. Many people were involved in carefully assessing opportunities and constraints for General Motors. Meticulous staff work culminated in committee discussions to evoke agreement and commitment to the mission statement. Through this process a vision was created which paved the way for the next phases of the transformation at GM.

At Chrysler, Lee Iacocca developed a vision without committee work or heavy staff involvement. Instead, he relied more on his intuitive and directive leadership, philosophy, and style. Both GM and Chrysler ended up with a new vision because of transformational leader proactively shaping a new organization mission and vision. . . .

*2. Mobilization of Commitment.* Here, the organization, or at least a critical mass of it, accepts the new mission and vision and makes it happen. At General Motors, Roger Smith took his top 900 executives on a five-day retreat to share and discuss the vision. The event lasted five days not because it takes that long to share a one-paragraph mission statement and eight objectives, but because the process of evolving commitment and mobilizing support requires a great deal of dialogue and exchange. It should be noted that mobilization of commitment must go well beyond five-day retreats; nevertheless, it is in the phase that transformational leaders get deeper understanding of their *followers*. . . . After transformational leaders create a vision and mobilize commitment, they must determine how to institutionalize the new mission and vision.

3. *Institutionalization of Change*. Organizations will not be revitalized unless new patterns of behavior within the organization are adopted. Transformational leaders need to transmit their vision into reality, their mission into action, their philosophy into practice. New realities, action, and practices must be shared throughout the organization. Alterations in communication, decision making, and problem-solving systems are tools through which transitions are shared so that visions become a reality. At a deeper level, institutionalization of change requires shaping and reinforcement of a new culture that fits with the revitalized organization. The human resource systems of selection, development, appraisal, and reward are major levers for institutionalizing change.

## INDIVIDUAL DYNAMICS OF CHANGE

The previous section outlined requisite processes for organizational revitalization. Although organizational steps are necessary, they are not sufficient in creating and implementing change. In managing transitions, a more problematic set of forces which focuses on individual psychodynamics of change must be understood and managed. Major transitions unleash powerful conflicting forces in people. The change invokes simultaneous positive and negative personal feelings of fear and hope, anxiety and relief, pressure and stimulation, leaving the old and accepting a new direction, loss of meaning and new meaning, threat to self-esteem and new sense of value. The challenge for transformational leaders is to recognize these mixed emotions, act to help people move from negative to positive emotions, and mobilize and focus energy that is necessary for individual renewal and organizational revitalization.

Figure 1 provides a set of concepts for understanding the individual dynamics of transitions. The concepts, drawn from the work by Bridges, propose a three-phase process of individual change: first come endings, followed by neutral zones, and then new beginnings.[6] During each of these phases, an identifiable set of psychological tasks can be identified which individuals need to successfully complete in order to accept change.

### The Three-Phase Process

*Endings*. All individual transitions start with endings. Endings must be accepted and understood before transitions can begin. Employees who refuse to accept the fact that traditional behaviors have ended will be unable to adopt new behaviors. The first task is to disengage, which often accompanies a physical transaction. For example, when transferring from one job to another, individuals must learn to accept the new physical setting and disengage from the old position: when transferred employees continually return to visit former colleagues, this is a sign that they have inadequately disengaged. The second task is to disidentify. Individual selfidentity is often tied to a job position in such a way that when a plant manager is transferred to corporate staff to work in the marketing department, he or she must disidentify with the plant and its people and with the self-esteem felt as a plant manager. At a deeper personal level, individual transactions require disenchantment. Disenchantment entails recognizing that the enchantment or positive feelings associated with past situations will not be possible to replicate in the future. . . . Finally, individuals need to experience and work through disorientation which reflects the loss of familiar trappings. As mature organizations become revitalized, individuals must disengage, disidentify, disenchant, and disorient with past practices and discover in new organizations a new sense of worth or value.

To help individuals cope with endings, transformational leaders need to replace past glories with future opportunities. However, leaders must also acknowledge individual resistances and senses of loss in a transitional period while encouraging employees to face and accept failures as learning opportunities. Holding on to past accomplishments and memories without coming to grips with failure and the need to change may be why companies such as W. T. Grant, International Harvester, and Braniff were unsuccessful at revitalization. There is a sense of dying in all endings, and it does not help to treat transactions as if the past can be buried without effort. Yet, one should see the past as providing new directions.

*Neutral Zone.* The key to individuals being able to fully change may be in the second phase which Bridges terms the neutral zone.[7] This phase can be interpreted as a seemingly unproductive "time out" when individuals feel disconnected from people and things of the past and emotionally unconnected with the present. In reality, this phase is a time of reorientation where individuals complete-endings and begin new patterns of behavior. Often Western culture, especially in the U.S., avoids this experience and treats the neutral zone like a busy street, to be crossed as fast as possible and certainly not a place to contemplate and experience. However, running across the neutral zone too hurriedly does not allow the ending to occur nor the new beginning to properly start. A death and rebirth process is necessary so that organizational members can work through the disintegration and reintegration. To pass through the neutral zone requires taking the time and thought to gain perspective on both the endings— what went wrong, why it needs to be changed, and what must be overcome in both attitude and behavioral change— and the new beginning—what the new priorities are, why they are needed, and what new attitudes and behaviors will be required. It is in this phase that the most skillful transformational leadership is called upon. . . .

Failure to lead individuals through the neutral zone may result in aborted new beginnings. In 1983, International Harvester appeared to be stuck in the neutral zone. In order for International Harvester to make a new beginning, it must enable people to find a new identification with the future organization while accepting the end of the old organization. Such a transformation has successfully occurred at Chrysler Corporation where morale and esprit de corps grew with the new vision implanted by Lee Iacocca. In the end, organizational revitalization can only occur if individuals accept past failures and engage in new behaviors and attitudes.

*New Beginnings.* After individuals accept endings by working through neutral zones, they are able to work with new enthusiasm and commitment. New beginnings are characterized by employees learning from the past rather than reveling in it, looking for new scripts rather than acting out old ones, and being positive and excited about current and future work opportunities rather than dwelling on past successes or failures. When Mr. Iacocca implemented his vision at Chrysler, many long-term employees discovered new beginnings. They saw the new Chrysler as an opportunity to succeed, and they worked with a renewed vigor.

## WHAT QUALITIES DO TRANSFORMATIONAL LEADERS POSSESS?

So what does it take to transform an organization's technical, political, and cultural systems? The transformational leader must possess a deep understanding, whether it be intuitive or learned, of organizations and their place both in society at large and in the lives of individuals. The ability to build a new institution requires the kind of political dialogue our founding fathers had when Jefferson, Hamilton, Adams, and others debated issues of justice, equity, separation of powers, checks and balances, and freedom. This language may sound foreign to corporate settings but when major organization revitalization is being undertaken, all of these concepts merit some level of examination. At Chrysler, issues of equity, justice, power, and freedom underlay many of Mr. Iacocca's decisions. Thus, as a start, transformational leaders need to understand concepts of equity, power, freedom, and the dynamics of decision making. In addition to modifying systems, transformational leaders must understand and realign cultural systems.

In addition to managing political and cultural systems, transformational leaders must make difficult decisions quickly. Leaders need to know when to push and

when to back off. Finally, transformational leaders are often seen as creators of their own luck. These leaders seize opportunities and know when to act so that casual observers may perceive luck as a plausible explanation for their success; whereas, in reality it is a transformational leader who knows when to jump and when not to jump. Again, Mr. Iacocca can be viewed either as a very lucky person or as the possessor of a great ability to judge when to act and when not to act.

## THE SIGNIFICANCE OF CORPORATE CULTURES

Much has been written about organizational cultures in recent years.[8]. . .

Culture plays two central roles in organizations. First, it provides organizational members with a way of understanding and making sense of events and symbols. Thus, when employees are confronted with certain complex problems, they "know" how to approach them the "right" way. Like the Eskimos who have a vocabulary that differentiates the five types of snow, organizations create vocabularies to describe how things are done in the organization. At IBM, it is very clear to all insiders how to form a task force and to solve problems since task forces and problem solving are a way of life in IBM's culture.

Second, culture provides meaning. It embodies a set of values which helps justify why certain behaviors are encouraged at the exclusion of other behaviors. Companies with strong cultures have been able to commit people to the organization and have them identify very personally and closely with the organization's success. Superficially, this is seen in the "hoopla" activities associated with an IBM sales meeting, a Tupperware party, or an Amway distributor meeting. Outsiders often ridicule such activities, yet they are part of the process by which some successful companies manage cultural meaning. On one level, corporate culture is analogous to rituals carried out in religious groups. The key point in assessing culture is to realize that in order to transform an organization the culture that provides meaning must be assessed and revamped. The transformational leader needs to articulate new values and norms and then to use multiple change levers ranging from role modeling, symbolic acts, creation of rituals, and revamping of human resource systems and management processes to support new cultural messages.

## CONCLUSION

Based on the premise that the pressure for basic organizational change will intensify and not diminish, we strongly believe that transformational leadership, not transactional management, is required for revitalizing our organizations. Ultimately, it is up to our leaders to choose the right kind of leadership and corporate lifestyle.

## REFERENCES

1. See J. M. Burns, *Leadership* (New York: Harper & Row, 1978).

2. See N. M. Tichy, *Managing Strategic Change: Technical, Political and Cultural Dynamics* (New York: John Wiley & Sons, 1983).

3. Ibid.

4. See K. H. Blanchard and S. Johnson, *The One Minute Manager* (New York: Berkeley Books, 1982).

5. See T. J. Peters and R. J. Waterman, Jr., *In Search of Excellence* (New York: Harper & Row, 1982).

6. See W. Bridges, *Making Sense of Life's Transitions* (New York: Addison-Wesley, 1980).

7. Ibid.

8. See: T. E. Deal and A. A. Kennedy, *Corporate Cultures* (Reading, MA: Addison-Wesley, 1982); "Corporate Culture: The Hard-to-Change Values That Spell Success or Failure," *Business Week*, 27 October 1980, pp. 148–160; W. Ulrich, "HRM and Culture: History, Rituals, and Myths," *Human Resource Management* (23/2) Summer 1984.

# 19
# Why Leaders Can't Lead
*Warren G. Bennis*

## THE UNCONSCIOUS CONSPIRACY CONTINUES

Thirteen years ago, I wrote *The Unconscious Conspiracy: Why Leaders Can't Lead*. It stirred up a bit of a commotion at the time. I was pleased to learn last summer that university presidents had named it (along with another book of mine—*Leaders* [1985]) as one of their favorite books on leadership. I was pleased and disturbed, actually, since its continuing popularity suggests that while the players have changed, as the world has, their predicament has not—except perhaps for the worse. In America today, it is harder than ever to lead. One of my favorite social barometers, the bumper sticker, corroborates this. There has been a resurgence lately of such exhortations as "Don't Vote—It Will Only Encourage Them." For at least the second time, "Impeach Someone" is popular. Though we need leaders as much as ever, we have never held them in lower regard. Circumstances conspire against them. And so—without meaning to—do the American people.

Writers and teachers like to think that once they have identified a problem and offered some solutions, the problem is on its way to being solved. Having named the leadership problem in 1976, and having pointed out the direction in which I thought solutions might lurk, I moved on to fresh pastures. One such verdant field was an extensive study of leaders and the characteristics of leader-

ship, which (with my coauthor Burt Nanus) I described in *Leaders*.

My next project was to have been a book titled *Managing the Dream*, in which I planned to focus on the application of leadership, spotlighting a variety of leaders and their organizations. As often happens, however, I had to go back before I could go forward. I needed to look again at the context of leadership—at our organizations and at society itself—because leaders do not emerge from or function in a vacuum, and there has never been a more challenging context than the one in which we live today.

My intent at that juncture was simply to update *The Unconscious Conspiracy* to reflect the changed circumstances. Almost immediately, however, I saw that much more was needed. In tone and temper, the 1980s were totally different from the 1970s. Indeed, the 1980s were less an extension of the 1970s than they were the *result* of both the 1960s and the 1970s. In the 1960s, we wanted to make the world better. In the 1970s, we wanted only to make ourselves better. Now, at the start of the 1990s, we seem to be uncertain about whether we can make anything better.

The business world is turbulent, its waters roiled by continuing scandals and violent stock market shifts. The political world is in upheaval, fueled by a growing fear that our leaders and institutions are failing to cope and, in fact, are frozen by the complexity of the problems we face.

*Source:* Adapted from *Why Leaders Can't Lead: The Unconscious Conspiracy Continues*, by Warren Bennis, Jossey-Bass, Inc., Publishers, pp. xi–xiv, 14–24. Copyright 1989 by Warren Bennis. Reprinted by permission.

The very fabric of our society is being unraveled by unchecked crime and drug traffic, increasing poverty and illiteracy, and unprecedented cynicism toward possible solutions. Who's in charge here? The answer seems to be, no one.

An unconscious conspiracy in contemporary society prevents leaders—no matter what their original vision—from taking charge and making changes. Within any organization, an entrenched bureaucracy with a commitment to the status quo undermines the unwary leader. To make matters worse, certain social forces—the increasing tension between individual rights and the common good, for example—discourage the emergence of leaders. The narcissistic children of the Me Decade seem unwilling to embrace any vision but their own—a narrow one that excludes the possibility of sacrificing a little bit today to gain something better tomorrow. A corollary of this unwillingness to sacrifice is an unwillingness to cooperate with neighbors. Americans are now going through a self-imposed isolation phase: Each individual feels helpless to affect anything beyond the immediate environment and so retreats into an ever-contracting private world—a phenomenon that manifests itself among the affluent as "cocooning" and among the poor as drug addiction. Activism is on the decline, including the simplest form of activism—voting. People float, but they don't dream. And people without a dream are less easily inspired by a leader's vision.

So the bad news is, the arena in which leadership is exercised has deteriorated. The good news is, we have, I believe, a better grasp of the problems and a better sense of the solutions than we did a dozen years ago. . . .

*Why Leaders Can't Lead* is an analysis of the problems facing anyone who tries to take charge of an organization—of whatever kind—and effect change. The book offers those engaged in the day-to-day tasks of leadership specific suggestions—not only on how to counter the turmoil and inertia that threaten the best-laid plans, but also on how to keep *routine*, which absorbs time and energy like a sponge, from sapping their ability to make a real impact.

The book is not overly optimistic. But I do think change is possible—even change for the better. Change begins slowly, however, as, one by one, individuals make the conscious choice to live up to their potential.

. . . While my description of our current circumstances may seem grim, I hope it will make the reader aware of the possibilities for change. In fact, I hope it will spur the reader on to take responsibility for change. Abraham Maslow said, "Each time one takes responsibility, this is an actualization of the self." It is also the first step in taking charge, in becoming a leader.

The best hope I have for this book is that twelve years from now I will look back on it and muse, "Where have all the leaders come from?"

## LEARNING SOME BASIC TRUISMS ABOUT LEADERSHIP

A moment of truth came to me toward the end of my first ten months as president of the University of Cincinnati. The clock was moving toward four in the morning, and I was still in my office, still mired in the incredible mass of paper stacked on my desk. I was bone weary and soul-weary, and I found myself muttering, "Either I can't manage this place, or it's unmanageable." I reached for my calendar and ran my eyes down each hour, half hour, quarter hour, to see where my time had gone that day, the day before, the month before.

Nobel laureate James Franck has said he always recognizes a moment of discovery by "the feeling of terror that seizes me." I felt a trace of it that morning. My discovery was this: *I had become the victim of a vast, amorphous, unwitting, unconscious conspiracy to prevent me from doing anything whatever to change the university's status quo.* Even those of my associates who fully shared my hopes to set new goals, new directions, and to work toward creative change were unconsciously often doing the most to make sure that I would never find the time to begin. I found myself thinking of a friend and former colleague who had taken over one of our top universities with goals and plans that fired up all those around him and who said when he left a few years later, "I never could get around to doing the things I wanted to do."

This discovery, or rediscovery, led me to formulate what might be called Bennis's First Law of Academic Pseudodynamics: Routine work drives out nonroutine work and smothers to death all creative planning, all fundamental change in the university—or any institution.

These were the illustrations facing me: To start, there were 150 letters in the day's mail that required a response. About 50 of them concerned our young dean of the School of Education, Hendrik Gideonse. His job was to bring about change in the teaching of teachers, in our university's relationship to the public schools and to students in the deprived and deteriorating neighborhood around us. Out of these urban schools would come the bulk of our students of the future—as good or as bad as the schools had shaped them.

But the letters were not about education. They were about a baby, the dean's ten-week-old son. Gideonse felt very strongly about certain basic values. He felt especially so about sex roles, about equality for his wife, about making sure

she had the time and freedom to develop her own potentials fully. So he was carrying the baby into his office two days a week in a little bassinet, which he kept on his desk while he did his work. The daily *Cincinnati Enquirer* heard about it, took a picture of Hendrik, baby, and bassinet, and played it on page one. TV splashed it across the nation. And my "in" basket began to overflow with letters that urged his arrest for child abuse or at least his immediate dismissal. My only public comment was that we were a tax-supported institution, and if Hendrik could engage in that form of applied humanism and still accomplish the things we both wanted done in education, then, like Lincoln with Grant's whiskey, I'd gladly send him several new babies for adoption.

Hendrik was, of course, simply a man a bit ahead of his time. Today, his actions would be applauded—maybe even with a Father of the Year award. Then, however, Hendrik and his baby ate up quite a bit of my time.

. . . The track coach wanted me to come over to see for myself how bad the track was. An alumnus couldn't get the football seats he wanted. Another wanted a coach fired. A teacher had called to tell me the squash court was closed at 7 P.M. when he wanted to use it.

Perhaps 20 percent of my time that year had been taken up by a problem at the general hospital, which was city-owned but administered by the university and served as the teaching hospital of the university medical school. Some terminal-cancer patients, with their consent, had been subjected to whole-body radiation as possibly beneficial therapy. Since the Pentagon saw this as a convenient way to gather data that might help protect civilian populations in nuclear warfare, it provided a series of subsidies for the work.

When this story broke and was pursued in such a way as to call up comparisons with the Nazis' experiments on human guinea pigs, it became almost impossible for me or anybody else to separate the essential facts from the fantasized distortions. The problem eventually subsided, after a blue-ribbon task force recommended significant changes in the experiment's design. But I invested endless time in a matter only vaguely related to the prime purposes of the university—and wound up being accused by some of interfering with academic freedom.

The radiation experiment and Hendrik's baby illustrate how the media, particularly TV, make the academic cloister a goldfish bowl. By focusing on the lurid or the superficial, they can disrupt a president's proper activities while contributing nothing to the advancement of knowledge. This leads me to Bennis's Second Law of Academic Pseudodynamics: Make whatever grand plans you will, you may be sure the unexpected or the trivial will disturb and disrupt them.

In my moment of truth, that weary 4 A.M. in my trivia-cluttered office, I began trying to straighten out in my own mind what university presidents should be doing and not doing, what their true priorities should be, how they must lead.

*Lead,* not *manage:* There is an important difference. Many an institution is very well managed and very poorly led. It may excel in the ability to handle each day all the routine inputs yet may never ask whether the routine should be done at all.

All of us find ourselves acting on routine problems because they are the easiest things to handle. We hesitate to get involved too early in the bigger ones—we collude, as it were, in the unconscious conspiracy to immerse us in routine.

My entrapment in routine made me realize another thing: People were following the old army game. They did not want to take the responsibility for or bear the consequences of decisions they properly should make. The motto was, "Let's push up the tough ones." The consequence was that everybody and anybody was dumping his "wet babies" (as the old State Department hands call them) on my desk, when I had neither the diapers nor the information to take care of them. So I decided that the president's first priority—the sine qua non of effective leadership—was to create an "executive constellation" to run the office of the president. It could be a mixed bag, some vice-presidents, some presidential assistants. The group would have to be compatible in the sense that its members could work together but neither uniform nor conformist—a group of people who knew more than the president about everything within their areas of competency and could attend to daily matters without dropping their wet babies on the president's desk.

What should the president him- or herself do? The president should be a *conceptualist.* That's something more than being just an "idea man." It means being a leader with entrepreneurial vision and the time to spend thinking about the forces that will affect the destiny of the institution. The president must educate board members so that they not only understand the necessity of distinguishing between leadership and management but also can protect the chief executive from getting enmeshed in routine machinery.

Leaders must create for their institutions clear-cut and measurable goals based on advice from all elements of the community. They must be allowed to proceed toward those goals without being crippled by bureaucratic machinery that saps their strength, energy, and initiative. They must be allowed to take risks, to embrace error, to use their creativity to the hilt and encourage those who work with them to use theirs.

These insights gave me the strength to survive my acid test: whether I, as a "leading theorist" of the principles of creative leadership, actually could prove myself a leader. However, the sum total of my experiences as president of the University of Cincinnati convinced me that most of the academic theory on leadership was useless.

After leaving the university, I spent nearly five years researching a book on leadership. I traveled around the country spending time with ninety of the most effective, successful leaders in the nation, sixty from corporations and thirty from the public sector. My goal was to find these leaders' common traits, a task that required more probing than I had expected. For a while, I sensed much more diversity than commonality among them. The group included both left-brain and right-brain thinkers; some who dressed for success and some who didn't; well-spoken, articulate leaders and laconic, inarticulate ones; some John Wayne types and some who were definitely the opposite.

I was finally able to come to some conclusions, of which perhaps the most important is the distinction between leaders and managers: Leaders are people who do the right thing; managers are people who do things right. Both roles are crucial, but they differ profoundly. I often observe people in top positions doing the wrong thing well.

This study also reinforced my earlier insight—that American organizations (and probably those in much of the rest of the industrialized world) are underled and overmanaged. They do not pay enough attention to doing the right thing, while they pay too much attention to doing things right. Part of the fault lies with our schools of management; we teach people how to be good technicians and good staff people, but we don't train people for leadership.

The group of sixty corporate leaders was not especially different from any profile of top leadership in America. The median age was fifty-six. Most were white males, with six black men and six women in the group. The only surprising finding was that all the CEOs not only were still married to their first spouses but also seemed enthusiastic about the institution of marriage. . . .

After several years of observation and conversation, I defined four competencies evident to some extent in every member of the group: management of attention; management of meaning; management of trust; and management of self. The first trait apparent in these leaders is their ability to draw others to them, not just because they have a vision but because they communicate an extraordinary focus of commitment. Leaders manage attention through a compelling vision that brings others to a place they have not been before.

One of the people I most wanted to interview was one of the few I could not seem to reach—Leon Fleischer, a well-known child prodigy who grew up to become a prominent pianist, conductor, and musicologist. I happened to be in Aspen, Colorado, one summer while Fleischer was conducting the Aspen Music Festival, and I tried again to reach him, even leaving a note on his dressing-room door. Driving back through downtown Aspen, I saw two perspiring young cellists carrying their instruments, and I offered them a ride to the music tent. They hopped in the back of my jeep, and as we rode I questioned them about Fleischer. "I'll tell you why he's so great," said one. "He doesn't waste our time."

Fleischer finally agreed not only to be interviewed but to let me watch him rehearse and conduct music classes. I linked the way I saw him work with that simple sentence, "He doesn't waste our time." Every moment Fleischer was before the orchestra, he knew exactly what sound he wanted. He didn't waste time because his intentions were always evident. What united him with the other musicians was their concern with intention and outcome.

When I reflected on my own experience, it struck me that when I was most effective, it was because I knew what I wanted. When I was ineffective, it was because I was unclear about it.

So the first leadership competency is the management of attention through a set of intentions or a vision, not in a mystical or religious sense but in the sense of outcome, goal, or direction.

The second leadership competency is management of meaning. To make dreams apparent to others and to align people with them, leaders must communicate their vision. Communication and alignment work together. Consider, for example, the contrasting styles of Presidents Reagan and Carter. Ronald Reagan is called "the Great Communicator"; one of his speech writers said that Reagan can read the phone book and make it interesting. The reason is that Reagan uses metaphors with which people can identify. In his first budget message, for example, Reagan described a trillion dollars by comparing it to piling up dollar bills beside the Empire State Building. Reagan, to use one of Alexander Haig's coinages, "tangibilitated" the idea. Leaders make ideas tangible and real to others, so they can support them. For no matter how marvelous the vision, the effective leader must use a metaphor, a word or a model to make that vision clear to others.

In contrast, President Carter was boring. Carter was one of our best-informed presidents; he had more facts at his fingertips than almost any other president. But he never made the meaning come

through the facts. I interviewed an assistant secretary of commerce appointed by Carter, who told me that after four years in his administration, she still did not know what Jimmy Carter stood for. She said that working for him was like looking through the wrong side of a tapestry; the scene was blurry and indistinct.

The leader's goal is not mere explanation or clarification but the creation of meaning. My favorite baseball joke is exemplary: In the ninth inning of a key playoff game, with a three-and-two count on the batter, the umpire hesitates a split second in calling the pitch. The batter whirls around angrily and says, "Well, what was it?" The umpire snarls back, "It ain't *nothing* until *I* call it!"

The third competency is management of trust. Trust is essential to all organizations. The main determinant of trust is reliability, what I call *constancy*. When I talked to the board members or staffs of these leaders, I heard certain phrases again and again: "She is all of a piece." "Whether you like it or not, you always know where he is coming from, what he stands for."

When John Paul II visited this country, he gave a press conference. One reporter asked how the pope could account for allocating funds to build a swimming pool at the papal summer palace. He responded quickly, "I like to swim. Next question." He did not rationalize about medical reasons or claim that he got the money from a special source. A recent study showed that people would much rather follow individuals they can count on, even when they disagree with their viewpoint, than people they agree with but who shift positions frequently. I cannot emphasize enough the significance of constancy and focus. Margaret Thatcher's reelection in Great Britain is another excellent example. When she won office in 1979, observers predicted that she quickly would revert to defunct

Labor Party policies. She did not. She has not turned; she has been constant, focused, and all of a piece.

The fourth leadership competency is management of self, knowing one's skills and deploying them effectively. Management of self is critical; without it, leaders and managers can do more harm than good. Like incompetent doctors, incompetent managers can make life worse, make people sicker and less vital. There is a term—*iatrogenic*—for illnesses caused by doctors and hospitals. There should be one for illnesses caused by leaders, too. Some give themselves heart attacks and nervous breakdowns; still worse, many are "carriers," causing their employees to be ill.

Leaders know themselves; they know their strengths and nurture them. They also have a faculty I think of as the Wallenda Factor. The Flying Wallendas are perhaps the world's greatest family of aerialists and tightrope walkers. I was fascinated when, in the early 1970s, seventy-one-year-old Karl Wallenda said that for him living was walking the tightrope, and everything else was waiting. I was struck with his capacity for concentration on the intention, the task, the decision. I was even more intrigued when, several months later, Wallenda fell to his death while walking a tightrope without a safety net between two high-rise buildings in San Juan, Puerto Rico. Wallenda fell still clutching the balancing pole he had warned his family never to drop lest it hurt somebody below. Later, Wallenda's wife said that before her husband had fallen, for the first time since she had known him he had been concentrating on falling, instead of on walking the tightrope. He had personally supervised the attachment of the guide wires, which he had never done before.

Like Wallenda before his fall, the leaders in my group seemed unacquainted with the concept of failure.

What you or I might call a failure, they referred to as a mistake. I began collecting synonyms for the word *failure* mentioned in the interviews, and I found more than twenty: *mistake, error, false start, bloop, flop, loss, miss, foul-up, stumble, botch, bungle* . . . but not *failure.* One CEO told me that if she had a knack for leadership, it was the capacity to make as many mistakes as she could as soon as possible, and thus get them out of the way. Another said that a mistake is simply "another way of doing things." These leaders learn from and use something that doesn't go well; it is not a failure but simply the next step.

Leadership can be felt throughout an organization. It gives pace and energy to the work and empowers the work force. Empowerment is the collective effect of leadership. In organizations with effective leaders, empowerment is most evident in four themes:

- *People feel significant.* Everyone feels that he or she makes a difference to the success of the organization. The difference may be small—prompt delivery of potato chips to a mom-and-pop grocery store or developing a tiny but essential part for an airplane. But where they are empowered, people feel that what they do has meaning and significance.
- *Learning and competence matter.* Leaders value learning and mastery, and so do people who work for leaders. Leaders make it clear that there is no failure, only mistakes that give us feedback and tell us what to do next.
- *People are part of a community.* Where there is leadership, there is a team, a family, a unity. Even people who do not especially like each other feel the sense of community. When Neil Armstrong talks about the Apollo explorations, he describes how a team carried out an almost unimaginably complex set of interdependent tasks. Until there were women astronauts, the men referred to this feeling as "brotherhood." I suggest they rename it "family."

- *Work is exciting*. Where there are leaders, work is stimulating, challenging, fascinating, and fun. An essential ingredient in organizational leadership is pulling rather than pushing people toward a goal. A "pull" style of influence attracts and energizes people to enroll in an exciting vision of the future. It motivates through identification, rather than through rewards and punishments. Leaders articulate and embody the ideals toward which the organization strives.

People cannot be expected to enroll in just any exciting vision. Some visions and concepts have more staying power and are rooted more deeply in our human needs than others. I believe the lack of two such concepts in modern organizational life is largely responsible for the alienation and lack of meaning so many experience in their work. One of these is the concept of quality. Modern industrial society has been oriented to quantity, providing more goods and services for everyone. Quantity is measured in money; we are a money-oriented society. Quality often is not measured at all but is appreciated intuitively. Our response to quality is a feeling. Feelings of quality are connected intimately with our experience of meaning, beauty, and value in our lives.

Closely linked to the concept of quality is that of dedication to, even love of, our work. This dedication is evoked by quality and is the force that energizes high-performing systems. When we love our work, we need not be managed by hopes of reward or fears of punishment. We can create systems that facilitate our work, rather than being preoccupied with checks and controls of people who want to beat or exploit the system.

Ultimately, in great leaders and the organizations surrounding them, there is a fusion of work and play to the point where, as Robert Frost says, "Love and need are one." How do we get from here to there? I think we must start by studying change.

# 20
# The Learning Leader as Culture Manager
*Edgar H. Schein*

Leadership can occur anywhere in the organization. Leadership is the attitude and motivation to examine and manage culture. Accomplishing this goal is more difficult lower down in the organization but by no means impossible in that subcultures can be managed just as can overall organizational cultures.

The issues that make the most difference to the kind of leadership required are twofold. First, different stages of organizational development require different kinds of culture management. Second, different strategic issues require a focus on different kinds of cultural dimensions. Each of these points is briefly examined below.

## LEADERSHIP IN CULTURE CREATION

In a growing organization leaders externalize their own assumptions and embed them gradually and consistently in the mission, goals, structures, and working procedures of the group. Whether we call these basic assumptions the guiding beliefs, the theories-in-use, the mental models, the basic principles, or the guiding visions on which founders operate, there is little question that they become major elements of the organization's emerging culture (for example, Argyris, 1976; Bennis, 1989; Davis, 1984; Donaldson and Lorsch, 1983; Dyer, 1986; Kotter and Heskett, 1992; Pettigrew, 1979; Schein, 1983).

In a rapidly changing world, the learning leader/founder must not only have vision but must be able to impose it and to develop it further as external circumstances change. Inasmuch as the new members of an organization arrive with prior organizational and cultural experiences, a common set of assumptions can only be forged by clear and consistent messages as the group encounters and survives its own crises. The culture creation leader therefore needs persistence and patience, yet as a learner must be flexible and ready to change.

As groups and organizations develop, certain key emotional issues arise. These have to do with dependence on the leader, with peer relationships, and with how to work effectively. Leadership is needed to help the group identify the issues and deal with them. During this process leaders must often absorb and contain the anxiety that is unleashed when things do not work as they should (Hirschhorn, 1988; Schein, 1983). Leaders may not have the answer, but they must provide temporary stability and emotional reassurance while the answer is being worked out. This anxiety-containing function is especially relevant during periods of learning, when old habits must be given up before new ones are learned. Moreover, if the world is increasingly changing, such anxiety may be perpetual, requiring learning leaders to assume a perpetual supportive role. The traumas of growth appear to be so constant and so powerful that unless a strong leader takes the role of anxiety and risk absorber, the group cannot get through its early stages of growth and fails. Being in an ownership position helps because everyone then realizes that the founder is in fact taking a greater personal financial risk; however, ownership does not automatically create the ability to absorb anxiety. For many leaders this is one of the most important things they have to learn.

When leaders launch new enterprises, they must be mindful of the power they have to impose on those enterprises their own assumptions about what is right and proper, how the world works, and how things should be done. Leaders should not apologize for or be cautious about their assumptions. Rather, it is intrinsic to the leadership role to create order out of chaos, and leaders are expected to provide their own assumptions as an initial road map into the uncertain future. The more aware leaders are of this process, the more consistent and effective they can be in implementing it.

The process of culture creation, embedding, and reinforcement brings with it problems as well as solutions. Many organizations survive and grow but at the same time operate inconsistently or do things that seem contradictory. One explanation of this phenomenon that has been pointed out repeatedly is that leaders not only embed in their organizations what they intend consciously to get across, but they also convey their own inner conflicts and the inconsistencies in their own personal makeup (Schein, 1983; Kets de Vries and Miller, 1984; Miller, 1990). The most powerful signal to which subordinates respond is what catches leaders' attention consistently, particularly what arouses them emotionally. But many of the things to which leaders respond emotionally reflect not so much their conscious intentions as their unconscious conflicts. The

organization then either develops assumptions around these inconsistencies and conflicts and they become part of the culture, or the leader gradually loses a position of influence if the behavior begins to be seen as too disruptive or actually destructive. In extreme cases the organization isolates or ejects the founder. In doing so, however, it is not rejecting all of the founder's assumptions but only those that are inconsistent with the core assumptions on which the organization was built.

The period of culture creation, therefore, puts an additional burden on founders—to obtain enough self-insight to avoid unwittingly undermining their own creations. Founding leaders often find it difficult to recognize that the very qualities that made them successful initially, their strong convictions, can become sources of difficulty later on and that they also must learn and grow as their organizations grow. Such insights become especially important when organizations face issues of leadership succession because succession discussions force into the open aspects of the culture that may not have been previously recognized.

What all of this means for leaders of developing organizations is that they must have tremendous self-insight and recognize their own role not only in creating the culture but also their responsibility in embedding and developing culture. Inasmuch as the culture is the primary source of identity for young organizations, the culture creation and development process must be handled sensitively with full understanding of the anxieties that are unleashed when identity is challenged.

## LEADERSHIP AT ORGANIZATIONAL MIDLIFE

As the organization develops a substantial history of its own, its culture becomes more of a cause than an effect. As subgroups develop their own subcultures, the opportunities for constructive use of cultural diversity and the problems of integration both become greater. The leader must be able to pay attention to diversity and assess clearly how much of it is useful for further organizational development and how much of it is potentially dysfunctional. The culture is now much less tied to the leader's own personality, which makes it easier to assess objectively, though there are likely to be sacred cows, holdovers from the founding period, that have to be delicately handled.

The leader at this stage must be able to detect how the culture influences the strategy, structure, procedures, and ways in which the group members relate to one another. Culture is a powerful influence on members' perceptions, thinking, and feeling, and these predispositions, along with situational factors, influence members' behavior. Because culture serves an important anxiety-reducing function, members cling to it even if it becomes dysfunctional in relationship to environmental opportunities and constraints.

Leaders at this stage need diagnostic skill to figure out not only what the cultural influences are, but also what their impact is on the organization's ability to change and learn. Whereas founding leaders most need self-insight, midlife leaders most need the ability to decipher the surrounding culture and subcultures. To help the organization evolve into whatever will make it most effective in the future, leaders must also have culture management skills. In some instances this may mean increasing cultural diversity, allowing some of the uniformity that may have been built up in the growth stage to erode. In other instances it may mean pulling together a culturally diverse set of organizational units and

attempting to impose new common assumptions on them. In either case the leader needs (1) to be able to analyze the culture in sufficient detail to know which cultural assumptions can aid and which ones will hinder the fulfillment of the organizational mission and (2) to possess the intervention skills to make desired changes happen.

Most of the prescriptive analyses of how to maintain the organization's effectiveness through this period emphasize that the leader must have certain insights, clear vision, and the skills to articulate, communicate, and implement the vision, but these analyses say nothing about how a given organization can find and install such a leader. In U.S. organizations in particular, the outside board members probably play a critical role in this process. If the organization has had a strong founding culture, however, its board may be composed exclusively of people who share the founder's vision. Consequently, real changes in direction may not become possible until the organization experiences serious survival difficulties and begins to search for a person with different assumptions to lead it.

One area to explore further here is the CEO's own role in succession. Can the leader of a midlife organization perceive the potential dysfunctions of some aspects of the culture to a sufficient extent to ensure that his or her successor will be able to move the culture in an appropriate new direction? CEOs have a great deal of power to influence the choice of their successor. Do they use that power wisely in terms of cultural issues? For example, it is alleged that one of the main reasons why Reginald Jones as CEO of General Electric "chose" Jack Welch to be his successor was because he recognized in Welch a person who would create the kinds of changes that were necessary for GE to remain viable. Similarly, Steve Jobs "chose" John Sculley to head Apple even though at some level he must have sensed that this choice might eventually lead to the kind of conflict that in the end forced Jobs to leave. The ultimate paradox here is that truly learning leaders may have to face the conclusion that they must replace themselves, that they do not have the vision needed to bring the midlife organization into alignment with a rapidly changing world.

## LEADERSHIP IN MATURE AND POTENTIALLY DECLINING ORGANIZATIONS

In the mature stage if the organization has developed a strong unifying culture, that culture now defines even what is to be thought of as leadership, what is heroic or sinful behavior, and how authority and power are to be allocated and managed. Thus, what leadership has created now either blindly perpetuates itself or creates new definitions of leadership, which may not even include the kinds of entrepreneurial assumptions that launched the organization in the first place. The first problem of the mature and possibly declining organization, then, is to find a process to empower a potential leader who may have enough insight to overcome some of the constraining cultural assumptions.

What the leader must do at this point in the organization's history depends on the degree to which the culture of the organization has, in fact, enabled the group to adapt to its environmental realities. If the culture has not facilitated adaptation, the organization either will not survive or will find a way to change its culture. If it is to change its culture, it must be led by someone who can, in effect, break the tyranny of the old culture. This requires not only the insight and diagnostic skill to determine what the old culture is, but to realize what

alternative assumptions are available and how to start a change process toward their acceptance.

Leaders of mature organizations must, as has been argued repeatedly, make themselves sufficiently marginal in their own organization to be able to perceive its assumptions objectively and nondefensively. They must, therefore, find many ways to be exposed to their external environment and, thereby facilitate their own learning. If they cannot learn new assumptions themselves, they will not be able to perceive what is possible in their organizations. Even worse, they may destroy innovative efforts that arise within their organizations if those innovative efforts involve countercultural assumptions.

Leaders capable of such managed culture change can come from inside the organization if they have acquired objectivity and insight into elements of the culture. Such culture objectivity appears to be related to having had a nonconventional career or exposure to many subcultures within the organization (Kotter and Heskett, 1992). However, the formally designated senior managers of a given organization may not be willing or able to provide such culture change leadership. Leadership then may have to come from other boundary spanners in the organization or from outsiders. It may even come from a number of people in the organization, in which case it makes sense to talk of turnaround teams or multiple leadership.

If a leader is imposed from the outside, she or he must have the skill to diagnose accurately what the culture of the organization is, what elements are well adapted and what elements are problematic for future adaptation, and how to change that which needs changing. In other words the leader must be a skilled change manager who first learns what the present state of the culture is, unfreezes it, redefines and changes it, and then refreezes the new assumptions. Talented turnaround managers seem to be able to manage all phases of such changes, but sometimes different leaders will be involved in the different steps over a considerable period of time. They will use all the mechanisms previously discussed in the appropriate combinations to get the job done provided that they have the authority and power to use extreme measures, such as replacing the people who perpetuate the old cultural assumptions.

In summary, leaders play a critical role at each developmental stage of an organization, but that role differs as a function of the stage. Much of what leaders do is to perpetually diagnose the particular assumptions of the culture and figure out how to use those assumptions constructively or to change them if they are constraints.

## LEADERSHIP AND CULTURE IN STRATEGY FORMULATION

Many companies have found that they or their consultants can think of new strategies that make sense from a financial, product, or marketing point of view, yet they cannot implement those strategies because such implementation requires assumptions, values, and ways of working that are too far out of line with the organization's existing assumptions. In some cases, the organization cannot even conceive of certain strategic options because they are too out of line with shared assumptions about the mission of the organization and its way of working, what Lorsch (1985) has aptly called "strategic myopia."

. . . We must remember that cultural assumptions are the product of past successes. As a result they are increasingly taken for granted and operate as silent filters on what is perceived and thought about. If the organization's environment changes and new responses are required, the danger is that the changes will not be noticed or, even if noticed, that the organization will not be able to adapt because of embedded routines based on past success. Culture constrains strategy by limiting what the CEO and other senior managers are able to think about and what they perceive in the first place.

*One of the critical roles of learning leadership, then, is first of all to notice changes in the environment and then to figure out what needs to be done to remain adaptive.* I am defining leadership in this context in terms of the role, not the position. The CEO or other senior managers may or may not be able to fulfill the leadership role, and leadership in the sense that I am defining it can occur anywhere in the organization. However, if real change and learning are to take place, it is probably necessary that the CEO or other very senior managers be able to be leaders in this sense.

Leaders must be somewhat marginal and must be somewhat embedded in the organization's external environment to fulfill this role adequately. At the same time, leaders must be well connected to those parts of the organization that are themselves well connected to the environment—sales, purchasing, marketing, public relations and legal, finance, and R & D. Leaders must be able to listen to disconfirming information coming from these sources and to assess the implications for the future of the organization. Only when they truly understand what is happening and what will be required in the way of organizational change can they begin to take action in initiating a learning process.

Much has been said about the need for vision in leaders, but too little has been said about their need to listen, to absorb, to search the environment for trends, and to build the organization's capacity to learn. Especially at the strategic level, the ability to see and acknowledge the full complexity of problems becomes critical. The ability to acknowledge complexity may also imply the willingness and emotional strength to admit uncertainty and to embrace experimentation and possible errors as the only way to learn. In our obsession with leadership vision, we may have made it possible for learning leaders to admit that their vision is not clear and that the whole organization will have to learn together. Moreover, as I have repeatedly argued, vision in a mature organization only helps when the organization has already been disconfirmed and members feel anxious and in need of a solution. Much of what learning leaders must do occurs before vision even becomes relevant.

To summarize, the critical roles of leadership in strategy formulation and implementation are (1) to perceive accurately and in depth what is happening in the environment, (2) to create enough disconfirming information to motivate the organization to change without creating too much anxiety, (3) to provide psychological safety by either providing a vision of how to change and in what direction or by creating a process of visioning that allows the organization itself to find a path, (4) to acknowledge uncertainty, (5) to embrace errors in the learning process as inevitable and desirable, and (6) to manage all phases of the change process, including especially the management of anxiety as some cultural assumptions are given up and new learning begins. . . .

## IMPLICATIONS FOR THE SELECTION AND DEVELOPMENT OF LEADERS

A dynamic analysis of organizational culture makes it clear that leadership is intertwined with culture formation, evolution, transformation, and destruction. Culture is created in the first instance by the actions of leaders; culture is embedded and strengthened by leaders. When culture becomes dysfunctional, leadership is needed to help the group unlearn some of its cultural assumptions and learn new assumptions. Such transformations sometimes require what amounts to conscious and deliberate destruction of cultural elements. This in turn requires the ability to surmount one's own taken-for-granted assumptions, seeing what is needed to ensure the health and survival of the group, and orchestrating events and processes that enable the group to evolve toward new cultural assumptions. Without leadership in this sense, groups will not be able to adapt to changing environmental conditions. Let us summarize what is really needed to be a leader in this sense.

## Perception and Insight

First, the leader must be able to perceive the problem, to have insight into himself or herself and into the culture and its dysfunctional elements. Such boundary-spanning perception can be difficult because it requires one to see one's own weaknesses, to perceive that one's own defenses not only help in managing anxiety but can also hinder one's efforts to be effective. Successful architects of change must have a high degree of objectivity about themselves and their own organizations, and such objectivity results from spending portions of their careers in diverse settings that permit them to compare and contrast different cultures. International experience is therefore one of the most powerful ways of learning.

Individuals often are aided in becoming objective about themselves through counseling and psychotherapy. One might conjecture that leaders can benefit from comparable processes such as training and development programs that emphasize experiential learning and self-assessment. From this perspective one of the most important functions of outside consultants or board members is to provide the kind of counseling that produces cultural insight. It is therefore far more important for the consultant to help the leader figure out for himself or herself what is going on and what to do than to provide recommendations on what the organization should do. The consultant also can serve as a "cultural therapist," helping the leader figure out what the culture is and what parts of it are more or less adaptive.

## Motivation

Leadership requires not only insight into the dynamics of the culture but the motivation and skill to intervene in one's own cultural process. To change any elements of the culture, leaders must be willing to unfreeze their own organization. Unfreezing requires disconfirmation, a process that is inevitably painful for many. The leader must find a way to say to his or her own organization that things are not all right and, if necessary, must enlist the aid of outsiders in getting this message across. Such willingness requires a great ability to be concerned for the organization above and beyond the self, to communicate dedication or commitment to the group above and beyond self-interest.

If the boundaries of organization become looser, a further motivational issue arises in that it is less and less clear where a leader's ultimate loyalty should lie— with the organization, with industry, with country, or with some broader professional community whose ultimate responsibility is to the globe and to all of humanity.

## Emotional Strength

Unfreezing an organization requires the creation of psychological safety, which means that the leader must have the emotional strength to absorb much of the anxiety that change brings with it and the ability to remain supportive to the organization through the transition phase even if group members become angry and obstructive. The leader is likely to be the target of anger and criticism because, by definition, he or she must challenge some of what the group has taken for granted. This may involve closing down the company division that was the original source of the company's growth and the basis of many employees' sense of pride and identity. It may involve laying off or retiring loyal, dedicated employees and old friends. Worst of all, it may involve the message that some of the founder's most cherished assumptions are wrong in the contemporary context. It is here that dedication and commitment are especially needed to demonstrate to the organization that the leader genuinely cares about the welfare of the total organization even as parts of it come under challenge. The leader must remember that giving up a cultural element requires one to take some risk, the risk that one will be very anxious and in the end worse off, and yet the leader must have the strength to forge the way into this unknown territory.

## Ability to Change the Cultural Assumptions

If an assumption is to be given up, it must be replaced or redefined in another form, and it is the burden of leadership to make that happen. In other words, the leader must have the ability to induce cognitive redefinition by articulating and selling new visions and concepts. The leader must be able to bring to the surface, review, and change some of the group's basic assumptions. . . .

## Ability to Create Involvement and Participation

A paradox of culture change leadership is that the leader must be able not only to lead but also to listen, to emotionally involve the group in achieving its own insights into its cultural dilemmas, and to be genuinely participative in his or her approach to learning and change. The leaders of social, religious, or political movements can rely on personal charisma and let the followers do what they will. In an organization, however, the leader has to work with the group that exists at the moment, because he or she is dependent on the group members to carry out the organization's mission. The leader must recognize that, in the end, cognitive redefinition must occur inside the heads of many members and that will happen only if they are actively involved in the process. The whole organization must achieve some degree of insight and develop motivation to change before any real change will occur, and the leader must create this involvement.

The ability to involve others and to listen to them also protects leaders from attempting to change things that should not be changed. When leaders are brought in from the outside this becomes especially important because some of the assumptions operating in the organization may not fit the leader's own assumptions yet be critical to the organization's success. To illustrate the kinds of mistakes that are possible, we need remember only the period in the Atari Company's history when Warner Communications, the parent company, decided to improve Atari's marketing by bringing in as president an experienced marketing executive from the food industry. This executive brought with him the assumption that the key to success is high motivation and high rewards based on individual performance. He created and imposed an incentive system designed to select the engineers who were doing the best job in inventing and designing new computer games and gave them large monetary rewards. Soon some of the best engineers were leaving,

and the company was getting into technical difficulty. What was wrong?

The new executive had created and articulated clear symbols, and everyone had rallied around them. Apparently, what was wrong was the assumption that the incentives and rewards should be based on individual effort. What the president failed to understand, coming from the food industry with its individualistic product management orientation, was that the computer games were designed by groups and teams and that the engineers considered the assignment of individual responsibility to be neither possible nor necessary. They were happy being group members and would have responded to group incentives, but unfortunately, the symbol chosen was the wrong symbol from this point of view. The engineers also noted that the president, with his nontechnical background, was not adept at choosing the best engineers, because their key assumption was that "best" was the product of group effort, not individual brilliance. Given the incompatible assumptions, it is no surprise that the president did not last long. Unfortunately, damage in terms of the loss of employees and in esprit had been done.

## Ability to Learn a New Culture

Culture change leaders often have to take over a company in which they did not previously have any experience. If they are to diagnose and possibly change the culture they have entered, it is, of course, mandatory that they first learn what the essence of that culture is. This point raises the question of how much an individual can learn that is totally new. My hypothesis, based on various streams of research on leadership and management, is that leaders can cross boundaries and enter new organizational cultures fairly easily if they stay within a given industry, as defined by a core technology. A manager growing up in one chemical company can probably become the successful CEO of another chemical company and can learn the culture of that company. What appears to be much more difficult is to cross industry or national boundaries, because cognitive frames that are built up early in the manager's career are fundamentally more embedded. The ability of a John Sculley to become a successful leader of Apple is unusual. . . .

In any case, the leader coming into a new organization must be very sensitive to his or her own need to truly understand the culture before assessing it and possibly changing it. A period of learning lasting a year or more, if the situation allows that much time, is probably necessary. If the situation is more critical, the leader could speed up his or her own learning by systematically involving the layers of the organization below him or her in culture deciphering exercises. . . .

## SUMMARY AND CONCLUSIONS

It seems clear that the leaders of the future will have to be perpetual learners. This will require (1) new levels of perception and insight into the realities of the world and also into themselves; (2) extraordinary levels of motivation to go through the inevitable pain of learning and change, especially in a world with looser boundaries in which one's own loyalties become more and more difficult to define; (3) the emotional strength to manage their own and others; anxiety as learning and change become more and more a way of life; (4) new skills in analyzing and changing cultural assumptions; (5) the willingness and ability to involve others and elicit their participation; and (6) the ability to learn the assumptions of a whole new organizational culture.

Learning and change cannot be imposed on people. Their involvement and participation are needed diagnosing what is going on, figuring out what to do, and actually doing it. The more turbulent, ambiguous, and out of control the world becomes, the more the learning process will have to be shared by all the members of the social unit doing the learning. If the leaders of today want to create organizational cultures that will themselves be more amenable to learning they will have to set the example by becoming learners themselves and involving others in the learning process.

The essence of that learning process will be to give organizational culture its due. Can we as individual members of organizations and occupations, as managers, teachers, researchers, and, sometimes, leaders recognize how deeply our own perceptions, thoughts, and feelings are culturally determined? Ultimately, we cannot achieve the cultural humility required to live in a turbulent culturally diverse world unless we can see cultural assumptions within ourselves. In the end, cultural understanding and cultural learning start with self-insight.

## REFERENCES

Argyris, C. *Increasing Leadership Effectiveness.* New York: Wiley-Interscience, 1976.

Bennis, W. *On Becoming a Leader.* Reading, Mass.: Addison-Wesley, 1989.

Davis, S. M. *Managing Corporate Culture.* New York: Ballinger, 1984.

Donaldson, G., and Lorsch, J. W. *Decision Making at the Top.* New York: Basic Books, 1983.

Dyer, W. G., Jr. *Culture Change in Family Firms.* San Francisco: Jossey-Bass, 1986.

Hirschhorn, L. *The Workplace Within: Psychodynamics of Organizational Life.* Cambridge, Mass.: MIT Press, 1988.

Kets de Vries, M. F. R., and Miller, D. *The Neurotic Organization: Diagnosing and Changing Counterproductive Styles of Management.* San Francisco: Jossey-Bass, 1984.

Kotter, J. P., and Heskett, J. L. *Corporate Culture and Performance.* New York: Free Press, 1992.

Lorsch, J. W. "Strategic Myopia: Culture as an Invisible Barrier to Change." In R. H. Kilmann, M. J. Saxton, R. Serpa, and others, *Gaining Control of the Corporate Culture.* San Francisco: Jossey-Bass, 1985.

Miller, D. *The Icarus Paradox.* New York: Harper & Row, 1990.

Pettigrew, A. M. "On Studying Organizational Cultures." *Administrative Science Quarterly,* 1979, 24, 570–581.

Schein, E. H. "The Role of the Founder in Creating Organizational Culture." *Organizational Dynamics,* Summer 1983, pp. 13–28.

# 21

# Leadership and the New Science: Searching for a Simpler Way to Lead Organizations

*Margaret J. Wheatley*

I am not alone in wondering why organizations aren't working well. Many of us are troubled by questions that haunt our work. Why do so many organizations feel dead? Why do projects take so long, develop ever-greater complexity, yet so often fail to achieve any truly significant results? Why does progress, when it appears, so often come from unexpected places, or as a result of surprises or serendipitous events that our planning had not considered? Why does change itself, that event we're all supposed to be "managing," keep drowning us, relentlessly reducing any sense of mastery we might possess? And why have our expectations for success diminished to the point that often the best we hope for is staying power and patience to endure the disruptive forces that appear unpredictably in the organizations where we work?

These questions had been growing within me for several years, gnawing away at my work and diminishing my sense of competency. The busier I became with work and the more projects I took on, the greater my questions grew. Until I began a journey.

Like most important journeys, mine began in a mundane place—a Boeing 757, flying soundlessly above America. High in the air as a weekly commuter between Boston and Salt Lake City, with long stretches of reading time broken only by occasional offers of soda and peanuts, I opened my first book on the new

science—Fritjof Capra's *The Turning Point*, which described the new world view emerging from quantum physics. This provided my first glimpse of a new way of perceiving the world, one that comprehended its processes of change and patterns of connections.

I don't think it accidental that I was introduced to a new way of seeing at 37,000 feet. The altitude only reinforced the message that what was needed was a larger perspective, one that took in more of the whole of things. From that first book, I took off, seeking out as many new science books as I could find in biology, evolution, chaos theory, and quantum physics. Discoveries and theories of new science called me away from the details of my own field of management inquiry and up to a vision of the inherent orderliness of the universe, of creative processes and dynamic, continuous change that still maintained order. This was a world where order and change, autonomy and control were not the great opposites that we had thought them to be. It was a world where change and constant creation signalled new ways of maintaining order and structure.

I don't believe I could have grasped these ideas if I had stayed on the ground. . . .

Somewhere—I knew then and believe even more firmly now—there is a simpler way to lead organizations, one that requires less effort and produces less stress than the current practices. For me, this new knowledge is only beginning to crystallize into applications, but I no longer believe that organizations are inherently unmanageable in our world of constant flux and unpredictability. Rather, I believe our present ways of understanding organizations are skewed, and that the longer we remain entrenched in our ways, the farther we move from those wonderful breakthroughs in understanding that the world of science calls "elegant." The layers of complexity, the sense of things being beyond our control and out of control, are but signals of our failure to understand a deeper reality of organizational life, and of life in general.

We are all searching for this simplicity. In many different disciplines, we live today with questions for which our expertise provides no answers. At the turn of the century, physicists faced the same unnerving confusion. There is a frequently told story about Niels Bohr and Werner Heisenberg, two founders of quantum theory. This version is from *The Turning Point:*

> In the twentieth century, physicists faced, for the first time, a serious challenge to their ability to understand the universe. Every time they asked nature a question in an atomic experiment, nature answered with a paradox, and the more they tried to clarify the situation, the sharper the paradoxes became. In their struggle to grasp this new reality, scientists became painfully aware that their basic concepts, their language, and their whole way of thinking were inadequate to describe atomic phenomena. Their problem was not only intellectual but involved an intense emotional and existential experience, as vividly described by Werner Heisenberg; "I remember discussions with Bohr which went through many hours till very late at night and ended almost in despair; and when at the end of the discussion I went alone for a walk in the neighboring park I repeated to myself again and

> again the question: Can nature possibly be so absurd as it seemed to us in these atomic experiments?"

> It took these physicists a long time to accept the fact that the paradoxes they encountered are an essential aspect of atomic physics. . . . Once this was perceived, the physicists began to learn to ask the right questions and to avoid contradictions . . . and finally they found the precise and consistent mathematical formulation of [quantum] theory.

> . . . Even after the mathematical formulation of quantum theory was completed, its conceptual framework was by no means easy to accept. Its effect on the physicists' view of reality was truly shattering. The new physics necessitated profound changes in concepts of space, time, matter, object, and cause and effect; and because these concepts are so fundamental to our way of experiencing the world, their transformation came as a great shock. To quote Heisenberg again: "The violent reaction to the recent development of modern physics can only be understood when one realizes that here the foundations of physics have started moving; and that this motion has caused the feeling that the ground would be cut from science." (In Capra 1963, 76–77. Used with permission.)

For the past several years, I have found myself often relating this story to groups of managers involved in organizational change. The story speaks with a chilling authority. Each of us recognizes the feelings this tale describes, of being mired in the habit of solutions that once worked yet are now totally inappropriate, of having rug after rug pulled from beneath us, whether by a corporate merger, reorganizations, downsizing, or a level of personal disorientation. But the story also gives great hope as a parable teaching us to embrace our despair as a step on the road to wisdom, encouraging us to sit in the unfamiliar seat of not knowing and open ourselves to radically new ideas. If we bear the confusion, then one day, the story promises, we will begin to see a whole new landscape, one of bright illumination that will dispel the oppressive shadows of our current ignorance. I still tell Heisenberg's story. It never fails to speak to me from this deep place of reassurance.

I believe that we have only just begun the process of discovering and inventing the new organizational forms that will inhabit the twenty-first century. To be responsible inventors and discoverers, though, we need the courage to let go of the old world, to relinquish most of what we have cherished, to abandon our interpretations about what does and doesn't work. As Einstein is often quoted as saying: "No problem can be solved from the same consciousness that created it. We must learn to see the world anew.

. . . Like many social scientists, I am at heart a lapsed scientist, still hoping that the world will yield up its secrets to me in predictable formulations.

But my focus on science is more than a personal interest. Each of us lives and works in organizations designed from Newtonian images of the universe. We manage by separating things into parts, we believe that influence occurs as a direct result of force exerted from one person to another, we engage in complex planning for a world that we keep expecting to be predictable, and we search continually for better methods of objectively perceiving the world. These assumptions come to us from seventeenth-century physics, from Newtonian mechanics. They are the base from which we design and manage organizations, and from which we do research in all of the social sciences. Intentionally or not, we work from a world view that has been derived from the natural sciences.

But the science has changed. If we are to continue to draw from the sciences to create and manage organizations, to design research, and to formulate

hypotheses about organizational design, planning, economics, human nature, and change processes (the list can be much longer), then we need to at least ground our work in the science of our times. We need to stop seeking after the universe of the seventeenth century and begin to explore what has become known to us in the twentieth century. We need to expand our search for the principles of organization to include what is presently known about the universe.

The search for the lessons of new science is still in progress, really in its infancy, but what I hope to convey in these pages is the pleasure of sensing those first glimmers of a new way of thinking about the world and its organizations. The light may be dim, but its potency grows as the door cracks wider and wider. Here there are scientists who write about natural phenomena with a poetry and a lucidity that speak to dilemmas we find in organizations. Here there are new images and metaphors for thinking about our own organizational experiences. This is a world of wonder and not knowing, where scientists are as awestruck by what they see as were the early explorers who marvelled at new continents. In this realm, there is a new kind of freedom, where it is more rewarding to explore than to reach conclusions, more satisfying to wonder than to know, and more exciting to search than to stay put.

This is not about conclusions, cases, or exemplary practices of excellent companies. It is deliberately *not* for two reasons. First, I no longer believe that organizations can be changed by imposing a model developed elsewhere. So little transfers to, or even inspires, those trying to work at change in their own organizations. Second, and much more important, the new physics cogently explains that there is no objective reality out there waiting to reveal its secrets. There are no recipes or formulae, no checklists or advice that describe "reality." There is only what we create through our engagement with others and with events. Nothing really transfers; everything is always new and different and unique to each of us.

. . . The ideas I have chosen to think about focus on the meta-issues that concern those of us who work in large organizations: What are the sources of order? How do we create organizational coherence, where activities correspond to purpose? How do we create structures that move with change, that are flexible and adaptive, even boundaryless, that enable rather than constrain? How do we simplify things without losing both control and differentiation? How do we resolve personal needs for freedom and autonomy with organizational needs for prediction and control?

Scientists in many different disciplines are questioning whether we can adequately explain how the world works by using the machine imagery created in the seventeenth century, most notably by Sir Isaac Newton. In the machine model, one must understand parts. Things can be taken apart, dissected literally or representationally (as we have done with business functions and academic disciplines), and then put back together without any significant loss. The assumption is that by comprehending the workings of each piece, the whole can be understood. The Newtonian model of the world is characterized by materialism and reductionism—a focus on things rather than relationships and a search, in physics, for the basic building blocks of matter.

In new science, the underlying currents are a movement toward holism, toward understanding the system as a system and giving primary value to the relationships that exist among seemingly discrete parts. Donella Meadows, a systems thinker, quotes an ancient Sufi teaching that captures this shift in focus: "You think because you understand *one* you must understand *two*, because one and one makes two. But you must also understand *and*" (1982, 23). When we view systems from this perspective, we enter an entirely new landscape of connections, of phenomena that cannot be reduced to simple cause and effect, and of the constant flux of dynamic processes. . . .

The quantum mechanical view of reality strikes against most of our notions of reality. Even to scientists, it is admittedly bizarre. But it is a world where *relationship* is the key determiner of what is observed and of how particles manifest themselves. Particles come into being and are observed only in relationship to something else. They do not exist as independent "things." Quantum physics paints a strange yet enticing view of a world that, as Heisenberg characterized it, "appears as a complicated tissue of events, in which connections of different kinds alternate or overlap or combine and thereby determine the texture of the whole" (1958, 107). These unseen *connections* between what were previously thought to be separate entities are the fundamental elements of all creation. . . .

New understandings of change and disorder are also emerging from chaos theory. Work in this field, which keeps expanding to take in more areas of inquiry, has led to a new appreciation of the relationship between order and chaos. These two forces are now understood as mirror images, one containing the other, a continual process where a system can leap into chaos and unpredictability, yet within that state be held within parameters that are well-ordered and predictable.

New science is also making us more aware that our yearning for simplicity is one we share with natural systems. In many systems, scientists now understand that order and conformity and shape are created not by complex controls, but by the presence of a new guiding formulae or principles. The survival and growth of systems that range in size from large ecosystems down to tiny leaves are made possible by the combination of key patterns or principles that express the system's overall identity and great levels of autonomy for individual system members.

The world described by new science is changing our beliefs and perceptions in many areas, not just in the natural sciences. I see new science ideas beginning to percolate in my own field of management theory. One way to see their effect is to look at the problems that plague us most in organizations these days or, more accurately, what we *define* as the problems. Leadership, an amorphous phenomenon that has intrigued us since people began studying organizations, is being examined now for its relational aspects. More and more studies focus on followership, empowerment, and leader accessibility. And ethical and moral questions are no longer fuzzy religious concepts but key elements in our relationships with staff, suppliers, and stakeholders. If the physics of our universe is revealing the primacy of relationships, is it any wonder that we are beginning to reconfigure our ideas about management in relational terms?

In motivation theory, our attention is shifting from the enticement of external rewards to the intrinsic motivators that spring from the work itself. We are refocusing on the deep longings we have for community, meaning, dignity, and love in our organizational lives. We are beginning to look at the strong emotions that are part of being human, rather than segmenting ourselves (love is for home, discipline is for work) or believing that we can confine workers into narrow roles, as though they were cogs in the machinery of production. As we let go of the machine models of work, we begin to step back and see ourselves in new ways, to appreciate our wholeness, and to design organizations that honor and make use of the totality of who we are.

The impact of vision, values, and culture occupies a great deal of organizational attention. We see their effects on organizational vitality, even if we can't quite define why they are such potent forces. We now sense that some of the best ways to create continuity of behavior are through the use of forces that we can't really see. Many scientists now work with the concept of fields—invisible forces that structure space or behavior. I have come to understand organizational vision as a field—a force of unseen connections that influences employees' behavior—rather than as an evocative message about some desired future state. Because of field theory, I believe I can better explain why vision is so necessary, and this leads me to new activities to strengthen its influence.

Our concept of organizations is moving away from the mechanistic creations that flourished in the age of bureaucracy. We have begun to speak in earnest of more fluid, organic structures, even of boundaryless organizations. We are beginning to recognize organizations as systems, construing them as "learning organizations" and crediting them with some type of self-renewing capacity. These are our first, tentative forays into a new appreciation for organizations. My own experience suggests that we can forgo the despair created by such common organizational events as change, chaos, information overload, and cyclical behaviors if we recognize that organizations are conscious entities, possessing many of the properties of living systems.

Some believe that there is a danger in playing with science and abstracting its metaphors because, after a certain amount of stretch, the metaphors lose their relationship to the tight scientific theories that gave rise to them. But others would argue that all of science is metaphor—a hopeful description of how to think of a reality we can never fully know. I share the sentiments of physicist Frank Oppenheimer who says: "If one has a new way of thinking, why not apply it wherever one's thought leads to? It is certainly entertaining to let oneself do so, but it is also often very illuminating and capable of leading to new and deep insights" (in Cole 1985, 2).

## REFERENCE

Capra, Fritjof. *The Tao of Physics*. New York: Bantam Books, 1976.

—*The Turning Point: Science, Society, and the Rising Culture*. New York. Bantam Books, 1983.

Cole, K. C. *Sympathetic Vibrations: Reflections on Physics as a Way of Life*. New York: Bantam Books, 1985.

Heisenberg, Werner. *Physics and Philosophy*. New York: Harper Torchbooks, 1958.

Meadows, Donella. "Whole Earth Models and Systems." *Co-Evolution Quarterly* (Summer 1982): 98–108.

# CHAPTER IV

# Teamwork and Empowerment

Productivity in private and public sector organizations has became the overriding issue in corporate boardrooms as well as in the legislative corridors of power. Virtually all of the "new" approaches to management that are being advocated—the attempts to find solutions to the "productivity problem"—have blended traditional and experimental management methods with new forms of employee involvement and participative management. For the past two decades we have witnessed a never-ending series of "new" management approaches, particularly approaches that emphasize organizational flexibility through the development and empowerment of individuals and work groups.

"Japanese management," with its long-term commitment to employees and its emphasis on communications through quality circles (Ouchi 1981; Pascale & Athos, 1981), was the first major participative/empowerment approach to clearly emerge from the post World War II Japanese industrial experience. By the 1970s, impressive productivity gains were attributed primarily to highly goal-oriented group activity within organizations (Hyde, 1991). For the most part, quality circles—voluntary work groups that attempt to recommend solutions to organizational problems—have been merged into and given way to successively more comprehensive management approaches, including:

- the "search for excellence" (Peters & Waterman, 1982),
- the "M-form society" (Ouchi, 1984),
- "total quality management" or "TQM" (Crosby, 1984; Deming, 1986, 1993; Juran, 1992),
- "reinventing government" (Gore, 1993; Osborne & Gaebler, 1992),
- "Socio-technical systems" or "Quality of Work Life (QWL)" (Weisbord, 1991),
- "productivity management" (Hyde, 1991; M.I.T. Commission on Industrial Productivity, 1989),
- "organizational architecture" (Nadler, Gerstein, & Shaw, 1992), and
- "reengineering," "process reengineering," or "business reengineering" (Hammer & Champy, 1993).

These management approaches share some common elements but also differ in emphasis, assumptions, and specific methods—as well as in their commitment to individual and work team empowerment. For example, "reengineering" is a radical change strategy, not an incremental "grass-roots" employee involvement approach. Reengineering literally means what its name implies. "When someone asks us for a quick definition of business reengineering, we say that it means 'starting over.' It *doesn't* mean tinkering with what already exists or making incremental changes that leave basic structures intact. . . . It involves going back to the beginning and inventing a better way of doing work" (Hammer & Champy, 1993, p. 31).

In contrast to reengineering's radical change approach, Quality of Work Life (QWL) has as its central themes, dignity, meaning of work and life, and community in the workplace. "We hunger for community in the workplace and are a great deal more productive when we find it. To feed this hunger in ways that preserve democratic values of individual dignity, opportunity for all, and mutual support is to harness energy and productivity beyond imagining" (Weisbord, 1991, p. xiv).

"Organizational architecture," an approach that uses physical architecture as an analogy for how managers should manage, falls in between process reengineering and QWL. Some of the principles of architecture that are applicable to this new-style management of organizations include (Gerstein, 1992, pp. 14, 15):

- Architecture is a "practical art." "Ordinary people" are its consumers. Because people have to work and live in that which is created, the ultimate test of any architecture is its utility measured in human terms.
- Architecture provides a framework for the conduct of life, not a specification for what that life should be. Architecture should facilitate, guide, and provide a context; it should not provide a blueprint for conduct.
- Unlike a painting that is produced by a single artist, architecture is produced by large numbers of people working together to achieve the vision of the architect.

Organizational architecture can be seen as the art of forming organizational space to meet human needs and aspirations. "Organizational architects work in the 'behavioral space' . . . creating opportunities for action, which we often call *empowerment*, and creating constraints to action which are central to the organizational architect's job" (Gerstein, 1992, p. 15). Thus, proponents of organizational architecture apply principles from applied physical sciences and art to the empowerment—and steering—of work teams and individuals.

Despite their differences, process reengineering, organizational architecture, and QWL all share common elements, including: an acknowledged need for organizations to be more flexible and innovative; recognition that people who actually do the work are the most knowledgeable about it and often have the best ideas about how to improve it; and an unwavering belief that major productivity gains cannot be achieved in bureaucracies that are top-heavy with rules and administrators. These common elements are the core themes of the readings in this chapter.

The readings in Chapter II, "Group and Intergroup Behavior," provide an excellent foundation for this chapter's exploration of group and individual empowerment. After all, an understanding and appreciation of group and intergroup behavior is essential for creating and maintaining effective work teams, and well-functioning work teams are at the core of most of the new management approaches that have been advocated since the mid-1980s. Virtually all of these flexibility- and productivity-increasing management approaches assume that groups provide individuals with opportunities for personal and professional growth and development, self-expression and creativity, and work satisfaction. They also assume that these opportunities cannot become available to workers in traditional hierarchical organizations. Also essential to the approaches, however, is the assumption that groups can and will provide structure and discipline for individuals at work. Therefore, organizations that permit empowerment do not need multiple levels and layers of supervisors and managers to coordinate, control, and monitor production and the behavior of individual workers. Work groups can and will accept responsibility for their processes and products—as well as the behavior of other group members.

The first selection in this chapter is the pioneering analysis of self-managing work teams written by J. Richard Hackman and Greg R. Oldham, "The Design of Work for Groups and Groups for Work" (1980). In this selection from their book *Work Redesign*, Hackman and Oldham focus on the design of work for groups. This approach, which originated in systems theories of organization, requires managers to give consideration to the design of groups as performing units, as well as organizational tasks and the people who perform them. Hackman and Oldham define self-managing work groups as "intact (if small) social systems whose members have the authority to handle internal processes as they see fit in order to generate a specific group product, service, or decision." Four aspects of group composition have strong influences on the amount of talent a group is able to use in its work:

1. The groups should include members who have high levels of task-relevant expertise;
2. The group should be large enough to do the work—but not much larger;
3. Group members should have at least a moderate level of interpersonal skill in addition to their task-relevant skills; and
4. The group should be composed to balance between homogeneity and heterogeneity of membership.

Hackman and Oldham's self-managing group model focuses on three aspects of the design of the group: task, composition, and norms. Each of the three aspects is susceptible to planned change activities. "What 'works' [however] depends on the kind of work that is being done. And whether it makes sense to proceed with the design of work for groups depends jointly on the demands of the work itself, the characteristics of the people, and the properties of the broader organizational context."

Ian Mitroff's selection, "Business Not as Usual: Building the Organization of the Future Now," which is reprinted here from his 1987 book, focuses on the design of jobs and organizations that are compatible with the technical and social needs of individuals and groups. He asserts that only in this manner can organizations develop and maintain fluidity and adaptability. Mitroff describes several cases in which bureaucratic structures and work flows were converted into organizations of teams. In a small company, virtually everyone who was interviewed had described the organization as "small, isolated groups, which they referred to as 'clumps.' The term 'clump' was so uppermost in people's minds that a number of individuals remarked with frustration that their organization practiced the 'clumponian' theory of management." If the values of service and quality were to be achieved, the main theme had to become integration—"tearing down the barriers and finding ways to foster teamwork and cooperation." Eventually, people began to envision the company as a "team of teams."

Mitroff uses the NASA space shuttle disaster as an example of managers high in the bureaucracy (who are primarily responsible for pleasing customers) choosing to distance themselves from—to void—the knowledge of lower levels of management (who are foremost responsible for solving technical problems). "The lesson is straightforward: *to do business in a tightly interconnected world, an organization must take on the properties of the complex environment in which it exists.*" Structure and environment must be matched, which requires integration, fluidity, and shared responsibility. Well designed and functioning work teams are essential ingredients.

"Self-Directed Work Teams: The New American Challenge" (1990), by Orsburn, Moran, Musselwhite, Zenger and Perrin (included in this chapter), updates and extends the Hackman and Oldham analysis. Orsburn *et al.* describe a self-directed work team as a "highly trained group of employees, from 6 to 18, on average, fully responsible for turning out a well-defined segment of finished work. Therefore, self-directed work teams differ in several "revolutionary" ways from conventional work groups:

- *Fewer Job Categories*: Each member of a self-directed work team performs multiple tasks. "When a conventional machine shop converts to self-direction, for example, 10 or so job categories may collapse into 1 or 2."
- *Authority*: Because self-directed work teams handle tasks that historically have been the purview of management, the teams need adequate authority. First-level supervisors usually work at a distance or their roles are changed to facilitator.
- *Reward System*: If self-directed teams are to produce their potential benefits, the organization needs to reward individual behaviors that promote team flexibility. This usually means compensating team members for mastering a range of skills. Gain-sharing and profit-sharing programs often are introduced.

Orsburn *et al.* explain that teams that are successful use self-directing teams for "downloading" duties to the lower levels. "Work teams release their managers to perform duties now exercised by managers at the level above." Executives have more time for strategic planning, and mid-managers have time to engage in activities such as coaching, championing innovative ideas, and working with vendors or customers. In all, self-directing work teams lead to organizational productivity, streamlining, flexibility, quality, commitment, and customer satisfaction.

All work groups pass through five stages in their progress toward "mature self-direction." (Orsburn *et al.*'s stages are quite similar to the stages of group development described by Hersey and Blanchard in Chapter II.):

Stage 1: Start-Up
Stage 2: State of Confusion
Stage 3: Leader-Centered Teams
Stage 4: Tightly Formed Teams
Stage 5: Self-Directed Teams

Ongoing training is the "engine that drives the transition." Training provides team members with operational know-how and also helps them to cope with the five predictable stages.

Marvin R. Weisbord's chapter, "Transforming Teamwork: Work Relationships in a Fast-Changing World" argues that productive workplaces need both individual effort and teamwork. He contends, however, that teams are business cliches that only receive "lip service." Teams need to be developed in two ways: (1) to unlearn "deeply ingrained, self-limiting assumptions about individualism, authority, and responsibility that defeat cooperation and, paradoxically, individual success; (2) to look outward toward the wider social and business networks that shape their mutual effort." People at work need to be cognizant of relationships and the environment in order to move from individualism and competition toward cooperation and wholeness.

Weisbord describes a theory of teamwork transformation that highlights the differences between managing a problem one-on-one and managing a group in which people depend on each other. "To do the latter requires an appreciation of task and process applied to teamwork in an unpredictable world." The objective for applying the teamwork transformation theory in practice, "is to reduce passivity and put people more firmly in charge of their own lives."

Most of the experience with employee involvement, empowerment, and self-directed teams to date has been in manufacturing industries. Service industry and government applications have largely been overlooked in practice and in the literature. David E. Bowen and Edward E. Lawler III's 1992 article, "The Empowerment of Service Workers: What, Why, How, and When," examines the benefits and costs of empowering employees in service industries, the range of management practices available for empowering employees to varying degrees, and the key business characteristics that affect the desirability of using empowerment approaches. Bowen and Lawler contend that managers need to be certain that there is a good fit between their organizational needs and their approach to front-line service workers. For Bowen and Lawler, "empowerment" is the sharing of four organizational "ingredients" with front-line service employees: (1) information about the organization's performance, (2) rewards based on organizational perfor-mance, (3) information and knowledge, and (4) power to make decisions.

"The Empowerment of Service Workers" uses Federal Express and UPS to demonstrate the need for fit between organizational needs and practices, and man-agement approach. Federal Express and UPS are both "excellent" service industry companies. Federal Express is totally committed to excellence through high involve-ment, self-managing work teams, horizontal coordination, gainsharing, employee empowerment, and customer-driven service. In contrast, UPS is a traditionally controlled, top-down organization that is characterized by "rules, a detailed union contract, carefully studied work methods, and rigid operational guidelines . . . in which employees are directed by policies and procedures based on industrial engineering studies of how all service delivery aspects should be carried out and how long they should take."

Possible gains or benefits to be realized from empowerment include: fast re-sponses to customer needs, better-quality employee relations with customers, em-ployees who feel better about themselves and their jobs, and ideas for service improvement. Some possible costs of employee empowerment include: a greater dollar investment in selection and training, higher labor costs, slower or inconsistent service delivery, inequities in service delivery, and bad decisions and needless "give aways." In summary, "before service organizations rush into empowerment programs, they need to determine whether and how empowerment fits their situation."

## REFERENCES

Barzelay, M. (1992). *Breaking through bureaucracy: A new vision for managing in govern-ment.* Berkeley, CA: University of California Press.

Bowen, D. E., & Lawler, E. E. III. (Spring 1992). The empowerment of service workers: What, why, how, and when. *Sloan Management Review*, 31–39.

Crosby, P. B. (1979). *Quality is free.* New York: McGraw-Hill.

Crosby, P. B. (1984). *Quality without tears.* New York: McGraw-Hill.

Daft, R. L., Bettenhausen, K. R., & Tyler, B. B. (1993). Implications of top managers' communication choices for strategic decisions. In G. P. Huber & W. H. Glick (Eds.), *Organizational change and redesign: Ideas and insights for improving performance* (pp. 112–146). New York: Oxford University Press.

Deming, W. E. (1986). *Out of the crisis.* Cambridge, MA: Massachusetts Institute of Tech-nology Press.

Deming, W. E. (1993). *The new economics.* Cambridge, MA: Massachusetts Institute of Technology Press.

Fink, S. L. (1992). *High commitment workplaces.* New York: Quorum Books.

Gerstein, M. S. (1992). From machine bureaucracies to networked organizations: An ar-chitectural journey. In D. A. Nadler, M. S. Gerstein, & R. B. Shaw (Eds.), *Organiza-tional architecture: Designs for changing organizations* (pp. 11–38). San Francisco: Jossey-Bass.

Gore, A. (1993). *The Gore report on reinventing government.* New York: Times Books.

Hackman, J. R., & Oldham, G. R. (1980). *Work redesign*. Reading, MA: Addison-Wesley.

Hammer, M., & Champy J. (1993). *Reengineering the corporation*. New York: Harper-Collins.

Hyde, A. C. (1991). Productivity management for public sector organizations. In J. S. Ott, A. C. Hyde, & J. M. Shafritz (Eds.), *Public management: The essential readings*. Chicago: Lyceum Books/Nelson-Hall.

Juran, J. M. (1992). *Juran on quality by design*. New York: The Free Press.

Juran, J. M., & Gryna, F. M. (Eds.). (1988). *Juran's quality control handbook* (4th ed.). New York: McGraw-Hill.

Katzenbach, J. R., & Smith, D. K. (1993). *The wisdom of teams: Creating the high-performance organization*. Boston: Harvard Business School Press.

Lawler, E. E. III, Mohrman, S. A., & Ledford, G. E., Jr. (1992). *Employee involvement and total quality management*. San Francisco: Jossey-Bass.

M.I.T. Commission on Industrial Productivity. (1989). *Made in America: Regaining the productive edge*. Cambridge, MA: Massachusetts Institute of Technology Press.

Mitroff, I. I. (1987). *Business not as usual*. San Francisco: Jossey-Bass.

Nadler, D. A., Gerstein, M. S., & Shaw, R. B. (Eds.). (1992). *Organizational architecture: Designs for changing organizations*. San Francisco: Jossey-Bass.

Orsburn, J. D., Moran, L., Musselwhite, E., Zenger, J. H. (with C. Perrin). (1990). *Self-directed work teams: The New American Challenge*. Homewood, IL: Business One Irwin.

Osborne, D., & Gaebler, T. (1992). *Reinventing government: How the entrepreneurial spirit is transforming the public sector*. Reading MA: Addison-Wesley.

Ouchi, W. G. (1981). *Theory Z: How American business can meet the Japanese challenge*. Reading, MA: Addison-Wesley.

Ouchi, W. G. (1984). *The M-form society: How American teamwork can recapture the competitive edge*. Reading MA: Addison-Wesley.

Pascale, R. T., & Athos, A. G. (1981). *The art of Japanese management*. New York: Simon & Schuster.

Peters, T. J., & Waterman, R. H., Jr. (1982). *In search of excellence*. New York: Harper & Row.

Weisbord, M. R. (1991). *Productive workplaces: Organizing and managing for dignity, meaning, and community*. San Francisco: Jossey-Bass.

## 22

# The Design of Work for Groups and Groups for Work

## *J. Richard Hackman and Greg R. Oldham*

## SELF-MANAGING WORK GROUPS: A DEFINITION

There are many kinds of work groups in organizations. Probably most common are what are called "coacting" groups. People in coacting groups may report to the same supervisor and work close to one another, but they have individually defined tasks. Even if group members meet together periodically to discuss how the work is going, or occasionally help one another out, it is still a coacting group.

We will *not* be dealing here with coacting groups. . . .

What we *are* dealing with in this chapter can be termed "self-managing work groups" (Hackman, 1978). These are intact (if small) social systems whose members have the authority to handle internal processes as they see fit in order to generate a specific group product, service, or decision. Such groups have the following three attributes.[1]

1. They are *real* groups. The group must be an intact and identifiable social system, even if small or temporary. At minimum, this requires that members have interdependent relations with one another, that they develop differentiated roles over time, and that the group be perceived as

such both by members and nonmembers (Alderfer, 1977).

2. They are *work* groups. The group must have a defined piece of work to do that results in a product, service, or decision whose acceptability is at least potentially measurable. If a group does not generate productive output, then we do not consider it to be a work group.

3. They are *self-managing* groups. Group members must have the authority to manage their own task and interpersonal processes as they carry out their work. If control over who does what when is instead retained by management, then a group would be self-managing in name only.

Only groups that meet all three of these conditions will be dealt with here. This includes groups that sometimes are called "autonomous work groups" (Bucklow, 1972) or "self-regulating work groups" (Cummings, 1978), as well as temporary task forces set up to solve specific problems, decision-making committees, many kinds of management teams, and so on. . . .

## A MODEL OF WORK GROUP EFFECTIVENESS[2]

. . . Here are the three criteria of group effectiveness that will guide our discussion in the pages to follow.

---

[1] These defining characteristics were developed collaboratively with Mary Dean Lee.

[2] Material in the remainder of this chapter is adapted from Hackman (1978).

*Source:* From J. Richard Hackman and Greg R. Oldham, *Work Redesign* (Excerpted from pages 164–190), © 1980 by Addison-Wesley Publishing Co., Inc. Reprinted by permission of the publisher.

1. The productive output of the work group meets or exceeds organizational standards of quantity and quality. If the work of the group is not acceptable to those who receive it and use it . . . then the group cannot be considered effective.

2. The group experience serves more to satisfy than frustrate the personal needs of group members. Sometimes groups develop patterns of interpersonal behavior that are destructive to the well-being of group members. If most members find that their experiences in the group serve to frustrate their needs, and to block them from achieving personal goals, then it would be hard to argue that the group is a successful social unit.

3. The social process used in carrying out the work maintains or enhances the capability of members to work together on subsequent team tasks. Some groups operate in ways that destroy the integrity of the group itself, that is, the group "burns itself up" in the process of performing the task. Even if the product of such a group is acceptable, we would not define as successful a group that generates so much divisiveness and conflict among members that they are unwilling or unable to work together on future occasions.

These criteria are, we believe, modest. They do not demand extraordinary accomplishment or exemplary social processes from group members. Yet neither are they easy to achieve. Just how would one proceed to design a work group that "passes" these three criteria of effectiveness?

It would be lovely if there were a simple and straightforward answer to that question, but unfortunately there is not. It is necessary, therefore, to work backwards from the criteria to understand what group conditions are most closely associated with effectiveness, and then to determine how groups can be set up to satisfy those conditions. In effect, we must build a *model* that specifies what is required for self-managing work groups to be effective.

## Intermediate Criteria of Effectiveness

The first step in building the model is illustrated in Fig. 1. There we specify three "intermediate" criteria of team effectiveness. While not themselves final indicators of effectiveness, these criteria do relate closely to the ultimate success or failure of a work group. They are: (1) the level of *effort* that group members bring to bear on the task, (2) the amount of *knowledge and skill* applied by group members to task work, and (3) the appropriateness of the *task performance strategies* used by the group in doing its work.

If by some magic we could set all three of these intermediate criteria at an appropriate level, we would be able to help almost any group, working on virtually any task, become effective. We could, for example, ensure that members work hard enough to get the task completed, correctly and on time. We could tinker with the amount of talent in the group, including the mix of skills held by different group members, to make sure that there is ample talent available to meet the demands of the task. We could adjust the performance strategies used by the group in its work, the ways members go about working together on the task, to make sure that these strategies are fully appropriate for the kind of work being done and consistent with the personal needs of group members.[3]

---

[3] For certain kinds of work, one or two of the intermediate criteria may be particularly salient in determining group effectiveness, and the other(s) less salient. As will be seen later in this chapter, the *work technology* plays an important role in affecting the salience of the intermediate criteria and therefore which aspects of the group design are most critical to effectiveness. In the pages to follow, we will assume that all three intermediate criteria are salient, which is usually the case when complex tasks are assigned to work teams in organizational settings.

## FIGURE 1 · THE INTERMEDIATE CRITERIA OF WORK GROUP EFFECTIVENESS.

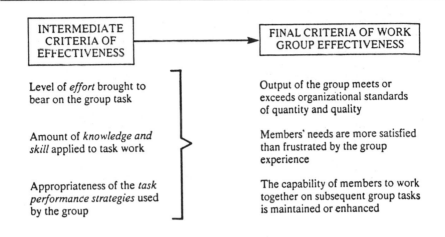

| INTERMEDIATE CRITERIA OF EFFECTIVENESS | FINAL CRITERIA OF WORK GROUP EFFECTIVENESS |
|---|---|
| Level of *effort* brought to bear on the group task | Output of the group meets or exceeds organizational standards of quantity and quality |
| Amount of *knowledge and skill* applied to task work | Members' needs are more satisfied than frustrated by the group experience |
| Appropriateness of the *task performance strategies* used by the group | The capability of members to work together on subsequent group tasks is maintained or enhanced |

The problem, of course, is that such magic cannot be performed: it usually is not possible to manipulate directly the effort, knowledge and skill, and performance strategy that members use in performing a task. What can be done, however, is to create conditions when the work group is designed that favor the achievement of the intermediate criteria. We discuss how this might be accomplished next.

### Key Design Features

While the standing of a self-managing work group on the three intermediate criteria is affected by many factors, three features of the basic design of the group warrant special attention. They are: (1) the design of the group task, (2) the composition of the group, and (3) group norms about performance processes. As is shown in Fig. 2, each of these design features is especially closely related to one of the three intermediate criteria.

*Design of the Group Task.* The motivational structure of the group task affects the amount of effort group members put into their work.[4] . . . We would expect group members to experience high motivation in their work (and therefore to exert high effort) when the following conditions are met:

1. The group task requires the use of many different skills for successful completion (skill variety).
2. The group task is a whole and meaningful piece of work (task identity).
3. The outcomes of the group's work on the task "make a difference" to other people either inside or outside the organization (task significance).
4. The group task provides substantial latitude for members to decide together

[4] It should be noted that member effort also is affected by relationships among members and by aspects of the organizational context (such as the reward system, performance objectives, supervisory expectations, and so on). The present focus is on the *design* of the work group; the roles of interpersonal and contextual factors are addressed in the next chapter.

FIGURE 2 · RELATIONSHIP BETWEEN THE DESIGN FEATURES AND THE
INTERMEDIATE CRITERIA.

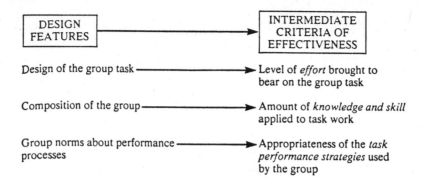

how they will carry out the work, including the methods to be used, the assignment of priorities to various subtasks, the pace of the work, and so on (autonomy).[5]

5. The group as a whole receives trustworthy information, preferably from doing the work itself, about the adequacy of group performance (feedback).

To generate ideas for creating a group task high on these properties, one can use "implementing principles" for enriching individual jobs: combining subtasks into a larger whole, forming natural work units, establishing client relationships, vertically loading the job, and opening feedback channels. However, it is important to make sure that the focus remains on the overall task of the *group*,

not on the tasks of individual group members, when these principles are applied.

Similarly, it is essential that members of the group clearly understand that it is a group task that is being performed. Confusion on this point can develop, since only rarely will the task be done in concert by group members. Instead, various individuals typically assume responsibility for different subtasks, and members coordinate with one another to complete the entire piece of work. All members must understand, therefore, that how the subtasks are divided up, how they are assigned to members, and how member activities are coordinated is a *group* decision.

If a group task is well designed according to the criteria set forth above, then members are likely to agree that the work is meaningful; they will understand that they collectively (not individually) are responsible for the results of the work; and they will agree that the group as a whole is the proper recipient of feedback about performance effectiveness. . . .

While it is true that individuals differ in energy level and in how hard they

[5] Earlier in this chapter we pointed out that a group cannot be considered "self-managing" unless management has given members substantial authority for handling their own affairs. That was definitional. But having formal authority for internal group processes is only the prerequisite for creating high motivation in work groups. The level of autonomy built into the task itself determines the degree to which members will be able to *use* that authority to generate products that they "own" and for which they feel responsible.

typically work on the job, there is not a great deal that anyone can do about people's personalities. And while norms clearly do develop in many groups that encourage especially high or low member effort, any attempts to *directly* alter group norms to improve member effort are probably doomed to failure. The reason is that group norms do not develop by chance. Instead, they are formed and shaped as devices *for dealing with particular problems or opportunities that confront the group.* And one common impetus for the development of norms about effort is the nature of the work the group is doing, that is, the design of the group task.

Consider, for example, a group task that is very low in motivating potential. Members find work on the task boring, frustrating, and generally unpleasant. As they share with one another their private reactions to the work, eventually they may develop an informal agreement that the best way to minimize their shared negative feelings is simply not to work so hard. When members begin to enforce such an agreement, they have developed a group norm that restricts work effort. Any attempt to alter that norm that does not also deal with the *reason* the norm developed probably will be futile and may even backfire.

On the other hand, if a group task is high in motivating potential, such that members find the work exciting, fulfilling, or otherwise rewarding, these experiences also are likely to be shared among group members, and a norm encouraging high effort on the task is likely to emerge. The implication, then, is that altering the design of the group task may be a better way to affect the effort expended by group members than would be direct attacks on productivity norms them-

selves. To do the latter, in many cases, would be to address the outcropping of the problem rather than the problem itself.[6]

*Composition of the Group.* How a group is composed—that is, who is in the group—directly affects the amount of knowledge and skill that can be applied to work on the group task. Four aspects of group composition have particularly strong influences on the amount of talent a group is actually able to use in its task work.

1. *The group should include members who have high levels of task-relevant expertise.* It is obvious that far and away the most efficient means of increasing the complement of knowledge and skill available for work on a group task is simply to put very talented people in the group. . . . Relatively sophisticated procedures currently are available for assessing the skill requirements of tasks and for measuring the capabilities of people to meet those requirements. Such procedures should be used in staffing work groups just as they are for selecting and placing people on individual jobs.

---

[6] It should be emphasized, however, that high motivation in response to a well-designed task will come about for groups, just as for individuals, *only* if the group is composed of people who collectively have sufficient knowledge and skill to complete the task successfully. If not, the same kind of frustration and withdrawal observed for individuals with insufficient task-relevant skills will be observed for a group. A basketball team is a good case in point: by all standards the task of a basketball team is well designed (that is, it is high on four of the five motivating task characteristics: skill variety, task identity, autonomy, and feedback). And if a team is skilled enough to be competitive with its opponents on the court and to play *together* competently, then motivation invariably is high. But if a team loses almost all of its games because of a lack of skill, then psychological (and sometimes behavioral) withdrawal of team members is a common outcome.

2. *The group should be large enough to do the work—but not much larger.* If a task requires three pairs of hands for successful completion, then obviously there should be at least three people in the group. Sometimes groups are understaffed, and those responsible for the design of work groups should be alert to this risk.

Far more dangerous, however, is the risk of overstaffing a work group. Indeed, adding additional members to a group sometimes can even decrease the productivity of the group. . . .

Nevertheless, large work groups (and especially decision-making committees) are widely used in organizations. The reasons, we believe, have less to do with considerations of group effectiveness than with emotional issues (such as using large numbers to share responsibility and spread accountability) or political considerations (like ensuring that all relevant specialties and functions are represented in the group so they will accept its product). So, in many cases, representatives of various constituencies are appointed to the group one-by-one or even two-by-two, creating a large group, a safe group, a politically "corrrect" group—and a group that may find itself incapable of generating even a satisfactory outcome, let alone one that shows signs of creativity. In our view, it usually is better to make groups and committees no larger than they absolutely must be to get the task accomplished, and to use alternative means for dealing with concerns about accountability and acceptance.

3. *Group members should have at least a moderate level of interpersonal skill in addition to their task-relevant skills.* As Argyris (1969) and others have shown, most individuals in organizations are not highly competent in managing complex and anxiety-arousing interpersonal situations. Yet if the group task is challenging and requires high member interde-

pendence, then at least moderate interpersonal skills are needed simply to bring the *task* skills of members effectively to bear on the work of the group. This requirement becomes especially salient when the group is demographically diverse (composed of people who differ in age, gender, race and so on) and when a work group consists of representatives of *other* organizational groups (such as functional departments) who may have a conflicting or competitive relationship with one another.

4. *The group should be composed to balance between homogeneity and heterogeneity of membership.* On the one hand, if the members are too much alike, some of the special advantages of having a team are lost, including the special expertise and perspectives that different individuals can bring to the task and the chance for people in the group to learn new skills from their co-workers. Yet excessive heterogeneity also can impair group effectiveness, because insufficient "common ground" among members makes communication difficult and provides for less-than-needed interchangeability among members.

Even when the heterogeneity of member skills is at about the right level problems can develop, particularly around the reluctance of members to share their knowledge and skill with one another. Individuals in a work group often have a vested interest in keeping to themselves special expertise they have developed, because their distinctiveness and status at work is based on that expertise. Only if the task of the group is highly motivating and involving are such individuals likely to be willing to sacrifice their "special" status in the interest of the group as a whole. . . .

Yet if well-composed teams can be created within existing organizational units, they can often assume increasing responsibility for the selection and training of members who subsequently join the group. When someone departs, for example, the team might be given responsibility for interviewing possible replacements. And once a replacement is chosen, members could have charge of that person's training and socialization. In many instances, the result will be an improvement in selection decisions since group members often are more knowledgeable than external managers about the special skills that are needed for the work and about the kind of person who is most likely to fit well with other members.

Moreover, group members should experience heightened responsibility for developing the persons that they (not management) chose to join the group. And perhaps most important is the fact that the group would be reaffirmed as a truly self-managing organizational unit. There is little that is more important to the life of a group than decision making about who becomes and remains a member. Being given responsibility for those decisions is a sign of trust from management that is sure to have great significance to group members.

*Group Norms About Performance Processes.* As shown in Fig. 2, the norms of a group can affect the appropriateness of the performance strategies that are used by a work group in carrying out its task. By performance strategies we mean the choices members make about how they will go about performing a given group task. For example, a group might decide to focus its energy on checking and rechecking for errors, in the interest of a high-quality product. Or members might choose to free associate about ideas for proceeding with work on a new task before starting to perform it. Or the group might decide to divide itself into two subgroups, each of which would do part of the overall task.

All of the above are choices about performance strategy, and those choices can be very important in determining how well a group actually performs. If, for example, successful completion of a certain task requires close coordination among members, with the contributions of each member made in a specific order at a specific time, then a group that has developed an explicit strategy for queuing and coordinating members inputs will probably perform better than a group that proceeds with the task using *ad hoc* or laissez-faire procedures. What specific strategy will work best for a given group task, of course, depends heavily on the particular requirements of that task.

Performance strategies generally are under the control of group norms. Members reach agreement early in their time together about how they will proceed with work on the task. Indeed, for familiar tasks members may not need to talk at all about their strategy, since all are familiar with "standard" procedures for doing the work. A group of senior managers composed to decide who will be selected for a lower-level management position, for example, would be unlikely to talk much about performance processes, simply because all members would have worked in similar groups with similar tasks many times before.

Once a strategy is agreed upon, whether explicitly or implicitly, then members routinely behave according to that strategy and enforce adherence to it. The way the group is working, or what it is attempting to achieve, may never again be addressed by members (Hackman and Morris, 1975). And individuals who deviate from group expectations about how the work is to be done are likely to be brought quickly back into line by fellow members.

The advantage to a group in having clear norms about performance strategies is that the need to manage and coordinate group member behavior on a continuous basis is minimized: everyone knows how things are to be done, and everyone does them in that way with little fuss and bother. More time therefore becomes available to the group for actual productive work.

The risk, of course, is that the performance strategies being enforced may not be terribly appropriate for the group task. Worse, members may be so intent on executing them that no one notices that they are flawed. This is particularly a problem when task requirements or constraints *change* after questions of strategy have been settled. If, for example, the "market" for a group's product were to gradually change from a seller's market to a buyer's market, the group might proceed far too long using its traditional strategy and discover that things had changed only when submerged in products that no one wanted.

The challenge in designing a work group, then, is to help members develop norms that reinforce the use of strategies that are uniquely appropriate to the group task, and that are amenable to change when task requirements or constraints change. How can this be done? One approach is for an outside agent (such as a manager or consultant) to independently diagnose the requirements of the task and to suggest to the group a way of operating that is particularly appropriate for that task. Group members, presumably, will be grateful for the help provided and (assuming the strategy is in fact workable) adopt it as their own. The problem is that reliance on an "outsider" does not help group members learn to manage their own performance processes or increase their readiness to change how they operate when task or organizational circumstances change. Instead, the group remains dependent on outside guidance and direction.

An alternative approach, and one that is more consistent with group self-management, is to help group members learn how to develop and monitor their *own* norms about performance strategy. When a work group is being formed, the person responsible for designing the group might meet with group members to discuss explicitly how they want to develop their performance strategies. Merely talking through this issue may foster a climate in which strategic questions can be openly discussed—both when initial norms about strategy are developed and in the future when circumstances change. In effect, the manager or consultant would be helping members develop a *general* norm that encourages open and self-conscious discussion of *specific* norms about how group members work together on the task. . . .

## THE FEASIBILITY OF DESIGNING WORK FOR GROUPS

. . . Here, then, are two general questions that we believe to be critical in assessing the feasibility of creating self-managing work groups in organizations.

### Question One: Would Self-Managing Work Groups Fit with the People and the Context?

Self-managing work groups are a social form that may or may not fit with the people who would compose them and with the organizational context in which they would function.

Consider first the needs of the group members. When employees have strong needs for *both* personal growth and significant social relationships, a team design would be appropriate. People with high needs for growth tend to respond more favorably to enriched individual tasks than do people with low growth need strength. Following the same reasoning, it appears that a challenging *group* task (such as those created for self-managing work groups) would be especially attractive to people who are high both in growth and social needs because the group provides an opportunity to satisfy both sets of needs simultaneously as the work is being done.

It would, however, be risky to form work teams if most members were high in social need strength but *low* in growth need strength. In this case, members might use the group experience to obtain desired social satisfactions, but at the expense of work on the task. Similarly, if the prospective group members are high in growth need strength but low in social need strength, then designing enriched work for *individuals* would seem to be the more appropriate alternative. If would be difficult for team members to maintain the considerable energy required to develop an effective group in such circumstances because of individual apathy to working in social situations.

Regarding the organizational context, it should be recognized that self-managing work groups sometimes will clash with the overall climate and managerial style of the surrounding organization. Consider, for example, an organization with a highly "individualistic" climate: personal achievement and interpersonal competition for rewards are paramount, and "group work" is generally viewed by managers as collectivistic nonsense that protects the weak and holds back the strong. Would self-managing work groups prosper in such a setting? Hardly. Nor would they be appropriate in a highly mechanistic organization where organizational rules and procedures are clearly defined and vigorously enforced, with power and authority firmly centralized at the top.

Self-managing work teams are a powerful social invention. In a moderately supportive organizational context they can prompt significant alterations in how work gets done and how the organization itself is managed. But if the people or the managerial climate and style of the organization are clearly unsympathetic to a group design for work, the potential benefits of such groups are unlikely to be realized.

## Question Two: How Hospitable Are Organizational Systems to Needed Changes?

Sometimes it just isn't possible to form self-managing work groups. It is hard to imagine, for example, how a group of cab drivers, each of whom works alone in response to radioed instructions from a dispatcher, could be formed into a meaningful self-managing group. Or consider a dozen industrial employees strung out at fixed locations on a noisy assembly line, all tending their parts of the machinery. Could work teams be formed in such circumstances that would meet the minimal criteria for self-managing groups we set forth earlier in this chapter?[7] Almost certainly they could not be, and it would be unwise to "force" the creation of self-managing groups in settings such as these.

When organizational circumstances do permit the *formation* of self-managing work groups, the question then becomes whether they can be *well designed* as performing units. To answer this question, it is necessary first to determine which of the design features that we have been discussing in this chapter are most criti-

---

[7] Those criteria, it will be recalled, are (1) that the group be an intact and identifiable—if sometimes small or temporary—social system, (2) that the group be charged with generating an identifiable product whose acceptability is potentially measurable, and (3) that the group have the authority to determine how members will go about working together to accomplish their task.

cal for group effectiveness and, second, to assess whether those features can be built into the design of the group.

*Identifying Critical Design Features.* What features of the design of a self-managing work group are most critical to its effectiveness? This depends on which intermediate criteria are most important for the work being done (see Fig. 1). If effort is salient in determining effectiveness, then one would attend especially carefully to the design of the group task; if knowledge and skill are salient, then group composition would receive special attention; and if performance strategies are salient, the focus would be on group norms about performance processes.

Throughout this chapter, we have assumed that all three of the intermediate criteria are of equal importance in determining group effectiveness. In fact, the importance of the intermediate criteria varies from task to task. For some, . . . all three of the intermediate criteria need to be high. Producing large quantities of high-quality driers requires great effort, a good deal of knowledge and skill, and a relatively sophisticated performance strategy that efficiently sequences and coordinates the work of members.

In other cases, only one or two of the intermediate criteria are salient in determining how effectively the group performs. Consider, for example, a group of park workers who have responsibility for maintaining a specified section of the park grounds. No complex knowledge or skill is required for satisfactory performance, as the work basically involves only picking up debris and raking. Neither is there much room for group decision making about performance strategy: how members go about the task is mostly determined by what needs to be done on a given day. In this case, how well the group performs will be affected mainly by

how much effort members expend on their group task.[8]

What, then, determines how salient each of the intermediate criteria is for a given group task? The nature of the *technology* (equipment, materials, and prescribed work procedures) appears to have a strong effect, as illustrated in our summary model in Fig. 3. Usually it is possible to determine which of the intermediate criteria are important in affecting group performance for a given technology simply by asking, "If greater effort (or different levels of knowledge and skill, or different performance strategies) were brought to bear on this task, would group performance effectiveness be likely to change markedly?" If the answer is "yes" for the intermediate criterion being considered, then it is salient in influencing group effectiveness. . . .

*Testing for Systemic Constraints.* Is it possible to build into the design of a self-managing work group those features that are most critical to its effectiveness? If not, the risk is that the group will not be a substantial enough innovation to bring about real alterations in personal or organizational outcomes. . . .

Once again we direct attention to three key organizational systems: the

---

[8] The point can be stated more generally as an equation:

$$\text{Overall Group Effectiveness} = S_1\left[\text{Level of effort}\right]$$
$$+ S_2\left[\text{Amount of knowledge and skill}\right]$$
$$+ S_3\left[\begin{array}{l}\text{Appropriateness of task}\\\text{performance strategies}\end{array}\right]$$

where $S_1$, $S_2$, and $S_3$ are the importances or the *saliences* of the three intermediate criteria in influencing group task effectiveness. How the work technology may affect the saliences of the intermediate criteria is explored in greater detail elsewhere (Hackman, 1978).

FIGURE 3 • A MODEL OF WORK GROUP EFFECTIVENESS.

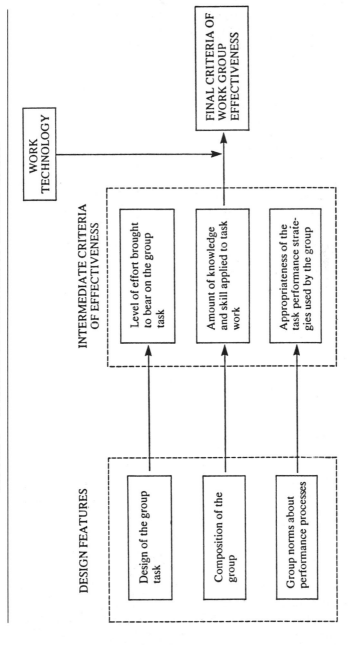

technological system, the personnel system, and the control system. The technological system may place constraints on the type of *group task* that can be designed. . . .

Finally, the control system may constrain *norms about performance processes*. To what extent are work processes preprogrammed and enforced by control system measures? How much "room" is there for group members to invent and implement performance strategies that they find uniquely appropriate for the work on the task? For example, could the group devise and implement its own procedures for handling quality control? Could members divide up the work in nontraditional ways? Or would such deviations throw the control system into disarray and control system managers into panic? Are there ways the control system itself could be modified to allow work groups greater latitude in managing their own performance processes?

## CONCLUSION

The conception of self-managing work groups presented in this chapter is both simpler and more complex than other treatments of work group behavior and effectiveness. It is simpler, in that it focuses on three key aspects of the design of the group—task, composition, and norms—each of which is assumed to control considerable variation in group effectiveness, and each of which is potentially open to planned change. It is more complex, in that the three design features are not posited as having consistent effects on performance across all circumstances. What "works" depends on the kind of work that is being done. And whether it makes sense to proceed with the design of work for groups depends jointly on the demands of the work itself, the characteristics of the peo-

ple, and the properties of the broader organizational context.

Ours is not a model that specifies what "causes" good group performance in the traditional sense of cause-effect relations. Instead, we emphasize how one can *create conditions* that will support high team effectiveness. By creating a motivating group task, a well-composed group, and group norms favoring open discussion of performance strategies, we believe, the *chances* are increased that group members will invest themselves in their work and perform it relatively well. Moreover, we expect that under such conditions group members will find the group experience more satisfying than frustrating and that group processes will be relatively healthy and constructive.[9]

Yet there is still more to the story. So far we have dealt only with the up-front *design* of self-managing work groups. The long-term success of such groups also is affected by how they are supported and managed after they have been formed. . . .

## REFERENCES

Alderfer, C. P. Group and intergroup relations. In J. R. Hackman and J. L. Suttle (eds.), *Improving life at work: Behavioral science approaches to organizational change.* Santa Monica, CA: Goodyear, 1977.

Argyris, C. The incompleteness of social psychological theory: Examples from small group, cognitive consistency, and attribution research. *American Psychologist,* 1969, *24,* 893–908.

[9] It must be re-emphasized here that our expectations are *only* expectations. The major tenets of our model are based on existing research findings about task-oriented groups, and we have found the model useful in analyzing self-managing work groups in organizations (and, in some cases, in predicting problems such groups are likely to encounter). But the model itself is new and has not yet been subjected to systematic research testing.

Bucklow, M. A new role for the work group. In L. E. Davis and J. C. Taylor (eds.), *Design of jobs*. Middlesex, England: Penguin, 1972.

Cummings, T. G. Self-regulating work groups: A socio-technical synthesis. *Academy of Management Review*, 1978, 3, 625–634.

Hackman, J. R. The design of self-managing work groups. In B. King, S. Streufert, and F. E. Fiedler (eds.), *Managerial control and organizational democracy*. Washington, D.C.: Winston and Sons, 1978.

Hackman, J. R., and C. G. Morris. Group tasks, group interaction process, and group performance effectiveness: A review and proposed integration. In L. Berkowitz (ed.), *Advances in experimental social psychology* (Vol. 8). New York: Academic Press, 1975.

# 23

# Business NOT as Usual: Building the Organization of the Future Now

## Ian I. Mitroff

An article in a Harvard Business School research colloquium provides a good summary of old versus new organizing assumptions underlying the design of jobs and organizations (Mills and Lovell, 1985, p. 467).

*Old Organizing Assumptions*

1. Jobs are performed best if they are constituted narrowly

2. Employee skills do not have to be matched to the complexity of the products; thus, specialization of employees is warranted.

3. Pay should be for specific job content.
4. Evaluation should be by direct supervision
5. Work must be closely supervised.

6. Assignment of overtime or transfer is by the rule book.
7. There is no need for career development.
8. The supervisor must deal primarily with employees as individuals.
9. There is no need for employees to be knowledgeable about the business as a whole.

*New Organizing Assumptions*

1. Jobs must be broadly defined if America is to produce the high-quality goods and products that are necessary to compete in a world economy.

2. Employee and management skills/ systems have to be closely matched to the complexity and systemic nature of the products necessary for a global economy.

3. Pay should be for skills mastered.
4. Evaluation should be encouraged by peers.
5. Self-supervision or peer supervision promotes better-quality products and work relationships.

6. Teams can be used to cover vacancies.
7. Concern for learning and growth must be central.
8. The supervisor must deal with employees as members of a team.
9. Everyone must have an overview of the entire business and feel they are a vital part of it in some fundamental way.

*Source:* Adapted from *Business NOT As Usual: Rethinking Our Individual, Corporate, and Industrial Strategies for Global Competition,* by Ian I. Mitroff, pp. 47–61. Copyright 1992 by Jossey-Bass, Inc., Publishers. Reprinted by permission.

## SEEING BEYOND THE INDIVIDUAL TREES: MANAGING THE WHOLE FOREST

A recent experience of Mitroff illustrates the problems confronting the outworn structure of many of today's organizations. Not too long ago, he had both the opportunity and the pleasure of working with a research unit of the U.S. Forest Service. On the surface at least, its mission was clear: to provide systematic and detailed research so that the region of the United States in which the unit was located could be managed effectively. Barely beneath the surface, however, were symptoms that indicated all was not well. Not only were there multiple, conflicting notions as to what the unit's "true," overall mission should be, but there was also significant conflict within particular notions.

The unit had been established to serve the needs of a variety of conflicting interests. It was charged with providing the basic research necessary (1) to *preserve* the forest and wildlands; (2) to *manage* the land for proper harvesting, for example, timbering; and (3) to *provide* proper recreational facilities for the thousands of people who annually flocked there. Thus, the unit was torn between conservation and preservation, on the one hand, and land use and economic development, on the other. What kind of research program should it enact under these conditions? The decision to carry out a specific program would support a particular policy of land use.

The real source of the problem lurked deeper beneath the surface. The unit had been organized around specific scientific disciplines that had now become so specialized and fragmented that they made no sense in the particular environment. Thus, the unit was finely subdivided into scientists who were "doctors of bugs and beetles," "doctors of tree bark and pine-cone needles," and "doctors of various kinds of small animals and creatures." Despite the multiple conflicting goals and multiple perspectives of Forest Service personnel, the region had to be managed as an integrated, coordinated entity. Although this had always been true, it now was more pressing. The increasing ecological problems affected whole regions, not isolated segments. Therefore, the unit would have to challenge and go beyond the *constraints* of its current organizational structure, that is, the separate scientific specialties would have to join together to build a model of the whole forest.

In many ways, the story of this one unit is the story of organizational America. Whether public or private, large organizations everywhere are struggling to free themselves from the type of structure that is no longer suited to the kind of environment we have discussed in the first three chapters. We find that the problem of change is thus generic. In the remainder of this chapter, we examine several cases that demonstrate some of the nuances of the changes that will be required of our organizations as they adapt to the global economy.

## REDESIGNING ORGANIZATIONAL STRUCTURES

Recent experience with a company that designs electronic systems was particularly helpful to us in demonstrating the tensions inherent in thinking systemically within organizations bounded by traditional assumptions. The company is a division of a large, well-known, and very successful electronics corporation. Like so many others, this corporation was staring at the potential for its own precipitous decline. Previously the master of a large niche, it had watched foreign competitors invade its markets with less expensive, better-quality products. And it was becoming painfully aware of its own rigidity because of its difficulty, despite monumental funding, in successfully entering the quick-paced and highly systemic world of automation.

Meanwhile, this company's small (approximately 500 people), often forgotten, somewhat sleepy, but highly sophisticated systems group was searching for its identity in the emerging new order. Sensing that his group was poorly organized to assume a role more responsive to the emerging needs of the corporation, the director of engineering spearheaded an effort to redesign the organization. What was especially interesting about this effort was that it was carried out by design teams composed of key individuals representing the different disciplines, projects, and perspectives in the division. Most of these representatives were from the various engineering and scientific disciplines, but the design teams also included representation from other functional areas, such as production, marketing, contracts, finance, and human resources. For years these people had been frustrated in designing, marketing, and selling systems from within the confines of the nonsystemic corporation. They had now been asked to set up a systems organization, and they responded to the opportunity with enthusiasm.

The effort began with Mitroff and Mohrman conducting in-depth diagnostic interviews with a cross section of key people in the organization. Summary data were shared with the design teams to stimulate early discussion and provide a foundation. Most notable about the interviews was that virtually everyone had the same perception of the organization and its problems. They described the organization as small, isolated groups, which they referred to as "clumps." The term "clump" was so uppermost in people's minds that a number of individuals remarked with frustration that their organization practiced the "clumponian" theory of management. People in the various clumps communicated with one another with extreme difficulty and, at best, were loyal to their clumps. They had little sense of belonging to the organization, let alone the parent corporation. Individuals with twenty years' tenure admitted to not knowing the names of co-workers in this small organization, even those who inhabited the same halls.

In reality, the company was an organization in name only. It was fractionated along very tight, specialized lines. People were suspicious of, and hostile to, one another, and there was a dearth of communication across complex technological projects and among the various functional groups whose coordinated energies were required for effective functioning in the marketplace. As a consequence, this division was unable to devise, produce, or sell the products that increasingly sophisticated customers demanded. Thus, the design teams were challenged to restructure the organization into one that could devise, produce, and deliver high-quality, complex electronic systems in a timely manner. To promote the values of service and quality in a marketplace in which customer needs were rapidly changing and becoming more complex, they found it necessary to propose changes in almost all aspects of the organization.

The main theme was integration—tearing down the barriers and finding ways to foster teamwork and cooperation. The rigid bureaucracy, with its built-in roadblocks to open, fast communication, couldn't respond in time any longer. Many felt that the company had lost sight of its mission, that customers, marketplace, quality, and productivity had become incidental. Its main purposes had become to protect turf, to build fiefdoms, and to control others but avoid being controlled. This philosophy applied to the internal functioning of the company, as well as to its role within the larger corporation, where it was one of many units, each wanting to coordinate with others only if *it* could call the shots. Indeed, one of the major legitimate complaints about bureaucracies is that they serve themselves instead of their intended clients. Unfortunately, this is true of both private and public organizations.

Teamwork became the integrating theme in the redesign. The company was envisioned as a "team of teams." To foster such teamwork, rewards and awards would go to teams, who would then determine whether individuals deserved special rewards. Each project team would be self-contained, in the sense that the necessary skills and functions would be represented; however, in line with the most interesting design feature, individuals would be able to move between levels of teams, between types of teams, and between functional assignments within teams as skills, knowledge, and need permitted. The same individual could be a technical contributor on one team and a leader on another team and, thus, alternate the roles of worker and manager. An individual would be allowed (indeed encouraged) to work on quality assurance on one project and design engineering on another project. Ongoing education and development of breadth as well as depth were to be fostered and rewarded. Where appropriate, "apprenticeships" would be established to enable cross-training on the job. It seemed that people in this organization feared stagnation, that is, becoming locked into a narrow technical specialty, into a role with

limited responsibility on a particular project, or into a role that permitted only a partial understanding of the many aspects of the business.

The team concept would be enhanced by creating a two-tier hierarchy in which project teams reported to a multidiscipline management team rather than one individual reporting to one manager. The separate functional areas would be represented in this higher-level body of appeal, but decisions would be made on the basis of multidiscipline considerations. In a sense, all decisions would be made on the basis of systemic considerations.

Thus, the design teams had envisioned a radically different organization—a fluid organization not constrained by rigid, permanent walls. The new organization would comprise teams as well as individuals. *The predominant image was lateral, not vertical.* The key behavioral principles would be to enable rather than constrain, to facilitate rather than control, to coordinate rather than segment, and to share responsibility rather than hoard power.

Unfortunately, however promising and beneficial, this design was not implemented. Independent of the redesign, this division had been merged with a sister division by the corporation and had lost its autonomy. Even before the merger, however, the design teams had encountered considerable negative reaction from authority figures in the organization. Leaders charged with redirecting the business feared loss of control and hence chaos. Functional managers feared the loss of distinct career tracks protected by specialized knowledge bases. The new design flew in the face of the underlying assumptions about how organizations should function. The ideas for change were challenged by defenders of the status quo who attributed problems to the weakness of individuals rather than to the inherent structure of the organization. Members of the design teams, originally chosen because they were considered to be key organizational players, suddenly became branded as "malcontents." And so, the bureaucracy did what it does best—protect its integrity by rejecting new ideas.

Could the new design have worked? Certainly it departed in many ways from tradition. Yet, the cry for new, more *systemic* visions of organization is heard in many quarters; ironically, the parent corporation is one of the leaders advocating change. Thus, customer demand for product compatibility has led such computer manufacturers as Hewlett-Packard and Xerox to reorganize to promote technical interchange and integration in diverse, previously autonomous businesses. AT&T, TRW, and others seek to eliminate expensive redundancy and to use their basic research laboratories to find new approaches to the development and transfer of technology within the organization. Such corporations have decided that they cannot afford to support large sophisticated basic research units, the activities of which may be remote from the business or in conflict with customers.

Perhaps the most public and sobering demonstration of the need for organizations to oversee systems is the 1986 space shuttle disaster. The presidential commission investigating this disaster found that systemic management and organizational problems in the National Aeronautics and Space Administration (NASA) had contributed to weaknesses leading to the technical failure of the shuttle and other accidents (Smith, 1986). The commission recommended establishment of management procedures to improve coordination among the four geographically dispersed space agency centers. One commissioner was quoted as follows: "The centers are little

kingdoms unto themselves, and each kingdom has its own king and each kingdom runs its affairs differently. . . . And there are very few ambassadors" (Dolan, 1986, p. 1). The commission further recommended that suppliers and astronauts participate in launch decisions.

Surely the accomplishments of NASA over the past decades must be heralded as among the greatest technical and social achievements in history; yet, even there, bureaucracy became paramount. The elaborate puzzle that must be completed to launch satellites, rockets, and shuttles had become segmented into small, isolated pieces. Higher levels in the bureaucracy had chosen to void the knowledge of lower levels. Managers responsible for pleasing customers had distanced themselves from managers responsible for solving technical problems.

The lesson is straightforward: *to do business in a tightly interconnected world, an organization must take on the properties of the complex environment in which it exists.* Its organizational structure and its products must be matched to its environment. The specific characteristics of the forms of organization needed are not yet fully known, but the broad characteristics—integration, fluidity, and shared responsibility—are obvious. Organizations have become so segmented that they have lost sight of their main purpose. To regain this vision is the *pivotal challenge* before American organizations. . . .

Earlier, we indicated that the design teams realized that a total redesign of the electronics company was necessary. The changes could not be confined to the systems group. The systems group was already dependent on the sales, marketing, finance, accounting, personnel, and manufacturing groups; it would be even more dependent on these groups if it wanted to produce truly integrated products. The *reward* system of the entire company was "out of sync." The company had to shift from rewarding people for being competent in narrow specialties to rewarding people for sharing competency across specialties and, in short, for forming a broader conception of the organization and its products. At the same time, the organization needed to change its *information* structure. Integrated products require manufacturing and marketing data different from those required by more specialized products. In addition, this information, which results from intense cooperation *in the field* among people from sales, engineering, marketing, manufacturing, and finance groups, must be obtained and integrated much faster than before to ensure that the right products are available at the right time for the right customers at the right price.

It became clear that in the long run the organization needed to recruit different kinds of *people*—integrators, or systems thinkers—and, at the same time, retrain its current employees to think systemically across traditional lines of responsibility.

Next, the individual *tasks* needed to be changed and/or combined differently to reflect greater integration.

Finally, the basic *structure* of the organization needed to change drastically. What was required was a structure that contained fewer, but different, levels that were well integrated.

Perhaps the most difficult part of the challenge is to alter the behavior of the millions of hardworking, competent, and conscientious Americans who have become used to, and good at, functioning in large, bureaucratic organizations. To get some sense of what this might take, we next examine the efforts of another company attempting to align its human resource management with the needs of a systems environment.

## DOES THE SYSTEM SUPPORT ITSELF?

The U.S. aerospace and defense industry is going through its own readjustment period. Such companies have been somewhat buffered from the global economy because their work often is done within the United States for security reasons. In the past, these companies have been relatively buffered from competition as well. Recently, however, the government has cut down on practices that it feels engender waste and inefficiency within government contracting firms, including cost-plus contracts and noncompetitive bidding. Thus the industry is now faced with a competitive environment.

In addition to these changes in the marketplace, there had been a dramatic increase in the sophistication of the products, reflecting the rapid rate of development of technology. Demands for integration skyrocketed; hundreds of thousands of lines of software had to be matched to intricate electronic hardware that must then fit together with components and codes generated from several companies, each of which was authorized to design and manufacture a specific part of the final product.

Recent work with firms in this industry has enabled us to take a close look at the human and organizational sides of the problem. One firm, in particular, decided to examine its reward systems to determine if they fit the needs of the business. The symptoms in this company were similar to those in other large companies. As in the electronics firm we described earlier, there were barriers between parts of the organization. Engineers were accused of "throwing" the finished design over the wall to production. Cost overruns and nonproducible designs led to accusations between two groups with divergent views of the business. These symptoms are well known in many technology-based companies. More fundamentally, however, individuals seemed distanced from the business. Results of a diagnostic survey indicated that although more than 85 percent of the people in the company felt that they were personally doing an outstanding job, a much smaller percentage reported that the projects on which they worked were performing well. Thus, there was a disconnection—individuals could feel good personally about contributions to projects that were in trouble, partly, at least, because the problems were the other guy's fault.

After we examined the systems that were in place to manage performance, it became apparent how this disconnection could exist. First, the majority of people did not feel that they benefited personally from the company's success. In this company, as in many others, the pay system was geared to meeting the external market and achieving internal equity. Thus, base pay depended on what people with similar skills and experience made elsewhere, and what people at similar levels of responsibility made within the company. Pay increases depended on individual merit as measured in the yearly performance appraisal, to which project performance was a negligible contributor. In fact, because there was a fixed pot of merit money, individuals saw themselves as being in competition with one another for their share of the pot. Second, although the individuals in this firm were clustered into interdisciplinary project teams, team performance was believed to contribute little to the reward and appraisal process. Indeed, the notion of team was an interesting one. In this company, teams were essentially large groups whose members had individual assignments that contributed to the project. Except for the top management, the team members did not really work to-

gether to accomplish a goal. The management met regularly to review the program, but team members reported that they received very little feedback on the status of the project. Thus, there was again a disconnection, this time between those who were *responsible* for the project and those who *did the work*.

In summary, the entire performance system in this company (and in many other companies as well) enabled, and indeed encouraged, individuals to see their own performance as separable from the enterprise as a whole. Individuals pursued their own assignments and were appraised and rewarded for how well they completed these assignments. In effect, each piece of a complex technical system was treated as a separate concept. Only managers possessed the information needed to fit the pieces together and to solve problems when the pieces didn't fit. Therefore, individuals disowned responsibility for the success of the final product.

One could almost say that certain behaviors were "locked in place" by the human resource systems. Risk taking was low, individuals worked in relative isolation, and the major concern in the company regarding pay was that people be treated equitably. To change this cycle would require major alterations in the goal-setting, decision-making, problem-solving, appraisal, and reward practices of the organization. In fact, this firm and many others are now engaged in such change. They are experimenting with systems that recognize the team as the unit of analysis. Goals have become team goals, problems are solved collectively, and individuals are appraised and rewarded, to a large extent, on how well the team meets its goal. Part of the reward still depends on how the business performed. Companies such as Motorola, Honeywell, McDonnell-Douglas, *what company is this?*

and TRW are the industry's leaders in this area. . . .

From the early pioneers in this area, we have learned that it takes more than minor readjustment. In fact, every system of an organization must be examined. The opposition is intense and in some cases compelling. Individually based job design, performance appraisal, and reward systems have been developed by decades of work by industrial psychologists both within companies and within universities. Criteria of equity, validity, and individual motivational impact have been almost universally applied in evaluating these systems. Court cases regarding discrimination and unfair treatment are resolved on the basis of the same criteria. Thus, there is truly a formidable institutional barrier to change. However, it is encouraging that there is a crack in the edifice, and that there is now widespread experimentation with new systems. An alternative vision is beginning to develop, and approaches congruent with that vision are being forged (Lawler, 1986). More businesses appear to be facing the fact that they can no longer afford to separate their internal management systems from the final product.

The move to overcome this reluctance and make the transition is beginning to spread. A large number of companies have experimented with quality circles and other group problem-solving approaches. Other companies are seriously examining their technologies with an eye to redesigning work to facilitate teamwork. Frequently new plants are designed to promote teamwork and integration (Lawler, 1986).

## REFERENCES

Dolan, M. "Poor management for Shuttle Charged." *Los Angeles Times*, June 4, 1986, p. 1.

Lawler, E. E. III. *High-Involvement Management.* San Francisco: Jossey-Bass, 1986.

Mills, D. Q., and Lovell, M. R., Jr. "Enhancing Competitiveness: The Contribution of Employee Relations." In B. R. Scott and G. C. Lodge (eds.), *U.S. Competitiveness in the World Economy.* Boston: Harvard Business School Press, 1985, pp. 455–478.

Smith, R. J. "Inquiry Faults Shuttle Management." *Science*, 1986, *232*, 1488–1489.

## 24
# Self-Directed Work Teams: The New American Challenge
*Jack D. Orsburn, Linda Moran, Ed Musselwhite, John H. Zenger with Craig Perrin*

## WHAT *IS* A SELF-DIRECTED WORK TEAM?

A self-directed work team is a highly trained group of employees, from 6 to 18, on average, fully responsible for turning out a well-defined segment of finished work. The segment could be a final product, like a refrigerator or ball bearing; or a service, like a fully processed insurance claim. It could also be a complete but intermediate product or service, like a finished refrigerator motor, an aircraft fuselage, or the circuit plans for a television set. Because every member of the team shares equal responsibility for this finished segment of work, self-directed teams represent the conceptual opposite of the assembly line, where each worker assumes responsibility for a narrow technical function.

Although work-team members demonstrate classic team-work, they're much more than simply good team players. For one thing, they have more resources at their command than traditional teams do: a wider range of cross-functional skills within the team itself, much greater decision-making authority, and better access to the information they need for making sound decisions. Work teams plan, set priorities, organize, coordinate with others, measure, and take corrective action—all once considered the exclusive province of supervisors and managers. They solve problems, schedule and assign work, and in many cases handle personnel issues like absenteeism or even team member selection and evaluation. To make sure all this happens smoothly, each team member receives extensive training in the administrative, interpersonal, and technical skills required to maintain a self-managing group.

Here are a few examples of work teams in action:

- An insurance company team takes responsibility for all phases of customer service (applications, claims, and payments) in a given geographic area. Traditionally, a separate group performs each of these activities.
- An electronics assembly team preps components, stuffs and solders circuit boards, tests and repairs boards, sets and monitors inventory levels, inspects, ships, receives, and processes paperwork. Not all team members perform all tasks, but they've all mastered several and understand the rest.
- A team of six assembles, paints, and tests automobile engines on traveling stands wheeled from station to station. Supporting the team are conventional work groups that do machining and purchasing at the front end and shipping and billing at the back.

*Source:* Adapted from *Self-Directed Work Teams: The New American Challenge,* by Jack Orsburn, *et al,* pp. 8–23. © 1990 by Richard D. Irwin, Inc. Used by permission of the publisher.

# CONVENTIONAL WORK GROUPS AND SELF-DIRECTED TEAMS

Since self-directed teams are accountable for producing a finished product or service, they differ in several "revolutionary" ways from conventional groups accountable only for performing specified tasks:

## Job Categories

Companies using conventional groups divide work into narrow jobs employees can handle with minimal training and effort. But because hundreds of people may contribute to an overall process, individual employees often see little relationship between their own efforts and the finished product. This detachment plus the narrowness of their jobs add up to the apathy and alienation so many companies experience. In contrast, each member of a self-directed work team performs many activities, and managers leave the team alone, so long as the team's product or service meets or exceeds established expectations. When a conventional machine shop converts to self-direction, for example, 10 or so job categories may collapse into 1 or 2. All team members then get appropriate cross-training so they can share in the challenging, as well as the routine, activities.

## Authority

Since members of a self-directed team perform many of the tasks usually handled by supervisors—communicating, planning, monitoring, scheduling, problem solving—every team needs the authority to initiate a broad range of actions. The first level of supervision over the teams usually functions at a distance to enable rather than directly control team activities. In companies where a supervisor or manager remains in close daily contact with each team, that person's title often changes to "facilitator" to reflect a new, nontraditional role. Further, because the conventional activities of some support groups (e.g., cost accounting, quality assurance, or maintenance) turn out to inhibit rather than promote team productivity, many teams absorb some of those functions as well. And even when support groups play their role more or less as before, the teams have more say about the specific services these groups provide.

## Reward System

While executives and managers retain authority over strategies of "why" and "what" for the business, the teams assume substantial authority over the tactics of "how." To realize the benefits of self-directed teams, a company has to reinforce individual behaviors that promote the flexibility of the team as a whole, usually by paying team members for mastering a range of skills required to reach team performance goals. Pay for knowledge (instead of pay for seniority and pay for a single narrow skill) promotes the flexibility teams need to respond quickly to changing conditions. Pay may increase as a team member acquires new skills, or may decrease if old skills begin to erode. Many companies also institute gain-sharing or profit sharing programs to encourage team members to keep finding new ways to improve productivity.

Table 1–1 summarizes these fundamental differences between conventional work groups and self-directed teams.

Many U.S. companies, like some of their European and Japanese counterparts, have found that shifting ownership of the work processes to the employees themselves promotes employee commitment and, as a result, promotes continuous improvement of quality and productivity. . . .

TABLE 1–1 • SELF-DIRECTED TEAMS: THE KEY DIFFERENCES

| Issue | Conventional Group | Self-Directed Team |
|-------|-------------------|-------------------|
| Job categories | Many narrow categories | One or two broad categories |
| Authority | Supervisor directly controls daily activities | Through group decisions, team controls daily activities |
| Reward system | Tied to type of job, individual performance, and seniority | Tied to team performance and individual breadth of skills |

## The Paranoia and the Promise

To the many people with a hip-pocket interest in the status quo, at any level, these fundamental changes in the way work gets done can look pretty threatening. Many fear that their expertise will no longer be valued, that they will no longer perform important duties, or even that they will no longer have a job. When they hear about self-directed teams, people typically suspect that the company will use them to justify "downsizing," and indeed, some companies do reassign people and restructure to eliminate entire organizational layers. The most successful companies, however, use self-directed teams for "downloading." As the first-line teams assume responsibility for daily operations, support personnel and managers all the way up to the CEO are able to delegate, or "download," some of their duties to the level just below them. In effect, work teams release their managers to perform duties now exercised by managers at the level above, who in turn release those above them, and so on. At the top, the executives gain additional time for strategic planning, highly profitable time, because operational functions are now managed by the people who understand them best.

Once they get through the unavoidable trauma of transition, most people find themselves playing a new, vital role in the long-term health of the company. Mid-managers, for example, now have time to act on new and long-neglected opportunities, such as:

- Coaching the teams
- Developing an overall strategy for the teams
- Interfacing between the teams and the larger organization
- Championing innovative ideas
- Paying more attention to the technology side of the business
- Attending to team resource needs
- Working with vendors and customers
- Making critical improvements long left on the back burner

Former supervisors, now often facilitators or team leaders, learn new skills and take pride in helping the teams achieve rising standards of quality and productivity. And front-line employees demonstrate energy and commitment all but unheard of in conventional operations. The result is improved overall performance, which typically translates as increased job security and increased opportunity for anyone who learns to contribute in new ways.

## THE ROAD TO SELF-DIRECTION

The cautious Princeton economist Alan S. Blinder sees great promise in a conspicuous but widely ignored way to accelerate "our miserably slow pace of productivity improvement."[1] At a 1989 conference that Blinder organized for the Brookings Institution (the prestigious Washington, D.C., think-tank), researchers presented 5 major studies and summarized 15 others on productivity in the American workplace. "To me," Blinder says in a recent essay in *Business Week*, "all this [research] adds up to a stronger and rather different message than I had expected. . . . Institutionalized participation by workers can raise productivity as well as increase the effectiveness of other productivity-enhancing measures." Blinder's judgment and a wealth of recent research confirm the practical experience of innovative companies all over the country:

> Self-directed work teams improve productivity, because deep employee involvement builds intense commitment to corporate success.

That realization, obvious as it seems, was a long time coming. Formal involvement programs caught the public eye only in the 1960s, when many American workers started demanding a bigger say over how they were managed. One early response, the "Quality of Work Life" movement, began by devising ways to make work more enjoyable: recreation facilities, spruced-up work areas, and the like. Even if these efforts begged the question of participation, they signaled the end of a frigid epoch in labor-management relations. Later decades brought more effective measures— jointly established work standards, work climate surveys, and multilevel task forces—but in this country the notion of workers as thoughtful, responsible contributors is only now coming into its own.

Many people think self-directed work teams are a recent import from Japan;

in fact, they were pioneered in Britain and Sweden during the 1950s. (Volvo, for example, is now so advanced that, in their new Uddevalla plant, self-directed work teams assemble entire cars.) In the United States, Procter & Gamble and a few other forward-thinking companies implemented work teams in the early 1960s with profitable results. Much later, the Japanese introduced their own highly successful teams, which emphasize quality, safety, and productivity. In the States, as Table 1–2 shows, it took a brutal decade in the global marketplace, as well as the spectacular success of Japanese teams, to build a mainstream following for self-directed teams.

These days, no U.S. company is totally unaffected by the movement toward increased involvement. Even so, very few companies are willing to grant workers the power to say yes, the power to make something happen. Certainly, more companies allow employees to say no, but being allowed to halt production to fix a problem is quite different from being empowered to improve production. Blinder is one more in a growing chorus of researchers, consultants, and top executives saying more or less the same thing: To carve their niche in the world marketplace, U.S. companies must give employees the authority and resources to carry out positive actions in the technical areas they know best.

Multilevel participation is an idea whose time has come. Its most promising tool is the self-directed work team.

## THE PAYOFFS OF SELF-DIRECTION

What do companies hope to gain through self-directed work teams? The answer varies depending on strategic goals, but companies typically cite one or more of the following critical benefits:

TABLE 1–2 · MAJOR COMPANIES USING SELF-DIRECTED WORK TEAMS[2]

| Company | Year Started | Company | Year Started |
|---|---|---|---|
| Boeing | 1987 | GE | 1985 |
| Caterpillar | 1986 | General Motors | 1975 |
| Champion International | 1985 | LTV Steel | 1985 |
| Cummins Engine | 1973 | Procter & Gamble | 1962 |
| Digital Equipment | 1982 | A. O. Smith | 1987 |
| Ford | 1982 | Tektronix | 1983 |

## Productivity

A recent *Business Week* cover story documented a GE plant in Salisbury, North Carolina, that used work teams and process innovations to achieve a staggering 250 percent increase in productivity (compared to conventional plants producing the same products in 1985).[3] And while that degree of improvement is the exception, most companies moving to teams report 20 to 40 percent gains in productivity after 18 months. To cite another common occurrence, factories routinely report an 800 percent reduction in set-up and tear-down time—say, from a day-and-a-half to an hour-and-a-half—because self-directed teams find shortcuts that have absolutely no deleterious effect on productivity or the quality of finished work. Anything that brings gains like these is something that no responsible manager can dismiss out of hand.

## Streamlining

Since first-line teams assume many of the functions formerly exercised by supervisors, mid-managers, and support staff, self-direction creates new options for flattening the organization—by redeveloping supervisors as facilitators or team members, or through attrition. Work teams also provide a simple way to trim other forms of redundant bureaucracy: Anything that does not support

the teams is a candidate for elimination. For example, a number of companies reduce the flow of paper with a process they call "work-out." Every piece of paperwork handled by the teams is reviewed periodically. If it's not directly useful to the teams, it's modified, eliminated, or dealt with in some other way.

## Flexibility

Economists have been saying for years that to succeed in a world market, companies must be capable of producing small batches of tailored products on a tight schedule to meet growing demands of emerging markets. This practice—a creed really, among the dominant foreign competitors—calls for innovative technical procedures and workers who move easily from job to job. Because self-directed work teams have the skills, the information, and the motivation to adapt to change, the company as a whole can respond quickly to changing conditions in both the organization and the marketplace.

## Quality

Self-directed work teams help drive a quality improvement effort into every fiber of the organization. When teams assume more operational responsibility, they develop a deep affinity for the technical nuances of their work. As a result, it becomes a matter of professional pride with them to seek and act on opportunities for quality improvement. Analyzing their own work processes in search of improvements is a way of life for work teams. And since team members perform both technical and administrative functions, they gain the experience they need to improve the interface between those functions.

## Commitment

Company after company implementing self-directed teams has found that increased involvement breeds increased commitment to corporate-wide goals. Commitment tends to remain high as well, partly because companies reward skills and contributions, not just seniority, and partly because team members take enormous satisfaction in managing their piece of the business. . . .

## Customer Satisfaction

The energy and flexibility of self-directed work teams promote customer satisfaction through quick response and improved quality. Customer satisfaction, of course, brings repeat business, which in turn brings growth, increased market share, and expanded opportunities for both employees and the community. What self-direction means to the customer is clearly illustrated by two groups of teams in a midwestern plant producing engines for heavy-duty trucks. One group of conventional teams worked assembly-line style, each installing one component of the finished engines. Another group of self-directed teams worked autonomously, each assembling entire engines from start to finish. Although the conventional teams met standards in every way, managers soon realized the work of these groups didn't match up to the higher standards achieved by the self-directed teams. When someone inadvertently shipped the conventional teams' engines to people who normally received engines produced by the self-directed teams, these formerly privileged customers besieged the plant with bitter complaints about "the sudden decline in quality."

## HOW EMPLOYEES BECOME SELF-DIRECTED TEAMS

Picture the far-too-typical U.S. organization: Executives get bogged down in tactical decisions, managers retain most of the control, supervisors make most of the operational decisions, and workers do only as much as it takes to meet externally imposed performance standards. Now picture the same organization with fully vested work teams: Executives focus on strategic decisions, and managers and team facilitators clear the way for motivated workers to exceed ambitious team standards they've set for themselves. This second is a pretty picture, but the transformation implies profound changes that many executives, managers, and supervisors find deeply unsettling. So, like Hamlet, many would rather bear the ills they have, than fly to others they know not of.

The antidote to this quandary is foresight. If executives and other decision makers can visualize the path toward self-direction, challenging as it may seem, they're far more likely to endorse the journey. Indeed, when a company gives up and turns back, it's usually because naive guides failed to forewarn people about the predictable perils of transition.

### No Train, No Gain

It takes a group of employees from two to five years to become a mature self-directed work team. During that period, teams normally experience both progress and regression as they struggle to escape the comfort and safety of their old ways. Without proper skills and understanding, virtually any team will bog down permanently in mid-process. That's why—both during and after the transition to full self-direction—an organization must provide intensive training in three critical areas:

*Technical Skills.* Technical cross-training, which allows team members to move from job to job within the team itself, is the foundation for the flexibility and productivity of the team as a whole. After a thorough review of all of the tasks performed by the team, individual team members receive training in the specific skills that will broaden their personal contributions to the overall effort.

*Administrative Skills.* Self-directed teams, as the name implies, perform many tasks formerly handled by supervisors. At first, the teams will need training in recordkeeping, reporting procedures, and other aspects of working with the larger organization. Later, depending on the team's charter, they will need to learn procedures for budgeting, scheduling, monitoring, and even hiring and evaluating team members.

*Interpersonal Skills.* With their broader responsibilities, members of a self-directed work team must communicate more effectively than conventional workers, both one on one and in groups, with each other and with people outside the team. Conventional workers rely on the boss to ensure good communication, set priorities, and handle interpersonal conflict. The peers who make up a self-directed team must handle these critical, often explosive matters on

their own, and since these skills rarely come naturally, team members will need skill-building training in several areas. Day-to-day interactions can be chaotic unless team members master the basics of listening and giving feedback. Cooperative decision making within and among teams demands the skills of group problem solving, influencing others, and resolving conflicts. In short, every team member must learn to collaborate in getting the right information, sending the right information, and using that information to increase productivity.

# THE STAGES OF TRANSITION TO SELF-DIRECTED TEAMS

The engine that drives the transition is ongoing training in the three skill areas—technical, administrative, and interpersonal. Not only does training give team members the operational know-how they need to turn out a finished product or service, it also helps them to cope with five predictable stages[4] in their long-term progress toward mature self-direction:

Stage 1: Start-Up
Stage 2: State of Confusion
Stage 3: Leader-Centered Teams
Stage 4: Tightly Formed Teams
Stage 5: Self-Directed Teams

What follows is a map of this five-stage transition to fully self-directed teams—a quick sketch that will give you some idea of the magnitude, the excitement, and the inevitable perils of the actual journey.

## Stage 1: Start-Up
The charged atmosphere and high hopes of this honeymoon phase last a few months at most. Prior to start-up, an executive steering committee has estab-

lished the feasibility of teams and developed a mission statement, and a multi-level design team has fleshed out a plan, selected the initial work team sites, done their pre-work with mid-managers and employees, and fired the starting gun. Then, at start-up, the optimistic teams and wary supervisors begin figuring out, and acting out, what they believe to be their new roles. Even people with serious reservations, often members of support groups, either pitch in cautiously or toe the line under the watchful eyes of senior managers. "Most of us wanted this thing to work," says one facilitator in a North Carolina nuclear fuels plant. "But even with the awareness training—which was very good—I'd say we had a pretty vague idea of what we were getting into."

The dominant feature of start-up is intensive training for all involved. Team members learn the ABCs of communication and group dynamics, begin using administrative procedures, and expand their repertoire of technical skills. Supervisors, who may see themselves as having the most to lose, also receive focused training and, if they've been carefully selected, generally do their best to facilitate, rather than control, the operational and decision-making efforts of the teams.

## Stage 2: State of Confusion

After the initial enthusiasm, a period of confusion is predictable, normal, and perhaps necessary. Informing people of what to expect during this stage reduces the agony, but even then foot-dragging and outright obstruction can exacerbate the problems teams have in adapting to their new roles. With the supervisor fading as a clear authority figure, new teams often have difficulty reaching cooperative decisions. An older team member, now retired from a New England insurance company, was a mainstay for her team during this period: "I'd seen the

same kind of thing before, just after the big war started. People get scared, confused. They work like crazy but they're not quite sure if they're doing the right thing. The horrible part is nobody can tell if what they're doing is gonna make things better or worse."

Some teams fret about higher work standards or wait sullenly for hypothetical disasters. Job security is Topic A, and many speculate about the "real reasons" for the move to self-direction. Now is the time when nonteam members may openly express their opposition, and unions (if any) may predict the return of the sweat shop. Struggling managers contemplate their shrinking role in day-to-day operations and wonder if executives will delegate enough responsibilities to fill the void. More than one group secretly hopes the transition will collapse.

## Stage 3: Leader-Centered Teams

If managers and facilitators continue to demonstrate their faith in the ability of teams to manage themselves, positive signs appear. Support groups begin responding more quickly and openly to requests from the teams. Confidence grows as teams master new skills, find better ways to accomplish the work, and meet ambitious goals. Lines between salaried and hourly people begin to blur. Finally, one team member steps forward as the primary source of direction and information within each team. Far from making a power play, this person usually emerges because the team wants one of their own to interface with the organization, clarify work assignments, and referee internal disputes. "The teams want a coach," says a long-time team leader in a midwestern clothing factory. "Somebody that can draw everybody else into group decisions—which is what you have to do as a team. And they sure don't want any 'deputy boss.' "

The chief danger in Stage 3 is the team that becomes too reliant on its internal leader. So, to make sure everyone continues to learn and eventually exercise leadership skills, teams often rotate the leadership role or allow anyone to exercise leadership functions as needed (e.g., to deal with someone doing substandard work).

Also significant at this stage: Conflict declines between the teams and their managers; norms evolve for team meetings, assignments, and interactions with the organization; managers withdraw further from daily operations to work on external matters affecting team performance; and productivity expands dramatically.

## Stage 4: Tightly Formed Teams

This next stage of the transition is deceptive because teams appear to be flying high. They manage their own scheduling, clearly express their needs, and meet challenging goals with limited resources. But at least one major kink remains: an intense team loyalty that can mask internal unrest and outright dysfunction. "Our main problem at this point was the teams' hiding a poorly performing member to protect the person from outside discipline," says an area manager in a California computer components company. "They also had trouble accepting a new team member or—even worse— letting a long-time person go who, for some reason, had to move to another team." Another common Stage 4 phenomenon: The teams become extremely defensive if the organization fails to meet their needs for information or resources.

These fierce loyalties often give rise to fierce competition among the teams. While friendly rivalry enhances productivity and job satisfaction, overzealous teams can withhold information and as-sistance in order to undermine the efforts of other teams. At this point, managers must refocus the teams on cross-team and organization-wide goals, often through councils of elected team members who review issues of mutual concern.

## Stage 5: Self-Directed Teams

After the firestorm of narrow loyalties comes the period of true self-direction. Mature teams develop a powerful commitment to achieving corporate and team goals, even if those goals require reconfiguration of the teams themselves. "We really couldn't believe what was happening," reports a vice president in a midwestern consumer goods company. "People on the floor were talking about world markets, customer needs, competitors' products, making process improvements—all the things managers are supposed to think about. Now they're like a satellite, in orbit, and sending back information all the time. They just keep going without much help from people on the ground." During Stage 5, all team members routinely acquire new skills, take on new technical tasks, seek out and respond to internal customer needs, improve support systems, handle administrative duties, and refine work processes, using detailed information about contracts, competitors, and external customers.

For the manager, mature teams are a new kind of challenge. Teams have now learned to think for themselves about strategically vital information, so they need to understand the rationale behind important management decisions. Further, to maintain the competitive advantage of multilevel involvement, managers must continuously seek new ways to foster the commitment, trust, and responsible involvement of team members. The system does not evolve into a perpetual motion machine. It must be constantly energized with training and information. . . .

## NOTES

1. Alan S. Blinder, "Want to Boost Productivity? Try Giving Workers a Say," *Business Week*, 17 April 1989, 10.

2. John Hoerr, "The Payoff from Teamwork," *Business Week*, 10 July 1989, 58.

3. John Hoerr, "The Payoff from Teamwork," *Business Week*, 10 July 1989, 58.

4. Linda Moran and Ed Musselwhite, *Self-Directed Workteams: A Lot More Than Just Teamwork*, (San Jose, CA: Zenger-Miller, Inc. 1988), 13–18.

# 25

# Transforming Teamwork: Work Relationships in a Fast-Changing World

## Marvin R. Weisbord

Teamwork has been a contradiction in American society clear back to Alexis de Tocqueville, that astute French observer who coined the phrase "habits of the heart" to describe our folkways. "Each man is forever thrown back on himself alone," wrote de Tocqueville in the 1830s, "and there is danger that he may be shut up in the solitude of his own heart." He called this tendency—lest you wonder where we got that word—"individualism" (de Tocqueville, in Bellah and others, 1985, p. 37). It is our great strength, the bedrock of the entrepreneurial spirit and innovation. Overused, it becomes our strongest weakness.

Productive workplaces need both individual effort and teamwork. And teams get much lip service. We call every work group a team even if they rarely see each other. "Team" rivals "quality" as a business cliché. "I have to see my team about that," says a company president. "Individually, of course," she adds. "I don't want to open a can of worms."

Sometimes people develop teamwork spontaneously, like schoolyard kids in a basketball game. That's what many self-managing teams did in the 1960s. Serving customers, rather than a boss, drove them to cooperate. Sometimes teams need help. In third-wave managing I think this help must include two perspectives: (1), unlearning deeply ingrained, self-limiting assumptions about individualism, authority, and responsibility that defeat cooperation and, paradoxically, individual success; (2), looking outward toward the wider social and business networks that shape their mutual effort. People need both perspectives—relationships *and* environment—to make sense of the workplace. Integrating both to move from competition and individualism toward cooperation and wholeness is what I mean by transforming teamwork. There is no more important task for third-wave managers.

## TEAMS AND TEAM BUILDING

Teamwork can be transformed using a particular learning structure a few times a year. It derives from the most widely used and predictably helpful tool in the OD kit: team building. . . . There is no standard procedure. Team building evolved in the early 1960s as a solution to the transfer-of-training dilemma—how to use workshop learning in real life. A T-group was (and is) an education in self-awareness. For willing members it offers learning that simply can't be got any other way. The exchange of perceptions of self and others unites groups in powerful ways. People learn to accept themselves, to trust one another, and to resolve their differences.

Two insights emerged, however, from efforts to repeat these results in compa-

*Source:* Adapted from *Productive Workplaces: Organizing and Managing for Dignity, Meaning, and Community,* by Marvin R. Weisbord, pp. 296–310. Copyright 1987 by Marvin Weisbord and Jossey-Bass, Inc., Publishers. Reprinted with permission.

nies in the 1960s. One, people who attended learning laboratories with strangers had powerful *ah-ha*'s that they could not describe to co-workers, or translate into new organizational policies or procedures. Two, when they sought to remedy this defect by running T-groups *within* organizations, they found people dredging up emotional issues too remote from the tasks at hand to be properly dealt with in that setting.

Developing self-awareness remains an essential but not sufficient activity for changing companies. A T-group changes by observing its own behavior as a temporary system. To use this knowledge, we don't transfer T-groups to the workplace, but only the learning principle. Teams benefit from observing together their own behavior *in the organization they wish to change*, in all its richness of environment, economics, and technology. Group norms and interpersonal feelings are pieces of a large jigsaw puzzle.

Businesspeople, aware that process skills could help them put the puzzle together faster, sought a format that would make these skills learnable in the workplace. Organizational realities had to be worked with—formal leadership, for example. That meant validating mutual goals, both personal and organizational. It meant opening the agenda to past, present, and future, instead of keeping it only "here and now." It meant giving the decision to proceed over to the whole team. And it required task structures different from, but not alien to, real life. The T-group was a closed system by design, so that each person could focus inward. To transform team building requires inquiry into the team's open system—personal, companywide, global, past, present, and future. It takes in every agenda.

Not everyone defines it that way. Team building has come to mean everything from interpersonal encounter among co-workers (a format I do not recommend), to joint work on tasks of mutual importance for the future (a format I strongly support). The earliest modes used an exchange of interpersonal feedback as the key building block. In my practice now I am more committed to helping each team member take a public stand on critical issues the team faces, the ones most likely to shape the future. The most powerful team building occurs in the mutual revisiting of an organization's future, its central tasks, the design of its jobs, policies, and systems—and how people move toward or away from these tasks.

*Many Methods.* Modern methods are available from many sources—everything from self-guided workbooks and cassette tapes to facilitators and consultants. Team building remains durable, flexible, and broadly useful in a wide range of situations: starting new teams and task forces, reorganizing, untangling conflicts between departments, setting goals, strategy planning, cultural change—any activity people cannot do alone. In such team meetings well-motivated groups routinely learn how to manage with less frustration and higher output. They usually report more openness, more mutual respect, higher trust and cooperation over time.

I stress well-motivated because that is the building block for all constructive change. You can't play winning football if half the team doesn't give a hoot. The same is true for producing, selling, or managing. That's not to say it takes no work. Even the best-intentioned groups find they must flounder for a while the first time they endeavor to have this sort of meeting. You can't get to Renewal without crossing into Confusion. After that, maintenance requires perhaps two meetings a year, during which team processes are part of the agenda. This becomes more important if, as is common, the team gets new members.

*Conditions for Success.* Team building succeeds under four conditions:

1. Interdependence. The team is working on important problems in which each person has a stake. In other words, teamwork is central to future success, not an expression of ideology or some misplaced "ought-to."
2. Leadership. The boss wants so strongly to improve group performance that he or she will take risks.
3. Joint decision. All members agree to participate.
4. Equal influence. Each person has a chance to influence the agenda.

In one typical scenario, the boss calls a meeting, states some personal goals, and asks for discussion. When (as is common) a consultant has been asked to help, the parties need a get-acquainted meeting. (I will describe the meeting from both consultant's and manager's perspectives. I think you will find them often interchangeable.) Often the consultant interviews team members to discover their concerns and wishes. Questions might include each person's objectives, tasks, problems, and the extent of help needed from others. Responses always encompass costs, markets, innovation, and other business-related issues.

Clients (some consultants too) often treat interviews as if their main purpose is for the consultant (doctor) to learn enough to prescribe the right cure. An experienced team-building consultant, however, knows that the prescription is voluntary dialogue. Interviews have two other purposes more important than the consultant's education. One, they help team members collect their thoughts and feelings, zero in on what they really want to say. Two, they reduce the fantasy about the consultant's motives and working methods. The consultant will learn about the organization in any case. What the consultant wants most to know is how much each team member will take responsibility for the meeting's success.

*Deciding to Proceed.* The consultant presents a summary of interview themes to the team, inviting discussion of the pros and cons of continuing. If the team decides to proceed, it schedules a two- or three-day offsite event. This meeting has a dual focus that makes it different from typical staff meetings. The team works directly on an important task identified by members: strategy formation, reorganizing, dealing with technologies, costs, or markets, quality or consumer problems. Here a future scenario—"X Corporation Five Years Hence"—can be a powerful lightning rod for attracting constructive dialogue. Team members also specify what it is about their own processes they wish to improve. This makes it possible for them to periodically step back and observe what they are doing that helps or hinders progress. This discussion can be helped by process-analysis forms like that in "Rating Teamwork," a grandchild of early group dynamics.

Such forms are easily constructed. You can spend days in the library tracking down the issues that decades of research have shown go hand in hand with output and satisfaction. Or you can ask the team members, and get roughly the same list in ten minutes. Nine times out of ten one item on the list will be "trust"— a validation of Jack Gibb's contention (1978) that without it nothing else of consequence is likely to happen.

Making such a list is a focusing device, a learning tool. It is useful when used once or twice to help people internalize key processes. Done by rote, it becomes a meaningless ritual, the social analogy to turning out reams of numbers in a quarterly rollout nobody pays attention to.

A more powerful way to help people experience their own processes is with videotape. Reviewing ten minutes of a meeting and asking people to recall what they were thinking or feeling is probably the simplest way to facilitate team learning (the same way sports teams, tennis players, skiers learn by watching themselves on tape).

The dual focus on task *and* process is the team-building meeting's unique contribution to productive workplaces. I have three success criteria.

1. The team resolves important dilemmas, often ones on which little progress was made before.
2. People emerge more confident of their ability to influence the future.
3. Members learn the extent to which output is linked to their own candor, responsibility for themselves, and willingness to cooperate with others.

## PRACTICAL THEORY

I want to describe the underlying theory in business terms, borrowing from an extraordinary consultant, the late Mike Blansfield, who pioneered the method years ago with TRW and other companies. He called his concept "Team Effectiveness Theory," outlined on the accompanying chart. Blansfield's method, which I will not describe, was based largely on interpersonal feedback. Yet he had a strong practical grasp of business issues that is reflected in his theory. I think it is a major contribution to the transformation of teamwork, fitting in with any agenda you can name. The key to team building, I believe, is its *dual* focus on task and process under conditions of rapid external change, not a narrowly interpersonal focus.

Blansfield's concept highlights universal processes that work teams rarely connect to results. The chart makes the linkages by bringing together a managerial vocabulary for output with a vocabulary for teamwork. Most managers define positive results as higher productivity, better quality, more profits, and lower costs, listed at the bottom of the chart.

When something on that bottom list goes wrong, people often feel out of control and (secretly) incompetent. They initiate a search for mistakes in techniques, policies, systems, plans (the middle list), or they seek to finger a villain. In extreme cases, if they have the power, they may fire somebody. Few consider the impact of their own behavior on the *key processes* affected by the situation. These are the three factors on the top list.

From Taylor to Lewin to McGregor to Emery and Trist, observers have identified management's own behavior as *the* starting place for improving anything— systems, labor-management relations, output, work satisfaction, culture, whatever. Blansfield's model highlights the differences between managing a problem one on one and managing a group in which people depend on one another. To do the latter requires an appreciation of task and process applied to teamwork in an unpredictable world.

I quickly learned to appreciate this model because of my management experiences years ago. About 1960, in the days of the eighty-column punch card and key verifier (remember when, senior citizens?), I installed a computerized order processing system. . . . Outside systems analysts told us what we needed. Programmers instructed the computer. The rest of us waited expectantly for results. I never considered that this new technology would change everybody's job, including mine, reduce our control over customer policy, and force us to rethink many nonroutine problems. I had never seen a computer before. Hardly anybody had. In the days before

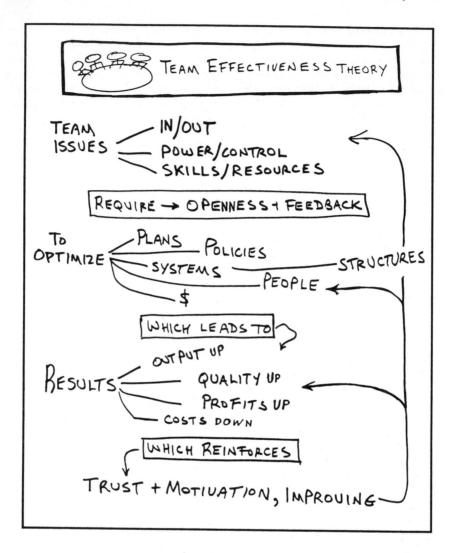

user friendliness, it was an aggravating initiation.

Little did I appreciate what strong feelings this innovation would stir, or how feelings, attitudes, and actions would combine to frustrate my intended result. It never occurred to me to get together the people affected and plan the implementation. I simply instructed all to carry out their assigned tasks, never imagining that people so instructed have

an unerring tendency to thwart one another unless they plan together.

I vividly recall the disruption, missed deadlines, angry customers, tearful order processing clerks, bewildered systems analyst, and general turmoil that cost two resignations and several lost customers. Who knows what our collective blood pressures were, how many got ulcers, how many smokers and drinkers stepped up their intake? I fell prey to a common tendency of task-driven managers. When things started to go wrong, I did what I knew best harder and faster. I pressured people to work overtime. I chided the office force for not cooperating. I reiterated my goals for rapid implementation. I fiddled with the system, rerouting Form A from Desk B and Desk C, with a carbon copy to Person D. I checked up and made sure that a copy went to Accounting. In short, I belabored the daylights out of the effectiveness factors, as if feelings and motivation had nothing to do with it. Managing one on one like a whirling dervish, I drove everybody nuts, including myself.

## ADDING TEAMWORK TO EFFECTIVENESS

My motor had a missing cylinder. I thought I was managing computer system technology and acted as if each person were a cog in the machine. I triggered a set of social dynamics about which I knew nothing—the factors listed at the top of Blansfield's model. Each person in a work group continually struggles with three questions that are never answered "once and for all." They are in jeopardy at every turning point, and must be resolved over and over again.

1. Am I in or out?
2. Do I have any power and control?
3. Can I use, develop, and be appreciated for my skills and resources?

*In or Out.* Most of us want to belong, to be valued, to have tasks that matter, and to be recognized as insiders by others. The more "in" we feel, the better we cooperate. The more we feel "out," the more we withdraw, work alone, daydream, defeat ourselves and other people. When I sought single-handedly to patch up the computer system, I drove everybody else out.

*Power and Control.* Power and control need little explaining after Taylor, McGregor, and the astronauts. We all want power. Faced with changes we can't influence, we feel impotent and in turn, lose self-esteem. It doesn't matter how smart we are, how skilled, or how far up the ladder of success we have climbed. Faced with something we can't influence, we may work harder and do worse, losing self-esteem until we gain control again. That happened to me in the 1960s, and I made it worse for everybody else.

*Skills and Resources.* Tremendous skills, experience, and common sense exist in every workplace. What keeps us from tapping them are outdated assumptions about who can and should do what. Often, jobs are defined so narrowly people can't use the brains they were born with, or even the training they have received. During my computer installation, I thought that people's years of experience with the old system were irrelevant. I pressured folks to turn on a dime and learn something nobody had any experience with. Lacking a team concept, I saw no way to help people support one another over the learning hump. In short, I was not only managing a computer installation, I was managing the destruction of a social system of trust, motivation, and commitment built up over many years.

Here is the simple truth: there was no way, in the face of the interdependent changes we were making, to manage this changeover successfully one on one. The three team process issues can be resolved only when the tasks are seen as team tasks, not the boss's problem to be solved. That is not to say they automatically *will* be resolved. They won't—unless two things occur. We need to learn how to be open about what's on our minds, and responsive to others. We need to give and get feedback.

*Candor and Feedback.* These two processes, openness and feedback, link team issues with results. We need a place where we can talk over what each person needs to do and our anxiety about doing it. We need a chance to own up to uncertainty and express differences of opinion constructively. We need to discover that others are in the same boat. We need one thing more. I've been in dozens of these meetings. Sooner or later somebody *always* brings up the importance of trust. Commitment is built on a foundation of mutual trust, and everybody knows it. Trusting one another is the most secure way to manage through tough times. The team-building meeting is one way people learn how to develop trust.

Feelings about membership, control, and skills influence our motivation, which in turn determines the quality of our work. If we talk *only* about results, tasks, and plans, without observing our ability to listen and hear, to discuss differences, to solve problems and decide in a way that builds commitment, we ultimately defeat the results we claim to value. It's all one system. Pull on any thread and you untangle the whole net—the task of a dual-focus meeting.

*Structure.* Such a meeting is helped along by structure. Usually a team-building meeting starts with a discussion of goals and agenda. Often there is considerable discussion just to get a meeting of the minds about the major agenda: why, how, what, who. Sometimes there are prearranged "stop-action" points when people fill out a process observation form or review the videotape. Sometimes a consultant will call time out if people are fighting or running away from the task. Usually a short process

discussion is enough to get things tracking again. Sometimes it takes several hours of dialogue. Each team's *own* process requirements should be kept front and center.

If people identify interpersonal conflicts or difficulty in communicating as sources of frustration, some device on personal style (maybe a self-report paper-and-pencil survey) may trigger half a day's discussion. In such exercises people learn to value their differences, to accept their strengths, and to express themselves more clearly.

Sometimes teams engage in role negotiation, a procedure devised by consultant Roger Harrison (1972). Each team member writes down what he or she wants each of the others to do less or more of, and what to keep doing the same. These requests are posted and negotiated. For example, "I'll give you at least a week's notice of schedule changes, if you'll refer customer complaints directly to me." There's no deal unless both parties agree.

Another useful format, responsibility charting, is indicated if the team's self-diagnoses is that important tasks are falling between the cracks. An "R" chart (see flip chart) lists who makes which decisions, who must be informed, who must support, and who has the power to veto (Galbraith, 1977). All these activities increase communication, provide feedback, take account of each person's needs, more equitably distribute influence, and promote orderly procedures for managing interdependence.

*Leadership and Consensus.* Nearly every team gets around to how the boss makes decisions. . . .

The boss laments, "They act like children, bucking everything to me." The team members echo, "He treats us like children and does too much himself."

The "R" CHART

R = RESPONSIBLE    A = APPROVE
C = CONSULT        I = INFORM

| DECISIONS | ACTORS | | | | |
| --- | --- | --- | --- | --- | --- |
| | GENERAL MANAGER | PROJECT MANAGER | FINANCE DIRECTOR | MARKETING MANAGER | HUMAN RESOURCES |
| CHANGE BUDGET | | | | | |
| ASSIGN PEOPLE | | | | | |
| CHANGE SCHEDULE | | | | | |
| CALL RE-VIEWS | | | | | |

The commonest discovery on both sides is how each acts to reinforce the others' perceptions—unconsciously accepting (even relishing) their roles in this age-old parent/child drama. Inevitably this triggers talk about the meaning of individual versus group decisions, when each is appropriate, what the practical limits of formal power really are, what the risks and payoffs can be when acting without consulting others, and whether consensus means "doing what the group wants."

I find consensus decision making the least understood and most useful dimension of teamwork. Consensus means support derived when each person feels heard and understood. Unanimous decision is a desirable goal. With or without it, a boss has the responsibility to decide. This task is made easier if each team member feels free to speak openly on important matters. Indeed, the simplest team-building technique is the "go-around," where all participants have a chance to say how they see it and what they would do. Bosses can facilitate this task by openly sharing their own dilemmas and willingness to hear people out. To maintain team cohesiveness, all should be satisfied that they had a chance to influence the decision and declare their willingness to support it. When any team member can't do that, the team has a serious problem.

## THE FUTURE OF TEAM BUILDING

A team-building meeting can become a procedural nightmare of consultant-orchestrated exercises. It also can be run simply, directly, and to the point. My partner Tony Petrella (1974), for example, has evolved many procedures to put responsibility firmly in members' hands. In one variation the consultant interviews each person in front of the others, asking questions all have agreed to in advance. Everybody takes notes. People review their notes in subgroups and diagnose their team's needs and priorities. The diagnoses are discussed, an agenda built, and the remaining time spent solving problems, working out new relationships, or improving policies and procedures. In another variation Petrella and Mike DiLorenzo interviewed managers and wrote down everything they heard—the traditional approach. In a followup meeting, before unveiling their notes, they simply asked people to repeat for one another what was already said, a request carried out with enthusiasm.

The objective of these simpler procedures is to reduce passivity and put people more firmly in charge of their own lives. The consultant's role is to help people talk constructively about their work, to learn, and to act. I share Petrella's conviction that most folks can discuss, learn, and act as readily with a little structure as with a lot. If you consider the "right" answer the best one that is implementable, this less-is-more approach will be welcome in many situations where participation and commitment are important to success.

Teamwork is essential to large system success. Team building is useful at some point in any change program. Most team members come away feeling more "in," more influential, more competent, more supported, and more committed to their common enterprise. They may also have solved some problems, devised a new strategy, moved toward a new structure, consolidated a future vision. . . .

## REFERENCES

Bellah, R. N., and others. *Habits of the Heart: Individualism and Commitment in American Life.* Berkeley and Los Angeles: University of California Press, 1985.

Galbraith, J. R. *Organization Design.* Reading, Mass.: Addison-Wesley, 1977.

Gibb, J. R. *Trust: A New View of Personal and Organizational Development.* Los Angeles: Guild of Tutors Press, 1978.

Harrison, R. "Role Negotiation: A Tough-Minded Approach to Team Development." In W. W. Burke and H. A. Hornstein (eds.), *The Social Technology of Organizational Development.* La Jolla, Calif.: University Associates, 1972.

Petrella, T. "Managing with Teams." Plainfield, N.J.: Block Petrella Associates, 1974.

## 26

# The Empowerment of Service Workers: What, Why, How, and When

## *David E. Bowen & Edward E. Lawler III*

Empowering service workers has acquired almost a "born again" religious fervor. Tom Peters calls it "purposeful chaos." Robert Waterman dubs it "directed autonomy." It has also been called the "art of improvisation."

Yet in the mid-1970s, the production-line approach to service was the darling child of service gurus. They advocated facing the customer with standardized, procedurally driven operations. Should we now abandon this approach in favor of empowerment?

Unfortunately, there is no simple, clear-cut answer. In this article we try to help managers think about the question of whether to empower by clarifying its advantages and disadvantages, describing three forms that empower employees to different degrees, and presenting five contingencies that managers can use to determine which approach best fits their situation. We do not intend to debunk empowerment, rather we hope to clarify why to empower (there are costs, as well as benefits), how to empower (there are alternatives), and when to empower (it really does depend on the situation).

## THE PRODUCTION-LINE APPROACH

In two classic articles, the "Production-Line Approach to Service" and the "In-dustrialization of Service," Theodore Levitt described how service operations can be made more efficient by applying manufacturing logic and tactics.[1] He argued:

> Manufacturing thinks technocratically, and that explains its success. . . . By contrast, service looks for solutions in the performer of the task. This is the paralyzing legacy of our inherited attitudes: the solution to improved service is viewed as being dependent on improvements in the skills and attitudes of the performers of that service.
>
> While it may pain and offend us to say so, thinking in humanistic rather than technocratic terms ensures that the service sector will be forever inefficient and that our satisfactions will be forever marginal.[2]

He recommended (1) simplification of tasks, (2) clear division of labor, (3) substitution of equipment and systems for employees, and (4) little decision-making discretion afforded to employees. In short, management designs the system, and employees execute it.

McDonald's is a good example. Workers are taught how to greet customers and ask for their order, including a script for suggesting additional items. They learn a set procedure for assembling the order (for example, cold drinks first, then hot ones), placing items on the tray, and placing the tray where the customer need not reach for it. There is a script and a procedure for collecting money and giving change. Finally, there is a script for saying thank you and asking the customer to come again.[3] This production-line approach makes customer-service interactions uniform and gives the organization control over them. It is easily learned; workers can be quickly trained and put to work.

What are the gains from a production-line approach? Efficient, low-cost, high-volume service operations, with satisfied customers.

## THE EMPOWERMENT APPROACH

Ron Zemke and Dick Schaaf, in *The Service Edge: 101 Companies That Profit from Customer Care*, note that empowerment is a common theme running through many, even most, of their excellent service businesses, such as American Airlines, Marriott, American Express, and Federal Express. To Zemke and Schaaf, empowerment means "turning the front line loose," encouraging and rewarding employees to exercise initiative and imagination: "Empowerment in many ways is the reverse of doing things by the book."[4]

The humanistic flavor of empowerment pervades the words of advocates such as Tom Peters:

> It is necessary to "dehumiliate" work by eliminating the policies and procedures (almost always tiny) of the organization that demean and belittle human dignity. It is impossible to get people's best efforts, involvement, and caring concern for things you believe important to your customers and the long-term interests of your organization when we write policies and procedures that treat them like thieves and bandits.[5]

And from Jan Carlzon, CEO of Scandinavian Airlines Systems (SAS):

> To free someone from rigorous control by instructions, policies, and orders, and to give that person freedom to take responsibility for his ideas, decisions, and actions is to release hidden resources that would otherwise remain inaccessible to both the individual and the organization.[6]

In contrast to the industrialization of service, empowerment very much looks to the "performer of the tasks" for solutions to service problems. Workers are asked to suggest new services and products and to solve problems creatively and effectively.

What, then, does it really mean—beyond the catchy slogans—to empower employees? We define empowerment as sharing with frontline employees four organizational ingredients: (1) information about the organization's performance, (2) rewards based on the organization's performance, (3) knowledge that enables employees to understand and contribute to organizational performance, and (4) power to make decisions that influence organizational direction and performance. We will say more about these features later. For now, we can say that with a production-line approach, these features tend to be concentrated in the hands of senior management; with an empowerment approach, they tend to be moved downward to frontline employees.

## WHICH APPROACH IS BETTER?

In 1990, Federal Express became the first service organization to win the Malcolm Baldrige National Quality Award. The company's motto is "people, service, and profits." Behind its blue, white, and red planes and uniforms are self-managing work teams, gainsharing plans, and empowered employees seemingly consumed with providing flexible and creative service to customers with varying needs.

At UPS, referred to as "Big Brown" by its employees, the philosophy was stated by founder Jim Casey: "Best service at low rates." Here, too, we find turned-on people and profits. But we do not find empowerment. Instead we find controls, rules, a detailed union contract, and carefully studied work methods. Nor do we find a promise to do all things for customers, such as handling off-schedule pickups and packages that don't fit size and weight limitations. In fact, rigid operational guidelines help guarantee the customer reliable, low-cost service.

Federal Express and UPS present two different faces to the customer, and behind these faces are different management philosophies and organizational cultures. Federal Express is a high-involvement, horizontally coordinated organization that encourages employees to use their judgment above and beyond the rulebook. UPS is a top-down, traditionally controlled organization, in which employees are directed by policies and procedures based on industrial engineering studies of how all service delivery aspects should be carried out and how long they should take.

Similarly, at Disney theme parks, ride operators are thoroughly scripted on what to say to "guests," including a list of preapproved "ad libs"! At Club Med, however, CEO Jacques Giraud fervently believes that guests must experience *real* magic, and the resorts' GOs (*gentils organisateurs*, "congenial hosts") are set free to spontaneously create this feeling for their guests. Which is the better approach? Federal Express or UPS? Club Med or Disney?

At a recent executive education seminar on customer service, one of us asked. "Who thinks that it is important for their business to empower their service personnel as a tool for improving customer service?" All twenty-seven participants enthusiastically raised their hands. Although they represented diverse services—banking, travel, utilities, airlines, and shipping—and they disagreed on most points, they all agreed that empowerment is key to customer satisfaction. But is it?

## EMPOWERING SERVICE EMPLOYEES: WHY, HOW, AND WHEN

### Why to Empower: The Benefits

What gains are possible from empowering service employees?

• **Quicker On-Line Responses to Customer Needs during Service Delivery.** Check-in time at the hotel begins at 2 P.M., but a guest asks the desk clerk if she can check in at 1:30 P.M. An airline passenger arrives at the gate at 7:30 A.M., Friday, for a 7:45 A.M. departure and wants to board the plane with a travel coupon good Monday through Thursday, and there are empty seats on the plane. The waitress is taking an order in a modestly priced family restaurant; the menu says no substitutions, but the customer requests one anyway.

The customer wants a quick response. And the employee would often like to be able to respond with something other than "No, it is against our rules," or "I will have to check with my supervisor." Empowering employees in these situations can lead to the sort of spontaneous, creative rule-breaking that can turn a potentially frustrated or angry customer into a satisfied one. This is particularly valuable when there is little time to refer to a higher authority, as when the plane is leaving in fifteen minutes. Even before greeting customers, empowered employees are confident that they have all the

necessary resources at their command to provide customers with what they need.
• **Quicker On-Line Responses to Dissatisfied Customers during Service Recovery.** Customer service involves both delivering the service, such as checking a guest into a hotel room, and recovering from poor service, such as relocating him from a smoking floor to the nonsmoking room he originally requested. Although delivering good service may mean different things to different customers, all customers feel that service businesses ought to fix things when service is delivered improperly.

Fixing something after doing it wrong the first time can turn a dissatisfied customer into a satisfied, even loyal, customer. But service businesses frequently fail in the act of recovery because service employees are not empowered to make the necessary amends with customers. Instead, customers hear employees saying, "Gee, I wish there was something I could do, but I can't," "It's not my fault," or "I could check with my boss, but she's not here today." These employees lack the power and knowledge to recover, and customers remain dissatisfied.
• **Employees Feel Better about Their Jobs and Themselves.** Earlier we mentioned Tom Peters' thinking on how strict rules can belittle human dignity. Letting employees call the shots allows them to feel "ownership" of the job; they feel responsible for it and find the work meaningful. Think of how you treat your car as opposed to a rented one. Have you ever washed a rental car? Decades of job design research show that when employees have a sense of control and of doing meaningful work they are more satisfied. This leads to lower turnover, less absenteeism, and fewer union organizing drives.
• **Employees Will Interact with Customers with More Warmth and Enthusiasm.** Research now supports

our long-standing intuition that customers' perceptions of service quality are shaped by the courtesy, empathy, and responsiveness of service employees.[7] Customers want employees to appear concerned about their needs. Can empowerment help create this? One of us has done customer service research in branch banks that showed that when the tellers reported feeling good about how they were supervised, trained, and rewarded, customers thought more highly of the service they received.[8] In short, when employees felt that management was looking after their needs, they took better care of the customer.

In service encounters, employees' feelings about their jobs will spill over to affect how customers feel about the service they get. This is particularly important when employee attitudes are a key part of the service package. In banking, where the customer receives no tangible benefits in the exchange other than a savings deposit slip, a sour teller can really blemish a customer's feelings about the encounter.
• **Empowered Employees Can Be a Great Source of Service Ideas.** Giving frontline employees a voice in "how we do things around here" can lead to improved service delivery and ideas for new services. The bank study showed that the tellers could accurately report how customers viewed overall service quality and how they saw the branches' service climate (e.g., adequacy of staff and appearance of facilities).[9]

Frontline employees are often ready and willing to offer their opinion. When it comes to market research, imagine the difference in response rates from surveying your employees and surveying your customers.
• **Great Word-of-Mouth Advertising and Customer Retention.** Nordstrom's advertising budget is 1.5 percent of sales, whereas the industry average is 5 per-

cent. Why? Their satisfied-no-matter-what customers spread the word about their service and become repeat customers.

## The Costs

What are the costs of empowerment?

• **A Greater Dollar Investment in Selection and Training.** You cannot hire effective creative problem solvers on the basis of chance or mere intuition. Too bad, because the systematic methods necessary to screen out those who are not good candidates for empowerment are expensive. For example, Federal Express selects customer agents and couriers on the basis of well-researched profiles of successful performers in those jobs.

Training is an even greater cost. The production-line approach trains workers easily and puts them right to work. In contrast, new hires at SAS are formally assigned a mentor to help them learn the ropes; Nordstrom department managers take responsibility for orienting and training new members of the sales team; customer service representatives at Lands' End and L.L. Bean spend a week in training before handling their first call. They receive far more information and knowledge about their company and its products than is the norm.

The more labor intensive the service, the higher these costs. Retail banking, department stores, and convenience stores are labor intensive, and their training and selection costs can run high. Utilities and airlines are far less labor intensive.

• **Higher Labor Costs.** Many consumer service organizations, such as department stores, convenience stores, restaurants, and banks, rely on large numbers of part-time and seasonal workers to meet their highly variable staffing needs. These employees typically work for short periods of time at low wages. To em-power these workers, a company would have to invest heavily in training to try to quickly inculcate the organization's culture and values. This training would probably be unsuccessful, and the employees wouldn't be around long enough to provide a return on the investment. Alternatively, the organization could pay higher wages to full-time, permanent employees, but they would be idle when business was slow.

• **Slower or Inconsistent Service Delivery.** Remember the hotel guest wanting to check in early and the airline passenger requesting special treatment at the gate? True, there is a benefit to empowering the employee to bend the rules, but only for the person at the front of the line! Customers at the back of the line are grumbling and checking their watches. They may have the satisfaction of knowing that they too may receive creative problem solving when and if they reach the counter, but it is small consolation if the plane has already left.

Based on our experiences as both researchers and customers, we believe that customers will increasingly value speed in service delivery. Purposeful chaos may work against this. We also believe that many customers value "no surprises" in service delivery. They like to know what to expect when they revisit a service business or patronize different outlets of a franchise. When service delivery is left to employee discretion, it may be inconsistent.

The research data show that customers perceive reliability—"doing it right the first time"—as the most important dimension of service quality. It matters more than employees' responsiveness, courtesy, or competency, or the attractiveness of the service setting.[10] Unfortunately, in the same research, a sample of large, well-known firms was more deficient on reliability than on these other dimensions. Much of the touted appeal of the production-line approach was that procedurally and technocratically driven operations could deliver service more reliably and consistently than service operations heavily dependent upon the skills and attitudes of employees. The production-line approach was intended to routinize service so that customers would receive the "best outcome" possible from their service encounters—service delivery with no glitches in the first place.

We feel that service managers need to guard against being seduced into too great a focus on recovery, at the expense of service delivery reliability. We say "seduced" because it is possible to confuse good service with inspiring stories about empowered employees excelling at the art of recovery. Recovery has more sex appeal than the nitty-gritty detail of building quality into every seemingly mundane aspect of the service delivery system, but an organization that relies on recovery may end up losing out to firms that do it right the first time.

• **Violations of "Fair Play."** A recent study of how service businesses handle customer complaints revealed that customers associate sticking to procedures with being treated fairly.[11] Customers may be more likely to return to a business if they believe that their complaint was handled effectively because of company policies rather than because they were lucky enough to get a particular employee. In other words, customers may prefer procedurally driven acts of recovery. We suspect that customers' notions of fairness may be violated when they see employees cutting special deals with other customers.

• **Giveaways and Bad Decisions.** Managers are often reluctant to empower their employees for fear they will give too much away to the customer. Perhaps they have heard the story of Willie, the doorman at a Four Seasons Hotel, who left work and took a flight to return a briefcase left behind by a guest. Or they have heard of too many giveaways by empowered Nordstrom employees. For some services, the costs of giveaways are far outweighed by enhanced customer loyalty, but not for others.

Sometimes creative rule breaking can cause a major problem for an organization. There may be a good reason why no substitutions are allowed or why a coupon cannot be used on a certain day (e.g., an international airfare agreement). If so, having an empowered employee break a rule may cause the organization serious problems, of which the employee may not even be aware.

These are some of the costs and benefits of empowerment. We hope this discussion will help service businesses use empowerment knowledgeably, not just because it is a fad. But we must add one more caveat: There is still precious little research on the consequences of empowerment. We have used anecdotal evidence, related research (e.g., in job design), and our work on service. More systematic research must assess whether this array of costs and benefits fully captures the "whys" (and "why nots") of empowerment.

## How to Empower: Three Options

Empowering service employees is less understood than industrializing service delivery. This is largely because the production-line approach is an example of the well-developed control model of organization design and management, whereas empowerment is part of the still evolving "commitment" or "involvement" model. The latter assumes that most employees can make good decisions if they are properly socialized, trained, and informed. They can be internally motivated to perform effectively, and they are capable of self-control and self-direction. This approach also assumes that most employees can produce good ideas for operating the business.[12]

The control and involvement models differ in that four key features are concentrated at the top of the organization in the former and pushed down in the organization in the latter. As we have discussed above, these features are the following: (1) information about organizational performance (e.g., operating results and competitor performance); (2) rewards based on organizational performance (e.g., profit sharing and stock ownership); (3) knowledge that enables employees to understand and contribute to organizational performance (e.g., problem-solving skills); and (4) power to make decisions that influence work procedures and organizational direction (e.g., through quality circles and self-managing teams).

Three approaches to empowering employees can be identified (see Figure 1).[13] They represent increasing degrees of empowerment as additional knowledge, information, power, and rewards are pushed down to the front line. Empower-

ment, then, is not an either/or alternative, but rather a choice of three options:

**1. Suggestion Involvement** represents a small shift away from the control model. Employees are encouraged to contribute ideas through formal suggestion programs or quality circles, but their day-to-day work activities do not really change. Also, they are only empowered to recommend; management typically retains the power to decide whether or not to implement.

Suggestion involvement can produce some empowerment without altering the basic production-line approach. McDonald's, for example, listens closely to the front line. The Big Mac, Egg McMuffin, and McDLT all were invented by employees, as was the system of wrapping burgers that avoids leaving a thumbprint in the bun. As another example, Florida Power and Light, which won the Deming quality award, defines empowerment in suggestion-involvement terms.

**2. Job Involvement** represents a significant departure from the control model because of its dramatic "opening up" of job content. Jobs are redesigned so that employees use a variety of skills. Employees believe their tasks are significant, they have considerable freedom in deciding how to do the work, they get more feed-

## FIGURE 1 · LEVELS OF EMPOWERMENT

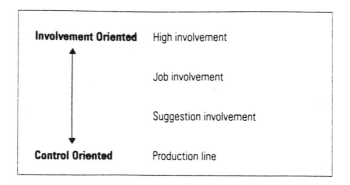

back, and they handle a whole, identifiable piece of work. Research shows that many employees find enriched work more motivating and satisfying, and they do higher-quality work.[14]

Often job involvement is accomplished through extensive use of teams. Teams are often appropriate in complex service organizations such as hospitals and airlines because individuals cannot offer a whole service or handle a customer from beginning to end of service delivery. Teams can empower back-office workers in banks and insurance companies as well.

Employees in this environment require training to deal with the added complexity. Supervisors, who now have fewer shots to call, need to be reoriented toward supporting the front line, rather than directing it. Despite the heightened level of empowerment it brings, the job involvement approach does not change higher-level strategic decisions concerning organization structure, power, and the allocation of rewards. These remain the responsibility of senior management.

3. **High-Involvement** organizations give their lowest-level employees a sense of involvement not just in how they do their jobs or how effectively their group performs, but in the total organization's performance. Virtually every aspect of the organization is different from that of a control-oriented organization. Business performance information is shared. Employees develop skills in teamwork, problem solving, and business operations. They participate in work-unit management decisions. There is profit sharing and employee ownership.

High-involvement designs may be expensive to implement. Perhaps most troublesome is that these management techniques are relatively undeveloped and untested. People Express tried to operate as a high-involvement airline, and the ongoing struggle to learn and develop this new organizational design contributed to its operating problems.

Today, America West is trying to make the high-involvement design work. New hires spend 25 percent of their first year's salary on company stock. All employees receive annual stock options. Flight attendants and pilots develop their own work procedures and schedules. Employees are extensively cross-trained to work where they are needed. Only time will tell if America West can make high-involvement work as it struggles with its financial crisis stemming from high fuel costs and rapid growth.

Federal Express displays many high-involvement features. A couple of years ago, it began a companywide push to convert to teams, including the back office. It organized its 1,000 clerical workers in Memphis into superteams of five to ten people and gave them the authority and training to manage themselves. These teams helped the company cut customer service problems, such as incorrect bills and lost packages, by 13 percent in 1989.

## When to Empower: A Contingency Approach

Management thought and practice frequently have been seduced by the search for the "one best way to manage." Unfortunately, business does not lend itself to universal truths, only to "contingency theories" of management. For example, early job enrichment efforts in the 1960s assumed that all employees would prefer more challenging work and more autonomy. By the 1970s it was clear that only those employees who felt the need to grow at work responded positively to job enrichment.[15] As the research on it is still thin, it is at least possible that empowerment is a universal truth, but historical evidence weighs against its being the best way to manage in all situations.

We believe that both the empowerment and production-line approaches have their advantages, and that each fits certain situations. The key is to choose the management approach that best meets the needs of both employees and customers.

Table 1 presents five contingencies that determine which approach to adopt. Each contingency can be rated on a scale of 1 to 5 to diagnose the quality of fit between the overall situation and

### TABLE 1 · THE CONTINGENCIES OF EMPOWERMENT

| Contingency | Production-Line Approach | | Empowerment |
|---|---|---|---|
| Basic business strategy | Low cost, high volume | 1 2 3 4 5 | Differentiation, customized, personalized |
| Tie to customer | Transaction, short time period | 1 2 3 4 5 | Relationship, long time period |
| Technology | Routine, simple | 1 2 3 4 5 | Nonroutine, complex |
| Business environment | Predictable, few surprises | 1 2 3 4 5 | Unpredictable, many surprises |
| Types of people | Theory X managers, employees with low growth needs, low social needs, and weak interpersonal skills | 1 2 3 4 5 | Theory Y managers, employees with high growth needs, high social needs, and strong interpersonal skills |

the alternative approaches. The following propositions suggest how to match situations and approaches. Matching is not an exact science, but the propositions suggest reasonable rules of thumb. Proposition 1: The higher the rating of each contingency (5 being the highest), the better the fit with an empowerment approach; the lower the rating (1 being the lowest), the better the fit with a production-line approach.

Proposition 2: The higher the total score from all five contingencies, the better the fit with an empowerment approach; the lower the total score, the better the fit with a production-line approach. A production-line approach is a good fit with situations that score in the range of 5 to 10. For empowerment approaches, suggestion involvement is a good fit with situations that score in the range of 11 to 15, job involvement with scores that range from 16 to 20, and high involvement with scores that range from 21 to 25.

Proposition 3: The higher the total score, the more the benefits of increasing empowerment will outweigh the costs.

In what follows, we describe each contingency's implications for a production-line or empowerment approach.

**Basic Business Strategy.** A production-line approach makes the most sense if your core mission is to offer high-volume service at the lowest cost. "Industrializing" service certainly leverages volume. The question is: what is the value-added from spending the additional dollars on employee selection, training, and retention necessary for empowerment? This question is especially compelling in labor-intensive services (e.g., fast food, grocery stores, and convenience stores) and those that require part-time or temporary employees.

The answer depends on what customers want from the service firm, and what they are willing to pay for. Certain customer segments are just looking for cheap, quick, reliable service. They do want quality—a warm hamburger rather than a cold one. But they are not necessarily expecting tender loving care. Even if they wanted it, they wouldn't pay for it.

These customers prefer a production-line approach. A recent study of convenience stores actually found a negative relationship between store sales and clerks being friendly with customers.[16] Customers wanted speed, and friendly clerks slowed things down. The point is that customers themselves may prefer to be served by a nonempowered employee.

At Taco Bell, counter attendants are expected to be civil, but they are not expected or encouraged to be creative problem solvers. Taco Bell wants to serve customers who want low-cost, good quality, fast food. Interestingly, the company believes that as more chains move to customized, service-oriented operations, it has more opportunities in the fast, low-price market niche.

The production-line approach does not rule out suggestion involvement. As mentioned earlier, employees often have ideas even when much of their work is routinized. Quality circles and other approaches can capture and develop them.

An empowerment approach works best with a market segment that wants the tender loving care dimension more than speed and cost. For example, SAS targets frequent business travellers (who do not pay their own way). The SAS strategy was to differentiate itself from other airlines on the basis of personalized service. Consequently, the company looked at every ingredient of its service package to see if it fit this segment's definition of service quality, and, if so, whether or not customers would pay for it.

**Tie to the Customer.** Empowerment is the best approach when service delivery involves managing a relationship, as opposed to simply performing a transaction. The service firm may want to establish relationships with customers to build loyalty or to get ideas for improving the service delivery system or offering new services. A flexible, customized approach can help establish the relationship and get the ideas flowing.

The returns on empowerment and relationship-building are higher with more sophisticated services and delivery systems. An employee in the international air freight industry is more likely to learn from a customer relationship than is a gasoline station attendant.

The relationship itself can be the principal valued commodity that is delivered in many services. When no tangibles are delivered, as in estate planning or management consulting, the service provider often is the service to the customer, and empowerment allows the employee to customize the service to fit the customer's needs.

The more enduring the relationship, and the more important it is in the service package, the stronger the case for empowerment. Remember the earlier comparison between Disney, which tightly scripts its ride operators, and Club Med, which encourages its GOs to be spontaneous? Giraud, Club Med's CEO, explains that Disney employees relate to their guests in thousands of brief encounters; GOs have week-long close relationships with a limited number of guests. The valuable service they sell is "time."

**Technology.** It is very difficult to build challenge, feedback, and autonomy into a telephone operator's job, given the way the delivery technology has been designed. The same is true of many fast-food operations. In these situations, the technology limits empowerment to only suggestion involvement and ultimately may almost completely remove individuals from the service delivery process, as has happened with ATMs.

When technology constrains empowerment, service managers can still support frontline employees in ways that enhance their satisfaction and the service quality they provide. For example, managers can show employees how much their jobs matter to the organization's success and express more appreciation for the work they do. In other words, managers can do a better job of making the old management model work!

Routine work can be engaging if employees are convinced that it matters. Volunteers will spend hours licking envelopes in a fundraising campaign for their favorite charity. Disney theme park employees do an admirable job of performing repetitive work, partly because they believe in the values, mission, and show business magic of Disney.

**Business Environment.** Businesses that operate in unpredictable environments benefit from empowerment. Airlines face many challenges to their operations: bad weather, mechanical breakdowns, and competitors' actions. They serve passengers who make a wide variety of special requests. It is simply impossible to anticipate many of the situations that will arise and to "program" employees to respond to them. Employees trained in purposeful chaos are appropriate for unpredictable environments.

Fast-food restaurants, however, operate in stable environments. Operations are fairly fail-safe; customer expectations are simple and predictable. In this environment, the service business can use a production-line approach. The stability allows, even encourages, management with policies and procedures, because managers can predict most events and identify the best responses.

**Types of People.** Empowerment and production-line approaches demand different types of managers and employees. For empowerment to work, particularly in the high-involvement form, the company needs to have Theory Y managers who believe that their employees can act independently to benefit both the organization and its customers. If the management ranks are filled with Theory X types who believe that employees only do their best work when closely supervised, then the production-line approach may be the only feasible option unless the organization changes its managers. Good service can still be the outcome. For example, most industry observers would agree that Delta and American Airlines are managed with a control orientation rather than a strong empowerment approach.

Employees will respond positively to empowerment only if they have strong needs to grow and to deepen and test their abilities—at work. Again, a checkered history of job enrichment efforts has taught us not to assume that everyone wants more autonomy, challenge, and responsibility at work. Some employees simply prefer a production-line approach.

Lastly, empowerment that involves teamwork requires employees who are interested in meeting their social and affiliative needs at work. It also requires that employees have good interpersonal and group process skills.

## THE FUTURE OF SERVICE WORK

How likely is it that more and more service businesses will choose to face the customer with empowered employees? We would guess that far more service organizations operate at the production-line end of our continuum than their business situations call for. A recent survey of companies in the "Fortune 1000" offers some support for this view.[17] This survey revealed that manufacturing firms tend to use significantly more employee-involvement practices than do service firms. Manufacturing firms use quality circles, participation groups, and self-managing work teams far more than service firms.

Why is this so? We think that the intense pressure on the manufacturing sector from global competition has created more dissatisfaction with the old control-oriented way of doing things. Also, it can be easier to see the payoffs from different management practices in manufacturing than in service. Objective measures of productivity can more clearly show profitability than can measures of customer perceptions of service quality. However, these differences are now blurring as service competition increases and service companies become more sophisticated in tracking the benefits of customer service quality.

As service businesses consider empowerment, they can look at high-involvement manufacturing organizations as labs in which the various empowerment approaches have been tested and developed. Many lessons have been learned in manufacturing about how to best use quality circles, enriched jobs, and so on. And the added good news is that many service businesses are ideally suited to applying and refining these lessons. Multisite, relatively autonomous service operations afford their managers an opportunity to customize empowerment programs and then evaluate them.

In summary, the newest approaches to managing the production line can serve as role models for many service businesses, but perhaps not all. Before service organizations rush into empowerment programs, they need to determine whether and how empowerment fits their situation.

# REFERENCES

1. T. Levitt, "Production-Line Approach to Service," *Harvard Business Review*, September-October 1972, pp. 41–52; and T. Levitt, "Industrialization of Service," *Harvard Business Review*, September-October 1976, pp. 63–74.

2. Levitt (1972).

3. D. Tansik, "Managing Human Resource Issues for High-Contact Service Personnel," in *Service Management Effectiveness*, eds. D. Bowen, R. Chase, and T. Cummings (San Francisco: Jossey-Bass, 1990).

4. R. Zemke and D. Schaaf, *The Service Edge: 101 Companies That Profit from Customer Care* (New York: New American Library, 1989), p. 68.

5. As quoted in Zemke and Schaaf (1989), p. 68.

6. J. Carlzon, *Moments of Truth* (New York: Ballinger, 1987).

7. V. Zeithaml, A. Parasuraman, and L. L. Berry, *Delivering Quality Service: Balancing Customer Perceptions and Expectations* (New York: The Free Press, 1990). See also: B. Schneider and D. Bowen, "Employee and Customer Perceptions of Service in Banks: Replication and Extension," *Journal of Applied Psychology* 70 (1985): 423–433.

8. Schneider and Bowen (1985).

9. Ibid.

10. Zeithaml, Parasuraman, and Berry (1990).

11. C. Goodwin and I. Ross, "Consumer Evaluations of Responses to Complaints: What's Fair and Why," *Journal of Services Marketing* 4 (1990): 53–61.

12. See E. E. Lawler III, *High-Involvement Management* (San Francisco: Jossey-Bass, 1986).

13. See E. E. Lawler III, "Choosing an Involvement Strategy," *Academy of Management Executive* 2 (1988): 197–204.

14. See for example J. R. Hackman and G. R. Oldham, *Work Redesign* (Reading, Massachusetts: Addison-Wesley, 1980).

15. Ibid.

16. R. J. Sutton and A. Rafaeli, "Untangling the Relationship between Displayed Emotions and Organizational Sales: The Case of Convenience Stores," *Academy of Management Journal* 31 (1988): 461–487.

17. E. E. Lawler III, G. E. Ledford, Jr., and S. A. Mohrman, *Employee Involvement in America: A Study of Contemporary Practice* (Houston: American Productivity & Quality Center, 1989).

# CHAPTER V

# *EFFECTS OF THE WORK ENVIRONMENT ON INDIVIDUALS*

In 1959, Warren Bennis observed that such classical organization theorists as Frederick Winslow Taylor, Henry Gantt, and Henri Fayol (see Shafritz & Ott, 1996, Chapter I) were fixated on structural variables (such as the chain of command, centralization and decentralization, and span of control) to the extent that they almost seem to think about "organizations without people." In contrast, the human relations-oriented organizational behaviorists of the late 1950s and 1960s were so enamored with people and groups (with personal growth, group development, sensitivity training groups, and human relations training) that they seemed to think only about "people without organizations." Bennis's observation was equally applicable to the early industrial/organizational psychologists—to the pre-Hawthorne and pre-Theory X and Theory Y value system-based social scientists who worked with organizational behavior, but not from an organizational behavior perspective (see the *Introduction*). However, between the 1930s and the 1950s and 1960s, *organizational behavior* reversed its field and in the process almost forgot (or at least ignored) the substantial influences that organization systems and structures have on the people and groups in and around them.

Many things in the organizational context influence and are influenced by organizational behavior. To list only a few:

- *The type of business in which an organization is engaged.* The business of banking places different demands on and yields different rewards to employees than does making and marketing new television game shows.
- *The legal relationship between an organization and people who work for it.* Typically, there are different impacts on organizational behavior in, for example, a family-owned business, a publicly held investor-owned company, a nonprofit organization, and a government agency.
- *The nature of the perceived relationships between an organization and its environment at large.* The prevailing perception in some organizations seems to be that they exist in a hostile world, where the media, general public, other types of organizations (such as government agencies, legislatures, or private corporations), and sometimes even clientele or customers (as well as direct

competitors) all are immediate or potential enemies or threats. In contrast, the prevailing view in other organizations is more one of the organization existing in harmony with its environment.

- *The structure of the organization*—this is the first subject of this chapter.

When someone refers to organization structure, usually he or she is talking about the relatively stable relationships among the positions or groups of positions (such as the units, divisions, and departments) that comprise an organization, along with the organized procedures and methods that define how things are designed for work to flow through it. Structure is the design of an organization, its units, and its production processes. It is the set of specific patterns of differentiation and integration of tasks and activities in an organization (Thompson, 1967; Miles, 1980). Differentiation is the (conceptual) dividing up of a total system into its component parts (units, groups, and people) which perform specialized tasks. (In essence, *differentiation* is a more sophisticated way of saying *division of labor*). Integration is how the divided-up parts and specialized tasks are linked together to form a coordinated whole.

To be more concrete, a widely read article by Lyman Porter and Edward Lawler (1965) identifies the properties of organization structure that, according to an extensive search of the then published literature, most affect individual and group attitudes and on-the-job behavior. Their list of structural properties includes:

- *Organization levels* (the number of levels and in which one—or how high—one is situated),
- *Line or staff* roles of organization units,
- *Span of control*,
- *Size of units*,
- *Size of the total organization*,
- *Organization shape* (flat or tall), and
- *Centralized or decentralized* authority and responsibility.

The structure—an organization's shape, size, procedures, production technology, position descriptions, reporting arrangements, and coordinating relationships—affects the feelings and emotions, and therefore the behavior of the people and groups inside them. There are incongruencies between the needs of a mature personality and of formal organization—between the growth trends of healthy people and the requirements of organizations (Argyris, 1957b). The impacts of structure on behavior partially result from the unique functions structure performs. In each organization, structure defines the unique ways labor is divided, how specialized roles and functions are to be coordinated (related to each other and to other organizational levels and functions), how information is to flow among people and groups, and how the system of controls (how tasks are measured, evaluated, and altered) is to work (Organ & Bateman, 1986). Structure establishes how *roles*, *expectations*, and *resource allocations* are defined for people and groups in any given organization. Structure is a primary reason why *organizational behavior* differs from mere *behavior*, and thus why organizational behavior developed as a separate field of study within the applied behavioral sciences.

Structure, however, is only one of several forces that affect the behavior of people in organizations. Attitudes and behaviors also are shaped by, for example: *Peer group pressure* (Asche, 1951; Janis, 1971), *group norms*—the standards that develop, are shared and enforced by the members of groups (Cohen, Fink, Gadon, & Willits, 1988 [Chapter 3]; Feldman, 1984; Roy, 1960), the particular blending of social and technical aspects of work tasks—the *socio-technical systems* (Thorsrud, 1968; Trist, 1960; Trist & Bamforth, 1951), and the *organizational culture* (Ott, 1989; Schein, 1992; Whyte, 1956).

To an extent, all formal and informal groups (see Chapter II) require and expect people to conform to norms—prescriptions for behavior. Norms are behavioral blueprints that provide organizations with coherence. Acceptance of and adherence to group norms permit people to know what to expect from each other and to predict what other members will do in different circumstances. Norms cause people to behave in patterned and predictable ways, "because their behaviors are guided by common expectations, attitudes and understandings . . . norms are strong stabilizers of organizational behavior" (Schmuck, 1971, pp. 215–216). Norms establish some conformity, stability, and predictability—states that are both necessary and desirable.

On the other hand, too much adherence to norms causes overconformance and can hurt or destroy individualism (Merton, 1957; Whyte, 1956). Potential damage, though, is not limited to individuals who work in organizations. Excessive conformity also results in organizational rigidity (Ott, 1989). Organizations must be open to divergent information, viewpoints, realities, and value systems. Indeed, organizations must seek diversity and reward individuals and groups who succeed in injecting diversity into strategic decision processes (Cox, 1993).

The readings in this chapter examine ways in which structure, socio-technical systems, group norms and pressures to conform, and organizational culture influence the behavior of individuals and groups in organizations. The focus is on how norms, group pressure, socio-technical systems and organizational culture combine to shape organizational behavior. Several of the selections also examine ways in which the forces that lead to conformity potentially damage individual and organizational performance.

The first reading describes research in the problematic area of group effects on individuals' decisions. In "Effects of Group Pressure Upon the Modification and Distortion of Judgments, "Solomon Asch (1951) describes his famous investigations into ways individuals cope when a group's majority opinion is directly contrary to the facts of a situation. Asch put lone experimental subjects (college students) in rooms with people who had been instructed to give blatantly wrong answers to factual questions. Only the experimental subjects did not know what was going on. Although a slim majority of experimental subjects retained their independence and reported the facts accurately, a sizable minority of subjects *altered their judgment to match that of the majority.* When faced with a group opinion that was obviously wrong, they were not willing to report their observations as they saw them. They changed their judgments. Asch attributes peoples' decisions to retain independence of judgment or to yield to the majority, to several factors. The two most important factors are:

- The size of the majority and the extent of unanimity among members of the majority; and
- Identifiable, enduring differences among individuals, particularly character differences involving social relations.

Asch's experiments provide dramatic evidence of group impacts on people in organizations. From a managerial perspective, they show why it is extremely important to focus attention on the group's beliefs, values, composition, and activities. Nevertheless, for the most part, *informal groups* are outside of the formal organization's direct sphere of influence.

*Sociotechnical systems* is commonly used to mean the interactive relationships or the *fit* between work technology, organization structure, and social interactions of the workplace. Most sociotechnical system studies involve investigations of how work processes (technology) and work teams (social systems) can be structured (organization) to maximize productivity and at the same time satisfy employees' desires for affiliation and, in some work settings, needs for safety that only close groups can provide. The Tavistock Institute of London has been closely identified with *sociotechnical systems* research and consulting since the 1950s. The best known of the Tavistock sociotechnical systems studies have been set in British coal mines (Trist and Bamforth, 1951; Trist, Higgin, Murray & Pollock, 1965) and weaving mills of India (Rice, 1953). These studies became the forerunners of many widely publicized sociotechnical systems-style work reorganization efforts, such as in the Scandinavian automobile industry (Thorsrud, 1968); "Procter & Gamble's plant in Lima, Ohio; Alcan's cold rolling mill in Quebec; Shell's refinery in Teesport, England; and Norsk Hydro's fertilizer plant in Porsgrunn, Norway" (Walton, 1975, p. 117).

Eric Trist, Kenneth Bamforth, and their associates at the Tavistock Institute studied the links between work technology, organization structure, and social structure. In their famous 1951 article, "Some Social and Psychological Consequences of the Longwall Method of Coal-Getting" (reprinted in this chapter), Trist and Bamforth found that management's attempts to increase coal mining productivity by moving to the *longwall method* (a technology analogous to mass production) had negative repercussions. At the time of its introduction in the late 1940s, the longwall method of coal-getting represented a major technological improvement. Prior to that time, coal had been mined by self-selecting, highly mutually supportive, self-regulating small groups (often pairs) who performed the entire cycle of extraction operations. The pairs faced grave dangers together working far under the earth, watched out for each other, and jointly decided when to change working places and procedures in the face of dangers. The pair system also provided each man with someone to talk with about fears and anxieties.

The longwall method changed everything. Miners no longer worked in long-established small groups. They worked in long lines, using new machinery that required them to face the wall, with a substantial distance between each man. When work pressure increased, there was no close associate to talk with about stress and anxiety or even people close enough for bantering. Introduction of the new structural and technological systems destroyed important social systems; hence, productivity and morale became major problems. "It is difficult to see how these problems can be solved effectively without restoring responsible autonomy to primary groups throughout the system and ensuring that each of these groups has a satisfying subwhole as its work task, and some scope for flexibility in workpace" (Trist & Bamforth, 1951, p. 38). The longwall coal study, along with several other socio-technical system studies that appeared at about the same time (for example, Jaques, 1950; Rice, 1953; Rice, Hill & Trist, 1950), represented a major turning point in the *practice* of organizational behavior. The coal companies *listened* to the workers (through the reporting of the behavioral scientists) and modified the technical system to mesh with the workers' social system needs.

In an article that follows, Robert Merton questions the long-term impacts of organizations' conformity requirements on the personalities—*the beingness*—of organization members. The concluding chapter of *The Organization Man* (1956), by William H. Whyte, Jr., which is reprinted here, leads us to Merton's question. In 1954, the United States had been shaken, perhaps as never before, by the apparent ease with which the Chinese had succeeded in "brainwashing" U.S. prisoners of war in Korea. For the first time in this nation's history, some of our soldiers, who were only required to provide captors with their "name, rank, and serial number" (under international agreement), aided their Chinese captors by identifying informal leaders among their fellow prisoners, revealing prisoner escape plans, confessing to illegal and immoral actions supposedly taken against the Chinese, and publicly denouncing the United States. Two years later Whyte's book, which culminated several years of research into the willingnesss of several hundred young U.S. managers to conform to organizational and role expectations, exploded onto the national scene. Where was America's rugged individualism? Had we become a nation of sheep?

Whyte quotes from Alexis de Tocqueville's *Democracy in America* (1847): If America ever destroyed its genius, "it would be . . . by making the individual come to regard himself as a hostage to prevailing opinion, by creating, in sum, a tyranny of the majority" (Whyte, 1956, p. 396). Whyte asserts this is occurring with the *Corporate American, the organization man of today:* "He is not only other-directed, to borrow David Riesman's concept, he is articulating a philosophy which tells him it is right to be that way" (p. 396). When Whyte wrote *The Organization Man*, he was not pessimistic about peoples' abilities to withstand pressures to conform. Quite the contrary—despite the evidence of his research. His solution lies in:

- Increased consciousness of the worth of individualism;
- Reexamination of the worth of designing work to allow individuals to be involved in a total effort, not just to increase efficiency or effectiveness, but also to allow individuals to build self-respect;
- Reduced amounts of time people at work spend in meetings. Require people to think creatively at least some of the time; and
- Reduced emphasis on professionals being "company men"—on organizational commitment. Instead, increase peoples' allegiances to their career.

Despite Whyte's professed lack of pessimism, he concludes on a less than optimistic note. "[The organization man] must *fight* the organization . . . for the demands for his surrender are constant and powerful, and the more he has come to like the life of organization the more difficult does he find it to resist these demands, or even to recognize them. . . . The peace of mind offered by organization remains a surrender, and no less so for being offered in benevolence. That is the problem" (p. 404). Thirty years later, in the 1980s, many of Whyte's themes and warnings are reappearing in the literature of the *organizational culture perspective* of organization theory (Ott, 1989).

In "Bureaucratic Structure and Personality," Robert Merton (1940, 1957) analyzes how one form of organization structure—*bureaucracy*—impinges on the personalities of people who work inside them. Merton uses *bureaucracy* to mean the pervasive form of organization that Max Weber (1922) described in *Wirtschat und Gesellschaft*. In this use, *bureaucracy* is neither an epithet per se, nor is it limited in applicability to government agencies. According to Merton, bureaucracy exerts constant pressures on people to be methodical and disciplined, to conform to patterns of obligations. These pressures eventually cause people to adhere to rules as an end rather than a means—as a matter of blind conformance. Bureaucratic structure also stresses depersonalized relations, and power and authority gained by virtue of organizational position rather than by thought or action. Without question, Merton sees bureaucratic structure as more than *affecting* organizational behavior and thinking: it also *determines and controls*. As a form of organization, bureaucracy has its advantages: order, predictability, stability, professionalism, and consistency (Shafritz & Ott, 1996, Chapter 1). Nevertheless, the behavioral consequences of bureaucratic structure are mostly negative, including reduced organizational flexibility and efficiency and, adapting a phrase coined by Merton, eventually *bureaupathological personalities* of members.

Twenty years after Solomon Asch's experiments, Irving Janis published the equally well-known study, "Groupthink," which is reprinted in this chapter. Like Asch, Janis explores pressures for conformance—the reasons why social conformity is encountered frequently in groups. But unlike Asch's experimental use of college students, Janis looked at high-level decision makers in times of real major fiascoes: the 1962 Bay of Pigs, the 1950 decision to send General MacArthur to the Yalu River, and the 1941 failure to prepare for the attack on Pearl Harbor. *Groupthink* is "the mode of thinking that persons engage in when *concurrence seeking* becomes so dominant in a cohesive in-group that it tends to override realistic appraisal of alternative courses of action . . . the desperate drive for consensus at any cost that suppresses dissent among the mighty in the corridors of power" (p. 44). Janis identifies eight symptoms of groupthink that are relatively easy to observe:

- An illusion of invulnerability;
- Collective construction of rationalizations which permit group members to ignore warnings or other forms of negative feedback;
- Unquestioning belief in the morality of the in-group;
- Strong, negative, stereotyped views about the leaders of enemy groups;
- Rapid application of pressure against group members who express even momentary doubts about virtually any illusions the group shares;
- Careful, conscious, personal avoidance of deviation from what appears to be a group consensus;
- Shared illusions of unanimity of opinion;
- Establishment of *mindguards*—people who "protect the leader and fellow members from adverse information that might break the complacency they shared about the effectiveness and morality of past decisions" (p. 74).

Janis concludes with an assessment of the negative influence of groupthink on executive decision making (including overestimation of the group's capability and self-imposed isolation from new or opposing information and points of view), and some preventive and remedial steps for groupthink.

Porter, Lawler, and Hackman's chapter, "Social Influences on Work Effectiveness," from their 1975 book, *Behavior in Organizations* (reprinted in this chapter), analyzes in depth how groups and other members of a person's role set exert influence on individuals in organizations, and how these social influences affect work effectiveness. This piece focuses particularly on the "notion that the nature and degree of such social influences depend crucially on the type of work being performed and thus on the demands that the work makes on the person" (Porter, Lawler, & Hackman, 1975, p. 403). The chapter specifically examines dysfunctional aspects of eliminating deviance from group norms, why high group cohesiveness can be dysfunctional, and ways that groups influence individual work effectiveness. "The point is that the people who surround an individual at work can facilitate as well as hinder . . . performance effectiveness—and that any serious attempt to diagnose the social environment in the interest of improving work performance should explicitly address unrealized possibilities for enhancing performance as well as issues for which remedial action may be required" (p. 421).

Chapter V concludes with an optimistic view of peoples' abilities to control their environments in organizations. Nancy E. Bell and Barry M. Straw (1989), in "People as Sculptors versus Sculpture: The Roles of Personality and Personal Control in Organizations," try to "knock organizational influence down a peg or two and to build up the role of the individual" (p. 239). They outline a model in which personality and personal control are the means by which people are able to resist pressures to conform and thereby maintain a degree of control over their work environments. Their model posits three types of personal control that are available to individuals: control over outcomes, control over behavior, and the ability to redirect outcomes and behavior. People in organizations thereby are able to be "sculptors" as well as "sculpture."

# REFERENCES

Argyris, C. (1957a). *Personality and organization*. New York: Harper.

Argyris, C. (1957b). The individual and organization: Some problems of mutual adjustment. *Administrative Science Quarterly, 2,* 1–24.

Asche, S. E. (1951). Effects of group pressure upon the modification and distortion of judgments. In, H. S. Guetzkow (Ed.), *Groups, leadership, and men* (pp. 177–190). Pittsburgh: Carnegie Press.

Bell, N. E., & Staw, B. M. (1989). People as sculptors versus sculpture: The roles of personality and personal control in organizations. In M. B. Arthur, D. T. Hall, & B. S. Lawrence (Eds.), *Handbook of career theory* (pp. 232–241). Cambridge, UK: Cambridge University Press.

Cohen, A. R., Fink, S. L., Gadon, H., & Willits, R. D. (1988). *Effective behavior in organizations* (4th ed.). Homewood, IL: Irwin.

Cox, T. H., Jr. (1993). *Cultural diversity in organizations: Theory, research & practice.* San Francisco: Berrett-Koehler.

Dill, W. R. (1958). Environment as an influence on managerial autonomy. *Administrative Science Quarterly, 2,* 409–443.

Feldman, D. C. ( January, 1984). The development and enforcement of group norms. *Academy of Management Review,* 47–53.

Janis, I. L. (1971). Groupthink. *Psychology Today,* 44–76.

Jaques, E. (1950). Collaborative group methods in a wage negotiation situation (The Glacier Project—I). *Human Relations, 3*(3).

Katz, D., & Kahn, R. L. (1966). *The social psychology of organizations*. New York: John Wiley & Sons.

Merton, R. K. (1957). Bureaucratic structure and personality. In, R. K. Merton, *Social theory and social structure* (rev. & enl. ed.). New York: The Free Press. A revised version of an article of the same title that appeared in *Social Forces,* 18 (1940).

Miles, R. H. (1980). *Macro organizational behavior.* Santa Monica, CA: Goodyear Publishing.

Mills, T. (October, 1976). Altering the social structure in coal mining: A case study. *Monthly Labor Review,* 3–10.

Organ, D. W., & Bateman, T. (1986). *Organizational behavior: An applied psychological approach* (3rd ed.). Plano, TX: Business Publications, Inc.

Ott, J. S. (1989). *The organizational culture perspective.* Belmont, CA: Wadsworth.

Porter, L. W., & Lawler, E. E., III. (1965). Properties of organization structure in relation to job attitudes and job behavior. *Psychological Bulletin, 64*(1), 23–51.

Porter, L. W., & Lawler, E. E., III (1964). The effects of tall vs. flat organization struc-tures on managerial job satisfaction. *Personnel Psychology, 17*, 135–148.

Porter, L. W., Lawler, E. E. III, & Hackman, J. R. (1975). Social influences on work effec-tiveness. In, L. W. Porter, E. E. Lawler III, & J. R. Hackman, *Behavior in organizations* (pp. 403–422). New York: McGraw-Hill.

Rice, A. K. (1953). Productivity and social organization in an Indian weaving shed: An examination of some aspects of the sociotechnical system of an experimental auto-matic loom shed. *Human Relations, 6*, 297–329.

Rice, A. K., Hill, J. M. M., & Trist, E. L. (1950). The representation of labour turnover as a social process (The Glacier Project—II). *Human Relations, 3*(4).

Roy, D. F. (1960). "Banana time": Job satisfaction and informal interaction. *Human Orga-nization, 18*, 158–168.

Schein, E. H. (1992). *Leadership and organizational culture* (2d. ed.). San Francisco: Jossey-Bass.

Schein, E. H. (1980). *Organizational psychology* (3d. ed.). Englewood Cliffs, NJ: Prentice-Hall.

Schmuck, R. A. (1971). Developing teams of organizational specialists. In R. A. Schmuck & M. B. Miles (Eds.), *Organization development in schools* (pp. 213–230). Palo Alto, CA: National Press Books.

Shafritz, J. M., & Ott, J. S. (1996). *Classics of organization theory* (4th ed.). Belmont CA: Wadsworth.

Thayer, F. C. (1981). *And end to hierarchy and competition: Administration in the post–affluent world* (2d ed.). New York: New Viewpoints.

Thompson, J. D. (1967). *Organizations in action*. New York: McGraw-Hill.

Thorsrud, D. E. (1968). Sociotechnical approach to job design and organization develop-ment. *Management International Review, 8*, 120–131.

Tocqueville, A. de (1847). *Democracy in America*. New York: Walker.

Trist, E. L. (1960). *Socio-technical systems*. London: Tavistock Institute of Human Rela-tions.

Trist, E. L., & Bamforth, K. (1951). Some social and psychological consequences of the longwall method of coal-getting. *Human Relations, 4*, 3–38.

Trist, E. L., Higgin, G. W., Murray, H., & Pollock, A. B. (1965). *Organizational choice*. London: Tavistock Institute of Human Relations.

Walton, R. E. (1975). From Hawthorne to Topeka and Kalmar. In, E. L. Cass & F. G. Zimmer (Eds.), *Man and work in society* (pp. 116–129). New York: Western Electric Co.

Weber, M. (1922). Bureaucracy. In, H. Gerth & C. W. Mills (Eds.), *Max Weber: Essays in sociology*. Oxford, U.K.: Oxford University Press.

Whyte, W. F. (1961). *Men at work*. Homewood, IL: The Dorsey Press.

Whyte, W. H., Jr. (1956). *The organization man*. New York: Simon and Schuster.

Worthy, J. C. (1950). Organizational structure and employee morale. *American Sociological Review, 15*, 169–179.

# 27
# Effects of Group Pressure Upon the Modification and Distortion of Judgments
*Solomon E. Asch*

. . . Our immediate object was to study the social and personal conditions that induce individuals to resist or to yield to group pressures when the latter are perceived to be *contrary to fact*. The issues which this problem raises are of obvious consequence for society; it can be of decisive importance whether or not a group will, under certain conditions, submit to existing pressures. Equally direct are the consequences for individuals and our understanding of them, since it is a decisive fact about a person whether he possesses the freedom to act independently, or whether he characteristically submits to group pressures. . . .

Basic to the current approach has been the axiom that group pressures characteristically induce psychological changes *arbitrarily*, in far-reaching disregard of the material properties of the given conditions. This mode of thinking has almost exclusively stressed the slavish submission of individuals to group forces, has neglected to inquire into their possibilities for independence and for productive relations with the human environment, and has virtually denied the capacity of men under certain conditions to rise above group passion and prejudice. It was our aim to contribute to a clarification of these questions, important both for theory and for their human implications, by means of direct observation of the effects of groups upon the decisions and evaluations of individuals.

## THE EXPERIMENT AND FIRST RESULTS

To this end we developed an experimental technique which has served as the basis for the present series of studies. We employed the procedure of placing an individual in a relation of radical conflict with all the other members of a group, of measuring its effect upon him in quantitative terms, and of describing its psychological consequences. A group of eight individuals was instructed to judge a series of simple, clearly structured perceptual relations—to match the length of a given line with one of three unequal lines. Each member of the group announced his judgments publicly. In the midst of this monotonous "test" one individual found himself suddenly contradicted by the entire group, and this contradiction was repeated again and again in the course of the experiment. The group in question had, with the exception of one member, previously met with the experimenter and received instructions to respond at certain points with wrong—and unanimous—judgments. The errors of the majority were large (ranging between ½″ and 1¾″) and of an order not encountered under control conditions. The outstanding person— the critical subject—whom we had placed in the position of a *minority of one* in the midst of a *unanimous majority*—was the object of investigation. He

*Source:* From "Effects of Group Pressure Upon the Modification and Distortion of Judgments" by Solomon E Asch, in *Groups, Leadership, and Men,* edited by Harold S. Guetzkow (Pittsburgh: Carnegie Press, 1951, pp. 177–190). Reprinted by permission from Carnegie Mellon University.

faced, possibly for the first time in his life, a situation in which a group unanimously contradicted the evidence of his senses.

This procedure was the starting point of the investigation and the point of departure for the study of further problems. Its main features were the following: (1) The critical subject was submitted to two contradictory and irreconcilable forces—the evidence of his own experience of an utterly clear perceptual fact and the unanimous evidence of a group of equals. (2) Both forces were part of the immediate situation; the majority was concretely present, surrounding the subject physically. (3) The critical subject, who was requested together with all others to state his judgments publicly, was obliged to declare himself and to take a definite stand vis-à-vis the group. (4) The situation possessed a self-contained character. The critical subject could not avoid or evade the dilemma by reference to conditions external to the experimental situation. (It may be mentioned at this point that the forces generated by the given conditions acted so quickly upon the critical subjects that instances of suspicion were rare.)

The technique employed permitted a simple quantitative measure of the "majority effect" in terms of the frequency of errors in the direction of the distorted estimates of the majority. At the same time we were concerned from the start to obtain evidence of the ways in which the subjects perceived the group, to establish whether they became doubtful, whether they were tempted to join the majority. Most important, it was our object to establish the grounds of the subject's independence or yielding— whether, for example, the yielding subject was aware of the effect of the majority upon him, whether he abandoned his judgment deliberately or compulsively. To this end we constructed a comprehensive set of questions which served

as the basis of an individual interview immediately following the experimental period. Toward the conclusion of the interview each subject was informed fully of the purpose of the experiment, of his role and of that of the majority. The reactions to the disclosure of the purpose of the experiment became in fact an integral part of the procedure. We may state here that the information derived from the interview became an indispensable source of evidence and insight into the psychological structure of the experimental situation, and in particular, of the nature of the individual differences. Also, it is not justified or advisable to allow the subject to leave without giving him a full explanation of the experimental conditions. The experimenter has a responsibility to the subject to clarify his doubts and to state the reasons for placing him in the experimental situation. When this is done most subjects react with interest and many express gratification at having lived through a striking situation which has some bearing on wider human issues.

Both the members of the majority and the critical subjects were male college students. We shall report the results for a total of fifty critical subjects in this experiment. In Table 1 we summarize the successive comparison trials and the majority estimates. The quantitative results are clear and unambiguous.

1. There was a marked movement toward the majority. One-third of all the estimates in the critical group were errors identical with or in the direction of the distorted estimates of the majority. The significance of this finding becomes clear in the light of the virtual absence of errors in control groups the members of which recorded their estimates in writing. . . .
2. At the same time the effect of the majority was far from complete. The preponderance of estimates in the critical group (68 per cent) was correct despite the pressure of the majority.

### TABLE 1 · LENGTHS OF STANDARD AND COMPARISON LINES

| Trials | Length of Standard Line (in inches) | Comparison Lines (in inches) | | | Correct Response | Group Response | Majority Error (in inches) |
|---|---|---|---|---|---|---|---|
| | | 1 | 2 | 3 | | | |
| 1 | 10 | 8¾ | 10 | 8 | 2 | 2 | — |
| 2 | 2 | 2 | 1 | 1½ | 1 | 1 | — |
| 3 | 3 | 3¾ | 4¼ | 3 | 3 | 1* | + ¾ |
| 4 | 5 | 5 | 4 | 6½ | 1 | 2* | −1.0 |
| 5 | 4 | 3 | 5 | 4 | 3 | 3 | — |
| 6 | 3 | 3¾ | 4¼ | 3 | 3 | 2* | +1¼ |
| 7 | 8 | 6¼ | 8 | 6¾ | 2 | 3* | −1¼ |
| 8 | 5 | 5 | 4 | 6½ | 1 | 3* | +1½ |
| 9 | 8 | 6¼ | 8 | 6¾ | 2 | 1* | −1¾ |
| 10 | 10 | 8¾ | 10 | 8 | 2 | 2 | — |
| 11 | 2 | 2 | 1 | 1½ | 1 | 1 | — |
| 12 | 3 | 3¾ | 4¼ | 3 | 3 | 1* | + ¾ |
| 13 | 5 | 5 | 4 | 6½ | 1 | 2* | −1.0 |
| 14 | 4 | 3 | 5 | 4 | 3 | 3 | — |
| 15 | 3 | 3¾ | 4¼ | 3 | 3 | 2* | +1¼ |
| 16 | 8 | 6¼ | 8 | 6¾ | 2 | 3* | −1¼ |
| 17 | 5 | 5 | 4 | 6½ | 1 | 3* | +1½ |
| 18 | 8 | 6¼ | 8 | 6¾ | 2 | 1* | −1¾ |

* Starred figures designate the erroneous estimates by the majority.

3. We found evidence of extreme individual differences. There were in the critical group subjects who remained independent without exception, and there were those who went nearly all the time with the majority. (The maximum possible number of errors was 12, while the actual range of errors was 0–11.) One-fourth of the critical subjects was completely independent; at the other extreme, one-third of the group displaced the estimates toward the majority in one-half or more of the trials.

The differences between the critical subjects in their reactions to the given conditions were equally striking. There were subjects who remained completely confident throughout. At the other extreme were those who became disoriented, doubt-ridden, and experienced a powerful impulse not to appear different from the majority. . . .

## A FIRST ANALYSIS OF INDIVIDUAL DIFFERENCES

On the basis of the interview data described earlier, we undertook to differentiate and describe the major forms of reaction to the experimental situation, which we shall now briefly summarize.

Among the *independent* subjects we distinguished the following main categories:

1. Independence based on *confidence* in one's perception and experience. The most striking characteristic of these subjects is the vigor with which they withstand the group opposition. Though they are sensitive to the group, and experience the conflict, they show a resilience in coping with it, which is expressed in their continuing reliance on their perception and the effectiveness with which

they shake off the oppressive group opposition.

2. Quite different are those subjects who are independent and *withdrawn*. These do not react in a spontaneously emotional way, but rather on the basis of explicit principles concerning the necessity of being an individual.

3. A third group of independent subjects manifest considerable tension and *doubt*, but adhere to their judgments on the basis of a felt necessity to deal adequately with the task.

The following were the main categories of reaction among the *yielding* subjects, or those who went with the majority during one-half or more of the trials.

1. *Distortion of perception* under the stress of group pressure. In this category belong a very few subjects who yield completely, but are not aware that their estimates have been displaced or distorted by the majority. These subjects report that they came to perceive the majority estimates as correct.

2. *Distortion of judgment*. Most submitting subjects belong to this category. The factor of greatest importance in this group is a decision the subjects reach that their perceptions are inaccurate, and that those of the majority are correct. These subjects suffer from primary doubt and lack of confidence; on this basis they feel a strong tendency to join the majority.

3. *Distortion of action*. The subjects in this group do not suffer a modification of perception nor do they conclude that they are wrong. They yield because of an overmastering need not to appear different from or inferior to others, because of an inability to tolerate the appearance of defectiveness in the eyes of the group. These subjects suppress their observations and voice the majority position with awareness of what they are doing.

The results are sufficient to establish that independence and yielding are not psychologically homogeneous, that submission to group pressure (and freedom from pressure) can be the result of different psychological conditions. It should also be noted that the categories described above, being based exclusively on the subjects' reactions to the experimental conditions, are descriptive, not presuming to explain why a given individual responded in one way rather than another. The further exploration of the basis for the individual differences is a separate task upon which we are now at work.

## EXPERIMENTAL VARIATIONS

The results described are clearly a joint function of two broadly different sets of conditions. They are determined first by the specific external conditions, by the particular character of the relation between social evidence and one's own experience. Second, the presence of pronounced individual differences points to the important role of personal factors, of factors connected with the individual's character structure. We reasoned that there are group conditions which would produce independence in all subjects, and that there probably are group conditions which would induce intensified yielding in many, though not in all. Accordingly we followed the procedure of *experimental variation*, systematically altering the quality of social evidence by means of systematic variation of group conditions. . . .

### The Effect of Nonunanimous Majorities

Evidence obtained from the basis experiment suggested that the condition of being exposed *alone* to the opposition of a "compact majority" may have played a decisive role in determining the course and strength of the effects observed. Accordingly we undertook to investigate in a series of successive variations the effects of *nonunanimous* majorities. The technical problem of altering the uniformity of a majority is, in terms of our procedure, relatively simple. In most instances, we merely directed one or more members of the instructed group to deviate from the majority in prescribed ways. It is obvious that we cannot hope to compare the performance of the same individual in two situations on the assumption that they remain independent of one another. At best we can investigate the effect of an earlier upon a later experimental condition. . . . The following were some of the variations we studied:

1. *The presence of a "true partner."* (a) In the midst of the majority were *two* naive, critical subjects. The subjects were separated, spatially, being seated in the fourth and eighth positions, respectively. Each therefore heard his judgment confirmed by one other person (provided the other person remained independent), one prior to, the other subsequently to announcing his own judgment. In addition, each experienced a break in the unanimity of the majority. There were six pairs of critical subjects. (b) In a further variation the "partner" to the critical subject was a member of the group who had been instructed to respond correctly throughout. This procedure permits the exact control of the partner's responses. The partner was always seated in the fourth position; he therefore announced his estimates in each case before the critical subject.

The results clearly demonstrate that a disturbance of the unanimity of the majority markedly increased the independence of the critical subjects. The frequency of pro-majority errors dropped to 10.4 per cent of the total number of

estimates in variation (a), and to 5.5 per cent in variation (b). These results are to be compared with the frequency of yielding to the unanimous majorities in the basic experiment, which was 32 per cent of the total number of estimates. It is clear that the presence in the field of *one other* individual who responded correctly was sufficient to deplete the power of the majority, and in some cases to destroy it. This finding is all the more striking in the light of other variations which demonstrate the effect of even small minorities provided they are unanimous. Indeed, we have been able to show that a unanimous majority of three is, under the given conditions, far more effective than a majority of eight containing one dissenter. That critical subjects will under these conditions free themselves of a majority of seven and join forces with one other person in the minority is, we believe, a result significant for theory. It points to a fundamental psychological difference between the condition of being alone and having a minimum of human support. It further demonstrates that the effects obtained are not the result of a summation of influences proceeding from each member of the group; it is necessary to conceive the results as being relationally determined.

2. *Withdrawal of a "true partner."* What will be the effect of providing the critical subject with a partner who responds correctly and then withdrawing him? The critical subject started with a partner who responded correctly. The partner was a member of the majority who had been instructed to respond correctly and to "desert" to the majority in the middle of the experiment. This procedure permits the observation of the same subject in the course of transition from one condition to another. The withdrawal of the partner produced a powerful and unexpected result. We had

assumed that the critical subject, having gone through the experience of opposing the majority with a minimum of support, would maintain his independence when alone. Contrary to this expectation, we found that the experience of having had and then lost a partner restored the majority effect to its full force, the proportion of errors rising to 28.5 per cent of all judgments, in contrast to the preceding level of 5.5 per cent. Further experimentation is needed to establish whether the critical subjects were responding to the sheer fact of being alone, or to the fact that the partner abandoned them.

3. *Late arrival of a "true partner."* The critical subject started as a minority of one in the midst of a unanimous majority. Toward the conclusion of the experiment one member of the majority "broke" away and began announcing correct estimates. This procedure, which reverses the order of conditions of the preceding experiment, permits the observation of the transition from being alone to being a member of a pair against a majority. It is obvious that those critical subjects who were independent when alone would continue to be so when joined by another partner. The variation is therefore of significance primarily for those subjects who yielded during the first phase of the experiment. The appearance of the late partner exerts a freeing effect, reducing the level to 8.7 per cent. Those who had previously yielded also became markedly more independent, but not completely so, continuing to yield more than previously independent subjects. The reports of the subjects do not cast much light on the factors responsible for the result. It is our impression that having once committed himself to yielding, the individual finds it difficult and painful to change his direction. To do so is tantamount to a public admission that he has not acted rightly. He therefore follows the precari-

ous course he has already chosen in order to maintain an outward semblance of consistency and conviction.

4. *The presence of a "compromise partner."* The majority was consistently extremist, always matching the standard with the most unequal line. One instructed subject (who, as the other variations, preceded the critical subject) also responded incorrectly, but his estimates were always intermediate between the truth and the majority position. The critical subject therefore faced an extremist majority whose unanimity was broken by one more moderately erring person. Under these conditions the frequency of errors was reduced but not significantly. However, the lack of unanimity determined in a strikingly consistent way the *direction* of the errors. The preponderance of the errors, 75.7 per cent of the total, was moderate, whereas in a parallel experiment in which the majority was unanimously extremist (*i.e.*, with the "compromise" partner excluded), the incidence of moderate errors was reduced to 42 per cent of the total. As might be expected, in a unanimously moderate majority, the errors of the critical subjects were without exception moderate.

## The Role of Majority Size

To gain further understanding of the majority effect, we varied the size of the majority in several different variations. The majorities, which were in each case unanimous, consisted of 16, 8, 4, 3, and 2 persons, respectively. In addition, we studied the limited case in which the critical subject was opposed by one instructed subject. . . .

With the opposition reduced to one, the majority effect all but disappeared. When the opposition proceeded from a group of two, it produced a measurable though small distortion, the errors being 12.8 per cent of the total number of estimates. The effect appeared in full force with a majority of three. Larger majorities of four, eight, and sixteen did not produce effects greater than a majority of three.

The effect of a majority is often silent, revealing little of its operation to the subject, and often hiding it from the experimenter. To examine the range of effects it is capable of inducing, decisive variations of conditions are necessary. An indication of one effect is furnished by the following variation in which the conditions of the basic experiment were simply reversed. Here the majority, consisting of a group of sixteen, was naive; in the midst of it we placed a single individual who responded wrongly according to instructions. Under these conditions the members of the naive majority reacted to the lone dissenter with amusement and disdain. Contagious laughter spread through the group at the droll minority of one. Of significance is the fact that the members lack awareness that they draw their strength from the majority, and that their reactions would change radically if they faced the dissenter individually. In fact, the attitude of derision in the majority turns to seriousness and increased respect as soon as the minority is increased to three. These observations demonstrate the role of social support as a source of power and stability, in contrast to the preceding investigations which stressed the effects of withdrawal of social support, or to be more exact, the effects of social opposition. Both aspects must be explicitly considered in a unified formulation of the effects of group conditions on the formation and change of judgments.

### The Role of the Stimulus-Situation

It is obviously not possible to divorce the quality and course of the group forces which act upon the individual from the specific stimulus-conditions. Of neces-

sity the structure of the situation molds the group forces and determines their direction as well as their strength. Indeed, this was the reason that we took pains in the investigations described above to center the issue between the individual and the group around an elementary and fundamental matter of fact. And there can be no doubt that the resulting reactions were directly a function of the contradiction between the objectively grasped relations and the majority position. . . .

We have also varied systematically the structural clarity of the task, including in separate variations judgments based on mental standards. In agreement with other investigators, we find that the majority effect grows stronger as the situation diminishes in clarity. Concurrently, however, the disturbance of the subjects and the conflict-quality of the situation decrease markedly. We consider it of significance that the majority achieves its most pronounced effect when it acts most painlessly.

### SUMMARY

We have investigated the effects upon individuals of majority opinions when the latter were seen to be in a direction contrary to fact. By means of a simple technique we produced a radical divergence between a majority and a minority, and observed the ways in which individuals coped with the resulting difficulty. Despite the stress of the given conditions, a substantial proportion of individuals retained their independence throughout. At the same time a substantial minority yielded, modifying their judgments in accordance with the majority. Independence and yielding are a joint function of the following major factors: (1) The character of the stimulus situation. Variations in structural clarity have a decisive effect: With diminishing clarity of the stimulus-conditions the majority effect increases. (2) The character of the group forces. Individuals are highly sensitive to the structural qualities of group opposition. In particular, we demonstrated the great importance of the factor of unanimity. Also, the majority effect is a function of the size of group opposition. (3) The character of the individual. There were wide, and indeed, striking differences among individuals within the same experimental situation. The hypothesis was proposed that these are functionally dependent on relatively enduring character differences, in particular those pertaining to the person's social relations.

## BIBLIOGRAPHY

1. Asch, S. E. Studies in the principles of judgments and attitudes: II. Determination of judgments by group and by ego-standards. *J. soc. Psychol.*, 1940, *12*, 433–465.

2. ———. The doctrine of suggestion, prestige and imitation in social psychology. *Psychol. Rev.*, 1948, *55*, 250–276.

3. Asch, S. E., Block, H., and Hertzman, M. Studies in the principles of judgments and attitudes. I. Two Basic principles of judgment. *J. Psychol.* 1938, *5*, 219–251.

4. Coffin, E. E. Some conditions of suggestion and suggestibility: A study of certain attitudinal and situational factors influencing the process of suggestion. *Psychol. Monogr.* 1941, *53*, No. 4.

5. Lewis, H. B. Studies in the principles of judgments and attitudes: IV. The operation of prestige suggestion. *J. soc. Psychol.*, 1941, *14*, 229–256.

6. Lorge, I. Prestige, suggestion, and attitudes. *J. soc. Psychol.*, 1936, *7*, 386–402.

7. Miller, N. E. and Dollard, J. *Social Learning and Imitation.* New Haven: Yale University Press, 1941.

8. Moore, H. T. The comparative influence of majority and expert opinion. *Amer. J. Psychol.*, 1921, *32*, 16–20.

9. Sherif, M. A study of some social factors in perception. *Arch. Psychol.*, N. Y. 1935, No. 187.

10. Thorndike, E. L. *The Psychology of Wants, Interests, and Attitudes.* New York: D. Appleton-Century Company, Inc., 1935.

# 28

# Some Social and Psychological Consequences of the Longwall Method of Coal-Getting[1]

## An Examination of the Psychological Situation and Defences of a Work Group in Relation to the Social Structure and Technological Content of the Work System

## *E. L. Trist & K. W. Bamforth*[2]

### INTRODUCTION: A PERSPECTIVE FROM RECENT INNOVATIONS

A number of innovations in work organization at the coal-face have been making a sporadic and rather guarded appearance since the change-over of the industry to nationalization. During the past two years the authors have been following the course of these developments. Though differing from each other, they have had the common effect of increasing productivity, at least to some extent, and sometimes the increase reported has reached a level definitely above the upper limit customarily achieved by good workmen using similar equipment under conventional conditions. They have been accompanied by impressive changes in the social quality of the work-life of face teams. Greater cohesiveness has appeared in groups, and greater personal satisfaction has been reported by individuals. Decreases have also been indicated in sickness and absenteeism.

In the account to follow, the longwall method will be regarded as a technological system expressive of the prevailing outlook of mass-production engineering and as a social structure consisting of the occupational roles that have been institutionalized in its use. These interactive technological and sociological patterns will be assumed to exist as forces having psychological effects in the life-space of the face-worker, who must either take a role and perform a task in the system they compose or abandon his attempt to work at the coal-face. His own contribution to the field of determi-

[1] The study reported here is one part of a larger project on which the Tavistock Institute of Human Relations has for some time been engaged, concerned with the conditions likely to increase the effectiveness of the "dissemination of information" about new social techniques developed in industry. This project was initiated by the Human Factors Panel of the Committee on Industrial Productivity set up by the Lord President of the Council under the Scientific Adviser to the Government. It has been administered by the Medical Research Council. No responsibility, however, attaches to either of these bodies for the contents of this paper, a shortened version of which has been discussed by the Medical Research Subcommittee of the National Coal Board.

[2] The field work necessary for this study has been lessened by the fact that Mr. K. W. Bamforth was himself formerly a miner and worked at the coal-face for 18 years.

*Source:* From "Some Social and Psychological Consequences of the Longwall Method of Coal-Getting" by E. L. Trist and K. W. Bamforth in *Human Relations,* 4 (1951). Reprinted by permission of Plenum Publishing Corporation.

nants arises from the nature and quality of the attitudes and relationships he develops in performing one of these tasks and in taking one of these roles. Together, the forces and their effects constitute the psycho-social whole which is the object of study.

## THE CHARACTER OF THE PRE-MECHANIZED EQUILIBRIUM AND THE NATURE OF ITS DISTURBANCE

### 1. Hand-got Systems and the Responsible Autonomy of the Pair-Based Work Group

The outstanding feature of the social pattern with which the pre-mechanized equilibrium was associated is its emphasis on small group organization at the coal-face. The groups themselves were interdependent working pairs to whom one or two extra individuals might be attached. It was common practice for two colliers—a hewer and his mate—to make their own contract with the colliery management and to work their own small face with the assistance of a boy "trammer." This working unit could function equally well in a variety of engineering layouts both of the advance and retreat type, whether step-wise or direct. Sometimes it extended its numbers to seven or eight, when three or four colliers, and their attendant trammers, would work together.[3]

A primary work-organization of this type has the advantage of placing responsibility for the complete coal-getting task squarely on the shoulders of a single, small, face-to-face group which experiences the entire cycle of opera-

tions within the compass of its membership. For each participant the task has total significance and dynamic closure. Though the contract may have been in the name of the hewer, it was regarded as a joint undertaking. Leadership and "supervision" were internal to the group, which had a quality of *responsible autonomy*. The capacity of these groups for self-regulation was a function of the wholeness of their work task, this connection being represented in their contractual status. A whole has power as an independent detachment, but a part requires external control.

Within these pair-based units was contained the full range of coal-face skills; each collier being an all-round workman, usually able to substitute for his mate. Though his equipment was simple, his tasks were multiple. The "underground skill" on which their efficient and safe execution depended was almost entirely person-carried. He had craft pride and artisan independence. These qualities obviated status difficulties and contributed to responsible autonomy.

Choice of workmates posed a crucial question. These choices were made by the men themselves, sociometrically, under full pressure of the reality situation and with long-standing knowledge of each other. Stable relationships tended to result, which frequently endured over many years. In circumstances where a man was injured or killed, it was not uncommon for his mate to care for his family. These work relationships were often reinforced by kinship ties, the contract system and the small group autonomy allowing a close but spontaneous connection to be maintained between family and occupation, which avoided tying the one to the other. In segregated mining communities the link between kinship and occupation can be oppressive as well as supportive; against this

---

[3] Hand-got methods contained a number of variants, but discussion of these is beyond present scope.

danger, "exogamous" choice was a safe-guard. But against too emotional a rela-tionship, more likely to develop between non-kin associates, kinship barriers were in turn a safeguard. . . .

## 2. The Adaptability of the Small Group to the Underground Situation

Being able to work their own short faces continuously, these pair, or near pair, groups could stop at whatever point may have been reached by the end of a shift. The flexibility in work pace so allowed had special advantages in the under-ground situation; for when bad condi-tions were encountered, the extraction process in a series of stalls could proceed unevenly in correspondence with the uneven distribution of these bad condi-tions, which tend to occur now in one and now in another section along a seam. Even under good conditions, groups of this kind were free to set their own targets, so that aspirations levels with respect to production could be ad-justed to the age and stamina of the indi-viduals concerned.

In the underground situation external dangers must be faced in darkness. Dark-ness also awakens internal dangers. The need to share with others anxieties aroused by this double threat may be taken as self-evident. In view of the re-stricted range of effective communica-tion, these others have to be immedi-ately present. Their number therefore is limited. These conditions point to the strong need in the underground worker for a role in a small primary group.

A second characteristic of the under-ground situation is the wide dispersal of particular activities, in view of the large area over which operations generally are extended. The small groups of the hand-got systems tended to become isolated from each other even when working in the same series of stalls; the isolation of

the group, as of the individual, being intensified by the darkness. Under these conditions there is no possibility of con-tinuous supervision, in the factory sense, from any individual external to the pri-mary work group.

The small group, capable of responsi-ble autonomy, and able to vary its work pace in correspondence with changing conditions, would appear to be the type of social structure ideally adapted to the underground situation. It is instruc-tive that the traditional work systems, evolved from the experience of succes-sive generations, should have been founded on a group with these attri-butes. . . .

## 3. The Counter Balance of the Large Undifferentiated Collectivity

The psychological disadvantages of a work system, the small group organiza-tion of which is based on pair relation-ships, raises issues of a far-reaching kind only recently submitted to study in group dynamics (4). It would appear that the self-enclosed character of the relation-ship makes it difficult for groups of this kind to combine effectively in differenti-ated structures of a somewhat larger so-cial magnitude, though this inability does not seem to hold in respect of much larger collectivities of a simpler mass character. . . .

In the pre-mechanized pattern, the pair-based primaries and the large re-latively undifferentiated collectivities composed a dynamically interrelated sys-tem that permitted an enduring social balance. The intense reciprocities of the former, with their personal and family significance, and the diffuse identifica-tions of the latter, with their community and class connectedness, were mutually supportive. The face teams could bear the responsibility of their autonomy through the security of their dependence on the united collectivity of the pit.

Difficulties arose largely from rivalries and conflicts between the various pairs and small teams. . . . All this was accepted as part of the system.

Inter-team conflict provided a channel for aggression that preserved intact the loyalties on which the small group depended. In the large group aggression received structured expression in trade union resistance. If the struggle was harsh, it was at least direct and understandable. It was not the insidious kind that knocked the bottom out of life, leaving those concerned without a sense of a scheme in things—the "anomie" described by Halliday (2) after the transition to the longwall. The system as a whole contained its bad in a way that did not destroy its good. The balance persisted, albeit that work was of the hardest, rewards often meagre, and the social climate rough at times and even violent.

## 4. Mechanization and the Problem of Intermediate Organization

With the advent of coal-cutters and mechanical conveyors, the degree of technological complexity of the coal-getting task was raised to a different level. Mechanisation made possible the working of a single long face in place of a series of short faces. . . .

The associated characteristics of mechanized complexity, and of largeness as regards the scale of the primary production unit, created a situation in which it was impossible for the method to develop as a technological system without bringing into existence a work relationship structure radically different from that associated with hand-got procedures. The artisan type of pair, composed of the skilled man and his mate, assisted by one or more labourers, was out of keeping as a model for the type of work group required. Need arose for a unit more of the size and differentiated complexity of a small factory department. A structure of intermediate social magnitude began therefore to emerge. The basic pattern round which the work relationships of the longwall production unit were organized became the cycle group of 40–50 men, their shot-firer and shift "deputies," who were responsible to the pit management for the working as a whole. Only in relation to this total cycle group could various smaller subgroups secure function and acquire social form.

This centring of the new system on a differentiated structure of intermediate social magnitude disturbed the simple balance that had existed between the very small and very large traditional groups, and impaired the quality of responsible autonomy. The psychological and sociological problems posed by the technological needs of the longwall system were those with respect to which experience in the industry was least, and towards which its traditions were antithetical. . . .

## 5. The Lack of Recognition of the Nature of the Difficulties

Anyone who has listened to the talk of older miners who have experienced in their own work-lives the change-over to the longwall cannot fail to be impressed by the confused mourning for the past that still goes on in them together with a dismay over the present coloured by despair and indignation. To the clinical worker the quality of these talks has at times a ring that is familiar. Those with rehabilitation experience will recognize it as similar to the quality of feeling expressed by rehabilitees when ventilating the aftermath in themselves of an impairment accepted as irreversible.

## THE STRESS OF MASS PRODUCTION IN THE UNDERGROUND SITUATION

### 1. The Interaction of Bad Conditions and Bad Work

Differentiated, rigidly sequenced work systems, organized on mass-production lines to deal with large quantities of material on a multi-shift cycle, are a basic feature of the factory pattern. . . . It [is] virtually impossible to establish the kind of constant background to the task that is taken for granted in the factory. A very large variety of unfavourable and changing environmental conditions is encountered at the coal-face, many of which are impossible to predict. Others, though predictable, are impossible to alter.

### 2. The Strain of Cycle Control

. . . In view of the darkness and the spread out character of the work, there is no possibility of close supervision. Responsibility for seeing to it that bad work is not done, however bad the conditions, rests with the face-workers themselves. But the responsible autonomy of some, especially, of the occupational subgroups has been impaired in the longwall method. This problem will be taken up in succeeding sections.

As a result, management complain of lack of support from the men, who are accused of being concerned only with their own fractional tasks and unwilling to take broader cycle responsibility. The parallel complaint of the workers is of being driven and tricked by management, who are resented as outsiders— intermittent visitors and "stick" men, who interfere without sharing the hard, physical work and in-group life of the face. . . .

The strain of cycle control tends to produce a group "culture" of angry and suspicious bargaining over which both

management and men are in collusion. There is displacement both upwards and downwards of the tensions generated. The "hell" that breaks loose in the under-manager's office when news comes in that the fillers are unlikely to fill off in one or more faces resounds through the pit.

### 3. The Norm of Low Productivity

In all work at the coal-face two distinct tasks are simultaneously present; those that belong to the production cycle being always to some extent carried out on the background of a second activity arising from the need to contend with interferences, actual or threatened, emanating from the underground situation.

. . . The crises of cycle stoppages and the stress of the deputy's role are but symptoms of a wider situation characterized by the establishment of a norm of low productivity, as the only adaptive method of handling, in the contingencies of the underground situation, a complicated, rigid, and large-scale work system, borrowed with too little modification from an engineering culture appropriate to the radically different situation of the factory. . . .

## THE SPECIAL SITUATION OF THE FILLING SHIFT

### 1. Isolated Dependence

Relationships between members of the filling shift are characterized by an absence of functional interdependence, which arises from the absence of role differentiation in the twenty identical tasks performed by the shift aggregate. . . .

The effect of the introduction of mechanized methods of face preparation and conveying, along with the retention of manual filling, has been not only to isolate the filler from those with whom he formerly shared the coal-getting task as a whole, but to make him one of a large aggregate serviced by the same small group of preparation workers. In place of an actually present partner, who belonged to him solely as the second member of an interdependent pair, he has acquired an "absent group," whom he must share with nineteen others. . . .

The absent, internally disconnected group on which he is dependent takes no functional cognizance of the existence of the filler as an individual. In view of the far-reaching community, as well as work, separation that exists between the preparation and the filling shifts (produced by the time-table arrangements), actual cognizance tends also to be minimal. . . .

## 2. Unequal Men with Equal Stints under Unequal Conditions

The fillers, as has been shown, have no secure relationships in face of the differential incidence of the bad conditions they may encounter or of the bad work they may inherit from the preparation workers on whom they are dependent. The men who face these unequal conditions are themselves unequal; but the lengths of face they clear are the same. . . .

The local arrival of certain types of bad conditions, such as rolls that move across the face, can be anticipated, so that anxiety piles up. . . . As regards bad work left by the other shifts, the filler is in the situation of never knowing what he may find, so that anxiety of a second kind arises that tends to produce chronic uncertainty and irritation. There is little doubt that these two circumstances contribute to the widespread incidence of psycho-somatic and kindred neurotic disorders among those concerned.

The degree of stress arising when men experience the full weight of this situation could have been explored only in a therapeutic relationship. But many instances were given of neurotic episodes occurring on shift—of men sitting in their lengths in stony silence, attacking their coal in towering rage, or leaving the face in panic. In a situation of dependent isolation with the odds unequal both as regards his own resources and what is required of him, the individual inevitably erects protective defences, and these are elaborated and shared in the work group. An account of the main pattern of group defences will now be given. These defences are reactive rather than adaptive. Their effectiveness therefore is only partial. But without them life at the longwall would be intolerable for all but those whose level of personal adjustment is rather better than that attained by most individuals in the course of their development.

## FOUR TYPES OF GROUP DEFENCE

### 1. Informal Organization

The functional isolation of the filler within his own group, which leaves him "officially" alone with his "coals," is met by an attempt to develop informal, small-group organization in which private arrangements to help each other out are made among neighbours, in twos, threes, or fours. But these solely interpersonal arrangements are undependable and open to manipulation for anti-social and competitive as well as for mutually protective ends. A number of isolates is left over. The total face group is incapable, except defensively, of acting as a socially responsible whole, since not even private allegiances are owed outside the small informal groups. These in turn are without responsible autonomy; the absence of institutionalized mutual obligation means that there are no statutory group tasks, and each individual can be held ultimately responsible only for clearing his own length. Internal "rows" the more easily break up the informal "coalitions," whose morale tends to be of the clique type. . . .

Isolates, it appears, are either individualists—who "won't even share timber"—or men with bad reputations, with whom others refuse to work. Amongst these are the unconscientious—who "won't help out at the end of a shift" and who are frequently absent—and the helpless—who "cannot learn to look after themselves under bad conditions." Others, whose stamina is deficient (whether through age, illness, or neurosis) and whose lengths are often uncleared in consequence, are dropped from the informal groups.

Only to a very limited extent, therefore, does his informal group organization meet the filler's need for a secure role in a primary group within his own shift. In view of the extent of his dependence on the performance of those in the other two shifts, his need for this foundation is greater than that of any of the other occupational groups, while the resources available to him are fewer.

## 2. Reactive Individualism

His small group failing, the filler is thrown on to himself and against others. The second defence against isolation is the development of a reactive individualism, in which a reserve of personal secrecy is apt to be maintained. Among his own shift mates there is competitive intrigue for the better places—middle positions are avoided; from these "it is a long way to creep"—and for jobs in workings where conditions are good there is a scramble.

On some faces described to the writers, fear of victimization was rife, particularly in the form of being sent to work in a "bad place"; the deputy being more easily turned into a persecutor in view of the guilt arising from the intrigue and deception which the men practised both against him and against each other. Against the deputy, advantage is taken of the scope afforded in the underground situation for petty deception over such matters as time of leaving the pit, or the "measure that is sent up" (amount of coal filled on to the conveyor). With the deputy, however, men are also prepared to enter into alliance against each other, often for very good reasons—to stop mates from going absent and by so doing throwing more work on to the others.

As regards outside groups, practices of bribing members of the other shifts in the hope of getting a "good deal" in one's own length were mentioned by several informants. Tobacco is taken to the cutter; gummers are stood a pint on Sunday. These practices are to be regarded as symptoms of a state of affairs rather than as widespread in themselves.

The effect of this defensive individualism is to reduce the sense of secure identification in the larger pit collectivity, which was the second principle on which the older equilibrium was based. . . .

The competition, intrigue, unwillingness to put allegations to the test and the reserve of personal secrecy, are parts of one pattern. Whatever their personal wishes, men feel under pressure to be out for themselves, since the social structure in which they work denies them membership in any group that can legitimize interdependence. In this respect reactive individualism makes a basic interpretation of the social structure of the filling shift and is the only form of authorized behaviour.

## 3. Mutual Scapegoating

Fillers almost never see those who work on the "back shifts," and this absence of contact gives full scope for mutual and irresponsible scapegoating. When there is a crisis, and the filling shift is unable to fill off, the "buck" is passed to the other shifts—or vice versa if disorganization has occurred elsewhere. It is frequently also passed to the deputy, who is blamed for not finding substitutes, and to repair men, brought in, but too old to stand the pace.

For these to pass the buck back to the fillers is fruitless. As they do not exist as a responsible whole, they, as a group, are not there to take the blame, and the individual filler can always exempt himself. Since bad conditions and bad work interact so closely, it is usually difficult to pin blame specifically. Mutual scapegoating is a self-perpetuating system, in which nothing is resolved and no one feels guilty. For all concerned to remain in collusion with such a system is a defence which allows each to make his "anonymous contribution" to the "group mentality," (4) which sabotages both the goal of cycle productivity and the needs of the individual for a membership in a satisfying work-group. So far as this pattern obtains, all strike at each other in a mock war in which no one is hurt yet all suffer.

This defence can also be seen as a "back-handed" attempt to recover the supportive unity lost through reactive individualism in a way that is consistent with it. For all to be "in the bad" together is at least a way of being together. . . .

Not that the system is felt as entirely bad since it is the means by which a living is earned. Moreover, under present conditions this living is a good one, both in terms of wages and of community status. But the benefits which these "goods" bring are not realized in the work activities of the group. They lie outside the work system, which is tolerated as a means to external ends rather than accepted also as an end in itself, worthy of whole-hearted pursuit in virtue of the internal satisfactions it affords. . . .

## 4. Self-Compensatory Absenteeism

Withdrawal is the fourth form of defence, complementing mutual scapegoating, and absenteeism is to be regarded as a recognized social technique within this pattern. . . .

When conditions on a face deteriorate, especially in ways that are predictable, absenteeism among fillers sometimes piles up to a point where the remainder have to stay down an extra two or three hours in order to clear the face. Should this situation repeat itself for more than a day or two, those coming on shift often meet at the pit-head baths before presenting themselves for work. If less than a certain number arrive, all go home.

Absenteeism of this self-compensatory type, though carried out as an act of aggrieved defiance against a system, felt in these circumstances as persecutory, is an attempt on the part of the individual to prolong his work life at the coal-face. For without the respite of occasional absences, he feels that he would soon become unable to carry on. In view of the accentuated differences both in wages and in status between face workers and repair, haulage, or surface personnel, the goal of remaining at the coal-face for as long as possible would appear to operate as a powerful motivational force in determining the behaviour of the ordinary face-worker. . . .

This, and the other three defences discussed, play a dynamically interrelated part in forming the culture[4] of the work group, though naturally the intensity to which the pattern is present varies widely, and there are faces where the group atmosphere remains for long periods relatively immune from these influences. These are apt, however, to be "fair-weather" faces.

The danger is that habituation to working in a bad system has the compensation of enabling those concerned to leave too much both of their own and of their group's "badness" *in the system*. It then ties them to it through the fact that it does this, despite their hatred of it. As well as its faults, it is their own hatred that they hate in the system— and there is usually stubborn refusal to recognize such projections in work—no less than in therapy-groups. A characteristic of faces with a bad group atmosphere is the protesting yet excited collusion of all concerned with the state of affairs. This is in contrast to the more independently critical and realistic attitude of those in groups where the pattern is less complete and less intense.

[4] The concept of "culture" as a psycho-social technique developed by a group in a structurally determined situation has been outlined by Trist, "Culture as a Psycho-Social Process," contributed to a symposium on The Concept of Culture, British Association, Section (H), Anthropology and Archeology, Birmingham Meeting, 1950. This viewpoint develops that of Curle, and Curle and Trist, "Transitional Communities and Social Reconnection," *Human Relations*, Vol. I, No. 1, pp. 42–68, and No. 2, pp. 240–288; and is akin to that of Ruesch, "Experiments in Psychotherapy, II: Individual Social Techniques," *The Journal of Social Psychology*, 1949, 29, 3–28; and Ruesch and Bateson, "Structure and Process in Social Relations," *Psychiatry*, 1949, Vol. XII, 2, pp. 105–124.

## REFERENCES

1. Dickson, D. E. "The Morbid Miner," *Edin. Med. J.*, 1936, p. 696.

2. Halliday, J. L. *Psychosocial Medicine: A Study of the Sick Society*, Heinemann, London, 1949.

3. Morris, J. N. "Coal Miners," *Lancet*, Vol. II, 1947, p. 341.

4. Bion, W. R. "Experiences in Groups, III," *Human Relations*, Vol. II, No. 1, January, 1949, pp. 13–22.

## 29

# The Organization Man: Conclusion

*William H. Whyte, Jr.*

Here, finally, is the apotheosis of the Social Ethic. Some might summarize the suburban temper in different terms—pragmatism, perhaps, or utilitarianism—and their intonation would depend on their own outlook. But the dominant motif is unmistakable. Not just as something expedient, but as something right, the organization transients have put social usefulness at the core of their beliefs. Adaptation has become more than a necessity; in a life in which everything changes, it has become almost a constant.

Since I am using suburbia as a vehicle to bring together many strands, it can be asked if it is fair to generalize from such places to organization man in general. I am talking about values, and the suburbanites themselves provide evidence that their values are a great deal more than a function of the physical environment. That they respond to the pressure of the court or the tight-knit block is not so significant. They have to. What is significant is how they feel about these pressures—and how, ideally, they think a person should feel about them. . . .

Let us now broaden our view to organization man in general and ask what this climate of thought portends. If, as I believe, the people I have been examining in this book are representative of the main stream of organization life, one thing seems clear. If ever there was a generation of technicians, theirs is it. No generation has been so well equipped, psychologically as well as technically, to cope with the intricacies of vast organizations; none has been so well equipped to lead a meaningful community life; and none probably will be so adaptable to the constant shifts in environment that organization life is so increasingly demanding of them. In the better sense of the word, they are becoming the interchangeables of our society and they accept the role with understanding. They are all, as they say, in the same boat.

But where is the boat going? No one seems to have the faintest idea; nor, for that matter, do they see much point in even raising the question. Once people liked to think, at least, that they were in control of their destinies, but few of the younger organizational people cherish such notions. Most see themselves as objects more acted upon than acting—and their future, therefore, determined as much by the system as by themselves.

In a word, they *accept*, and if we do not find this comforting at least we should recognize that it would be odd if they did not feel this confidence. For them society has in fact been good—very, very good—for there has been a succession of fairly beneficent environments: college, the paternalistic, if not always pleasant, military life, then, perhaps, graduate work through the G.I. Bill of Rights, a corporation apprenticeship during a pe-

*Source:* From *The Organization Man* (pp. 392–404) by William H. Whyte, Jr., New York: Simon & Schuster, Inc. Copyright © 1956, 1984 by William H. Whyte, Jr. Reprinted by permission of Simon & Schuster, Inc.

riod of industrial expansion and high prosperity, and, for some, the camaraderie of communities like Park Forest. The system, they instintively conclude, is essentially benevolent.

No one should begrudge them the prosperity that has helped make them feel this way. If we have to have problems, after all, the adversities of good times are as worthy as any to have to worry about. Nor should we regard the emphasis on co-operation as a reversal of our national character. When the suburbanites speak of re-establishing the spirit of the frontier communities, there is a truth in their analogy. Our country was born as a series of highly communal enterprises, and though the individualist may have opened the frontier, it was the co-operative who settled it. So throughout our history. Our national genius has always lain in our adaptability, in our distrust of dogma and doctrine, in our regard for the opinion of others, and in this respect the organization people are true products of the American past. "The more equal social conditions become," de Tocqueville, no friend of conformity, presciently observed, "the more men display this reciprocal disposition to oblige each other."

And there is the crux. When de Tocqueville wrote this a century ago it was the double-edged nature of this disposition that haunted him. He understood its virtue; he was an aristocrat and he confessed that he missed the excellence of the few in the good of the many, but he saw clearly that our egalitarianism and our ease of social co-operation were the great fruits of democracy. We could not sustain these virtues without suffering their defects. But could we keep them in balance? de Tocqueville made a prophecy. If America ever destroyed its genius it would be by intensifying the social virtues at the expense of others, by making the individual come to regard

himself as a hostage to prevailing opinion, by creating, in sum, a tyranny of the majority.

And this is what the organization man is doing. He is doing it for what he feels are good reasons, but this only makes the tyranny more powerful, not less. At the very time when the pressures of our highly organized society make so stringent a demand on the individual, he is himself compounding the impact. He is not only other-directed, to borrow David Riesman's concept, he is articulating a philosophy which tells him it is right to be that way.

My charge against the Social Ethic, then, is on precisely the grounds of contemporary usefulness it so venerates. It is not, I submit, suited to the needs of "modern man," but is instead reinforcing precisely that which least needs to be emphasized, and at the expense of that which does. Here is my bill of particulars.

*It is redundant.* In some societies individualism has been carried to such extremes as to endanger the society itself, and there exist today examples of individualism corrupted into a narrow egotism which prevents effective co-operation. There is a danger, there is no question of that. But is it today as pressing a danger as the obverse—a climate which inhibits individual initiative and imagination, and the courage to exercise it against group opinion? Society is itself an education in the extrovert values, and I think it can be rightfully argued that rarely has there been a society which has preached them so hard. No man is an island unto himself, but how John Donne would writhe to hear how often, and for what reasons, the thought is so tiresomely repeated.

*It is premature.* To preach technique before content, the skills of getting along isolated from why and to what end the getting along is for, does not produce maturity. It produces a sort of permanent prematurity, and this is true not only of the child being taught life adjustment but of the organization man being taught well-roundedness. This is a sterile concept, and those who believe that they have mastered human relations can blind themselves to the true bases of co-operation. People don't co-operate just to co-operate; they co-operate for substantive reasons, to achieve certain goals, and unless these are comprehended the little manipulations for morale, team spirit, and such are fruitless.

And they can be worse than fruitless. Held up as the end-all of organization leadership, the skills of human relations easily tempt the new administrator into the practice of a tyranny more subtle and more pervasive than that which he means to supplant. No one wants to see the old authoritarian return, but at least it could be said of him that what he wanted primarily from you was your sweat. The new man wants your soul.

*It is delusory.* It is easy to fight obvious tyranny; it is not easy to fight benevolence, and few things are more calculated to rob the individual of his defenses than the idea that his interests and those of society can be wholly compatible. The good society is the one in which they are most compatible, but they never can be completely so, and one who lets The Organization be the judge ultimately sacrifices himself. Like the good society, the good organization encourages individual expression, and many have done so. But there always remains some conflict between the individual and The Organization. Is The Organization to be the arbiter? The Organization will look to its own interests, but it will look to the individual's *only as The Organization interprets them.*

*It is static.* Organization of itself has no dynamic. The dynamic is in the individual and thus he must not only question how The Organization interprets

his interests, he must question how it interprets its own. The bold new plan he feels is necessary, for example. He cannot trust that The Organization will recognize this. Most probably, it will not. It is the nature of a new idea to confound current consensus—even the mildly new idea. It might be patently in order, but, unfortunately, the group has a vested interest in its miseries as well as its pleasures, and irrational as this may be, many a member of organization life can recall instances where the group clung to known disadvantages rather than risk the anarchies of change.

*It is self-destructive.* The quest for normalcy, as we have seen in suburbia, is one of the great breeders of neuroses, and the Social Ethic only serves to exacerbate them. What is normalcy? We practice a great mutual deception. Everyone knows that they themselves are different—that they are shy in company, perhaps, or dislike many things most people seem to like—but they are not sure that other people are different too. Like the norms of personality testing, they see about them the sum of efforts of people like themselves to seem as normal as others and possibly a little more so. It is hard enough to learn to live with our inadequacies, and we need not make ourselves more miserable by a spurious ideal of middle-class adjustment. Adjustment to what? Nobody really knows—and the tragedy is that they don't realize that the so-confident-seeming other people don't know either.

Now let us ask if these defects are inevitable. Does The Organization *have* to require acquiescence? Many critics of American civilization, European critics in particular, see our spiritual conformities as an unavoidable consequence of an industrial society, and further growth and prosperity of our kind, they believe, will lead to the ultimate dehumanization of man. The external similarities of

American life, in short, they hold as inextricably related to the inner similarities.

We should never allow ourselves to be complacent about the external similarities of American life, or use prosperity as an apologia for Babbittry. But it is a retrograde point of view that fails to recognize that these similarities are in great part a consequence of making the benefits of our civilization available to more people. The monotonous regularity of ranch-type houses that can so easily appall us is not the product of an inner desire for uniformity so much as the fact that modular construction is a condition of moderate-cost housing. This kind of housing is no more or less a pressure for inner conformity than the rows of identical brownstones of the 1890s or, for that matter, the identical brick fronts of the 1700s.

Science and technology do not have to be antithetical to individualism. To hold that they must be antithetical, as many European intellectuals do, is a sort of utopianism in reverse. For a century Europeans projected their dreams into America; now they are projecting their fears, and in so doing they are falling into the very trap they accuse us of. Attributing a power to the machine that we have never felt, they speak of it almost as if it were animistic and had a will of its own over and above the control of man. Thus they see our failures as inevitable, and those few who are consistent enough to pursue the logic of their charge imply that there is no hope to be found except through a retreat to the past.*

---

* In *Tomorrow Is Already Here*, to cite one example, Robert Jungk touches on many of the things I have gone into in this book, but his underlying premise seems to be that it is morally wrong for man to try to control his environment the way Americans are doing. In this indictment he fails to distinguish between the kinds of control, and with little qualification he

This is a hopelessly pessimistic view. The fault is not in the pressures of industrial society—an agrarian society has pressures as powerful—but in the stance we assume before these pressures. If we reverse our current emphases, we will not reverse progress, for individualism is more necessary, not less, than it ever was.

This does not mean a "return" to the Protestant Ethic as preached a century ago. It is futile to speak of individualism as if unrestrained self-interest will somehow produce the greater good. It is for this reason, perhaps, that the right wing has remained a comparatively negative force in American thought. Even more than those who preach the Social Ethic slough over the individual's rights against society, the right sloughs over the individual's obligations to society— and the lack of realism is sensed by the middle as well as the left.

---

equates aberrations like "soul engineering" with such activities as trying to find better air medicine techniques, scientific agriculture, etc. This is very sloppy thinking. One kind of activity represents man's attempt to control his physical environment; the other is an attempt at social manipulation, and its relation to science lies only in its pretensions.

Where man uses science to control the physical, the result is to enlarge the area of his potential freedom. This point shouldn't need to be labored, but some of our own critics similarly fail to distinguish between control of the physical and control of the social, with the result that they see the I.B.M. machine, fluorescent lighting, and the like as symbols of spiritual decline. This false personalization of the inanimate seems to me a very sentimental viewpoint and one that militates against any comprehension of the real problems. The I.B.M. machine has no ethic of its own; what it does is enable one or two people to do the amount of computing work that formerly required many more people. If people often use it stupidly, it is their stupidity, not the machine's, and a return to the abacus would not exorcise the failing. People can be treated as drudges just as effectively without modern machines.

The pendulum analogy that suggests itself would be misleading, for it implies a return to some ideal state of balance. What we need is not to return but to reinterpret, to apply to our problems the basic idea of individualism, not ancient particulars. The doctrines of the nineteenth-century businessman and our modern society are disparate, but that they are disparate is little cause for us to assume that individualism must be too. The central ideal—that the individual, rather than society, must be the paramount end—animated Western thought long before the Industrial Revolution, or Calvinism, or Puritanism, and it is as vital and as applicable today as ever.

But what is the "*solution*"? many ask. There is no solution. The conflict between individual and society has always involved dilemma; it always will, and it is intellectual arrogance to think a program would solve it. Certainly the current experience does suggest a few steps we can profitably take, and I would like to suggest several. Common to all, however, must be a fundamental shift of emphasis, and if this is evaded, any change will exist largely on the level of language. The organization man has a tremendous affinity for vogue words by which the status quo can be described as dynamic advance, and "individualism," alas, is such a word. Let us beware, then, the hard-sell, twelve-point program. Many have been touted as in the name of individual expression, but as those suppressed by them will sense, they are usually organization-serving loyalty devices that fool only those who administrate them.

This caveat made, let me suggest several areas where constructive proposals are in order. First, "human relations." We need by all means to continue to experiment and study. Whatever we call human relations, they are central to the problem of The Organization and the individual, and the more we find out about the effect of the one on the other the better we can find more living room for the individual. But it's not going to be done if many of those who propagate the doctrine cling to self-proving assumptions about the overriding importance of equilibrium, integration, and adjustment. The side of the coin they have been staring at so intently is a perfectly good one, but there is another side and it should not be too heretical at least to have a peek at it. Thousands of studies and case histories have dwelled on fitting the individual to the group, but what about fitting the group to the person? What about *individual* dynamics? The tyranny of the happy work team? The adverse effects of high morale?

One does not have to be in favor of unhappiness to explore such hypotheses, and now, encouragingly, a few whose good will is unquestionable are showing more disposition to do so. The Harvard Business School, which almost grew old with human relations, has been using the word *administrator* less, the word *leader* more, and lately its best research seems directed at the matter of individual initiative more than of group happiness. Rensis Likert, the leader of the "group dynamics" school, has announced that recent studies of organization are leading him and his colleagues to question their earlier conclusions that good morale necessarily produces high productivity. They still believe that the work group should be supervised as a group rather than on a man-to-man basis, but they do warn that the supervisor who concentrates on making the group happy may produce belongingness but not very much else.

Another fruitful approach would be a drastic re-examination of the now orthodox view that the individual should be given less of the complete task, the team more of it. For a century we have been breaking down tasks into the components and sub-components, each to be performed by a different cell member, and this assembly-line mentality has affected almost everything that men do for a living, including the arts. We can grant that to a degree the benefits of compartmentalized work have surpassed the disadvantages. But do we have to grant that progress demands more of same? That the monotony, the sacrifice of individual accomplishment are inevitable? On the assembly line itself, where specialization would seem most necessary, some companies have found that a reversal of emphasis can actually lead to more productivity. Instead of trying to offset the monotony of a task with externals, such as bowling alleys and "economic education," they have enlarged the task itself. By giving the worker more of the total job to do—asking him to wire the whole set, for example, instead of just one relay—they have given him that wonderful thing that is challenge, and he has responded with more effort, more skill, more *self-respect*.

Is there not a moral here for all organization life? If we truly believe the individual is more creative than the group, just in day-to-day routine there is something eminently practical we can do about it. Cut down the amount of time the individual has to spend in conferences and meetings and team play. This would be a somewhat mechanical approach to what is ultimately a philosophical problem, but if organization people would take a hard look at the different types of meetings inertia has accumulated for The Organization, they might find that the ostensibly negative act of cutting out many of them would lead to some very positive benefits over and above the time saved. Thrown more on their own resources, those who have nothing to offer but the skills of compro-

mising other people's efforts might feel bereft, but for the others the climate might be invigorating. Of itself such a surface change in working conditions would not give them more freedom, but it would halt a bad momentum, it would force organization to distinguish between what are legitimate functions of the group and what are not, and even if it yielded only a few more hours, this would be no small blessing. Once enjoyed, room to move around in is sweet indeed, and men partially liberated might be tantalized into demanding more.

In fighting the incubus of team work, we need to look more understandingly at the frustrations of those involved. Let's go back a moment to the situation of the professional employee. Studies have now convinced organization people that engineers and scientists in industry make up its most disaffected group, and that something should be done about it. The diagnosis is valuable. But how does organization interpret it? Organization people have concluded that the trouble is that the professional tends to be career-oriented rather than company-oriented. What The Organization must do, they believe, is to direct its efforts at integrating him by giving him more company status, indoctrinating him more effectively in the "big picture," by making him, in short, a company man.

How futile, how destructive is this solution! Why should the scientist be company-oriented? Is he to be called maladjusted because he does not fit the administrator's Procrustean bed? And of what profit would be his integration? It is not to his self-interest, neither is it to that of The Organization. Leave him his other allegiance. It is his work that must be paramount, and efforts to divert him into contentment are the efforts best calculated to bridle the curiosity that makes him productive.

Is it so practical? There is a magnificent piece of evidence that it is anything but. In the great slough of mediocrity that is most corporation research, what two laboratories are conspicuous exceptions in the rate of discovery? They are General Electric's research department and Bell Labs: exactly the two laboratories most famous for their encouragement of individualism—the most tolerant of individual differences, the most patient with off-tangent ideas, the least given to the immediate, closely supervised team project. By all accounts, the scientists in them get along quite well, but they do not make a business of it, and neither do the people who run the labs. They care not a whit if scientists' eyes fail to grow moist at company anthems; it is enough that the scientists do superbly well what they want to do, for though the consequences of profit for The Organization are secondary to the scientist, eventually there are these consequences, and as long as the interests of the group and the individual touch at this vital point, such questions as belongingness are irrelevant. Hard-boiled? No, tough-minded—and what more moral basis, it can be asked, for people working together, scientists or others?

It is not just for the scientist, not just for the brilliant, that the moral should be drawn, and this brings us to what ultimately is the single greatest vehicle for constructive change—education. The many points against the social adjustment emphases now prevailing are being vigorously sounded, and it is right that they should be, but one point needs to be made much more emphatically. The case for a rigorously fundamental schooling can be made on the utilitarians' own grounds: social usefulness. There are better reasons for the development of the individual, but until this

point is made more clearly we seem by default to leave the debate on the either/or grounds of "democratic education" versus a highly trained elite. This is false antithesis. The great bulk of people will face organization pressures as inhibiting for them as for the few, and they need, as much if not more, to have the best that is within them demanded early. Is it "democratic" to hold that the humanities can have no meaning for them? They do not have to be taught to shake hands with other people; society will attend to this lesson. They have to be taught to reach. All of them. Some will be outstanding, some not, but the few will never flourish where the values of the many are against them.

I have been speaking of measures organizations can take. But ultimately any real change will be up to the individual himself, and this is why his education is so central to the problem. For he must look to his discontents with different eye. It has been said that dominance of the group is the wave of the future and that, lament it or not, he might as well accept it. But this is contemporaryism at its worst; things are not as they are because there is some good reason they are. Nor is the reverse true. It may one day prove true, as some prophets argue, that we are in a great and dismal tide of history that cannot be reversed, but if we accept the view we will only prove it.

Whatever kind of future suburbia may foreshadow, it will show that at least we have the choices to make. The organization man is not in the grip of vast social forces about which it is impossible for him to do anything; the options are there, and with wisdom and foresight he can turn the future away from the dehumanized collective that so haunts our thoughts. He may not. But he can.

He must *fight* The Organization. Not stupidly, or selfishly, for the defects of individual self-regard are no more to be venerated than the defects of co-operation. But fight he must, for the demands for his surrender are constant and powerful, and the more he has come to like the life of organization the more difficult does he find it to resist these demands, or even to recognize them. It is wretched, dispiriting advice to hold before him the dream that ideally there need be no conflict between him and society. There always is; there always must be. Ideology cannot wish it away; the peace of mind offered by organization remains a surrender, and no less so for being offered in benevolence. That is the problem.

# 30
# Bureaucratic Structure and Personality
*Robert K. Merton*

## THE STRUCTURE OF BUREAUCRACY

The ideal type of . . . formal organization is bureaucracy and, in many respects, the classical analysis of bureaucracy is that by Max Weber.[1] As Weber indicates, bureaucracy involves a clear-cut division of integrated activities which are regarded as duties inherent in the office. A system of differentiated controls and sanctions is stated in the regulations. The assignment of roles occurs on the basis of technical qualifications which are ascertained through formalized, impersonal procedures (*e.g.*, examinations). Within the structure of hierarchically arranged authority, the activities of "trained and salaried experts" are governed by general, abstract, and clearly defined rules which preclude the necessity for the issuance of specific instructions for each specific case. The generality of the rules requires the constant use of *categorization*, whereby individual problems and cases are classified on the basis of designated criteria and are treated accordingly. The pure type of bureaucratic official is appointed, either by a superior or through the exercise of impersonal competition; he is not elected. A measure of flexibility in the bureaucracy is attained by electing higher functionaries who presumably express the will of the electorate (*e.g.*, a body of citizens or a board of directors).

The election of higher officials is designed to affect the purposes of the organization, but the technical procedures for attaining these ends are carried out by continuing bureaucratic personnel.[2]

Most bureaucratic offices involve the expectation of life-long tenure, in the absence of disturbing factors which may decrease the size of the organization. Bureaucracy maximizes vocational security.[3] The function of security of tenure, pensions, incremental salaries and regularized procedures for promotion is to ensure the devoted performance of official duties, without regard for extraneous pressures.[4] The chief merit of bureaucracy is its technical efficiency, with a premium placed on precision, speed, expert control, continuity, discretion, and optimal returns on input. The structure is one which approaches the complete elimination of personalized relationships and nonrational considerations (hostility, anxiety, affectual involvements, etc.).

With increasing bureaucratization, it becomes plain to all who would see that man is to a very important degree controlled by his social relations to the instruments of production. This can no longer seem only a tenet of Marxism, but a stubborn fact to be acknowledged by all, quite apart from their ideological persuasion. Bureaucratization makes readily visible what was previously dim and obscure. More and more people discover that to work, they must be employed. For to work, one must have tools and equipment. And the tools and equipment are increasingly available only in bureaucracies, private or public. Consequently, one must be employed by the bureaucracies in order to have access to tools in order to work in order to live. It is in this sense that bureaucratization entails separation of individuals from the instruments of production, as in modern capitalistic enterprise or in state communistic enterprise (of the midcentury variety), just as in the postfeudal army, bureaucratization entailed complete separation from the instruments of destruction. Typically, the worker no longer owns his tools nor the soldier, his weapons. And in this special sense, more and more people become workers, either blue collar or white collar or stiff shirt. So develops, for example, the new type of scientific worker, as the scientist is "separated" from his technical equipment—after all, the physicist does not ordinarily own his cyclotron. To work at his research, he must be employed by a bureaucracy with laboratory resources.

Bureaucracy is administration which almost completely avoids public discussion of its techniques, although there may occur public discussion of its policies.[5] This secrecy is confirmed neither to public nor to private bureaucracies. It is held to be necessary to keep valuable information from private economic competitors or from foreign and potentially hostile political groups. . . .

## THE DYSFUNCTIONS OF BUREAUCRACY

The transition to a study of the negative aspects of bureaucracy is afforded by the application of Veblen's concept of "trained incapacity," Dewey's notion of "occupational psychosis" or Warnotte's view of "professional deformation." Trained incapacity refers to that state of

affairs in which one's abilities function as inadequacies or blind spots. Actions based upon training and skills which have been successfully applied in the past may result in inappropriate responses *under changed conditions*. An inadequate flexibility in the application of skills, will, in a changing milieu, result in more or less serious maladjustments.[6] . . .

Dewey's concept of occupational psychosis rests upon much the same observations. As a result of their day to day routines, people develop special preferences, antipathies, discriminations and emphases.[7] (The term psychosis is used by Dewey to denote a "pronounced character of the mind.") These psychoses develop through demands put upon the individual by the particular organization of his occupational role. . . .

For reasons which we have already noted, the bureaucratic structure exerts a constant pressure upon the official to be "methodical, prudent, disciplined." If the bureaucracy is to operate successfully, it must attain a high degree of reliability of behavior, an unusual degree of conformity with prescribed patterns of action. Hence, the fundamental importance of discipline which may be as highly developed in a religious or economic bureaucracy as in the army. Discipline can be effective only if the ideal patterns are buttressed by strong sentiments which entail devotion to one's duties, a keen sense of the limitation of one's authority and competence, and methodical performance of routine activities. The efficacy of social structure depends ultimately upon infusing group participants with appropriate attitudes and sentiments. As we shall see, there are definite arrangements in the bureaucracy for inculcating and reinforcing these sentiments.

At the moment, it suffices to observe that in order to ensure discipline (the necessary reliability of response), these sentiments are often more intense than is technically necessary. There is a margin of safety, so to speak, in the pressure exerted by these sentiments upon the bureaucrat to conform to his patterned obligations, in much the same sense that added allowances (precautionary overestimations) are made by the engineer in designing the supports for a bridge. But this very emphasis leads to a transference of the sentiments from the *aims* of the organization onto the particular details of behavior required by the rules. Adherence to the rules, originally conceived as a means, becomes transformed into an end-in-itself; there occurs the familiar process of *displacement of goals* whereby "an instrumental value becomes a terminal value."[8] Discipline, readily interpreted as conformance with regulations, whatever the situation, is seen not as a measure designed for specific purposes but becomes an immediate value in the life-organization of the bureaucrat. This emphasis, resulting from the displacement of the original goals, develops into rigidities and an inability to adjust readily. Formalism, even ritualism, ensues with an unchallenged insistence upon punctilious adherence to formalized procedures.[9] This may be exaggerated to the point where primary concern with conformity to the rules interferes with the achievement of the purposes of the organization, in which case we have the familiar phenomenon of the technicism or red tape of the official. An extreme product of this process of displacement of goals is the bureaucratic virtuoso, who never forgets a single rule binding his action and hence is unable to assist many of his clients.[10] . . .

## STRUCTURAL SOURCES OF OVERCONFORMITY

Thus far, we have treated the ingrained sentiments making for rigorous discipline simply as data, as given. However,

definite features of the bureaucratic structure may be seen to conduce to these sentiments. The bureaucrat's official life is planned for him in terms of a graded career, through the organizational devices of promotion by seniority, pensions, incremental salaries, etc., all of which are designed to provide incentives for disciplined action and conformity to the official regulations.[11] The official is tacitly expected to and largely does adapt his thoughts, feelings and actions to the prospect of this career. But *these very devices* which increase the probability of conformance also lead to an over-concern with strict adherence to regulations which induces timidity, conservatism, and technicism. Displacement of sentiments from goals onto means is fostered by the tremendous symbolic significance of the means (rules).

Another feature of the bureaucratic structure tends to produce much the same result. Functionaries have the sense of a common destiny for all those who work together. They share the same interests, especially since there is relatively little competition in so far as promotion is in terms of seniority. In-group aggression is thus minimized and this arrangement is therefore conceived to be positively functional for the bureaucracy. However, the *esprit de corps* and informal social organization which typically develops in such situations often leads the personnel to defend their entrenched interests rather than to assist their clientele and elected higher officials. . . .

In a stimulating paper, Hughes has applied the concepts of "secular" and "sacred" to various types of division of labor; "the sacredness" of caste and *Stände* prerogatives contrasts sharply with the increasing secularism of occupational differentiation in our society.[12] However, as our discussion suggests, there may ensue, in particular vocations and in particular types of organization, the *process of sanctification* (viewed as the counterpart of the process of secularization). This is to say that through sentiment-formation, emotional dependence upon bureaucratic symbols and status, and affective involvement in spheres of competence and authority, there develop prerogatives involving attitudes of moral legitimacy which are established as values in their own right, and are no longer viewed as merely technical means for expediting administration. One may note a tendency for certain bureaucratic norms, originally introduced for technical reasons, to become rigidified and sacred, although, as Durkheim would say, they are *laïque en apparence*.[13] Durkheim has touched on this general process in his description of the attitudes and values which persist in the organic solidarity of a highly differentiated society.

## PRIMARY VERSUS SECONDARY RELATIONS

Another feature of the bureaucratic structure, the stress on depersonalization of relationships, also plays its part in the bureaucrat's trained incapacity. The personality pattern of the bureaucrat is nucleated about this norm of impersonality. Both this and the categorizing tendency, which develops from the dominant role of general, abstract rules, tend to produce conflict in the bureaucrat's contacts with the public or clientele. Since functionaries minimize personal relations and resort to categorization, the pecularities of individual cases are often ignored. But the client who, quite understandably, is convinced of the special features of *his* own problem often objects to such categorical treatment. Stereotyped behavior is not adapted to the exigencies of individual problems. The impersonal treatment of affairs which are at times of great personal significance

to the client gives rise to the charge of "arrogance" and "haughtiness" of the bureaucrat. . . .

Still another source of conflict with the public derives from the bureaucratic structure. The bureaucrat, in part irrespective of his position within the hierarchy, acts as a representative of the power and prestige of the entire structure. In his official role he is vested with definite authority. This often leads to an actually or apparently domineering attitude, which may only be exaggerated by a discrepancy between his position within the hierarchy and his position with reference to the public.[14] Protest and recourse to other officials on the part of the client are often ineffective or largely precluded by the previously mentioned *esprit de corps* which joins the officials into a more or less solidary in-group. This source of conflict *may* be minimized in private enterprise since the client can register an effective protest by transferring his trade to another organization within the competitive system. But with the monopolistic nature of the public organization, no such alternative is possible. Moreover, in this case, tension is increased because of a discrepancy between ideology and fact: the governmental personnel are held to be "servants of the people," but in fact they are often superordinate, and release of tension can seldom be afforded by turning to other agencies for the necessary service.[15] This tension is in part attributable to the confusion of the status of bureaucrat and client; the client may consider himself socially superior to the official who is at the moment dominant.[16]

. . . The conflict may be viewed, then, as deriving from the introduction of inappropriate attitudes and relationships. Conflict within the bureaucratic structure arises from the converse situation, namely, when personalized relationships are substituted for the structurally required impersonal relationships. This type of conflict may be characterized as follows.

The bureaucracy, as we have seen, is organized as a secondary, formal group. The normal responses involved in this organized network of social expectations are supported by affective attitudes of members of the group. Since the group is oriented toward secondary norms of impersonality, any failure to conform to these norms will arouse antagonism from those who have identified themselves with the legitimacy of these rules. Hence, the substitution of personal for impersonal treatment within the structure is met with widespread disapproval and is characterized by such epithets as graft, favoritism, neoptism, apple-polishing, etc. These epithets are clearly manifestations of injured sentiments.[17] The function of such virtually automatic resentment can be clearly seen in terms of the requirements of bureaucratic structure.

Bureaucracy is a secondary group structure designed to carry on certain activities which cannot be satisfactorily performed on the basis of primary group criteria.[18] Hence behavior which runs counter to these formalized norms becomes the object of emotionalized disapproval. This constitutes a functionally significant defence set up against tendencies which jeopardize the performance of socially necessary activities. . . .

## PROBLEMS FOR RESEARCH

A large number of specific questions invite our attention. To what extent are particular personality types selected and modified by the various bureaucracies (private enterprise, public service, the quasi-legal political machine, religious orders)? Inasmuch as ascendancy and submission are held to be traits of personality, despite their variability in different

stimulus-situations, do bureaucracies select personalities of particularly submissive or ascendant tendencies? And since various studies have shown that these traits can be modified, does participation in bureaucratic office tend to increase ascendant tendencies? Do various systems of recruitment (*e.g.*, patronage, open competition involving specialized knowledge or general mental capacity, practical experience) select different personality types?[19] Does promotion through seniority lessen competitive anxieties and enhance administrative efficiency? A detailed examination of mechanisms for imbuing the bureaucratic codes with affect would be instructive both sociologically and psychologically. Does the general anonymity of civil service decisions tend to restrict the area of prestige-symbols to a narrowly defined inner circle? Is there a tendency for differential association to be especially marked among bureaucrats?

The range of theoretically significant and practically important questions would seem to be limited only by the accessibility of the concrete data. . . .

## NOTES

1. Max Weber, *Wirtschaft und Gesellschaft* (Tübingen: J. C. B. Mohr, 1922), Pt. III, chap. 6; 650–678. For a brief summary of Weber's discussion, see Talcott Parsons, *The Structure of Social Action*, esp. 506 ff. For a description, which is not a caricature, of the bureaucrat as a personality type, see C. Rabany, "Les types sociaux: le fonctionnaire," *Revue générale d'administration* 88 (1907), 5–28.

2. Karl Mannheim, *Ideology and Utopia* (New York: Harcourt Brace Jovanovich, 1936), 18n., 105 ff. See also Ramsay Muir, *Peers and Bureaucrats* (London: Constable, 1910), 12–13.

3. E. G. Cahen-Salvador suggests that the personnel of bureaucracies is largely constituted by those who value security above all else. See his "La situation matérielle et

morale des fonctionnaires," *Revue politique et parlementaire* (1926), 319.

4. H. J. Laski, "Bureaucracy," *Encyclopedia of the Social Sciences*. This article is written primarily from the standpoint of the political scientist rather than that of the sociologist.

5. Weber, *op. cit.*, 671.

6. For a stimulating discussion and application of these concepts, see Kenneth Burke, *Permanence and Change* (New York: New Republic, 1935), pp. 50 ff.; Daniel Warnotte, "Bureaucratie et Fonctionnarisme," *Revue de l'Institut de Sociologie* 17 (1937), 245.

7. *Ibid.*, 58–59.

8. This process has often been observed in various connections. Wundt's *heterogony of ends* is a case in point; Max Weber's *Paradoxie der Folgen* is another. See also MacIver's observations on the transformation of civilization into culture and Lasswell's remark that "the human animal distinguishes himself by his infinite capacity for making ends of his means." See Merton, "The unanticipated consequences of purposive social action," *American Sociological Review* 1 (1936), 894–904. In terms of the psychological mechanisms involved, this process has been analyzed most fully by Gordon W. Allport, in his discussion of what he calls "the functional autonomy of motives." Allport emends the earlier formulations of Woodworth, Tolman, and William Stern, and arrives at a statement of the process from the standpoint of individual motivation. He does not consider those phases of the social structure which conduce toward the "transformation of motives." The formulation adopted in this paper is thus complementary to Allport's analysis; the one stressing the psychological mechanisms involved, the other considering the constraints of the social structure. The convergence of psychology and sociology toward this central concept suggests that it may well constitute one of the conceptual bridges between the two disciplines. See Gordon W. Allport, *Personality* (New York: Henry Holt & Co., 1937), chap. 7.

9. See E. C. Hughes, "Institutional office and the person," *American Journal of Sociology*, 43 (1937), 404–413; E. T. Hiller, "Social structure in relation to the person," *Social Forces* 16 (1937), 34–4.

10. Mannheim, *Ideology and Utopia*, 106.

11. Mannheim, *Mensch und Gesellschaft*, 32–33. Mannheim stresses the importance of the "Lebensplan" and the "Amtskarriere." See the comments by Hughes, *op. cit.*, 413.

12. E. C. Hughes, "Personality types and the division of labor," *American Journal of Sociology* 33 (1928), 754–768. Much the same distinction is drawn by Leopold von Wiese and Howard Becker, *Systematic Sociology* (New York: John Wiley & Sons, 1932), 22–25 et passim.

13. Hughes recognizes one phase of this process of sanctification when he writes that professional training "carries with it as a by-product assimilation of the candidate to a set of professional attitudes and controls, *a professional conscience and solidarity. The profession claims and aims to become a moral unit.*" Hughes, *op. cit.*, 762, (italics inserted). In this same connection, Sumner's concept of *pathos*, as the halo of sentiment which protects a social value from criticism, is particularly relevant, inasmuch as it affords a clue to the mechanism involved in the process of sanctification. See his *Folkways*, 180–181.

14. In this connection, note the relevance of Koffka's comments on certain features of the pecking-order of birds. "If one compares the behavior of the bird at the top of the pecking list, the despot, with that of one very far down, the second or third from the last, then one finds the latter much more cruel to the few others over whom he lords it than the former in this treatment of all members. As soon as one removes from the group all members above the penultimate, his behavior becomes milder and may even become very friendly. . . . It is not difficult to find analogies to this in human societies, and therefore one side of such behavior must be primarily the effects of the social groupings, and not of individual characteristics." K. Koffka, *Principles of Gestalt Psychology* (New York: Harcourt Brace Jovanovich, 1935), 668–9.

15. At this point the political machine often becomes functionally significant. As Steffens and others have shown, highly personalized relations and the abrogation of formal rules (red tape) by the machine often satisfy the needs of individual "clients" more fully than the formalized mechanism of governmental bureaucracy.

16. As one of the unemployed men remarked about the clerks at the Greenwich Employ-

ment Exchange: "'And the bloody blokes wouldn't have their jobs if it wasn't for us men out of a job either. That's what gets me about their holding their noses up.'" Bakke, *op. cit.*, 80. See also H. D. Lasswell and G. Almond, "Aggressive behavior by clients towards public relief administrators," *American Political Science Review* 28 (1934), 643–55.

17. The diagnostic significance of such linguistic indices as epithets has scarcely been explored by the sociologist. Sumner properly observes that epithets produce "summary criticisms" and definitions of social situations. Dollard also notes that "epithets frequently define the central issues in a society," and Sapir has rightly emphasized the importance of context of situations in appraising the significance of epithets. Of equal relevance is Linton's observation that "in case histories the way in which the community felt about a particular epi-

sode is, if anything, more important to our study than the actual behavior. . . ." A sociological study of "vocabularies of encomium and opprobrium" should lead to valuable findings.

18. *Cf.* Ellsworth Faris, *The Nature of Human Nature* (New York: McGraw-Hill, 1937), 41 ff.

19. Among recent studies of recruitment to bureaucracy are: Reinhard Bendix, *Higher Civil Servants in American Society* (Boulder: University of Colorado Press, 1949); Dwaine Marwick, *Career Perspectives in a Bureaucratic Setting* (Ann Arbor: University of Michigan Press, 1954); R. K. Kelsall, *Higher Civil Servants in Britain* (London: Routledge & Kegan Paul, 1955); W. L. Warner and J. C. Abegglen, *Occupational Mobility in American Business and Industry* (Minneapolis: University of Minnesota Press, 1955).

# 31

# Groupthink: The Desperate Drive for Consensus at Any Cost

*Irving L. Janis*

"How could we have been so stupid!" President John F. Kennedy asked after he and a close group of advisers had blundered into the Bay of Pigs invasion. For the last two years I have been studying that question, as it applies not only to the Bay of Pigs decision-makers but also to those who led the United States into such other major fiascos as the failure to be prepared for the attack on Pearl Harbor, the Korean War stalemate and the escalation of the Vietnam War.

Stupidity certainly is not the explanation. The men who participated in making the Bay of Pigs decision, for instance, comprised one of the greatest arrays of intellectual talent in the history of American Government—Dean Rusk, Robert McNamara, Douglas Dillon, Robert Kennedy, McGeorge Bundy, Arthur Schlesinger Jr., Allen Dulles and others.

It also seemed to me that explanations were incomplete if they concentrated only on disturbances in the behavior of each individual within a decision-making body: temporary emotional states of elation, fear, or anger that reduce a man's mental efficiency, for example, or chronic blind spots arising from a man's social prejudices or idiosyncratic biases.

I preferred to broaden the picture by looking at the fiascos from the standpoint of group dynamics as it has been explored over the past three decades, first by the great social psychologist Kurt Lewin and later in many experimental situations by myself and other behavioral scientists. My conclusion after poring over hundreds of relevant documents—historical reports about formal group meetings and informal conversations among the members—is that the groups that committed the fiascos were victims of what I call "groupthink."

"*Groupy*." In each case study, I was surprised to discover the extent to which each group displayed the typical phenomena of social conformity that are regularly encountered in studies of group dynamics among ordinary citizens. For example, some of the phenomena appear to be completely in line with findings from social-psychological experiments showing that powerful social pressures are brought to bear by the members of a cohesive group whenever a dissident begins to voice his objections to a group consensus. Other phenomena are reminiscent of the shared illusions observed in encounter groups and friendship cliques when the members simultaneously reach a peak of "groupy" feelings.

Above all, there are numerous indications pointing to the development of group norms that bolster morale at the expense of critical thinking. One of the most common norms appears to be that of remaining loyal to the group by sticking with the policies to which the group has already committed itself, even when

*Source:* Reprinted with permission from *Psychology Today Magazine*, Copyright © 1971 (Sussex Publishers, Inc.).

those policies are obviously working out badly and have unintended consequences that disturb the conscience of each member. This is one of the key characteristics of groupthink.

*1984.* I use the term groupthink as a quick and easy way to refer to the mode of thinking that persons engage in when *concurrence-seeking* becomes so dominant in a cohesive ingroup that it tends to override realistic appraisal of alternative courses of action. Groupthink is a term of the same order as the words in the newspeak vocabulary George Orwell used in his dismaying world of *1984.* In that context, groupthink takes on an invidious connotation. Exactly such a connotation is intended, since the term refers to a deterioration in mental efficiency, reality testing and moral judgments as a result of group pressures.

The symptoms of groupthink arise when the members of decision-making groups become motivated to avoid being too harsh in their judgments of their leaders' or their colleagues' ideas. They adopt a soft line of criticism, even in their own thinking. At their meetings, all the members are amiable and seek complete concurrence on every important issue, with no bickering or conflict to spoil the cozy, "we-feeling" atmosphere.

*Kill.* Paradoxically, soft-headed groups are often hard-hearted when it comes to dealing with outgroups or enemies. They find it relatively easy to resort to dehumanizing solutions—they will readily authorize bombing attacks that kill large numbers of civilians in the name of the noble cause of persuading an unfriendly government to negotiate at the peace table. They are unlikely to pursue the more difficult and controversial issues that arise when alternatives to a harsh military solution come up for discussion. Nor are they inclined to raise ethical issues that carry the implication that *this fine group of ours, with its humanitarianism and its high-minded principles, might be capable of adopting a course of action that is inhumane and immoral.*

*Norms.* There is evidence from a number of social-psychological studies that as the members of a group feel more accepted by the others, which is a central feature of increased group cohesiveness, they display less overt conformity to group norms. Thus we would expect that the more cohesive a group becomes, the less the members will feel constrained to censor what they say out of fear of being socially punished for antagonizing the leader or any of their fellow members.

In contrast, the groupthink type of conformity tends to increase as group cohesiveness increases. Groupthink involves nondeliberate suppression of critical thoughts as a result of internalization of the group's norms, which is quite different from deliberate suppression on the basis of external threats of social punishment. The more cohesive the group, the greater the inner compulsion on the part of each member to avoid creating disunity, which inclines him to believe in the soundness of whatever proposals are promoted by the leader or by a majority of the group's members.

In a cohesive group, the danger is not so much that each individual will fail to reveal his objections to what the others propose but that he will think the proposal is a good one, without attempting to carry out a careful, critical scrutiny of the pros and cons of the alternatives. When groupthink becomes dominant, there also is considerable suppression of deviant thoughts, but it takes the form of each person's deciding that his misgivings are not relevant and should be set aside, that the benefit of the doubt regarding any lingering uncertainties should be given to the group consensus.

*Stress.* I do not mean to imply that all cohesive groups necessarily suffer from groupthink. All ingroups may have a mild tendency toward groupthink, displaying one or another of the symptoms from time to time, but it need not be so dominant as to influence the quality of the group's final decision. Neither do I mean to imply that there is anything necessarily inefficient or harmful about group decisions in general. On the contrary, a group whose members have properly defined roles, with traditions concerning the procedures to follow in pursuing a critical inquiry, probably is capable of making better decisions than any individual group member working alone.

The problem is that the advantages of having decisions made by groups are often lost because of powerful psychological pressures that arise when the members work closely together, share the same set of values and, above all, face a crisis situation that puts everyone under intense stress.

The main principle of groupthink, which I offer in the spirit of Parkinson's Law, is this: *The more amiability and esprit de corps there is among the members of a policy-making ingroup, the greater the danger that independent critical thinking will be replaced by groupthink, which is likely to result in irrational and dehumanizing actions directed against outgroups.*

Symptoms. In my studies of high-level governmental decision-makers, both civilian and military, I have found eight main symptoms of groupthink.

1. INVULNERABILITY. Most or all of the members of the ingroup share an illusion of invulnerability that provides for them some degree of reassurance about obvious dangers and leads them to become over-optimistic and willing to take extraordinary risks. It also causes them to fail to respond to clear warnings of danger.

The Kennedy ingroup, which uncritically accepted the Central Intelligence Agency's disastrous Bay of Pigs plan, operated on the false assumption that they could keep secret the fact that the United States was responsible for the invasion of Cuba. Even after news of the plan began to leak out, their belief remained unshaken. They failed even to consider the danger that awaited them: a worldwide revulsion against the U.S. . . .

2. RATIONALE. As we see, victims of groupthink ignore warnings; they also collectively construct rationalizations in order to discount warnings and other forms of negative feedback that, taken seriously, might lead the group members to reconsider their assumptions each time they recommit themselves to past decisions. Why did the Johnson ingroup avoid reconsidering its escalation policy when time and again the expectations on which they based their decisions turned out to be wrong? James C. Thompson, Jr., a Harvard historian who spent five years as an observing participant in both the State Department and the White House, tells us that the policymakers avoided critical discussion of their prior decisions and continually invented new rationalizations so that they could sincerely recommit themselves to defeating the North Vietnamese.

In the fall of 1964, before the bombing of North Vietnam began, some of the policymakers predicted that six weeks of air strikes would induce the North Vietnamese to seek peace talks. When someone asked, "What if they don't?" the answer was that another four weeks certainly would do the trick. . . .

3. MORALITY. Victims of groupthink believe unquestioningly in the inherent morality of their ingroup; this belief inclines the members to ignore the ethical or moral consequences of their decisions.

Evidence that this symptom is at work usually is of a negative kind—the things that are left unsaid in group meetings. At least two influential persons had doubts about the morality of the Bay of Pigs adventure. One of them, Arthur Schlesinger Jr., presented his strong objections in a memorandum to President Kennedy and Secretary of State Rusk but suppressed them when he attended meetings of the Kennedy team. The other, Senator J. William Fulbright, was not a member of the group, but the President invited him to express his misgivings in a speech to the policymakers. However, when Fulbright finished speaking the President moved on to other agenda items without asking for reactions of the group.

David Kraslow and Stuart H. Loory, in *The Secret Search for Peace in Vietnam*, report that during 1966 President Johnson's ingroup was concerned primarily with selecting bomb targets in North Vietnam. They based their selections on four factors—the military advantage, the risk to American aircraft and pilots, the danger of forcing other countries into the fighting, and the danger of heavy civilian casualties. At their regular Tuesday luncheons, they weighed these factors the way school teachers grade examination papers, averaging them out. Though evidence on this point is scant, I suspect that the group's ritualistic adherence to a standardized procedure induced the members to feel morally justified in their destructive way of dealing with the Vietnamese people—after all, the danger of heavy civilian casualties from U.S. air strikes was taken into account on their checklists.

4. STEREOTYPES. Victims of groupthink hold stereotyped views of the leaders of enemy groups: they are so evil that genuine attempts at negotiating differences with them are unwarranted, or they are too weak or too stupid to deal effectively with whatever attempts the ingroup makes to defeat their purposes, no matter how risky the attempts are.

Kennedy's groupthinkers believed that Premier Fidel Castro's air force was so ineffectual that obsolete B-26s could knock it out completely in a surprise attack before the invasion began. They also believed that Castro's army was so weak that a small Cuban-exile brigade could establish a well-protected beachhead at the Bay of Pigs. In addition, they believed that Castro was not smart enough to put down any possible internal uprisings in support of the exiles. They were wrong on all three assumptions. Though much of the blame was attributable to faulty intelligence, the point is that none of Kennedy's advisers even questioned the CIA planners about these assumptions. . . .

5. PRESSURE. Victims of groupthink apply direct pressure to any individual who momentarily expresses doubts about any of the group's shared illusions or who questions the validity of the arguments supporting a policy alternative favored by the majority. This gambit reinforces the concurrence-seeking norm that loyal members are expected to maintain.

President Kennedy probably was more active than anyone else in raising skeptical questions during the Bay of Pigs meetings, and yet he seems to have encouraged the group's docile, uncritical acceptance of defective arguments in favor of the CIA's plan. At every meeting, he allowed the CIA representatives to dominate the discussion. He permitted them to give their immediate refutations in response to each tentative doubt that one of the others expressed, instead of asking whether anyone shared the doubt or wanted to pursue the implications of the new worrisome issue that had just been raised. And at the most crucial meeting, when he was calling on each member to give his vote for or against the plan, he did not call on Arthur Schlesinger, the one man there who was known by the President to have serious misgivings.

Historian Thomson informs us that whenever a member of Johnson's in-group began to express doubts, the group used subtle social pressures to "domesticate" him. To start with, the dissenter was made to feel at home provided that he lived up to two restrictions: 1) that he did not voice his doubts to outsiders, which would play into the hands of the opposition; and 2) that he kept his criticisms within the bounds of acceptable deviation, which meant not challenging any of the fundamental assumptions that went into the group's prior commitments. One such "domesticated dissenter" was Bill Moyers. When Moyers arrived at a meeting, Thomson tells us, the President greeted him with, "Well, here comes Mr. Stop-the-Bombing."

6. SELF-CENSORSHIP. Victims of groupthink avoid deviating from what appears to be group consensus; they keep silent about their misgivings and even minimize to themselves the importance of their doubts.

As we have seen, Schlesinger was not at all hesitant about presenting his strong objections to the Bay of Pigs plan in a memorandum to the President and the Secretary of State. But he became keenly aware of his tendency to suppress objections at the White House meetings. "In the months after the Bay of Pigs, I bitterly reproached myself for having kept so silent during those crucial discussions in the cabinet room," Schlesinger writes in *A Thousand Days*, "I can only explain my failure to do more than raise a few timid questions by reporting that one's impulse to blow the whistle on this nonsense was simply undone by the circumstances of the discussion."

7. UNANIMITY. Victims of groupthink share an illusion of unanimity within the group concerning almost all judgments expressed by members who speak in favor of the majority view. This symptom results partly from the preceding one,

whose effects are augmented by the false assumption that any individual who remains silent during any part of the discussion is in full accord with what the others are saying.

When a group of persons who respect each other's opinions arrives at a unanimous view, each member is likely to feel that the belief must be true. This reliance on consensual validation within the group tends to replace individual critical thinking and reality testing, unless there are clear-cut disagreements among the members. In contemplating a course of action such as the invasion of Cuba, it is painful for the members to confront disagreements within their group, particularly if it becomes apparent that there are widely divergent views about whether the preferred course of action is too risky to undertake at all. Such disagreements are likely to arouse anxieties about making a serious error. Once the sense of unanimity is shattered, the members no longer can feel complacently confident about the decision they are inclined to make. Each man must then face the annoying realization that there are troublesome uncertainties and he must diligently seek out the best information he can get in order to decide for himself exactly how serious the risks might be. This is one of the unpleasant consequences of being in a group of hardheaded, critical thinkers.

To avoid such an unpleasant state, the members often become inclined, without quite realizing it, to prevent latent disagreements from surfacing when they are about to initiate a risky course of action. The group leader and the members support each other in playing up the areas of convergence in their thinking, at the expense of fully exploring divergencies that might reveal unsettled issues. . . .

8. MINDGUARDS. Victims of groupthink sometimes appoint themselves as

mindguards to protect the leader and fellow members from adverse information that might break the complacency they shared about the effectiveness and morality of past decisions. At a large birthday party for his wife, Attorney General Robert F. Kennedy, who had been constantly informed about the Cuban invasion plan, took Schlesinger aside and asked him why he was opposed. Kennedy listened coldly and said, "You may be right or you may be wrong, but the President has made his mind up. Don't push it any further. Now is the time for everyone to help him all they can. . . ."

*Products.* When a group of executives frequently displays most or all of these interrelated symptoms, a detailed study of their deliberations is likely to reveal a number of immediate consequences. These consequences are, in effect, products of poor decision-making practices because they lead to inadequate solutions to the problems under discussion.

First, the group limits its discussions to a few alternative courses of action (often only two) without an initial survey of all the alternatives that might be worthy of consideration.

Second, the group fails to reexamine the course of action initially preferred by the majority after they learn of risks and drawbacks they had not considered originally.

Third, the members spend little or no time discussing whether there are nonobvious gains they may have overlooked or ways of reducing the seemingly prohibitive costs that made rejected alternatives appear undesirable to them.

Fourth, members make little or no attempt to obtain information from experts within their own organizations who might be able to supply more precise estimates of potential losses and gains.

Fifth, members show positive interest in facts and opinions that support their preferred policy, they tend to ignore facts and opinions that do not.

Sixth, members spend little time deliberating about how the chosen policy might be hindered by bureaucratic inertia, sabotaged by political opponents, or temporarily derailed by common accidents. Consequently, they fail to work out contingency plans to cope with foreseeable setbacks that could endanger the overall success of their chosen course.

*Support.* The search for an explanation of why groupthink occurs has led me through a quagmire of complicated theoretical issues in the murky area of human motivation. My belief, based on recent social psychological research, is that we can best understand the various symptoms of groupthink as a mutual effort among the group members to maintain self-esteem and emotional equanimity by providing social support to each other, especially at times when they share responsibility for making vital decisions.

Even when no important decision is pending, the typical administrator will begin to doubt the wisdom and morality of his past decisions each time he receives information about setbacks, particularly if the information is accompanied by negative feedback from prominent men who originally had been his supporters. It should not be surprising, therefore, to find that individual members strive to develop unanimity and esprit de corps that will help bolster each other's morale, to create an optimistic outlook about the success of pending decisions, and to reaffirm the positive value of past policies to which all of them are committed.

*Pride.* Shared illusions of invulnerability, for example, can reduce anxiety about taking risks. Rationalizations help members believe that the risks are really not so bad after all. The assumption of inherent morality helps the members to avoid feelings of shame or guilt. Negative stereotypes function as stress-reducing devices to enhance a sense of moral righteousness as well as pride in a lofty mission.

The mutual enhancement of self-esteem and morale may have functional value in enabling the members to maintain their capacity to take action, but it has maladaptive consequences insofar as concurrence-seeking tendencies interfere with critical, rational capacities and lead to serious errors of judgment. . . .

*Remedies.* To counterpoint my case studies of the major fiascos, I have also investigated two highly successful group enterprises, the formulation of the Marshall Plan in the Truman Administration and the handling of the Cuban missile crisis by President Kennedy and his advisers. I have found it instructive to examine the steps Kennedy took to change his group's decision-making processes. These changes ensured that the mistakes made by his Bay of Pigs ingroup were not repeated by the missile-crisis ingroup, even though the membership of both groups was essentially the same.

The following recommendations for preventing groupthink incorporate many of the good practices I discovered to be characteristic of the Marshall Plan and missile crisis groups:

1. The leader of a policy-forming group should assign the role of critical evaluator to each member, encouraging the group to give high priority to open airing of objections and doubts. This practice needs to be reinforced by the leader's acceptance of criticism of his own judgments in order to discourage members from soft-pedaling their disagreements and from allowing their striving for concurrence to inhibit critical thinking.

2. When the key members of a hierarchy assign a policy-planning mission to any group within their organization, they should adopt an impartial stance instead of stating preferences and expectations at the beginning. This will encourage open inquiry and impartial probing of a wide range of policy alternatives.

3. The organization routinely should set up several outside policy-planning and evaluation groups to work on the same policy question, each deliberating under a different leader. This can prevent the insulation of an ingroup.

4. At intervals before the group reaches a final consensus, the leader should require each member to discuss the group's deliberations with associates in his own unit of the organization— assuming that those associates can be trusted to adhere to the same security regulations that govern the policymakers—and then to report back their reactions to the group.

5. The group should invite one or more outside experts to each meeting on a staggered basis and encourage the experts to challenge the views of the core members.

6. At every general meeting of the group, whenever the agenda calls for an evaluation of policy alternatives, at least one member should play devil's advocate, functioning as a good lawyer in challenging the testimony of those who advocate the majority position.

7. Whenever the policy issue involves relations with a rival nation or organization, the group should devote a sizable block of time, perhaps an entire session, to a survey of all warning signals from the rivals and should write alternative scenarios on the rivals' intentions.

8. When the group is surveying policy alternatives for feasibility and effectiveness, it should from time to time divide into two or more subgroups to meet separately under different chairmen, and then come back together to hammer out differences.

9. After reaching a preliminary consensus about what seems to be the best policy, the group should hold a "second-chance" meeting at which every member expresses as vividly as he can all his residual doubts, and rethinks the entire issue before making a definitive choice.

*How.* These recommendations have their disadvantages. To encourage the open airing of objections, for instance, might lead to prolonged and costly debates when a rapidly growing crisis requires immediate solution. It also could cause rejection, depression and anger. A leader's failure to set a norm might create cleavage between leader and members that could develop into a disruptive power struggle if the leader looks on the emerging consensus as anathema. Setting up outside evaluation groups might increase the risk of security leakage. Still, inventive executives who know their way around the organizational maze probably can figure out how to apply one or another of the prescriptions successfully, without harmful side effects. . . .

In this era of atomic warheads, urban disorganization and ecocatastrophes, it seems to me that policymakers should collaborate with behavioral scientists and give top priority to preventing groupthink and its attendant fiascos.

# 32
# Social Influences on Work Effectiveness

*Lyman W. Porter, Edward E. Lawler III,*
*& J. Richard Hackman*

## CONDITIONS WITHIN GROUPS THAT MODERATE THEIR IMPACT ON WORK EFFECTIVENESS

Before proceeding to consider (in the next section) the ways that groups can influence the work effectiveness of individuals, we should first take into account certain conditions within groups that can affect how much and what kind of impact they will have. Uppermost among these are a group's characteristic reactions to deviance and the degree of cohesiveness that exists within the group.

### Deviance and Group Effectiveness

The experimental work on how groups react to members who engage in behaviors which are inconsistent with group norms . . . reveals a fairly primitive type of group process. Caricatured a bit, the process operates as follows: Uniformity, conformity to norms, and adherence to one's role is the rule. When someone steps out of line, other members provide him with potent doses of discretionary stimuli designed to persuade or coerce him back to "normal." This pressure continues until the would-be deviant (1) gives in and ceases expressing his deviant thoughts or exhibiting his deviant behavior; (2) is psychologically or bodily rejected by the group or becomes

institutionalized by the group as the "house deviant"; or (3) finally convinces the other group members of the rightness of his thoughts or the appropriateness of his behavior.

The more the group has control of discretionary stimuli which are important to group members, the more it can effectively eliminate most appearances of deviance on the part of its members. The members, in such circumstances, may faithfully behave in accord with their roles in the group, refrain from violating group norms, and express their endorsement of the "right" attitudes and beliefs. And from all visible indicators, at least in the short term, everything seems well with the group.

### Dysfunctional Aspects of Eliminating Deviance from Group Norms

It can be argued, however, that this pattern of dealing with deviance is highly dysfunctional for the long-term effectiveness of a group, for at least two reasons (Hackman, 1975). First, if members comply primarily because of the application of pressure from the group (or the expected application of that pressure), the result may be public compliance *at the expense of* private acceptance and personal commitment to what is being done (cf. Kelman, 1961; Kiesler, 1969; pp. 279–295). And when a group is heavily populated by individuals who are saying

*Source:* Lyman W. Porter, Edward E. Lawler III, and J. Richard Hackman, "Social Influences on Work Effectiveness." Pages 404–422 in Porter, Lawler and Hackman, *Behavior in Organizations* (McGraw-Hill, 1975). Reprinted by permission of the publisher.

and doing one thing but thinking and feeling another, high effectiveness in the long haul is unlikely.

Second, to the extent that a group uses its control of discretionary stimuli to swiftly extinguish any signs of deviance, it loses the opportunity to explore the usefulness and ultimate validity of the very attitudes, beliefs, norms and roles it is enforcing. For example, if compliance to a given norm about work behavior is enforced so effectively that deviance from that norm virtually never occurs, the group will be unable to discover whether that norm is actually helpful or detrimental to the achievement of the goals of the group. In essence, it may be that an unexamined norm is not worth enforcing—at least if high group effectiveness is aspired to in the long run.

Despite these and other dysfunctions of excessive pressures against deviance, the research literature suggests that groups have a strong tendency to stamp out (or at least sweep under the rug) behaviors which are not congruent with traditional standards of acceptability in the group. Apparently groups rarely attempt to work through the more basic problems of why people deviate from the group, what the consequences of such deviance for the group are, and how deviance can be most effectively dealt with for the good of both individual members and the group as a whole. . . .

It is emotionally quite stressful and difficult for group members to deal openly with core questions of conformity, deviation, and interpersonal relationships in a group. Indeed, research (Bion, 1959; Argyris, 1969) suggests that it may be impossible for a group to break out of a traditional pattern of interpersonal behavior without outside professional assistance. Even with such assistance, it may take a great deal of time and effort before a group can overcome the basic assumptions which guided its

early behavior and develop into an effective and truly interdependent work group (Bion, 1959). When a group becomes able to make more open and conscious choices about the use of those discretionary stimuli under its control to deal with issues of conformity and deviance, the long-term effectiveness of the group should be greatly enhanced.

## Why High Group Cohesiveness Can Be Dysfunctional

In general, as the cohesiveness of a work group increases, the overall level of member conformity to the norms of the group would also be expected to increase—for two different but mutually reinforcing reasons: First, . . . there tend to be stronger group-generated pressures toward uniformity and conformity in groups which are highly cohesive than in groups which are not (cf. Festinger et al., 1950). And second, group members are likely to value especially strongly the interpersonal rewards which are available in highly cohesive groups—precisely because of the strong positive feelings members have for one another in such groups. Therefore, group members are unlikely to risk losing those rewards by ignoring or defying pressures to conform to group norms. And, in fact, research evidence confirms that conformity is especially high in cohesive groups (cf. Tajfel, 1969; pp. 334–347; Lott & Lott, 1965, pp. 292–296; Hackman, 1975).

The problem is that conformity to group norms which occurs in highly cohesive groups may *not* be functional for group or individual productivity. Indeed, cohesiveness may be strongly dysfunctional for effectiveness in some situations for several reasons, which are discussed below.

*Deviance Is Dealt with Ineffectively.* As noted previously, groups tend in general to stamp out deviant behavior on the part of individual group members—

rather than use such deviance to increase either the learning of individual group members or the capability of the group as a whole to respond effectively to a changing or turbulent state of affairs. Since pressures toward uniformity are highest in highly cohesive groups, the risk of quick and ill-considered elimination of all appearances of deviance in the group also are likely to be highest in cohesive groups—even though exploration of such deviant behaviors might actually be helpful to the group in the long run.

*Norms Are Strong, but Their Direction May Be Negative.* While it is generally true that cohesive groups are able to effectively control members such that their behavior closely approximates that specified by the group norm, the *direction* of the group norm itself (i.e., toward high versus low performance) has been found to be unrelated to the level of cohesiveness (Schachter et al., 1951; Berkowitz, 1954; Seashore, 1954; Darley et al., 1952).

For example, in several studies (e.g., Schachter et al., 1951; Berkowitz, 1954) conditions of high versus low cohesiveness and high- versus low-productivity norms were created by experimental manipulation. It was found that member productivity was indeed closer to the group norm in the high- than in the low-cohesiveness groups—for both the high- *and* the low-production norms. There have been similar findings in industrial situation using survey techniques (Seashore, 1954). In this study of over 200 work groups in a machinery factory, no correlation was found between cohesiveness and productivity—but, as would be expected, when cohesiveness was high, the amount of *variation* in the productivity of group members was low, and vice versa.

*Groupthink May Develop.* One of the seeming advantages of having a great

deal of uniformity or conformity in a group is that members do not have to deal with the thorny interpersonal problems which can arise when members behave in nonuniform ways—e.g., when each member of a work group is allowed to select his own level of production and the levels selected turn out to vary a good deal from member to member. This "group-maintenance" function of uniformity may be especially important to members of highly cohesive groups, since members of such groups typically value strongly the rewards controlled by their fellows—and would be particularly upset to receive negative interpersonal reactions from them.

It has been suggested, however, that as a group becomes excessively close-knit and develops a strong feeling of "we-ness," it becomes susceptible to a pattern of behavior known as "groupthink" (Janis, 1972). Among the several symptoms of groupthink are an excessive concern with maintaining uniformity among members, a marked decrease in the openness of the group to discrepant or unsettling information (from sources either inside or outside the group), and a simultaneous unwillingness to examine seriously and process such negative information if it ever is brought to the attention of the group.

These social processes may often serve immediate group-maintenance functions and help perpetuate the warm and cohesive feelings which characterize the group. In addition, however, they result in an increased likelihood that the group, in a spirit of goodwill and shared confidence, will develop and implement a course of action which is grossly inappropriate and ineffective. It has been shown (Janis, 1972), for example, how the groupthink phenomenon may have contributed substantially to a number of historical fiascoes planned and executed by groups of government officials (e.g., the Bay of Pigs invasion and Britain's appeasement policy toward Hitler prior to World War II).

## Should Cohesiveness Be Avoided?

It might appear from the above discussion that high cohesiveness of groups in organizations is something that should be avoided—to minimize the possibility of enforced low-production norms in work settings or the likelihood that groupthink-like phenomena will develop among decision makers. Such a conclusion would be a very pessimistic one: low cohesiveness among members of work groups or decision-making groups would indeed lower the possibility of obtaining the negative outcomes mentioned but also would require that the positive potential of cohesive groups be forgone as well—such as the increased capability of such groups to regulate behavior so as to *increase* the attainment of group and organizational goals.

The question, then, becomes how the norms of highly cohesive groups can be changed such that they encourage careful examination of the task environment (including negative or unsettling information which may be present), exploration of interpersonal issues, which may be impairing group performance, and high rather than low levels of group and member productivity. Although presently little is known about what factors affect the kinds of norms developed by work groups in organizations (cf. Vroom, 1969, pp. 226–227), two general approaches to the problem are discussed briefly below.

*Fostering Intergroup Competition.* One frequently espoused tactic for developing simultaneously high work-group cohesiveness and commitment to organizational goals can be referred to as the "best damn group in the whole damn organization ploy." Many managers realize that if they can get their subordinates, as a group, to experience themselves in competition with other groups in the organization, a kind of team spirit often develops which results in high group cohesiveness and great member commitment to be the "best" in whatever it is that defines the competition. And, in fact, there is considerable research evidence that when groups enter into competitive relationships with other groups, internal cohesiveness and high individual task commitment do increase—often dramatically (cf. Sherif, 1965; Blake & Mouton, 1964).

The problem is that such intergroup competitiveness often actually works against the best interests of the total organization in the long run. For example, in the interest of "winning," information which really should be shared *among* groups for optimal organizational functioning often is withheld—and at times even misinformation is communicated up and down the line in a way intended to make sure that "our group looks best." The pervasive line-staff and interdepartment (e.g., sales versus production) conflicts in contemporary organizations often reflect exactly this type of intergroup competition.

One common means of attempting to overcome such problems of dysfunctional intergroup competition within organizations (while maintaining high commitment within groups) is to introduce or make especially salient a superordinate goal which all groups share. Research evidence does support the idea that a superordinate goal can reduce or eliminate hostilities between groups (Sherif, 1965). And, in fact, many business organizations use the idea of the superordinate goal in their attempts to get employees in diverse groups to pull together for the good of the organization as a whole—for example, by prominently posting the number of trunkets sold this month by one's own company versus the number sold by the chief competitor. The problem, of course, is that it is not likely that a lower-level employee who hates his job and feels he is grossly and unfairly underpaid is going to *care* very much about whether or not his own organization is ahead in the trunket-selling competition—regardless of the attempts of the company employee-relations department to make that competition an organizing theme of the company.

*Basing Cohesiveness on Task Rather Than Social Rewards.* It may be that one of the major reasons for the failure of many cohesive groups to work as effectively as they might toward group and organizational goals has to do with the basis of the cohesiveness itself—i.e., the reasons why the group members have a strong desire to stick together.

In virtually all the research which has been discussed here, cohesiveness was based upon the *interpersonal rewards* present or potentially present in the group. The "stake" of most group members in such situations, then, would be to refrain from behaviors that might disrupt the interpersonal satisfactions which are obtained from group membership. The control of the group over its members in such cases rests largely upon its capability to provide or withhold such valued social satisfactions. In the groupthink situation, for example, such control results in interpersonal strategies characterized by lessened vigilance for new and potentially disruptive information, acceptance of the views of "high-status others" as the doctrine of the group, and suppression of any interpersonal unpleasantries—all of which can severely impair the work effectiveness of the group.

If the basis for the cohesiveness were a shared commitment to the *task* of the group (instead of a commitment to

maintaining the interpersonal rewards received in the group), the picture might change considerably. The criterion for when to accept information and direction from others in the group, for example, might change from something like "Will questioning what is being said by the leader risk my being rejected or ridiculed by the group?" to "Will such questioning contribute to our succeeding in the task?" Conformity, then, should remain high in such groups, but the norms to which conformity is enforced would focus on facilitating the group's task performance activities rather than on maintaining interpersonal comfortableness. This change in orientation also would bear on the question of the *direction* of norms for individual production in work groups: if one of the major reasons for the cohesiveness of the group were a shared commitment to succeeding in the task, then that commitment should in most cases lead to group norms oriented toward high rather than low task effectiveness. . . .

The problem in attempting to develop task-based cohesiveness in real-world work groups is twofold. First, many tasks (and perhaps most production tasks) in organizations are not such as to generate genuine group commitment. Instead, the reverse may often be true: the task may be so uninteresting that the group accepts as an alternative a task of "getting" management or of avoiding hard work. In such cases, the power resident in the group cohesiveness may be exceptionally dysfunctional for organizational goals. Second, it is quite difficult, even for objectively important tasks, for group members to overcome their orientation to interpersonal rewards and rejections. The group of Kennedy advisors during the Bay of Pigs crisis, for example, certainly had an important task; but the heavy investment of each member toward remaining a member of the high-status, high-prestige group apparently was so strong that "not rocking the interpersonal boat" overwhelmed "doing the task well" as a behavioral criterion for most group members.

Thus, while there appears to be much to be said for the development of tasks which can provide a strong positive basis for group cohesiveness, few guidelines for designing such tasks currently exist. The crux of the problem, it seems, is to create conditions such that the rewards from genuinely shared task activities become as salient and as attractive to group members as are the more skin-surface interpersonal satisfactions, which, unfortunately, currently typify relationships within most "cohesive" groups in organizations.

## WAYS GROUPS INFLUENCE INDIVIDUAL WORK EFFECTIVENESS

Now we are in a position to turn to the question of how groups can in fact have an impact on how hard and how well their members work. . . . The major direct determinants of the work behavior of organization members can be summarized in terms of four major classes of variables:

1. The job-relevant knowledge and skills of the individual
2. The level of psychological arousal the individual experiences while working
3. The performance strategies the individual uses doing his work
4. The level of effort the individual exerts in doing his work

Which (or which combination) of the four classes of variables can contribute substantially to increased individual work *effectiveness*, of course, very much depends upon the nature of the task or job being performed. On a routine and simple clerical job, for example, where the sole performance criterion is quantity of acceptable output, only effort is likely to be of real importance in influencing measured work effectiveness. On a more complex job, where there are many ways to go about performing it (e.g., most managerial jobs), the performance *strategies* used may critically influence effectiveness. For yet other jobs, arousal and/or the job-relevant skills of the individual may be critical.* . . .

## Group Influences by Affecting Member Knowledge and Skills

Performance on many tasks and jobs in organizations is strongly affected by the job-relevant knowledge and skills of the individuals who do the work. Thus, even if an employee has both high commitment toward accomplishing a particular piece of work and a well-formed strategy about how to go about doing it, the implementation of that plan can be constrained or terminated if he does not know how to carry it out, or if he knows how but is incapable of doing so. While ability is relevant to the performance of jobs at all levels in an organization, its impact probably is somewhat reduced for lower-level jobs. The reason is that such jobs often are not demanding of high skill levels. Further, to the extent that organizational selection, placement, and promotion practices are adequate, *all* jobs should tend to be occupied by individuals who possess the skills requisite for adequate performance.

---

* The characteristics of tasks or jobs which identify which classes of variables are of most importance in determining work effectiveness have been termed "critical task contingencies," i.e., those contingencies which specify what behaviors are critical to effective or successful performance for the job in question. Depending upon what the critical task contingencies are for a given task or job, it is possible to determine on an a priori basis which variables must be dealt with in any attempt to improve performance effectiveness on that job. This notion is developed more completely by Hackman (1975).

. . . The impact of groups on member performance effectiveness by improving member knowledge and skill probably is one of the lesser influences groups can have—both because employees on many jobs tend already to have many or all of the skills needed to perform them effectively and because there are other sources for improving skills which may be more useful and more potent than the work group, such as formal job training programs and self-study programs.

## Group Influences by Affecting Member Arousal Level

It was shown in the last chapter how a group can substantially influence the level of psychological arousal experienced by a member—through the mere presence of the other group members and by those others sending the individual messages which are directly arousal-enhancing or arousal-depressing. The conditions under which such group-promoted changes in arousal level will lead to increased performance effectiveness, however, very much depend upon the type of task being worked on (Zajonc, 1965).

In this case, the critical characteristics of the job have to do with whether the initially *dominant task responses* of the individual are likely to be correct or incorrect. Since the individual's output of such responses is facilitated when he is in an aroused state, arousal should improve performance effectiveness on well-learned tasks (so-called performance tasks) in which the dominant response is correct and needs merely to be executed by the performer. By the same token, arousal should impair effectiveness for new or unfamiliar tasks (learning tasks) in which the dominant response is likely to be incorrect. . . .

Groups can, of course, increase member arousal in ways other than taking an evaluative stance toward the individual.

Strongly positive, encouraging statements also should increase arousal in some performance situations—for example, by helping the individual become personally highly committed to the group goal, and making sure he realizes that he is a very important part of the team responsible for reaching that goal. What must be kept in mind, however, is that such devices represent a double-edged sword: while they may facilitate effective performance for well-learned tasks, they may have the opposite effect for new and unfamiliar tasks.

What, then, can be said about the effects on performance of group members when their presence (and interaction) serves to *decrease* the level of arousal of the group member—as, for example, when individuals coalesce into groups under conditions of high stress? When the other members of the group are a source of support, comfort, or acceptance to the individual (and serve to decrease his arousal level), it would be predicted that performance effectiveness would follow a pattern exactly opposite to that described above: the group would impair effectiveness for familiar or well-learned performance tasks (because arousal helps on these tasks, and arousal is being lowered) and facilitate effectiveness for unfamiliar or complicated learning tasks (because in this case arousal is harmful, and it is being lowered).

. . . As the group becomes increasingly threatening, evaluative, or strongly encouraging, effectiveness should increase for performance tasks and decrease for learning tasks. When the group is experienced as increasingly supportive, comforting, or unconditionally accepting, effectiveness should decrease for performance tasks and increase for learning tasks. And when no meaningful relationship at all is experienced by the individual between himself and the group, performance should not be affected. While some of these predictions have been tested and confirmed in small group experimental settings, others await research. . . .

It is well known that overly routine jobs can decrease a worker's level of arousal to such an extent that his performance effectiveness is impaired. It seems quite possible, therefore, that the social environment of workers on such jobs can be designed so as to compensate partially for the deadening effects of the job itself and thereby lead to an increment in performance on well-learned tasks.

Finally (as discussed in a subsequent section), the supervisor probably has a more powerful effect on the level of arousal of a worker than any other single individual in his immediate social environment. By close supervision (which usually results in the worker's feeling more or less constantly evaluated) supervisors can and do increase the level of arousal experienced by workers. While this may, for routine jobs, have some potential for improving performance effectiveness, it also is quite likely that the worker's negative reactions to being closely supervised ultimately will result in his attention being diverted from the job itself and focused instead on ways he can either get out from "under the gun" of the supervisor or somehow get back at the supervisor to punish him for his unwanted close supervision.

## Group Influences by Affecting Level of Member Effort and Member Performance Strategies

The level of effort a person exerts in doing his work and the performance strategies he follows are treated together here because both variables are largely under the performer's *voluntary* control.

*Direct Versus Indirect Influences on Effort and Strategy.* Throughout this book we have used a general "expectancy the-

ory" approach to analyze those aspects of a person's behavior in organizations which are under his voluntary control. From this perspective, a person's choices about his effort and work strategy can be viewed as hinging largely upon (1) his *expectations* regarding the likely consequences of his choices and (2) the degree to which he *values* those expected consequences. Following this approach, it becomes clear that the group can have both a direct and an indirect effect on the level of effort a group member exerts at his job and his choices about performance strategy.

The *direct* impact of the group on effort and strategy, of course, is simply the enforcement by the group of its own norms regarding what is an "appropriate" level of effort to expend on the job and what is the "proper" performance strategy. We previously discussed in some detail how groups use their control of discretionary stimuli to enforce group norms, and thereby affect such voluntary behaviors. Thus, if the group has established a norm about the level of member effort or the strategies members should use in going about their work, the group can control individual behavior merely by making sure that individual members realize that their receipt of valued group-controlled rewards is contingent upon their behaving in accord with the norm.

The *indirect* impact of the group on the effort and performance strategies of the individual involves the group's control of information regarding the state of the organizational environment outside the boundaries of the group. Regardless of any norms the group itself may have about effort or strategy, it also can communicate to the group member "what leads to what" in the broader organization, and thereby affect the individual's *own* choices about his behavior. . . .

Moreover . . . groups can affect the *personal preferences and values* of individual members—although such influences tend to occur relatively slowly and over a long period of time. When such changes do occur, the level of desire (or the valence) individuals have for various outcomes available in the organizational setting will change as well. And as the kinds of outcomes valued by the individual change, his behavior also will change to increase the degree to which the newly valued outcomes are obtained at work. The long-term result can be substantial revision of the choices made by the individual about the work he will expend and the performance strategies he will use at work.

It should be noted, however, that such indirect influences on member effort and performance strategy will be most potent early in the individual's tenure in the organization when he has not yet had a chance to develop through experience his own personal "map" of the organization. When the individual becomes less dependent upon the group for data about "what leads to what" and "what's good" in the organization, the group may have to revert to direct norm enforcement to maintain control of the work behavior of individual members.

In summary, the group can and does have a strong impact on both the level of effort exerted by its members and the strategies members use in carrying out their work. This impact is realized both directly (i.e., by enforcement of group norms) and indirectly (i.e., by affecting the beliefs and values of the members). When the direct and indirect influences of a group are congruent—which is often the case—the potency of the group's effects on its members can be quite strong. For example, if at the same time that a group is enforcing its *own* norm of, say, moderately low production, it also is providing a group member with data regard-ing the presumably *objective* negative consequences of hard work in the particular organization, the group member will experience two partially independent and mutually reinforcing influences aimed at keeping his rate of production down.

*Effort, Strategy, and Performance Effectiveness.* What, then, are the circumstances under which groups can improve the work *effectiveness* of their members through influences on individual choices about level of effort and about strategy? Again, the answer depends upon the nature of the job. Unless a job is structured so that effort level or performance strategy actually can make a real difference in work effectiveness, group influences on effort or strategy will be irrelevant to how well individual members perform.

Strategy: In general, groups should be able to facilitate member work effectiveness by influencing strategy choices more for complex jobs than for simple, straightforward, or routine ones. The reason is that on simple jobs, strategy choices usually cannot make much of a difference in effectiveness; instead, how well one does is determined almost entirely by how hard one works. On jobs characterized by high variety and autonomy, on the other hand, the work strategy used by the individual usually is of considerable importance in determining work effectiveness. By helping an individual develop and implement an appropriate work strategy—of where and how to put in his effort—the group should be able to substantially facilitate his effectiveness.

Effort: In the great majority of organizational settings, most jobs are structured such that the harder one works, the more effective his performance is likely to be. Thus, group influences on the effort expended by members on their jobs are both very pervasive and very potent de-

terminers of individual work effectiveness. There are, nevertheless, some exceptions to this generalization: the
success of a complicated brain operation,
for example, is less likely to depend upon
effort expended than it is upon the strategies used and the job-relevant knowledge and skills of the surgeon.

When either effort or strategy or both
are in fact important in determining performance effectiveness, the individual
has substantial personal control over
how well he does in his work. In such
cases, the degree to which the group facilitates (rather than hinders) individual
effectiveness will depend jointly upon
(1) the degree to which the group has
accurate information regarding the task
and organizational contingencies which
are operative in that situation and makes
such information available to the individual and (2) the degree to which the
norms of the group are congruent with
those contingencies and reinforce them.

*Participation.* One management practice which in theory should contribute
positively to meeting both of the above
conditions is the use of group participation in making decisions about work
practices. Participation has been widely
advocated as a management technique,
both on ideological grounds and as a
direct means of increasing work effectiveness. And, in fact, some studies have
shown that participation can lead to
higher work effectiveness (e.g., Coch &
French, 1948; Lawler & Hackman,
1969). In the present framework, participation should contribute to increased
work effectiveness in two different ways.

1 Participation can increase the
amount and the accuracy of information
workers have about work practices and
the environmental contingencies associated with them. . . .

2 Participation can increase the degree to which group members feel they
"own" their work practices—and there-

fore the likelihood that the group will
develop a norm of support for those practices. In the participative groups in the
study cited above, for example, the nature of the work-related communication
among members changed from initial
"shared warnings" about management
and "things management proposes" to
helping members (especially new members) come to understand and believe
in "our plan." In other words, as group
members come to experience the work
or work practices *as under their own control or ownership,* it becomes more likely
that informal group norms supportive of
effective behavior vis-à-vis those practices will develop. Such norms provide
a striking contrast to the "group protective" norms which often emerge when
control is perceived to be exclusively and
unilaterally under management control.

We can see, then, that group participative techniques can be quite facilitative of individual work effectiveness—
but only under certain conditions:

1 The topic of participation must be
relevant to the work itself. There is no
reason to believe that participation involving task-irrelevant issues (e.g., preparing for the Red Cross Bloodmobile
visit to the plant) will have facilitative
effects on work productivity. While such
participation may indeed help increase
the cohesiveness of the work group, it
clearly will not help group members gain
information or develop norms which are
facilitative of high work effectiveness.
Indeed, such task-irrelevant participation may serve to direct the attention
and motivation of group members *away
from* work issues and thereby even lower
productivity (cf. French, Israel, & Ås,
1960).

2 The objective task and environmental contingencies in the work setting
must actually be supportive of more effective performance. That is, if through
participation group members learn more

about what leads to what in the organization, then it is increasingly important that there be real and meaningful positive outcomes which result from effective performance. If, for example, group members gain a quite complete and accurate impression through participation that "hard work around here pays off only in backaches," then increased effort as a consequence of participation is most unlikely. If, on the other hand, participation results in a new and better understanding that hard work can lead to increased pay, enhanced opportunities for advancement, and the chance to feel a sense of personal and group accomplishment, then increased effort should be the result.

3 Finally, the work must be such that increased effort (or a different and better work strategy) objectively can lead to higher work effectiveness. If it is true—as argued here—that the main benefits of group participation are (1) increased understanding of work practices and the organizational environment and (2) increased experienced "ownership" by the group of the work and work practices, then participation should increase productivity only when the *objective determinants of productivity are under the voluntary control of the worker*. There is little reason to expect, therefore, that participation should have a substantial facilitative effect on productivity when work outcomes are mainly determined by the level of skill of the worker and/or by his arousal level (rather than effort expended or work strategy used) or when outcomes are controlled by objective factors in the environment over which the worker can have little or no control (e.g., the rate or amount of work which is arriving at the employee's station).

## Implications for Diagnosis and Change

This section has focused on ways that the group can influence the performance effectiveness of individual group members. While it has been maintained throughout that the group has a substantial impact on such performance effectiveness, it has been emphasized that the nature and extent of this impact centrally depends upon the characteristics of the work being done.

To diagnose and change the direction or extent of social influences on individual performance in an organization, then, the following three steps might be taken.

1 An analysis of the task or job would be made to determine which of the four classes of variables (i.e., skills, arousal, strategies, effort) objectively affect measured performance effectiveness. This might be done by posing this analytical question: "If skills (or arousal, or effort, or strategies) were brought to bear on the work differently than is presently the case, would a corresponding difference in work effectiveness be likely to be observed as a consequence?" By scrutinizing each of the four classes of variables in this way, it usually is possible to identify which specific variables are objectively important to consider for the job. In many cases, of course, more than one class of variables will turn out to be of importance.

2 After one or more "target" classes of variables have been identified, the work group itself would be examined to unearth any ways in which the group was blocking effective individual performance. It might be determined, for example, that certain group norms were impeding the expression and use of various skills which individuals potentially could bring to bear on their work. Or it might turn out that the social environment of the worker created conditions which were excessively (or insufficiently) arousing for optimal performance on the task at hand. For effort and strategy, which are under the voluntary

control of the worker, there are two major possibilities to examine: (a) that norms are enforced in the group which coerce individuals to behave in ineffective ways or (b) that the group provides information to the individual members about task and environmental contingencies in an insufficient or distorted fashion, resulting in their making choices about their work behavior which interfere with task effectiveness. . . .

3 Finally, it would be useful to assess the group and the broader social environment to determine if there are ways that the "people resources" in the situation could be more fully utilized in the interest of increased work effectiveness. That is, rather than focusing solely on ways the group may be blocking or impeding performance effectiveness, attention should be given as well to any unrealized *potential* which resides in the group. It could turn out, for example, that some group members would be of great help to others in increasing the level of individual task-relevant skills, but these individuals have never been asked for help. Alternatively, it might be that the group could be assisted in finding new and better ways of ensuring that each group member has available accurate and current information about those task and environmental contingencies which determine the outcomes of various work behaviors.

The point is that the people who surround an individual at work can facilitate as well as hinder his performance effectiveness—and that any serious attempt to diagnose the social environment in the interest of improving work performance should explicitly address unrealized possibilities for enhancing performance as well as issues for which remedial action may be required.

What particular organizational changes will be called for on the basis of such a diagnosis—or what techniques should be used to realize these changes—will, of course, largely depend upon the particular characteristics of the organization and of the resources which are available there. The major emphasis of this section has been that there is *not* any single universally useful type of change or means of change—and that, instead, intervention should always be based on a thorough diagnosis of the existing social, organizational, and task environment. Perhaps especially intriguing in this regard is the prospect of developing techniques of social intervention which will help groups see the need for (and develop the capability of) making such interventions *on their own* in the interest of increasing the work effectiveness of the group as a whole. . . .

# BIBLIOGRAPHY

Argyris, C. The incompleteness of social psychological theory: Examples from small group, cognitive consistency and attribution research. *American Psychologist*, 1969, **24**, 893–908.

Berkowitz, L. Group standards, cohesiveness and productivity. *Human Relations*, 1954, **7**, 509–519.

Bion, W. R. *Experiences in groups*. New York: Basic Books, 1959.

Blake, R. R., & Mouton, J. S. *The Managerial Grid*. Houston: Gulf, 1964.

Blake, R. R., & Mouton, J. S. *Building a dynamic corporation through GRID organization development*. Reading, Mass.: Addison-Wesley, 1969.

Coch, L., & French, J. R. P., Jr. Overcoming resistance to change. *Human Relations*, 1948, **1**, 512–532.

Darley, J., Gross, N., & Martin, W. Studies of group behavior: Factors associated with the productivity of groups. *Journal of Applied Psychology*, 1952, **36**, 396–403.

Festinger, L. Informal social communication. *Psychological Review*, 1950, **57**, 271–282.

French, J. R. P., Jr., Israel, J., & Ås, D. An experiment on participation in a Norwegian factory. *Human Relations*, 1960, **13**, 3–19.

Hackman, J. R. Group influences on individuals in organizations. In M. D. Dunnette (Ed.), *Handbook of industrial and organizational psychology.* Chicago: Rand-McNally, 1975.

Janis, I. L. *Victims of groupthink: A psychological study of foreign-policy decisions and fiascos.* Boston: Houghton Mifflin, 1972.

Kelman, H. C. Processes of opinion change. *Public Opinion Quarterly,* 1961, **25,** 57–78.

Kiesler, C. A. Group pressure and conformity. In J. Mills (Ed.), *Experimental social psychology.* New York: Macmillan, 1969.

Lawler, E. E., & Hackman, J. R. The impact of employee participation in the development of pay incentive plans: A field experiment. *Journal of Applied Psychology,* 1969, **53,** 467–471.

Lott, A. J., & Lott, B. E. Group cohesiveness as interpersonal attraction: A review of relationships with antecedent and consequent variables. *Psychological Bulletin,* 1965, **64,** 259–309.

Schachter, S. Deviation, rejection and communication. *Journal of Abnormal and Social Psychology,* 1951, **46,** 190–207.

Seashore, S. *Group cohesiveness in the industrial work group.* Ann Arbor: Institute for Social Research, University of Michigan, 1954.

Sherif, M. Formation of social norms: The experimental paradigm. In H. Proshansky and B. Seidenberg (Eds.), *Basic studies in social psychology.* New York: Holt, Rinehart & Winston, 1965.

Tajfel, H. Social and cultural factors in perception. In G. Lindzey and E. Aronson (Eds.), *The handbook of social psychology* (2nd ed.) Reading Mass.: Addison-Wesley, 1969.

Vroom, V. H. Industrial social psychology. In G. Lindzey & E. Aronson (Eds.), *The handbook of social psychology* (2nd ed.) Reading Mass.: Addison-Wesley, 1969.

Zajonc, R. B. Social facilitation. *Science,* 1965, **149,** 269–274.

# 33

# People as Sculptors Versus Sculpture: The Roles of Personality and Personal Control in Organizations

## Nancy E. Bell & Barry M. Staw

The popular literature on careers advises individuals to take charge of their situations—to be active agents in shaping their work environments and career opportunities.

> We believe you will improve your effectiveness and your sense of yourself as a person 300% if you can learn to think (or if you already think) of yourself as an *active agent* helping to mould your own present environment and your future, rather than a passive agent, waiting for your environment to mould you. (Bolles 1980:74)

> You *have to* take over the management of your own job-hunt or career-change, if it is to be successful. (Bolles 1988:43)

> You can create opportunity for the future by putting yourself in charge of your career. Your initial commitment is to take full control of your actions. (Greco 1975:19)

In contrast, a major school of thought in the academic literature on careers, the socialization literature, views individuals as much more passive and malleable. Often, individuals are portrayed as if they join the organization practically as lumps of clay, ready to be shaped by all those around them, from co-worker to supervisor to mentor. As mainly *receivers* of influence, individuals attempt to "learn the ropes" in the organization, modeling not only their behaviors but also their attitudes on those who appear to be successful participants:

> Like a sculptor's mold, certain forms of socialization can produce remarkably similar outcomes no matter what individual ingredients are used to fill the mold. (Van Maanen and Schein 1979:231)

To be fair, we recognize that the academic literature does not toally ignore the individual in its treatment of careers. Researchers have given careful consideration to personality and other individual difference variables in examining the selection stage of the career process (e.g., Holland 1966, 1976, 1985; Neiner and Owens 1985; Owens 1976). In fact, the focus on organizational participants as sculpture, or as malleable receivers of influence, is a relatively recent phenomenon. Much of the early academic literature on careers took an explicitly psychological approach, emphasizing the fit between specific personality traits and particular careers (see, e.g., Hansen and Campbell 1985; Strong 1943).

Person variables have been given far less consideration in recent work. This may be due to the emphasis in the literature on the early stages of careers, when people are thought to be most open to organizational influence (Hall 1986). Because this literature is strongly rooted

*Source:* From "People as Sculptors versus Sculpture: The Roles of Personality and Personal Control in Organizations," by Nancy E. Bell and Barry M. Staw in *Handbook of Career Theory*, Arthur, *et al*, eds., Cambridge University Press, 1989, pp. 232–251. Reprinted with permission of the publisher.

in a socialization view of careers, the picture that emerges shows the organization as the dominant entity, much more of an "agent" than the individual. The individual is at best viewed as a diagnostician or planner, reacting to organizational contingencies rather than proactively shaping those contingencies. Sometimes the person is seen as negotiating a "psychological contract" (e.g., Schein 1970) with the organization; yet even in these cases, if such a contract proves difficult to negotiate, the individual's only alternative is to exit the organization. . . .

Our recent work, which we discuss later in this chapter, attempts to revitalize the dispositional view of job attitudes. We show how a person variable, affective disposition (a general tendency toward positive or negative evaluation of life stimuli), can predict job attitudes. In this chapter, we will argue for a similar emphasis on the person in the career/socialization literatures—for the individual to be viewed more as sculptor than sculpture. While we do not deny the significant contributions of "situational" approaches that look at how the organization shapes the person, we think that the field has swung too far in the situational direction. In our view, it is now time to pay more attention to the individualization of organizational life (cf. Jones 1983; Schneider 1983; Staw, Bell, and Claussen, 1986; Weiss and Adler 1984). This view is compatible with that of more psychologically oriented career theory, such as Hall's (1976) work on the self-directed "protean" career and Tiedeman and Miller-Tiedeman's (1984) notion of personal agency (or "'I' power") in the career. Thus we will focus on the roles of personality and personal control in organizations, hoping to balance the situational perspective so dominant in the current literature with a fresh perspective that emphasizes people as

the shapers of their own organizational fates.

In addressing the roles of personality and personal control, we first review an ongoing debate in psychology over the relative influence of person versus situation in determining behavior and attitudes. We consider some evidence that indicates that people may not be as open to organizational influence as they are often depicted to be. The person versus situation debate also offers some insights into what kinds of situations should promote individualistic, rather than conforming, behavior. After reviewing the evidence for a dispositional and proactive view of individual behavior, we propose a model of personal control in organizations. We contend that personal control is the mechanism by which individual differences get expressed in organizational and career settings. Finally, in order to highlight some explicit testable links in the model, we describe a process whereby power needs affect people's efforts at personal control as well as subsequent perceptions of self-efficacy.

## CAREERS AS PERSONALITY OR SITUATION

The question of whether career outcomes are due more to the person or to the organizational context is not a new one. Over the past fifty years, personality theorists as well as social psychologists have been engaged in a very similar debate over the relative influence of person versus situation in determining attitudes and behavior. . . .

A more recent form of this debate began in 1968 with the publication of a seminal book by Walter Mischel in which he took issue with the work of trait theorists. Mischel's argument was essentially that traits had proven to be poor predictors of behavior and showed little cross-situational consistency. Mischel argued that if we wish to predict behavior we should switch our emphasis away from traits and dispositions and instead look at the contingencies posed by the situations in which individuals find themselves.

There have been numerous replies to Mischel's critique of personality research. Bem and Allen (1974) pointed out that individuals differ from one another both in the way traits are related to each other within each person and in whether or not a given trait is even relevant for the person in question. . . .

Another rejoinder of the "personologists" to the "situationists" has to do with the nature of the dependent variables used in personality research. Most often, these dependent variables have been measured by single acts. However, researchers such as Epstein (1979) and Buss and Craik (1983) have argued that we must take multiple measures of our behavioral criteria. Epstein's argument is that while any one act may not show great consistency with personality, an index or aggregate of acts thought to be related to the personality construct in question will show a stronger relationship. Thus, careeers should be ideally suited to this method of research since they are, by definition, aggregates of people's experiences. While any one cross-sectional measure may show weak results, an aggregate of a person's work experiences should show a stronger relationship to measures of personality, especially if the personality measures are also based on aggregated data.

## Strong Versus Weak Situations

One of the most important concepts to emerge from the person versus situation debate is that of "strong versus weak situations" (Mischel 1977). A strong situation is one that (1) leads everyone to construe the situation in the same way, (2) induces uniform expectancies regarding appropriate response patterns, (3) provides incentives for the performance of certain response patterns, and (4) requires skills that everyone has (Mischel 1977:347). Weak situations, by contrast, are more ambiguous or less structured (Snyder and Ickes 1985). Weak situations exert few pressures for conformity and may not even provide cues as to what would constitute conforming behavior.

When we examine situations according to their relative strength we can begin to see why traits have proved to be such poor predictors of behavior in comparison with contexts. As a number of researchers have pointed out (Bowers 1973; Weiss and Adler 1984), the typical study offering support to the situationist position is a laboratory experiment. In the lab, the conditions for a strong situation are purposely created so as to have a "good" manipulation and "experimental control." In fact, the manipulation checks for an experiment often assess whether subjects heeded the four characteristics of strong situations noted, with variability due to individual differences considered as error variance. Thus, having reduced the possible variation due to people, it should come as no surprise that experimental studies usually show weak results for person variables (Schneider 1987). . . .

## Organizations as Strong or Weak Situations

Usually it is argued that organizational socialization provides entrants with a shared set of values and norms, with strong cues for conformity (Van Maanen and Schein 1979). It has also been argued that organizations are themselves mechanisms for behavioral control (Thompson 1967), where individuals receive behavioral instructions and act on these cues to perform their respective roles (Katz and Kahn 1978). Yet, are organizations such powerful situations, capable of homogenizing behavior in the face of individual differences?

To answer this question, first let us note that few situations are so compelling as to force behavior in a prescribed direction. Even in the famous Asch (1956) conformity experiments, those usually cited to illustrate the effects of situational pressure, only a minority—about one-third—of the subjects actually conformed. While one-third of the subjects is significant and provides us with a valuable insight into human nature, the fact that the majority did not conform suggests that people will often behave in ways that they believe to be "right," even at the expense of violating a norm that seems to be shared by everyone else in the situation.

Some scholars have also noted that organizations are not as strong and coherent as they might appear. Thompson (1967), for example, emphasized that although the technology of an organization's production may be relatively known, firms must deal with uncertainties in their interactions with customers, financial institutions, and social/legal institutions. The managers who must cope with such uncertainties rarely have routinized or prescribed roles where correct solutions are fully known. Instead, idiosyncratic styles and behavioral repertoires are used by managers in hopes of placing some structure or algorithmic solutions on the ambiguity (Miner and Estler, 1985). Consequently, when a successful manager leaves the organization, the firm often tries to replicate that person as closely as possible since the traits of the role occupant (e.g., aggressive yet friendly) may be better known than the specific skills necessary to solve the organization's problems. Thus, the unique "personal style" of a role occupant is subsequently used as a "pattern" to be

followed by later occupants of that role (Turner 1988:3).

Logically, as one proceeds up the hierarchy of a firm, it is expected that organizational roles increase in degrees of uncertainty. This ordering is implicit in Jaques's (1961) notion of "time span of discretion," the time period necessary to obtain feedback on one's performance. It is also implicit in Simon's (1957) notion of administration as the absorption of uncertainty and in the fact that the hiring of managers is frequently based more on commonality of values and personality than on a bundle of requisite skills (Kanter 1977). In addition, many authors have taken pains to note the power and discretionary influence of those at even the lowest levels (e.g., Crozier 1964; Mechanic 1962), with the assumption of organizational roles often being more a product of negotiation and mutual influence than the result of simple role sending and conformity (Graen 1976; Graen, Orris, and Johnson 1973). Thus, while one would expect the personality of the founder or top manager of a firm to be manifested more strongly in his or her role than that of a person on the shop floor, even at the lowest levels of the organization the influence process is not entirely one way, nor is conformity the only explanation of behavior.

The most extreme view of organizations as being characterized by ambiguity rather than by structure is taken by March and his associates (March 1978; March and Olsen 1976). They argue that much of organizational life is imbued with ambiguity and that, often, the workings of an organization more closely resemble a random process than some finely tuned vehicle of production. Alternatively, Pfeffer (1981) has noted that organizational contexts can differ in terms of their degree of uncertainty, and that the most uncertain situations are precisely those contexts where power can be exerted by individuals and organizational subunits. House (1988) has recently extended this argument by noting that personal dispositions for power will be most strongly expressed under conditions of greatest organizational ambiguity, in settings where routines are not in place or are undergoing large-scale change. Such a hypothesis is similar to saying that organizational situations can vary in strength and clarity, and that dispositions will be most strongly expressed in the weakest of these contexts.

## Uncovering the Person in Organizational Behavior

Some research has specifically shown that individual dispositions are expressed in organizational settings, rather than being swamped by forces for conformity. Research on need for achievement and power, for example, has shown that people high in these characteristics manage to climb the organizational ladder with more success than do others in the organization (McClelland and Boyatzis 1982). Research has also indicated a relationship between personality and satisfaction with career decisions, with those individuals high in trait anxiety exhibiting relatively low satisfaction with their career choices (Kimes and Troth 1974). Other work has shown that individuals high in internal control [using Rotter's (1966) I/E scale] make more money and assume occupations of higher status than individuals who score higher in external control (Andrisani and Nestel 1976). However, because much of this personality research is based on cross-sectional data, the results can be interpreted as evidence for situational rather than dispositional effects. That is, the association between personality and organization could be due to the power of the organizational situation in shaping the person. Like Pygmalion, individuals' personalities could be products of organizational socialization and the taking of particular roles.

Much stronger evidence for the expression of personal dispositions has recently come from two longitudinal studies on job attitudes. In one study, Staw and Ross (1985) found that individuals' job attitudes were somewhat impervious to objective job changes. They found job satisfaction to be consistent over time, regardless of whether individuals changed employers or occupations. They also found that initial job satisfaction was a far better predictor of subsequent job attitudes than were changes in job status or pay. Staw and Ross's results thus show the individual as rather resistant to organizational influence, with attitudes determined more by personal and dispositional characteristics than by the job situation. . . .

Parallel to these findings, recent work by personality psychologists has shown that individual differences are predictive of well-being across many areas of people's lives. In a longitudinal study of over 4,900 men and women, Costa, McCrae, and Zonderman (1987) found that both general well-being, and its component parts (positive affect, negative affect, and health concerns), were stable over time. In addition, this stability was as high for people who had experienced major changes in areas of their lives (e.g., changes in marital status, residence, or employment) as for those who had experienced relatively little situational change. In other words, stable individual differences were more predictive of people's well-being than were dramatic alterations in people's situations. In terms of people's careers, these findings imply that career satisfaction may be determined as much (or more) by individuals' stable predispositions as by the "objective" features of the career.

## A MODEL OF PERSONAL INFLUENCE IN ORGANIZATIONAL SETTINGS

So far we have tried to knock organizational influence down a peg or two and to build up the role of the individual. Although we would not argue that conformity is nonexistent, we think its degree and frequency have been overplayed. To say that personality has effects in the organization does not, of course, mean that individuals will dominate the work situation. It simply means that, when properly measured, it is possible to discern individualization rather than homogenization in the work force. It also means that socialization, role taking, and social influence are at best incomplete forces, not capable of smoothing out all the idiosyncrasies that people bring to the organization. Especially when traits or predispositions are strong, they will be less likely to be overriden by situational forces (Dweck and Leggett 1988). Organizational roles are far more ambiguous than scholars usually realize, and in the space created by such ambiguity, individuals are able to maneuver and express their own individuality. Thus, from our perspective, individuals are proactive and often significant forces in the way organizational roles are carried out.

The personality literature we have discussed certainly illustrates the potential for people to shape their own organizational outcomes, yet this literature does not address the *process* by which people act as sculptors. In the remainder of this chapter, we outline a model that uses personal control as the means by which individuals' personalities and traits influence work outcomes. By personal control, we refer to individuals' *proactive regulation of their work lives*. This definition is compatible with recent work by Greenberger and Strasser (1986; Greenberger, Strasser, and Lee 1988), who de-scribe personal control as "an individual's beliefs, at a given point in time, in his or her ability to affect a change, in a desired direction" (Greenberger and Strasser 1986:165). They observe that members of organizations are more likely to initiate action when they perceive themselves to have personal control, and our usage of personal control also emphasizes this action component. We believe personal control encompasses not only the expression of individuality in organizational settings but also how individuals manage to change their work situations. Thus, we posit that it is possible to take the arguments of the "personologists" a step further, by indicating how personality, through the process of personal control, can actually affect outcomes that are normally thought to be governed by environmental forces.

In an effort to show how work roles can be individualized, we will first present a general model of personal control in organizations. We will then provide an example of how one specific person variable, need for power, might lead to varying attempts at personal control as well as varying consequences for the individual.

### A General Model of Personal Control in Organizations

*Individual Characteristics.* The model depicted in Figure 1 shows that certain individual characteristics influence whether or not a person attempts to exert control in an organizational context. Several personality characteristics are posited to be related to the person acting as an agent (initiating control attempts), rather than reacting passively to his or her organizational situation. Each of the characteristics discussed here was chosen on the basis of its robustness in related research contexts and is therefore promising for future research. This is not, however, meant to represent an inclu-

## FIGURE 1 · GENERAL MODEL OF PERSONALITY AND PERSONAL CONTROL IN ORGANIZATIONS

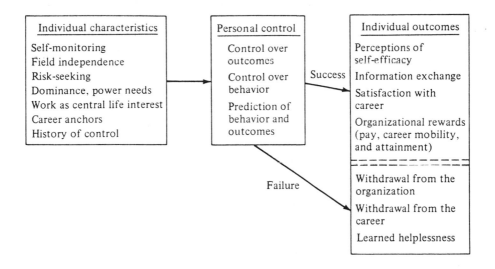

sive set of personality characteristics that might influence personal control, and we would hope that future research would expand on this set of traits.

First, whether a person is a high or a low self-monitor will influence the probability of personal control. Self-monitoring refers to an individual's tendency to rely on features of the situation when making behavioral choices (Snyder 1974; Snyder and Ickes 1985). High self-monitors are those individuals whose behavior is largely regulated by situational contingencies. Therefore, their behaviors tend to be situation-specific. Low self-monitors, by contrast, rely on their own inner states in making behavioral choices. Low self-monitors are more resistant to situational pressures or less inclined to view situations as strong or compelling. A closely related finding from the organizational literature is that people who are "field-dependent" are more susceptible to social influence at work than are people who are "field independent" (Weiss and Nowicki

1981; Weiss and Shaw 1979). We can hypothesize that low self-monitors or high field independents will therefore be more likely to initiate attempts at personal control. It should be noted that the model at this point does not assume that these attempts will necessarily be successful. (Both positive and negative outcomes will be considered later in this discussion.) It is conceivable that while low self-monitors (or high field independents) will be less hesitant about acting proactively, they may also attend less to situational cues that might be helpful in suggesting what *form* such influence attempts should take (e.g, rewards, ingratiation, persuasion, manipulation of information given to other organizational actors, and so on). Low self-monitors may therefore make relatively more errors in choosing among influence strategies than would other people.

Whether a person is risk seeking, versus risk averse, has been argued to be a factor in whether the individual will attempt upward political influence in an organization (Porter, Allen, and Angle 1981). We would expand this argument to include any attempt at personal control, whether the attempt is political or not. To the extent that a person is risk seeking, he or she should be more willing to test the environment by exerting attempts to change or control it.

Dominance and the need for power are almost by definition related to attempts at personal control. People with high needs for power are concerned with control over their environment and with influencing others (Porter, Allen, and Angle 1981). Managers who are high in dominance or need for power are thus more likely to engage in influence attempts than are others (for a review, see House 1988). For example, Mowday (1978) found that elementary school principals who were rated high in influence activity had high power motivation as well. Mowday also suggested that need for achievement should be related to influence attempts. While he reasoned that people with a high need for achievement would be more self-confident, and therefore more likely to risk an influence attempt, there is an even more direct reason for expecting need for achievement to be related to attempts at personal control. This is because people who are high in need for achievement are task oriented, and attempts to control contingencies in the environment may be necessary in order to succeed at many work tasks (cf. Kanter 1977; Staw 1986).

Another personality variable related to the likelihood of initiating an influence attempt would be whether or not the person holds work as a central life interest. Dubin and Champoux (1975) found that workers who held work, rather than nonwork activities, as a central life interest perceived themselves as being more decisive and as taking more initiative than did workers with other central life interests (either neutral, or nonwork). Insofar as individuals hold work (or work-related activities, such as union activism) as a central part of their identities, they should have a stake in controlling the course of their careers, as well as the outcomes.

A person's occupational self-concept, or "career anchor" (Schein 1978), should also be related to his or her likelihood of exerting personal control at work. Schein defines a career anchor as being composed of three types of self-perception, each of which is based on the person's actual work experiences. These are the person's self-perceived talents and abilities, the person's self-perceived motives and needs, and the person's self-perceived attitudes and values. Schein outlines five major career anchors. Of these, we would expect those individuals whose career anchor is "stability and security" to make relatively few efforts at personal control. This is similar to our predictions for risk-averse versus risk-seeking people. At the other extreme, those with the career anchor of "creativity" would be expected to engage in a lot of control activity.

Finally, the person's history of control should affect future influence attempts. To the extent that the person has made previous attempts at personal control, he or she should understand what is involved in making these attempts. Such an understanding or feeling of capability may be a prerequisite for many attempts at personal control. To the extent that these attempts have been rewarded in the past, the person will have learned which sorts of attempts have high probabilities of success, and that these attempts can indeed pay off.

*Forms of Personal Control.* Though individual characteristics can affect attempts at personal control, it is not clear what form these control attempts will take. Figure 1 therefore addresses three types of personal control: control over outcomes, control over behavior, and the ability to predict outcomes and behavior (Staw 1986). It is hypothesized that the most desirable form of influence is control over the distribution of outcomes. If people identify strongly with the organization, and/or occupy managerial roles, they may, for example, want to influence organizational outcomes, such as make-or-buy decisions or decisions to enter new markets. However, for most organizational participants, the primary concern will be influence over matters like pay, promotion, and benefits. Controlling these outcomes immediately affects participants' personal welfare.

Outcome control attempts can take many forms, from outright manipulation, to more subtle persuasion and ingratiation attempts. When the organizational member has legitimate power to specify outcomes, a control attempt could take the form of a direct order or outright manipulation of returns. For example, the supervisor who does the scheduling for shift work often has control over his or her own schedule as well. The outcome over which the individual has control in this case might be having desirable days off, such as the weekend. When individuals do not have the power to manipulate their outcomes directly, they may try persuasion. Again using the example of desirable time off, individuals might try to persuade the supervisor to schedule them according to their preferences, perhaps by suggesting that their preferred schedule will result in higher efficiency. Finally, individuals might try to gain control of outcomes more indirectly, through ingratiation. Here, it may be that individuals never directly state what they want; rather, they hope that by being in the good graces of more powerful others, positive outcomes will be

provided (Wortman and Linsenmeier, 1977).

Frequently, control over outcomes is impossible. An employee may desire a pay raise, but wages are frozen; more overtime may be wanted, but production is slow; a promotion may be yearned for, but the firm is not growing. In these cases, the next most desirable contingency to control would be control over behavior. Because most people want to feel efficacious, they are likely to attempt some measure of control over their environments. Thus, if control over outcomes is not possible, individuals may attempt a second kind of personal control, control over their own work behavior or inputs to the production process. Examples of behavioral control might include decisions about actual work methods, pace, amount of effort, dress, and even language and demeanor shown at work. These forms of behavioral control will often serve to satisfy desires for self-determination. They may also even affect people's *perceptions* of outcome control. In this vein, research has shown that individuals often cognitively confuse outcome and behavioral control (cf. Langer 1975, 1978, on the "illusion of control"). Thus, people who have some measure of behavioral control may come to believe that they possess outcome control as well.

The third kind of personal control depicted by the model is the ability to make sense of or predict one's environment. If real outcome control is not possible, and if the work is structured in a manner that leaves little room for people to exert control over their own behavior, people may gain a sense of efficacy by learning to *predict* their behavior and outcomes (Staw 1977). Being able to predict one's behavior means knowing what one is going to be asked to do, even though there may be little choice in the compliance with such role demands. Being able to predict outcomes refers to knowledge of rewards and punishments connected to the role, their occurrence and contingencies, even though the individual may have little power over the administration of these outcomes.

By reducing ambiguity and by clarifying the reinforcement contingencies in their environments, people gain some sense of control. As observed by Louis (1980), efforts toward predictive power, or what she calls "sensemaking," are especially prevalent during the early stages of organizational socialization. Extending this idea, we contend that the ability to predict one's environment is vital throughout one's career. Not only is this necessary for a sense of personal efficacy, but it may also increase people's future chances of upgrading their form of personal control to either behavioral or outcome control. For example, people who are in highly structured jobs may, through their knowledge of the job, be able to suggest more efficient ways of performing their tasks. The changes could also involve more discretion on the person's part. If the person is successful in persuading those higher up to approve the changes, then he or she will have successfully upgraded the form of control from predictive to behavioral control. At this point, the individual may be able to lobby successfully for greater pay or benefits, thereby moving from behavioral control to control over outcomes. Thus, the three forms of control shown in Figure 1 may be hierarchical in nature. Not only can individuals work their ways up the control ladder, but influence at each level is likely to include the forms of influence at the preceding level.

*Results of Control.* If the person finds that he or she cannot exert any of the three levels of control in Figure 1, the model shows two possible outcomes. Depending on the individual characteristics depicted in the first stage of the model, the person will either withdraw from the organization (and perhaps even from an entire career path) or enter a state of learned helplessness. If the person scores highly on the traits discussed earlier, it is predicted that these proactive tendencies will push him or her to change directions, either in terms of the organization or the career. By contrast, if the person is low on the traits depicted in the model, he or she is likely to react with increasing feelings of helplessness. This, in turn, can create a vicious cycle. When people have less motivation or energy for initiating control attempts of any sort (including withdrawing, as a more proactive person might do), they receive less and less opportunity for control, thus leading to even more feelings of helplessness.

What outcomes might we expect from successful attempts at personal control? First, any of the three types of personal control would likely increase people's senses of self-efficacy. In contrast to the learned helplessness that may be engendered by unsuccessful control attempts, people who have successfully exercised personal control should infer that they can be influential or efficacious in the organizational context. Personal control might also lead to greater information exchange with the organization. Through testing their environments, individuals should garner information with which to predict their future behavior and outcomes. In some cases, the individuals may provide the organization with valuable feedback on employee preferences as well as new and better ways to do the work. Of course, successful control attempts may not always result in an *even* exchange of information between the employee and the organization. This is because one way of controlling one's behavior may be to restrict information to others about one's work procedures. Katz (1980), for example, suggests that people in the adaptation stage of the socialization process may surround their work with secrecy and ritual so that others in the organization leave them alone to do their work as they please.

Control over work behavior and inputs should result in greater satisfaction with the career, and perhaps even in greater career involvement. This follows from research on job design, which shows that to the extent that people feel responsible for their work, they should have more positive affective reactions toward it (Hackman and Oldham 1980). Likewise, in the case of control over outcomes, individuals are also expected to feel greater career satisfaction and career involvement due to the self-efficacy that is created by successful personal control. In addition, if people manage to significantly improve their level or mix of organizational rewards, outcome control should have a rather direct effect on job attitudes. As shown in Figure 1, increased pay, career mobility, and attainment are just a few of the possible products that control over outcomes may provide. . . .

## CONCLUSION

We began this chapter by noting that there is a disparity between the popular and academic views of careers concerning the amount of control individuals can exert over their organizational lives. Drawing on a similar debate in psychology about the relative influence of person versus situation, we noted that people may not be as malleable or open to organizational influence as they are often depicted to be. We attempted to resolve the issue of individual versus organizational influence by discussing the concept of situational strength and by noting that many organizational contexts are weak or ambiguous enough to let personal dispositions shine through. People may shape their environments as much or more than they are shaped by their environments.

To suggest a process by which this individualization or modification of the environment might occur, we outlined a model of personal control in organizations. In our view, personal control is a primary mechanism by which individual dispositions come to be expressed in organizational settings. . . .

Our models of personal influence in organizations provide only a few of the ways in which personality and individual differences are likely to be expressed in career actions and outcomes. We have specified some of the simplest interrelationships, yet even these are, at present, based more on speculation than on concrete research. The effects of personality and personal control are thus prime candidates for future career research.

## REFERENCES

Andrisani, P. J., and Nestel, G. (1976). Internal-external control as contributor to and outcome of work experience. *Journal of Applied Psychology, 61*, 156–165.

Asch, S. E. (1956). Studies of independence and conformity. *Psychological Monographs, 70* (whole no. 416).

Bem, D. J., and Allen, A. (1974). On predicting some of the people some of the time: the search for cross-situational consistencies in behavior. *Psychological Review, 81*, 506–520.

Bolles, R. N. (1988). *What Color Is Your Parachute?* Berkeley, CA: Ten Speed.

Bowers, K. S. (1973). Situationism in psychology: an analysis and critique. *Psychological Bulletin, 80*, 307–336.

Buss, D. M., and Craik, K. H. (1983). The act frequency approach to personality. *Psychological Review, 90*, 105–126.

Costa, P. T., Jr., McCrae, R. R., and Zonderman, A. B. (1987). Environmental and dispositional influences on well-being: longitudinal followup of an American national sample. *British Journal of Psychology, 78,* 299–306.

Crozier, M. (1964). *The Bureaucratic Phenomenon.* Chicago: University of Chicago Press.

Dubin, R., and Champoux, J. E. (1975). Workers' central life interests and personality characteristics. *Journal of Vocational Behavior, 6,* 165–174.

Dweck, C. S., and Leggett, E. L. (1988). A social-cognitive approach to motivation and personality. *Psychological Review, 95,* 256–273.

Epstein, S. (1979). The stability of behavior: I. On predicting most of the people much of the time. *Journal of Personality and Social Psychology, 37,* 1097–1126.

Graen, G. (1976). Role-making processes within complex organizations. In M. D. Dunnette (ed.), *Handbook of Industrial and Organizational Psychology.* Chicago: Rand McNally.

Graen, G., Orris, J. B., and Johnson, T. (1973). Role assimilation processes in a complex organization. *Journal of Vocational Behavior, 3,* 395–420.

Greco, B. (1975). *How To Get the Job That's Right For You.* Homewood, IL: Dow Jones-Irwin.

Greenberger, D. B., and Strasser, S. (1986). The development and application of a model of personal control in organizations. *Academy of Management Review, 11,* 164–177.

Greenberger, D. B., Strasser, S., and Lee, S. (1988). Personal control as a mediator between perceptions of supervisory behaviors and employee reactions. *Academy of Management Journal, 31,* 405–417.

Hackman, J. R., and Oldham, G. R. (1980). *Work Redesign.* Reading, MA: Addison-Wesley.

Hall, D. T. (1976). *Careers in Organizations.* Pacific Palisades, CA: Goodyear.

Hall, D. T. (1986). Breaking career routines: midcareer choice and identity development. In D. T. Hall (ed.), *Career Development in Organizations.* San Francisco: Jossey-Bass.

Hansen, J., and Campbell, D. P. (1985). *Manual for the SVIB-SCII.* Palo Alto, CA: Consulting Psychology.

Holland, J. L. (1966). *The Psychology of Vocational Choice.* Waltham, MA: Blaisdell.

Holland, J. L. (1976). Vocational preferences. In M. D. Dunnette (ed.), *Handbook of Industrial and Organizational Psychology.* Chicago: Rand McNally.

Holland, J. L. (1985). *Making Vocational Choices: A Theory of Vocational Personalities and Work Environments,* 2nd ed. Englewood Cliffs, NJ: Prentice-Hall.

House, R. J. (1988). Power and personality in complex organizations. In B. M. Staw and L. L. Cummings (eds.), *Research in Organizational Behavior,* Vol. 10. Greenwich, CT: JAI.

Jaques, E. (1961). *Equitable Payment.* New York: Wiley.

Jones, G. R. (1983). Psychological orientation and the process of organizational socialization: an interactionist perspective. *Academy of Management Review, 8,* 464–474.

Kanter, R. M. (1977). *Men and Women of the Corporation.* New York: Basic Books.

Katz, D., and Kahn, R. L. (1978). *The Social Psychology of Organizations,* 2nd ed. New York: Wiley.

Katz, R. (1980). Time and work: toward an integrative perspective. In B. M. Staw and L. L. Cummings (eds.), *Research in Organizational Behavior,* Vol. 2, Greenwich, CT: JAI.

Kimes, H. G., and Troth, W. A. (1974). Relationship of trait anxiety to career decisiveness. *Journal of Counseling Psychology, 21,* 277–280.

Langer, E. J. (1975). The illusion of control. *Journal of Personality and Social Psychology, 32,* 311–328.

Langer, E. J. (1978). Rethinking the role of thought in social interaction. In J. H. Harvey, W. I. Ickes, and R. F. Kidd (eds.), *New Directions in Attribution Research,* Vol. 2, Hillsdale, NJ: Erlbaum.

Louis, M. R. (1980). Surprise and sense making: what newcomers experience in entering unfamiliar organizational settings. *Administrative Science Quarterly, 25,* 226–251.

McClelland, D. C., and Boyatzis, R. E. (1982). Leadership motive pattern and long term success in management. *Journal of Applied Psychology, 67,* 737–743.

March, J. G. (1978). Bounded rationality, ambiguity, and the engineering of choice. *Bell Journal of Economics, 9,* 587–608.

March, J. G., and Olsen, J. P. (1976). *Ambiguity and Choice in Organizations*. Bergen, Norway: Universitetsforlaget.

Mechanic, D. (1962). Sources of power of lower participants in complex organizations. *Administrative Science Quarterly*, 7, 349–364.

Miner, A. S., and Estler, S. E. (1985). Accrual mobility: job mobility in higher education through responsibility accrual. *Journal of Higher Education*, 56, 121–143.

Mischel, W. (1968). *Personality and Assessment*. New York: Wiley.

Mischel, W. (1977). The interaction of person and situation. In D. Magnusson and N. S. Endler (eds.), *Personality at the Crossroads: Current Issues in International Psychology*. Hillsdale, NJ: Erlbaum

Mowday, R. T. (1978). The exercise of upward influence in organizations. *Administrative Science Quarterly*, 23, 137–156.

Neiner, A. G., and Owens, W. A. (1985). Using biodata to predict job choice among college graduates. *Journal of Applied Psychology*, 70, 127–136.

Owens, W. A. (1976). Background data. In M. D. Dunnette (ed.), *Handbook of Industrial and Organizational Psychology*. Chicago: Rand McNally.

Pfeffer, J. (1981). *Power in Organizations*. Marshfield, MA: Pitman.

Porter, L. W., Allen, R. W., and Angle, H. L. (1981). The politics of upward influence in organizations. In B. M. Staw and L. L. Cummings (eds.), *Research in Organizational Behavior*, Vol. 3, Greenwich, CT: JAI.

Rotter, J. B. (1966). Generalized expectancies for internal versus external control of reinforcement. *Psychological Monographs*, 80 (whole No. 609).

Salancik, G. R., and Pfeffer, J. (1978). A social information processing approach to job attitudes and task design. *Administrative Science Quarterly*, 23, 224–253.

Schein, E. H. (1970). *Organizational Psychology*. Englewood Cliffs, NJ: Prentice-Hall.

Schein, E. H. (1978). *Career Dynamics: Matching Individual and Organizational Needs*. Reading MA: Addison-Wesley.

Schneider, B. (1983). Interactional psychology and organizational behavior. In B. M. Staw and L. L. Cummings (eds.), *Research in Organizational Behavior*, Vol. 5. Greenwich, CT: JAI.

Schneider, B. (1987). The people make the place. *Personnel Psychology*, 40, 437–453.

Simon, H. A. (1957). *Administrative Behavior*. New York: Macmillan.

Snyder, M. (1974). The self-monitoring of expressive behavior. *Journal of Personality and Social Psychology*, 30, 526–537.

Snyder, M., and Ickes, W. (1985). Personality and social behavior. In G. Lindzey and E. Aronson (eds.), *Handbook of Social Psychology*, 3rd ed., Vol. 2. New York: Random House.

Staw, B. M. (1977). Motivation in organizations: toward synthesis and redirection. In B. M. Staw and G. R. Salancik (eds.), *New Directions in Organizational Behavior*. Chicago: St. Clair.

Staw, B. M. (1986). Beyond the control graph: steps toward a model of perceived control in organizations. In R. N. Stern and S. McCarthy (eds.), *The Organizational Practice of Democracy*. Chichester: Wiley.

Staw, B. M., Bell, N. E., and Claussen, J. A. (1986). The dispositional approach to job attitudes: a lifetime longitudinal test. *Administrative Science Quarterly*, 31, 56–77.

Staw, B. M., and Ross, J. (1985). Stability in the midst of change: a dispositional approach to job attitudes. *Journal of Applied Psychology*, 70, 469–480.

Strong, E. K., Jr. (1943). *Vocational Interests of Men and Women*. Stanford, CA: Stanford University Press.

Thompson, J. D. (1967). *Organizations in Action*. New York: McGraw-Hill.

Tiedeman, D. V., and Miller-Tiedeman, A. (1984). Career decision making: an individualistic perspective. In D. Brown and L. Brooks (eds.), *Career Choice and Development*. San Francisco: Jossey-Bass.

Turner, R. H. (1988). Personality in society: social psychology's contribution to sociology. *Social Psychology Quarterly*, 51, 1–10.

Van Maanen, J., and Schein, E. H. (1979). Toward a theory of organizational socialization. In B. M. Staw and L. L. Cummings (eds.), *Research in Organizational Behavior*, Vol. 1. Greenwich, CT: JAI.

Weiss, H. M., and Adler, S. (1984). Personality and organizational behavior. In B. Staw and L. Cummings (eds.), *Research in Organizational Behavior*, Vol. 6, Greenwich, CT: JAI.

Weiss, H. M., and Nowicki, C. E. (1981). Social influences on task satisfaction: model competence and observer field dependence. *Organi-*

*zational Behavior and Human Performance, 27,* 345–366.

Weiss, H. M., and Shaw, J. B. (1979). Social influences on judgements about tasks. *Organizational Behavior and Human Performance, 24,* 126–140.

Wortman, C. B., and Linsenmeier, J. A. W. (1977). Interpersonal attraction and techniques of ingratiation in organizational settings. In B. M. Staw and G. R. Salancik (eds.), *New Directions in Organizational Behavior.* Chicago: St. Clair.

# CHAPTER VI

# *Power and Influence*

Power is the latent ability to influence others' actions, thoughts, or emotions. It is the potential to get people to do things the way you want them done—a social energy waiting to be used, to be transformed into influence or, as in the words of R. G. H. Siu, to be transformed from *potential power* into *kinetic power*. Power is influence over the beliefs, emotions, and behaviors of people and, according to Siu, "potential power is the capacity to do so, but kinetic power is the act of doing so. . . . One person exerts power over another to the degree that he is able to exact compliance as desired" (Siu, 1979, p. 31).

As we have seen throughout this book almost everything necessary for understanding organizational behavior is related to everything else, and *power* is no exception. The subject of power in organizations is inseparable from the topics and issues that have been the focuses of earlier chapters, most notably (but certainly not exclusively) *the organizational context* (including specialization, division of labor, and the functions of structure), *intergroup dynamics*, and *leadership*.

As a concept of organizational behavior, *power* is associated with several other organizational subjects which many people find distasteful. First, for most of us, power suggests an ability to overcome resistance. This "black side" of power is behind Rosabeth Moss Kanter's (1979, p. 65) observation: "Power is America's last dirty word. It is easier to talk about money—and much easier to talk about sex—than it is to talk about power. People who have it deny it; people who want it do not want to appear hungry for it; and people who engage in its machinations do so secretly." Second, power owes much of its existence to feelings of dependence. Power exists only when there is an unequal relationship between two people—where one of the two is dependent upon the other (Emerson, 1962).

## THE ORGANIZATIONAL CONTEXT

Power starts with structural issues. Although individual skill determines the effectiveness of the use of power, power is not fundamentally an issue of person or personality. "Power is first and foremost a structural phenomenon, and should be understood as such" (Pfeffer, 1981, p. x). *Specialization* and *division of labor*, two related subjects that were discussed rather extensively in the *Introduction*, are the most fundamental causes of dependence among individuals and organizational units.

With division of labor, people in organizations are dependent upon others for all sorts of things that are needed to accomplish their tasks: They are dependent for timely completion of prior tasks, accurate information, materials and supplies, competent people, and political support.

In this chapter we assert that structure establishes how *roles, expectations,* and *resource allocations* are defined for people and groups in any given organization. Thus, the structural forces caused by specialization and division of labor are extended (by the vital importance of these three functions of structure) to the people and groups in organizations. The functions of structure in the establishment of organizational roles, expectations, and resource allocations make it very clear why power is first and foremost a structural phenomenon, and why effective use of power in organizations is crucial for success. Jeffrey Pfeffer emphasizes this point in his "Preface" to *Power in Organizations* (1981): "Those persons and those units that have the responsibility for performing the more critical tasks in the organization have a natural advantage in developing and exercising power in the organization" (p. x). Resource allocation decisions have enormous impacts on a person's (or group's) ability to do its job, to "shine" or "excel." Structure affects resource allocations. A primary reason for using power is to affect resource allocations, and resource allocations affect the balance of power in organizations: The variables are inseparable. Power cannot be understood independent of the structural context, and vice versa.

## INTERGROUP DYNAMICS

Organizations are complex systems which often can be visualized most clearly as grids or spider webs of overlapping, interwoven, and competing *coalitions* of individuals, formal groups, and informal groups, each having its own interests, beliefs, values, preferences, perspectives, and perceptions. The coalitions compete with each other continuously for scarce organizational resources. Conflict is inevitable. Influence—and the power and political activities through which influence is acquired and maintained—is the primary "weapon" for use in competition and conflicts. Thus, power, politics, and influence are critically important and permanent facts of organizational life.

Returning for a moment to the subject of *organizational context*, power relations are permanent features of organizations primarily because specialization and the division of labor result in many interdependent organizational units with varying degrees of importance. The units compete with each other for scarce resources—as well as with the transitory coalitions. As James D. Thompson points out in *Organizations in Action* (1967), lack of balance in the interdependence among units sets the stage for the use of power relations.

## LEADERSHIP

Leadership involves "an interpersonal process through which one individual influences the attitudes, beliefs, and especially the behavior of one or more other people" (see Chapter IV). The parallels and overlappings among issues of *leadership* and of *power in organizations* are obvious, and this chapter attempts to emphasize the parallels and explain the overlappings.

Historically, power in organizations and authority were viewed as being essentially synonymous. Such "classical era" students of organization as Max Weber (1922) and Henri Fayol (1949, 1916) simply *assumed* that power and formal rules (promulgated and enforced by those in authority) flow downward through people who occupy offices to successively lower levels in hierarchical organizations. Even today, proponents of the "modern structural perspective of organization theory" (see Shafritz and Ott, 1996, Chapter IV) tend to see authority as the source of power in organizations (or, at least the primary source). From this perspective, *leader*, *supervisor*, and *manager* mean the same thing: people who possess power by virtue of the authority inherent in the organizational position they occupy. Power is legitimized by virtue of a person being in such a position. In fact, the aptly descriptive phrases *legitimate power* and *legitimate authority* gained common usage and still are seen and heard occasionally in today's management literature.

In contrast, most organizational behavioralists see power in a very different light. For example, John Kotter (1985) argues that in today's organizational world, the gap is increasing between the power one needs to get the job done and the power that automatically comes with the job (authority). Most organizational behavioralists view authority as only one of many available sources of organizational power, and power is aimed in *all* directions—not just down through the hierarchy. For example, Robert W. Allen and Lyman W. Porter divide their 1983 book of readings on *Organizational Influence Processes* into three major parts: downward influence (authority), lateral influence, and upward influence.

Authority-based power is far from being the only form of power in organizations. In fact, other forms of power and influence often prevail over authority-based power. Several of this chapter's selections identify different sources of power in organizations (particularly the second reading, "The Bases of Social Power," by John R. P. French and Bertram Raven), so only a few are listed here as examples:

- *Control over scarce resources*, for example, office space, discretionary funds, current and accurate information, and time and skill to work on projects;
- *Easy access to others who are perceived as having power*, important customers or clients, members of the board of directors, or someone else with formal authority or who controls scarce resources;
- *A central place in a potent coalition*;
- *Ability to "work the organizational rules*," such as knowing how to get things done or to prevent others from getting things done; and
- *Credibility*, for example, that one's word can be trusted.

The more that leadership issues in organizations are separated or differentiated from management issues, the more closely they become aligned with power issues—issues that extend beyond authority issues.

## SELECTIONS IN THIS CHAPTER

The readings on power that comprise this chapter span almost twenty-five years and address a spectrum of issues associated with power and behavior in organizations. The first, Dorwin Cartwright's "Power: A Neglected Variable in Social Psychology" (1959), is adapted from an address he delivered to the Society for the Psychological Study of Social Issues in 1953. The article is not organization-specific. Rather, it defines the historical place of power in the field of social psychology originating with "metaphysical era social psychologists" including Hobbes (1651) and Nietzsche (1912). However, "twentieth century social psychologists have been 'soft' on power" (p. 2), preferring to avoid it or to study it only in "safe or weak populations— witness the classical stature of research on pecking order among chickens and on dominance among children" (p. 2). Cartwright identifies leading social issues (phenomena which are social psychological in nature) that "cannot be adequately understood without the concept of power" (p. 3). They include leadership and social roles, public opinion, rumor, propaganda, prejudice, attitude change, morale, communications, race relations, and conflicts of value. Cartwright concludes that these phenomena raise questions about power in society which cannot be answered with our existing systems of knowledge.

"The Bases of Social Power," by John R. P. French and Bertram Raven (1959), reprinted here, accepts Dorwin Cartwright's challenge head on. In their often-cited analysis, French and Raven start from the premise that power and influence involve relations between at least two agents (they limit their definition of agents to individuals), and theorize that the reaction of the *recipient agent* is the more useful focus for explaining the phenomena of social influence and power. The core of French and Raven's piece, however, is their identification of five bases or sources of social power: reward power, the perception of coercive power, legitimate power (organizational authority), referent power (through association with others who possess power), and expert power (power of knowledge or ability).

French and Raven examine the effects of power derived from the five different bases on *attraction* (the recipient's sentiment toward the agent who uses power) and *resistance* to the use of power. Their investigations show that the use of power from the different bases has different consequences. For example, coercive power typically decreases attraction and causes high resistance, whereas reward power increases attraction and creates minimal levels of resistance. In what amounts to one of the earliest looks at ethical limits on the use of power, they conclude that "the more legitimate the coercion (is perceived to be) the less it will produce resistance and decreased attraction" (p. 165).

David Mechanic's influential 1962 *Administrative Science Quarterly* article, "Sources of Power of Lower Participants in Complex Organizations," which is reprinted here, examines sources of influence and power that can be aimed at targets who possess more formal authority than the potential "influencer" possesses. As John Kotter reminds us in the final selection in this chapter, power requires feelings of dependence, and lower-level organization members have an array of tools with which to make others dependent on them. These tools include expertise, effort and interest, attractiveness (or charisma), location and position in the organization, membership in intra- and inter-organizational coalitions, and knowledge of rules. All of this is a more formal way of saying something that we all know—some people are treated like prima donnas or "get away with murder" in organizations because they have some special skills that give them power in the context of their organizations. "Hawkeye" and "Trapper," from the MASH movie and television series, are ready examples. If they had not been badly needed surgeons at the battlefront, they would have been court-martialed years before.

From Dorwin Cartwright, French and Raven, and David Mechanic, it is a fifteen-year leap to Gerald Salancik and Jeffrey Pfeffer's 1977 widely respected analysis, "Who Gets Power—And How They Hold on to It: A Strategic-Contingency Model of Power." This article also reflects the field of organizational behavior's tremendous strides during the 1970s in accepting power as a legitimate subject for serious investigation.

Salancik and Pfeffer see power as one of the few mechanisms available for aligning an organization with the realities of its environment. Their assertion rests on the premise that power is derived from being essential to an organization's functional needs. According to Salancik and Pfeffer's notion (which they label *strategic-contingency theory*), power accrues to individuals and subunits that handle an organization's most critical problems. Effective use of power allows those subunits that are engaged in critical activities to "place allies in key positions," "control scarce critical resources," and thereby enhance the probability of their survival and expansion. Subunits engaged in critical functions prosper, and those engaged in noncritical functions wither, and the organization realigns itself. Because the most critical contingencies organizations face involve the environmental context, this power allocating process explains how organizations constantly readjust themselves with the needs of their external worlds.

Salancik and Pfeffer believe that power is shared in organizations "out of necessity more than out of concern for principles of organizational development or participatory democracy" (p. 7). It is shared out of structural-functional need. To repeat an earlier quotation: "Power is first and foremost a structural phenomen n, and should be understood as such" (Pfeffer, 1981, p. x).

Strategic-contingency theory has far-reaching consequences. If the use of po er by subunits helps organizations align themselves with their critical needs, then suppression of the use of power, for example to reduce unwanted *politics* and *conflicts*, reduces organizational adaptability. Thus, in the current literature of organizational behavior, one seldom sees the phrase *conflict resolution* used. It has been almost totally replaced with the concept of *conflict management*—using conflict (and power struggles) constructively for the organization's benefit.

"Who Gets Power—And How They Hold on to It," contains a second very important contribution to the understanding of power in organizations. Salancik and Pfeffer identify three contextual conditions under which the use of power by members of subunits can be expected to determine how important decisions are

decided. (For Salancik and Pfeffer, "important decisions" usually are resource allocation decisions.)

- The degree of resource scarcity,
- The criticalness of the resources to subunits' core activities, and
- The level of uncertainty existing about what or how an organization
  should do.

When these conditions are linked with Salancik and Pfeffer's identification of
subunits that are most likely to get and hold on to power, it is possible to predict
an organization's decision processes (under certain circumstances) by using a power
perspective of organizational behavior. When clear-cut criteria do not exist, the
use of power to control resource allocation decisions is likely to be most effective.

John P. Kotter's article, "Power, Dependence, and Effective Management"
(1977), which is reprinted in this chapter, focuses on the inexorable relationship
between power and dependence, and examines how an appreciation of this relationship permits effective managerial performance. Kotter's article attempts to answer
three questions:

1. Why are the dynamics of power necessarily an important part of managerial processes?
2. How do effective managers acquire power?
3. How and for what purposes do effective managers use power?

Kotter's answer to his first question is found in the dependency consequences
of "two organizational facts of life, division of labor and limited rsources" (p. 126).
Managers often are dependent on people over whom they have no control for
information, resources, and the performance of activities. Kotter makes an argument
which since has been popularized by Kanter (1979) and that is contrary to common
wisdom: The more formal authority managers possess, the less powerful and the
more vulnerable they are.

Kotter's answer to his second question is: Successful managers build their power
by creating a sense of obligation in others, creating images of expertise and skill,
"fostering others' unconscious identification with them or with ideas they 'stand
for'" (p. 131), and feeding peoples' beliefs that they are dependent on the manager.
Successful managers create perceptions of dependence by finding and acquiring
important resources and, more importantly, by influencing *perceptions* of their ability
to marshal resources. Kotter answers his third question: "How and for what purposes
do effective managers use power?" with a matrix-type analysis of the advantages
and disadvantages of face-to-face and indirect influence processes for different types
of purposes.

Power and influence are integral aspects of organizational behavior. Their
contributions to understanding the behavior of people in organizations can be
understood only in relationship to leadership, group and intergroup dynamics, the
organizational context, and motivational structures. In 1959, Dorwin Cartwright

wrote about power as a neglected variable in social psychology. In 1979, Rosabeth Moss Kanter called power "America's last dirty word," a word and a concept that people in organizations (and elsewhere) try to avoid. But power is a subject that cannot and should not be avoided. The importance of power will become even more clear in Chapter VII, *Organizational Change*.

## REFERENCES

Allen, R. W., Madison, D. L., Porter, L. W., Renwick, P. A., & Mayes, B. T. (1979). Organizational politics: Tactics and characteristics of its actors. *California Management Review, 22*, 77–83.

Allen, R. W., & Porter, L. W. (Eds.) (1983). *Organizational influence processes*. Glenview, IL.: Scott, Foresman.

Cartwright, D. (1959). Power: A neglected variable in social psychology. In, D. Cartwright (Ed.), *Studies in social power* (pp. 1–14). Ann Arbor, MI: University of Michigan, Institute for Social Research.

Emerson, R. M. (1962). Power-dependence relations. *American Sociological Review, 27*, 31–40.

Fayol, H. (1949). *General and industrial management* (C. Storrs, Trans.) London: Pitman Publishing Co. (Original work published 1916).

French, J. R. P., & Raven, B. (1959). The bases of social power. In, D. Cartwright & A. Zander (Eds.), *Studies in social power* (pp. 150–167). Ann Arbor, MI: University of Michigan, Institute for Social Research.

Haire, M. (1962). The concept of power and the concept of man. In, G. B. Strother (Ed.), *Social science approaches to business behavior* (pp. 163–183). Homewood, IL: Richard D. Irwin.

Hobbes, T. (1651). *Leviathan*. Reprinted in 1904, Cambridge, UK; University Press.

Kanter, R. M. (July–August, 1979). Power failure in management circuits. *Harvard Business Review, 57*, 65–75.

Korda, M. (1975). *Power*. New York: Ballantine Books.

Kotter, J. P. (March–April, 1976). Power, success, and organizational effectiveness. *Organizational Dynamics*, 27–40.

Kotter, J. P. (July–August, 1977). Power, dependence, and effective management. *Organizational Dynamics*, 125–136.

Kotter, J. P. (1985). *Power and influence*. New York: Free Press.

March, J. G. (1962). The business firm as a political coalition. *Journal of Politics, 24*, 662–678.

Mayes, B. T., & Allen, R. W. (1977). Toward a definition of organizational politics. *Academy of Management Review, 2*, 672–678.

McClelland, D., & Burnham, D. (March–April, 1976). Power is the great motivator. *Harvard Business Review*, 100–110.

Mechanic, D. (December, 1962). Sources of power of lower participants in complex organizations. *Administrative Science Quarterly, 7*(3), 349–364.

Mintzberg, H. (1983). *Power in and around organizations*. Englewood Cliffs, NJ: Prentice-Hall.

Nietzsche, F. (1912). *Der Wille zur Macht*. Book 3, sec. 702. In, F. Nietzsche, *Werke* (Vol. 16). Leipzig: Alfred Kroner.

Perrow, C. (1970). Departmental power and perspectives in industrial firms. In, M. N. Zald (Ed.), *Power in organizations* (pp. 59–89). Nashville. TN: Vanderbilt University Press.

Pfeffer, J. (1981). *Power in organizations*. Marshfield, MA: Pitman Publishing Co.

Pfeffer, J. (1992). *Managing with power: Politics and influence in organizations*. Boston: Harvard Business School Press.

Porter, L. W., Allen, R. W., & Angle, H. L. (1981). The politics of upward influence in organizations. In, L. L. Cummings & B. M. Staw (Eds.), *Research in organizational behavior* (Vol. 3) (pp. 408–422). Greenwich, CT: JAI Press.

Robbins, S. P. (1976). *The administrative process: Integrating theory and practice*. Englewood Cliffs, NJ: Prentice-Hall.

Salancik, G. R., & Pfeffer, J. (1977). Who gets power—and how they hold on to it: A strategic-contingency model of power. *Organizational Dynamics, 5*, 2–21.

Sennett, R. (1980). *Authority*. New York: Alfred A. Knopf, Inc.

Shafritz, J. M., & Ott, J. S. (1996). *Classics of organization theory* (4th ed.). Belmont, CA: Wadsworth.

Siu, R. G. H. (1979). *The craft of power*. New York: John Wiley & Sons.

Thompson, J. D. (1967). *Organizations in action*. New York: McGraw-Hill.

Tushman, M. L. (April, 1977). A political approach to organizations: A review and rationale. *The Academy of Management Review, 2*, 206–216.

Weber, M. (1922). Bureaucracy. In, H. Gerth & C. W. Mills (Eds.), *Max Weber: Essays in sociology*. Oxford, U.K.: Oxford University Press.

Yates, D., Jr. (1985). *The politics of management*. San Francisco: Jossey-Bass.

# 34
# Power: A Neglected Variable in Social Psychology[1]

## Dorwin Cartwright

Twentieth century social psychology can be traced back to the earliest philosophers, but its complexion is largely determined by developments in this century. Prior to World War I social psychology had failed by and large to meet those requirements of an abstract, positive science which Comte had laid down about the middle of the nineteenth century. Today, in sharp contrast, the spirit of positivism holds sway, and the only problems deemed worthy of attention are those susceptible to objective observation and, preferably, quantification. But this gain has not been made without cost, for scientific status has been achieved by neglecting any phenomena which do not lend themselves readily to the operation of science. . . .

Power is such a phenomenon. This topic received considerable attention in the metaphysical era of social psychology. The classic reference is Hobbes (14) who in 1651 analyzed the motivation for power and some of its social consequences. More recent discussions, still in the metaphysical era, are those of Nietzsche (27) and Adler (1). Many other philosophical and speculative treatments could, of course, be cited. . . .

Both early social psychology and modern society recognize the importance of power. If, however, we examine social psychology since the beginning of its scientific epoch, we search in vain for any concentrated attack on the problem. Surely this constitutes a weakness of modern social psychology. We can only conclude that twentieth century social psychologists have been "soft" on power. Direct investigation has been evaded in many ways. One mode of evasion has been to study power in safe or weak populations—witness the classical stature of research on pecking order among chickens and on dominance among children. Another has been to convert the problem of power into one of attitudes, expectations, and perceptions. Thus, there is more interest in authoritarianism than authority; expectations are made the critical element in the notion of role rather than behavioral restrictions or compulsions; prestige is studied because it can be investigated apart from any specific situation of interpersonal interaction and influence.

It is not here suggested that social psychologists have been cowardly; the fact is that the softer aspects of power have been more accessible to investigation. Nor is it implied that these softer aspects are irrelevant or psychologically uninteresting. The complaint is, rather, that

[1] This chapter is based on the presidential address delivered at the 1953 annual meeting of the Society for the Psychological Study of Social Issues.

*Source:* Dorwin Cartwright, "Power: A Neglected Variable in Social Psychology," in *Studies in Social Power*, edited by Dorwin Cartwright (Ann Arbor, MI: Institute for Social Research, The University of Michigan, 1959), pp. 1–14. Reprinted by permission of the publisher.

power is often seen as essentially not a psychological problem. When asked about power the social psychologist has typically referred the question to the political scientist, sociologist, or economist; or, worse, he has given answers based upon purely personal values. . . .

## SOME ILLUSTRATIVE PROBLEMS INVOLVING POWER

To document the point it is necessary to show how power is inevitably a part of the accepted phenomena of social psychology. This task is made difficult by the fact that there is considerable ambiguity concerning the boundaries of the field. Nevertheless, it is possible to identify certain phenomena (problem areas) as essentially social psychological in nature. Allport (2) has provided a list of these, not intended to be exhaustive, which contains the following: leadership, public opinion, rumor, propaganda, prejudice, attitude change, morale, communications, race relations, and conflicts of value. We shall attempt to show that phenomena of this sort cannot be adequately understood without the concept of power.

### Leadership and Social Roles

Empirical research has progressively forced a restatement of the problem of leadership from that of identifying personal traits of the leader to one of determining the causes and consequences of leadership behavior. In this analysis concepts like "social situation," "position," "function," and "role" have come to the fore. As long as leadership was viewed only as a particular combination of personality traits, properties of the social system could easily be ignored. A major advance in the study of leadership therefore came with the abandonment of this narrow point of view, mistakenly labeled "psychological". . . .

The gradually accumulating evidence from studies such as these fosters a dim view of supervisory training schemes which ignore the power structure of the organization; any theory of leadership which ignores power cannot be viewed more favorably.

If we turn our attention to the general theory of role, we are forced to conclude that here too power is inevitably involved. Since recent work on role, especially that of Newcomb (26), has broadened the scope of social psychology and increased its ability to deal with important phenomena in an integrated fashion, the significance of this conclusion is far-reaching. . . .

Strodtbeck (31, 32) has devised an ingenious experimental method for determining the relative influence of roles. He has used this method to study the roles of husband, wife, and son in different cultures. The procedure is to place members of a family in a situation where they will have a difference of opinion and then to record the ensuing events. He finds, for example, that among Navahos the wife wins 46 arguments to the husband's 34. But among Mormons it is husband 42 to 29! The son seldom wins except by forming coalitions. This research of Strodtbeck and that of others makes it clear that even in groups having no formal table of organization the power of one person to influence another depends upon the role he occupies.

The program of investigations by Shartle, Stogdill, Hemphill and others in the Ohio State Leadership Studies (30) is providing important documentation for our theories of role. In their work the concept of responsibility is assuming fundamental importance; each member of an organization is responsible for the performance of certain activities and is responsible to certain other individuals.

Positions in an organization can be described in terms of these two aspects of responsibility. What people in the organization do, with whom they interact, whom they like, from whom they receive recognition, and so forth—all these factors depend to a high degree upon the nature of the responsibility structure. Members of the organization may vary in the extent to which they accept this structure, but if a member does accept it, his behavior is then guided by certain other people and organizational requirements. Stated differently, the whole organizational structure acquires power over the member and consequently certain other people have power over him, the specific persons depending upon his position in the organization.

This raises the ancient sociological problem which Jaques (20) has analyzed in some detail and has referred to as the "sanctioning of authority." It seems that a group member cannot simply proclaim a new position of power with himself as the occupant. The authority of a position must be sanctioned by others if it is to possess power. In one of the earliest experiments upon the process of interpersonal influence, Frank (13) found that when students agreed to be subjects they automatically gave such authority to the role of experimenter that he could not get them to resist his efforts to have them perform very disagreeable tasks. He finally had to instruct them to resist before he could measure the relative effectiveness of his different techniques of pressure! In a study on changing mothers' behavior toward their children, Brim (7) found that mothers were more likely to try out advice given by a doctor the more they attributed high prestige to the role of doctor. Much of the research on the effects of prestige and credibility, it would seem, can best be interpreted in terms of the sanctioning of the authority of certain roles.

This line of theorizing raises an important question: what determines whether a person accepts the authority of a position occupied by others (or even by himself)? Although there is no research which answers this question directly, the work relating group cohesiveness to strength of group standards (discussed below) suggests that if the authority structure of a group is functionally equivalent to the standards of a group, then the more strongly members are attracted to the group the more will they accept its authority structure. This hypothesis could readily be tested.

The personality characteristics of individuals may also be expected to influence their readiness to sanction the authority of a role. Much of the work on authoritarianism can be interpreted as dealing with this problem. Another provocative approach is represented by the research of Jeanne and Jack Block (6) who, though not investigating directly the sanctioning of authority of a role, do show how the amount of influence exerted by a role on a person is related to certain of his personality characteristics. . . . The results show compliance to be related to (a) a trichotomy on "ego control" into over-controllers, appropriate controllers, and under-controllers; (b) scores on the California test of ethnocentrism; and (c) speed of establishing norms in an experiment on autokinetic movement. The Blocks propose that conforming to a suggestion from an authority is the expression of a more general "structuring" approach to an unpredictable environment. This predisposition, in turn, may be viewed as part of a larger syndrome of ego control which they term "over-control." The results of this one study do not, of course, tell us whether these over-controllers tend to accept the authority of all roles which might claim authority or whether they are inclined to give sanction only to certain sorts of potentially authoritative roles.

An experiment by Hoffman (15) should also be mentioned in this connection. He, too, related behavior in an experimental setting to personality variables. In his study, subjects were dichotomized into conformers and nonconformers on the basis of conformity to an announced group average of judgments of perceived distance. His results show that the conformers scored significantly higher on such measures as parental dominance, inability to tolerate impulses, overconcern for the well-being of parents, and strict moralism. . . .

This brief overview of research on role raises doubt that such soft properties as expectations and perceptions adequately characterize the actual phenomena of role. The harder properties of power are inextricably a part of the phenomena referred to by the concept of role.

## Communication

If we turn to research on communication, we find that power must be recognized here, too. In fact, it is the power aspect of communication which gives the concept such a central place in current social psychological theory. Communication is the mechanism by which interpersonal influence is exerted. Without communication there would be no group norms, group goals, or organized group action. Let us examine the evidence for these conclusions.

First, it is perfectly obvious as soon as one bothers to raise the question that all communications are not equally influential. This, of course, has been known for a long time, and there is a respectable literature on the effectiveness of different kinds of content in communications. We are not so well supplied, however, with findings concerning the way in which the relations between communicator and recipient influence

the effectiveness of communication. The work of Hovland and Weiss (16) and Kelman and Hovland (23) on source credibility dramatizes the importance of treating separately the content of a communication and its source. They have shown that the so-called "sleeper effect" depends upon the more rapid decay over time of the effects of the source than of the content. . . .

A program of research conducted at the Research Center for Group Dynamics adds further insight into the nature of communication. First, Festinger, Schachter, and Back (11) and Back (4) show that a communication between people in a group to which they are strongly attracted is more effective than a similar communication between people in a less attractive group. . . .

Second, the direction and content of the flow of communication in an organized group or community are not indifferent to the social position of the people involved. Orders, for example, seldom flow up a power hierarchy, but certain other types of communication are quite likely to do so. The studies by Hurwitz, Zander, and Hymovitch (18), Jackson (19), Kelley (22), and others are beginning to reveal how upward communication may serve an individual as a substitute for upward locomotion in a power hierarchy, how a person may use communication as a device for minimizing the dangers of hostile actions by those in higher positions, and how a person of superior power may tailor the content and direction of his communications to maintain the belief among others that his superior behavior justifies his position. Thus, we must specify the power relations among people to understand either the frequency and content of communications passing among them or the authority of such communications.

Third, even the study of rumor cannot safely ignore the power situation. . . .

Rumors are especially likely to flourish among people who see that their fates are in other people's hands.

If communication is to be a basic concept of social psychology, so too is power.

## Interpersonal and Intergroup Relations

A few years ago the Research Center for Group Dynamics was asked by a group of junior high school teachers to help them understand better the sources of conflict and irritation in the relations among teachers, parents, and students. A project was organized by Jenkins and Lippitt (21) which included interviews with a sample of each of these populations. Respondents were asked to indicate what they believed were the things that each group did that each other group liked (for example, "What are the things that parents do that teachers like?"). They were also asked parallel questions to indicate disliked behavior.

Consider, first, the teacher-student relationship. Of all categories of teacher behavior, the one having most significance for students is that the teacher be fair. This seems to imply that the teacher is a sort of judge who hands down decisions of importance, thus making fairness a matter of real concern. When we examine the other side of the relationship and consider the responses of teachers, we get further confirmation of the teacher's power over students. Seventy-three percent of the teachers mention as important student behavior "being respectful" and "accepting the teacher as authority." Forty-two per cent mention "obedience."

The relations between parents and students turn out to be much the same, but with different realms of behavior coming under the control of parents. Complaints about parents consists of a long list of things "they won't let us do" and of other things "they make us do."

Though parents tend not to mention the importance of obedience and respect as much as teachers, the students nonetheless report that parents do place major emphasis upon compliance to parental authority.

More subtle is the finding concerning teacher-parent relations. Here it is clear that teachers have strong needs for friendship with adults and for acceptance as members of the community. Parents chiefly control the fate of teachers in this respect; they can give or withhold gratification of these needs. This relation is, moreover, one way; there is no indication that parents would feel deprived without the friendship, recognition, or acceptance of teachers. Knowledge of this asymmetrical power relation is essential for understanding the behavior, attitudes, and feelings of teachers and parents.

Experience with intergroup discrimination and prejudice points the same lesson. Can we really hope to explain these phenomena or to build programs of social action solely with such variables as authoritarianism, ethnocentrism, displaced aggression, and attitude? How do these concepts help to understand the substantial improvement of conditions for Negroes in the automobile industry following certain union policy-decisions or the presence of a nonsegregated dining room at Montgomery, Alabama— on the Air Force Base? Kurt Lewin (24) recognized the importance of power in intergroup relations when he asserted that "discrimination against minorities will not be changed as long as forces are not changed which determine the decisions of the gatekeepers." (p. 186) With such a perspective social psychologists will take more than passing notice of such findings as that of Hunter (17) in his study of the power structure of Regional City—a medium sized city with a Negro population of nearly one-third the total. Through various devices he was able to construct a list of 40 people who could safely be called the city's most powerful; the approval of these people is required for the success of any community project. Those who wish to better intergroup relations in this city might be well advised to work with this group. They should know, however, that not a single Negro is on this list of influential people. (Only 3 could be considered even nominees on a list of 175.) . . .

## Social Determinants of Emotional Adjustment

The importance of the concept of power for social psychology may be illustrated with respect to one other social problem. What determines the mental health or illness of individuals? While it is clear that physiological determinants are important, it is now known that social situations differ significantly in their impact upon the emotional adjustment of all those involved in them. Perhaps one of the clearest demonstrations of such influences was provided by the experiment of Lewin, Lippitt, and White (25) on different styles of leadership. Here it was found that the aggressiveness of a given child depended upon the style of leadership provided by the adult in charge of the group. Although the different styles of leadership studied in this experiment differed from one another in a number of ways, it appears that the most critical aspects of leadership were the size of the space of free movement allowed the children and whether the leader's power was used to support or obstruct the behavior of the children. The leader's use of power basically affected the emotional climate of the group.

In any social situation, and especially in hierarchical ones, certain people have power to help or hinder the goal-directed behavior of others. Emotional security

depends rather directly upon the magnitude of this power and upon the benevolence of its use. . . .

Consistent with this general conception of the relation between security and power are the findings of a rather different sort of experiment conducted by Pepitone (29). He placed boys in a situation where the achievement of an attractive object was under the control of a panel of three judges. After a standardized interaction between the boy and the panel, each boy was asked to rate the relative power and relative benevolence of each member of the panel. In this setting Pepitone found perceptual distortions designed, as it were, to minimize the threatening power of the panel members—if a member was rated as powerful, his benevolence was rated higher; and if he was rated as malevolent, his power was rated lower.

From the findings of research of the sort reported here it seems clear that the impact of social situations upon emotional adjustment will be adequately understood only if power is explicitly recognized.

## SUMMARY

This brief overview of the field of social psychology leads to four conclusions:

1. A major deficiency of the theories of social psychology is that they have been soft on power.
2. The important social problems which demand our attention raise questions about power—questions which our systematic knowledge cannot answer.
3. Quite apart from any practical considerations, a social psychological theory without the concept of power (or its equivalent) is incomplete. Such concepts as communication, role, attitude, expectation, and norm cannot by themselves account realistically for the processes of influence to which they

refer, nor can they deal effectively with social change and resistance to change.

4. A concerted attack on the problem of power should produce a major advance in the field of social psychology. Such an advance will consist of an improved understanding of the proper subject-matter of social psychology and a reorganization of its conceptual systems.

# REFERENCES

1. Adler, A. A study of organ inferiority and its psychic compensations. *Trans. Nerv. ment. Dis. Monogr. Ser.*, 1917, **24.**

2. Allport, G. W. The historical background of modern social psychology. In G. Lindzey (Ed.), *Handbook of social psychology.* Cambridge: Addison-Wesley, 1954, 3–56.

3. Arsenian, J. M. Young children in an insecure situation. *J. abnorm. soc. Psychol.*, 1943, **38,** 225–249.

4. Back, K. W. Influence through social communication. *J. abnorm. soc. Psychol.*, 1951, **46,** 9–23.

5. Barnard, C. I. *The functions of the executive.* Cambridge: Harvard Univer. Press, 1938.

6. Block, J., & Block, J. An interpersonal experiment on reactions to authority. *Hum. Relat.*, 1952, **5,** 91–98.

7. Brim, O. G., Jr. The acceptance of new behavior in child-rearing. *Hum. Relat.*, 1954, **7,** 473–491.

8. Campbell, A. Administering research organizations. *Amer. Psychol.*, 1953, **8,** 225–230.

9. Deutsch, M., & Collins, M. E. *Interracial housing: A psychological evaluation of a social experiment.* Minneapolis: Univer. Minnesota Press, 1951.

10. Festinger, L., Cartwright, D., et al. A study of a rumor: Its origin and spread. *Hum. Relat.*, 1948, **1,** 464–486.

11. Festinger, L., Schachter, S., & Back, K. W. *Social pressures in informal groups.* New York: Harper, 1950.

12. Fleishman, E. A., Harris, E. F., & Burtt, H. E. *Leadership and supervision in industry: An evaluation of a supervisory training program.* Columbus: Ohio State University Bureau of Educational Research, 1955.

13. Frank, J. D. Experimental study of personal pressures and resistance: I. Experimental production of resistance. *J. gen. Psychol.*, 1944, **30,** 23–41.

14. Hobbes, T. *Leviathan.* Reprint of 1st (1651) Ed., Cambridge: Univer. Press, 1904.

15. Hoffman, M. L. Some psychodynamic factors in compulsive conformity. *J. abnorm. soc. Psychol.*, 1953, **48,** 383–393.

16. Hovland, C. I., & Weiss, W. The influence of source credibility on communication effectiveness. *Pub. Opin. Quart.*, 1952, **15,** 635–650.

17. Hunter, F. *Community power structure.* Chapel Hill: Univer. North Carolina Press, 1953.

18. Hurwitz, J. I., Zander, A. F., & Hymovitch. B. Some effects of power on the relations among group members. In D. Cartwright & A. Zander (Eds.), *Group dynamics: Research and theory.* Evanston: Row, Peterson, 1953, pp. 483–492.

19. Jackson, J. M. Analysis of interpersonal relations in a formal organization. Unpublished doctor's dissertation, Univer. Michigan, 1952.

20. Jaques, E. *The changing culture of a factory.* London: Tavistock, 1951.

21. Jenkins, D., & Lippitt, R. *Interpersonal perceptions of teachers, students and parents.* Washington: Nat. Train. Labor. Group Devel., 1951.

22. Kelley, H. H. Communication in experimentally created hierarchies. *Hum. Relat.*, 1951, **4,** 39–56.

23. Kelman, H. C., & Hovland, C. I. "Reinstatement" of the communicator in delayed measurement of opinion change. *J. abnorm. soc. Psychol.*, 1953, **48,** 327–335.

24. Lewin, K. *Field theory in social science.* New York: Harper, 1951.

25. Lewin, K., Lippitt, R., & White, R. K. Patterns of aggressive behavior in experimentally created "social climates." *J. soc. Psychol.*, 1939, **10,** 271–299.

26. Newcomb, T. *Social psychology.* New York: Dryden, 1950.

27. Nietzsche, F. *Der Wille zur Macht.* Book 3, sec. 702. In Nietzsche's complete *Werke,* vol. **16.** Leipzig: Alfred Kröner, 1912.

28. Pelz, D. C. Influence: A key to effective leadership in the first line supervisor. *Personnel*, 1952, **3,** 3–11.

29. Pepitone, A. Motivational effects in social perception. *Hum. Relat.*, 1950, **3,** 57–76.

30. Stogdill, R. M. Leadership, membership and organization. *Psychol. Bull.*, 1950, **47,** 1–14.

31. Strodtbeck, F. L. Husband-wife interaction over revealed differences. *Amer. sociol. Rev.*, 1951, **16,** 468–473.

32. Strodtbeck, F. L. The family as a three-person group. *Amer. sociol. Rev.*, 1954, **19,** 23–29.

33. Wright, M. E. The influence of frustration on the social relations of young children. *Charact. Pers.*, 1943, **12,** 111–122.

## 35

# The Bases of Social Power

## John R. P. French, Jr., & Bertram Raven

The processes of power are pervasive, complex, and often disguised in our society. Accordingly one finds in political science, in sociology, and in social psychology a variety of distinctions among different types of social power or among qualitatively different processes of social influence (1, 6, 14, 20, 23, 29, 30, 38, 41). Our main purpose is to identify the major types of power and to define them systematically so that we may compare them according to the changes which they produce and the other effects which accompany the use of power. The phenomena of power and influence involve a dyadic relation between two agents which may be viewed from two points of view: (a) What determines the behavior of the agent who exerts power? (b) What determines the reactions of the recipient of this behavior? We take this second point of view and formulate our theory in terms of the life space of P, the person upon whom the power is exerted. In this way we hope to define basic concepts of power which will be adequate to explain many of the phenomena of social influence, including some which have been described in other less genotypic terms. . . .

### POWER, INFLUENCE, AND CHANGE

#### Psychological Change

Since we shall define power in terms of influence, and influence in terms of psychological change, we begin with a discussion of change. We want to define change at a level of generality which includes changes in behavior, opinions, attitudes, goals, needs, values and all other aspects of the person's psychological field. We shall use the word "system" to refer to any such part of the life space.[1] Following Lewin (26, p. 305) the state of a system at time 1 will be noted $s_1(a)$.

Psychological change is defined as any alteration of the state of some system $a$ over time. The amount of change is measured by the size of the difference between the states of the system $a$ at time 1 and at time 2: $ch(a) = s_2(a) - s_1(a)$.

Change in any psychological system may be conceptualized in terms of psychological forces. But it is important to note that the change must be coordinated to the resultant force of all the forces operating at the moment. Change in an opinion, for example, may be determined jointly by a driving force induced by another person, a restraining force corresponding to anchorage in a group opinion, and an own force stemming from the person's needs.

### Social Influence

Our theory of social influence and power is limited to influence on the person, P, produced by a social agent, O, where O

[1] The word "system" is here used to refer to a whole or to a part of the whole.

Source: John R. P. French, Jr., and Bertram Raven, "The Bases of Social Power," in *Studies in Social Power*, edited by Dorwin P. Cartwright (Ann Arbor, MI: Institute for Social Research, The University of Michigan, 1959), pp. 150–167. Reprinted by permission of the publisher.

can be either another person, a role, a norm, a group or a part of a group. We do not consider social influence exerted on a group.

The influence of O on system *a* in the life space of P is defined as the resultant force on system *a* which has its source in an act of O. This resultant force induced by O consists of two components: a force to change the system in the direction induced by O and an opposing resistance set up by the same act of O.

By this definition the influence of O does not include P's own forces nor the forces induced by other social agents. Accordingly the "influence" of O must be clearly distinguished from O's "control" of P. O may be able to induce strong forces on P to carry out an activity (i.e., O exerts strong influence on P); but if the opposing forces induced by another person or by P's own needs are stronger, then P will locomote in an opposite direction (i.e., O does not have control over P). Thus psychological change in P can be taken as an operational definition of the social influence of O on P only when the effects of other forces have been eliminated. . . .

Commonly social influence takes place through an intentional act on the part of O. However, we do not want to limit our definition of "act" to such conscious behavior. Indeed, influence might result from the passive presence of O, with no evidence of speech, or overt movement. A policeman's standing on a corner may be considered an act of an agent for the speeding motorist. Such acts of the inducing agent will vary in strength, for O may not always utilize all of his power. The policeman, for example, may merely stand and watch or act more strongly by blowing his whistle at the motorist.

The influence exerted by an act need not be in the direction intended by O. The direction of the resultant force on

P will depend on the relative magnitude of the induced force set up by the act of O and the resisting force in the opposite direction which is generated by that same act. In cases where O intends to influence P in a given direction, a resultant force in the same direction may be termed positive influence whereas a resultant force in the opposite direction may be termed negative influence. . . .

## Social Power

The strength of power of O/P in some system *a* is defined as the maximum potential ability of O to influence P in *a*.

By this definition influence is kinetic power, just as power is potential influence. It is assumed that O is capable of various acts which, because of some more or less enduring relation to P, are able to exert influence on P.[2] O's power is measured by his maximum possible influence, though he may often choose to exert less than his full power.

An equivalent definition of power may be stated in terms of the resultant of two forces set up by the act of O: one in the direction of O's influence attempt and another resisting force in the opposite direction. Power is the maximum resultant of these two forces:

$$\text{Power of O/P}(a) = (f_{a,x} - f_{\overline{a,x}})^{\text{max}}$$

where the source of both forces is an act of O.

Thus the power of O with respect to system *a* of P is equal to the maximum

[2] The concept of power has the conceptual property of *potentiality*; but it seems useful to restrict this potential influence to more or less enduring power relations between O and P by excluding from the definition of power those cases where the potential influence is so momentary or so changing that it cannot be predicted from the existing relationship. Power is a useful concept for describing social structure only if it has a certain stability over time; it is useless if every momentary social stimulus is viewed as actualizing social power.

resultant force of two forces set up by any possible act of O: (a) the force which O can set up on the system *a* to change in the direction x, (b) the resisting force,[3] in the opposite direction. Whenever the first component force is greater than the second, positive power exists; but if the second component force is greater than the first, then O has negative power over P. . . .

For certain purposes it is convenient to define the range of power as the set of all systems within which O has power of strength greater than zero. A husband may have a broad range of power over his wife, but a narrow range of power over his employer. We shall use the term "magnitude of power" to denote the summation of O's power over P in all systems of his range.

## The Dependence of s(a) on O

We assume that any change in the state of a system is produced by a change in some factor upon which it is functionally dependent. The state of an opinion, for example, may change because of a change either in some internal factor such as a need or in some external factor such as the arguments of O. Likewise the maintenance of the same state of a system is produced by the stability or lack of change in the internal and external factors. In general, then, psychological change and stability can be conceptualized in terms of dynamic dependence. Our interest is focused on the special case of dependence on an external agent, O **(31)**.

In many cases the initial state of the system has the character of a quasistationary equilibrium with a central force field around $s_1(a)$ **(26, p. 106)**. In such cases we may derive a tendency toward retrogression to the original state as soon as the force induced by O is removed.[4]

Consider the example of three separated employees who have been working at the same steady level of production despite normal, small fluctuations in the work environment. The supervisor orders each to increase his production, and the level of each goes up from 100 to 115 pieces per day. After a week of producing at the new rate of 115 pieces per day, the supervisor is removed for a week. The production of employee A immediately returns to 100 but B and C return to only 110 pieces per day. Other things being equal, we can infer that A's new rate was completely dependent on his supervisor whereas the new rate of B and C was dependent on the supervisor only to the extent of 5 pieces. Let us further assume that when the supervisor returned, the production of B and of C returned to 115 without further orders from the supervisor. Now another month goes by during which B and C maintain a steady 115 pieces per day. However, there is a difference between them: B's level of production still depends on O to the extent of 5 pieces whereas C has come to rely on his own sense of obligation to obey the order of his legitimate supervisor rather than on the supervisor's external pressure for the maintenance of his 115 pieces per day. Accordingly, the next time the supervisor departs, B's production again drops to 110 but C's remains at 115 pieces per day. In cases like employee B, the degree

---

[3] We define resistance to an attempted induction as a force in the opposite direction which is set up by the same act of O. It must be distinguished from opposition which is defined as existing opposing forces which do not have their source in the same act of O. For example, a boy might resist his mother's order to eat spinach because of the manner of the induction attempt, and at the same time he might oppose it because he didn't like spinach.

[4] Miller (33) assumes that all living systems have this character. However, it may be that some systems in the life space do not have this elasticity.

of dependence is contingent on the perceived probability that O will observe the state of the system and note P's conformity (5, 6, 11, 12, 23). The level of observability will in turn depend on both the nature of the system (e.g., the difference between a covert opinion and overt behavior) and on the environmental barriers to observation (e.g., O is too far away from P). . . .

## THE BASES OF POWER

By the basis of power we mean the relationship between O and P which is the source of that power. It is rare that we can say with certainty that a given empirical case of power is limited to one source. Normally, the relation between O and P will be characterized by several qualitatively different variables which are bases of power (30, Chapter 11). Although there are undoubtedly many possible bases of power which may be distinguished, we shall here define five which seem especially common and important. These five bases of O's power are: (1) reward power, based on P's perception that O has the ability to mediate rewards for him; (2) coercive power, based on P's perception that O has the ability to mediate punishments for him; (3) legitimate power, based on the perception by P that O has a legitimate right to prescribe behavior for him; (4) referent power, based on P's identification with O; (5) expert power, based on the perception that O has some special knowledge or expertness. . . .

### Reward Power

Reward power is defined as power whose basis is the ability to reward. The strength of the reward power of O/P increases with the magnitude of the rewards which P perceives that O can mediate for him. Reward power depends on O's ability to administer positive valences and to remove or decrease negative valences. The strength of reward power also depends upon the probability that O can mediate the reward, as perceived by P. A common example of reward power is the addition of a piecework rate in the factory as an incentive to increase production.

The new state of the system induced by a promise of reward (for example the factory worker's increased level of production) will be highly dependent on O. Since O mediates the reward, he controls the probability that P will receive it. Thus P's new rate of production will be dependent on his subjective probability that O will reward him for conformity minus his subjective probability that O will reward him even if he returns to his old level. Both probabilities will be greatly affected by the level of observability of P's behavior. . . .

The utilization of actual rewards (instead of promises) by O will tend over time to increase the attraction of P toward O and therefore the referent power of O over P. As we shall note later, such referent power will permit O to induce changes which are relatively independent. Neither rewards nor promises will arouse resistance in P, provided P considers it legitimate for O to offer rewards.

The range of reward power is specific to those regions within which O can reward P for conforming. The use of rewards to change systems within the range of reward power tends to increase reward power by increasing the probability attached to future promises. However, unsuccessful attempts to exert reward power outside the range of power would tend to decrease the power; for example if O offers to reward P for performing an impossible act, this will reduce for P the probability of receiving future rewards promised by O.

### Coercive Power

Coercive power is similar to reward power in that it also involves O's ability to manipulate the attainment of valences. Coercive power of O/P stems from the expectation on the part of P that he will be punished by O if he fails to conform to the influence attempt. Thus negative valences will exist in given regions of P's life space, corresponding to the threatened punishment by O. The strength of coercive power depends on the magnitude of the negative valence of the threatened punishment multiplied by the perceived probability that P can avoid the punishment by conformity, i.e., the probability of punishment for nonconformity minus the probability of punishment for conformity (11). Just as an offer of a piecerate bonus in a factory can serve as a basis for reward power, so the ability to fire a worker if he falls below a given level of production will result in coercive power.

Coercive power leads to dependent change also; and the degree of dependence varies with the level of observability of P's conformity. An excellent illustration of coercive power leading to dependent change is provided by a clothes presser in a factory observed by Coch and French (3). As her efficiency rating climbed above average for the group the other workers began to "scapegoat" her. That the resulting plateau in her production was not independent of the group was evident once she was removed from the presence of the other workers. Her production immediately climbed to new heights.[5] . . .

The distinction between these two types of power is important because the

dynamics are different. The concept of "sanctions" sometimes lumps the two together despite their opposite effects. While reward power may eventually result in an independent system, the effects of coercive power will continue to be dependent. Reward power will tend to increase the attraction of P toward O; coercive power will decrease this attraction (11, 12). The valence of the region of behavior will become more negative, acquiring some negative valence from the threatened punishment. The negative valence of punishment would also spread to other regions of the life space. Lewin (25) has pointed out this distinction between the effects of rewards and punishment. In the case of threatened punishment, there will be a resultant force on P to leave the field entirely. Thus, to achieve conformity, O must not only place a strong negative valence in certain regions through threat of punishment, but O must also introduce restraining forces, or other strong valences, so as to prevent P from withdrawing completely from O's range of coercive power. Otherwise the probability of receiving the punishment, if P does not conform, will be too low to be effective.

## Legitimate Power

There has been considerable investigation and speculation about socially prescribed behavior, particularly that which is specific to a given role or position. Linton (29) distinguishes group norms according to whether they are universals for everyone in the culture, alternatives (the individual having a choice as to whether or not to accept them), or specialties (specific to given positions). Whether we speak of internalized norms, role prescriptions and expectations (34), or internalized pressures (15), the fact remains that each individual sees certain regions toward which he should locomote, some regions toward which he should not locomote, and some regions

[5] Though the primary influence of coercive power is dependent, it often produces secondary changes which are independent. Brainwashing, for example, utilizes coercive power to produce many primary changes in the life space of the prisoner, but these dependent changes can lead to identification with the aggressor and hence to secondary changes in ideology which are independent.

toward which he may locomote if they are generally attractive for him. This applies to specific behaviors in which he may, should, or should not engage; it applies to certain attitudes or beliefs which he may, should, or should not hold. The feeling of "oughtness" may be an internalization from his parents, from his teachers, from his religion, or may have been logically developed from some idiosyncratic system of ethics. He will speak of such behaviors with expressions like "should," "ought to," or "has a right to." In many cases, the original source of the requirement is not recalled.

Though we have oversimplified such evaluations of behavior with a positive-neutral-negative trichotomy, the evaluation of behaviors by the person is really more one of degree. This dimension of evaluation, we shall call "legitimacy." Conceptually, we may think of legitimacy as a valence in a region which is induced by some internalized norm or value. This value has the same conceptual property as power, namely an ability to induce force fields (**26**, p. 40–41). . . .

Legitimate power of O/P is here defined as that power which stems from internalized values in P which dictate that O has a legitimate right to influence P and that P has an obligation to accept this influence. We note that legitimate power is very similar to the notion of legitimacy of authority which has long been explored by sociologists, particularly by Weber (**42**), and more recently by Goldhammer and Shils (**14**). However, legitimate power is not always a role relation: P may accept an induction from O simply because he had previously promised to help O and he values his word too much to break the promise. In all cases, the notion of legitimacy involves some sort of code or standard, accepted by the individual, by virtue of which the external agent can assert his

power. We shall attempt to describe a few of these values here.

*Bases for legitimate power.* Cultural values constitute one common basis for the legitimate power of one individual over another. O has characteristics which are specified by the culture as giving him the right to prescribe behavior for P, who may not have these characteristics. These bases, which Weber (**42**) has called the authority of the "eternal yesterday," include such things as age, intelligence, caste, and physical characteristics. In some cultures, the aged are granted the right to prescribe behavior for others in practically all behavior areas. In most cultures, there are certain areas of behavior in which a person of one sex is granted the right to prescribe behavior for the other sex.

Acceptance of the social structure is another basis for legitimate power. If P accepts as right the social structure of his group, organization, or society, especially the social structure involving a hierarchy of authority, P will accept the legitimate authority of O who occupies a superior office in the hierarchy. Thus legitimate power in a formal organization is largely a relationship between offices rather than between persons. And the acceptance of an office as *right* is a basis for legitimate power—a judge has a right to levy fines, a foreman should assign work, a priest is justified in prescribing religious beliefs, and it is the management's prerogative to make certain decisions (**10**). However, legitimate power also involves the perceived right of the person to hold the office.

Designation by a legitimizing agent is a third basis for legitimate power. An influencer O may be seen as legitimate in prescribing behavior for P because he has been granted such power by a legitimizing agent whom P accepts. Thus a department head may accept the authority of his vice-president in a certain area because that authority has been specifically delegated by the president. An election is perhaps the most common example of a group's serving to legitimize the authority of one individual or office for other individuals in the group. The success of such legitimizing depends upon the acceptance of the legitimizing agent and procedure. In this case it depends ultimately on certain democratic values concerning election procedures. The election process is one of legitimizing a person's right to an office which already has a legitimate range of power associated with it.

*Range of legitimate power of O/P.* The areas in which legitimate power may be exercised are generally specified along with the designation of that power. A job description, for example, usually specifies supervisory activities and also designates the person to whom the jobholder is responsible for the duties described. Some bases for legitimate authority carry with them a very broad range. Culturally derived bases for legitimate power are often especially broad. It is not uncommon to find cultures in which a member of a given caste can legitimately prescribe behavior for all members of lower castes in practically all regions. More common, however, are instances of legitimate power where the range is specifically and narrowly prescribed. A sergeant in the army is given a specific set of regions within which he can legitimately prescribe behavior for his men.

The attempted use of legitimate power which is outside of the range of legitimate power will decrease the legitimate power of the authority figure. Such use of power which is not legitimate will also decrease the attractiveness of O (11, 12, 36).

*Legitimate power and influence.* The new state of the system which results from legitimate power usually has high dependence on O though it may become independent. Here, however, the degree of dependence is not related to the level of observability. Since legitimate power is based on P's values, the source of the forces induced by O include both these internal values and O. O's induction serves to activate the values and to relate them to the system which is influenced, but thereafter the new state of the system may become directly dependent on the values with no mediation by O. Accordingly this new state will be relatively stable and consistent across varying environmental situations since P's values are more stable than his psychological environment. . . .

## Referent Power

The referent power of O/P has its basis in the identification of P with O. By identification, we mean a feeling of oneness of P with O, or a desire for such an identity. If O is a person toward whom P is highly attracted, P will have a feeling of membership or a desire to join. If P is already closely associated with O he will want to maintain this relationship (39, 41). P's identification with O can be established or maintained if P behaves, believes, and perceives as O does. Accordingly O has the ability to influence P, even though P may be unaware of this referent power. A verbalization of such power by P might be, "I am like O, and therefore I shall behave or believe as O does," or "I want to be like O, and I will be more like O if I behave or believe as O does." The stronger the identification of P with O the greater the referent power of O/P. . . .

We must try to distinguish between referent power and other types of power which might be operative at the same time. If a member is attracted to a group and he conforms to its norms only because he fears ridicule or expulsion from the group for nonconformity, we would call this coercive power. On the other hand if he conforms in order to obtain praise for conformity, it is a case of reward power. . . . Conformity with majority opinion is sometimes based on a respect for the collective wisdom of the group, in which case it is expert power. It is important to distinguish these phenomena, all grouped together elsewhere as "pressures toward uniformity," since the type of change which occurs will be different for different bases of power.

The concepts of "reference group" **(40)** and "prestige suggestion" may be treated as instances of referent power. In this case, O, the prestigeful person or group, is valued by P; because P desires to be associated or identified with O, he will assume attitudes or beliefs held by O. Similarly a negative reference group which O dislikes and evaluates negatively may exert negative influence on P as a result of negative referent power.

It has been demonstrated that the power which we designate as referent power is especially great when P is attracted to O **(2, 7, 8, 9, 13, 23, 30)**. In our terms, this would mean that the greater the attraction, the greater the identification, and consequently the greater the referent power. In some cases, attraction or prestige may have a specific basis, and the range of referent power will be limited accordingly: a group of campers may have great referent power over a member regarding campcraft, but considerably less effect on other regions **(30)**. However, we hypothesize that the greater the attraction of P toward O, the broader the range of referent power of O/P. . . .

## Expert Power

The strength of the expert power of O/P varies with the extent of the knowledge or perception which P attributes to O within a given area. Probably P evaluates O's expertness in relation to his own knowledge as well as against an absolute standard. In any case expert power results in primary social influence on P's cognitive structure and probably not on other types of systems. Of course changes in the cognitive structure can change the direction of forces and hence of locomotion, but such a change of behavior is secondary social influence. Expert power has been demonstrated experimentally **(8, 33)**. Accepting an attorney's advice in legal matters is a common example of expert influence; but there are many instances based on much less knowledge, such as the acceptance by a stranger of directions given by a native villager.

Expert power, where O need not be a member of P's group, is called "informational power" by Deutsch and Gerard **(4)**. This type of expert power must be distinguished from influence based on the content of communication as described by Hovland et al. **(17, 18, 23, 24)**. The influence of the content of a communication upon an opinion is presumably a secondary influence produced after the *primary* influence (i.e., the acceptance of the information). Since power is here defined in terms of the primary changes, the influence of the content on a related opinion is not a case of expert power as we have defined it, but the initial acceptance of the validity of the content does seem to be based on expert power or referent power. . . .

The range of expert power, we assume, is more delimited than that of referent power. Not only is it restricted to cognitive systems but the expert is seen as having superior knowledge or ability in very specific areas, and his power will be limited to these areas, though some "halo effect" might occur. Recently, some of our renowned physical scientists have found quite painfully that their expert power in physical sciences does not extend to regions involving international politics. Indeed, there is some evidence that the attempted exertion of expert power outside of the range of expert power will reduce that expert power. An undermining of confidence seems to take place.

## SUMMARY

We have distinguished five types of power: referent power, expert power, reward power, coercive power, and legitimate power. These distinctions led to the following hypotheses.

1. For all five types, the stronger the basis of power the greater the power.
2. For any type of power the size of the range may vary greatly, but in general referent power will have the broadest range.
3. Any attempt to utilize power outside the range of power will tend to reduce the power.
4. A new state of a system produced by reward power or coercive power will be highly dependent on O, and the more observable P's conformity the more dependent the state. For the other three types of power, the new state is usually dependent, at least in the beginning, but in any case the level of observability has no effect on the degree of dependence.
5. Coercion results in decreased attraction of P toward O and high resistance; reward power results in increased attraction and low resistance.
6. The more legitimate the coercion the less it will produce resistance and decreased attraction.

## REFERENCES

1. Asch, S. E. *Social psychology.* New York: Prentice-Hall, 1952.
2. Back, K. W. Influence through social communication. *J. abnorm. soc. Psychol.,* 1951, **46,** 9–23.
3. Coch, L., & French, J. R. P., Jr. Overcoming resistance to change. *Hum. Relat.,* 1948, **1,** 512–32.
4. Deutsch, M., & Gerard, H. B. A study of normative and informational influences upon individual judgment. *J. abnorm. soc. Psychol.,* 1955, **51,** 629–36.
5. Dittes, J. E., & Kelley, H. H. Effects of different conditions of acceptance upon conformity to group norms. *J. abnorm. soc. Psychol.,* 1956, **53,** 100–107.
6. Festinger, L. An analysis of compliant behavior. In Sherif, M., & Wilson, M. O., (Eds.), *Group relations at the crossroads.* New York: Harper, 1953, 232–56.
7. Festinger, L. Informal social communication. *Psychol. Rev.,* 1950, **57,** 271–82.
8. Festinger, L., Gerard, H. B., Hymovitch, B., Kelley, H. H., & Raven, B. H. The influence process in the presence of extreme deviates. *Hum. Relat.,* 1952, **5,** 327–346.
9. Festinger, L., Schachter, S., & Back, K. The operation of group standards. In Cartwright, D., & Zander, A. *Group dynamics: research and theory.* Evanston: Row, Peterson, 1953, 204–23.
10. French, J. R. P., Jr., Israel, Joachim & Ås, Dagfinn. "Arbeidernes medvirkning i industribedriften. En eksperimentell undersøkelse." Institute for Social Research, Oslo, Norway, 1957.
11. French, J. R. P., Jr., Levinger, G., & Morrison, H. W. The legitimacy of coercive power. In preparation.
12. French, J. R. P., Jr., & Raven, B. H. An experiment in legitimate and coercive power. In preparation.
13. Gerard, H. B. The anchorage of opinions in face-to-face groups. *Hum. Relat.,* 1954, **7,** 313–325.
14. Goldhammer, H., & Shils, E. A. Types of power and status. *Amer. J. Sociol.,* 1939, **45,** 171–178.
15. Herbst, P. G. Analysis and measurement of a situation. *Hum. Relat.,* 1953, **2,** 113–140.
16. Hochbaum, G. M. Self-confidence and reactions to group pressures. *Amer. soc. Rev.,* 1954, **19,** 678–687.
17. Hovland, C. I., Lumsdaine, A. A., & Sheffield, F. D. *Experiments on mass communication.* Princeton: Princeton Univer. Press, 1949.
18. Hovland, C. I., & Weiss, W. The influence of source credibility on communication effectiveness. *Publ. Opin. Quart.,* 1951, **15,** 635–650.

19. Jackson, J. M., & Salzstein, H. D. The effect of person-group relationships on conformity processes. *J. abnorm. soc. Psychol.*, 1958, **57**, 17–24.

20. Jahoda, M. Psychological issues in civil liberties. *Amer. Psychologist*, 1956, **11**, 234–240.

21. Katz, D., & Schank, R. L. *Social psychology.* New York: Wiley, 1938.

22. Kelley, H. H., & Volkart, E. H. The resistance to change of group-anchored attitudes. *Amer. soc. Rev.*, 1952, **17**, 453–465.

23. Kelman, H. Three processes of acceptance of social influence: compliance, identification and internalization. Paper read at the meetings of the American Psychological Association, August 1956.

24. Kelman, H., & Hovland, C. I. "Reinstatement" of the communicator in delayed measurement of opinion change. *J. abnorm. soc. Psychol.*, 1953, **48**, 327–335.

25. Lewin, K. *Dynamic theory of personality.* New York: McGraw-Hill, 1935, 114–170.

26. Lewin, K. *Field theory in social science.* New York: Harper, 1951.

27. Lewin, K., Lippitt, R., & White, R. K. Patterns of aggressive behavior in experimentally created social climates. *J. soc. Psychol.*, 1939, **10**, 271–301.

28. Lasswell, H. D., & Kaplan, A. *Power and society: A framework for political inquiry.* New Haven: Yale Univer. Press, 1950.

29. Linton, R. *The cultural background of personality.* New York: Appleton-Century-Crofts, 1945.

30. Lippitt, R., Polansky, N., Redl, F., & Rosen, S. The dynamics of power. *Hum. Relat.*, 1952, **5**, 37–64.

31. March, J. G. An introduction to the theory and measurement of influence. *Amer. polit. Sci. Rev.*, 1955, **49**, 431–451.

32. Miller, J. G. Toward a general theory for the behavioral sciences. *Amer. Psychologist*, 1955, **10**, 513–531.

33. Moore, H. T. The comparative influence of majority and expert opinion. *Amer. J. Psychol.* 1921, **32**, 16–20.

34. Newcomb, T. M. *Social psychology.* New York: Dryden, 1950.

35. Raven, B. H. The effect of group pressures on opinion, perception, and communication. Unpublished doctoral dissertation, University of Michigan, 1953.

36. Raven, B. H., & French, J. R. P., Jr. Group support, legitimate power, and social influence. *J. Person.*, 1958, **26**, 400–409.

37. Rommetveit, R. *Social norms and roles.* Minneapolis: Univer. Minnesota Press, 1953.

38. Russell, B. *Power: A new social analysis.* New York: Norton, 1938.

39. Stotland, E., Zander, A., Burnstein, E., Wolfe, D., & Natsoulas, T. Studies on the effects of identification. University of Michigan, Institute for Social Research. Forthcoming.

40. Swanson, G. E., Newcomb, T. M., & Hartley, E. L. *Readings in social psychology.* New York: Henry Holt, 1952.

41. Torrance, E. P., & Mason, R. Instructor effort to influence: an experimental evaluation of six approaches. Paper presented at USAF-NRC Symposium on Personnel, Training, and Human Engineering. Washington, D.C., 1956.

42. Weber, M. *The theory of social and economic organization.* Oxford: Oxford Univer. Press, 1947.

## 36

# Sources of Power of Lower Participants in Complex Organizations

*David Mechanic*

It is not unusual for lower participants[1] in complex organizations to assume and wield considerable power and influence not associated with their formally defined positions within these organizations. In sociological terms they have considerable personal power but no authority. Such personal power is often attained, for example, by executive secretaries and accountants in business firms, by attendants in mental hospitals, and even by inmates in prisons. The personal power achieved by these lower participants does not necessarily result from unique personal characteristics, although these may be relevant, but results rather from particular aspects of their location within their organizations.

## INFORMAL VERSUS FORMAL POWER

### Clarification of Definitions

The purpose of this paper is to present some hypotheses explaining why lower participants in organizations can often assume and wield considerable power which is not associated with their positions as formally defined within these organizations. For the purposes of this analysis the concepts "influence," "power," and "control" will be used synonymously. Moreover, we shall not be concerned with type of power, that is, whether the power is based on reward, punishment, identification, power to veto, or whatever.[2] Power will be defined as *any force that results in behavior that would not have occurred if the force had not been present.* We have defined power as a force rather than a relationship because it appears that much of what we mean by power is encompassed by the normative framework of an organization, and thus any analysis of power must take into consideration the power of norms as well as persons.

I shall also argue, following Thibaut and Kelley,[3] that power is closely related

[1] The term "lower participants" comes from Amitai Etzioni, *A Comparative Analysis of Complex Organizations* (New York, 1961) and is used by him to designate persons in positions of lower rank: employees, rank-and-file, members, clients, customers, and inmates. We shall use the term in this paper in a relative sense denoting position vis-à-vis a higher-ranking participant.

[2] One might observe, for example, that the power of lower participants is based primarily on the ability to "veto" or punish. For a discussion of bases of power, see John R. P. French, Jr., and Bertram Raven, "The Bases of Social Power," in D. Cartwright and A. Zander, eds., *Group Dynamics* (Evanston, Ill., 1960), pp. 607–623.

[3] John Thibaut and Harold H. Kelley, *The Social Psychology of Groups* (New York, 1959). For a similar emphasis on dependence, see Richard M.

*Source:* Reprinted from "Sources of Power of Lower Participants in Complex Organizations," by David Mechanic, published in *Administrative Science Quarterly*, Volume 7 #3 (December 1962), pp. 349–365, by permission of *Administrative Science Quarterly*.

to dependence. To the extent that a person is dependent on another, he is potentially subject to the other person's power. Within organizations one makes others dependent upon him by controlling access to information, persons, and instrumentalities, which I shall define as follows:

   *a. Information* includes knowledge of the organization, knowledge about persons, knowledge of the norms, procedures, techniques, and so forth.

   *b. Persons* include anyone within the organization or anyone outside the organization upon whom the organization is in some way dependent.

   *c. Instrumentalities* include any aspect of the physical plant of the organization or its resources (equipment, machines, money, and so on).

Power is a function not only of the extent to which a person controls information, persons, and instrumentalities, but also of the importance of the various attributes he controls.[4] . . .

## A Classic Example

Like many other aspects of organizational theory, one can find a classic statement of our problem in Weber's discussion of the political bureaucracy. Weber indicated the extent to which bureaucrats may have considerable power over political incumbents, as a result, in part, of their permanence within the political bureaucracy, as contrasted to public officials, who are replaced rather frequently.[5] Weber noted how the low-ranking bureaucrat becomes familiar with the organization—its rules and operations, the work flow, and so on—which gives him considerable power over the new political incumbent, who might have higher rank but is not as familiar with the organization. While Weber does not directly state the point, his analysis suggests that bureaucratic permanence has some relationship to increased access to persons, information, and instrumentalities. To state the hypothesis suggested somewhat more formally:

   H1   Other factors remaining constant, organizational power is related to access to persons, information, and instrumentalities.

   H2   Other factors remaining constant, as a participant's length of time in an organization increases, he has increased access to persons, information, and instrumentalities. . . .

## IMPLICATIONS OF ROLE THEORY FOR THE STUDY OF POWER

Role theorists approach the question of influence and power in terms of the behavioral regularities which result from established identities within specific social contexts like families, hospitals, and business firms. The underlying premise of most role theorists is that a large proportion of all behavior is brought about through socialization within specific organizations, and much behavior is routine and established through learning the traditional modes of adaptation in dealing with specific tasks. Thus the positions persons occupy in an organization account for much of their behavior. Norms and roles serve as mediating forces in influence processes.

   While role theorists have argued much about vocabulary, the basic prem-

---

Emerson, Power-Dependence Relationships, *American Sociological Review*, 28(1962), 31–41.

[4] Although this paper will not attempt to explain how access may be measured, the author feels confident that the hypotheses concerned with access are clearly testable.

[5] Max Weber, "The Essentials of Bureaucratic Organization: An Ideal-Type Construction," in Robert Merton *et al.*, *Reader in Bureaucracy* (Glencoe, Ill., 1952), pp. 18–27.

ises underlying their thought have been rather consistent. The argument is essentially that knowledge of one's identity or social position is a powerful index of the expectations such a person is likely to face in various social situations. Since behavior tends to be highly correlated with expectations, prediction of behavior is therefore possible. The approach of role theorists to the study of behavior within organizations is of particular merit in that it provides a consistent set of concepts which is useful analytically in describing recruitment, socialization, interaction, and personality, as well as the formal structure of organizations. Thus the concept of role is one of the few concepts clearly linking social structure, social process, and social character. . . .

It should be clear that lower participants will be more likely to circumvent higher authority, other factors remaining constant, when the mandates of those in power, if not the authority itself, are regarded as illegitimate. Thus as Etzioni points out, when lower participants become alienated from the organization, coercive power is likely to be required if its formal mandates are to be fulfilled.[6]

Moreover, all organizations must maintain control over lower participants. To the extent that lower participants fail to recognize the legitimacy of power, or believe that sanctions cannot or will not be exercised when violations occur, the organization loses, to some extent, its ability to control their behavior. Moreover, in-so-far as higher participants can create the impression that they can or will exert sanctions above their actual willingness to use such sanctions, control over lower participants will increase. It is usually to the advantage of an organization to externalize and impersonalize controls, however, and if

possible to develop positive sentiments toward its rules.

In other words, an effective organization can control its participants in such a way as to make it hardly perceivable that it exercises the control that it does. It seeks commitment from lower participants, and when commitment is obtained, surveillance can be relaxed. On the other hand, when the power of lower participants in organizations is considered, it often appears to be clearly divorced from the traditions, norms, and goals and sentiments of the organization as a whole. Lower participants do not usually achieve control by using the role structure of the organization, but rather by circumventing, sabotaging, and manipulating it.

## SOURCES OF POWER OF LOWER PARTICIPANTS

The most effective way for lower participants to achieve power is to obtain, maintain, and control access to persons, information, and instrumentalities. To the extent that this can be accomplished, lower participants make higher-ranking participants dependent upon them. Thus dependence together with the manipulation of the dependency relationship is the key to the power of lower participants.

A number of examples can be cited which illustrate the preceding point. Scheff, for example, reports on the failure of a state mental hospital to bring about intended reform because of the opposition of hospital attendants.[7] He noted that the power of hospital attendants was largely a result of the dependence of ward physicians on attendants. This dependence resulted from the phy-

[6] Etzioni, *op. cit.*

[7] Thomas J. Scheff, Control over Policy by Attendants in a Mental Hospital, *Journal of Health and Human Behavior*, 2 (1961), 93–105.

sician's short tenure, his lack of interest in administration, and the large amount of administrative responsibility he had to assume. An implicit trading agreement developed between physicians and attendants, whereby attendants would take on some of the responsibilities and obligations of the ward physician in return for increased power in decision-making processes concerning patients. Failure of the ward physician to honor his part of the agreement resulted in information being withheld, disobedience, lack of co-operation, and unwillingness of the attendants to serve as a barrier between the physician and a ward full of patients demanding attention and recognition. When the attendant withheld co-operation, the physician had difficulty in making a graceful entrance and departure from the ward, in handling necessary paper work (officially his responsibility), and in obtaining information needed to deal adequately with daily treatment and behavior problems. When attendants opposed change, they could wield influence by refusing to assume responsibilities officially assigned to the physician.

Similarly, Sykes describes the dependence of prison guards on inmates and the power obtained by inmates over guards.[8] He suggests that although guards could report inmates for disobedience, frequent reports would give prison officials the impression that the guard was unable to command obedience. The guard, therefore, had some stake in ensuring the good behavior of prisoners without use of formal sanctions against them. The result was a trading agreement whereby the guard allowed violations of certain rules in return for co-

operative behavior. A similar situation is found in respect to officers in the Armed Services or foremen in industry. To the extent that they require formal sanctions to bring about co-operation, they are usually perceived by their superiors as less valuable to the organization. For a good leader is expected to command obedience, at least, if not commitment.

## FACTORS AFFECTING POWER

### Expertise

Increasing specialization and organizational growth has made the expert or staff person important. The expert maintains power because high-ranking persons in the organization are dependent upon him for his special skills and access to certain kinds of information. One possible reason for lawyers obtaining many high governmental offices is that they are likely to have access to rather specialized but highly important means to organizational goals.[9]

We can state these ideas in hypotheses, as follows:

> H3 Other factors remaining constant, to the extent that a low-ranking participant has important expert knowledge not available to high-ranking participants, he is likely to have power over them.

Power stemming from expertise, however, is likely to be limited unless it is difficult to replace the expert. This leads to two further hypotheses:

[8] Gresham M. Sykes, "The Corruption of Authority and Rehabilitation," in A. Etzioni, ed., *Complex Organizations* (New York, 1961), pp. 191–197.

[9] As an example, it appears that 6 members of the cabinet, 30 important subcabinet officials, 63 senators, and 230 congressmen are lawyers (*New Yorker*, April 14, 1962, p. 62). Although one can cite many reasons for lawyers holding political posts, an important one appears to be their legal expertise.

*H4* Other factors remaining constant, a person difficult to replace will have greater power than a person easily replaceable.

*H5* Other factors remaining constant, experts will be more difficult to replace than non-experts. . . .

The application of our hypothesis about expertise is clearly relevant if we look at certain organizational issues. For example, the merits of medical versus lay hospital administrators are often debated. It should be clear, however, that all other factors remaining unchanged, the medical administrator has clear advantage over the lay administrator. Where lay administrators receive preference, there is an implicit assumption that the lay person is better at administrative duties. This may be empirically valid but is not necessarily so. The special expert knowledge of the medical administrator stems from his ability legitimately to oppose a physician who contests an administrative decision on the basis of medical necessity. Usually hospitals are viewed primarily as universalistic in orientation both by the general public and most of their participants. Thus medical necessity usually takes precedence over management policies, a factor contributing to the poor financial position of most hospitals. The lay administrator is not in a position to contest such claims independently, since he usually lacks the basis for evaluation of the medical problems involved and also lacks official recognition of his competence to make such decisions. If the lay administrator is to evaluate these claims adequately on the basis of professional necessity, he must have a group of medical consultants or a committee of medical men to serve as a buffer between medical staff and the lay administration.

As a result of growing specialization, expertise is increasingly important in organizations. As the complexity of organizational tasks increases, and as organizations grow in size, there is a limit to responsibility that can be efficiently exercised by one person. Delegation of responsibility occurs, experts and specialists are brought in to provide information and research, and the higher participants become dependent upon them. Experts have tremendous potentialities for power by withholding information, providing incorrect information, and so on, and to the extent that experts are dissatisfied, the probability of organizational sabotage increases.

## Effort and Interest

The extent to which lower participants may exercise power depends in part on their willingness to exert effort in areas where higher-ranking participants are often reluctant to participate. Effort exerted is directly related to the degree of interest one has in an area.

*H6* Other factors remaining constant, there is a direct relationship between the amount of effort a person is willing to exert in an area and the power he can command.

For example, secretarial staffs in universities often have power to make decisions about the purchase and allocation of supplies, the allocation of their services, the scheduling of classes, and, at times, the disposition of student complaints. Such control may in some instances lead to sanctions against a professor by polite reluctance to furnish supplies, ignoring his preferences for the scheduling of classes, and giving others preference in the allocation of services. While the power to make such decisions may easily be removed from the jurisdiction of the lower participant, it can only be accomplished at a cost—the willingness to allocate time and effort to the decisions dealing with these matters. To the extent that responsibilities are delegated to lower participants, a certain degree of power is likely to accompany the responsibility. Also, should the lower participant see his perceived rights in jeopardy, he may sabotage the system in various ways. . . .

When an organization gives discretion to lower participants, it is usually trading the power of discretion for needed flexibility. The cost of constant surveillance is too high, and the effort required too great; it is very often much easier for all concerned to allow the secretary discretion in return for cooperation and not too great an abuse of power.

> H7   Other factors remaining constant, the less effort and interest high-ranking participants are willing to devote to a task, the more likely are lower participants to obtain power relevant to this task.

## Attractiveness

Another personal attribute associated with the power of low-ranking persons in an organization is attractiveness or what some call "personality." People who are viewed as attractive are more likely to obtain access to persons, and, once such access is gained, they may be more likely to succeed in promoting a cause. But once again dependence is the key to the power of attractiveness, for whether a person is dependent upon another for a service he provides, or for approval or affection, what is most relevant is the relational bond which is highly valued.

> H8   Other factors remaining constant, the more attractive a person, the more likely he is to obtain access to persons and control over these persons.

## Location and Position

In any organization the person's location in physical space and position in social space are important factors influencing access to persons, information, and instrumentalities.[10] Propinquity affects the opportunities for interaction, as well as one's position within a communication network. Although these are somewhat separate factors, we shall refer to their combined effect as centrality[11] within the organization.

> H9   Other factors remaining constant, the more central a person is in an organization, the greater is his access to persons, information, and instrumentalities.

Some low participants may have great centrality within an organization. An executive's or university president's secretary not only has access, but often controls access in making appointments and scheduling events. Although she may have no great formal authority, she may have considerable power.

## Coalitions

It should be clear that the variables we are considering are at different levels of analysis; some of them define attributes of persons, while others define attributes of communication and organization. Power processes within organizations are particularly interesting in that there are

[10] There is considerable data showing the powerful effect of propinquity on communication. For summary, see Thibaut and Kelley, *op. cit.*, pp. 39–42.

[11] The concept of centrality is generally used in a more technical sense in the work of Bavelas, Shaw, Gilchrist, and others. For example, Bavelas defines the central region of a structure as the class of all cells with the smallest distance between one cell and any other cell in the structure, with distance measured in link units. Thus the most central position in a pattern is the position closest to all others. Cf. Harold Leavitt, "Some Effects of Certain Communication Patterns on Group Performance," in E. Maccoby, T. N. Newcomb, and E. L. Hartley, eds., *Reading in Social Psychology* (New York, 1958), p. 559.

many channels of power and ways of achieving it.

In complex organizations different occupational groups attend to different functions, each group often maintaining its own power structure within the organization. Thus hospitals have administrators, medical personnel, nursing personnel, attendants, maintenance personnel, laboratory personnel, and so on. Universities, similarly, have teaching personnel, research personnel, administrative personnel, maintenance personnel, and so on. Each of these functional tasks within organizations often becomes the sphere of a particular group that controls activities relating to the task. While these tasks usually are coordinated at the highest levels of the organization, they often are not coordinated at intermediate and lower levels. It is not unusual, however, for coalitions to form among lower participants in these multiple structures. A secretary may know the man who manages the supply of stores, or the person assigning parking stickers. Such acquaintances may give her the ability to handle informally certain needs that would be more time-consuming and difficult to handle formally. Her ability to provide services informally makes higher-ranking participants in some degree dependent upon her, thereby giving her power, which increases her ability to bargain on issues important to her.

## Rules

In organizations with complex power structures lower participants can use their knowledge of the norms of the organization to thwart attempted change. In discussing the various functions of bureaucratic rules, Gouldner maintains that such rules serve as excellent substitutes for surveillance, since surveillance in addition to being expensive in time and effort arouses considerable hostility

and antagonism.[12] Moreover, he argues, rules are a functional equivalent for direct, personally given orders, since they specify the obligations of workers to do things in specific ways. Standardized rules, in addition, allow simple screening of violations, facilitate remote control, and to some extent legitimize punishment when the rule is violated. The worker who violates a bureaucratic rule has little recourse to the excuse that he did not know what was expected, as he might claim for a direct order. Finally, Gouldner argues that rules are "the 'chips' to which the company staked the supervisors and which they could use to play the game";[13] that is, rules established a punishment which could be withheld, and this facilitated the supervisors' bargaining power with lower participants.

While Gouldner emphasizes the functional characteristics of rules within an organization, it should be clear that full compliance to all the rules at all times will probably be dysfunctional for the organization. Complete and apathetic compliance may do everything but facilitate achievement of organizational goals. Lower participants who are familiar with an organization and its rules can often find rules to support their contention that they not do what they have been asked to do, and rules are also often a rationalization for inaction on their part. The following of rules becomes especially complex when associations and unions become involved, for there are then two sets of rules to which the participant can appeal.

What is suggested is that rules may be chips for everyone concerned in the game. Rules become the "chips" through which the bargaining process is main-

[12] Alvin W. Gouldner, *Patterns of Industrial Bureaucracy* (Glencoe, Ill., 1954).
[13] *Ibid.*, p. 173.

tained. Scheff, as noted earlier, observed that attendants in mental hospitals often took on responsibilities assigned legally to the ward physician, and when attendants refused to share these responsibilities the physician's position became extremely difficult.[14] . . .

Given the time-consuming formal chores of the physician, and his many other duties, he usually worked out an arrangement with the ward personnel, particularly the charge (supervisory attendant), to handle these duties. On several wards, the charge called specific problems to the doctor's attention, and the two of them, in effect, would have a consultation. The charge actually made most of the decisions concerning dosage change in the back wards. Since the doctor delegated portions of his formal responsibilities to the charge, he was dependent on her good will toward him.

If she withheld her co-operation, the physician had absolutely no recourse but to do all the work himself.[15] . . .

There are occasions, of course, when rules are regarded as illegitimate by lower participants, and they may disregard them. Gouldner observed that, in the mine, men felt they could resist authority in a situation involving danger to themselves.[16] They did not feel that they could legitimately be ordered to do anything that would endanger their lives. It is probably significant that in extremely dangerous situations organizations are more likely to rely on commitment to work than on authority. Even within nonvoluntary groups dangerous tasks are regarded usually as requiring task commitment, and it is likely that commitment is a much more powerful organizational force than coercive authority. . . .

---

[14] Scheff, *op. cit.*

[15] *Ibid.*, p. 97.

[16] Gouldner, *op. cit.*

# 37

# Who Gets Power—And How They Hold on to It: A Strategic-Contingency Model of Power

*Gerald R. Salancik & Jeffrey Pfeffer*

Power is held by many people to be a dirty word or, as Warren Bennis has said, "It is the organization's last dirty secret."

This article will argue that traditional "political" power, far from being a dirty business, is, in its most naked form, one of the few mechanisms available for aligning an organization with its own reality. However, institutionalized forms of power—what we prefer to call the cleaner forms of power: authority, legitimization, centralized control, regulations, and the more modern "management information systems" —tend to buffer the organization from reality and obscure the demands of its environment. Most great states and institutions declined, not because they played politics, but because they failed to accommodate to the political realities they faced. Political processes, rather than being mechanisms for unfair and unjust allocations and appointments, tend toward the realistic resolution of conflicts among interests. And power, while it eludes definition, is easy enough to recognize by its consequences—the ability of those who possess power to bring about the outcomes they desire.

The model of power we advance is an elaboration of what has been called strategic-contingency theory, a view that sees power as something that accrues to organizational subunits (individuals, departments) that cope with critical organizational problems. Power is used by subunits, indeed, used by all who have it, to enhance their own survival through control of scarce critical resources, through the placement of allies in key positions, and through the definition of organizational problems and policies. Because of the processes by which power develops and is used, organizations become both more aligned and more misaligned with their environments. This contradiction is the most interesting aspect of organizational power, and one that makes administration one of the most precarious of occupations.

## WHAT IS ORGANIZATIONAL POWER?

You can walk into most organizations and ask without fear of being misunderstood, "Which are the powerful groups or people in this organization?" Although many organizational informants may be *unwilling* to tell you, it is unlikely they will be *unable* to tell you. Most people do not require explicit definitions to know what power is.

Power is simply the ability to get things done the way one wants them to be done. For a manager who wants an increased budget to launch a project that he thinks is important, his power is measured by his ability to get that budget.

For an executive vice-president who wants to be chairman, his power is evidenced by his advancement toward his goal.

People in organizations not only know what you are talking about when you ask who is influential but they are likely to agree with one another to an amazing extent. . . .

## WHERE DOES ORGANIZATIONAL POWER COME FROM?

Earlier we stated that power helps organizations become aligned with their realities. This hopeful prospect follows from what we have dubbed the strategic-contingencies theory of organizational power. Briefly, those subunits most able to cope with the organization's critical problems and uncertainties acquire power. In its simplest form, the strategic-contingencies theory implies that when an organization faces a number of lawsuits that threaten its existence, the legal department will gain power and influence over organizational decisions. Somehow other organizational interest groups will recognize its critical importance and confer upon it a status and power never before enjoyed. This influence may extend beyond handling legal matters and into decisions about product design, advertising production, and so on. Such extensions undoubtedly would be accompanied by appropriate, or acceptable, verbal justifications. In time, the head of the legal department may become the head of the corporation, just as in times past the vice-president for marketing had become the president when market shares were a worrisome problem and, before him, the chief engineer, who had made the production line run as smooth as silk.

Stated in this way, the strategic-contingencies theory of power paints an appealing picture of power. To the extent that power is determined by the critical uncertainties and problems facing the organization and, in turn, influences decisions in the organization, the organization is aligned with the realities it faces. In short, power facilitates the organization's adaptation to its environment—or its problems. . . .

### Ignoring Critical Consequences

When organizational members are not aware of the critical contingencies they face, and do not share influence accordingly, the failure to do so can create havoc. In one case, an insurance company's regional office was having problems with the performance of one of its departments, the coding department. From the outside, the department looked like a disaster area. The clerks who worked in it were somewhat dissatisfied; their supervisor paid little attention to them, and they resented the hard work. Several other departments were critical of this manager, claiming that she was inconsistent in meeting deadlines. The person most critical was the claims manager. He resented having to wait for work that was handled by her department, claiming that it held up his claims adjusters. Having heard the rumors about dissatisfaction among her subordinates, he attributed the situation to poor supervision. He was second in command in the office, and therefore took up the issue with her immediate boss, the head of administrative services. They consulted with the personnel manager and the three of them concluded that the manager needed leadership training to improve her relations with her subordinates. The coding manager objected, saying it was a waste of time, but agreed to go along with the training and also agreed to give more priority to the claims department's work. Within a week after the training, the results showed that her workers were happier but that the performance of her department had decreased, save for the people serving the claims department.

About this time, we began, quite independently, a study of influence in this organization. We asked the administrative services director to draw up flow charts of how the work of one department moved on to the next department. In the course of the interview, we noticed that the coding department began or interceded in the work flow of most of the other departments and casually mentioned to him, "The coding manager must be very influential." He said "No, not really. Why would you think so?" Before we could reply he recounted the story of her leadership training and the fact that things were worse. We then told him that it seemed obvious that the coding department would be influential from the fact that all the other departments depended on it. It was also clear why productivity had fallen. The coding manager took the training seriously and began spending more time raising her workers' spirits than she did worrying about the problems of all the departments that depended on her. Giving priority to the claims area only exaggerated the problem, for their work was getting done at the expense of the work of the other departments. Eventually the company hired a few more clerks to relieve the pressure in the coding department and performance returned to a more satisfactory level.

Originally we got involved with this insurance company to examine how the influence of each manager evolved from his or her department's handling of critical organizational contingencies. We reasoned that one of the most important contingencies faced by all profit-making organizations was that of generating income. Thus we expected managers would be influential to the extent to which they contributed to this function. Such was the case. The underwriting managers, who wrote the policies that committed the premiums, were the most influential; the claims managers, who kept a lid on the funds flowing out, were a close second. Least influential were the managers of functions unrelated to revenue, such as mailroom and payroll managers. And contrary to what the administrative services manager believed, the third most powerful department head (out of 21) was the woman in charge of the coding function, which consisted of rating, recording, and keeping track of the codes of all policy applications and contracts. Her peers attributed more influence to her than could have been inferred from her place on the organization chart. And it was not surprising, since they all depended on her department. The coding department's records, their accuracy and the speed with which they could be retrieved, affected virtually every other operating department in the insurance office. The underwriters depended on them in getting the contracts straight; the typing department depended on them in preparing the formal contract document; the claims department depended on them in adjusting claims; and accounting depended on them for billing. Unfortunately, the "bosses" were not aware of these dependences, . . . while the coding manager, who was a hard-working but quiet person, did little to announce her importance.

The cases of this plant and office illustrate nicely a basic point about the source of power in organizations. The basis for power in an organization derives from the ability of a person or subunit to take or not take actions that are desired by others. . . . Whether power is used to influence anything is a separate issue. We should not confuse this issue with the fact that power derives from a social situation in which one person has a capacity to do something and another person does not, but wants it done.

## POWER SHARING IN ORGANIZATIONS

Power is shared in organizations, and it is shared out of necessity more than out of concern for principles of organizational development or participatory democracy. Power is shared because no one person controls all the desired activities in the organization. While the factory owner may hire people to operate his noisy machines, once hired they have some control over the use of the machinery. And thus they have power over him in the same way he has power over them. Who has more power over whom is a mooter point than that of recognizing the inherent nature of organizing as a sharing of power. . . .

Because power derives from activities rather than individuals, an individual's or subgroup's power is never absolute and derives ultimately from the context of the situation. The amount of power an individual has at any one time depends, not only on the activities he or she controls, but also on the existence of other persons or means by which the activities can be achieved and on those who determine what ends are desired and, hence, on what activities are desired and critical for the organization. One's own power always depends on other people for these two reasons. Other people, or groups or organizations, can determine the definition of what is a critical contingency for the organization and can also undercut the uniqueness of the individual's personal contribution to the critical contingencies of the organization.

Perhaps one can best appreciate how situationally dependent power is by examining how it is distributed. In most

societies, power organizes around scarce and critical resources. Rarely does power organize around abundant resources. In the United States, a person doesn't become powerful because he or she can drive a car. There are simply too many others who can drive with equal facility. In certain villages in Mexico, on the other hand, a person with a car is accredited with enormous social status and plays a key role in the community. In addition to scarcity, power is also limited by the need for one's capacities in a social system. While a racer's ability to drive a car around a 90° turn at 80 mph may be sparsely distributed in a society, it is not likely to lend the driver much power in the society. The ability simply does not play a central role in the activities of the society.

The fact that power revolves around scarce and critical activities, of course, makes the control and organization of those activities a major battleground in struggles for power. Even relatively abundant or trivial resources can become the bases for power if one can organize and control their allocation and the definition of what is critical. Many occupational and professional groups attempt to do just this in modern economies. Lawyers organize themselves into associations, regulate the entrance requirements for novitiates, and then get laws passed specifying situations that require the services of an attorney. Workers had little power in the conduct of industrial affairs until they organized themselves into closed and controlled systems. In recent years, women and blacks have tried to define themselves as important and critical to the social system, using law to reify their status. . . .

The power to define what is critical in an organization is no small power. Moreover, it is the key to understanding why organizations are either aligned with their environments or misaligned.

If an organization defines certain activities as critical when in fact they are not critical, given the flow of resources coming into the organization, it is not likely to survive, at least in its present form.

Most organizations manage to evolve a distribution of power and influence that is aligned with the critical realities they face in the environment. The environment, in turn, includes both the internal environment, the shifting situational contexts in which particular decisions get made, and the external environment that it can hope to influence but is unlikely to control.

## THE CRITICAL CONTINGENCIES

The critical contingencies facing most organizations derive from the environmental context within which they operate. This determines the available needed resources and thus determines the problems to be dealt with. That power organizes around handling these problems suggests an important mechanism by which organizations keep in tune with their external environments. The strategic-contingencies model implies that subunits that contribute to the critical resources of the organization will gain influence in the organization. Their influence presumably is then used to bend the organization's activities to the contingencies that determine its resources. This idea may strike one as obvious. But its obviousness in no way diminishes its importance. Indeed, despite its obviousness, it escapes the notice of many organizational analysts and managers, who all too frequently think of the organization in terms of a descending pyramid, in which all the departments in one tier hold equal power and status. This presumption denies the reality that departments differ in the contributions

they are believed to make to the overall organization's resources, as well as to the fact that some are more equal than others.

Because of the importance of this idea to organizational effectiveness, we decided to examine it carefully in a large midwestern university. A university offers an excellent site for studying power. It is composed of departments with nominally equal power and is administered by a central executive structure much like other bureaucracies. However, at the same time it is a situation in which the departments have clearly defined identities and face diverse external environments. Each department has its own bodies of knowledge, its own institutions, its own sources of prestige and resources. Because the departments operate in different external environments, they are likely to contribute differentially to the resources of the overall organization. Thus a physics department with close ties to NASA may contribute substantially to the funds of the university; and a history department with a renowned historian in residence may contribute to the intellectual credibility or prestige of the whole university. Such variations permit one to examine how these various contributions lead to obtaining power within the university.

We analyzed the influence of 29 university departments throughout an 18-month period in their history. Our chief interest was to determine whether departments that brought more critical resources to the university would be more powerful than departments that contributed fewer or less critical resources.

To identify the critical resources each department contributed, the heads of all departments were interviewed about the importance of seven different resources to the university's success. The seven included undergraduate students (the factor determining size of the state allocations by the university), national prestige, administrative expertise, and so on. The most critical resource was found to be contract and grant monies received by a department's faculty for research or consulting services. At this university, contract and grants contributed somewhat less than 50 percent of the overall budget, with the remainder primarily coming from state appropriations. The importance attributed to contract and grant monies, and the rather minor importance of undergraduate students, was not surprising for this particular university. The university was a major center for graduate education; many of its departments ranked in the top ten of their respective fields. Grant and contract monies were the primary source of discretionary funding available for maintaining these programs of graduate education, and hence for maintaining the university's prestige. The prestige of the university itself was critical both in recruiting able students and attracting top-notch faculty.

From university records it was determined what relative contributions each of the 29 departments made to the various needs of the university (national prestige, outside grants, teaching). Thus, for instance, one department may have contributed to the university by teaching 7 percent of the instructional units, bringing in 2 percent of the outside contracts and grants, and having a national ranking of 20. Another department, on the other hand, may have taught one percent of the instructional units, contributed 12 percent to the grants, and be ranked the third best department in its field within the country.

The question was: Do these different contributions determine the relative power of the departments within the university? Power was measured in several ways; but regardless of how measured, the answer was "yes." Those three

resources together accounted for about 70 percent of the variance in subunit power in the university.

But the most important predictor of departmental power was the department's contribution to the contracts and grants of the university. Sixty percent of the variance in power was due to this one factor, suggesting that the power of departments derived primarily from the dollars they provided for graduate education, the activity believed to be the most important for the organization.

## THE IMPACT OF ORGANIZATIONAL POWER ON DECISION MAKING

While it is perhaps not absolutely valid, we can generally gauge the relative importance of a department of an organization by the size of the budget allocated to it relative to other departments. Clearly it is of importance to the administrators of those departments whether they get squeezed in a budget crunch or are given more funds to strike out after new opportunities. And it should also be clear that when those decisions are made and one department can go ahead and try new approaches while another must cut back on the old, then the deployment of the resources of the organization in meeting its problems is most directly affected.

Thus our study of the university led us to ask the following question: Does power lead to influence in the organization? To answer this question, we found it useful first to ask another one, namely: Why should department heads try to influence organizational decisions to favor their own departments to the exclusion of other departments? While this second question may seem a bit naive to anyone who has witnessed the political realities of organizations, we posed it in a context of research on organizations that sees power as an illegitimate threat to the neater rational authority of modern bureaucracies. In this context, decisions are not believed to be made because of the dirty business of politics but because of the overall goals and purposes of the organization. In a university, one reasonable basis for decision making is the teaching workload of departments and the demands that follow from that workload. We would expect, therefore, that departments with heavy student demands for courses would be able to obtain funds for teaching. Another reasonable basis for decision making is quality. We would expect, for that reason, that departments with esteemed reputations would be able to obtain funds both because their quality suggests they might use such funds effectively and because such funds would allow them to maintain their quality. A rational model of bureaucracy intimates, then, that the organizational decisions taken would favor those who perform the stated purposes of the organization—teaching undergraduates and training professional and scientific talent—well.

The problem with rational models of decision making, however, is that what is rational to one person may strike another as irrational. For most departments, resources are a question of survival. . . . Thus goals rather than being clearly defined and universally agreed upon are blurred and contested throughout the organization. If such is the case, then the decisions taken on behalf of the organization as a whole are likely to reflect the goals of those who prevail in political contests, namely, those with power in the organization. . . .

We have examined three conditions that are likely to affect the use of power in organizations: scarcity, criticality, and uncertainty. The first suggests that subunits will try to exert influence when the resources of the organization are scarce. If there is an abundance of resources, then a particular department or a particular individual has little need to attempt influence. With little effort, he can get all he wants anyway.

The second condition, criticality, suggests that a subunit will attempt to influence decisions to obtain resources that are critical to its own survival and activities. Criticality implies that one would not waste effort, or risk being labeled obstinate, by fighting over trivial decisions affecting one's operations. . . .

The third condition that we believe affects the use of power is uncertainty: When individuals do not agree about what the organization should do or how to do it, power and other social processes will affect decisions. The reason for this is simply that, if there are no clear-cut criteria available for resolving conflicts of interest, then the only means for resolution is some form of social process, including power, status, social ties, or some arbitrary process like flipping a coin or drawing straws. Under conditions of uncertainty, the powerful manager can argue his case on any grounds and usually win it. Since there is no real consensus, other contestants are not likely to develop counter arguments or amass sufficient opposition. Moreover, because of his power and their need for access to the resources he controls, they are more likely to defer to his arguments.

Although the evidence is slight, we have found that power will influence the allocations of scarce and critical resources. In the analysis of power in the university, for instance, one of the most critical resources needed by departments is the general budget. First granted by the state legislature, the general budget is later allocated to individual departments by the university administration in response to requests from the department heads. Our analysis of the factors that contribute to a department getting more or less of this budget indicated that subunit power was the major predictor, overriding such factors as student demand for courses, national reputations of departments, or even the size of a department's faculty. Moreover, other research has shown that when the general budget has been cut back or held below previous uninflated levels, leading to monies becoming more scarce, budget allocations mirror departmental powers even more closely.

Student enrollment and faculty size, of course, do themselves relate to budget allocations, as we would expect since they determine a department's need for resources, or at least offer visible testimony of needs. But departments are not always able to get what they need by the mere fact of needing them. In one analysis it was found that high-power departments were able to obtain budget without regard to their teaching loads and, in some cases, actually in inverse relation to their teaching loads. In contrast, low-power departments could get increases in budget only when they could justify the increases by a recent growth in teaching load, and then only when it was far in excess of norms for other departments. . . .

When the four resources were arrayed from the most to the least critical and scarce, we found that departmental power best predicted the allocations of the most critical and scarce resources. In other words, the analysis of how power influences organizational allocations leads to this conclusion: Those subunits most likely to survive in times of strife are those that are more critical to the organization. Their importance to the organization gives them power to influence resource allocations that enhance their own survival.

## HOW EXTERNAL ENVIRONMENT IMPACTS EXECUTIVE SELECTION

Power not only influences the survival of key groups in an organization, it also influences the selection of individuals to key leadership positions, and by such a process further aligns the organization with its environmental context. . . .

As with the selection of administrators, the context of organizations has also been found to affect the removal of executives. The environment, as a source of organizational problems, can make it more or less difficult for executives to demonstrate their value to the organization. In the hospitals we studied, long-term administrators came from hospitals with few problems. They enjoyed amicable and stable relations with their local business and social communities and suffered little competition for funding and staff. The small city hospital director who attended civic and Elks meetings while running the only hospital within a 100-mile radius, for example, had little difficulty holding on to his job. Turnover was highest in hospitals with the most problems, a phenomenon similar to that observed in a study of industrial organizations in which turnover was highest among executives in industries with competitive environments and unstable market conditions. The interesting thing is that instability characterized the industries rather than the individual firms in them. The troublesome conditions in the individual firms were attributed, or rather misattributed, to the executives themselves.

It takes more than problems, however, to terminate a manager's leadership. . . . For those hospitals dependent upon private donations, the length of an administrator's term depended not at all on the status of the operating budget but was fairly predictable from the hospital's relations with the business community. On the other hand, in hospitals dependent on the operating budget for capital financing, the greater the deficit the shorter was the tenure of the hospital's principal administrators.

## CHANGING CONTINGENCIES AND ERODING POWER BASES

The critical contingencies facing the organization may change. When they do, it is reasonable to expect that the power of individuals and subgroups will change in turn. . . .

One implication of the idea that power shifts with changes in organizational environments is that the dominant coalition will tend to be that group that is most appropriate for the organization's environment, as also will the leaders of an organization. . . .

## THE NONADAPTIVE CONSEQUENCES OF ADAPTATION

From what we have said thus far about power aligning the organization with its own realities, an intelligent person might react with a resounding ho-hum, for it all seems too obvious: Those with the ability to get the job done are given the job to do.

However, there are two aspects of power that make it more useful for understanding organizations and their effectiveness. First, the "job" to be done has a way of expanding itself until it becomes less and less clear what the job is. Napoleon began by doing a job for France in the war with Austria and ended up Emperor, convincing many

that only he could keep the peace. Hitler began by promising an end to Germany's troubling postwar depression and ended up convincing more people than is comfortable to remember that he was destined to be the savior of the world. In short, power is a capacity for influence that extends far beyond the original bases that created it. Second, power tends to take on institutionalized forms that enable it to endure well beyond its usefulness to an organization.

There is an important contradiction in what we have observed about organizational power. On the one hand we have said that power derives from the contingencies facing an organization and that when those contingencies change so do the bases for power. On the other hand we have asserted that subunits will tend to use their power to influence organizational decisions in their own favor, particularly when their own survival is threatened by the scarcity of critical resources. The first statement implies that an organization will tend to be aligned with its environment since power will tend to bring to key positions those with capabilities relevant to the context. The second implies that those in power will not give up their positions so easily; they will pursue policies that guarantee their continued domination. In short, change and stability operate through the same mechanism, and, as a result, the organization will never be completely in phase with its environment or its needs. . . .

## MISTAKING CRITICAL CONTINGENCIES

One thing that allows subunits to retain their power is their ability to name their functions as critical to the organization when they may not be. Consider again our discussion of power in the university. One might wonder why the most critical tasks were defined as graduate education and scholarly research, the effect of which was to lend power to those who brought in grants and contracts. Why not something else? The reason is that the more powerful departments argued for those criteria and won their case, partly because they were more powerful.

In another analysis of this university, we found that all departments advocate self-serving criteria for budget allocation. Thus a department with large undergraduate enrollments argued that enrollments should determine budget allocations, a department with a strong national reputation saw prestige as the most reasonable basis for distributing funds, and so on. We further found that advocating such self-serving criteria actually benefited a department's budget allotments but, also, it paid off more for departments that were already powerful.

Organizational needs are consistent with a current distribution of power also because of a human tendency to categorize problems in familiar ways. An accountant sees problems with organizational performance as cost accountancy problems or inventory flow problems. A sales manager sees them as problems with markets, promotional strategies, or just unaggressive salespeople. But what is the truth? Since it does not automatically announce itself, it is likely that those with prior credibility, or those with power, will be favored as the enlightened. This bias, while not intentionally self-serving, further concentrates power among those who already possess it, independent of changes in the organization's context.

## INSTITUTIONALIZING POWER

A third reason for expecting organizational contingencies to be defined in fa-miliar ways is that the current holders of power can structure the organization in ways that institutionalize themselves. By institutionalization we mean the establishment of relatively permanent structures and policies that favor the influence of a particular subunit. While in power, a dominant coalition has the ability to institute constitutions, rules, procedures, and information systems that limit the potential power of others while continuing their own.

The key to institutionalizing power always is to create a device that legitimates one's own authority and diminishes the legitimacy of others. When the "Divine Right of Kings" was envisioned centuries ago it was to provide an unquestionable foundation for the supremacy of royal authority. There is generally a need to root the exercise of authority in some higher power. Modern leaders are no less affected by this need. Richard Nixon, with the aid of John Dean, reified the concept of executive privilege, which meant in effect that what the President wished not to be discussed need not be discussed.

In its simpler form, institutionalization is achieved by designating positions or roles for organizational activities. The creation of a new post legitimizes a function and forces organization members to orient to it. By designating how this new post relates to older, more established posts, moreover, one can structure an organization to enhance the importance of the function in the organization. . . .

The structures created by dominant powers sooner or later become fixed and unquestioned features of the organization. Eventually, this can be devastating. It is said that the battle of Jena in 1806 was lost by Frederick the Great, who died in 1786. Though the great Prussian leader had no direct hand in the disaster, his imprint on the army was so thorough, so embedded in its skeletal underpinnings, that the organization was inappropriate for others to lead in different times.

Another important source of institutionalized power lies in the ability to structure information systems. Setting up committees to investigate particular organizational issues and having them report only to particular individuals or groups, facilitates their awareness of problems by members of those groups while limiting the awareness of problems by the members of other groups. Obviously, those who have information are in a better position to interpret the problems of an organization, regardless of how realistically they may, in fact, do so.

Still another way to institutionalize power is to distribute rewards and resources. The dominant group may quiet competing interest groups with small favors and rewards. The credit for this artful form of cooperation belongs to Louis XIV. To avoid usurpation of his power by the nobles of France and the Fronde that had so troubled his father's reign, he built the palace at Versailles to occupy them with hunting and gossip. Awed, the courtiers basked in the reflected glories of the "Sun King" and the overwhelming setting he had created for his court.

At this point, we have not systematically studied the institutionalization of power. But we suspect it is an important condition that mediates between the environment of the organization and the capabilities of the organization for dealing with that environment. The more institutionalized power is within an organization, the more likely an organization will be out of phase with the realities it faces. President Richard Nixon's structuring of his White House is one of the better documented illustrations. . . .

One of the more interesting implications of institutionalized power is that executive turnover among the executives who have structured the organization is likely to be a rare event that occurs only under the most pressing crisis. If a dominant coalition is able to structure the organization and interpret the meaning of ambiguous events like declining sales and profits or lawsuits, then the "real" problems to emerge will easily be incorporated into traditional molds of thinking and acting. If opposition is designed out of the organization, the interpretations will go unquestioned. Conditions will remain stable until a crisis develops, so overwhelming and visible that even the most adroit rhetorician would be silenced.

## IMPLICATIONS FOR THE MANAGEMENT OF POWER IN ORGANIZATIONS

Instead of ending with homilies, we will end with a reversal of where we began. Power, rather than being the dirty business it is often made out to be, is probably one of the few mechanisms for reality testing in organizations. And the cleaner forms of power, the institutional forms, rather than having the virtues they are often credited with, can lead the organization to become out of touch. The real trick to managing power in organizations is to ensure somehow that leaders cannot be unaware of the realities of their environments and cannot avoid changing to deal with those realities. That, however, would be like designing the "self-liquidating organization," an unlikely event since anyone capable of designing such an instrument would be obviously in control of the liquidations. . . .

One conclusion you can, and probably should, derive from our discussion is that power—because of the way it develops and the way it is used—will always result in the organization suboptimizing its performance. However, to this grim absolute, we add a comforting caveat: If any criteria other than power were the basis for determining an organization's decisions, the results would be even worse.

# 38
# Power, Dependence, and Effective Management
*John P. Kotter*

Americans, as a rule, are not very comfortable with power or with its dynamics. We often distrust and question the motives of people who we think actively seek power. We have a certain fear of being manipulated. Even those people who think the dynamics of power are inevitable and needed often feel somewhat guilty when they themselves mobilize and use power. Simply put, the overall attitude and feeling toward power, which can easily be traced to the nation's very birth, is negative. In his enormously popular *Greening of America*, Charles Reich reflects the views of many when he writes, "It is not the misuse of power that is evil; the very existence of power is evil."[1] . . .

In this article I hope to clear up some of the confusion regarding power and managerial work by providing tentative answers to three questions:

1. Why are the dynamics of power necessarily an important part of managerial processes?
2. How do effective managers acquire power?

[1] Charles A. Reich. *The Greening of America: How the Youth Revolution Is Trying to Make America Liveable* (New York: Random House, 1970).

3. How and for what purposes do effective managers use power? . . .

## RECOGNIZING DEPENDENCE IN THE MANAGER'S JOB

One of the distinguishing characteristics of a typical manager is how dependent he is on the activities of a variety of other people to perform his job effectively.[2] Unlike doctors and mathematicians, whose performance is more directly dependent on their own talents and efforts, a manager can be dependent in varying degrees on superiors, subordinates, peers in other parts of the organization, the subordinates of peers, outside suppliers, customers, competitors, unions, regulating agencies, and many others.

These dependency relationships are an inherent part of managerial jobs because of two organizational facts of life: division of labor and limited resources. Because the work in organizations is divided into specialized divisions, departments, and jobs, managers are made di-

[2] See Leonard R. Sayles, *Managerial Behavior: Administration in Complex Organization* (New York: McGraw-Hill, 1964) as well as Rosemary Stewart, *Managers and Their Jobs* (London: Macmillan, 1967) and *Contracts in Management* (London: McGraw-Hill, 1976).

*Author's note:* This article is based on data from a clinical study of a highly diverse group of 26 organizations including large and small, public and private, manufacturing and service organizations. The study was funded by the Division of Research at the Harvard Business School. As part of the study process, the author interviewed about 250 managers.

rectly or indirectly dependent on many others for information, staff services, and cooperation in general. Because of their organization's limited resources, managers are also dependent on their external environments for support. Without some minimal cooperation from suppliers, competitors, unions, regulatory agencies, and customers, managers cannot help their organizations survive and achieve their objectives.

Dealing with these dependencies and the manager's subsequent vulnerability is an important and difficult part of a manager's job because, while it is theoretically possible that all of these people and organizations would automatically act in just the manner that a manager wants and needs, such is almost never the case in reality. All the people on whom a manager is dependent have limited time, energy, and talent, for which there are competing demands. . . .

Indeed, managers often find themselves dependent on many people (and things) whom they do not directly control and who are not "cooperating." . . .

As a person gains more formal authority in an organization, the areas in which he or she is vulnerable increase and become more complex rather than the reverse. As the previous example suggests, it is not at all unusual for the president of an organization to be in a highly dependent position, a fact often not apparent to either the outsider or to the lower level manager who covets the president's job.

A considerable amount of the behavior of highly successful managers that seems inexplicable in light of what management texts usually tell us managers do becomes understandable when one considers a manager's need for, and efforts at, managing his or her relation-

ships with others.[3] To be able to plan, organize, budget, staff, control, and evaluate, managers need some control over the many people on whom they are dependent. Trying to control others solely by directing them and on the basis of the power associated with one's position simply will not work—first, because managers are always dependent on some people over whom they have no formal authority, and second, because virtually no one in modern organizations will passively accept and completely obey a constant stream of orders from someone just because he or she is the "boss."

Trying to influence others by means of persuasion alone will not work either. Although it is very powerful and possibly the single most important method of influence, persuasion has some serious drawbacks too. To make it work requires time (often lots of it), skill, and information on the part of the persuader. And persuasion can fail simply because the other person chooses not to listen or does not listen carefully.

This is not to say that directing people on the basis of the formal power of one's position and persuasion are not important means by which successful managers cope. They obviously are. But, even taken together, they are not usually enough.

Successful managers cope with their dependence on others by being sensitive to it, by eliminating or avoiding unnecessary dependence, and by establishing power over those others. Good managers then use that power to help them plan, organize, staff, budget, evaluate, and so on. *In other words, it is primarily because of the dependence inherent in managerial*

---

[3] I am talking about the type of inexplicable differences that Henry Mintzberg has found; see his article "The Manager's Job: Folklore and Fact," *HBR* July–August 1975, p. 49.

*jobs that the dynamics of power necessarily form an important part of a manager's processes. . . .*

Not all management jobs require an incumbent to be able to provide the same amount of successful power-oriented behavior. . . . So long as our technologies continue to become more complex, the average organization continues to grow larger, and the average industry continues to become more competitive and regulated, that trend will continue; as it does so, the effective acquisition and use of power by managers will become even more important.

## ESTABLISHING POWER IN RELATIONSHIPS

To help cope with the dependency relationships inherent in their jobs, effective managers create, increase, or maintain four different types of power over others.[4] Having power based in these areas puts the manager in a position both to influence those people on whom he or she is dependent when necessary and to avoid being hurt by any of them.

### Sense of Obligation

One of the ways that successful managers generate power in their relationships with others is to create a sense of obligation in those others. When the manager is successful, the others feel that they should—rightly—allow the manager to influence them within certain limits.

---

[4] These categories closely resemble the five developed by John R. P. French and Bertram Raven; see "The Bases of Social Power" in *Group Dynamics: Research and Theory*, Dorwin Cartwright and Alvin Zandler, eds. (New York: Harper & Row, 1968), Chapter 20. Three of the categories are similar to the types of "authority"-based power described by Max Weber in *The Theory of Social and Economic Organization* (New York: Free Press, 1947).

Successful managers often go out of their way to do favors for people who they expect will feel an obligation to return those favors. As can be seen in the following description of a manager by one of his subordinates, some people are very skilled at identifying opportunities for doing favors that cost them very little but that others appreciate very much:

> "Most of the people here would walk over hot coals in their bare feet if my boss asked them to. He has an incredible capacity to do little things that mean a lot to people. Today, for example, in his junk mail he came across an advertisement for something that one of my subordinates had in passing once mentioned that he was shopping for. So my boss routed it to him. That probably took 15 seconds of his time, and yet my subordinate really appreciated it. To give you another example, two weeks ago he somehow learned that the purchasing manager's mother had died. On his way home that night, he stopped off at the funeral parlor. Our purchasing manager was, of course, there at the time. I bet he'll remember that brief visit for quite a while."

Recognizing that most people believe that friendship carries with it certain obligations ("A friend in need. . . ."), successful managers often try to develop true friendships with those on whom they are dependent. They will also make formal and informal deals in which they give something up in exchange for certain future obligations.

### Belief in a Manager's Expertise

A second way successful managers gain power is by building reputations as "experts" in certain matters. Believing in the manager's expertise, others will often defer to the manager on those matters. Managers usually establish this type of power through visible achievement. The larger the achievement and the more visible it is, the more power the manager tends to develop.

One of the reasons that managers display concern about their "professional reputations" and their "track records" is that they have an impact on others' beliefs about their expertise. These factors become particularly important in large settings, where most people have only secondhand information about most other people's professional competence, . . .

## Identification with a Manager

A third method by which managers gain power is by fostering others' unconscious identification with them or with ideas they "stand for." Sigmund Freud was the first to describe this phenomenon, which is most clearly seen in the way people look up to "charismatic" leaders. Generally, the more a person finds a manager both consciously and (more important) unconsciously an ideal person, the more he or she will defer to that manager.

Managers develop power based on others' idealized views of them in a number of ways. They try to look and behave in ways that others respect. They go out of their way to be visible to their employees and to give speeches about their organizational goals, values, and ideals. They even consider, while making hiring and promotion decisions, whether they will be able to develop this type of power over the candidates. . . .

## Perceived Dependence on a Manager

The final way that an effective manager often gains power is by feeding others' beliefs that they are dependent on the manager either for help or for not being hurt. The more they perceive they are dependent, the more most people will be inclined to cooperate with such a manager.

There are two methods that successful managers often use to create perceived dependence.

*Finding & Acquiring Resources.* In the first, the manager identifies and secures (if necessary) resources that another person requires to perform his job, that he does not possess, and that are not readily available elsewhere. These resources include such things as authority to make certain decisions; control of money, equipment, and office space; access to important people; information and control of information channels; and subordinates. Then the manager takes action so that the other person correctly perceives that the manager has such resources and is willing and ready to use them to help (or hinder) the other person. Consider the following extreme—but true—example.

When young Tim Babcock was put in charge of a division of a large manufacturing company and told to "turn it around," he spent the first few weeks studying it from afar. He decided that the division was in disastrous shape and that he would need to take many large steps quickly to save it. To be able to do that, he realized he needed to develop considerable power fast over most of the division's management and staff. He did the following:

- He gave the division's management two hours' notice of his arrival.
- He arrived in a limousine with six assistants.
- He immediately called a meeting of the 40 top managers.
- He outlined briefly his assessment of the situation, his commitment to turn things around, and the basic direction he wanted things to move in.
- He then fired the four top managers in the room and told them that they had to be out of the building in two hours.
- He then said he would personally dedicate himself to sabotaging the career of anyone

who tried to block his efforts to save the division.

- He ended the 60-minute meeting by announcing that his assistants would set up appointments for him with each of them starting at 7:00 A.M. the next morning.

Throughout the critical six-month period that followed, those who remained at the division generally cooperated energetically with Mr. Babcock.

*Affecting Perceptions of Resources.* A second way effective managers gain these types of power is by influencing other persons' perceptions of the manager's resources.[5] In settings where many people are involved and where the manager does not interact continuously with those he or she is dependent on, those people will seldom possess "hard facts" regarding what relevant resources the manager commends directly or indirectly (through others), what resources he will command in the future, or how prepared he is to use those resources to help or hinder them. They will be forced to make their own judgments.

Insofar as a manager can influence people's judgments, he can generate much more power than one would generally ascribe to him in light of the reality of his resources.

In trying to influence people's judgments, managers pay considerable attention to the "trappings" of power and to their own reputations and images. Among other actions, they sometimes carefully select, decorate, and arrange their offices in ways that give signs of power. They associate with people or organizations that are known to be powerful or that others perceive as powerful. Managers selectively foster rumors concerning their own power. Indeed, those who are particularly skilled at creating

[5] For an excellent discussion of this method, see Richard E. Neustadt, *Presidential Power* (New York: John Wiley, 1960).

power in this way tend to be very sensitive to the impressions that all their actions might have on others.

## Formal Authority

Before discussing how managers use their power to influence others, it is useful to see how formal authority relates to power. By *formal authority*, I mean those elements that automatically come with a managerial job—perhaps a title, an office, a budget, the right to make certain decisions, a set of subordinates, a reporting relationship, and so on.

Effective managers use the elements of formal authority as resources to help them develop any or all of the four types of power previously discussed, just as they use other resources (such as their education). Two managers with the same formal authority can have very different amounts of power entirely because of the way they have used that authority. For example:

- By sitting down with employees who are new or with people who are starting new projects and clearly specifying who has the formal authority to do what, one manager creates a strong sense of obligation in others to defer to his authority later.
- By selectively withholding or giving the high-quality service his department can provide other departments, one manager makes other managers clearly perceive that they are dependent on him.

On its own, then, formal authority does not guarantee a certain amount of power; it is only a resource that managers can use to generate power in their relationships.

## EXERCISING POWER TO INFLUENCE OTHERS

Successful managers use the power they develop in their relationships, along with persuasion, to influence people on whom they are dependent to behave in ways that make it possible for the managers to get their jobs done effectively. They use their power to influence others directly, face to face, and in more indirect ways.

## Face-to-face Influence

The chief advantage of influencing others directly by exercising any of the types of power is speed. If the power exists and the manager correctly understands the nature and strength of it, he can influence the other person with nothing more than a brief request or command. . . .

When used to influence others, each of the four types of power has different advantages and drawbacks. For example, power based on perceived expertise or on identification with a manager can often be used to influence attitudes as well as someone's immediate behavior and thus can have a lasting impact. It is very difficult to influence attitudes by using power based on perceived dependence, but if it can be done, it usually has the advantage of being able to influence a much broader range of behavior than the other methods do. When exercising power based on perceived expertise, for example, one can only influence attitudes and behavior within that narrow zone defined by the "expertise."

The drawbacks associated with the use of power based on perceived dependence are particularly important to recognize. A person who feels dependent on a manager for rewards (or lack of punishments) might quickly agree to a request from the manager but then not follow through— especially if the manager cannot easily find out if the person has obeyed or not. Repeated influence attempts based on perceived dependence also seem to encourage the other person to try to gain some power to balance the manager's. And perhaps most important, using power based on perceived dependence

in a coercive way is very risky. Coercion invites retaliation. . . .

Effective managers will often draw on more than one form of power to influence someone, or they will combine power with persuasion. In general, they do so because a combination can be more potent and less risky than any single method. . . .

It is also common for managers not to coercively exercise power based on perceived dependence by itself, but to combine it with other methods to reduce the risk of retaliation. In this way, managers are able to have a large impact without leaving the bitter aftertaste of punishment alone.

## Indirect Influence Methods

Effective managers also rely on two types of less direct methods to influence those on whom they are dependent. In the first way, the use any or all of the face-to-face methods to influence other people, who in turn have some specific impact on a desired person. . . .

This type of manipulation of the environments of others can influence both behavior and attitudes and can often succeed when other influence methods fail. But it has a number of serious drawbacks. It takes considerable time and energy, and it is quite risky. Many people think it is wrong to try to influence others in this way, even people who, without consciously recognizing it, use this technique themselves. If they think someone is trying, or has tried, to manipulate them, they may retaliate. Furthermore, people who gain the reputation of being manipulators seriously undermine their own capacities for developing power and for influencing others. Almost no one, for example, will want to identify with a manipulator. And virtually no one accepts, at face value, a manipulator's sincere attempts at persuasion. In extreme

## EXHIBIT · METHODS OF INFLUENCE

| Face-to-face methods | What they can influence | Advantages | Drawbacks |
|---|---|---|---|
| Exercise obligation-based power. | Behavior within zone that the other perceives as legitimate in light of the obligation. | Quick. Requires no outlay of tangible resources. | If the request is outside the acceptable zone, it will fail; if it is too far outside, others might see it as illegitimate. |
| Exercise power based on perceived expertise. | Attitudes and behavior within the zone of perceived expertise. | Quick. Requires no outlay of tangible resources. | If the request is outside the acceptable zone, it will fail; if it is too far outside, others might see it as illegitimate. |
| Exercise power based on identification with a manager. | Attitudes and behavior that are not in conflict with the ideals that underlie the identification. | Quick. Requires no expenditure of limited resources. | Restricted to influence attempts that are not in conflict with the ideals that underlie the identification. |
| Exercise power based on perceived dependence. | Wide range of behavior that can be monitored. | Quick. Can often succeed when other methods fail. | Repeated influence attempts encourage the other to gain power over the influencer. |
| Coercively exercise power based on perceived dependence. | Wide range of behavior that can be easily monitored. | Quick. Can often succeed when other methods fail. | Invites retaliation. Very risky. |
| Use persuasion. | Very wide range of attitudes and behavior. | Can produce internalized motivation that does not require monitoring. Requires no power or outlay of scarce material resources. | Can be very time-consuming. Requires other person to listen. |
| Combine these methods. | Depends on the exact combination. | Can be more potent and less risky than using a single method. | More costly than using a single method. |

(*continued*)

EXHIBIT • METHODS OF INFLUENCE (continued)

| Indirect methods | What they can influence | Advantages | Drawbacks |
|---|---|---|---|
| Manipulate the other's environment by using any or all of the face-to-face methods. | Wide range of behavior and attitudes. | Can succeed when face-to-face methods fail. | Can be time-consuming. Is complex to implement. Is very risky, especially if used frequently. |
| Change the forces that continuously act on the individual: Formal organizational arrangements. Informal social arrangements. Technology. Resources available. Statement of organizational goals. | Wide range of behavior and attitudes on a continuous basis. | Has continuous influence, not just a one-shot effect. Can have a very powerful impact. | Often requires a considerable power outlay to achieve. |

cases, a reputation as a manipulator can completely ruin a manager's career.

A second way in which managers indirectly influence others is by making permanent changes in an individual's or a group's environment. They change job descriptions, the formal systems that measure performance, the extrinsic incentives available, the extrinsic incentives available, the tools, people, and other resources that the people or groups work with, the architecture, the norms or values of work groups, and so on. If the manager is successful in making the changes, and the changes have the desired effect on the individual or group, that effect will be sustained over time.

Effective managers recognize that changes in the forces that surround a person can have great impact on that person's behavior. Unlike many of the other influence methods, this one

doesn't require a large expenditure of limited resources or effort on the part of the manager on an ongoing basis. Once such a change has been successfully made, it works independently of the manager.

This method of influence is used by all managers to some degree. Many, however, use it sparingly simply because they do not have the power to change the forces acting on the person they wish to influence. In many organizations, only the top managers have the power to change the formal measurement systems, the extrinsic incentives available, the architecture, and so on.

## GENERATING & USING POWER SUCCESSFULLY

Managers who are successful at acquiring considerable power and using it to manage their dependence on others tend to share a number of common characteristics:

1. They are sensitive to what others consider to be legitimate behavior in acquiring and using power. They recognize that the four types of power carry with them certain "obligations" regarding their acquisition and use. A person who gains a considerable amount of power based on his perceived expertise is generally expected to be an expert in certain areas. . . .

2. They have good intuitive understanding of the various types of power and methods of influence. They are sensitive to what types of power are easiest to develop with different types of people. They recognize, for example, that professionals tend to be more influenced by perceived expertise than by other forms of power. They also have a grasp of all the various methods of influence and what each can accomplish, at what costs, and with what risks. (See the *Exhibit* on pages 431 and 432.) They are good at recognizing the specific conditions in any situation and then at selecting an influence method that is compatible with those conditions.

3. They tend to develop all the types of power, to some degree, and they use all the influence methods mentioned in the exhibit. Unlike managers who are not very good at influencing people, effective managers usually do not think that only some of the methods are useful or that only some of the methods are moral. They recognize that any of the methods, used under the right circumstances, can help contribute to organizational effectiveness with few dysfunctional consequences. At the same time, they generally try to avoid those methods that are more risky than others and those that may have dysfunctional con-

sequences. For example, they manipulate the environment of others only when absolutely necessary.

4. They establish career goals and seek out managerial positions that allow them to successfully develop and use power. They look for jobs, for example, that use their backgrounds and skills to control or manage some critically important problem or environmental contingency that an organization faces. They recognize that success in that type of job makes others dependent on them and increases their own perceived expertise. They also seek jobs that do not demand a type or a volume of power that is inconsistent with their own skills.

5. They use all of their resources, formal authority, and power to develop still more power. To borrow Edward Banfield's metaphor, they actually look for ways to "invest" their power where they might secure a high positive return.[6] For example, by asking a person to do him two important favors, a manager might be able to finish his construction program one day ahead of schedule. That request may cost him most of the obligation-based power he has over that person, but in return he may significantly increase his perceived expertise as a manager of construction projects in the eyes of everyone in his organization.

6. Effective managers engage in power-oriented behavior in ways that are tempered by maturity and self-control.[7] They seldom, if ever, develop and use power in impulsive ways or for their own aggrandizement.

7. Finally, they also recognize and accept as legitimate that, in using these

---

[6] See Edward C. Banfield, *Political Influence* (New York: Free Press, 1965), Chapter II.

[7] See David C. McClelland and David H. Burnham, "Power Is the Great Motivator," *HBR* March–April 1976, p. 100.

methods, they clearly influence other people's behavior and lives. Unlike many less effective managers, they are reasonably comfortable in using power to influence people. They recognize, often only intuitively, what this article is all about—that their attempts to establish power and use it are an absolutely necessary part of the successful fulfillment of their difficult managerial role.

# CHAPTER VII

# *Organizational Change*

Organizational change requires the application of all of the other topics that have been addressed in this book. In order to confront organizational change in theory or in practice, one must tie together and use knowledge about human motivation, leadership, group and intergroup behavior, the relationship between people and their organizational contexts, and power and influence—all from the organizational behavior perspective. Thus, in examining the historical foundations and current practice of organizational change, this chapter incorporates contributions from:

- The Hawthorne experiments, as described by Fritz Roethlisberger (included in Chapter I, *Motivation*);
- Transformative leadership, as explained in the 1984 article by Noel Tichy and David Ulrich (reprinted in Chapter III, *Leadership*);
- The socio-technical systems-oriented group at the Tavistock Institute, as represented by Eric Trist and Kenneth Bamforth's article about the consequences of changing to the longwall method of coal mining, in Chapter V;
- Survey research and feedback techniques, that draw extensively from work done by Kurt Lewin and his associates (another piece by Lewin, on a different topic, "Group Decision and Social Change," appears in this chapter); and
- The development of sensitivity training (or T-groups), a phenomenon which in itself incorporates theory, research, and practice on leadership, group development and behavior, intergroup behavior, motivation, power and influence, and individual-organizational context impacts.

## ORGANIZATIONAL CHANGE FROM THE ORGANIZATIONAL BEHAVIOR PERSPECTIVE

The subject of organizational change has been receiving wide attention in the recent literature on organizational behavior and organizational theory. Like the Hugo Münsterberg (1913) and Henry Gantt (1908) work on behavior in organizations that preceded the development of the organizational behavior perspective, much of the new writing about change in organizations is not based on familiar humanistic-type assumptions. Change is perhaps the most visible and heated current battleground between proponents of the organizational behavior perspective (and its assumptions, values, and methods) and the advocates of change through manipulation of power and/or perceptions. (For more on this subject, see Shafritz & Ott, 1996.) So, the subject of organizational change provides a fitting, integrative subject with which to close this collection of classic readings in organizational behavior.

For more than thirty years (since about 1960), the organizational behavior perspective's interest in change has been riveted on *planned change*. The organizational behavior/planned change perspective assumptions have constituted the mainstream of organizational behavior literature and practice for so long that it sometimes is hard to think about any other. Thus, it is instructive to first take a brief glance at one of the more recent viewpoints on organizational change. A comparison between the 1960s-style "planned change" and the 1980s-style "transformational change," makes it easy to understand and appreciate the uniqueness of the planned organizational change assumptions.

## FOR COMPARISON: A DIFFERENT VIEW OF ORGANIZATIONAL CHANGE—TRANSFORMATION

The 1984 article by Noel Tichy and David Ulrich, "The Leadership Challenge— A Call for the Transformational Leader" provides an excellent example of the transformational view of organizational change (reprinted in Chapter III, *Leadership*). Tichy and Ulrich call for leaders who are able to manage *planned revolutionary organizational change* ("organizational transformations"). Transformational leaders (or as some authors call them, transformative leaders [Bennis, 1984; Bennis & Nanus, 1985]) are expected to accomplish different magnitudes of organizational change (qualitative and quantitative), using strategies and methods that are not compatible with the mores of the human relations/planned change perspective. Transformative leaders use *transformative power* (Bennis, 1984) or *transforming leadership* (Adams, 1986) literally to transform organizations and their cultures—to alter organizational norms, realities, beliefs, values and assumptions (Allaire & Firsirotu, 1985; Gemmill & Smith, 1985; Kilmann & Covin, 1988). In essence, transformative change is accomplished by violating organizational norms: by creating a new vision of the organization often through conscious manipulation of symbols, and then "selling" the new vision to important stakeholders. The best known model of a transformative leader who accomplished transformative change is Lee Iacocca (Iacocca, 1984).

## ASSUMPTIONS ABOUT CHANGE FROM THE ORGANIZATIONAL BEHAVIOR/PLANNED CHANGE PERSPECTIVE

Before transformational leadership and radical change started to attract attention (during the two decades from about 1960 to the early 1980s), the literature and practice of people-oriented organizational change had been dominated by the assumptions, beliefs, and tactics of the organizational behavior perspective. These assumptions, which provided the technological and normative direction for two decades of change-oriented organizational behavior theory and practice, were articulated most clearly by Chris Argyris in the first chapter of his seminal 1970 book, *Intervention Theory and Methods,* excerpts from which are reprinted here. Although Argyris's words are descriptive, his tone and his message are very prescriptive.

> Valid information, free choice, and internal commitment are considered integral parts of any intervention activity, no matter what the substantive objectives are (for a change). These three processes are called the primary intervention tasks (p. 17).

As Argyris lists his three primary intervention tasks, his normative assumptions become unmistakably evident:

1. Without valid, usable information (including knowledge of the consequences of alternatives), there can be no free informed choice.
2. Without free informed choice, there can be no personal responsibility for decisions.
3. Without personal responsibility for decisions there can be no internalized commitment to the success of a decision (no *psychological ownership*).

The organizational behavior perspective also embraces strong beliefs about what constitutes organizational effectiveness. These beliefs have further steered the pursuit of organizational improvement away from the manipulation of extrinsic variables such as systems of rewards and punishments. Under this line of reasoning, organizational effectiveness is not defined as *outcomes* but rather as *ongoing process states.* Warren Bennis uses the analogy of *health* or *healthy organization* to communicate his widely accepted concept of organizational process effectiveness. Bennis's criteria for assessing organizational health (or effectiveness) are (in Schein, 1980, p. 232):

1. *Adaptability:* The ability to solve problems and to react with flexibility to changing environmental demands.
2. A *sense of identity:* Knowledge and insight on the part of the organization of what it is, what its goals are, and what it is to do. . . .
3. *Capacity to test reality:* The ability to search out, accurately perceive, and correctly interpret the real properties of the environment, particularly those which have relevance for the functioning of the organization.
4. *Integration:* A fourth, often-cited criterion that in effect underlies the others is a state of "integration" among the subparts of the total organization, such that the parts are not working at cross-purposes.

In a philosophically consistent vein, Schein (1980) identifies the organizational coping processes that are necessary conditions for maintaining or increasing organizational effectiveness (health):

1. The ability to take in and communicate information reliably and validly.

2. . . . internal flexibility and creativity to make changes which are demanded by the information obtained.

3. . . . integration of and commitment to the multiple goals of the organization, from which comes the willingness to change when necessary.

4. . . . an internal climate of support and freedom from threat, since being threatened undermines good communications, reduces flexibility, and stimulates self-protection rather than concern for the total system.

5. . . . the ability to continuously redesign the organization's structure to be congruent with its goal and tasks (p. 249).

By comparing Bennis's and Schein's necessary conditions for organizational health/effectiveness with those of Hugo Münsterberg (1913) or Frederick Winslow Taylor (1911) (they are summarized in the *Introduction*), the vastness of the differences between these organizational perspectives becomes very evident. The organizational behavior perspective defines organizational effectiveness as a process state— not as it has been defined traditionally in terms of organizational outcomes such as market penetration, profitability, or quantity and/or quality levels of output.

## ORGANIZATION DEVELOPMENT

The most dynamic and energetic manifestation of organizational behavior-based change has been the subfield of *organization development* or simply O.D. O.D. is a particular form of planned organizational change (or development) that embodies the full set of premises, assumptions, values, and strategies of the organizational behavior perspective. Although all authors' definitions of organization development vary in emphasis, most are quite consistent in substance. For example:

> Organization development is an effort (1) *planned* (2) *organization-wide,* and (3) *managed* from the *top,* to (4) *increase organization effectiveness* and *health* through (5) *planned intervention* in the organization's "process," using *behavioral-science* knowledge (Beckhard, 1969). (Emphasis in original text.)

and

> Organization development is a long-range effort to improve an organization's problem-solving and renewal processes, particularly through a more effective and collaborative management of organizational culture . . . with the assistance of a change agent, or catalyst, and the use of the theory and technology of applied behavioral science, including action research (French and Bell, 1984).

Organization development is about planned organizational change as a process or strategy. O.D. is as concerned about *how* planned change is implemented as it is about specifically *where* change will lead an organization. Typically, the product or result of O.D. activities is an ongoing set of processes for organizational renewal that are *in-and-of-themselves defined as criteria of organizational effectiveness.* O.D. assumes that change is purposeful and dynamic, is accomplished through application of behavioral science knowledge, and is accomplished according to carefully prescribed ground rules that are derived from the assumptions of the organizational behavior perspective. Thus, for example, revolutionary and evolutionary change generally are not considered to be within the purview of O.D.

O.D. is concerned with deep, long-lasting, organization-wide change or improvement—not in superficial changes in isolated organizational pockets. This concern for the broad-based and long-term led O.D. practitioners to an interest in the concept of organizational culture long before it became a fashionable management topic in the 1980s (Ott, 1989).

O.D. practitioners have developed numerous strategies and techniques for improving organizations: Most of them utilize *interventions* facilitated by outsiders (often called *change agents*). Some of the most common strategies include organizational diagnosis, process consultation, team building (in many forms), action research, data feedback, job enlargement, job enrichment, and conflict management. But each author has his or her own preferred tactics. For example, in one of the best known such lists, Schmuck and Miles (1971) include: training and education, process consultation or coaching, confrontation meetings, data feedback, problem solving, goal setting, O.D. task force establishment, and techno-structural activity. Thus, organization development represents a very notable effort to apply an impressive array of research-based social science knowledge within a prescriptive value framework, to ongoing organizational improvement.

The origins of organization development can be traced to several events and movements that started in the 1930s and 1940s:

1.  *The Hawthorne* studies;
2.  *The sensitivity training* (or "T-group") *movement*, which originated in the late 1940s at the National Training Laboratories, under the leadership of such luminaries as Leland Bradford;
3.  *Developments in survey research and feedback techniques*, particularly through the work of Kurt Lewin (1952), which presaged creation of the basic *action research* model of organizational change; and
4.  *The socio-technical "school" of research and analysis*, pioneered at the Tavistock Institute by such pioneers as Eric Trist, Kenneth Bamforth, A. K. Rice, and Elliott Jaques.

*The Hawthorne studies* and their importance to understanding organizational behavior-oriented change processes, are discussed extensively in the *Introduction* and in Chapter III, *Leadership*. So, other than referring the reader to Fritz Roethlisberger's "The Hawthorne Experiments" (in Chapter I), we will move on to the remaining three historical trends and events that opened the way for organization development.

*The sensitivity training* (or "T-group") *movement* had its start in 1946 when Kurt Lewin, Leland Bradford, Ronald Lippitt, and Kenneth Benne collaboratively conducted a training workshop to help improve racial relations and community leadership in New Britain, Connecticut (Bradford, Gibb & Benne, 1964). During their evening staff meetings, they discussed the behavior of workshop participants and the dynamics of events. Several workshop participants asked to join the night discussions, and the results of the process eventually led to the initiation and institutionalization of *T-group technology.* Although the early T-groups focused primarily on individual growth and development, they quickly were adapted for organizational application. T-groups became the method by which organizational members learned how to communicate honestly and directly about facts and feelings (Argyris, 1962). (From the human relations perspective, *feelings are facts.*) Thus, T-groups became a keystone strategy for increasing organizational effectiveness by improving interpersonal communications (e.g., feedback), reducing defensiveness (and thus rigidity), and otherwise helping organizations achieve Bennis's criteria for organizational effectiveness—adaptability, sense of identity, capacity to test reality, and integration—through the development of coping processes that are necessary conditions for maintaining or increasing organizational effectiveness:

1. The ability to take in and communicate information reliably and validly;
2. The internal flexibility and creativity to make changes which are demanded by the information obtained;
3. The integration of and commitment to the multiple goals of the organization, from which comes the willingness to change when necessary;
4. An internal climate of support and freedom from threat; and
5. The ability to continuously redesign the organization's structure to be congruent with its goal and tasks (Schein, 1980, p. 249).

Without sensitivity training groups (T-groups) there probably would never have been a subfield of organization development.

*Survey research and feedback techniques* particularly characterized the work initiated by Kurt Lewin and his associates at the Research Center for Group Dynamics first at M.I.T. and, after his death, at the University of Michigan. Survey research methodology, when combined with feedback/communication techniques, and applied to planned organizational change, resulted in the development of the *action research* model of organizational change—another mainstay of O.D. practitioners and theorists. The action research model is a prescribed process for identifying needs for organizational improvement and creating improvement strategies that utilizes external consultation but creates psychological ownership of problems and solutions by organizational members. Briefly, action research involves:

- Collecting organizational diagnostic-type data, usually either by questionnaire or through consultant interviews;
- Systematically feeding back information to groups of people (organization members) who provided input;
- Discussing what the information means to members and its implications for the organization in order to be certain the "diagnosis" is accurate and to generate psychological ownership of the need for improvement actions;

- Jointly developing action-improvement plans, using the knowledge and skills of the consultant and the insider perspective of members; and generating psychological ownership of the improvement action plan.

The action research model is diagrammed in Figure 1.

*The socio-technical approach to research and analysis* made its appearance in the late 1940s and early 1950s through a group of organizational researchers at the Tavistock Institute in London who identified a tight link between human and technological factors in the workplace. They concluded that neither people nor

### FIGURE 1 · THE ORGANIZATION DEVELOPMENT ACTION RESEARCH MODEL

*Initial Diagnostic and Planning Phase*

Preliminary conceptualization of organizational problems by management and consultant
↓
Consultant gathers diagnostic data through, for example, questionnaires, interviews, and observations
↓
Consultant prepares the data for feedback to organization members
↓
Consultant feeds back diagnostic data to organization members
↓
Joint interpretation of the meaning and implications of the data, by organization members and the consultant
↓
Joint action planning by organization members and consultant
↓
*Implementation Phase 1* ←

Organization members implement action plans with assistance from consultant as desired or needed
↓
Consultant collects data on progress and effectiveness of action plan implementation
↓
Consultant feeds back data to organization members
↓
Joint interpretation of the meaning and implications of the data by organization members and the consultant
↓
Joint action planning by organization members and consultant
↓
*Implementation Phase n*

Organization members implement new action plans with assistance from consultant as desired or needed
↓
Repeat steps in Implementation Phase 1

work/technology takes precedence over the other. Once again, as was true with the Hawthorne studies, the socio-technical group does not assume that the task is to increase productivity by fitting people to the work. Eric Trist and Kenneth Bamforth found that changing the coal-mining technology from small group production to a physically spaced *long-wall* method, disrupts the social structure of the miners and in turn production. By modifying the work (technical) system to allow the social structure to reform, workers returned to helping each other, productivity and morale increased, and accidents and absenteeism decreased. (See "Some Social and Psychological Consequences of the Longwall Method of Coal-Getting," Article 28 in Chapter V.)

## INTRODUCTION TO THE ARTICLES IN THIS CHAPTER

This chapter's first selection is one of the best known and most frequently quoted experiments on the introduction of organizational change, Lester Coch and John R. P. French's 1948 *Human Relations* article, "Overcoming Resistance to Change." Coch and French studied the relationship between worker participation in design decisions leading to the introduction of changes in work process, and their resistance to changes. The authors used a research design complete with experimental and control groups of pajama folders, pressers, and examiners at the Harwood Manufacturing Corporation in Marion, Virginia. Using Kurt Lewin's concepts of quasi-stationary equilibriums and change force fields, Coch and French conclude that group participation in planning reduces workers' resistance to changes, decreases turnover during and following changes, and accelerates worker re-learning curves (the rapidity with which workers return to full-speed production following process changes).

Whether it is 1948 or 1996, whenever organizational change is discussed, Kurt Lewin heads everyone's list of people who have made invaluable and lasting contributions to our understanding of change processes and dynamics. His 1952 article that is reprinted here, "Group Decision and Social Change," is a condensed restatement of ideas Lewin put forth in one of his best known works, "Frontiers in Group Dynamics: Concept, Method and Reality in Social Science; Social Equilibria and Social Change" (1947). Lewin describes social organizations as resting in a state of stable quasi-stationary equilibrium. In order to effect social change, one must begin with an "analysis of the conditions for 'no change,' that is, for the state of equilibrium." Quite obviously, the now-familiar technique of *force field analysis* evolved from this concept, in which there are but two basic approaches for accomplishing change: "Adding forces in the desired direction, or by diminishing opposing forces." Lewin argues that the latter approach is less preferable because it tends to be accompanied by a "high state of tension" which in turn causes anger, aggressiveness and a lower propensity to be constructive. In this piece, Lewin articulates his well-known assertion that social change must be viewed as a three-step process of unfreezing, change, and refreezing. If one focuses only on the change process per se, change will be short-lived at best. . . .

Chris Argyris's 1970 book, *Intervention Theory and Methods* is a comprehensive, widely cited, and enduring work on organizational consulting for change written from an organizational behavior/organization development perspective. A portion of the first chapter from *Intervention Theory and Methods* is reprinted here. The book has remained central to the field because Argyris unambiguously lays out the fundamental tenets that undergird the organizational behavior perspective of change. (Argyris calls the tenets "the three primary intervention tasks." They are listed earlier in this chapter and in Article 41, so they are not repeated here.) These tenets define such fundamentals as the nature of the change-agent/client relationship, the necessity for valid and usable information, and necessary preconditions for oganization members to internalize change.

Whereas the article by Chris Argyris is about change processes in general, Herbert Kelman and Donald Warwick's (1978) "The Ethics of Social Intervention: Goals, Means, and Consequences" (which is reprinted here) analyzes one important organizational change issue: the ethics of intervening in ongoing social systems. The authors subsume Bennis's (1966) concepts of planned organizational change under the expanded topic of *social interventions*. Kelman and Warwick concentrate on four steps in any intervention in a social system that are likely to raise important ethical issues:

1. The choice of the change goal,
2. Definition of the change target,
3. Selection of intervention means, and
4. The assessment of the consequences of intervening in ongoing social systems.

Ethical issues inevitably arise during these steps because each involves questions about which competing values will take priority over others.

Rosabeth Moss Kanter has been among the most widely cited observers of organizational phenomena during the last 15 to 20 years. Her contribution to this chapter is from her 1983 bestselling book, *The Change Masters*, titled "The Architecture of Culture and Strategy Change." The core of Kanter's *architecture of change* is a set of five *building blocks of change* that permit change to progress beyond innovation to institutionalization (Kanter also sometimes refers to these building blocks as *forces*):

1. Departures from tradition,
2. A crisis or galvanizing event,
3. Strategic decisions,
4. Individual "prime movers," and
5. Action vehicles.

Kanter concludes that the "tools of change masters are creative and interactive; they have an intellectual, a conceptual, and a cultural aspect." Change masters are the right people (people with ideas), in the right place (integrative environments that support innovation), at the right time. According to Kanter, *right times* are:

> Those moments in the flow of organizational history when it is possible to reconstruct reality on the basis of accumulated innovations to shape a more productive and successful future (p. 306).

For Peter Senge, change *is* learning, and learning *is* change—for people and organizations. Thus, organizations that can learn to change are possible because "deep down, we are all learners." In Chapter One from *The Fifth Discipline: The Art and Practice of the Learning Organization* (1990) (reprinted here), Senge proposes that five new "component technologies" are gradually converging that will collectively permit the emergence of learning organizations. He labels these component technologies the "five disciplines": *systems thinking*—"systems" of the variety described by Margaret Wheatley in "Leadership and the New Science" (reprinted in Chapter III); *personal mastery*—people approaching life and work "as an artist would approach a work of art" (p. 7); *mental models*—deeply ingrained assumptions or mental images "that influence how we understand the world and how we take action" (p. 8); *building shared vision*—"when there is a genuine vision . . . people excel and learn, not because they are told to, but because they want to" (p. 9); and *team learning*—team members engaging in true dialogue with their assumptions suspended.

A learning organization employs the five disciplines in a never-ending quest to expand its capacity to create its future. As Senge explains, "systems thinking" is the fifth discipline—the integrative discipline that fuses the others into a coherent body of theory and practice. Learning organizations are organizations that are able to move past mere survival learning to engage in generative learning—"learning that enhances our capacity to create" (p. 14).

The concluding reading in this chapter is about "fundamental change" in organizations, changes in the essence or identity of an organization and its members. In "Focusing the Effort: Crucial Themes That Drive Change," Richard Beckhard and Wendy Pritchard (1992) identify five themes that underlie fundamental organizational change and that need to be its focus:

- Change in the mission or "reason to be";
- Change in the identity or outside image;
- Change in relationships to key stakeholders;
- Change in the way of work; and
- Change in the organizational culture (p. 37).

Beckhard and Pritchard advise that the five themes are interrelated. Although an effort to initiate fundamental change in an organization usually is focused on one of the five themes (for example, a change in mission or in organizational culture), all five will be affected and require attention.

Thus, organizational change involves the application of all of the other topics that have been addressed in this book about organizational behavior. Change requires the application of knowledge about motivation, group and intergroup dynamics, leadership, teamwork, empowerment, effects of the work environment on individuals at work, power, and influence. Change brings it all together—it is where "the rubber meets the road" for organizational behavior.

## REFERENCES

Adams, J. D. (Ed.). (1986). *Transforming leadership: From vision to results*. Alexandria, VA: Miles River Press.

Allaire, Y., & Firsirotu, M. (Spring, 1985). How to implement radical strategies in large organizations. *Sloan Management Review, 26*(3), 19–34.

Argyris, C. (1962). *Interpersonal competence and organizational effectiveness*. Homewood, IL: The Dorsey Press and Richard D. Irwin.

Argyris, C. (1970). *Intervention theory and methods*. Reading, MA: Addison-Wesley.

Argyris, C. (1993). *Knowledge for action: A guide to overcoming barriers to organizational change*. San Francisco: Jossey-Bass.

Beckhard, R. (1969). *Organization development: Strategies and models*. Reading, MA: Addison-Wesley.

Beckhard, R., & Harris, R. T. (1977). *Organizational transitions: Managing complex change*. Reading, MA: Addison-Wesley.

Beckhard, R., & Pritchard, W. (1992). *Changing the essence: The art of creating and leading fundamental change in organizations*. San Francisco: Jossey-Bass.

Bennis, W. G. (1966). Applying behavioral sciences to planned organizational change. In, W. G. Bennis, *Changing organizations* (pp. 81–94). New York: McGraw-Hill.

Bennis, W. G. (1969). *Organization development: Its nature, origins and prospects*. Reading, MA: Addison-Wesley.

Bennis, W. G. (1984). Transformative power and leadership. In, T. J. Sergiovanni & J. E. Corbally (Eds.), *Leadership and organizational culture* (pp. 64–71). Urbana, IL: University of Illinois Press.

Bennis, W. G., Benne, K. D., and Chin, R. (1961). *The planning of change*. New York: Holt, Rinehart & Winston.

Bennis, W. G., & Nanus, B. (1985). *Leaders*. New York: Harper & Row Publishers.

Bradford, L., Gibb, J. R., & Benne, K. D. (Eds.). (1964). *T-group theory and laboratory method; innovation in re-education*. New York: Wiley.

Coch, L., & French, J. R. P., Jr. (August, 1948). Overcoming resistance to change. *Human Relations*, 512–532.

French, W. L., & Bell, C. H., Jr. (1984). *Organization development* (3rd ed.). Englewood Cliffs, NJ: Prentice-Hall.

French, W. L., Bell, C. H., Jr. & Zawacki, R. A. (Eds.). (1983). *Organization development: Theory, practice, and research* (rev. ed.). Plano, TX: Business Publications, Inc.

Gantt, H. L. (1908). Training workmen in habits of industry and cooperation. Paper presented to the American Society of Mechanical Engineers.

Gemmill, G., & Smith, C. (1985). A dissipative structure model of organization transformation. *Human Relations, 38,* 751–766.

Gersick, C. (January 1991). Revolutionary change theories: A multilevel exploration of the punctuated equilibrium paradigm. *Academy of Management Review,* 10–36.

Huber, G. P., & Glick, W. H. (1993). *Organizational change and redesign: Ideas and insights for improving performance.* New York: Oxford University Press.

Iacocca, L. (1984). *Iacocca, an autobiography.* Toronto: Bantam Books.

Jaques, E. (1951). *The changing culture of a factory.* London, UK: Tavistock Publications.

Kanter, R. M. (1983). *The change masters.* New York: Simon & Schuster.

Kelman, H. C., & Warwick, D. (1978). The ethics of social intervention: Goals, means, and consequences. In, H. C. Bermant, H. C. Kelman, & D. P. Warwick, (Eds.), *The ethics of social intervention* (pp. 3–27). New York: Hemisphere Publishing Company.

Kilmann, R. H., & Covin, T. J. (Eds.). (1988). *Corporate transformation.* San Francisco: Jossey-Bass.

Kozmetsky, G. (1985). *Transformational management.* Cambridge, MA: Ballinger Publishing Company.

Leavitt, H. J. (1965). Applied organizational change in industry: Structural, technological, and humanistic approaches. In, J. G. March (Ed.), *Handbook of organizations* (pp. 1144–1170). Chicago: Rand McNally.

Lewin, K. (June, 1947). Frontiers in group dynamics: Concept, method and reality in social science; Social equilibria and social change. *Human Relations, 1*(1).

Lewin, K. (1952). Quasi-stationary social equilibria and the problem of permanent change. In, G. E. Swanson, T. N. Newcomb, & E. L. Hartley (Eds.), *Readings in social psychology* (rev. ed.) (pp. 207–211). New York: Holt, Rinehart & Winston.

McWhinney, W. (1992). *Paths of change: Strategic choices for organizations and society.* Newbury Park, CA: Sage.

Münsterberg, H. (1913). *Psychology and industrial efficiency.* Boston: Houghton Mifflin Company.

Ott, J. S. (1989). *The organizational culture perspective.* Belmont, CA: Wadsworth.

Rice, A. K. (1953). Productivity and social organization in an Indian weaving shed: An examination of some aspects of the socio-technical system of an experimental automatic loom shed. *Human Relations, 6,* 297–329.

Schein, E. H. (1988). *Process consultation: Its role in organization development* (2d. ed). Reading, MA: Addison-Wesley.

Schein, E. H. (1980). *Organizational psychology* (3rd ed.). Englewood Cliffs, NJ: Prentice-Hall, Inc.

Schmuck, R. A., & Miles, M. B. (Eds.). (1971). *Organization development in schools.* Palo Alto, CA: National Press Books.

Senge, P. M. (1990). *The fifth discipline: The art and practice of the learning organization.* New York: Doubleday Currency.

Shafritz, J. M., & Ott, J. S. (1996). *Classics of organization theory* (4th ed.). Belmont, CA: Wadsworth.

Taylor, F. W. (1911). *The principles of scientific management.* New York: W. W. Norton.

Tichy, N. M., & Ulrich, D. O. (Fall, 1984). The leadership challenge—A call for the transformational leader. *Sloan Management Review, 26*(1), 59–68.

Trist, E., & Bamforth, K. W. (1951). Some social and psychologial consequences of the longwall method of coal-getting. *Human Relations, 4,* 3–38.

Wheatley, Margaret, J. (1992). *Leadership and the new science: Learning about organization from an orderly universe.* San Francisco: Jossey-Bass.

# 39

# Overcoming Resistance to Change[1]

*Lester Coch & John R. P. French, Jr.*

## INTRODUCTION

It has always been characteristic of American industry to change products and methods of doing jobs as often as competitive conditions or engineering progress dictates. This makes frequent changes in an individual's work necessary. In addition, the markedly greater turnover and absenteeism of recent years result in unbalanced production lines which again makes for frequent shifting of individuals from one job to another. One of the most serious production problems faced at the Harwood Manufacturing Corporation has been the resistance of production workers to the necessary changes in methods and jobs. This resistance expressed itself in several ways, such as grievances about the piece rates that went with the new methods, high turnover, very low efficiency, restriction of output, and marked aggression against management. Despite these undesirable effects, it was necessary that changes in methods and jobs continue. . . .

[1] Grateful acknowledgements are made by the authors to Dr. Alfred J. Marrow, president of the Harwood Manufacturing Corporation, and to the entire Harwood staff for their valuable aid and suggestions in this study.
The authors have drawn repeatedly from the works and concepts of Kurt Lewin for both the action and theoretical phases of this study. Many of the leadership techniques used in the experimental group meetings were techniques developed at the first National Training Laboratory for Group Development held at Bethel, Maine, in the summer of 1947. Both authors attended this laboratory.

## BACKGROUND

The main plant of the Harwood Manufacturing Corporation, where the present research was done, is located in the small town of Marion, Virginia. The plant produces pajamas and, like most sewing plants, employs mostly women. The plant's population is about 500 women and 100 men. The workers are recruited from the rural, mountainous areas surrounding the town, and are usually employed without previous industrial experience. The average age of the workers is 23; the average education is eight years of grammar school.

The policies of the company in regard to labor relations are liberal and progressive. A high value has been placed on fair and open dealing with the employees and they are encouraged to take up any problems or grievances with the management at any time. Every effort is made to help foremen find effective solutions to their problems in human relations, using conferences and role-playing methods. Carefully planned orientation, designed to help overcome the discouragement and frustrations attending entrance upon the new and unfamiliar situation, is used. Plant-wide votes are conducted where possible to resolve problems affecting the whole working population. The company has invested both time and money in employee services such as industrial music, health services, lunchroom, and recreation programs. In the same spirit, the man-

*Source:* From "Overcoming Resistance to Change" by Lester Coch and John R. P. French, Jr., in *Human Relations* (1948), pp. 512–532. Reprinted by permission of Plenum Publishing Corporation.

agement has been conscious of the importance of public relations in the local community; they have supported both financially and otherwise any activity which would build up good will for the company. As a result of these policies, the company has enjoyed good labor relations since the day it commenced operations.

Harwood employees work on an individual incentive system. Piece rates are set by time study and are expressed in terms of units. One unit is equal to one minute of standard work: 60 units per hour equal the standard efficiency rating. Thus, if on a particular operation the piece rate for one dozen is 10 units, the operator would have to produce 6 dozen per hour to achieve the standard efficiency rating of 60 units per hour. The skill required to reach 60 units per hour is great. On some jobs, an average trainee may take 34 weeks to reach the skill level necessary to perform at 60 units per hour. Her first few weeks of work may be on an efficiency level of 5 to 20 units per hour. . . .

When it is necessary to change an operator from one type of work to another, a transfer bonus is given. This bonus is so designed that the changed operator who relearns at an average rate will suffer no loss in earnings after change. Despite this allowance, the general attitudes toward job changes in the factory are markedly negative. Such expressions as, "When you make your units (standard production), they change your job," are all too frequent. Many operators refuse to change, preferring to quit.

## THE TRANSFER LEARNING CURVE

An analysis of the after-change relearning curve of several hundred experienced operators rating standard or better prior to change showed that 38 per cent of

the changed operators recovered to the standard unit rating of 60 units per hour. The other 62 per cent either became chronically sub-standard operators or quit during the relearning period.

The average relearning curve for those who recover to standard production on the simplest type job in the plant (Figure I) is eight weeks long, and, when smoothed, provides the basis for the transfer bonus. The bonus is the percent difference between this expected efficiency rating and the standard of 60 units per hour. Progress is slow for the first two or three weeks, as the relearning curve shows, and then accelerates markedly to about 50 units per hour with an increase of 15 units in two weeks. . . .

It is interesting to note in Figure I that the relearning period for an experienced operator is longer than the learning period for a new operator. . . .

Figure II, which presents the relearning curves for 41 experienced operators who were changed to very difficult jobs, gives a comparison between the recovery rates for operators making standard or better prior to change, and those below standard prior to change. Both classes of operators dropped to a little below 30 units per hour and recovered at a very slow but similar rate. These curves show a general (though by no means universal) phenomenon; that the efficiency rating prior to change does not indicate a faster or slower recovery rate after change.

## A PRELIMINARY THEORY OF RESISTANCE TO CHANGE

The fact that relearning after transfer to a new job is so often slower than initial learning on first entering the factory would indicate, on the face of it, that the resistance to change and the slow relearning is primarily a motivational problem. The similar recovery rates of the skilled and unskilled operators

FIGURE I · A COMPARISON OF THE LEARNING CURVE FOR NEW,
INEXPERIENCED EMPLOYEES WITH THE RELEARNING CURVE FOR
ONLY THOSE TRANSFERS (38 PER CENT) WHO EVENTUALLY
RECOVER TO STANDARD PRODUCTION.

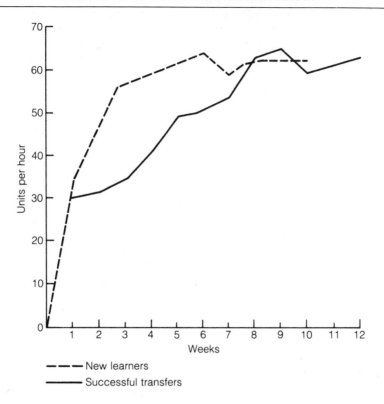

- - - New learners
——— Successful transfers

shown in Figure II tend to confirm the hypothesis that skill is a minor factor and motivation is the major determinant of the rate of recovery. Earlier experiments at Harwood by Alex Bavelas demonstrated this point conclusively. He found that the use of group decision techniques on operators who had just been transferred resulted in very marked increases in the rate of relearning, even though no skill training was given and there were no other changes in working conditions (2).

Interviews with operators who have been transferred to a new job reveal a common pattern of feelings and attitudes which are distinctly different from those of successful non-transfers. In addition to resentment against the management for transferring them, the employees typically show feelings of frustration, loss of hope of ever regaining their former level of production and status in the factory, feelings of failure, and a very low level of aspiration. In this respect these transferred operators are similar to the chronically slow workers studied previously.

Earlier unpublished research at Harwood has shown that the non-transferred employees generally have an explicit goal of reaching and maintaining an efficiency rating of 60 units per

### FIGURE II • THE DROP IN PRODUCTION AND THE RATE OF RECOVERY AFTER TRANSFER FOR SKILLFUL AND FOR SUBSTANDARD OPERATORS.

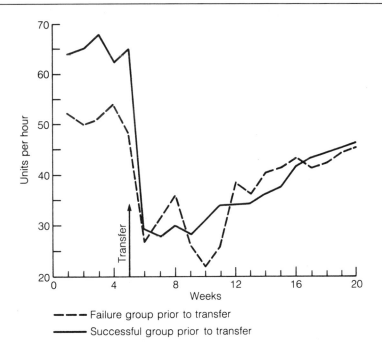

- - - - Failure group prior to transfer

——— Successful group prior to transfer

hour. A questionnaire administered to several groups of operators indicated that a large majority of them accept as their goal the management's quota of 60 units per hour. This standard of production is the level of aspiration according to which the operators measure their own success or failure; and those who fall below standard lose status in the eyes of their fellow employees. Relatively few operators set a goal appreciably above 60 units per hour.

The actual production records confirm the effectiveness of this goal of standard production. The distribution of the total population of operators in accordance with their production levels is by no means a normal curve. Instead there is a very large number of operators who rate 60 to 63 units per hour and relatively

few operators who rate just above or just below this range. Thus we may conclude that:

• Hypothesis (1): There is a force acting on the operator in the direction of achieving a production level of 60 units per hour or more. It is assumed that the strength of this drving force (acting on an operator below standard) increases as she gets nearer the goal—a typical goal gradient (see Figure 1).

On the other hand restraining forces operate to hinder or prevent her from reaching this goal. These restraining forces consist among other things of the difficulty of the job in relation to the operator's level of skill. Other things being equal, the faster an operator is sewing the more difficult it is to increase her speed by a given amount. Thus we may conclude that:

• Hypothesis (2): The strength of the restraining force hindering higher production increases with increasing level of production.

In line with previous studies, it is assumed that the conflict of these two opposing forces—the driving force corresponding to the goal of reaching 60 and the restraining force of the difficulty of the job—produces frustration. In such a conflict situation, the strength of frustration will depend on the strength of these forces. If the restraining force against increasing production is weak, then the frustration will be weak. But if the driving force toward higher production (i.e., the motivation) is weak, then the frustration will also be weak. Probably both of the conflicting forces must be above a certain minimum strength before any frustration is produced; for all goal-directed activity involves some degree of conflict of this type, yet a person is not usually frustrated so long as he is making satisfactory progress toward his goal. Consequently we assume that:

• Hypothesis (3): The strength of frustration is a function of the weaker of these two opposing forces, provided that the weaker force is stronger than a certain minimum necessary to produce frustration (Hypothesis [1]).

An analysis of the effects of such frustration in the factory showed that it resulted, among other things, in high turnover and absenteeism. The rate of turnover for successful operators with efficiency ratings above standard was much lower than for unsuccessful operators. Likewise, operators on the more difficult jobs quit more frequently than those on the easier jobs. Presumably the effect of being transferred is a severe frustration which should result in similar attempts to escape from the field.

In line with this theory of frustration, and the finding that job turnover is one resultant of frustration, an analysis was made of the turnover rate of transferred operators as compared with the rate among operators who had not been transfered recently. . . .

The results are given in Figure III. Both the levels of turnover and the form of the curves are strikingly different for the two groups. Among operators who have not been transferred recently the average turnover per month is about 4½ per cent; among recent transfers the monthly turnover is nearly 12 per cent. Consistent with the previous studies, both groups show a very marked drop in the turnover curve after an operator becomes a success by reaching 60 units per hour or standard production. However, the form of the curves at lower unit ratings is markedly different for the two groups. The nontransferred operators show a gradually increasing rate of turnover up to a rating of 55 to 59 units per hour. The transferred operators, on the other hand, show a high peak at the lowest unit rating of 30 to 34 units per hour, decreasing sharply to a low point at 45 to 49 units per hour. Since most changed operators drop to a unit rating of around 30 units per hour when changed and then drop no further, it is obvious that the rate of turnover was highest for these operators just after they were changed and again much later just before they reached standard. Why?

It is assumed that the strength of frustration for an operator who has *not* been transferred gradually increases because both the driving force towards the goal of reaching 60 and the restraining force of the difficulty of the job increase with increasing unit rating. This is in line with hypotheses (1), (2) and (3). For the transferred operator on the other hand the frustration is greatest immediately after transfer when the contrast of

## FIGURE III • THE RATE OF TURNOVER AT VARIOUS LEVELS OF PRODUCTION FOR TRANSFERS AS COMPARED WITH NONTRANSFERS.

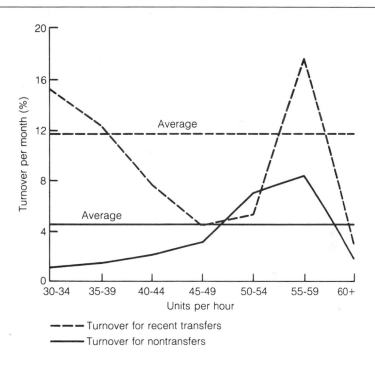

- - - Turnover for recent transfers
——— Turnover for nontransfers

her present status with her former status is most evident. At this point the strength of the restraining forces is at a maximum because the difficulty is unusually great due to proactive inhibition. Then as she overcomes the interference effects between the two jobs and learns the new job, the difficulty and the frustration gradually decrease and the rate of turnover declines until the operator reaches 45–49 units per hour. Then at higher levels of production the difficulty starts to increase again and the transferred operator shows the same peak in frustration and turnover at 55–59 units per hour. . . .

Another factor which seems to affect recovery rates of changed operators is the amount of we-feeling. Observations seem to indicate that a strong psychological sub-group with negative attitudes toward management will display the strongest resistance to change. On the other hand, changed groups with high we-feeling and positive cooperative attitudes are the best relearners. Collections of individuals with little or no we-feeling display some resistance to change but not so strongly as the groups with high we-feeling and negative attitudes toward management. However, turnover for the individual transfers is much higher than in the latter groups. This phenomenon of the relationship between we-feeling and resistance to change is so overt that for years the general policy of the management of the plant was never to change a group as a group but rather to scatter the individuals in different areas throughout the factory.

An analysis of turnover records for changed operators with high we-feeling showed a 4 per cent turnover rate per month at 30 to 34 units per hour, not significantly higher than in unchanged operators but significantly lower than in changed operators with little or no we-feeling. However, the acts of aggression are far more numerous among operators with high we-feeling than among operators with little we-feeling. Since both types of operators experience the same frustration as individuals but react to it so differently, it is assumed that the effect of the in-group feeling is to set up a restraining force against leaving the group and perhaps even to set up driving forces toward staying in the group. In these circumstances, one would expect some alternative reaction to frustration rather than escape from the field. This alternative is aggression. Strong we-feeling provides strength so that members dare to express aggression which would otherwise be suppressed.

One common result in a sub-group with strong we-feeling is the setting of a group standard concerning production. Where the attitudes toward management are antagonistic, this group standard may take the form of a definite restriction of production to a given level. This phenomenon of restriction is particularly likely to happen in a group that has been transferred to a job where a new piece rate has been set; for they have some hope that if production never approaches the standard, the management may change the piece rate in their favor.

A group standard can exert extremely strong forces on an individual member of a small sub-group. . . .

## THE EXPERIMENT

On the basis of the preliminary theory that resistance to change is a combina-

tion of an individual reaction to frustration with strong group-induced forces it seemed that the most appropriate methods for overcoming the resistance to change would be group methods. Consequently an experiment was designed employing two variations of democratic procedure in handling groups to be transferred. The first variation involved participation through representation of the workers in designing the changes to be made in the jobs. The second variation consisted of total participation by all members of the group in designing the changes. A third control group was also used. Two experimental groups received the total participation treatment. The three experimental groups and the control group were roughly matched with respect to: (a) the efficiency ratings of the groups before transfer; (b) the degree of change involved in the transfer; (c) the amount of we-feeling observed in the groups. . . .

The control group of hand pressers went through the usual factory routine when they were changed. The production department modified the job, and a new piece rate was set. A group meeting was then held in which the control group was told that the change was necessary because of competitive conditions, and that a new piece rate had been set. The new piece rate was thoroughly explained by the time study man, questions were answered, and the meeting dismissed.

Experimental group 1 was changed in a different manner. Before any changes took place, a group meeting was held with all the operators to be changed. The need for the change was presented as dramatically as possible, showing two identical garments produced in the factory; one was produced in 1946 and had sold for 100 per cent more than its fellow in 1947. The group was asked to identify the cheaper one and could not do it.

This demonstration effectively shared with the group the entire problem of the necessity of cost reduction. A general agreement was reached that a savings could be effected by removing the "frills" and "fancy" work from the garment without affecting the folders' opportunity to achieve a high efficiency rating. Management then presented a plan to set the new job and piece rate:

1. Make a check study of the job as it was being done.
2. Eliminate all unnecessary work.
3. Train several operators in the correct methods.
4. Set the piece rate by time studies on these specially trained operators.
5. Explain the new job rate to all the operators.
6. Train all operators in the new method so they can reach a high rate of production within a short time.

The group approved this plan (though no formal group decision was reached), and chose the operators to be specially trained. A sub-meeting with the "special" operators was held immediately following the meeting with the entire group. They displayed a cooperative and interested attitude and immediately presented many good suggestions. This attitude carried over into the working out of the details of the new job; and when the new job and piece rates were set, the "special" operators referred to the resultants as "our job," "our rate," etc. The new job and piece rates were presented at a second group meeting to all the operators involved. The "special" operators served to train the other operators on the new job.

Experimental groups 2 and 3 went through much the same kind of change meetings. The groups were smaller than experimental group 1, and a more intimate atmosphere was established. The need for a change was once again made dramatically clear; the same general plan was presented by management. However, since the groups were small, all operators were chosen as "special" operators; that is, all operators were to participate directly in the designing of the new jobs, and all operators would be studied by the time study man. It is interesting to note that in the meetings with these two groups, suggestions were immediately made in such quantity that the stenographer had great difficulty in recording them. The group approved of the plans, but again no formal group decision was reached.

## Results

. . . The control group improved little beyond their early efficiency ratings. Resistance developed almost immediately after the change occurred. Marked expressions of aggression against management occurred, such as conflict with the methods engineer, expression of hostility against the supervisor, deliberate restriction of production, and lack of cooperation with the supervisor. There were 17 per cent quits in the first forty days. Grievances were filed about the piece rate, but when the rate was checked, it was found to be a little "loose."

Experimental group 1 showed an unusually good relearning curve. At the end of fourteen days, the group averaged 61 units per hour. During the fourteen days, the attitude was co-operative and permissive. They worked well with the methods engineer, the training staff, and the supervisor. (The supervisor was the same person in the cases of the control group and experimental group 1.) There were no quits in this group in the first forty days. This group might have presented a better learning record if work had not been scarce during the first seven days. There was one act of aggression against the supervisor recorded in the first forty days. It is interesting to note that the three special representative operators in experimental group 1 recovered at about the same rate as the rest of their group.

Experimental groups 2 and 3 recovered faster than experimental group 1. After a slight drop on the first day of change, the efficiency ratings returned to a pre-change level and showed sustained progress thereafter to a level about 14 per cent higher than the prechange level. No additional training was provided them after the second day. They worked well with their supervisors and no indications of aggression were observed from these groups. There were no quits in either of these groups in the first forty days.

A fourth experimental group, composed of only two sewing operators, was transferred by the total participation technique. Their new job was one of the most difficult jobs in the factory, in contrast to the easy jobs for the control group and the other three experimental groups. As expected, the total participation technique again resulted in an unusually fast recovery rate and a final level of production well above the level before transfer. Because of the difficulty of the new job, however, the rate of recovery was slower than for experimental groups 2 and 3, but faster than for experimental group 1.

In the first experiment, the control group made no progress after transfer for a period of 32 days. At the end of this period the group was broken up and the individuals were reassigned to new jobs scattered throughout the factory. Two and a half months after their dispersal, the thirteen remaining members of the original control group were again brought together as a group for a second experiment.

This second experiment consisted of transferring the control group to a new job, using the total participation tech-

nique in meetings which were similar to those held with experimental groups 2 and 3. The new job was a pressing job of comparable difficulty to the new job in the first experiment. On the average it involved about the same degree of change. In the meetings no reference was made to the previous behavior of the group on being transferred.

The results of the second experiment were in sharp contrast to the first. With the total participation technique, the same control group now recovered rapidly to their previous efficiency rating, and, like the other groups under this treatment, continued on beyond it to a new high level of production. There was no aggression or turnover in the group for 19 days after change, a marked modification of their previous behavior after transfer. Some anxiety concerning their seniority status was expressed, but this was resolved in a meeting of their elected delegate, the union business agent, and a management representative. It should be noted that the pre-change level on the second experiment is just above 60 units per hour; thus the individual transfers had progressed to just above standard during the two and a half months between the two experiments.

## INTERPRETATION

. . . The first experiment showed that the rate of recovery is directly proportional to the amount of participation, and that the rates of turnover and aggression are inversely proportional to the amount of participation. The second experiment demonstrated more conclusively that the results obtained depended on the experimental treatment rather than on personality factors like skill or aggressiveness, for identical individuals yielded markedly different results in the control treatment as contrasted with the total participation treatment.

Apparently total participation has the same type of effect as participation through representation, but the former has a stronger influence. In regard to recovery rates, this difference is not unequivocal because the experiment was unfortunately confounded. Right after transfer, experimental group number 1 had insufficient material to work on for a period of seven days. Hence their slower recovery during this period is at least in part due to insufficient work. In succeeding days, however, there was an adequate supply of work and the differential recovery rate still persisted. Therefore we are inclined to believe that participation through representation results in slower recovery than does total participation. . . .

Where we are dealing with a quasi-stationary equilibrium, the resultant forces upward and the forces downward are opposite in direction and equal in strength at the equilibrium level. Of course either resultant forces may fluctuate over a short period of time, so that the forces may not be equally balanced at a given moment. However, over a longer period of time and on the average the forces balance out. Fluctuations from the average occur but there is a tendency to return to the average level.

Just before being transferred, all of the groups in both experiments had reached a stable equilibrium level at just above the standard production of 60 units per hour. This level was equal to the average efficiency rating for the entire factory during the period of the experiments. Since this production level remained constant, neither increasing nor decreasing, we may be sure that the strength of the resultant force upward was equal to the strength of the resultant force downward. This equilibrium of forces was maintained over the period of time when production was stationary at this level. But the forces changed markedly after

transfer, and these new constellations of forces were distinctly different for the control and the experimental groups.

For the control group the period after transfer is a quasi-stationary equilibrium at a lower level, and the forces do not change during the period of thirty days. The resultant force upward remains equal to the resultant force downward and the level of production remains constant. . . .

The situation for the experimental groups after transfer can be viewed as a quasi-stationary equilibrium of a different type. Figure IV gives a schematic diagram of the resultant forces for the experimental groups. At any given level of production, such as 50 units per hour or 60 units per hour, both the resultant forces upward and the resultant forces downward change over the period of thirty days. During this time the point of equilibrium, which starts at 50 units per hour, gradually rises until it reaches a level of over 70 units per hour after thirty days. Yet here again the equilibrium level has the character of a "central force field" where at any point in the total field the resultant of the upward and the downward forces is in the direction of the equilibrium level. . . .

There are three main component forces influencing production in a downward direction: (1) the difficulty of the job; (2) a force corresponding to avoidance of strain; (3) a force corresponding to a group standard to restrict production to a given level. The resultant force upward in the direction of greater production is composed of three additional component forces; (4) the force corresponding to the goal of standard production; (5) a force corresponding to pressures induced by the management through supervision; (6) a force corresponding to a group standard of competition. Let us examine each of these six component forces.

FIGURE IV • A SCHEMATIC DIAGRAM OF THE QUASI-
STATIONARY EQUILIBRIUM FOR THE EXPERIMENTAL GROUPS
AFTER TRANSFER.

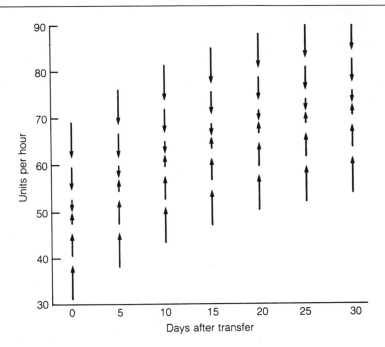

1. *Job Difficulty.* For all operators the difficulty of the job is one of the forces downward on production. The difficulty of the job, of course, is relative to the skill of the operator. The given job may be very difficult for an unskilled operator but relatively easy for a highly skilled one. In the case of a transfer a new element of difficulty enters. For some time the new job is much more difficult, for the operator is unskilled at that particular job. In addition to the difficulty experienced by any learner, the transfer often encounters the added difficulty of proactive inhibition. Where the new job is similar to the old job there will be a period of interference between the two similar but different skills required. . . .
2. *Strain Avoidance.* The force toward lower production corresponding to the difficulty of the job (or the lack of skill of the person) has the character of a restraining force—that is, it acts to prevent locomotion rather than as a driving force causing locomotion. However, in all production there is a closely related driving force towards lower production, namely "strain avoidance." We assume that working too hard and working too fast is an unpleasant strain; and corresponding to this negative valence there is a driving force in the opposite direction, namely towards taking it easy or working slower. The higher the level of production the greater will be the strain and, other things being equal, the stronger will be the downward force of strain avoidance. Likewise, the greater the difficulty of the job the stronger will be the force corresponding to strain

avoidance. But the greater the operator's skill the smaller will be the strain and the strength of the force of strain avoidance. Therefore:

• Hypothesis (4): The strength of the force of strain avoidance =

$$\frac{job\ difficulty \times production\ level}{skill\ of\ operator}$$

The differential recovery rates of the control group in both experiments and the three experimental groups in Experiment I cannot be explained by strain avoidance because job difficulty, production level, and operator skill were matched at the time immediately following transfer. . . .

4. *The Goal of Standard Production.* In considering the negative attitudes toward transfer and the resistance to being transferred, there are several important aspects of the complex goal of reaching and maintaining a level of 60 units per hour. For an operator producing below standard, this goal is attractive because it means success, high status in the eyes of her fellow employees, better pay, and job security. On the other hand, there is a strong force against remaining below standard because this lower level means failure, low status, low pay, and the danger of being fired. Thus it is clear that the upward force corresponding to the goal of standard production will indeed be strong for the transfer who has dropped below standard.

It is equally clear why any operator, who accepts the stereotype about transfer, shows such strong resistance to being changed. She sees herself as becoming a failure and losing status, pay, and perhaps the job itself. The result is a lowered level of aspiration and a weakened force toward the goal of standard production.

Just such a weakening of the force toward 60 units per hour seems to have occurred in the control group in Experiment I. The participation treatments, on the other hand, seem to have involved the operators in designing the new job and setting the new piece rates in such a way that they did not lose hope of regaining the goal of standard production. Thus the participation resulted in a stronger force toward higher production. However, this force alone can hardly account for the large differences in recovery rate between the control group and the experimental groups; certainly it does not explain why the latter increased to a level so high above standard.

5. *Management Pressure.* On all operators below standard the management exerts a pressure for higher production. This pressure is not harsh and autocratic treatment involving threats. Rather it takes the form of persuasion and encouragement by the supervisors. They attempt to induce the low rating operator to improve her performance and to attain standard production. . . .

The reaction of a person to an effective induced force will vary depending, among other things, on the person's relation to the inducing agent. A force induced by a friend may be accepted in such a way that it acts more like an own force. An effective force induced by an enemy may be resisted and rejected so that the person complies unwillingly and shows signs of conflict and tension. Thus in addition to what might be called a "neutral" induced force, we also distinguish an *accepted* induced force and a *rejected* induced force. Naturally the acceptance and the rejection of an induced force can vary in degree from zero (i.e., a neutral induced force) to very strong acceptance or rejection. To account for the difference in character between the acceptance and the rejection of an induced force, we make the following assumptions:

• Hypothesis (5): The acceptance of an induced force sets up additional own forces in the same direction.
• Hypothesis (6): The rejection of an induced force sets up additional own forces in the opposite direction.

The grievances, aggression, and tension in the control group in Experiment I indicate that they rejected the force toward higher production induced by the management. The group accepted the stereotype that transfer is a calamity, but the control procedure did not convince them that the change was necessary and they viewed the new job and the new piece rates set by management as arbitrary and unreasonable.

The experimental groups, on the contrary, participated in designing the changes and setting the piece rates so that they spoke of the new job as "our job" and the new piece rates as "our rates." Thus they accepted the new situation and accepted the management induced force toward higher production. . . .

6. *Group Standards.* Probably the most important force affecting the recovery under the control procedure was a group standard, set by the group, restricting the level of production to 50 units per hour. Evidently this explicit agreement to restrict production is related to the group's rejection of the change and of the new job as arbitrary and unreasonable. Per-

haps they had faint hopes of demonstrating that standard production could not be attained and thereby obtain a more favorable rate. In any case there was a definite group phenomenon which affected all the members of the group. We have already noted the striking example of the presser whose production was restricted in the group situation to about half the level she attained as an individual. In the control group, too, we would expect the group to induce strong forces on the members. The more a member deviates above the standard the stronger would be the group-induced force to conform to the standard, for such deviations both negate any possibility of management's increasing the piece rate and at the same time expose the other members to increased pressure from management. Thus individual differences in levels of production should be sharply curtailed in the control group after transfer.

An analysis was made for all groups of the individual differences within the group in levels of production. In Experiment I the 40 days before change were compared with the 30 days after change; in Experiment II the 10 days before change were compared to the 17 days after change. As a measure of variability, the standard deviation was calculated each day for each group. The average daily standard deviations *before* and *after* change were as follows:

| Group | Variability | | |
|---|---|---|---|
| Experiment I | Before Change | | After Change |
| Control group | 9.8 | . . . | 1.9 |
| Experimental 1 | 9.7 | . . . | 3.8 |
| Experimental 2 | 10.3 | . . . | 2.7 |
| Experimental 3 | 9.9 | . . . | 2.4 |
| **Experiment II** | | | |
| Control group | 12.7 | . . . | 2.9 |

There is indeed a marked decrease in individual differences within the control group after their first transfer. In fact the restriction of production resulted in a lower variability than in any other group. . . .

The table of variability also shows that the experimental treatments markedly reduced variability in the other four groups after transfer. In experimental group 1 (participation by representation) this smallest reduction of variability was produced by a group standard of individual competition. Competition among members of the group was reported by the supervisor soon after transfer. This competition was a force toward higher production which resulted in good recovery to standard and continued progress beyond standard.

Experimental groups 2 and 3 showed a greater reduction in variability following transfer. These two groups under total participation were transferred on the same day. Group competition developed between the two groups. This group competition, which evidently resulted in stronger forces on the members than did the individual competition, was an effective group standard. The standard gradually moved to higher and higher levels of production with the result that the groups not only reached but far exceeded their previous levels of production.

## Turnover and Aggression

Returning now to our preliminary theory of frustration, we can see several revisions. The difficulty of the job and its relation to skill and strain avoidance has been clarified in hypothesis (4). It is now clear that the driving force toward 60 is a complex affair; it is partly a negative driving force corresponding to the negative valence of low pay, low status, failure, and job insecurity. Turnover results not only from the frustration produced by the conflict of these two forces, but also as a direct attempt to escape from

the region of these negative valences. For the members of the control group, the group standard to restrict production prevented escape by increasing production, so that quitting their jobs was the only remaining escape. In the participation groups, on the contrary, both the group standards and the additional own forces resulting from the acceptance of management-induced forces combined to make increasing production the distinguished path of escape from this region of negative valence. . . .

The control procedure had the effect for the members of setting up management as a hostile power field. They rejected the forces induced by this hostile power field, and group standards to restrict production developed within the group in opposition to management. In this conflict between the power field of management and the power field of the group, the control group attempted to reduce the strength of the hostile power field relative to the strength of their own power field. This change was accomplished in three ways: (a) the group increased its own power by developing a more cohesive and well-disciplined group, (b) they secured "allies" by getting the backing of the union in filing a formal grievance about the new piece rate, (c) they attacked the hostile power field directly in the form of aggression against the supervisor, the time study engineer, and the higher management. Thus the aggression was derived not only from individual frustration but also from the conflict between two groups. Furthermore, this situation of group conflict both helped to define management as the frustrating agent and gave the members strength to express any aggressive impulses produced by frustration.

## CONCLUSIONS

It is possible for management to modify greatly or to remove completely group resistance to changes in methods of work and the ensuing piece rates. This change can be accomplished by the use of group meetings in which management effectively communicates the need for change and stimulates group participation in planning the changes.

For Harwood's management, and presumably for managements of other industries using an incentive system, this experiment has important implications in the field of labor relations. A majority of all grievances presented at Harwood have always stemmed from a change situation. By preventing or greatly modifying group resistance to change, this concomitant to change may well be greatly reduced. The reduction of such costly phenomena as turnover and slow relearning rates presents another distinct advantage.

## REFERENCES

1. French, John R. P., Jr. The Behaviour of Organized and Unorganized Groups under Conditions of Frustration and Fear, Studies in Topological and Vector Psychology, III, *University of Iowa Studies in Child Welfare*, 1944, Vol. XX, pp. 229–308.

2. Lewin, Kurt. Frontiers in Group Dynamics, *Human Relations*, Vol. I, No. 1, 1947, pp. 5–41.

# 40

# Group Decision and Social Change

*Kurt Lewin*

## QUASI-STATIONARY SOCIAL EQUILIBRIA AND THE PROBLEM OF PERMANENT CHANGE

*1. The Objective of Change.* The objective of social change might concern the nutritional standard of consumption, the economic standard of living, the type of group relation, the output of a factory, the productivity of an educational team. It is important that a social standard to be changed does not have the nature of a "thing" but of a "process." A certain standard of consumption, for instance, means that a certain action—such as making certain decisions, buying, preparing, and canning certain food in a family—occurs with a certain frequency within a given period. Similarly, a certain type of group relations means that within a given period certain friendly and hostile actions and reactions of a certain degree of severity occur between the members of two groups. Changing group relations or changing consumption means changing the level at which these multitude of events proceed. In other words, the "level" of consumption, of friendliness, or of productivity is to be characterized as the aspect of an ongoing social process.

Any planned social change will have to consider a multitude of factors characteristic for the particular case. The change may require a more or less unique combination of educational and organizational measures; it may depend upon quite different treatments or ideology, expectation and organization. Still, certain general formal principles always have to be considered.

*2. The Conditions of a Stable Quasi-stationary Equilibrium.* The study of the conditions for change begins appropriately with an analysis of the conditions for "no change," that is, for the state of equilibrium.

From what has been just discussed, it is clear that by a state of "no social change" we do not refer to a stationary but to a quasi-stationary equilibrium; that is, to a state comparable to that of a river which flows with a given velocity in a given direction during a certain time interval. A social change is comparable to a change in the velocity or direction of that river.

A number of statements can be made in regard to the conditions of quasi-stationary equilibrium. (These conditions are treated more elaborately elsewhere.[1])

A. The strength of forces which tend to lower that standard of social life should

[1] K. Lewin, "Frontiers in Group Dynamics: Concept, Method and Reality in Social Science; Social Equilibria and Social Change," *Human Relations*, I, 1, June, 1947, pp. 5–42.

*Source:* "Group Decision and Social Change" by Kurt Lewin from *Readings in Social Psychology*, Revised Edition by Guy E. Swanson, Theodore M. Newcomb and Eugene L. Hartley, Copyright © 1952 and renewed 1980 by Holt, Rinehart and Winston, Inc., reprinted by permission of the publisher.

## FIGURE 1 • GRADIENTS OF RESULTANT FORCES (f*).

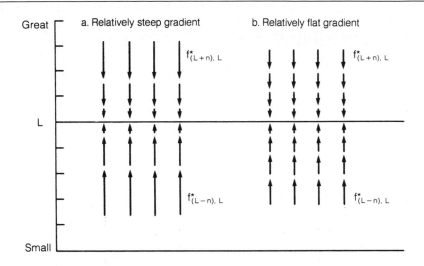

be equal and opposite to the strength of forces which tend to raise its level. The resultant of forces on the line of equilibrium should therefore be zero.

B. Since we have to assume that the strength of social forces always shows variations, a quasi-stationary equilibrium presupposes that the forces against raising the standard increase with the amount of raising and that the forces against lowering increase (or remain constant) with the amount of lowering. This type of gradient which is characteristic for a "positive central force field"[2] has to hold at least in the neighborhood of the present level (Fig. 1).

C. It is possible to change the strength of the opposing forces without changing the level of social conduct. In this case the tension (degree of conflict) increases.

*3. Two Basic Methods of Changing Levels of Conduct.* For any type of social management, it is of great practical importance that levels of quasi-stationary

equilibria can be changed in either of two ways: by adding forces in the desired direction, or by diminishing opposing forces. If a change from the level $L_1$ to $L_2$ is brought about by increasing the forces toward $L_2$, the secondary effects should be different from the case where the same change of level is brought about by diminishing the opposing forces.

In both cases the equilibrium might change to the same new level. The secondary effect should, however, be quite different. In the first case, the process on the new level would be accompanied by a state of relatively high tension; in the second case, by a state of relatively low tension. Since increase of tension above a certain degree is likely to be paralleled by higher aggressiveness, higher emotionality, and lower constructiveness, it is clear that as a rule the second method will be preferable to the high pressure method.

The group decision procedure which is used here attempts to avoid high pressure methods and is sensitive to resistance to change. In the experiment by Bavelas on changing production in factory work (as noted below), for instance, no attempt was made to set the new production goal by majority vote because a majority vote forces some group members to produce more than they consider appropriate. These individuals are likely to have some inner resistance. Instead a procedure was followed by which a goal was chosen on which everyone could agree fully.

It is possible that the success of group decision and particularly the permanency of the effect is, in part, due to the attempt to bring about a favorable decision by removing counterforces within the individuals rather than by applying outside pressure.

The surprising increase from the second to the fourth week in the number of mothers giving cod liver oil and orange juice to the baby can probably be explained by such a decrease of counterforces. Mothers are likely to handle their first baby during the first weeks of life somewhat cautiously and become more ready for action as the child grows stronger.

*4. Social Habits and Group Standards.* Viewing a social stationary process as the result of a quasi-stationary equilibrium, one may expect that any added force will change the level of the process. The idea of "social habit" seems to imply that, in spite of the application of a force, the level of the social process will not change because of some type of "inner resistance" to change. To overcome this inner resistance, an additional force seems to be required, a force sufficient to "break the habit," to "unfreeze" the custom.

Many social habits are anchored in the relation between the individuals and certain group standards. An individual P may differ in his personal level of conduct ($L_P$) from the level which represents group standards ($L_{Gr}$) by a certain amount. If the individual should try to diverge "too much" from group standards, he would find himself in increasing difficulties. He would be ridiculed, treated severely and finally ousted from the group. Most individuals, therefore, stay pretty close to the standard of the groups they belong to or wish to belong to. In other words, the group level itself acquires value. It becomes a positive valence corresponding to a central force field with the force $f_{P,L}$ keeping the individual in line with the standards of the group.

*5. Individual Procedures and Group Procedures of Changing Social Conduct.* If the resistance to change depends partly on the value which the group standard has for the individual, the resistance to change should diminish if one diminishes the strength of the value of the group standard or changes the level perceived by the individual as having social value.

This second point is one of the reasons for the effectiveness of "group carried" changes[3] resulting from procedures which approach the individuals as part of face-to-face groups. Perhaps one might expect single individuals to be more pliable than groups of like-minded individuals. However, experience in leadership training, in changing of food habits, work production, criminality, alcoholism, prejudices, all indicate that it is usually easier to change individuals formed into a group than to change any one of them separately.[4] As long as group standards are unchanged, the individual will resist changes more strongly the farther he is to depart from group standards. If the group standard itself is changed, the resistance which is due to the rela-

[3] N. R. F. Maier, *Psychology in Industry* (Boston: Houghton Mifflin Co., 1946).

[4] K. Lewin and P. Grabbe (eds.) *op. cit.*

tion between individual and group standard is eliminated.

6. *Changing as a Three-step Procedure: Unfreezing, Moving, and Freezing of a Level.* A change toward a higher level of group performance is frequently short lived: after a "shot in the arm," group life soon returns to the previous level. This indicates that it does not suffice to define the objective of a planned change in group performance as the reaching of a different level. Permanency of the new level, or permanency for a desired period, should be included in the objective. A successful change includes therefore three aspects: unfreezing (if necessary) the present level $L_1$, moving to the new level $L_2$, and freezing group life on the new level. Since any level is determined by a force field, permanency implies that the new force field is made relatively secure against change.

The "unfreezing" of the present level may involve quite different problems in different cases. Allport[5] has described the "catharsis" which seems to be neces-

[5] G. W. Allport, "Catharsis and the Reduction of Prejudice" in K. Lewin and P. Grabbe (eds.), *op. cit.*, 3–10.

FIGURE 2 · EFFECT OF GROUP DECISION ON
SEWING-MACHINE OPERATORS.

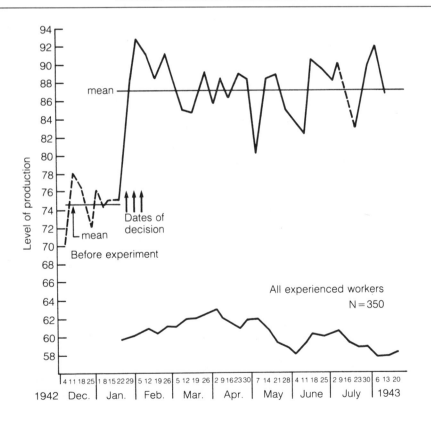

sary before prejudices can be removed. To break open the shell of complacency and self-righteousness, it is sometimes necessary to bring about deliberately an emotional stir-up.

Figure 2 presents an example of the effect of three group decisions of a team in a factory reported by Bavelas[6] which illustrates an unusually good case of permanency of change measured over nine months.

The experiments on group decision reported here cover but a few of the necessary variations. Although in some cases the procedure is relatively easily executed, in others it requires skill and presupposes certain general conditions. Managers rushing into a factory to raise

production by group decisions are likely to encounter failure. In social management as in medicine there are no patent medicines and each case demands careful diagnosis.

One reason why group decision facilitates change is illustrated by Willerman.[7] Figure 3 shows the degree of eagerness to have the members of a students' eating cooperative change from the consumption of white bread to whole wheat. When the change was simply requested the degree of eagerness varied greatly with the degree of personal preference for whole wheat. In case of group decision the eagerness seems to be relatively independent of personal preference; the

[6] N. R. F. Maier, *op. cit.*

[7] K. Lewin "Forces behind Food Habits . . . ," *op. cit.*

**FIGURE 3 · RELATION BETWEEN OWN FOOD PREFERENCES AND EAGERNESS TO SUCCEED.**

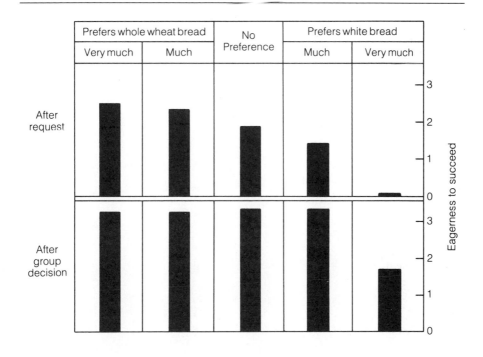

individual seems to act mainly as a "group member."

## SUMMARY

Group decision is a process of social management or self management of groups. It is related to social channels, gates and gatekeepers; to the problem of social perception and planning; and to the relation between motivation and action, and between the individual and the group.

Experiments are reported in which certain methods of group decision prove to be superior to lecturing and individual treatment as means of changing social conduct.

The effect of group decision can probably be best understood by relating it to a theory of quasi-stationary social equilibria, to social habits and resistance to change, and to the various problems of unfreezing, changing and freezing social levels.

## 41
# Intervention Theory and Methods
*Chris Argyris*

## A DEFINITION
## OF INTERVENTION

To intervene is to enter into an ongoing system of relationship, to come between or among persons, groups, or objects for the purpose of helping them. There is an important implicit assumption in the definition that should be made explicit: the system exists independently of the intervenor. There are many reasons one might wish to intervene. These reasons may range from helping the clients make their own decisions about the kind of help they need to coercing the clients to do what the intervenor wishes them to do. Examples of the latter are modern black militants who intervene to demand that the city be changed in accordance with their wishes and choices (or white racists who prefer the same); executives who invite interventionists into their system to manipulate subordinates for them; trade union leaders who for years have resisted systematic research in their own bureaucratic functioning at the highest levels because they fear that valid information might lead to entrenched interests—especially at the top—being unfrozen.

The more one conceives of the intervenor in this sense, the more one implies that the client system should have little autonomy from the intervenor; that its boundaries are indistinguishable from those of the intervenor; that its health

or effectiveness are best controlled by the intervenor.

In contrast, our view acknowledges interdependencies between the intervenor and the client system but focuses on how to maintain, or increase, the client system's autonomy; how to differentiate even more clearly the boundaries between the client system and the intervenor; and how to conceptualize and define the client system's health independently of the intervenor's. This view values the client system as an ongoing, self-responsible unity that has the obligation to be in control over its own destiny. An intervenor, in this view, assists a system to become more effective in problem solving, decision making, and decision implementation in such a way that the system can continue to be increasingly effective in these activites and have a decreasing need for the intervenor.

Another critical question the intervenor must ask is, how is he helping—management or employees, black militants or Negro moderates, white racists or white moderates? Several chapters of the book are concerned with this question. At this point, it is suggested that the intervenor must be concerned with the system as a whole even though his initial contact may be made with only a few people. He therefore focuses on those intervention activities that eventually (not necessarily immediately) will provide *all* the members' opportunities

*Source:* Chris Argyris, *Intervention Theory and Methods: A Behavioral Science View* © 1980, Addison-Wesley Publishing Co., Inc., Reading, Massachusetts, pp. 15–20. Reprinted by permission of the publisher.

to enhance their competence and effectiveness. If any individual or subsystem wishes help to prevent other individuals or subsystems from having these opportunities, then the intervenor may well have to question seriously his involvement in the project.[1]

## BASIC REQUIREMENTS FOR INTERVENTION ACTIVITY

Are there any basic or necessary processes that must be fulfilled regardless of the substantive issues involved, if intervention activity is to be helpful with any level of client (individual, group, or organizational)? One condition that seems so basic as to be defined axiomatic is the generation of *valid information*. Without valid information, it would be difficult for the client to learn and for the interventionist to help.

A second condition almost as basic flows from our assumption that intervention activity, no matter what its substantive interests and objectives, should be so designed and executed that the client system maintains its discreteness and autonomy. Thus *free, informed choice* is also a necessary process in effective intervention activity.

Finally, if the client system is assumed to be ongoing (that is, existing over time), the clients require strengthening to maintain their autonomy not only vis-

à-vis the interventionist but also vis-à-vis other systems. This means that their commitment to learning and change has to be more than temporary. It has to be so strong that it can be transferred to relationships other than those with the interventionist and can do so (eventually) without the help of the interventionist. The third basic process for any intervention activity is therefore the client's *internal commitment* to the choices made.

In summary, valid information, free choice, and internal commitment are considered integral parts of any intervention activity, no matter what the substantive objectives are (for example, developing a management performance evaluation scheme, reducing intergroup rivalries, increasing the degree of trust among individuals, redesigning budgetary systems, or redesigning work). These three processes are called the primary intervention tasks.

## PRIMARY TASKS OF AN INTERVENTIONIST

Why is it necessary to hypothesize that in order for an interventionist to behave effectively and in order that the integrity of the client system be maintained, the interventionist has to focus on three primary tasks, regardless of the substantive problems that the client system may be experiencing?

### Valid and Useful Information

First, it has been accepted as axiomatic that valid and useful information is the foundation for effective intervention. Valid information is that which describes the factors, plus their interrelationships, that create the problem for the client system. There are several tests for checking the validity of the information. In increasing degrees of power they are public verifiability, valid prediction,

---

[1] There is an important function within the scope of responsibility of the interventionist that will not be discussed systematically in this volume. It is the public health function. There are many individuals who do not ask for help because they do not know they need help or that help could be available to them. The societal strategy for developing effective intervention activity must therefore include a function by which potential clients are educated about organizational health and illness as well as the present state of the art in effecting change. The writer hopes that this volume plays a role in facilitating this function.

and control over the phenomena. The first is having several independent diagnoses suggest the same picture. Second is generating predictions from the diagnosis that are subsequently confirmed (they occurred under the conditions that were specified). Third is altering the factors systematically and predicting the effects upon the system as a whole. All these tests, if they are to be valid, must be carried out in such a way that the participants cannot, at will, make them come true. This would be a self-fulfilling prophecy and not a confirmation of a prediction. The difficulty with a self-fulfilling prophecy is its indication of more about the degree of power an individual (or subset of individuals) can muster to alter the system than about the nature of the system when the participants are behaving without knowledge of the diagnosis. For example, if an executive learns that the interventionist predicts his subordinates will behave (a) if he behaves (b), he might alter (b) in order not to lead to (a). Such an alteration indicates the executive's power but does not test the validity of the diagnosis that if (a), then (b).

The tests for valid information have important implications for effective intervention activity. First, the interventionist's diagnoses must strive to represent the total client system and not the point of view of any subgroup or individual. Otherwise, the interventionist could not be seen only as being under the control of a particular individual or subgroup, but also his predictions would be based upon inaccurate information and thus might not be confirmed.

This does not mean that an interventionist may not begin with, or may not limit his relationship to, a subpart of the total system. It is totally possible, for example, for the interventionist to help management, blacks, trade union leaders, etc. With whatever subgroup he works he simply should not agree to limit his diagnosis to its wishes.

It is conceivable that a client system may be helped even though valid information is not generated. Sometimes changes occur in a positive direction without the interventionist having played any important role. These changes, although helpful in that specific instance, lack the attribute of helping the organization to learn and to gain control over its problem-solving capability.

The importance of information that the clients can use to control their destiny points up the requirement that the information must not only be valid, it must be useful. Valid information that cannot be used by the clients to alter their system is equivalent to valid information about cancer that cannot be used to cure cancer eventually. An interventionist's diagnosis should include variables that are manipulable by the clients and are complete enough so that if they are manipulated effective changes will follow.

## Free Choice

In order to have free choice, the client has to have a cognitive map of what he wishes to do. The objectives of his action are known at the moment of decision. Free choice implies voluntary as opposed to automatic; proactive rather than reactive. The act of selection is rarely accomplished by maximizing or optimizing. Free and informed choice entails what Simon has called "satisficing," that is, selecting the alternative with the highest probability of succeeding, given some specified cost constraints. Free choice places the locus of decision making in the client system. Free choice makes it possible for the clients to remain responsible for their destiny. Through free choice the clients can maintain the autonomy of their system.

It may be possible that clients prefer to give up their responsibility and their autonomy, especially if they are feeling a sense of failure. They may prefer, as we shall see in several examples, to turn over their free choice to the interventionist. They may insist that he make recommendations and tell them what to do. The interventionist resists these pressures because if he does not, the clients will lose their free choice and he will lose his own free choice also. He will be controlled by the anxieties of the clients.

The requirement of free choice is especially important for those helping activities where the processes of help are as important as the actual help. For example, a medical doctor does not require that a patient with a bullet wound participate in the process by defining the kind of help he needs. However, the same doctor may have to pay much more attention to the processes he uses to help patients when he is attempting to diagnose blood pressure or cure a high cholesterol. If the doctor behaves in ways that upset the patient, the latter's blood pressure may well be distorted. Or, the patient can develop a dependent relationship if the doctor cuts down his cholesterol—increasing habits only under constant pressure from the doctor— and the moment the relationship is broken off, the count goes up.

Effective intervention in the human and social spheres requires that the processes of help be congruent with the outcome desired. Free choice is important because there are so many unknowns, and the interventionist wants the client to have as much willingness and motivation as possible to work on the problem. With high client motivation and commitment, several different methods for change can succeed.

A choice is free to the extent the members can make their selection for a course of action with minimal internal defensiveness; can define the path (or paths) by which the intended consequence is to be achieved; can relate the choice to their central needs; and can build into their choices a realistic and challenging level of aspiration. Free choice therefore implies that the members are able to explore as many alternatives as they consider significant and select those that are central to their needs.

Why must the choice be related to the central needs and why must the level of aspiration be realistic and challenging? May people not choose freely unrealistic or unchallenging objectives? Yes, they may do so in the short run, but not for long if they still want to have free and informed choice. A freely chosen course of action means that the action must be based on an accurate analysis of the situation and not on the biases or defenses of the decision makers. We know, from the level of aspiration studies, that choices which are too high or too low, which are too difficult or not difficult enough will tend to lead to psychological failure. Psychological failure will lead to increased defensiveness, increased failure, and decreased self-acceptance on the part of the members experiencing the failure. These conditions, in tun, will tend to lead to distorted perceptions by the members making the choices. Moreover, the defensive members may unintentionally create a climate where the members of surrounding and interrelated systems will tend to provide carefully censored information. Choices made under these conditions are neither informed nor free.

Turning to the question of centrality of needs, a similar logic applies. The degree of commitment to the processes of generating valid information, scanning, and choosing may significantly vary according to the centrality of the choice to the needs of the clients. The more central the choice, the more the system will strive to do its best in developing valid information and making free and informed choices. If the research from perceptual psychology is valid, the very perception of the clients is altered by the needs involved. Individuals tend to scan more, ask for more information, and be more careful in their choices when they are making decisions that are central to them. High involvement may produce perceptual distortions, as does low involvement. The interventionist, however, may have a greater probability of helping the clients explore possible distortion when the choice they are making is a critical one.

## INTERNAL COMMITMENT

Internal commitment means the course of action or choice that has been internalized by each member so that he experiences a high degree of ownership and has a feeling of responsibility about the choice and its implications. Internal commitment means that the individual has reached the point where he is acting on the choice because it fulfills his own needs and sense of responsibility, as well as those of the system.

The individual who is internally committed is acting primarily under the influence of his own forces and not induced forces. The individual (or any unity) feels a minimal degree of dependence upon others for the action. It implies that he has obtained and processed valid information and that he has made an informed and free choice. Under these conditions there is a high probability that the individual's commitment will remain strong over time (even with reduction of external rewards) or under stress, or when the course of action is challenged by others. It also implies that the individual is continually open to reexamination of his position because he believes in taking action based upon valid information.

# 42
# The Ethics of Social Intervention: Goals, Means, and Consequences
*Herbert C. Kelman & Donald P. Warwick*

Social intervention is any act, planned or unplanned, that alters the characteristics of another individual or the pattern of relationships between individuals. The range of acts covered in this definition is intentionally broad. It includes such macro phenomena as national planning, military intervention in the affairs of other nations, population policy, and technical assistance. It also applies to psychotherapy, sensitivity training, neighborhood action programs, experiments done with human beings, and other micro changes. . . .

We prefer to subsume planned change efforts under a broader definition of social intervention that provides for the ethical evaluation of institutional structures and practices with critical social effects, as well as of situations with more readily identifiable change agents. We can thus explore the ethical implications of government policies or intellectual traditions, for example, even though these are not explicitly geared toward producing social change and are not associated with a single individual or agency. The major focus of this book, however, is on deliberate interventions. In this book, while keeping the broad definition in mind, we use social intervention more narrowly to refer to deliberate attempts by professionals to change the characteristics of individuals or groups, or to influence the pattern of relationships between individuals and/or groups. The last clause in this working definition is designed to cover such interventions as mediation, where the intent is not to change individuals and groups as such, but to shape the course of their relationships and interactions on a short-term or long-term basis.

## VALUE PREFERENCES AND VALUE CONFLICTS

There are four aspects of any social intervention that are likely to raise major ethical issues: (1) the choice of goals to which the change effort is directed, (2) the definition of the target of the change, (3) the choice of means used to implement the intervention, and (4) the assessment of the consequences of the intervention. At each of these steps, the ethical issues that arise may involve conflicting values, that is, questions about what values are to be maximized at the expense of what other values. (We define *values* as individual or shared conceptions of the desirable—"goods" considered worth pursuing.)

Thus, values determine the choice of goals to which a change effort is directed. Clearly, an intervention is designed to maximize a particular set of values. But those setting the goals of the intervention are equally concerned with minimizing the loss of certain other values.

*Source:* Reprinted by permission of the Human Affairs Research Centers of the Battelle Memorial Institute from "The Ethics of Social Intervention: Goals, Means, and Consequences." by H. C. Kelman and D. P. Warwick from *The Ethics of Social Intervention*, 1978 (pp. 3–33).

These imperiled values thus serve as criteria of tolerable and intolerable costs in a given intervention. Under pressures of rapid demographic growth and limited resources, for example, a government might contemplate a set of coercive population control measures, such as involuntary sterilization. The benefit to be promoted by this program would be the common welfare or, in extreme cases, even the physical survival of the country. At the same time, the policy makers might be concerned about the effects of this program on two other values: freedom and justice. These values would be seen as social goods to be preserved—benefits that should not fall below some minimal threshold. Values may influence the choice of goals not only in such explicit, conscious ways, but also in a covert way. This may happen, as we shall see, when a change program departs from a value-based but unquestioned definition of a problem.

[Second,] the definition of the target of change is often based on just this kind of implicit, unexamined conception of where the problem lies. . . .

Third, values play a central role in an ethical evaluation of the means chosen to implement a given intervention. Questions about the morality of coercion, manipulation, deception, persuasion, and other methods of inducing change typically involve a conflict between the values of individual freedom and self-determination, on the one hand, and the values of social welfare, economic progress, or equal opportunity, on the other. For example, to what extent and under what conditions is a government justified in imposing limits on the freedom to reproduce for the sake of presumed long-run improvements in the quality of life?

Finally, conflicting values enter into assessment of the consequences of a social intervention. One of the consequences of industrialization, for example, may be a weakening of traditional authority structures or family bonds. The extent to which we are willing to risk these consequences depends on whether we are more committed to traditional values or to those values that industrialization is designed to enhance. In other words, our assessment of the consequences of an intervention depends on what values we are willing or unwilling to sacrifice in the interest of social change.

Analysis of the ethical problems that may arise at each of these four points in the change process, and of the value conflicts from which they derive, presupposes consideration of some more general procedural issues that must be faced in any effort at applied ethics. These refer to the procedures to be followed in deriving the values that apply in a social intervention, in determining whose values should be given what weight, and in adjudicating value conflicts.[1]

First, an analysis of the ethics of social intervention presumes some notion of what values should apply and how they are to be derived. The problem is simplified, of course, if the analyst simply accepts the values held by the initiators of the change. Thus, if a government agency says that it undertook a population control program in order to promote the general welfare and that it also considered the costs of the program for individual freedom, an analyst might simply confine his or her attention to the values of freedom and welfare. Few students of ethics, however, would be content to let the individual or group initiating a change be the sole judge of the relevant values at stake. The human inclination toward selective perception and self-deception, not to mention the protec-

---

[1] These procedural issues are discussed in greater detail in Warwick and Kelman (1973). Much of the discussion in this chapter is derived from that earlier publication.

tion of vested political interests, is simply too great to justify this approach. In this example, the concerned observer might also wish to examine the effects of the population program on other values, such as justice, dignity, or the self-esteem of minority groups. To leave the definition of the ethical situation to the sponsor of a program would be to abdicate one's moral judgment. . . .

A second fundamental procedural question concerns the weights assigned to the different, and often competing, sets of values held by different groups. . . . Thus, at the national level, decisions about social intervention must weigh the claims and concerns of diverse groups within the society. The problem of "whose values" becomes even more complex in international programs of development or technical assistance. Such programs are often planned and carried out by individuals and agencies external to the society in which the changes are to be introduced. Therefore, there is a real possibility that the values of the change agents may deviate from those of the local population. The question of whose values determine the goals, targets, and means of change takes on special importance in such cases. The issue is not only whose interests are being served by the program, but whose conceptual framework generates the definition of the problem and the setting of goals. This issue persists even when representatives of the local society are fully involved in the planning and execution of the change program because these representatives, who are often trained abroad, may have adopted the conceptual framework of the external agency. Since the writings of social scientists often provide the conceptual frameworks for development programs, it is particularly important to scrutinize them in terms of whose values they reflect and to balance them by assuring that proper weight is given to competing points of view.

Third, deliberate attention to the content and derivation of values and to the different groups whose values are engaged by a given action often reveals value conflicts. Different values held within the same group and differences in value priorities set by different groups may present incompatible claims. For example, advocates of a noninterventionist population policy typically stress the value of freedom, while those who favor strong measures of population control emphasize the values of welfare and survival of the human species. The critical question is not which of the two sets of values to pick, but what is the optimum balance between them. How much freedom, in other words, ought to be sacrificed in the interests of welfare and survival? Debates on national development often array advocates of cultural diversity, of the right of all peoples to determine their own destinies, and of the importance of traditional values as a matrix for the development of self-identity and self-esteem, against those who feel that traditional values are by definition obstacles to development and must, therefore, be changed as rapidly and efficiently as possible. Again the question concerns the most desirable trade-offs between conflicting values: How much traditional culture ought to be sacrificed for the sake of modernization?

Perhaps the most difficult challenge for ethical analysis is in providing some approximate guidelines for adjudicating such competing claims. Though no neat formulas or mechanistic answers are possible, one can try to establish a rough order of ethical priorities. . . .

With these procedural issues in mind, we now turn to some of the specific ethical questions raised by the four aspects of social intervention: the choice of goals, the definition of the target, the choice of means, and the assessment of consequences.

## CHOICE OF GOALS

Social scientists and others writing about social change continually make explicit or implicit assumptions about the nature and the end-points of the changes that are necessary and desirable. These assumptions are influenced not only by the values that individual writers bring to their research but also by the interests and orientations that surround the general issue of social change in their societies. The choice of goals for social intervention thus depends on the particular intellectual and political perspectives from which the change agents and their advisors view the situation. Biased views cannot be avoided, but they can be counteracted insofar as they are made explicit and confronted with analyses based on alternative perspectives. . . .

The first and frequently neglected step, then, in an ethical analysis of social intervention is the recognition that the choice of goals for intervention is determined by the value perspective of the chooser, which is not necessarily shared by all interested parties. The goals to be pursued in social change are by no means self-evident. They depend very much on what we consider a desirable outcome and what costs in terms of other values we are prepared to bear for the achievement of this outcome—a complex judgment about which there may be considerable disagreement.

The role of cultural and ideological biases in the choice of goals is often ignored because the change effort may have a hierarchy of values built into its very definition. These values may simply be taken for granted without questioning their source and their possibly controversial nature. . . .

In recognizing the role of their own value preference, change agents (or social scientists who conceptualize the process of social change) do not abandon their values or attempt to neutralize them. It is neither possible nor desirable to do so. But being aware of their own value perspectives can allow change agents to bring other perspectives to bear on the choice of goals, which reduces the likelihood that they will impose their own values on the population in whose lives they are intervening. This process of relating our own values to those of others in the choice of goals for intervention—without either abandoning or imposing our own values—can often be aided by a distinction between general goals and specific institutional arrangements designed to give expression to these goals. It may be possible to identify certain broad, basic end-points that are widely shared across different cultures and ideological systems—at least among groups and individuals operating within a broadly humanistic framework. These groups or individuals may at the same time disagree about the specific political, social, and economic institutions that they regard as most conducive to the realization of these ends. Thus, one may be able to define the goals for intervention in more or less universal terms, while recognizing that these goals may be achieved through a variety of specific arrangements and that different cultures and ideologies may differ sharply in their preferences among these arrangements.

Ethical issues in the choice of goals for intervention revolve around the question of what values are to be served by the intervention and whether these are the right values for the target population. Since answers to these questions are likely to differ for different individuals—and to differ systematically for groups with different cultural backgrounds and positions in society—the question of *what* values inevitably brings up the question of *whose* values are to be served by the intervention.

Any society, community, or organization in which a change program is introduced contains different segments, with differing needs and interests that may be affected by the intervention. Thus, a key issue concerns the extent to which the values of these different population segments are reflected in the goals that govern the intervention and the extent to which they participate in the goal-setting process. The question of who decides on the goals often has implications for who ultimately benefits from the outcome of the intervention. Since the interests and values of different groups may, to varying degrees, be incompatible, the change program usually involves some compromise between competing preferences. Representation and participation in goal setting may thus have an important bearing on how the values of a given group are weighted in the final outcome.

The problem of competing interests and values in the goal-setting process is complicated by the fact that the change agents and those to whom the change effort is directed usually represent different segments of the population. . . . The change agents are in some sense outsiders to the target population in terms of social class, national affiliation, or both. Moreover, they are usually not disinterested outsiders: Social change programs may have important implications for the wealth, power, and status of their own groups. The problem is further exacerbated by the fact that the agents and the targets of change usually represent groups that differ along a power dimension. The change agents come from the more powerful classes and nations, the targets from the less powerful ones.

The change agents are in a strong position to influence the choice of goals for the intervention. Those who formulate and run the program clearly play a direct role in goal setting. Those who provide the conceptual frameworks may have a more subtle, yet highly pervasive, impact in that they establish the perspective from which the goal setting proceeds and thus the way in which the problem is defined and the range of choices seen as available. It is therefore quite possible that the change agents will view the problem from the perspective of their own group and set goals that will, often unintentionally, accrue to the benefit of their group at the expense of the target population. Given the power differential, their intervention may in fact strengthen the status quo and increase the impotence of those who are already disadvantaged. It is not surprising, therefore, that population control or educational programs sponsored by white middle-class agencies in black ghettoes, or by U.S. agencies in developing countries, are sometimes greeted with suspicion by the target populations. Whatever the merits of the specific case may be, there are sound structural bases for fearing that such programs may end up serving the purposes of the advantaged group at the expense of the disadvantaged.

The ethical problems created by the value and power differentials between change agents and target groups are not easily resolved. Clearly, the more the target group participates in the process of goal setting, the greater the likelihood that the change program will indeed reflect its values. But bringing in representatives of the target group or turning the program over to indigenous agents may not go very far in correcting power imbalances. . . .

Despite the ambiguities that often remain when an outside, more powerful change agent involves representatives of the less powerful target population in the change effort, such involvement constitutes the best protection against the imposition of foreign values. . . .

## DEFINITION OF THE TARGET

Social intervention usually begins as an effort to solve a problem. A decision to undertake a program of organization development, for example, may spring from a concern about poor communication, intraorganizational conflicts, or underutilization of employee abilities. The adoption of population controls may be an effort to deal with the problem of scarce resources or an attempt to preserve the quality of life. In every case, identification of the problem represents, in large part, a value judgment. What we consider to be problematic—that is, what we see as falling short of some ideal state and requiring action—depends very much on our particular view of the ideal state. Moreover, identification of the problem depends on the perspective from which we make this evaluation. . . .

Identification of the problem has important ethical implications because it determines selection of the target to which change efforts are directed. Where we intervene depends on where we, with our personal value preferences and perspectives, perceive the problem to lie. Thus, those who see social unrest as a breakdown of social order are likely to define the protesters as the proper targets of change. . . .

Definition of the target of change has important consequences for the competing interests of different groups within a society.

Social scientists play a major role in identifying, or at least articulating, the problems to which change efforts are to be directed and thus in defining the targets for social intervention. . . .

Far from being ethically neutral, the models with which social scientists work may play a major role in determining the problems and targets for social intervention. In defining their research problems, choosing their models, and communicating their findings, therefore, social scientists have a responsibility to consider the consequences for the populations affected. More broadly, they have the responsibility to ensure that all segments of the population have the opportunity to participate in the research enterprise, which influences the definition of the problems for intervention, and have access to the research findings, which influence the setting of policy.

## CHOICE OF MEANS

The most difficult ethical choices in deliberate social intervention usually concern the selection of means. Is it ever morally justified, for example, to force individuals to accept a program under the threat of death, physical harm, or other severe deprivation? What ethical problems are posed by manipulating the environment so that people are more likely to choose one alternative over others? Should a change program make full use of group pressures for conformity, or attempt to tamper with basic attitudes and motives? These are real questions in most change programs, and there are no easy answers.

It is possible, however, to clarify some of the issues at stake by relating the various means to the value of freedom. Warwick (1971) has defined freedom as the capacity, the opportunity, and the incentive to make reflective choices and to act on these choices. Individuals are thus free when:

1. The structure of the environment provides them with options for choice.
2. They are not coerced by others or forced by circumstances to elect only

certain possibilities among those of which they are aware.

3. They are, in fact, aware of the options in the environment and possess knowledge about the characteristics and consequences of each. Though such knowledge may be less than complete, there must be enough to permit rational deliberation.

4. They are psychologically able to weigh the alternatives and their consequences. In practice this means not only possessing information but being able to use it in coming to a decision.

5. Having weighed the relative merits of the alternatives, they can choose among them. Rollo May (1969) has argued that one of the pathologies of modern existence is an inability to choose—a deficiency of will. A person who cannot pass from deliberation to choice must be considered less than free.

6. Having chosen an alternative, they are able to act on it. Among the conditions that may prevent them from doing so is a lack of knowledge about how to implement the choice, anxiety about acting at all, or a low level of confidence in their abilities, even when they have sufficient knowledge to act.

This discussion of freedom suggests a typology of means used in implementing social interventions. At the "least free" end is coercion, a situation in which people are forced to do something they do not want to do, or are prevented from doing something they do want to do. Next comes manipulation, then persuasion, and finally, at the "most free" end, facilitation.

## Coercion

In simple terms, coercion takes place when one person or group uses the threat of severe deprivation to induce other people or groups either to carry out actions that they desire not to perform or normally would not perform, or to refrain from carrying out actions that they

want to perform or, in the normal course of events, would perform. It is difficult to arrive at precise definitions of "threat" or "deprivation," but basically these refer to the loss of highly valued goods, such as one's life, means of livelihood, or the well-being of one's relatives. Coercion should be distinguished from compliance that occurs within the framework of legitimate authority. In a certain sense, tax laws may be coercive because they force people to do things that they would prefer not to do under the threat of penalties. However, insofar as people comply with the law out of a belief that it is right to do so, since they see the law as rooted in consensual processes, their behavior would not be coerced.

Coercion forms an integral part of many programs of social intervention. Some clear examples would be the nationalization of a foreign-owned petroleum refinery or the outright confiscation of land in agrarian reform programs. . . .

Is coercion ever ethically justified in social intervention and, if so, under what conditions? Two broad conditions are commonly invoked to defend coercive methods. The first is a grave threat to basic societal values. Thus, highly coercive population control programs are frequently recommended on the grounds that excessive fertility jeopardizes the continued survival of the human race or the material welfare of a nation's citizens. The second justification is the need for prompt and positive action to accomplish the goals of a change program, even when there is no threat to such values as physical survival. . . .

In the first case, an ethical justification of coercion requires the change agent to demonstrate, rather than assume, the threat to basic values. The population field is punctuated with dire predictions of disaster offered to the public with little supporting evidence. The legal concept of "clear and present danger" would seem to be an appropriate test of any proposal for coercion. Even then, however, coercion may not be justified. In the second case, the defense of coercion usually rests on personal evaluations of the system in question. In gross terms, those who favor a given regime will generally support its use of coercion to promote rapid change, while those who oppose it will reject its coercive methods.

Since the justification of coercive tactics often rests on the legitimacy of those who use them, determinations of legitimacy become an important part of ethical analysis. The legitimacy of a regime, in Western democratic tradition, is evidenced by the fact that its major officials have been duly elected, but there are other ways of establishing that a regime is representative of the population and governs with its consent. Even if the regime is seen as generally legitimate, some of its specific policies and programs may be considered illegitimate by various segments of the population because they exceed the regime's range of legitimate authority, because they are discriminatory, or because they violate certain basic values. . . .

## Environmental Manipulation

Individual freedom has two core components: the availability of options in the environment, and the person's capacity to know, weigh, choose, and act on those options. Manipulation is a deliberate act of changing either the structure of the alternatives in the environment (environmental manipulation) or personal qualities affecting choice without the knowledge of the individuals involved (psychic manipulation). The cardinal feature of this process is that it maintains the semblance of freedom while modifying the framework within which choices are made. No physical compulsion or

threats of deprivation are applied, and the individuals may be no more than dimly aware that they or the environment have been changed. Somewhat different ethical considerations are raised by environmental and psychic manipulation.

The term *environmental manipulation*, though it carries sinister overtones, applies to a broad range of activities generally regarded as necessary and desirable. These include city planning; governmental intervention in the economy through means such as taxation and control of interest rates; the construction of roads, dams, or railroads; and the addition of new consumer goods to the market. In each case a deliberate attempt is made to alter the structure of opportunities available, whether through addition, subtraction, or other modifications. . . .

Clearly, people make distinctions between justifiable and unjustifiable control of opportunities. But what are the limits of justifiable manipulation and what ethical calculus should be used to establish these limits? Is it morally justified, for example, to attempt to shape an entire cultural environment in the interest of promoting happiness and survival, as Skinner (1971) has proposed? Perhaps the key question raised by Skinner's proposals is who decides on the shape of the new environment and the controls to be instituted. . . .

Daniel Callahan (1971) has raised several questions about environmental manipulation, pointing to the ironic possibility that people can be manipulated by increasing their freedom.

Similar questions arise in any strategy for social change that relies on creating new realities that make it more necessary—or at least more possible—for people to change their behavior. In the field of race relations, for example, observers have noted that an effective way of changing individual attitudes and practices is to introduce a fait accompli: If an antidiscrimination law or policy is established without too much ado, people will be confronted with a new social reality that, for both practical and normative reasons, they are more likely to accept than to resist. . . .

In sum, if human freedom, and dignity are taken as critical values, there is reason for concern about deliberate attempts to manipulate one person's environment to serve the needs of another. The value of freedom requires not only the availability of options for choice at a given point in time, but an awareness of major changes in the structure of these alternatives. . . . Assuming that this awareness will always be less than complete, who should have the right to tamper with the environment without our knowledge and what conditions should govern such intervention? Some thought has been given to criteria for an ethical evaluation of environmental manipulation. For example, manipulation would seem more acceptable to the extent that the people affected participate in the process, are free to enter and leave the program, and find their range of choices broadened rather than narrowed. Manipulation also seems more acceptable if the manipulators are not the primary beneficiaries of the manipulation, are reciprocally vulnerable in the situation, and are accountable to public agencies.

## Psychic Manipulation

Even within a constant environment of choice, freedom can be affected through the manipulation of its psychological components: for example, knowledge of the alternatives and their consequences; motives; and the ability to reason, choose, and implement one's choices. Recent decades have seen dramatic developments in the techniques of psychic

manipulation. These include insight therapies; the modification of brain functioning through surgery, chemicals, or electrical stimulation; hypnosis; sensitivity training; and programs of attitude change (cf. London, 1969). The emergence of behavior control technology raises fundamental questions about human nature and the baseline assumptions for ethical analysis.

The ethical questions raised by psychic manipulation are similar to those presented by environmental control, and the same criteria for ethical evaluation are applicable. In many interventions of this type, however, particular attention must be paid to moral problems of deception and incomplete knowledge of effects—conditions on which these programs often rely for their success. The use of deception in such programs is based on considerations similar to those used to justify deceptive methods in psychological experiments and other forms of social research. It is assumed that some of the phenomena that the investigator is trying to create or observe would be destroyed if people were aware of the precise nature of the experimental manipulation or of the behavior under study. The moral problems posed by the use of deception in social research have received increasing attention in recent years (cf. Kelman, 1968, 1972; Warwick, 1973, 1975). . . . Similar issues arise in all efforts at psychic manipulation.

In some situations, the ethical problem is not outright deception, but the participant's incomplete or distorted knowledge of the effects of an intervention. . . . The basic ethical question, however, concerns the right of the participant to be informed, not only of probable benefits, but also of potential dangers resulting from psychic manipulation. This question applies to other forms of psychic manipulation, such as brain stimulation or drug experimentation, as much as it does to group experiences.

Often change agents are unaware that they are engaged in manipulative efforts or that these efforts have ethical implications. They may be convinced that all they are doing is conveying information or providing a setting in which self-generated change processes are allowed to emerge. They may thus fail to recognize the situational and structural factors that enhance their power over their clients and the subtle ways in which they communicate their expectations of them. Even if they are aware of their manipulative efforts, they may be so convinced that what they are doing is good for the clients that they fail to recognize the ethical ambiguity of the control they exercise (cf. Kelman, 1968, Chapter 1). Such dangerous blindspots on the part of change agents, which preclude their even raising the ethical questions, are particularly likely to arise in the more subtle forms of psychic manipulation.

## Persuasion

. . . At first blush, persuasion seems highly consistent with the value of freedom—almost its exemplification, in fact. The communication process appears to be carried out in the open, all parties appear to be free to consider the arguments, apparently have free choice whether to reject or accept them, and no coercion is consciously practiced. Quite clearly, when compared with outright coercion or the more gross forms of manipulation, persuasion emerges as a relatively free method of intervention. But at the same time, its seeming openness may sometimes mask covert and far-reaching efforts at personality change.

Insight therapies such as psychoanalysis would generally be regarded as persuasive means of attitude and behavior change. Through such therapy, individuals are led to a better understanding of the sources of their complaints—why they think, act, and feel as they do. The guiding assumption is that self-knowledge will take them a long way toward dealing with the problems. The techniques used to promote understanding are generally nondirective, and the client is urged to assume major responsibility for talking during the therapy sessions.

In principle, at least, insight therapy shows a high degree of respect for people's freedom. The patients do most of the talking, the therapist does not impose his or her personal values, and the process can be ended by the patient at any time. . . . The ethical problem posed by psychotherapy, however, is that the values guiding the influence process are hidden behind global notions such as mental health, self-actualization, and normality. The problem is mitigated to the extent that therapists recognize that they are bringing their own values into the relationship and label those values properly for their patients. "Among other things, such a recognition would allow the patient, to a limited extent, to 'talk back' to the therapist, to argue about the appropriateness of the values that the therapist is introducing" (Kelman, 1968, pp. 25–26).

When we move from persuasion in the one-to-one context to efforts at mass persuasion, the question of who has the opportunity and the capacity to mount a persuasion campaign takes on central importance. Since such opportunities and capacities are not equally distributed in any society, this question is fraught with ethical implications. . . . The question is, who should be responsible for deciding when and where persuasive campaigns are necessary? Should the interested parties from a community be involved in the decision about whether a campaign should be launched, as well as in the later stages of the intervention? Furthermore, how can illiterate villagers argue on an equal plane with sophisticated national planners armed with charts, statistics, debating skills, and prestige? Those in power are usually in a much better position to launch a persuasion campaign and to carry it out effectively. Thus, even though persuasion itself may be more consistent than other means of intervention with the principles of democratic dialogue and popular participation, it often occurs in a context where some are more equal than others.

## Facilitation

Some strategies of intervention may simply be designed to make it easier for individuals to implement their own choices or satisfy their own desires. An underlying assumption in these strategies is that people have some sense of what they want to do and lack only the means to do it. Though facilitation, like persuasion, seems highly consistent with freedom, it too can move close to the borders of manipulation.

An example from the field of family planning can illustrate the different degrees of manipulativeness that a facilitation effort might involve. At the least manipulative extreme, a program providing a regular supply of contraceptive pills to a woman who is highly informed about the possibilities of contraception and strongly motivated to limit her family size, and who knows that she wants to use the pill but simply lacks the means to obtain it, would be a case of almost pure facilitation. At the other extreme would be the case of a woman who vaguely feels that she has too many children, but is not strongly motivated to limit her family size, and who possesses no information on contraception. . . .

The ethical problems of intervention increase as one moves from more or less pure facilitation to cases in which facilitation occurs as the last stage of a manipulative or persuasive strategy. But ethical questions can be raised even about seemingly pure facilitation. The most vexing problem is that the selective reinforcement of an individual's desires, even when these are sharply focused and based on adequate information, can be carried out for someone else's purposes. Here we face a critical question about the ethics of planned change: It is right for party A to assist party B in attaining B's own desires when the reason for this assistance is that B's actions will serve A's interests? In other words, does any kind of facilitation also involve elements of environmental manipulation through the principle of selective reinforcement? . . .

Some have tried to handle the charge of manipulation through facilitation by being completely honest and open. Consider the case of a church-related action group that approaches a neighborhood organization with an offer of assistance. In such a relationship, open dialogue about why each party might be interested in the other, joint setting of goals, and complete liberty on both sides to terminate the relationship would certainly represent ethically laudable policies, but they would not remove the possibility of manipulation. The fact remains that the church group is making its resources available to one organization rather than another. It thereby facilitates the attainment of the goals associated with that organization and may weaken the influence and bargaining position of competing groups. In cases where there are numerous organizations claiming to represent essentially the same constituency, as among Puerto Ricans in the United States, the receipt of outside aid may give one contender for leadership considerable advantage over the others. Moreover, since the church group retains ultimate control of the resources provided, it can exercise great leverage in setting goals by the implicit threat of withdrawing its support. It is therefore essential to distinguish between honesty in the process by which an intervention is carried out and the underlying power relationships operating in the situation.

## ASSESSMENT OF CONSEQUENCES

A final set of ethical concerns arises from the consequences of a change program—its products as well as its by-products. Questions that might be raised about a specific case include: Who benefits from the change, in both the short and the long run? Who suffers? How does the change affect the distribution of power in the society, for example, between elites and masses, or between competing social groups? What is its impact on the physical environment? Which social values does it enhance and which does it weaken? Does the program create a lasting dependency on the change agent or on some other sponsor? What will its short-term and long-term effects be on the personalities of those involved? Many of these questions can be grouped under the heading of *direct* and *indirect consequences*.

An ethical analysis of the direct consequences, which flow immediately from the substance or contents of the intervention, would relate them to the set of basic values used as criteria for assessing the intervention. . . .

In addition to its direct consequences, almost any change program creates by-products or side effects in areas of society and personality beyond its immediate intentions or scope of influence. These indirect effects must form part of any serious ethical evaluation. Such an evaluation requires a guiding theory of change, of how one part of a system af-

fects another. Unfortunately, many efforts at social intervention completely ignore these systems effects, or discover them too late. Among the most common unanticipated effects are the destruction or weakening of integrative values in the society, change in the balance between aspirations and achievement, and strengthening the power of one group at the expense of another.

One of the latent consequences of many programs of modernization is to undercut or challenge existing values and norms, particularly in rural areas. The introduction of a new road, building of an industrial plant, teaching literacy, or even selling transistor radios may expose isolated villagers to a variety of new stimuli that challenge their traditional world view. Though the direct effects of such programs often serve the values of welfare, justice, and freedom, the indirect effects may generate abundant confusion and a search for new alternatives. . . .

Another common side-effect of change involves a shift in the balance between individual aspirations and the opportunities for achieving them. The delicate ethical question in this case concerns the degree to which a change agent is justified in tampering with aspirations. The dilemma is often severe. On the one hand, to do nothing implies an endorsement of the status quo. On the other hand, in raising aspirations to stir up motivation for change, a program may overshoot its mark. The unintended result may be a rise in frustration. Questions of this type could be raised about the innovative method of literacy instruction developed by Paulo Freire (1971), which attempts to develop not only an ability to read, but also a heightened consciousness of one's position in society and the forces shaping one's destiny. One can certainly argue that this experience enhances the person's freedom. But a change in critical consciousness and political aspirations without a corresponding modification of the social environment may also be a source of profound frustration. Where collective action to change the system is impossible, either because of strong political repression or other barriers to organization, the net effect may be short-term enthusiasm followed by long-term depression. In fact, the experience of having been stimulated and then frustrated may lead to a lower probability of future action than existed before the intervention. One must then ask if it is morally justifiable to raise political aspirations without ensuring that there are opportunities for implementing those aspirations. . . .

# REFERENCES

Bennis, W. G., Benne, K. D., Chin, R., & Corey, K. E. (Eds.). *The planning of change* (3rd ed.). New York: Holt, Rinehart and Winston, 1976.

Blake, J. Population policy for Americans: Is the government being misled? *Science*, 1969, 164, 522–529.

Callahan, D. Population limitation and manipulation of familial roles. Unpublished manuscript. Hastings-on-Hudson, N.Y.: Institute of Society, Ethics, and the Life Sciences, 1971.

Freire, P. *Pedagogy of the oppressed.* New York: Herder and Herder, 1971.

Gottschalk, L. A., & Pattison, E. M. Psychiatric perspectives on T-groups and the laboratory movement: An overview. *American Journal of Psychiatry*, 1969, 126, 823–840.

Goulet, D. *The cruel choice.* New York: Atheneum, 1971.

Gustafson, J. M. Basic ethical issues in the biomedical fields. *Soundings*, 1970, 53(2), 151–180.

Kelman, H. C. *A time to speak: On human values and social research.* San Francisco: Josey-Bass, 1968.

Kelman, H. C. The relevance of social research to social issues: Promises and pitfalls. In P. Halmos (Ed.), *The sociology of sociology* (The Sociological Review: Monograph No. 16). Keele: University of Keele, 1970.

Kelman, H. C. The rights of the subject in social research: An analysis in terms of relative power and legitimacy. *American Psychologist*, 1972, 27, 989–1016.

Lippitt, R., Watson, J., & Westley, B. *The dynamics of planned change.* New York: Harcourt Brace Jovanovich, 1958.

London, P. *The modes and morals of psychotherapy.* New York: Holt, Rinehart and Winston, 1964.

London, P. *Behavior control.* New York: Harper & Row, 1969.

May, R. *Love and will.* New York: Norton, 1969.

Population Task Force of the Institute of Society, Ethics, and the Life Sciences. *Ethics, population, and the American tradition.* A study prepared for the Commission on Population Growth and the American Future. Hastings-on-Hudson, N.Y.: Institute of Society, Ethics, and the Life Sciences, 1971.

Rostow, W. W. *The stages of economic growth.* New York: Cambridge University Press, 1960.

Skinner, B. F. *Beyond freedom and dignity.* New York: Knopf, 1971.

Warwick, D. P. Freedom and population policy. In Population Task Force, *Ethics, population, and the American tradition.* Hastings-on-Hudson, N.Y.: Institute of Society, Ethics, and the Life Sciences, 1971.

Warwick, D. P. Tearoom trade: Means and ends in social research. *Hastings Center Studies*, 1973, 1(1), 27–38.

Warwick, D. P. Social scientists ought to stop lying. *Psychology Today*, 1975, 8(9), 38–40, 105–106.

Warwick, D. P., & Kelman, H. C. Ethical issues in social intervention. In G. Zaltman (Ed.), *Processes and phenomena of social change.* New York: Wiley, 1973.

# 43

# The Architecture of Culture and Strategy Change

*Rosabeth Moss Kanter*

It is hard to imagine anything more frustrating to middle-level corporate entrepreneurs and their teams than doing everything right to develop an innovation, only to have it melt away because higher-level executives fumble their part in the change process—by failing to design and construct the new "platform" to support the innovation.

Corporate change—rebuilding, if you will—has parallels to the most ambitious and perhaps most noble of the plastic arts, architecture. The skill of corporate leaders, the ultimate change masters, lies in their ability to envision a new reality and aid in its translation into concrete terms. Creative visions combine with the building up of events, floor by floor, from foundation to completed construction. How productive change occurs is part artistic design, part management of construction.

All the pieces can be right—new product prototypes already test-marketed, new work methods measured and found effective, new systems and structures piloted in local areas—and still an organization can fail to incorporate them into new responses to changing demands. . . .

The ultimate skill for change mastery works on just that larger context surrounding the innovation process. It consists of the ability to conceive, construct, and convert into behavior a new view of organizational reality.

I find it interesting that organizational theorists have produced much more work, and work of greater depth and intellectual sophistication, on the recalcitrance of organizations and their people—how and why they resist change—than on the change process. Maybe the first is easier, because "change" is an elusive concept. Not only is it notoriously hard to measure accurately—so how do we know when we have one?—but it can connote an abrupt disjunction, a separation of one set of organizational events and activities from others, in a way that does not match reality.

*Many* kinds of activities or tendencies are present in an organization at any one time. Some of these cohere and are called "the" structure or "the" strategy or "the" culture. But there may be other activities which contradict this core or begin to depart from it. Thus, at another time we could simply reconceptualize what the pattern is, emphasizing some activities in place of others *which may still linger*, and decide that the organization has "changed." Indeed, the act of making changes may involve merely reconceptualizing and repackaging coexisting organizational tendencies, as the balance tips from the dominance of one tendency to the dominance of another. The historian Barbara Tuchman once used the image of a kaleidoscope to describe this: when the cylinder is shaken, the same set of fragments form a new picture.

*Source:* From *The Change Masters* by Rosabeth Moss Kanter, 1983, New York: Simon & Schuster, Inc. (pp. 278–306). Copyright © 1983 Rosabeth Moss Kanter. Reprinted by permission of Simon & Schuster, Inc.

Acknowledging the elusiveness of "change," I use a modest definition of it here, one that stays close to the idea of innovation. Change involves the crystallization of new action possibilities (new policies, new behaviors, new patterns, new methodologies, new products, or new market ideas) based on reconceptualized patterns in the organization. The architecture of change involves the design and construction of new patterns, or the reconceptualization of old ones, to make new, and hopefully more productive, actions possible.[1]

It is important to remember that organizations change by a variety of methods, not all of them viewed as desirable by the people involved. The innovations implemented by entrepreneurial managers by participative methods or those designed and carried out by employee teams may reflect more *constructive* and *productive* methods of change, but they do not exhaust the possibilities, nor are they even typical in organizations with a high degree of segmentation and segmentalism. . . . Changes may also be brought about by internal political actions: for example, a "*coup d'état,*" in which officials plot to remove the chief executive; a rebellion, in which some members refuse to abide by the directives of the top and act according to their own rules; or a mass movement, in which grass-roots groups of activists mobilize to protest organizational policies or actions.[2]

The choice of methods—participative, authoritarian, or political—may be independent of the source of the pressure for change, although there is a strong likelihood that participative methods will be used when an organization's prime movers see the impetus for change as internally driven, based on choice and responsiveness, rather than externally imposed, based on coercion and resistance. In contrast, in a cascade-down effect, a change demand seen as imposed from without and not embraced by the organization's leaders may be handled in authoritarian or political fashion by the organization. (Both are segmentalist in nature.) To put it another way, organization leaders who are not sure they really want to change—whether in response to market pressures, government regulation, or the actions of competitors—may be more likely to restrict the chance for members to participate in shaping the kinds of changes that could occur, thus missing the opportunity to transfer potential threat into innovation.

The external world surrounding an organization and poking and prodding it in numerous ways is obviously important in stimulating change. But since the "environment" is itself made up of numerous organizations and groups—stakeholders and constituencies—pressing numerous claims, with varying degrees of power, and since a company is made up of numerous action possibilities not always expressed in official policy or strategy at any moment, any assumption of correspondence between what the environment "does" and what the company "does" has to be simpleminded and misleading, especially in the short run. If in the long run there appears to be adjustment by the company in predictable ways, that might be *mutual* adjustment—parties in the environment shifting in response to the organization's actions.[3]

But the fact that the environment is important—and its "discovery" represents one of the important developments for both real organizations and organization theory in the last two decades—does not mean that it "causes" change either automatically or directly.

This is a subtle point. Organizational change is stimulated not by *pressures* from the environment, resulting in a buildup of problems triggering an automatic response, but by the *perceptions* of that environment and those pressures held by key actors. Organizations may not respond to environments so much as "enact" them—create them by the choice to selectively define certain things as important. When an organization tries to "see" its environment, as Cornell social psychologist Karl Weick put it, what might it do to create the very displays it sees? And how might the environment change when it "knows" it is being "watched"?[4]

Clearly, decision makers, via their patterns of attention and inattention, intervene between a company and its environment. And this, of course, means that a company with a diverse group in the "dominant coalition" at the top— more fields and functions represented, more diversity in sex, race, and culture—is more likely to pick up on more external cues, as did the task forces at Honeywell or the management committees at J. C. Penney, than a company with a smaller, more homogeneous set of top decision makers or with a single function—whether finance, marketing, or any other—having disproportionate power to define the appropriate focuses of attention.

Furthermore, even if the "environment" looks objective and real in an industry, so that companies in it share *perceptions* of strategic issues, strategy does not automatically follow, and leaders may sometimes make strategic choices based on their own areas of competence and career payoff, rather than on what the best response might be to the anticipated character of the environment. A chief executive with a financial background might have more knowledge of balance sheets than operations and might get more credit in the press for acquiring and merging than for technical advances in manufacturing methods—

and so long-term investment in productivity may be neglected.[5]

Innovation and change, I am suggesting, are bound up with the meanings attached to events and the action possibilities that flow from those meanings. But that very recognition—of the symbolic, conceptual, cultural side of change—makes it more difficult to see change as a mechanical process and extract the "formula" for producing it.

## "TRUTH" IS IMPOSSIBLE— AND THEREIN LIES A "TRUTH": ACCOUNTS OF CORPORATE CHANGE

It is hard to tell the "truth" about organizational changes, and thus to learn what "really" makes them happen. I am not referring to something mundane and mechanical like the limits of participant perception and memory, but to rather more profound systematic forces built into the nature of organizational change itself. In understanding why change accounts are often distorted, we understand some important things about the architecture of change itself.

One limitation on the accuracy of models of change and even accounts of specific changes is shared by all historical analysis: the problem of when the clock starts running. In trying to reconstruct how a particular company got from state A to state B, we are also assuming there were a Time I and a Time II. But what is called Time I? Many current models of strategic planning or planned change begin at the point at which strategic decisions were made to seek an alternative course; recognizing a problem, leaders set out to mobilize the search for solutions or to move the organization in an envisioned direction. This, of course, reflects the rational-planning bias so nicely critiqued by business analyst James Brian Quinn on the basis of his examination of important strategic shifts at major companies like General Mills and Texas Instruments.[6] It also reflects a bias toward "official" history—the assumption that only leadership actions "count."

Generally, however, by the time high-level organizational odometers are set at zero to record change, a large number of other—perhaps less public—events have already occurred that set the stage for the "official" decision process, that indeed make it possible, like a successful experiment by a corporate entrepreneur. And still other events may have occurred that contradict the direction of change.

Thus, lack of awareness of this "prehistory" of change makes any conclusions about how a particular organization managed a change suspect, to say the least, and perhaps impossible to replicate elsewhere, a point to which I shall return. Most of us—and corporate actors are no exception—begin the recording of "history" at the moment at which we become conscious of our own strategic actions, neglecting the groundwork already laid before we became aware of it. What seems to us the "beginning" is, in another sense, a mid-point of a longer process, and not seeing this "prehistory" we may not understand the dynamism of the process already in motion, and we may be haunted later by some of its ghosts. Or we may try to repeat someone else's success based on his/her account of what he/she did "first," as I have seen many companies do, finding that little of it works, because the supposed "first step" was in reality preceded by a large number of other events that set the stage but go unreported because no "intelligent strategy" was involved.

In conceiving of a different future, change masters have to be historians as well. When innovators begin to define a project by reviewing the issues with people across areas, they are not only seeing what is possible, they may be learning more about the past; and one of the prime uses of the past is in the construction of a story that makes the future seem to grow naturally out of it in terms compatible with the organization's culture.

The architecture of change thus requires an *awareness of foundations*—the bases in "prehistory," perhaps below the surface, that make continued construction possible. And if the foundations will not support the weight of what is about to be built, then they must be shored up before any other actions can take place. . . .

Often the foundations enabling innovations to occur are positive ones: some experience with similar events that provides at least some skilled, knowledgeable people; a history of joint planning by the leaders who are going to have to act as a team to manage the innovation; preexisting relationships of cooperation and trust cross segments involved in the change. Changes really "start" there. If those foundations do not exist, they have to be constructed first, and if they do exist, they may need to become part of the story that is told about the change, because foundations not only make change possible, they also provide security and stability—"grounding"—in the midst of it.

The complicated question of "beginning" is only one issue that can distort change accounts. The other is more subtle and complex: the *rewriting of corporate history* is often part of the innovation-and-change process itself.

The actual events in a change sequence (as seen by a detached on-the-spot observer) may seem very different from how they are rendered in retrospective public accounts, especially "official" ones.[7] The reconstruction itself serves important organizational purposes. For example, if the changes are ones that

require many people's support to implement, then we are likely to see these
well-intentioned "distortions" in official accounts:

*Individuals disappear into collectives.*
What was initiated and pushed by one
person may be redefined, because the
person was successful in involving others
and getting them to take ownership, as
the will and the act of the group.

For example, one of my high-level corporate informants was concerned that I
not make him too central in one of the
accomplishments I recount or give him
too much credit as an individual, because he pushed new concepts through
the system by working with others to
make them feel they had initiated and
owned the change—"planting seeds"
and then letting the harvest be reaped
collectively. For organizational purposes,
the whole group had done it, and to
assert otherwise would be destructive of
the new reality that had been built
together. . . .

In American companies, this transformation smooths power relations. The
use of "power" is made possible partly
by the power user's tacit agreement to
keep his or her power invisible once others have agreed to participate. Others'
participation may be contingent on a
feeling that they are involved out of
commitment or conviction—not because power is being exercised over
them. Successful innovators know this,
and so they often downplay their own
role in an accomplishment in official organizational communications in favor of
credit's going to the whole team. Or they
spend time "convincing" their subordinates and giving them a piece of the
action even if they could in fact apply
visible power.

*Early events and people disappear into
the background as later events and people
come forward.* I saw this repeatedly in the
course of managerial innovations. The
account of a change at any particular
moment has to feature most prominently
those actors whose actions are most immediately connected to the foundations
of the next necessary development. And
so the earlier people and events may appear to be forgotten—not because memory fades with time, but because there is
little to be gained in terms of continuing
the momentum of the change by remembering them. . . .

*Conflicts disappear into consensuses.*
Just as in the treaties after a war, "losers"
may disappear into allies. Pain, suffering,
trauma, and resistance may disappear
into "necessary evils." What was highly
contentious at the time eventually gets
worked out, and the price of the final
agreement is to forget that conflict had
existed, as in political systems where the
final vote has to be unanimous despite
the acrimony of the debate. The organizational memory, at least, cannot afford
grudges, especially in integrative systems; segmentalist ones seem to nurse
old wounds longer. One gets cooperation
by agreeing to save the face of those
who were critical or opposed and not
embarrass them by reminding them of
it. And the survivors of pain and trauma
may, in their turn, agree to forget in
exchange for some of the benefits of
the change.

*Equally plausible alternatives disappear
into obvious choices.* To get commitment
and support for a course of action may
require that it appear essential—not as
one of a number of possibilities. By the
time a decision is announced, it may
need to be presented as the *only* choice,
even if there are many people aware of
how much debate went into it or how
many other options looked just as good.

The announcers—the champions of
the idea—have to look unwaveringly
convinced of the rightness of their
choice to get other people to accept the
change. Unambivalent and unequivocal

communication—once a variety of alternatives have been explored—provides security. One CEO of my acquaintance is not particularly good at this; he presents decisions about new procedures tentatively, expressing ambivalence about the favored option in the light of plausible alternatives—and others say to themselves, "If *he* isn't convinced, then why should we do anything about this?" The consequence is that change is stalled; no one ever does seem to get around to using the new procedures.

*Accidents, uncertainties, and muddleheaded confusions disappear into clearsighted strategies.* There is a long philosophic tradition arguing that action precedes thought; a "reconstructed logic" helps us make sense out of events, and they always sound more strategic and less accidental or fortuitous later. Some analysts are even willing to go so far as to say that organizations formulate strategy *after* they implement it.[8]

But the importance of defining a clear direction, even if one is already almost at the destination, is to build commitment by reducing the plausibility of other directions, to reinforce the pride people take in the intelligence of the system, or to reward those leading the pack by crediting their vision, to remove any lingering doubts about what the direction is, and to signal to critics that the time for opposition is over. Thus, it may be organizationally important to present the image of strategy in the accounts that are constructed whether or not this rational model conveys the "truth." For the innovators to get the coalition to chip in with investments, for example, they have to feel that the entrepreneur knows what he or she is doing; strategic plans are one of those symbols which are highly reassuring to investors.[9]

*Multiple events disappear into single thematic events.* How a story about change is constructed also comes to reflect what the organization needs to symbolize, what images it wishes to create or preserve, what lessons it wants to draw to permit the changes to be reinforced or the next actions to be taken. Sometimes this reflects the preservation of power: e.g., creating the appearance that the leader did something that was really the result of a great deal of behind-the-scenes staff work, eliminating the messy events and focusing on the outstanding success, or telling about only the times when the leaders showed their commitment to quality of work life and ignoring the times they did not. Sometimes this simply reflects the human reality that too much complexity and detail cannot be grasped and remembered easily and thus interferes with a clear conception of what the situation now *is*. So a large number of things that might have occurred are reduced to just a few critical ones which tell a story that gives people a common image of what is now the right thing to do.

*The fragility of changes (that exist alongside the residues of the old system) disappear into images of solidity and full actuality.* Multiple organizational tendencies, including contradictory ones, often coexist, but these are ignored in favor of insistence that an innovation has taken hold simply because it exists at all. In some companies, this helps reward the innovators, builds commitment, and disarms the critics. But in others, where innovation is still threatening even when successful and productive, I suspect that this represents a kind of collective sigh of relief that "now we've done it; we don't have to think about change anymore"; some organizations are too ready to believe that all the hard work is over when *one* example is in place.

As if all these "distortions" were not enough, the organization's culture also influences the stories that must be constructed about change. Some prefer to submerge changes into continuity; others like to turn continuities into change. I have pointed out that segmented organizations may promote change-aversiveness and, thus, a preference for denying that major change has occurred. This makes it easy, of course, for the rest of the system to avoid adjusting in response; if the official story says that nothing much has happened any differently from what the system already knew, then no one has to move out of the safety of his or her segment. . . .

There are tactical uses to these ways of constructing change, too. For example, announcing "change!" in one part of an organization's world to make clear the need for change in others is a stimulus to action in a way that stressing continuity is not. It is a power move, used well by leaders of social movements to rally the troops as well as by corporate staffs to influence the line organization. And younger people invoke change to show the older ones in power that their wisdom no longer fits, and they should step aside. In contrast, in "cultures of age," denial of change preserves the power of the establishment.

All of this tells us something important about the essence of the change process: *Organizational change consists in part of a series of emerging constructions of reality, including revision of the past, to correspond to the requisites of new players and new demands.* Organizational history *does* need to be rewritten to permit events to move on. (In a sense, change is partly the construction of such reconstructions.) To use a physical analogy: as each floor of a building is built, the supports need to be made invisible to permit focusing on the important current thing—the *use* of the space. Simi-

larly, as an innovator "sells" each member of her coalition on the worth of her project, the influence process and perhaps even the origin of the idea may have to be "forgotten" and not revealed outside the group to permit attention to go to the people whose role is critical now. Official histories of changes, reports about projects, and even the way organization members tell one another about what happened to move the system from A to B always serve a present function.

The art and architecture of change, then, also involves *designing reports about the past to elicit the present actions required for the future*—to extract the elements necessary for current action, to continue to construct and reconstruct participants' understanding of events so that the next phase of activity is possible. "Power" may need to remain less than fully visible; "prime movers" may need to make sure others are equally credited; room at center stage may need to be given over to those people and activities that are now necessary to go on from here—e.g., the marketing people instead of the product developers becoming the "heroes" of the account.

Change masters should understand these phenomena and work with them; they should know how to create and use myths and stories.[10] But we should not confuse the results—an official, retrospective account of organizational actions—with lessons about guiding organizational change. We need to understand what goes on behind and beyond official accounts, to create models that are closer to events-as-they-happened than to events-as-they-are-retold.

In short, those who master change know that they can never tell the "truth," but they also know what the "truth" is. In their actions they exhibit knowledge at both levels, recapturing those aspects of a change process which have faded or disappeared in official accounts and rational models. Thus:

- Where groups or organizations appear to "act," there are often strong individuals persistently pushing.
- Where recent events seem the most important in really bringing the change about, a number of less obvious early events were probably highly important.
- Where there is apparent consensus, there was often controversy, dissent, and bargaining.
- Where the ultimate choice seems the only logical one, unfolding naturally and inevitably from what preceded it, there were often a number of equally plausible alternatives that might have fitted too.
- Where clear-sighted strategies are formulated, there was often a period of uncertainty and confusion, of experiment and reaching for anyone with an answer, and there may have been some unplanned events or "accidents" that helped the strategy to emerge.
- Where single leaders or single occurrences appear to be the "cause" of the change, there were usually many actors or many events.
- Where an innovation appears to have taken hold, there may be contradictory tendencies in the organization that can destroy or replace it, unless other things have occurred to solidify—institutionalize—the change.
- And where there appears to be only continuity, there was probably also change. Where there appears to be only change, there was probably also continuity.

These realizations constitute part of the "architecture" of change. But there are also a set of building blocks that together constitute the structure behind the process of change.

## THE BUILDING BLOCKS OF CHANGE: FROM INNOVATION TO INSTITUTIONALIZATION

It is important to see how micro-innovations and macro-changes come to be joined together, how major change is constructed out of the actions of numerous entrepreneurs and innovators as well as top decision makers.

"Breakthrough" changes that help a company attain a higher level of performance are likely to reflect the interplay of a number of smaller changes that together provide the building blocks for the new construction. . . .

An organization's "total" strategy is defined by the interaction of major subsystem strategies, each reflecting the unique needs, capacities, and power requirements of local units. Even when it is impossible to fully guide the organization from the top—i.e., predict in advance how these units will evolve—the right kinds of integrative mechanisms, including communication between areas, can ensure the coordination among these substrategies and micro-innovations that ultimately results in a company's strategic posture. In short, effective organizations benefit from integrative structures and cultures that promote innovation below the top and learn from them. . . .

In short, action first, thought later; experience first, making a "strategy" out of it second. Strategy may not so much drive structure as exist in an interdependent relationship with it.[11] In many cases new structural possibilities out of experiments by middle-level innovators make possible the formulation of a new strategy to meet a sudden external challenge of which even the middle-level innovators might have been unaware. Then the new strategy, in effect, elevates the innovators' experiments to the level of policy.

I see a combination of five major building blocks present in productive corporate changes, changes that increase the company's capacity to meet new challenges.

### Force A. Departures from Tradition

First, activities occur, generally at the grass-roots level, that deviate from organizational expectations. Either these are driven by entrepreneurial innovators, or they "happen" to the organization in a more passive fashion.[12]

Some departures may be random or chance events reflecting "loose coupling" in the system—i.e., no one does everything entirely according to plan even if he or she intends to, and slight local variations on procedures may result in new ideas. They may be the result of "accidents"—i.e., events occur for which there is no contingency plan, or the organization's traditional sources are exhausted, so the company innovates by default, turning to a new idea or a new person just to fill a gap. Or a "hole" in the system may open up because another change is taking place: a changeover of bosses leaving a temporary gap, a new system being installed that does not yet work perfectly. All these constitute the "unplanned opportunities" that permit entrepreneurs to step forward even in highly segmented, noninnovating companies; they may work best at the periphery, in "zones of indifference" where no one else cares enough to prevent a little occasional deviance. The ideas or experiences resulting from deviant events then constitute "solutions looking for problems"[13]—models that can be applied elsewhere.

In innovating companies, in contrast to their less receptive counterparts, a high proportion of these departures from tradition are brought about through the actions of entrepreneurs who seek to move beyond the job-as-given. . . .

Departures from tradition provide the organization with a *foundation in experience* to use to solve new problems as they arise or to replace existing methods with more productive ones. This foundation in experience suggests the possibility of a new strategy—one that could not be developed as easily without the existence of organizational experiences. At the same time, those experiences condi-

tion the direction of any new strategies. In effect, it is hard to see where you want to go until you have a few options, but those options do not limit later choices.

One lesson is straightforward: an organization that wants to innovate to stay ahead of change should be just loosely enough controlled to promote local experiments, variations on a plan. It should make it easy for ambitious innovators to grab the power to experiment—within bounds, of course. It is those variations—sometimes more than the plan itself—which may be the keys to future successes. And there need to be enough experiments for organizational policymakers to have choices when it comes to reformulating strategies. This constitutes the internal equivalent of a "diversified portfolio" for turbulent times.

There is another important value that successful experiments or small-scale innovations have for the change process: they prove the organization's capacity to take productive action. An unfortunate number of change efforts seem to begin with the negative rather than the positive: a catalogue of problems, a litany of woes. But identification of potential, description of strengths, seems to be a better—and faster—way to begin. . . .

But deviant events do not by themselves produce major change. Large systems are capable of containing many contradictions, many departures from tradition that do not necessarily affect the organization's central tendency. . . .

"Deviant" events result in overall change only under one or more of these circumstances: Perhaps enough similar instances of the event or idea accumulate slowly over time so that at some point, definition of the organization's central tendency changes in response to the new reality—a very slow process. (But these are much more common in integrative than segmentalist organizations.) Or, as a second possibility, the organization has mechanisms for the transmission of positive innovations to other sectors which might take advantage of them—e.g., informal or formal communication mechanisms for cross-fertilization. Or, finally, impending crisis or obvious problems that cannot be solved by traditional means lead the organization to search for a solution to grab, and so the deviant idea is pushed forward. The first circumstance is too slow and leaves too much to chance for today's competitive business environment. The second circumstance is more characteristic of high-innovation organizations than of noninnovating ones. But the crisis factor is central to major changes at both ends of the spectrum.

## Force B. Crisis or Galvanizing Event

The second set of forces in the change process involves "external" ones, changes elsewhere that appear to require a response. By external-in-quotes I mean that they do not necessarily come from outside the organization—e.g., a lawsuit, an abrupt market downturn, the oil embargo, a competitor's new-product introduction—but may also be events within an organization's borders that are outside current operating frameworks—e.g., a new demand from a higher-level official, a change of technology, a recognition of change in the work force. The change-stimulating-change chain is one reason it is so hard to develop an orderly model of the change process; overlapping events intrude on one another. What is "external" to any change sequence we are trying to describe—or *manage*—may be the A force (tradition departure) or C force (strategic decision) in some other change sequence.

The critical point for the people involved is that the event or crisis has a demand quality and seems to require a response. If the crisis is defined as insoluble by traditional means, or if traditional solutions quickly exhaust their value, or if the external parties pushing indicate that they will not be satisfied by the same old response—then a nontraditional solution may be pushed forward. One of the grass-roots experiments or local innovations may be grabbed.

I propose that organizations with segmentalist approaches to problems will be less "externally" responsive. A tendency to isolate problems—more accurately, pieces of problems—in segmented subunits, and a reluctance on the part of each subunit to admit to being unable to handle its piece adequately, will result in less ability to perceive earlier crises before they add up to full-blown disasters. The "seen it all before" syndrome in a culture of age may result in few things being seen as "crises." Danger signals may simply not be attended to as events requiring response. And even if one unit—perhaps assigned to scan a particular part of the environment—sees the signs, there may be few mechanisms for transmitting this information to other units, or for getting others to cooperate in a response. Thus, perception may be restricted, and so may action.

On the other hand, integrative approaches may mean that an organization "sees" more galvanizing events in general and "sees" them earlier. A tendency to tie problems to larger wholes is one aspect of this. Rather than writing off potential external problems, an organization characterized by this approach may instead see small crises as symptomatic of larger dangers and prepare earlier preventive responses. Since information flows more freely across integrative structures, and since the culture encourages identification with larger units and issues rather than smaller units and specialities, it is easier for the signals of "external" change seen by one part of the system to be added to those seen by others, helping to define a "crisis" demanding response. In addition, the culture of change we saw in innovating companies may promote in people the desire to define events as "crises" that can be used to mobilize others around the search for an innovative response. . . .

## Force C. Strategic Decisions

At last we get to the point in the process familiar in most of the "change management" or "strategic planning" literature. This is the point at which leaders enter, and strategies are developed that use Force A to solve the problems inherent in Force B. A new definition of the situation is formulated, a new set of plans, that lifts the experiments of innovators from the periphery to center stage, that reconceptualizes them *as* the emergent tradition rather than as departures from it. . . .

While "strategic" is clearly an overused word, and many companies are dropping it as an automatic modifier to "planning," it does express an important idea for this part of the change process: deliberate and conscious articulation of a direction. Strong leaders articulate direction and save the organization from change via "drift." They create a vision of a possible future that allows themselves and others to see more clearly the steps to take, *building on present capacities and strengths, on the results of Force A and Force B,* to get there.[14]

If one can never get the leaders together to do that kind of strategy formulation, to build on a set of innovations, then it is likely that the innovations will drift away. Or that so many kinds of innovations will float by that none of them will even gain the momentum and force to take hold. But what makes the leaders ready to engage in this formulation is the experience the organization has already had.

It may be more accurate to speak of a series of smaller decisions made over time than a single dramatic strategic decision, but I am stressing the symbolic aspects of strategy after events are already in motion. Thus, there may be key meetings at which a critical piece of what later became "the" strategy was formulated, a plan or mission statement generated that articulated a commitment, or an important "go-ahead" directive issued. . . . Leaders' articulation of what may have been only embryonic up to that point represents "change" to the organization. Such leader action is important to crystallize change potential once departures from tradition have given the organization some experience with the new way.

Not surprisingly, more integrative systems have an advantage here too. More entrepreneurs, pushing more innovations, create pressure to do something with them. More overlaps and communication channels and team mechanisms keep more ideas circulating. And the existence of teams at the top, drawing together many areas and exchanging ideas among them—as contrasted with segmented officials running fiefdoms—are in a better position to engage in forward planning to tie together external circumstances and grass-roots experience. The preexistence of coalitions and cooperative traditions makes it easier to get moving; precious time does not have to be expended forming the coalitions that will make the strategic decisions. . . .

Innovating organizations can sometimes try to keep so many possibilities alive that they avoid strategic decisions, avoid strong leadership that imposes focusing mechanisms to promote some actions over others. The key is to allow a continual creative tension between grass-roots innovation in a free-wheeling environment and periodic strategic decisions by strong central leaders.

So now new strategies are defined that build new methods, products, structures, into official plans. The crystallized plans serve many purposes other than the obvious. . . . In short, strategic decisions help set into motion the next two major forces in "change."

## Force D. Individual "Prime Movers"

Any new strategy, no matter how brilliant or responsive, no matter how much agreement the formulators have about it, will stand a good chance of not being implemented fully—or sometimes, at all—without someone with power pushing it. We have all had the experience of going to a meeting where many excellent ideas are developed, everyone agrees to a plan, and then no one takes any responsibility for doing anything about it, and again the change opportunity drifts away. Even assigning accountabilities does not always guarantee implementation if there is not a powerful figure concerned about pushing the accountable party to live up to it. Hence the importance of the corporate entrepreneur who remains steadfast in his or her vision and keeps up the momentum of the action team even when its effort wanes, or of a powerful sponsor of "idea champion" for innovations that require a major push beyond the actions of the innovating team. Empowering champions is one way leaders solidify commitment to a new strategy.[15]

Prime movers push in part by repetition, by mentioning the new idea or the new practice on every possible occasion, in every speech, at every meeting. Perhaps there are catchphrases that become "slogans" for the new efforts; John De Butts, the former AT&T chairman, used to repeat "the system is the solution" and built it into Bell's advertising, and Tom Jones, the CEO of Northrup, liked to reiterate, "everybody at Northrup is

in marketing."[16] At Honeywell, then-President (now Vice-Chairman) James Renier instituted the "Winning Edge Program," a remarkably long-lasting corporatewide motivation program, and the slogan "We are the Winning Edge" has found it way onto everything from memo pads to coffee mugs. It is currently fashionable to draft "corporate philosophies" or compile lists of seven or eight "management principles" which stimulate the executive team and sometimes employee groups, to discuss the key phrases that represent a shared vision, phrases that can then be tacked on every wall and woven into every speech.

What is important about such communications is certainly not that they rest on pat phrases but that they are part of unequivocal messages about the firm commitment of the prime movers to the changes. It is easy for the people in the company to make fun of the slogans if they are unrelated to other actions or not taken seriously by the leaders themselves. Prime movers pushing a new strategy have to make clear that they *believe* in it, that it is oriented toward getting something that they want, because it is good for the organization. They might, for example, visit local units, ask questions about implementation, praise efforts consistent with the thrusts. The personal tour by a top executive is an important tool of prime movers.

This is especially important for changes that begin with pressures in the environment and were not sought by the corporation—changes in response to regulatory pressures, shifts to counter a competitor's strategy. The drive for change must become internalized even if it originated externally, or prime movers cannot push with conviction, and the people around them can avoid wholehearted implementation. I have seen numerous instances of this around affirmative action, for example; those companies where prime movers found a way to see the changes as meeting *organizational* needs and convey an unwavering commitment have a better track record with respect to women and minorities than places with weak or equivocating leadership.

People in organizations are constantly trying to figure out what their leaders *really* mean—which statements or plans can be easily ignored and which have command value. Leaders say too many things, suggesting too many courses of action, for people to act on all of them. Thus, prime movers have to communicate strategic decisions forcefully enough, often enough, to make their intentions clear, or they can run into the problems that arise when zealous subordinates, trying to interpret vague statements from the top, take strong action in the *wrong* direction. . . .

A few clear signals, consistently supported, are what it takes to change an organzation's culture and direction: signposts in the morass of organizational messages. The job of prime movers is not only to "talk up" the new strategy but also to manipulate those symbols which indicate commitment to it. The devices which can be used to signal that organizational attention is redirected include such mundane tools as: the kinds of reports required, what gets on the agenda at staff meetings, the places at which key events are held, or the reporting level of people responsible for the new initiatives.[17] . . .

Prime movers push—but to complete the process they need ways to embody the change in action.

## Force E. Action Vehicles

The last critical force for guiding productive change involves making sure there are mechanisms that allow the new action possibilities to be expressed. The actions implied by the changes cannot reside on the level of ideas, as abstractions, but must be concretized in actual procedures or structures or communication channels or appraisal measures or work methods or rewards.

"The map is not the territory," philosophers warn us—but we cannot even begin to find our way around the territory to the people with whom we must interact *without* a map. This is not quite an obvious point—or at least, not obvious to all managers. I have seen too many ideas adopted by organizations as matters of policy while members at lower levels scratch their heads wondering what this means they should *do*. . . .

The problem is not the association of an idea with a program, but rather the existence of *too few* programs expressing the idea. Changes take hold when they are reflected in multiple concrete manifestations throughout the organization. After all, people's behavior in organizations is shaped by their place in structures and by the patterns those structures imply. It is when the structures surrounding a change also change to support it that we say that a change is "institutionalized"—that it is now part of legitimate and ongoing practice, infused with value and supported by other aspects of the system.

"Institutionalization" requires other changes to support the central innovation, and thus it must touch, must be integrated with, other aspects of the organization.[18] If innovations are isolated, in segmentalist fashion, and not allowed to touch other parts of the organization's structure and culture, then it is likely that the innovation will never take hold, fade into disuse, or produce a lower level of benefits than it potentially could.

The first step, of course, is that something has to work; premature diffusion of an innovation is a mistake some companies make—trying to solidify something before it has proved its value. The new practices implied by an innovation need to produce results and a success experience for the people using them. Then the new practices can become defined and known to people. They take on an identity and perhaps a name, balancing the dangers of faddism with the need for identity. People can see their presence, recognize their absence, attribute results to them, and evaluate their use.

A number of integrative actions can help weave the innovation into the fabric of the organization's expected operations. Changes in training and communication are important. People need to learn how to use or incorporate the new structure or method or opportunity. This is aided by training for any new skills required, help provided for people to make the transition—why companies with successful employee-involvement programs invest so much in consultants and training, . . . Then communication vehicles (e.g., conferences, networks, informal visits) spread information about them, help transfer experiences from earlier users to newer ones. At Honeywell a variety of conferences, floating resources (staff available from a Center), training tapes, brochures, and traveling road shows are spreading the idea of participative management.

Furthermore, it is important that rewards change to support the new practices. Successes in using them get publicity and recognition or maybe even formal rewards, like the way parallel-organization participation was written into job descriptions and appraisals at Chipco. This can mean the development of measures of their use and accountability for doing so—e.g., in performance appraisals. . . . Leaders or prime movers have to demonstrate that they want the changes and continue to push for them even when it looks as if things might slide back. In successful change efforts there is a continuing series of reinforcing messages from leaders, both explicit and symbolic. And individuals find that using the new practices clearly creates benefits for them: more of something they have always wished they could have or do.[19]

Other structures and patterns also need to change to support the new practices: the flow of information, the division of responsibilities, what regular meetings are held and who comes to them, the composition of teams, and so forth. Furthermore, incorporation of innovations is further aided when people are encouraged to look for broader applications, so that the new practices move from being confined to a few "experimental" areas off to the side to being broadly relevant to tasks of all sorts.

All of these ways of embodying change in the structure create *momentum* and critical mass: more and more people use the new practices, their importance is repeated frequently and on multiple occasions. It becomes embarrassing, "out-of-sync," not to use them.

It is also possible to go even further to build strength into the change that has been constructed. For example, new practices can become "contractual": a written or implied guarantee to customers, a written or implied condition of work in the organization, etc. They can become a basis for the selection of people for work in the organization: Can they use the new practices? Do they fit with the new posture? And there can be mechanisms for educating new people who enter the organization in the practices. By this time, the practices are no longer "new" but, rather, simply "the way we do things around here."

The "failure" of many organizational change efforts has more to do with the lack of these kinds of integrating, institutionalizing mechanisms than with inherent problems in an innovation itself.[20] We have seen that some very positive innovations . . . are never taken advantage of because of oversegmentation and hence, overisolation of the innovation. Some new product or technological process ideas are never developed, as in the small steel company that sold an ultimately important invention to the Japanese rather than exploiting it— to its later regret. And even in innovations embraced by the organization as important strategies, like the QWL effort at General Motors, neighboring systems may not change to support them, such as selection systems, reward systems, and extension to other kinds of tasks (salaried workers or middle managers).

In short, innovations are built into the structure of the organization when they are made to touch—and change— a variety of supporting systems. But the action vehicles also need to be derived from a good theory, in order to avoid the "roast pig" problem.

## The "Roast Pig" Problem

Pervading the time of institutionalizing innovations, when leaders want to ensure that their benefits can be derived repeatedly, is the nagging question of defining accurately the practice or method or cluster of attributes that is desired. Out of all the events and elements making up an innovation, what is the core that needs to be preserved? What *is* the essence of the innovation? This is a problem of theory, an intellectual problem of understanding exactly *why* something works.

I call this the "Roast Pig" problem after Charles Lamb's classic 1822 essay "A Dissertation on Roast Pig," a satirical account of how the art of roasting was discovered in a Chinese village that did not cook its food. A mischievous child accidentally set fire to a house with a pig inside, and the villagers poking around in the embers discovered a new delicacy. This eventually led to a rash of house fires. The moral of the story is: when you do not understand how the pig gets cooked, you have to burn a whole house down every time you want a roast-pork dinner.

The "Roast Pig" problem can plague any kind of organization that lacks a solid understanding of itself. . . .

In many companies, management practices are much more vulnerable to the Roast Pig problem than products, because the depth of understanding of technology and markets sometimes far exceeds the understanding of organizational behavior and organizational systems. So among a dozen failures to diffuse successful work innovations were a number that did not spread because of uncertainty or confusion about what the "it" was that was to be used elsewhere.[21] Or I see "superstitious behavior," the mindless repetition of unessential pieces of a new practice in the false belief that it will not work without them—e.g., in the case of quality circles which companies often burden with excessive and unnecessary formulas for their operation from which people become afraid to depart.

Beliefs may indeed help something work, but beliefs can also be modified by information and theory. The consequences of failing to perform this intellectual task are twofold: first, as one innovation gets locked rigidly into place, further experimentation may be discouraged—house burning may become so ritualistic that the search for other cooking methods is stifled; and perhaps more important, the company may waste an awful lot of houses.

The other extreme also poses problems, of course: reductionism, or the stripping down to apparent "essentials," thus missing some critical piece out of the cluster of elements that makes the innovation work. This fallacy of understanding also needs to be corrected by theory and analysis. As usual, the issue is balance between inclusion of unnecessary rituals and the elimination of key supports.

Thus, the task of conceptualization is as important at the "end" of a change sequence, when the time comes to institutionalize an innovation, as it was at the beginning. Behind every institutionalized practice is a theory about why things work as they do; the success and efficiency of the organization's use of the practice depend on the strength of that theory.

## THE VISIONS AND BLUEPRINTS OF CHANGE MASTERS

It has become fashionable among organizational-behavior theorists to apply the word "art" to management practice, setting it up in opposition to the idea of "technique." Thus, Richard Pascale and Anthony Athos speak of the "art" of Japanese management, covering a range of human sensibilities and sensitivities quite different from the analytic skills taught in business schools. "Great companies make meaning," they said, showing us that leadership deals with values and superordinate goals and not merely with technical matters. Warren Bennis has made a similar point in his discussion of the "artform" of leadership; leadership involves creating larger visions and engaging people's imaginations in pursuit of them. Even discussions of corporate strategic planning are beginning to stress the intuitive side, the artful crafting of an image of possibilities out of the materials provided by organizational subunits—dealing in symbols,

creating coalitions with shared understandings, building comfort levels. Indeed, among the most popular models of the policymaking process today are those which focus on "accident" of circumstance more than rationality or even intelligent intuition; decision makers are shown as "muddling through" instead of rationally calculating.[22]

Such discussions add an important dimension to our understanding of how to guide organizations to achieve higher levels of success. They clearly do not replace the need for rational, analytic techniques such as budgets; reporting and control systems; objective setting and reviews; financial, production, and related quantitative measures; market analyses and environmental scans; and other tools in the modern manager's bag. But the role of such tools has to be seen in perspective. They are part of the management of ongoing operations, keeping the organization on course. They may even suggest areas where changes or improvements are necessary, and they provide the data to back up the argument and get a change effort moving. But overused to guide organizations, they may also stifle innovation, reduce creativity, and prevent organizations from benefiting from the departures from plan that produce entirely new strategies.

The art and architecture of change works through a different medium than the management of the ongoing, routinized side of an organization's affairs. Most of the rational, analytic tools *measure what already is* (or make forecasts as a logical extrapolation from data on what is). But change efforts have to *mobilize people around what is not yet known*, not yet experienced. They require a leap of imagination that cannot be replaced by reference to all the "architect's sketches," "planner's blueprints" or examples of similar buildings that can be mustered. They require a leap of faith that cannot be eliminated by presentation of all the forecasts, figures, and advance guarantees that can be accumulated. . . .

Blueprints and forecasts are important tools and should be provided as much and as frequently as possible. But they are only approximations, and they may be modified dramatically as events unfold. And they are fundamentally different from the emotional appeal—the appeal to human imagination, human faith, and sometimes human greed—that needs to be made to get people on board. And of course, to the extent that change efforts raise concerns about loss and displacement—the negatives that people can easily imagine—architects of change also have to take these issues into account. They have to manage the politics and the anxiety with inclusive visions that give everyone a sense of both the direction of action and their piece of it.[23]

Thus, it is not surprising that I find myself concentrating on the symbolic or conceptual aspects of the change process—on new understandings, on the communication of those, and then on the inevitable reformulations as events move forward. The architects of change have to operate on a symbolic as well as a practical level, choosing, out of all possible "truths" about what is happening, those "truths" needed at the moment to allow the next step to be taken. They have to operate integratively, bringing other people in, bridging multiple realities, and reconceptualizing activities to take account of this new, shared reality. I know exactly how managers feel who come into a meeting with an excellent plan reflecting long hours of toil, only to find it reshaped by their colleagues in small respects even when there are no major flaws; I have been disquieted when my "perfect" proposal for a participative team has been revised

by that very team. Here's the paradox: there needs to be a plan, and the plan has to acknowledge that it will be departed from.

In short, the tools of change masters are creative and interactive; they have an intellectual, a conceptual, and a cultural aspect. Change masters deal in symbols and visions and shared understandings as well as the techniques and trappings of their own specialties.

Thus, those of us interested in promoting change should be wary of excessively logical "how-to" approaches, whether in the form of strategic-planning models or that of other one-two-three guides. Those kinds of models can be extremely useful as a discipline and a structure for discussions resulting in plans—I say this not as a throwaway line but out of my own experience running top-executive strategy sessions. But they fit only one piece of the change process and, by themselves, provide no guarantee that action will *fit* the plans. Many companies, even very sophisticated ones, are much better at generating impressive plans on paper than they are at getting "ownership" of the plans so that they actually guide operational activities. Instead of a formal model of change, then, or a step-by-step rational guide, an outline of patterns is more appropriate and realistic, a set of guiding principles that can help people understand not how it *should* be done but how to understand what might fit the situation they are in.

Perhaps a key to the use of others' experience with change—indeed, a key to the process of innovation itself—is to learn to ask questions rather than assume there are preexisting answers, to trust the process of operating in the realm of faith and hope and embryonic possibility. Repeating the past works fine for routine events in a static environment, but it runs counter to the ability to change. What an innovating organization does is open up action possibilities rather than restrict them and thus trusts to faith as well as formal plans. A well-managed innovating organization clearly has plans—mission, strategies, structure, central thrust, a preference for some activities/products/markets over others—but it also has a willingness to reconceptualize the details and even sometimes the overarching frameworks on the basis of a continual accumulation of new ideas—innovations—produced by its people, both as individuals and as members of participating teams.

Change masters are—literally—the right people in the right place at the right time. The *right people* are the ones with the ideas that move beyond the organization's established practice, ideas they can form into visions. The *right places* are the integrative environments that support innovation, encourage the building of coalitions and teams to support and implement visions. The *right times* are those moments in the flow of organizational history when it is possible to reconstruct reality on the basis of accumulated innovations to shape a more productive and successful future.

The concepts and visions that drive change must be both inspiring and realistic, based on an assessment of that particular corporation's strengths and traditions. Clearly there is no "organizational alchemy" capable of transmuting an auto company into an electronics firm; there is only the hard work of searching for those innovations which fit the life stage and thrust of each company. But all companies can create more of the internal conditions that empower their people to carry out the search for those appropriate innovations. And in that search might lie the hope of the American economic future.

# NOTES

1. As the noted anthropologist Clifford Geertz commented, "What we call our data are re-

ally our own constructions of other people's constructions of what they or their compatriots are up to . . . Explanation often consists of substituting complex pictures for simple ones while striving somehow to retain the persuasive clarity that went with the simple ones." Geertz, *The Interpretation of Cultures*, New York: Oxford, 1975. For a similar perspective in a larger context see Peter Berger and Thomas Luckmann, *The Social Construction of Reality*, Garden City, N.Y.: Anchor Books, 1967.

2. Mayer N. Zald and M. A. Berger, "Social Movements in Organizations," *American Journal of Sociology*, 83 (1978): 823–61.

3. William H. Starbuck, "Organizations and Their Environments," in M. D. Dunnette, ed., *Handbook of Industrial and Organizational Psychology*, Chicago: Rand McNally, 1976, pp. 1069–1123.

4. Karl Weick, *The Social Psychology of Organizing*, second edition, Reading, Mass.: Addison Wesley, 1979, especially page 178.

5. Robert J. Litschert and T. W. Bonham, "Strategic Responses to Different Perceived Strategic Challenges," *Journal of Management*, 5 (1979): 91–105. Robert H. Hayes and William J. Abernathy, "Managing Our Way to Economic Decline," *Harvard Business Review*, 58 (July–August 1980): 67–77.

6. James Brian Quinn, *Strategies for Change: Logical Incrementalism*, Homewood, Ill.: Richard D. Irwin, 1980.

7. Howard Aldrich called my attention to research by Baruch Fischoff on reinterpreting the past. He shows, through experiments, that people cannot disregard what they already know about something, when it comes to constructing an explanation about why something happened in the past. That is, once they know the outcome, people build stories which lead, inevitably, to that outcome. The researchers investigated this by altering historical outcomes, using cases most people don't know much about. They took real historical data, and simply changed the outcome of some series of events. When people were asked to estimate the probability with which they could have successfully predicted the outcome of the events, given knowledge only of the past, they constantly overestimated their ability to successfully predict. They also, in writing up stories about the justification of their prediction, were able to put together a very coherent and compelling story line. Of course,

they were historically wrong! See Fischoff, "For Those Condemned to Study the Past . . ." in D. Kahneman, P. Slovic, and A. Tversky, eds., *Judgment Under Uncertainty*, New York: Cambridge University Press, 1982.

8. Weick, *The Social Psychology of Organizing*, pp. 158, 165. The philosopher Abraham Kaplan is associated with this position.

9. For arguments about the symbolic functions of various aspects of organizational structure, see John W. Meyer and Brian Rowan, "Institutionalized Organizations: Formal Structure as Myth and Ceremony," *American Journal of Sociology*, 83 ( July 1977): 340–63.

10. It has become fashionable to urge the management of organizational myths and stories. See Ian I. Mitroff and Ralph H. Kilmann, "Stories Managers Tell: A New Tool for Organizational Problem Solving," *Management Review*, July 1975; David M. Boje, Donald B. Fedor, and Kendrith M. Rowland, "Myth Making: A Qualitative Step in OD Interventions," *Journal of Applied Behavioral Science*, 18 (1982): 17–28.

11. Weick, *Social Psychology of Organizing*.

12. The idea of random or planned deviance setting a change cycle in motion is consistent with the idea that organizational, like human, evolution begins with "variations," as captured in what has become known as the "population ecology" model. This is well explicated in Howard Aldrich, *Organizations and Environments*, Englewood Cliffs, N.J.: Prentice-Hall, 1979. I am suggesting that the evolutionary view is useful but requires a cognitive model of conscious and directed human action to flesh it out.

13. Michael D. Cohen, James March, and Johan P. Olsen, "A Garbage Can Model of Organizational Choice," *Administrative Science Quarterly*, 17 (1972): 1–25.

14. For a similar idea see Richard D. Beckhard and Reuben Harris, *Organizational Transitions: Managing Complex Change*, Reading, Mass.: Addison-Wesley, 1977.

15. See Modesto A. Mardique, "Entrepreneurs, Champions, and Technological Innovation," *Sloan Management Review*, 21 (Winter 1980). Edward Roberts of the Sloan School at MIT is one of the first innovation researchers to identify the importance of champions; there is also a similar idea in Quinn, *Strategies*.

16. Thomas J. Peters, "Symbols, Patterns, and Settings: An Optimistic Case for Getting Things Done," in H. J. Leavitt, L. R. Pondy, and D. M. Boje, *Readings in Managerial Psychology*, 3rd ed., Chicago: University of Chicago Press, 1980.

17. See Peters, *ibid.*, for other examples.

18. For an account of one of the most elaborate attempts at institutionalizing a system for organizational strategy and change by tying it to every unit—Texas Instruments' OST system—see Mariann Jelinek, *Institutionalizing Innovation*, New York: Praeger, 1979.

19. In a recent study of a large number of employee-involvement programs, one of the strongest predictors of new-program adoption was the staff's expectation of benefits. Philip H. Mirvis, "Assessing Factors Influencing Success and Failure in Organizational Change Programs," in S. Seashore, E. Lawler, P. Mirvis, and C. Cammann, eds., *Observing and Measuring Organizational Change*, New York: Wiley, in press.

20. In evolutionary theory ("population ecology") this is a "failure of retention." See Aldrich, *Organizations and Environments*.

21. Richard Walton, "The Diffusion of New Work Structures: Explaining Why Success Didn't Take," *Organizational Dynamics*, 4 (Winter 1975): 3–21.

22. Richard Pascale and Anthony Athos, *The Art of Japanese Management*, New York: Simon and Schuster, 1980. Warren Bennis, *More Power to You*, New York: Doubleday, forthcoming. Quinn, *Strategies*. Charles E. Lindblom, "The Science of Muddling Through," *Public Administration Review*, 19 (1959): 78–88. Cohen, March, and Olsen, "Garbage Can Model."

23. David Nadler includes politics and anxiety as two of his three key tasks of change management. The third is control: ensuring ongoing organizational maintenance while change is still in process. His solution to politics is the use of teams and visionary leaders; to anxiety, a clear vision; and to control, breaking the change down into a series of smaller, shorter, and thus more manageable transitions. Nadler, "Managing Transitions to Uncertain Future States," *Organizational Dynamics*, 11 (Summer 1982): 37–45. Noel Tichy has provided a full picture of the political-management tasks in change efforts in his *Managing Strategic Change*, New York: Wiley, 1983.

# 44

# The Fifth Discipline: The Art and Practice of The Learning Organization

*Peter M. Senge*

From a very early age, we are taught to break apart problems, to fragment the world. This apparently makes complex tasks and subjects more manageable, but we pay a hidden, enormous price. We can no longer see the consequences of our actions; we lose our intrinsic sense of connection to a larger whole. When we then try to "see the big picture," we try to reassemble the fragments in our minds, to list and organize all the pieces. But, as physicist David Bohm says, the task is futile—similar to trying to reassemble the fragments of a broken mirror to see a true reflection. Thus, after a while we give up trying to see the whole altogether.

. . . When we give up this illusion— we can then build "learning organizations," organizations where people continually expand their capacity to create the results they truly desire, where new and expansive patterns of thinking are nurtured, where collective aspiration is set free, and where people are continually learning how to learn together.

As *Fortune* magazine recently said, "Forget your tired old ideas about leadership. The most successful corporation of the 1990s will be something called a learning organization." "The ability to learn faster than your competitors," said Arie De Geus, head of planning for Royal Dutch/Shell, "may be the only sustainable competitive advantage." As the world becomes more interconnected and

business becomes more complex and dynamic, work must become more "learningful." It is no longer sufficient to have one person learning for the organization, a Ford or a Sloan or a Watson. It's just not possible any longer to "figure it out" from the top, and have everyone else following the orders of the "grand strategist." The organizations that will truly excel in the future will be the organizations that discover how to tap people's commitment and capacity to learn at *all* levels in an organization.

Learning organizations are possible because, deep down, we are all learners. No one has to teach an infant to learn. In fact, no one has to teach infants anything. They are intrinsically inquisitive, masterful learners who learn to walk, speak, and pretty much run their households all on their own. Learning organizations are possible because not only is it our nature to learn but we love to learn. Most of us at one time or another have been part of a great "team," a group of people who functioned together in an extraordinary way—who trusted one another, who complemented each others' strengths and compensated for each others' limitations, who had common goals that were larger than individual goals, and who produced extraordinary results. I have met many people who have experienced this sort of profound teamwork—in sports, or in the performing arts, or in business. Many say that they have spent much of their life looking for that experience again. What they experienced was a learning organization. The team that became great didn't start off great—it *learned* how to produce extraordinary results. . . .

There is also another, in some ways deeper, movement toward learning organizations, part of the evolution of industrial society. Material affluence for the majority has gradually shifted people's orientation toward work—from what Daniel Yankelovich called an "instrumental" view of work, where work was a means to an end, to a more "sacred" view, where people seek the "intrinsic" benefits of work.[1] Our grandfathers worked six days a week to earn what most of us now earn by Tuesday afternoon," says Bill O'Brien, CEO of Hanover Insurance. "The ferment in management will continue until we build organizations that are more consistent with man's higher aspirations beyond food, shelter and belonging."

Moreover, many who share these values are now in leadership positions. I find a growing number of organizational leaders who, while still a minority, feel they are part of a profound evolution in the nature of work as a social institution. "Why can't we do good works at work?" asked Edward Simon, president of Herman Miller, recently. "Business is the only institution that has a chance, as far as I can see, to fundamentally improve the injustice that exists in the world. But first, we will have to move through the barriers that are keeping us from being truly vision-led and capable of learning."

Perhaps the most salient reason for building learning organizations is that we are only now starting to understand the capabilities such organizations must possess. For a long time, efforts to build learning organizations were like groping in the dark until the skills, areas of knowledge, and paths for development of such organizations became known.

What fundamentally will distinguish learning organizations from traditional authoritarian "controlling organizations" will be the mastery of certain basic disciplines. That is why the "disciplines of the learning organization" are vital.

## DISCIPLINES OF THE LEARNING ORGANIZATION

On a cold, clear morning in December 1903, at Kitty Hawk, North Carolina, the fragile aircraft of Wilbur and Orville Wright proved that powered flight was possible. Thus was the airplane invented; but it would take more than thirty years before commercial aviation could serve the general public.

Engineers say that a new idea has been "invented" when it is proven to work in the laboratory. The idea becomes an "innovation" only when it can be replicated reliably on a meaningful scale at practical costs. If the idea is sufficiently important, such as the telephone, the digital computer, or commercial aircraft, it is called a "basic innovation," and it creates a new industry or transforms an existing industry. In these terms, learning organizations have been invented, but they have not yet been innovated. . . .

Today, I believe, five new "component technologies" are gradually converging to innovate learning organizations. Though developed separately, each will, I believe, prove critical to the others' success, just as occurs with any ensemble. Each provides a vital dimension in building organizations that can truly "learn," that can continually enhance their capacity to realize their highest aspirations:

### Systems Thinking

A cloud masses, the sky darkens, leaves twist upward, and we know that it will rain. We also know that after the storm, the runoff will feed into groundwater miles away, and the sky will grow clear by tomorrow. All these events are distant in time and space, and yet they are all connected within the same pattern. Each has an influence on the rest, an influence that is usually hidden from view. You can only understand the system of a rainstorm by contemplating the whole, not any individual part of the pattern.

Business and other human endeavors are also systems. They, too, are bound by invisible fabrics of interrelated actions, which often take years to fully play out their effects on each other. Since we are part of that lacework ourselves, it's doubly hard to see the whole pattern of change. Instead, we tend to focus on snapshots of isolated parts of the system, and wonder why our deepest problems never seem to get solved. Systems thinking is a conceptual framework, a body of knowledge and tools that has been developed over the past fifty years, to make the full patterns clearer, and to help us see how to change them effectively.

Though the tools are new, the underlying worldview is extremely intuitive; experiments with young children show that they learn systems thinking very quickly.

## Personal Mastery

Mastery might suggest gaining dominance over people or things. But mastery can also mean a special level of proficiency. A master craftsman doesn't dominate pottery or weaving. People with a high level of personal mastery are able to consistently realize the results that matter most deeply to them—in effect, they approach their life as an artist would approach a work of art. They do that by becoming committed to their own lifelong learning.

Personal mastery is the discipline of continually clarifying and deepening our personal vision, of focusing our energies, or developing patience, and of seeing reality objectively. As such, it is an essential cornerstone of the learning organization—the learning organization's spiritual foundation. An organization's commitment to and capacity for learning can be no greater than that of its members. The roots of this discipline lie in both Eastern and Western spiritual traditions, and in secular traditions as well.

But surprisingly few organizations encourage the growth of their people in this manner. This results in vast untapped resources: "People enter business as bright, well-educated, high-energy people, full of energy and desire to make a difference," says Hanover's O'Brien. "By the time they are 30, a few are on the "fast track" and the rest 'put in their time' to do what matters to them on the weekend. They lose the commitment, the sense of mission, and the excitement with which they started their careers. We get damn little of their energy and almost none of their spirit."

And surprisingly few adults work to rigorously develop their own personal mastery. When you ask most adults what they want from their lives, they often talk first about what they'd like to get rid of: "I'd like my mother-in-law to move out," they say, or "I'd like my back problems to clear up." The discipline of personal mastery, by contrast, starts with clarifying the things that really matter to us, of living our lives in the service of our highest aspirations.

Here, I am most interested in the connections between personal learning and organizational learning, in the reciprocal commitments between individual and organization, and in the special spirit of an enterprise made up of learners.

## Mental Model

"Mental models" are deeply ingrained assumptions, generalizations, or even pictures or images that influence how we understand the world and how we take action. Very often, we are not consciously aware of our mental models or the effects they have on our behavior. For example, we may notice that a co-worker dresses elegantly, and say to ourselves, "She's a country club person." About someone who dresses shabbily, we may feel, "He doesn't care about what others think." Mental models of what can or cannot be done in different management settings are no less deeply entrenched. Many insights into new markets or outmoded organizational practices fail to get put into practice because they conflict with powerful, tacit mental models.

Royal Dutch/Shell, one of the first large organizations to understand the advantages of accelerating organizational learning, came to this realization when they discovered how pervasive was the influence of hidden mental models, especially those that become widely shared. Shell's extraordinary success in managing through the dramatic changes and unpredictability of the world oil business in the 1970s and 1980s came in large measure from learning how to surface and challenge manager's mental models. (In the early 1970s Shell was the weakest of the big seven oil companies; by the late 1980s it was the strongest.) Arie de Geus, Shell's recently retired Coordinator of Group Planning, says that continuous adaptation and growth in a changing business environment depends on "institutional learning, which is the process whereby management teams change their shared mental models of the company, their markets, and their competitors. For this reason, we think of planning as learning and of corporate planning as institutional learning."[2]

The discipline of working with mental models starts with turning the mirror inward; learning to unearth our internal pictures of the world, to bring them to the surface and hold them rigorously to scrutiny. It also includes the ability to carry on "learningful" conversations that balance inquiry and advocacy, where people expose their own thinking effectively and make that thinking open to the influence of others.

## Building Shared Vision

If any one idea about leadership has inspired organizations for thousands of years, it's the capacity to hold a shared picture of the future we seek to create. One is hard pressed to think of any organization that has sustained some measure of greatness in the absence of goals, values, and missions that become deeply shared throughout the organization. IBM had "service", Polaroid had instant photography, Ford had public transportation for the masses, and Apple had computing power for the masses. Though radically different in content and kind, all these organizations managed to bind people together around a common identity and sense of destiny.

When there is a genuine vision (as opposed to the all-too-familiar "vision statement"), people excel and learn, not because they are told to, but because they want to. But many leaders have personal visions that never get translated into shared visions that galvanize an organization. All too often, a company's shared vision has revolved around the charisma of a leader, or around a crisis that galvanizes everyone temporarily. But, given a choice, most people opt for pursuing a lofty goal, not only in times of crisis but at all times. What has been lacking is a discipline for translating individual vision into shared vision—not a "cookbook" but a set of principles and guiding practices.

The practice of shared vision involves the skills of unearthing shared "pictures of the future" that foster genuine commitment and enrollment rather than compliance. In mastering this discipline, leaders learn the counterproductiveness of trying to dictate a vision, no matter how heartfelt.

## Team Learning

How can a team of committed managers with individual IQs above 120 have a collective IQ of 63? The discipline of team learning confronts this paradox. We know that teams can learn; in sports, in the performing arts, in science, and even, occasionally, in business, there are striking examples where the intelligence of the team exceeds the intelligence of the individuals in the team, and where teams develop extraordinary capacities for coordinated action. When teams are truly learning, not only are they producing extraordinary results but the individual members are growing more rapidly than could have occurred otherwise.

The discipline of team learning starts with "dialogue," the capacity of members of a team to suspend assumptions and enter into a genuine "thinking together." To the Greeks *dia-logos* meant a free-flowing of meaning through a group, allowing the group to discover insights not attainable individually. Interestingly, the practice of dialogue has been preserved in many "primitive" cultures, such as that of the American Indian, but it has been almost completely lost to modern society. Today, the principles and practices of dialogue are being rediscovered and put into a contemporary context. (Dialogue differs from the more common "discussion," which has its roots with "percussion" and "concussion," literally a heaving of ideas back and forth in a winner-takes-all competition.)

The discipline of dialogue also involves learning how to recognize the patterns of interaction in teams that undermine learning. The patterns of defensiveness are often deeply engrained in how a team operates. If unrecognized, they undermine learning. If recognized and surfaced creatively, they can actually accelerate learning.

Team learning is vital because teams, not individuals, are the fundamental learning unit in modern organizations. This is where "the rubber meets the road"; unless teams can learn, the organization cannot learn.

If a learning organization were an engineering innovation, such as the airplane or the personal computer, the components would be called "technologies." For an innovation in human behavior, the components need to be seen as *disciplines*. By "discipline," I do not mean an "enforced order" or "means of punishment," but a body of theory and technique that must be studied and mastered to be put into practice. A discipline is a developmental path for acquiring certain skills or competencies. As with any discipline, from playing the piano to electrical engineering, some people have an innate "gift," but anyone can develop proficiency through practice.

To practice a discipline is to be a life-long learner. You "never arrive"; you spend your life mastering disciplines. You can never say, "We are a learning organization," any more than you can say, "I am an enlightened person." The more you learn, the more acutely aware you become of your ignorance. Thus, a corporation cannot be "excellent" in the sense of having arrived at a permanent excellence; it is always in the state of practicing the disciplines of learning, of becoming better or worse.

That organizations can benefit from disciplines is not a totally new idea. After all, management disciplines such as accounting have been around for a long time. But the five learning disciplines differ from more familiar management disciplines in that they are "personal" disciplines. Each has to do with how we think, what we truly want, and how we interact and learn with one another. In this sense, they are more like artistic disciplines than traditional management disciplines. Moreover, while accounting is good for "keeping score," we have never approached the subtler tasks of building organizations, of enhancing their capabilities for innovation and creativity, of crafting strategy and designing policy and structure through assimilating new disciplines. Perhaps this is why, all too often, great organizations are fleeting, enjoying their moment in the sun, then passing quietly back to the ranks of the mediocre.

Practicing a discipline is different from emulating "a model." All too often, new management innovations are described in terms of the "best practices" of so-called leading firms. While interesting, I believe such descriptions can often do more harm than good, leading to piecemeal copying and playing catch-up. I do not believe great organizations have ever been built by trying to emulate another, any more than individual greatness is achieved by trying to copy another "great person."

When the five component technologies converged to create the DC-3 the commercial airline industry began. But the DC-3 was not the end of the process. Rather, it was the precursor of a new industry. Similarly, as the five component learning disciplines converge they will not create *the* learning organization but rather a new wave of experimentation and advancement.

## THE FIFTH DISCIPLINE

It is vital that the five disciplines develop as an ensemble. This is challenging because it is much harder to integrate new tools than simply apply them separately. But the payoffs are immense.

This is why systems thinking is the fifth discipline. It is the discipline that integrates the disciplines, fusing them into a coherent body of theory and practice. It keeps them from being separate gimmicks or the latest organization change fads. Without a systemic orientation, there is no motivation to look at how the disciplines interrelate. By enhancing each of the other disciplines, it continually reminds us that the whole can exceed the sum of its parts.

For example, vision without systems thinking ends up painting lovely pictures of the future with no deep understanding of the forces that must be mastered to move from here to there. This is one of the reasons why many firms that have jumped on the "vision bandwagon" in recent years have found that lofty vision alone fails to turn around a firm's fortunes. Without systems thinking, the seed of vision falls on harsh soil. If nonsystemic thinking predominates, the first condition for nurturing vision is not met: a genuine belief that we can make our vision real in the future. We may say "We can achieve our vision" (most American managers are conditioned to this belief), but our tacit view of current reality as a set of conditions created by somebody else betrays us.

But systems thinking also needs the disciplines of building shared vision, mental models, team learning, and personal mastery to realize its potential. Building shared vision fosters a commitment to the long term. Mental models focus on the openness needed to unearth shortcomings in our present ways of seeing the world. Team learning develops the skills of groups of people to look for the larger picture that lies beyond individual perspectives. And personal mastery fosters the personal motivation to continually learn how our actions affect our world. Without personal mastery, people are so steeped in the reactive mindset ("someone/something else is creating my problems") that they are deeply threatened by the systems perspective.

Lastly, systems thinking makes understandable the subtlest aspect of the learning organization—the new way individuals perceive themselves and their world. At the heart of a learning organization is a shift of mind—from seeing ourselves as separate from the world to connected to the world, from seeing problems as caused by someone or something "out there" to seeing how our own actions create the problems we experience. A learning organization is a place where people are continually discovering how they create their reality. And how they can change it. As Archimedes has said, "Give me a lever long enough . . . and single-handed I can move the world."

## METANOIA—A SHIFT OF MIND

When you ask people about what it is like being part of a great team, what is most striking is the meaningfulness of the experience. People talk about being part of something larger than themselves, of being connected, of being generative. It becomes quite clear that, for many, their experiences as part of truly great teams stand out as singular periods of life lived to the fullest. Some spend the rest of their lives looking for ways to recapture that spirit.

The most accurate word in Western culture to describe what happens in a learning organization is one that hasn't had much currency for the past several hundred years. It is a word we have used in our work with organizations for some ten years, but we always caution them, and ourselves, to use it sparingly in public. The word is "metanoia" and it means a shift of mind. The word has a rich history. For the Greeks, it meant a fundamental shift or change, or more literally transcendence (*"meta"*—above or beyond, as in "metaphysics") of mind ("noia," from the root *"nous,"* of mind). In the early (Gnostic) Christian tradition, it took on a special meaning of awakening shared intuition and direct knowing of the highest, of God. "Metanoia" was probably the key term of such early Christians as John the Baptist. In the Catholic corpus the word metanoia was eventually translated as "repent."

To grasp the meaning of "metanoia" is to grasp the deeper meaning of "learning," for learning also involves a fundamental shift or movement of mind. The problem with talking about "learning organizations" is that the "learning" has lost its central meaning in contemporary usage. Most people's eyes glaze over if you talk to them about "learning" or "learning organizations." Little wonder—for, in everyday use, learning has come to be synonymous with "taking in information." "Yes, I learned all about

that at the course yesterday." Yet, taking in information is only distantly related to real learning. It would be nonsensical to say, "I just read a great book about bicycle riding—I've now learned that."

Real learning gets to the heart of what it means to be human. Through learning we re-create ourselves. Through learning we become able to do something we never were able to do. Through learning we reperceive the world and our relationship to it. Through learning we extend our capacity to create, to be part of the generative process of life. There is within each of us a deep hunger for this type of learning. It is, as Bill O'Brien of Hanover Insurance says, "as fundamental to human beings as the sex drive."

This, then, is the basic meaning of a "learning organization"—an organization that is continually expanding its capacity to create its future. For such an organization, it is not enough merely to survive. "Survival learning" or what is more often termed "adaptive learning" is important—indeed it is necessary. But for a learning organization, "adaptive learning" must be joined by "generative learning," learning that enhances our capacity to create.

A few brave organizational pioneers are pointing the way, but the territory of building learning organizations is still largely unexplored. It is my fondest hope that this book can accelerate that exploration. . . .

## NOTES

1. Daniel Yankelovich, *New Rules: Searching for Self-fulfillment in a World Turned Upside Down* (New York: Random House), 1981.

2. Arie de Geus, "Planning as Learning," *Harvard Business Review* (March/April 1988): 70–74.

## 45

# Focusing the Effort: Crucial Themes That Drive Change

## Richard Beckhard & Wendy Pritchard

What underlies fundamental change in addition to its being vision-driven? We have identified five themes that may serve as the focus of fundamental change:

- Change in the mission or "reason to be"
- Change in the identity or outside image
- Change in relationships to key stakeholders
- Change in the way of work
- Change in the culture

Leaders need to think about the themes or foci that describe the change effort being undertaken. For example, if they decide to change their *key relationship* with their suppliers in some way that becomes a fundamental change, all the points we have made about fundamental change will follow. At the same time, other changes will occur that leaders must consider. For example, a change in their relationship with suppliers from "friendly adversary" to "partner" may also require some changes in the *mission* or reason to be, including a change in the public *identity* of the organization or in the basic *way in which work within the organization is done*. It probably will also affect the *culture*. Although one focus of change may lead, others will inevitably follow. All these perspectives are connected, and yet effective change will be facilitated if top management can identify and manage the change with one of

these perspectives as a pulling force (see Figure 1).

We will look in more detail at each of the five themes, examples of their use, and implications for the management of change.

## CHANGE IN THE MISSION OR "REASON TO BE"

This theme is the driving force when leadership decides that the "reason to be" or purpose of the organization must be changed. Such a decision then requires subsequent decisions about changes in the way of work, outside image, and organizational design and structure.

A change in mission resulted when the leaders of Federal Express decided that they were in the transportation business rather than in the package delivery business. In addition to choosing a primary theme—change in mission—they decided that two other themes flowed from this choice: change in the way of work and change in the culture.

To implement these themes, several major changes in functioning were designed and put in place. The leaders of Federal Express changed the basic assumption governing their delivery mechanism. Under the old assumption, their strategy was the same as their competitors': best results were achieved by a delivery system that trans-

*Source:* From *Changing the Essence: The Art of Creating and Leading Fundamental Change in Organizations,* Richard Beckhard and Wendy Pritchard pp. 37–48. Copyright 1992 by Jossey-Bass, Inc., Publishers. Reprinted by permission.

FIGURE 1 • FOCUS FOR FUNDAMENTAL CHANGE.

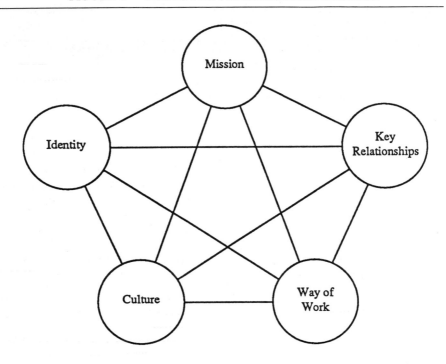

ported from pickup point to delivery point by the shortest direct route. Under the new assumption, the transportation policies and practices were based on the "hub concept" adopted by many airlines. In this mode, a package was flown from its starting city to a hub city (Memphis, Tennessee, was chosen). All packages from everywhere in the United States arrived in the hub city before 10 P.M., every day. A large staff of handlers (part-time employees, mostly college students) sorted all the incoming materials and redirected them to their final destinations. From 2 A.M. onward, planes left Memphis and flew to these locations for final ground delivery.

In addition to this change, Federal Express developed a new and dedicated information system that allowed the company to have constant real-time information on the whereabouts of every package.

The clear choice by management of the primary theme, and its consequential requirements for action, ensured that the organization would be aligned in its implementation of the decision.

Awareness of the need for a current and clear statement of mission as a part of setting a vision and goals is growing and is causing many large organizations to reexamine their traditional statements for relevance.

## CHANGE IN IDENTITY

We propose this as a separate category because it often starts from a different motivation from a change in mission. Changes in mission usually flow from the energy of leaders that is directed toward reexamining and restating the fundamental purpose, whereas identity change usually flows from the need to recoup or regain competitive leadership. It is usually the result of some major outside force or technological breakthrough. Well-documented examples of this are the changes in identity of many financial institutions from "banks" to "financial services" organizations.

Sears, Roebuck & Co. is a dramatic example of an organization whose goal was to change its identity from a retail business to a one-stop service, by way of a financial services group. The achievement of that goal had mixed results. We would speculate that part of the reason for its less than fantastic success was that the identity change did not register with the consumer. Most consumers still preferred to think of Sears as a high-quality, low-cost, easily accessible retail company. We would further speculate that the staff members who interacted with customers did not reflect the change, but worked hard to maintain their traditional identity as retailers.

A change in identity not only involves outside expressions such as logos, symbols, and advertising strategies. It also involves a well-planned effort to address the attitudes and resistances that are likely to occur in the organization itself. Unless there is visible behavior from the top leaders indicating the importance of implementing this change, it is unlikely that high commitment will occur with members of the organization. Wally Olins (1989), who has been described as the "doyen" of the corporate identity business, states in the introduction to his recent book *Corporate Identity:* "The identity of the corporation must be so clear that it becomes the yardstick against which its products, behavior and actions are measured." He further states: "It [the book] takes the view that the corporation's actions are indivisible: that how it behaves, what it says, how it treats people, what it makes and sells are part of a single whole."

## CHANGE IN RELATIONSHIPS TO KEY STAKEHOLDERS

Most large consumer organizations are reexamining their marketing or selling strategies. They are forced into these examinations by changes in consumer habits, but even more by changes in the purchasing policies and practices of large customers. It is no longer acceptable to have fifteen or twenty salespersons calling on one purchasing department.

A large manufacturing company had a history of satisfactory relationships, which could be described as "friendly adversarial," with its suppliers. The leaders of the company decided that if they could change the nature of the relationships to "partnerships," both the company's performance and its competitive position would be improved.

The leadership initiated a program of establishing new arrangements with all of the company's major suppliers. These arrangements were based on the assumption that the company and its suppliers would jointly create new working relationships that would ensure maximum profits for all.

The managers quickly discovered that this program was in effect a fundamental change and that a number of related changes would be required to make it work. For example, changes were required in the functioning of purchasing agents and in the relationship between purchasing and product management. The criteria for "high performance" needed to be revised. New personnel and compensation practices had to be developed.

The organization instituted a series of discussions with its major suppliers in which the agenda was an inquiry into the possibility of this different "partner" relationship. Operationally, suppliers and purchasers would collaborate in working out the procedures that would provide the best chance of increasing profit for both organizations—a "win-win" deal.

There was tremendous resistance from many quarters to this change. Some suppliers felt that they would be losing their power in the negotiation. The purchasing agents in the manufacturing organization saw a loss of control over their own work and noticed changed perceptions of their role by other parts of the company. Employees in manufacturing were threatened by the potential new role of the purchasing employees. The top management of the organization had to bring together the managers of the purchasing and manufacturing functions as well as several others to design an internal strategy that would support the new external relationship with the suppliers.

The organizational implications of such a change are tremendous. Issues include:

- A change in the role of the purchasing agent
- New information systems co-located in both suppliers' and purchasers' space
- New policies concerning company secrets and openness toward the customer
- Changed accounting practices
- Redesigned relationships between purchasing, manufacturing, and distribution
- The effect on control of all costs by business units

As a result of these changing customer requirements and policies, manufacturers are reexamining their purchasing and selling practices. If the organization's leaders are aware of the complexity of this process, they will set up a change management system that will take into account all of the smaller changes mandated by the basic decision.

As companies scramble to increase their competitive edge by implementing these changes, some result-oriented companies are shooting themselves in the foot.

In one such case, the management of a large consumer-oriented company misjudged the complexity of outside pressures and devised a change strategy that was incremental rather than fundamental.

The outside impetus was a change in buying policies of several large customers. The customers were dissatisfied with the organization's sales policies, which required that the purchasers deal with a number of salespeople from the company, each selling individual products or product lines. The customers wanted to deal with many fewer salespeople representing significantly larger numbers of products.

This was an industry-wide problem. The company's management was aware that all its competitors were giving high priority to finding an effective organizational response. Management also knew that it had to define the nature of the problem to be solved. It was finally determined that the company's sales practices—and consequently, the sales department—had to be radically reorganized in order to win the competition for best performance and provide highest customer satisfaction.

What management did not recognize was that the problem required rethinking the company's relationships to key customers, and not a change in the sales function. Major changes were required in the internal relationship between sales and product lines and between functional organizations and product organizations. A new information system was needed; compensation practices had to be revised. A fundamental change strategy was required.

Given the force of the demands and the necessity for a basic change in the conduct of business, the leaders' definition of the problem and their strategies for dealing with it doomed the effort from the start. Had management seen this as a systems problem, the issue would have been redefined as requiring a major change in the company's relationships with one of its key constituencies.

## CHANGE IN THE WAY OF WORK

In this category we place changes in the way the organization looks and works. The concern here is that the change should be fundamental to the organization. As in any fundamental change, the consequences may affect both the organization and its outside constituencies. However, unlike changes in identity, where what is important is the way the organization is perceived by the world, these changes are aimed at the way the business and the work are organized.

An increasingly common cause of changes in the way of work is a decision to become a global enterprise. Most organizations are country-based, even if they do business in several countries. In recent years, however, many enterprises have changed to a multinational posture, which involves such strategies as manufacturing in low-wage countries or developing regional sales or distribution centers and administrative headquarters.

Moving to a global enterprise is a fundamental change decision that affects the entire organization. New items to be considered include the criteria for location of the global headquarters; the roles, functions, and powers of the central executive; and the worldwide management structure. The relationships and power distribution between product or business heads, territorial heads, and functions will be different. Financial and personnel policies must be reexamined and quite probably changed. This type of force is driving many of the massive change programs we see today. British Petroleum, Imperial Chemical Industries, Norsk Hydro, and Statoil are examples of this phenomenon.

Changes from technology-driven to customer-driven businesses may lead to associated changes in the way of work—for example, in the way the business is governed. If an organization is going global, the role of the broad will be different from its role in other types of business. Changes in posture are needed from executive management to strategic management.

A business decision to become a global enterprise, followed by an internal diagnosis, is likely to lead to changes in the way the organization works. A dramatic illustration of this may be given by one of several global companies.

The "before-change" condition was one in which the raw materials were acquired by the purchasing function, and both the products and the machinery on which they were made were designed and monitored by the engineering function. The actual manufacture was under the control of the manufacturing function, but the distribution of finished products was the property of the distribution function.

After a diagnosis, the technical management instituted a new concept called "product supply," based on the flow of products from the time they came into the organization until they were on the customers' shelves. The paradigm changed to one process and the subparts, such as purchasing and manufacturing, involved one team rather than four individual functions.

When this change was announced, colossal resistance occurred. The constellation of changes included changes in the relationships between (1) product supply and product business areas, (2) information and product supply and sales, and (3) parts purchasing, manufacturing, and personnel policies and practices. A separate management system was required to manage and integrate all of the changes and the people who had to carry them out.

Changes in the way of work are visible and immediate to organization members; therefore, management must be doubly vigilant to see that the changes are managed in a climate where learning is honored and where there is explicit management of the change. Top management's unique role of managing the change effort should be particularly visible in this case.

## CHANGE IN THE CULTURE

This is the most subtle theme of the five, in the sense that all changes imply and often mandate a "culture" change. What we are addressing here is the condition that occurs when a change in the culture is the basic goal.

By culture we mean:

- The set of values (what is good or bad) and assumptions (beliefs about human nature) that distinguishes a particular organization from others
- Norms (ground rules for behavior) and artifacts (such as who gets the corner office) that guide actions in the organization

In the case of Xerox, one of the major subgoals was a change in the cultural norms—replacing "big-win" values with improvement and learning.

A commonly *stated* change goal today is to become more customer and/or service oriented. One can watch any two hours of television and see a minimum of three corporate commercials touting this goal for their companies. For this to be achieved in *reality* requires massive changes within the organization in attitudes, behavior, and rewards.

Whatever decision the top management takes, it must have a follow-up change management plan. Resistance to this type of change is usually strong, even if it may be covert. It is important for management to define the specific changes to be implemented in recruiting policies and practices, career planning mechanisms, and financial and other rewards. An explicit communication strategy is needed when such a change takes place.

Even more than other themes, a culture change usually requires the organization to set up supporting educational activities. A current example consists of the changes made in the training and education programs at the General Electric Company to support the position of CEO Jack Welch that a change in the "genetic code" is required to produce a different kind of leader-manager in the future. This position was described by Noel Tichy of the University of Michigan, who took leave from the university to be manager of GE's Management Development Operation from 1985 to 1987 (Tichy):

Radically altering the genetic code of a large successful corporation requires revolutionary action. Since 1981 John F. Welch has been struggling to break the company's old genetic code. The code was built around a core set of principles based on growth in sales greater than GNP [gross national product], with many strategic business units relying on financial savvy, meticulous staff work and a domestically focused company. The new genetic code is to build shareholder value in a slow-growth environment through operating competitive advantage with transformational leadership throughout the organization.

Five years of this effort includes downsizing GE by over 100,000 employees, divesting $6 billion and acquiring $13 billion in businesses which moved GE to No. 3 in the United States in market value from No. 10.

To accomplish the quantum change in GE, a new breed of leader was required. These are leaders who can:

1. Transform the organization, that is creatively destroy and remake an organization around new visions, supported by revamping the social architecture of the organization.
2. Develop global product and services strategies. This means changes in product and service design production, distribution and marketing. Leaders must be able to create new forms of design teams, make strategic use of sourcing, drive world class standards for design, service and performance.
3. Develop strategic alliances.
4. Global co-ordination and integration. Better communication and cultural integration will be required.
5. Global staffing and development. Present systems are outmoded and undergoing total revamping.

These were not just "motherhood" statements. They provided the basis and the context for a massive development and retraining effort for all GE management. They also provided the stimulus for a significant reexamination of policies and practices by managers throughout the GE world.

Practically all fundamental change involves all five of the themes we have been discussing. Each fundamental change has one particular focus, such as change in mission, identity, or way of work. One of the major tasks of leaders is to understand these themes and their relationships and to determine the focus of a particular change effort and ensure that the organization is designed to implement it.

## BIBLIOGRAPHY

Argyris, C. *Reasoning, Learning, and Action: Individual and Organizational.* San Francisco: Jossey-Bass, 1982.

Beer, M. *Organization Change and Development.* Santa Monica, Calif.: Goodyear, 1980.

Bennis, W. *On Becoming a Leader.* Reading, Mass.: Addison-Wesley, 1989.

Bushe, G. R. and Shani, A. B. *Parallel Learning Structures.* Reading, Mass.: Addison-Wesley, 1991.

Ciompo, D. *Total Quality.* Reading, Mass.: Addison-Wesley, 1991.

Cohen, B. D. *Influence Without Authority.* New York: Wiley, 1990.

De Pree, M. *Leadership Is an Art.* New York: Doubleday, 1989.

Drucker, P. F. *Innovation and Entrepreneurship.* New York: Harper-Collins, 1986.

Fritz, R. *The Path of Least Resistance.* New York: Fawcett-Columbine, 1989.

Gardner, J. *On Leadership.* New York: Free Press, 1989.

Hanna, D. P. *Designing Organizations for High Performance.* Reading, Mass.: Addison-Wesley, 1988.

Hirschorn, C. *Managing in the New Team Environment.* Reading, Mass.: Addison-Wesley, 1991.

Hornstein, H. A. *Managerial Courage.* New York: Wiley, 1986.

Kanter, R. M. and Stein, B. *The Tale of "O": On Being Different in an Organization.* New York: HarperCollins, 1986.

McGregor, D. *The Human Side of Management.* New York: McGraw-Hill, 1960.

Maslow, A. H. *Eupsychian Management.* Homewood, Ill.: Dow Jones-Irwin, 1965.

Mitroff, I. *Break-Away Thinking.* New York: Wiley, 1988.

Mohrman, S. A. and Cummings, T. G. *Self-Designing Organizations.* Reading, Mass.: Addison-Wesley, 1989.

Morgan, G. *Creative Organization Theory.* Newbury Park, Calif.: Sage, 1989.

Pettigrew, A. *The Awakening Giant.* Oxford: Basil Blackwell, 1986.

Renesch, J. (ed.) *New Traditions in Business.* San Francisco: New Leaders Press, 1991.

Schein, E. *Organizational Culture and Leadership: A Dynamic View.* San Francisco: Jossey-Bass, 1985.

Tichy, N. M. *Managing Strategic Change.* New York: Wiley, 1983.

Weisbord, M. *Productive Workplaces: Organizing and Managing for Dignity, Meaning, and Community.* San Francisco: Jossey-Bass, 1987.